SECOND EDITION

Principles and Practices of AGRONOMY

P. BALASUBRAMANIYAN

Professor of Agronomy
Agricultural College and Research Institute
Tamil Nadu Agricultural University
Madurai, Tamil Nadu

SP. PALANIAPPAN

Dean & Director (Retd.)
Tamil Nadu Agricultural University
Coimbatore

AGROBIOS (INDIA)

Published by:
Agrobios (India)
Agro House, Behind Nasrani Cinema
Chopasani Road, Jodhpur 342 003
Phone: 91-0291-2643993
E. Mail: agrobiosindia@gmail.com
Website: www.agrobiosonline.com

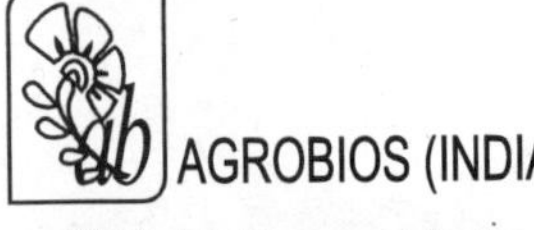

First Published, 2000
Reprinted: 2001-2003
Second Edition, 2004
Reprint, 2005-2020
Reprint, 2026

Published by: Dr. Updesh Purohit for Agrobios (India), Jodhpur
Laser typeset at: Yashee Computers, Jodhpur
Cover Design by: Reena
Printed at: Agrobios Digitals, Jodhpur

Preface to Second Edition

In this age of information technology quiet a lot of information is available in all the fields. In agriculture front and particularly in the subject of agronomy, the information is vast. Choosing the required information is difficult especially for the young graduate students who initiate into the subject. It is the prime duty of the teachers to compile the subject in a comprehensive manner so that the students can easily understand them. The chapters have been chosen and arranged in such a manner that it will explore the entire gamut of agronomy. Some of the chapters such as Agroforestory and Wasteland Development, Post-harvest Management and Information Technology in Agronomy are exclusive to this book.

In this period of competitiveness, one has to be updated with the latest knowledge. Hence in this second edition, efforts have been made to update the available information. The first chapter, field crops-overview, has been completely revised incorporating the latest available data. Additional information has been provided in the chapters such as Nutrient Management mainly organic farming, Watershed management, Farming system. Information Technology in the field of Agronomy has been added in the last chapter.

We hope that this book will serve as a textbook for the graduate students and teachers in agricultural institutions and those who are interested in the subject. We always welcome valuable suggestions to improve the text which will be very well incorporated during the next revision. The authors thank profusely the publishers, Agrobios (India), to bring the second edition nicely and mainly for the cheaper paper back copies exclusively for the students.

January 29, 2004

P. BALASUBRAMANIYAN
SP. PALANIAPPAN

Preface to First Edition

This is the age of information technology. Information is exploding on all fronts. Sometimes one is totally confounded and clueless about sieving the mass of information and choosing the one required by him/her. This is especially so for the young undergraduate students and those who are initiated into a subject. It is important for the teachers to process the mass of information and make it available to the students in an easily understandable manner. The information provided should not only be simple to understand but also to comprehend in an integrated manner. With the expanding horizon of knowledge in agriculture, particularly crop production, there have been several attempt in this direction keeping in view the undergraduate syllabus of agronomy for the agriculture students followed in agricultural universities, as recommended by the Deans Committee of the Indian Council of Agricultural Research. We believe that the book will be useful to the undergraduate students in agriculture, teachers in agricultural institutions and those who are interested in the subject. The chapters have been arranged in such a manner as to lead the students through the entire gamut of agronomy, supported by suitable examples and diagrams. There may still be some lacuna in the book. If these are brought to our knowledge, we will attempt to make the necessary corrections in the subsequent editions. In writing the book, we have freely used the materials provided by our colleagues. We are extremely thankful to them for permitting us to use the information. The authors wish to thank Tamil Nadu Agricultural University and the Vice-Chancellor of the university for providing all the encouragement and help in bringing out the book. The first author wishes to thank his colleagues in the Department of Agronomy, Agricultural College and Research Institute, Madurai, for their co-operation and help. The authors place on record the support given by their families while writing the book. Finally, the publishers of the book, Agrobios (India), are profusely thanked for bringing the book nicely.

August 14, 2000

P. BALASUBRAMANIYAN
SP. PALANIAPPAN

Contents

CHAPTER 1

Field Crops : An Overview

Field crops are classified into different groups based on various criteria. The most useful classification is from the agronomic standpoint based on their usage. Field crops are classified as cereals, pulses, oilseeds, fibre crops, sugars, forage crops, narcotics, tuber crops, plantation crops, spices, etc. Roots and tubers, plantation crops, flowers, spices, fruit trees and vegetables are generally referred to as horticultural crops. Among the field crops, cereals and pulses are called as food crops; the others as cash or commercial crops. At present only 200 species are used as food and 80 % of the food supply come from eight species only.

FOOD PRODUCTION

Food grain production in India has steadily increased from 50.8 m. t in 1950-51 to 176 m. t in 1990-91 and 196.8 m. t in 2000-01. There was decline in production during 1965-67, 1972-73, 74-75, 1979-80 and 1987-88 due to drought. The estimated food grain production in 2001-02 is 212 m. t. The productivity level of food grain production also increased steadily from 1950 to 1996. Analysis of 5 year average productivity of all food grains indicates that from just 582 kg/ha during 1950-55, productivity increased to 1454 kg/ha during 1990-95 and 1598 kg/ha during 96-2000s (Table 1.1).

TABLE 1.1: Production and productivity of food grains in India

Year	Production (m.t.)	Yield (kg/ha)	Year	Production (m.t.)	Yield (kg/ha)
1950-51	50.8	552	1976-77	111.2	894
52	52.0	536	78	126.4	991
53	59.2	580	79	131.9	1022
54	69.8	640	80	109.7	876
55	68.0	631	81	129.6	1023
56	68.9	605	82	133.3	1032
57	69.9	629	83	129.5	1035
58	64.3	587	84	152.4	1162
59	77.1	672	85	145.5	1149
60	76.7	662	86	150.4	1175
61	82.0	710	87	143.4	1128

Year	Production (m.t.)	Yield (kg/ha)	Year	Production (m.t.)	Yield (kg/ha)
62	82.7	705	88	140.4	1173
63	80.2	680	89	169.9	1331
64	80.6	687	90	171.0	1349
65	89.4	757	91	176.4	1380
66	72.3	629	92	168.4	1382
67	74.2	644	93	179.5	1457
68	95.1	783	94	184.3	1501
69	93.0	781	95	191.5	1548
70	99.5	805	96	185.0	1499
71	108.4	872	97	199.4	1614
72	105.2	858	98	192.3	1552
73	97.0	813	99	203.6	1627
74	104.7	827	2000	209.8	1704
75	99.8	824	01	196.8	1626
76	121.0	944	02	212.0	1739

Source: Agricultural statistics at a glance-2003. Ministry of Agriculture, New Delhi

Higher production and productivity were achieved mainly due to increase in irrigated area, wide adoption of high yielding varieties and enhanced use of fertilizers and plant protection chemicals. Gross irrigated area in 1950-51 was only 22.6 m.ha which was almost doubled in 1980-81 (49.8 m.ha). The irrigated area further increased to 76.3 m. ha in 1999-2000. From almost no use of fertilizers in 1950-51 (0.07 m. t), fertilizer consumption increased to 12.5 m. t in 1990-91 and further increased to 18.1 m. t. in 1999-2000 (Table 1.2).

TABLE 1.2: Irrigated area and fertilizer consumption in India

Year	Gross Irrigated area (m. ha)	Fertilizer consumption (m. t)
1950-51	22.6	0.07
1960-61	28.0	0.3
1970-71	38.0	2.2
1980-81	49.1	5.5
1990-91	63.2	12.5
1999-00	76.3	18.1

Source: Agricultural statistics at a glance-2003

FOOD SECURITY

Food security means that all people at all times have access to safe and nutritious food to maintain healthy and active life. This definition implies availability, access and stability at various levels viz., global, national and household and the individual.

Food security is defined as both physical and economic access to food. The concept of nutritional security involves physical and economic access to balanced diets and safe drinking water. Without nutritional security, it will not be possible to provide newborn children with an opportunity for the full expression of their innate genetic potential for physical and mental development (Swaminathan, 1993).

There has been consistent production of more food to keep pace with the ever-increasing world population growth. It has been forecasted that global population will rise from a little under 6.0 billion today to 7.0 billion in 2010 and stabilize at 10-11 billion around 2050. In the World Food Summit at Rome in 1996, it was brought out that the number of chronically undernourished people in the developing world would be 840 million. Along with this, children under the age of five were estimated to be malnourished due to inadequate intake of dietary protein. It was agreed in the Summit that food would not be used as a political weapon and each country should be as self reliant as possible in the availability of food.

FOOD GRAIN AVAILABILITY

The amount of calories available every day per each person (per capita availability) varies among different countries. South Korea and Mexico have the highest intake. In India consumption behaviour indicates 47.7 % households have caloric inadequacy and 19.8 % have protein inadequacy. About 19.9 % have both caloric and protein inadequacy. The per capita cereal consumption has declined over the years resulting in the aggregate energy intake of 1859 kcal per capita as against 2200 kcal recommended. The per capita supply of protein in the countries like South Korea, Mexico, Malaysia and Chile is fairly good. With respect to per capita availability of food grains in India, it was 394.9 g in 1950-51 and it increased to 510.1 g in 1990-91 and in 1997-98 it was only 450.3 g/day. Though the food grain availability steadily increased from 1951 to 1991 there was steady decline in the availability of pulses from 60.7 g to 41.6 g/day during this period (Table 1.3).

TABLE 1.3: Per capita availability of food grains in India

Year	Availability (g /day)		
	Cereal	Pulses	Food Grains
1950-51	334.2	60.7	394.9
1960-61	399.7	69.0	468.7
1970-71	417.6	51.2	468.8
1980-81	417.3	37.5	454.8
1990-91	468.5	41.6	510.1
1997-98	417.3	33.0	450.3

Source: Agricultural statistics at a glance-2003

In India, food grain availability (rice and wheat) is ensured through a net work of Fair Price Shops (FPSs). Central Government operates the food stocks and has three important functional components: food security reserve, operational stocks and market intervention stocks. Each month the stocks are released for distribution to the State Governments. They, in-turn, supply the food grains to the people through Public Distribution System (PDS). The PDS is an important constituent of the strategy for poverty alleviation. PDS continues to be a major instrument of Government's economic policy for ensuring food security to the poor. The Targetted Public Distribution System (TPDS) replaced the erstwhile PDS from June 1997. Under the new system, a two tier susidised pricing system was introduced to the benefit the poor. The essential features of TPDS are: Government of India is committed to making available food grains to the States to meet the requirement of food grains at the scale of 10 kg per month per family at specially susidised prices to population falling below the officially estimated poverty line (BPL). The states would also receive the quantity needed for transitory allocation to Above Poverty Line (APL) population. The state governments were to streamline the PDS by issuing special cards to BPL families and selling essential articles under TPDS to them at specially subsidised prices with better monitoring of the delivery system. About 10.1 m.t of wheat and 15.1 m.t of rice has been allotted under PDS (1996-97).

CEREALS

The word 'cereal' is derived from '*cereas*', the Roman Goddess of grain. A cereal crop is a grass grown for its edible grain, rich in starch. Cereals are the most important food crops. The common cereal crops are wheat, rice, maize, barley, oats and rye. Commercially, the cereals other than wheat and rice are known as coarse cereals. Globally 2029 m.t. of cereals are produced from 658.5 m.ha with the average productivity of 3083 kg/ha. In India, the cereal grain production has increased from 42.4-m. t. in 1950-51 to 185.2 m. t. in 2000-01. Average yield of the cereals has increased three folds during this period (Table 1.4).

TABLE 1.4: Production and productivity of cereals in India

Year	Production (m.t)	Yield (kg/ha)
1950-51	42.4	542
1960-61	69.3	753
1970-71	96.6	949
1980-81	119.0	1142
1990-91	162.1	1571
2000-01	185.7	

Source: Agricultural statistics at a glance-2003

Nutritive value

Cereal grains provide the world with a majority of its food calories and about half its protein. They are the staple food in the diets of most population. The grains contain 58-72 % carbohydrate, 8-13 % protein, 2-5 % fat and 2-10 % indigestible fibre. They also contain about 310-350 k.cal/100 g of grain (Table 1.5).

TABLE 1.5: Percentage composition of cereal grains

Cereals	Calories (k.cal/100 g)	CHO	Protein	Fat	Fibre
Wheat	340	69	13	2	3
Rice	310	65	8	2	9
Maize	352	72	10	4	2
Barley	320	63	12	2	6
Rye	321	71	12	2	2
Oats	317	58	10	5	10

Source: Potter and Hotchkiss, (1996)

Rice (*Oryza sativa* L.)

Rice is the most widely cultivated crop in the world occupying an area of about 154 m. ha. Total rice output is 603 m.t and the average yield is 3.9 t/ha. During the last 30 years, area under rice has increased only to a small extent from 135.4 m. ha in 1970 to 153.9 m.ha in 2000. However, rice production increased greatly from 307 m.t to 602.6 m.t (Table 1.6).

TABLE 1.6: Rice production trend in the world

Year	Area (m.ha)	Production (m.t)	Yield (kg/ha)
1970	135.4	306.6	2280
1975	143.7	359.6	2521
1980	143.5	397.6	2770
1985	144.5	472.7	3272
1990	146.7	521.1	3553
1995	149.2	550.2	3689
2000	153.9	602.6	3917

Source: FAO, 2003

World demand for rice in 2025 is estimated to be about 765 m. t. Rice is the crop of tropical climate. However, it is grown successfully in humid regions of sub-tropics and temperate climate. Rice growing countries include those in Asia, West and North Africa, South and Central Latin America, Australia and the United States of America. More than 90 % of the world's rice area is in Asia, which is the home for more than half of world's poor and more than half of worlds rice cultivators. Out of 2.4 billion consuming rice in the world, more than 95 % live in Asia. China and India are the two major countries producing rice in Asia. These two countries together have 46.3 % of the world rice area (68.1 m.ha) with the 50.9 % of world production (293.2 m.t.). Though China has three fourth of area than India, its production is high. Other important rice growing Asian countries are Indonesia, Bangladesh, Thailand, Vietnam, Myanmar, Philippines, Japan, Pakistan, etc (Table 1.7 and 1.8).

TABLE 1.7: Rice production in different continents of the world, 2002

Countries/Continent	Area (m.ha)	Production (m.t.)	Yield (kg/ha)
World	147.1	576.3	3916
Asia	130.8	523.0	3998
Africa	8.6	17.0	1991
North & Central America	1.9	11.9	6229
South America	5.9	18.3	3108
Europe (Former)	0.4	2.6	6421
Oceania	0.1	1.3	8193

Source: FAO, 2003

TABLE 1.8: Rice production in the Asian countries, 2002

Country	Area (m.ha)	Production (m.t)	Productivity (kg/ha)
Bangladesh	11.59	38.1	3448
China	28.2	176.6	6266
India	40.0	116.8	2915
Indonesia	11.6	51.6	4433
Japan	1.7	11.1	6582
Myanmar	6.2	21.9	3532
Nepal	1.5	4.1	2667
Pakistan	2.2	6.3	2882
Philippines	4.0	13.3	3280
Republic of Korea	1.0	6.7	6315
Sri Lanka	0.7	2.8	3827
Thailand	9.9	25.9	2597
Vietnam	7.5	34.1	4551
World	**147.1**	**576.3**	**3916**

Source: FAO, 2003

In India, the area under rice has increased from 30.8 m ha in 1950- 51 to 45.2 m. ha in 2000-01. There was also a steady increase in the production of rice. Production doubled from 20.6 m. t. in 1950-51 and to 40 m.t. in 1970. It has again doubled to 80 m.t. in 1995-96. The current production level is 93 m. t. The yield level also increased from 668 kg/ha in 1950 to 2086 kg / ha in 2002 (Table 1.9). However, comparing the world average (3917 kg/ha), there is enormous scope to further push the yield level. Rice is cultivated in almost all states in India. However, the states having large area under rice are West Bengal, Uttar Pradesh, Andhra Pradesh, Punjab, Orissa, Tamil Nadu, Bihar, Chattisgarh, Assam, Karnataka, Haryana,

Maharashtra, Madhya Pradesh, Jharkhand, etc. These states contribute about 90 % of the area and production (Table 1.10).

TABLE 1.9: Area, production and productivity of rice in India

Year	Area (m. ha)	Production (m.t)	Productivity (kg /ha)
1950 –51	30.8	20.6	668
51-52	29.8	21.3	714
52-53	29.9	22.9	764
53-54	31.3	21.2	902
54-55	30.8	25.2	820
55-56	31.5	27.6	874
56-57	32.3	29.0	800
57-58	32.3	25.5	790
58-59	33.2	30.8	930
59-60	33.8	31.7	937
60-61	34.1	34.6	1013
61-62	34.7	35.7	1028
62-63	35.7	33.2	931
63-64	35.8	36.9	1034
64-65	34.5	39.3	1078
65-66	35.5	30.6	862
66-67	35.3	30.4	863
67-68	36.4	37.6	1032
68-69	36.9	39.8	1076
69-70	37.7	40.4	1073
70-71	37.6	42.2	1123
71-72	37.8	43.1	1141
72-73	36.7	39.2	1070
73-74	38.3	44.1	1151
74-75	37.9	39.6	1045
75-76	39.5	48.5	1235
76-77	38.5	41.9	1088
77-78	40.3	52.7	1308
78-79	40.5	53.8	1328
79-80	39.4	42.3	1074
80-81	40.2	53.6	1336
81-82	40.7	53.2	1308
82-83	38.3	47.1	1231
83-84	41.2	60.1	1457
84-85	41.2	58.3	1417
85-86	41.1	63.8	1552
86-87	41.2	60.6	1471
87-88	38.8	56.9	1465
88-89	41.7	70.5	1689

Year	Area (m. ha)	Production (m.t)	Productivity (kg /ha)
89-90	42.2	73.6	1745
90-91	42.7	74.3	1740
91-92	42.6	74.7	1751
92-93	41.8	72.9	1744
93-94	42.5	80.3	1888
94-95	42.8	81.8	1911
95-96	42.9	79.6	1855
96-97	43.4	81.7	1882
97-98	43.5	82.5	1900
98-99	44.8	86.1	1921
99-00	45.16	89.7	1986
2000-01	45.7	84.9	1901
2001-02	44.6	93.1	2086

Source: Agricultural statistics at a glance-2003

TABLE 1.10: Rice production in different states in India, 2001-02

States	Area ('000 ha)	Production ('000 tonnes)	Yield (kg/ha)
Andhra Pradesh	3.83	11.39	2978
Assam	2.53	3.85	1524
Bihar	3.57	5.28	1480
Chhattishgarh	3.73	5.13	1374
Gujarat	0.66	1.03	1549
Haryana	1.03	2.72	2652
Jharkhand	1.48	1.64	1111
Karnataka	1.42	3.17	2236
Kerala	0.32	0.72	2218
Madhya Pradesh	1.76	1.66	948
Maharashtra	1.51	2.65	1751
Orissa	4.50	7.15	1589
Panjab	2.49	8.82	3545
Tamil Nadu	2.11	6.87	3263
Uttar Pradesh	5.88	12.46	2514
West Bengal	6.07	15.26	2514
All India	**44.62**	**93.08**	**2086**

Source: Agricultural statistics at a glance-2003

India has the potential to become the number one rice producer in the world. India has reached a plateau in its irrigated rice yield, yet in the coming years it is expected to play a crucial role in the international rice production and technology. The focus is to be on tapping the production potential in the North Eastern region. New varieties will have to be bred to enhance the yield per hectare. Area under hybrid rice should be extended beyond the frontiers of South India, where it has been adapted more favorably than in the North.

Nutritive value of rice

Rough rice (paddy) consists of about 20 % hull and 80 % grain (hulled or brown rice). There is loss of about 10 % of brown rice while milling as bran and germ. Some part of the endosperm is also removed at polishing. Rice has a high calorific and nutritional value and rich in easily digestible starch and carbohydrates. Whole rice contains high amount of vitamin B (thiamin, riboflavin and niacin). Most of the vitamins are removed while polishing in the modern rice mills. The grains contain appreciable amount of K, P, Mg and I.

All parts of the rice are used economically. The husk is used as fuel and rice grains are used for making starch and vinegar. In many rice growing Asian countries, alcohol beverages are also brewed from rice.

Rice genotypes

Vavillov considered that India and Burma would be the centers of origin of cultivated rice. Rice belongs to the family *Gramineae* and the genus *Oryza*. Two cultivated species of rice are *O. sativa* (L) and *O. glaberrima* (steud). *Oryza sativa* is widely grown in Asia, parts of Europe and America. Cultivation of *O. glaberrima* is restricted to Africa. The cultivated species of *O. sativa* are further divided into *japonica, javanica* and *indica,* based on the morphological and physiological characteristics. These sub-species also differ in their geographical distribution.

Indica rices are indigenous to the humid regions of the tropics and sub-tropics of Asia. The japonica types are limited to temperate zones and sub-tropics. Javanicas are mainly grown in parts of Indonesia.

Varietal improvement

Rice Breeding programme in India was started as early as 1911. The Imperial Council of Agricultural Research established the Central Rice Research Institute (CRRI) at Cuttack, Orissa in 1946 primarily for developing high yielding rice varieties and technologies for different parts of the country (Ramaiah, 1953). In 1965, the All-India Co-ordinated Rice Improvement Project (AICRIP) was established to accelerate and co-ordinate rice research at national level for rapid generation and identification of varieties and management techniques appropriate to different agro-ecological situations in partnership with state Agricultural universities and departments of agricultural and Central agricultural research institutes. A major break-through was made in rice breeding with the release of IR8 in 1966 from the introduced material of the IRRI. This variety bestowed practical expression to the concept of ideotypes. A number of such high yielding varieties have been released subsequently through selection and hybridization. Varieties are released for different purposes such as earliness, deep water and flood resistance, lodging resistance, drought resistance, non-shedding of grains, disease resistance and high response to heavy manuring. Varieties are also available with good quality and aromatic characters. Hybrids have been released recently by for higher productivity.

Early maturing varieties

Early maturing rice varieties play greater role in intensive cropping systems. Farmers could fit them in varied cropping systems and increase productivity. Early maturing high yielding dwarf cultivars of rice replaced large area under millets and oil seeds in the 1970's. Some of the quick maturing varieties are Pusa 2-21, Pusa 33, Saket - 4 and Annapurna. These varieties are capable of yielding as high as 90 % of medium duration varieties under irrigated conditions.

Resistance to pests and diseases

In rice about 25-30 % yield loss occurs due to pest and disease incidence. The problem became serious after the introduction of high yielding, semi-dwarf varieties. These varieties provide a favourable host environment due to their genetic homogeneity. Large areas are planted with a few high yielding varieties. Changes in the cropping pattern, crop intensification and high input management also added to the problem. Of late, varieties have been released for specific or multiple resistances to biotic and abiotic stresses. The impact of host- plant resistance is visible through reduced crop losses and less frequent recurrence of pest epidemics. Their resistance could also be assessed with stable yield in pest endemic areas.

Insect resistance

Varieties resistant to some predominant insect pests:

- ***Gall midge:*** Phalguna, Surekha, Pothana, Abhaya, Suraksha, Triguna
- ***Brown plant hopper (BPH):*** Krishnaveni, Chaitanya Jyothi, Sonasali, Kanakam
- ***Stem borer:*** TKM 6, Sasyasri, Vikas, Ratna

Disease resistance

Important diseases in rice are bacterial leaf blight (BLB), sheath blight, rice tungro virus (RTV). The estimated yield loss is about 10%. Varieties resistant to the diseases are:

- ***BLB:*** Ajaya, PR 110, PR 111, Pantdhan 12
- ***RTV:*** Vikramarya, Nidhi, Bharani, Vasundhara
- ***Blast:*** CO 25, CO 29, CO 30, CO 38, Mtu 17
- ***Helminthosporium:*** Ch13, Ch 45, IET 1328

Special situations

Drought tolerance

Tolerance to drought is generally associated with

i) high germination in polyethylene glycol,
ii) less starch disintegration in root and low destruction of chlorophyll,

iii) tillering in quick succession before the onset of drought,
iv) longer root length (> 25 cm),
v) high leaf moisture content and greater accumulation of reducing sugars.

Varieties: CO 31, Mtu 17, Ch 45, Bala, Kiran, CRM 13-3241, PMK®-3.

Tolerance to water logging

Tolerance to water logged situations is associated with (i) fast, early tillering, (ii) liberation of more oxygen from the root, (iii) moderate pectin-methyl esterase activity in the culm and (iv) greater chlorophyll b and higher photosynthetic rate of the top leaves above water level.

Varieties: CR 1014, Mashsuri, Pankaj, Jaganath, Gauthami, Visishta.

Deep water condition

The standing water in the field for a significant period of time is more than 50 cm. In Huntra area of Thailand, water usually remains on the fields for four months or longer. Deep water areas are found in deltas, estuaries and river valleys of India, Bangladesh, Burma, Thailand, Vietnam, Kampuchea and Indonesia. In India there is a large deep water rice area in west Bengal, Assam, Orissa and Kerala. Drought at the early phase, weed competition, poor stand establishment and submergence of rice at various growth stages are some of the problems encounted in deep water rice. Varieties should have good seedling vigour, ability to elongate if the water level increases, intermediate plant height (about 100 cm), submergence tolerance and with kneeing ability. The duration of the varieties varies from 150 to 240 days.

Varieties: Jaladhi I, Jaladhi II, PLA-2, ARC- 353 – 146, Jaisuria, Jalmagna, Ptb 15, Ptb 16, TNR 1, TNR 2.

- ***Post-flood situation:*** Heera, Luit, Kalinga III
- ***Saline and alkaline tolerance:*** CST 7-1, Lunishree, CSR 10, Panvel 1, Panvel 2, Vytilla 2, Vytilla 3, Vytilla 4 and CSR 5 tolerate saline conditions.
- For alkaline areas, Vikas, CSR 5, TRY 1, TRY 2 are suitable.
- ***Hilly regions:*** VL_Dhan 163, VL Dhan 206, VL Dhan 221.

Scented rice varieties

Scented rice varieties are known for their characteristic fragrance when cooked. There are several scented varieties of rice which emit aroma and form a group by themselves. Genetic studies showed that single dominant gene controls fragrance at flowering (Jodon, 1944). The aroma inheritance reportedly depends on one to three complementary factors. However, little is known about the influence of environment on the intensity of aroma. Studies on flavour component in scented rice varieties showed their higher content of carboryl component than ordinary varieties.

'Basmati' rices are an elite group among rice varieties characterised by aroma and specific cooking and eating quality. They fetch highest premium since they are priced about three times than that of high quality non-Basmati type. The traditional scented varieties are Krishnabhog, Prasadbhog, Bhadshabhog, Rajbhog, etc. All these traditional scented varieties are tall, most of them are weak-strawed, lodge heavily and are poor yielders. The most popular scented varieties in the North India are Basmati 370 and 217. Dwarf aromatic varieties (Pusa Basmati I, Kasturi) are dwarf, high yielding and comparable with highly prized Basmati varieties like 'Basmati 370'. Medium slender and medium bold grains without belly are preferred. Aroma and fluffiness on cooking are other desirable traits. Pusa Basmati 1 is an example of fine grain scented with a potential of 5 t/ha.

In Punjab, Haryana and Western U.P., Basmati is cultivated in about 7-8 lakh ha. About 60 % of the basmati rice produced are exported. Major markets for this scented rice are the middle East and the Gulf (Saudi Arabia, U.A.E. and Kuwait). Scented rice varieties are normally grown in smaller areas due to low yield (1.5 to 2.0 t/ha).

Timely harvest is important for obtaining high milling %age. Harvest is to be taken up at 25 days from general flowering when the last few grains at the base of the panicle are still green but in their hard dough stage. Further drying in shade will increase the head rice recovery by avoiding sun-cracks which will increase the %age of broken rice.

Hybrid rice

Hybrid rice is a land mark technology development in China. Professor Yuvan Long Ping, the father of hybrid rice revolution in China, developed the first hybrid rice. He started the work on hybrid rice with the idea of exploiting heterosis in rice. Since 1976, hybrid rice is being cultivated on a commercial scale in China. Hybrid rice cultivation has helped China to increase rice production by nearly 200 m.t from 1976 to 1991. Hybrid rice technology has enabled China to improve rice yields by 15-20% over the commercial rice varieties. China's success with hybrid rice technology has generated great interest in the other Asian countries.

International Rice Research Institute, Philippines, started work on hybrid rice in the 1980's. The other countries such as India, Indonesia, Korea, Thailand and Vietnam have also joined in this pursuit. Having recognized heterosis breeding of rice as one of the most feasible methods to increase the productivity and production of rice in the country in 1989, Government of India initiated a goal-oriented, time-bound project entitled, "The Development and use of Hybrid Rice Technology". This ICAR project has been further strengthened by financial support from the United Nations Development Programme (UNDP) and by technical support from FAO since September 1991. As a result of extensive evaluation, hybrids have been released in the states of Andhra Pradesh, Tamil Nadu, Karnataka, West Bengal, Uttar Pradesh (Table 1.11). The hybrids released are capable of producing 16-44 % additional yield per hectare than the best variety.

TABLE 1.11: Hybrids released in India

Hybrids	Duration (days)	Adaptability
APHR 1	130-135	Telengana and Rayalseema region, AP
APHR 2	120-125	Telengana and Rayalseema region, AP
DRRH1	125-130	AP, TN, Karnataka
CORH 1	110-115	*Kuruvai* (June-Sep) in Tamil Nadu
CORH2	120-125	Late *Thaladi* (Oct-Dec) in Tamil Nadu
ADTRH 1	115-120	Cauvery delta zone of Tamil Nadu
KRH 1	120-125	Irrigated areas of Karnataka
KRH2	130-135	Irrigated areas of Karnataka
KRH 4	130-135	Irrigated areas of Karnataka
CNHR 3	125-130	*Boro* season in West Bengal
Narendra Sankar Dhan-2	125-130	Uttar Pradesh
Pro Agro-6201	125-130	Eastern & some parts of South India

Most of the rice hybrids developed in and outside China are based on cytoplasmic male sterility (CMS) and fertility restoration system. The basic problem encountered with hybrid rice production is developing male sterile lines adapted to tropical countries. A CMS line must possess stable pollen sterility, adaptability to target environment, good crossing potential and good combining ability. Seed production is the major constraint in commercializing rice hybrids.

GM rice (Golden rice)

Another technology innovation is genetically engineered beta carotene rice, popularly known as 'golded rice'. It was engineered save millions of children from vision impairment (over 50000 children go blind every year in South Asia due to deficiency of Vitamin A). Considering that beta carotene can supplement vitamin A needs by 30 per cent and that The U.S. Food and Drug Administration has classified it as 'genetically acceptable as safe' (Siddiq, 2002).

Wheat (*Triticum* sp)

Among the cereals, wheat ranks first in area and production in the world. Wheat production in the world has steadily increased from 312 m.t. in 1970 to 586 m.t. in 2000. The increase was 87.5 % compared to 1970. Productivity also increased from 1.5 t/ha in 1970 to 2.7 t/ha in 2000. The area increase was not substantial (only 3% as compared to 1970). (Table 1.12).

TABLE 1.12: Wheat production in the world

Year	Area (m. ha)	Production (m. t.)	Yield (kg/ha)
1970	210.3	311.6	1480
1975	228.9	354.7	1550
1980	236.9	446.0	1877
1985	230.6	550.7	2193
1990	231.7	592.9	2559
1995	220.6	541.1	2453
2000	215.5	585.9	2720

Source: FAO, 2003

South and East Asia greatly contributed towards increase in global wheat production. Area and production of wheat in most important wheat growing countries are given in Table 1.13. The countries such as China, United States, India, Russia Federation, Canada, European union and Australia account for 60.9 % of total area and 67.6 % of global production.

TABLE 1.13: Wheat cultivating area and production in different countries, 2002

Country	Area (m. ha.)	Production (m.t)
Australia	11.0	9.4
Canada	8.9	15.7
China	23.5	91.3
European union	18.0	104.8
India	25.9	71.8
Russian Federation	22.4	50.6
United states of America	18.5	43.9
World	**210.6**	**572.9**

Source: FAO, 2003

Wheat is an important winter cereal contributing about 32 % of the total food grain production in India. Since the introduction of high yielding dwarf varieties in 1965, there has been continuous increase in both the production and productivity. India now occupies the third position in wheat production. About one tenth of the global wheat production is from India. The area under wheat was only 9.7 m.ha in 1950-51 which has increased to 25.7 m.ha in 2000-01. This increase was only 2.7 times; however, there was about 10 times increase in grain production. The production was only 6.5 m.t. in 1950-51 which has tremendously increased to 69.7 m.t. in 2000-01. The increase in production was about 5.6 times during the first 30 years (1950-81). During the later period, production was almost doubled. With respect to yield, there was 4 times increase from 1950 to 2000. (From 663 kg /ha to 2708 kg/ha) (Table 1.14).

TABLE 1.14: Area, production and productivity of wheat in India

Year	Area (m.ha)	Production (m.t)	Yield (kg/ha)
1950-51	9.7	6.5	663
52	9.5	6.2	653
53	9.8	7.5	763
54	10.7	8.0	750
55	11.3	9.0	803
56	12.4	8.8	708
57	13.5	9.4	695
58	11.7	8.0	682
59	12.6	10.0	789
60	13.4	10.3	772
61	12.9	10.9	851
62	13.6	12.1	890
63	13.6	10.8	793
64	13.5	9.9	730
65	13.4	12.3	913
66	12.6	10.4	827
67	12.8	11.4	887
68	15.0	16.5	1103
69	15.9	18.6	1169
70	16.6	20.1	1202
71	18.2	23.8	1307
72	19.1	26.4	1380
73	19.5	24.7	1271
74	18.6	21.8	1172
75	18.0	24.1	1388
76	20.5	28.8	1410
77	20.9	29.0	1387
78	21.5	31.3	1480
79	22.6	35.5	1568
80	22.2	31.8	1436
81	22.3	36.3	1630
82	22.1	37.5	1691
83	23.6	42.8	1816
84	24.7	45.5	1843
85	23.6	44.1	1870
86	23.0	47.1	2048
87	23.1	44.3	1916
88	23.1	46.2	2002
89	24.1	54.1	2244
90	23.5	49.9	2121
91	24.2	55.1	2281
92	23.3	55.7	2394

Year	Area (m.ha)	Production (m.t)	Yield (kg/ha)
93	24.6	57.2	2327
94	25.1	59.8	2380
95	25.7	65.8	2559
96	25.1	62.6	2493
97	25.9	69.4	2679
98	26.7	66.4	2485
99	27.5	71.3	2590
2000	27.5	76.4	2778
01	25.7	69.7	2708
02	25.9	71.8	2770

Source: Agricultural statistics at a glance-2003

Continuous varietal improvements and their adoption have pushed the productivity to high levels, almost equal to the world average yield (2.7 t/ha). The projected wheat grain production is around 109 m.t by the year 2020 AD. Providing copious water at the right time can increase wheat productivity. Improper nutrient application, poor crop stand and wrong sowing time are some of the major hurdles in increasing the yield.

Wheat is mainly grown in the northern part of India. Major wheat growing states are Uttar Pradesh, Madhya Pradesh, Punjab, Bihar and Haryana. These states contribute almost 80 % of wheat area and production. The yield level in the states of Punjab and Haryana are high to the tune of 4.0-4.5 t/ha Other states like Gujarat, West Bengal, Himachal Pradesh and Karnataka also have significant area under wheat cultivation (Table 1.15).

TABLE 1.15: State-wise area, production and yield of wheat, 2001-02

States	Area (m.ha)	Production (m. t)	Yield (kg/ha)
Bihar	2.13	4.38	2056
Gujarat	0.47	1.15	2435
Haryana	2.30	9.44	4103
Himachal Pradesh	0.37	0.60	1609
Karnataka	0.26	0.19	754
Madhya Pradesh	3.43	5.63	1642
Maharashtra	0.78	1.08	1388
Punjab	3.42	15.49	4532
Rajasthan	2.29	6.39	2793
Uttar Pradesh	9.08	25.02	2755
West Bengal	0.43	0.96	2215
All India	**25.92**	**71.81**	**2770**

Source: Agricultural statistics at a glance-2003

Usage of wheat

Bulk of the wheat is produced and consumed in northern and western India. Wheat is consumed in the form of roti, puri, paratha or suji halwa prepared from atta, maida or suji. In North India, 75 % of the households eat more than 40 kg wheat products per month. Wheat is eaten as atta in the North and West, in the South and East as maida and suji. Rava is consumed mainly in the South. Pasta is a mixture of flour and salt. Pasta products comprise vermicelli, noodles, macaroni and spaghetti. Europe is the major consumer of pasta products. The main bakery products of wheat are biscuits, bread and cake/ pastry.

Types of wheat

Cultivation of wheat is older than the history of man. The common wheat would have originated in southwestern Asia and the durum wheat probably in the region of Abyssinia. Wheat comprises several species of Triticum, having diploids, tetraploids, and hexaploids with 7, 14 and 21 pairs of chromosomes respectively.

Out of 12 cultivated species of Triticum, four species are important: *T. aestivum, T. durum* (Desf.), *T. dicoccum* (schub L.) and *T. sphaerococcum.* Among them, *T. aestivum* and *T. durum* are known as spring wheat and adapted to sub- tropical and temperate regions. The spring types are characterised by a relatively much shorter duration (well below 175 days). Under most situations, the duration varies between 100 to 150 days depending on temperature.

In major parts of India, the spring type of wheat is grown. The other type of wheat, *T. dicoccum* and *T. sphaerococcum* are grown in temperate countries and are called winter wheat. They have long duration of around 250 days. These species have an obvious advantage of higher productivity due to the longer duration. However, these types cannot be grown in all parts of the world. Because of the longer duration only one crop can be cultivated in a year.

Bread wheat (T. aestivum)

This is the most important species cultivated in India occupying about 90 % of the total area under wheat. This is said to be mexican dwarf type introduced in India by Dr. N.E. Borlaug. This has 42 chromosomes. Varieties 'Sharbati Sonora' was introduced in 1965 and subsequently 'Kalyansona' in 1970. Important varieties of wheat developed by All India Co-ordinated Wheat Improvement Project (AICWIP) are:

Sonalika, Lerma Roja, Chhoti Lerma, Arjun, e. 306, WL 711, UP 2003, UP 262, LoK 1, HUW 206, HUW 234, HD 2189, HD2329, HD2285, Raj 3077, PBW 34, Raj 1555, WH 147, HP 1209, Sujatha, VL 421, VL 616, HS 240, HS 295, etc.

Wheat varieties recommended for different situation are listed below:

Irrigated condition	Normal sown	Sonalika, Kalyansona, Arjun, Girija, UP 301, UP 310, UP 319, Moti, HD 2122, Pratap, Choti Lerma and Safed Lerma
	Late sown	Sonalika, Janak, Sharbati Sonora and Shera
Rainfed	Normal sown	Kalyansona, Sonalika, Girija, Pratap and Janak
condition	Late sown	Kalyansona, Ridley, Janak, Mukta, and Girija

Durum wheat (T. durum Desf.)

It is the second major species of Triticum having 28 chromosomes. About 10 % of the total wheat production in the world is from durum type. In India, durum wheat production is estimated to be about 3-4 % of the total production. The kernels are typically larger, harder and heavier than the kernels of bread wheat. Varying environmental conditions and cultural practices influence the grain quality considerably. The crop cultivated on sandy soils and with less N fertilizers have much higher mottled grains. The crop is cultivated in dry and hot environment in Madhya Pradesh, Gujarat, Maharashtra, Karnataka and Southern Rajasthan. Though its productivity is less, the grain quality is good. Central and Peninsular India are favourable for the production of good quality grain with good hectoliter value, high protein and less yellow berry. Durum wheat cultivated in Punjab has high productivity; however, its quality is not very good. The ambient temperature during the crop season is comparatively cooler but the humidity is higher. Such a weather condition reduces the lustrousness of the grain and grain mottling increases. The grain is often rated unfit for exports. Durum wheat is extensively used for making instant foods such as semolina, macaroni, noodles and snack foods. In view of the limited availability of durum and greater demand for the valve- added products, always the FOB price of durum is higher than that of bread wheat. Globally, the U.S. and Canada are the major durum exporters.

Varieties: PDW 215, PDW 233, PDW 273, WH 896, Raj 1555, HI 8381, HI 8498, GW 1139.

Maize (*Zea mays*)

Maize or Indian corn is one of the most important cereals of the world. Physiologically maize is one of the most efficient species domesticated by man. Globally maize is cultivated in an area of 136.4 m.ha with the production of 602.6 m. t. (2002). The area, production and productivity over last 30 years are given in Table 1.16. Among the cereals, the productivity of maize is the highest (4.1 t/ha) as compared to rice (3.7 t/ha) and wheat (2.5 t/ha). About 40% of world maize production is from the United States followed by China. About 58% of the world maize production is in the developed countries with the USA as the major producer and exporter while about 22% is from developing countries. Other corn producing counties are China, Brazil, Mexico, Russia, India,

Indonesia and Philippines (Table 1.17).

TABLE 1.16: Maize production in the world

Year	Area (m.ha)	Production (m.t)	Yield (kg/ha)
1970	110.8	266.8	2410
1975	113.8	327.3	2849
1980	128.8	394.1	3060
1985	129.2	4848	3787
1990	127.4	479.1	3760
1995	136.2	514.5	3776
2000	138.2	592.3	4343

Source: FAO, 2003

TABLE 1.17: Maize production in the world, 2002

Country	Area (m.ha)	Production (m.t)	Yield (kg/ha)
Brazil	11.9	35.5	2989
China	24.5	123.2	5022
India	6.2	10.6	1705
Indonesia	3.3	9.3	2819
Mexico	7.2	17.5	2437
Philippines	2.4	4.3	1803
United States	28.1	228.8	8157
World	**136.4**	**602.6**	**4343**

Source: FAO, 2003

In India, maize occupies the third place among the cereals after wheat and rice. In 2000-01, it occupied 6.56 m.ha with the production of 12.1 m. t. The average productivity of maize in India is much lower (1.8 t/ha) than the world average (4.3 t/ha). The important states growing maize are Uttar Pradesh, Rajasthan, Madhya Pradesh, Bihar, Himachal Pradesh, Karnataka, Andhra Pradesh and Jammu & Kashmir.

These states account for about more than 80 % of the area and production (Table 1.18). According to some experts, India may have to produce 20 m.t of maize to meet its reqirement for human consumption, piggery, pharma industries and fodder by 2020 (Singhal, 1999).

TABLE 1.18: Production of maize in important states of India, 2000-01

States	Area (m.ha)	Production (m.t)	Yield (kg/ha)
Andhra Pradesh	0.52	1.43	2727
Bihar	0.64	1.46	723
Himachal Pradesh	0.29	0.68	2293
Jammu & Kashmir	0.33	0.53	1592
Karnataka	0.67	2.11	3157

States	Area (m.ha)	Production (m.t)	Yield (kg/ha)
Madhya Pradesh	0.82	1.20	1192
Rajasthan	0.97	1.02	1047
Uttar Pradesh	0.91	0.49	1633
All India	**6.56**	**12.07**	**1841**

Source: Agricultural statistics at a glance-2003

Usage of maize

Maize is largely consumed as food in various forms. It is also used as animal feed, particularly for poultry. Green maize plants are used as succulent fodder. Popping the corn is a method of starch cookery. Maize is a raw material for a number of products viz., starch, glucose, dextrose, sorbitol, dextrine, high fructose syrup, maltodextrine, germ oil, germ meal, fibre and gluten products which have application in industries such as alcohol, textile, paper, pharmaceuticals, organic chemicals, cosmetics and edible oil. Maize-based industry is the driving force of the U.S. economy.

Maize Types

Maize is the native of the Americas. It is classified into seven groups based largely on the character of the kernels. They are pod corn, pop corn, flint corn, dent corn, flour corn, sweet corn and waxy corn.

1. **Pod corn (*Zea mays tunicata*):** The kernel is enclosed in a pod or husk; the ear formed is also enclosed in husk. Pod corn is also known as cow corn, forage corn and husk corn. It is not grown commercially.
2. **Pop corn (*Zea mays everta*):** The kernels are small and posses a higher %age of hard endosperm starch. The ability to pop is due to rapid expansion of moisture in each individual starch grain upon the application of heat.
3. **Flint corn (*Zea mays indurata*):** The kernels consist of endosperm with soft starch in the centre and completely enclosed by a very hard outer layer. The kernels shrink uniformly as they mature.
4. **Dent corn (*Zea mays indentata*):** The kernels are characterized by a depression or dent in the crown due to shrinkage during ripening in a deposit of soft starch at the crown. This group is most widely cultivated corn.
5. **Flour corn (*Zea mays amylacea*):** The kernels consist almost entirely of soft starch with a very thin layer of hard starch on the sides. They are also known as soft corn.
6. **Sweet corn (*Zea mays saccharata*):** The kernels are translucent, horny and more or less wrinkled in appearance when dry. They have a large proportion of sugar to starch and hence sweeter than other corns.
7. **Waxy corn (*Zea mays ceratina*):** The endosperm looks waxy when the kernel is cut or broken. These types are used for making adhesives and for textile and paper sizing.

Important varieties of maize

- ***Very early maturing types:*** Sathi, Kathri, Teen Pakhia
- ***Medium early maturing:*** Basi, KT 41, Jaunpur, Rudrapur Local
- ***Late maturing:*** Malan

Hybrids and composites

- ***Hybrids:*** Ganga 1, Ganga 101, Ranjit, Deccan, Ganga 5, Ganga safed -2, Hi-Starch, Ganga -4, Himalayan 123, Ganga 3, V.L. 54, Shakti 1
- ***Composites:*** Vijay, Amber, Sona, Kisan, Jawahar, Vikram, Ageti 76, Pratap, Navjot, Prabhat
- ***Nutritionally superior maize composites:*** Shakti, Rattan, Protina
- The composite seeds can be used for subsequent sowing.

Barley (*Hordeum* spp.)

Barley is believed to have originated in Abyssinia and Southeastern Asia. It is an important cereal crop in the world cultivated in temperate and sub-tropical areas. It ranks fourth with respect to area and production among cereals after wheat, rice and maize. It occupies about 9.4% of the total cereal acreage with about 7.8% of the total cereal production in the world. In 2002, production was 132.2 m. t. from an area of 52.2 m. ha. The average productivity is 2.5 t/ha. Barley is cultivated in Russia, Canada, France, Spain, U.K. Germany, Turkey, Australia, Morocco and Ethiopia. In India, it is an important *rabi* (winter) cereal cultivated in an area of 0.67 m.ha with the annual production of 1.42 m.t. The average productivity of barley is 2.1 t/ha. Barley is predominantly grown in Uttar Pradesh. Other states are Rajasthan, Madhya Pradesh, Haryana, Punjab, Bihar and Himachal Pradesh.

Barley grains are mainly used for the purpose of malting. Barley is highly nutritious containing 10% protein, 64% CHO, minerals and fibres. They are also used as feed for cattle and horses and the straw is also fed to cattle.

Types of barley

Based on the number of rows of grain and their arrangement, barley is grouped into three types (Aberg and wiebe): *Hordeum vulgare* (six - row barley); *H. distichum* (two -row type barley); and *H. irregulare* (irregular barley with tough rachis). Among them, *H. vulgare* is the most important group that is grown widely in the United States.

Based on the season of cultivation, it is grouped as spring and winter barley. Spring barley is mostly grown in many parts the world. Winter barley is of longer duration than spring types. Barley is highly drought-tolerant and can be grown with less soil moisture.

Varieties: C 164, Kailash, Amber, Vijaya, Ratna, Jyoti, R.S. 6, Azad, Himani, Dolma, K 169, K 125, K 141, Lokhan.

Oats (*Avena sativa*)

The common oats in its cultivated form is believed to be of Asiatic origin. Among the cereals, oats ranks fifth in position after wheat, rice, maize and barley. It is cultivated in an area of 13.5 m.ha with a production of 25.5 m.t in 2002. The average productivity of oats is 1897 kg/ha. Oats is widely grown in cooler and more temperate countries like Russia, USA, Canada, Germany, Poland, France, Sweden, Australia, Finland and Spain. About 50% of production is from USA and Canada.

In India, it is cultivated in Punjab, Haryana and Uttar Pradesh. Oats is mainly used as feed and for preparation of breakfast cereal. Oats is a valuable food grain for all classes of livestock, particularly for horses, poultry and breeding stock. A liquid aldehyde, furfural, is the most valuable industrial product from the oats hulls. The hulls are used to make pharmaceutical products.

Rye (*Secale cereale*)

Rye is believed to have originated from Asia minor. The crop is highly frost - hardy and can withstand cold better than other cereals. Rye is an important bread grain, particularly in parts of northern Europe with poor soils and severe winters. The leading countries growing rye are the Russia, Poland, Germany, Czech Republic, Slovakia, Hungary and USA. Bread made from rye is cheap and widely consumed in northern Europe. Rye grain is fed to livestock mixed with other cereals. Straw is a useful bedding material.

MILLETS

A group of cereal crops is called millets. They are warm weather cereals with small grains. They are grouped into major and minor millets. Sorghum and pearl millet are known as major millets. Millets serve as the staple food for the people in the arid and semi-arid tropics.

Millets are grown for food and fodder. Small millets are the staple food crops of the working class. These crops are risk alleviating for the small farmers. Cultivation of small millets stretches from sea level to almost 1828 metres above mean sea level. Finger millet, kodo and barnyard millets have the capacity to produce more than 2000 kg/ha. The small millets have a wide adaptability and can be grown in extreme soil and climatic conditions. In all small millet-growing states (Tamil Nadu, Madhya Pradesh, Orissa and Bihar), the crops are extremely important to tribal farmers because of their earliness and providing grain as well as fodder. Small millets are practically devoid of grain storage pests and have long storage life. Bread could be prepared from finger millet for diabetic patients. Small millets could be popped or flaked. Finger millet is used for malting and brewing. Malted finger millet is used in infant food and in milk thickness formulations. Finger millet malt brewed with an equal proportion produces beer of commercial standards.

Nutritional value: Millet grains are highly nutritious and even superior to major cereals (rice and wheat) in many respects. They provide cheap protein, minerals and vitamins to the poorest of the poor where the need for such ingredients is the maximum. The dehusked prosomillet has a protein content of 12. 5 % compared to wheat (11.8 %). Finger millet contains high amount of Ca (344 mg/100 g) as that of wheat grain (41 mg/100 g).

Sorghum (*Sorghum bicolor*)

Sorghum is called as 'camel of crops' since it can withstand drought greatly. It is also known as great millet. It is believed that cultivated sorghum originated in east central Africa. Sorghum is mainly cultivated in the Semi-Arid Tropics and is extensively grown in Africa, Asia and north America.

It is cultivated in an area of 42.6 m. ha with an annual production of 69.0 m.t. The average yield is 1.5 t/ha. Africa and Asia alone contribute 82 % area and 45% of world production. India contributes about 83 % area in South East Asia and 22 % of world acreage (Table 1.19).

TABLE 1.19: Area and production of sorghum in the world, 2002

Continent/Country	Area (m. ha)	Production (m.t)	Yield (kglha)
Africa	23.6	20.3	861
North America	2.9	9.4	3179
Asia	11.4	10.9	959
India	9.5	7.1	743
World	**42.6**	**69.0**	**1463**

Source: FAO, 2003

In India, the share of sorghum out of total cropped area is about 7% and it contributes about 6.2 % of total food grain production. Among the cereals, it ranks third in area and production after rice and wheat in India. Though cultivated area of sorghum has remained static, production and productivity have almost doubled in 1980-81 compared to 1950's. Currently it is cultivated in an area of 9.93 m.ha with an annual production of 7.8 m. t. Maharashtra, Karnataka, Madhya Pradesh, Andhra Pradesh, Rajasthan, Tamil Nadu, Uttar Pradesh and Gujarat are the important states growing sorghum (Table 1.20 and 1.21).

TABLE 1.20: Area, production and productivity of sorghum in India

Year	Area (m. ha)	Production (m.t)	Yield (kglha)
1950-51	15.6	5.5	353
1960-61	18.4	9.8	533
1970-71	17.4	8.1	466
1980-81	15.8	10.4	660
1990-91	14.4	11.7	814
2000-01	8.86	7.63	764

Source: Agricultural statistics at a glance-2003

TABLE 1.21: Important states growing sorghum in India, 2001-02

States	Area (m. ha)	Production (m. t)	Yield (kg/ha)
Andhra Pradesh	0.64	0.63	992
Gujarat	0.18	0.17	928
Karnataka	1.79	1.44	804
Madhya Pradesh	0.64	0.59	918
Maharashtra	5.14	3.91	761
Rajasthan	0.61	0.25	414
Tamil Nadu	0.47	0.46	978
Uttar Pradesh	0.31	0.30	949
All India	**9.93**	**7.79**	**785**

Source: Agricultural statistics at a glance-2003

Sorghum is grown both in *kharif* and *rabi* seasons. *Rabi* sorghum is grown under receding moisture condition leading to terminal drought in Maharashtra, Karnataka and Andhra Pradesh where winter is relatively warmer. Moisture stress, poor soil fertility and susceptibility to shoot fly, lodging, charcoal rot and cold are the major yield constraints.

Sorghum types

Sorghum is broadly classified into four agronomic groups: grain sorghum, sorgos, broomcorn and grass sorghum. Grain sorghum is mainly used for grain purpose and also for forage and silage. Sorgos is otherwise called as sweet sorghum. Broomcorn is used for the manufacture of brooms. Grass sorghum may be annual or perennial and is used for hay or pasture.

Grain sorghum

Sorghum grain is used as food in India but used as cheap source of feed for poultry and cattle industry. They also serve as raw material for industrial starch and alcohol production.

Varieties: CSV–1 (Swarna), CSV-2 (302), CSV–3 (CS3541), CSV-4 (168), CSV-5, CSV-6, CSV-7.

Hybrids: CSH-1, CSH-2, CSH-3, CSH-4, CSH-5, CSH-6, CSH-7, CSH-8, CSH-9, CSH-10, CSH-11, CSH -13, CSH -15 R (CSH-9-ruling *Kharif* hybrid, CSH-15R-ruling *rabi* hybrid)

Sweet sorghum (*Sorghum bicolor*)

It has a juicy pitch and produces small amount of grain as compared to grain sorghum. Grains are used for making flour. Stalks are rich in sugar and used for alcohol preparation. The straw residue after extracting sugary juice is used as livestock feed. Jaggery and crystalline sugar can also be made from sweet sorghum.

A sweet - stalked variety 'SSV 84'was released in 1992 with 51. 4 t/ ha green cane yield, 17.8% brix content and 1.88 t/ha grain yield. This variety could be utilized only for raw sugar (jaggery) production due to crystallization problem. Such sorghum is a best alternative for sugarcane in areas where sugarcane cannot be economically grown. It is also possible to produce ethanol from grains and juice of sweet sorghum.

Forage sorghum

The average yield in the demonstration plots in farmers' fields is 40-50 t/ ha green fodder with best yield upto 60 t/ha. Multicut varieties: Pusa chari (PC 23), Haryana Chari (JS 73/53), SL 44, Meeti Sudan (SSG 59-3). Hybrids: Proagro Chari, MFSH-3; Hara Sona, PC 106. Recently released cultivars, CSH 13 and CSH 15 offer distinctly both high fodder and grain yield.

Pearl millet (*Pennisetum glaucum*)

It is also known as cattail millet or bulrush millet. This is an important crop in arid regions of Africa and Asia. It probably originated in tropical Africa. In USA, it is raised as a pasture crop. Pearl millet is the fourth important food crop in India next to rice, wheat and sorghum and the second major coarse cereal grain after sorghum. Pearl millet is extensively cultivated in poor fertile and water- deficit soils, mostly under low and erratic rainfall. Pearlmillet is grown in semi-arid and arid climate of tropical and sub-tropical regions. Globally it is cultivated in an area of 36.5 m.ha with the total production of 29.6 m.t. The average productivity is 745 kg/ha (1995-96). India is the largest producer of pearl millet in the world. Area under pearl millet was 9.0 m. ha during 1950-51 and increased to 12.9 m. ha during 1970-71. The area, however, decreased to 9.83 m. ha during 2000-01. However, the production increased from 2.6 m.t. in 1950-51 to 8.0 m.t. in 1970-71. There was significant increase in yield from 288 kg/ha in 1950-51 to 688 kg/ha in 2000-01 (Table 1.22).

Principal pearl millet growing states are Rajasthan, Maharashtra, Gujarat, Uttar Pradesh, Haryana and Karnataka which account for 90 % of the total area and 86 % of production (Table 1.23). Pearl millet is cultivated in areas with the rainfall of 150 to 700 mm. It is largely grown for home and local consumption and the marketable surplus is limited. Pearl millet can substitute wheat and rice in processed foods. The development of alternative foods adds value to commercial exploitation of this millet.

TABLE 1.22: Area, production and productivity of pearl millet, India

Year	Area (m.ha)	Production (m.t)	Yield (kg/ha)
1950-51	9.0	2.6	288
1960-61	11.5	3.3	286
1970-71	12.9	8.0	622
1980-81	11.7	5.3	458
1990-91	10.5	6.9	658
2000-01	9.83	6.76	688

Source: Agricultural statistics at a glance-2003

TABLE 1.23: Major states growing pearl millet in India, 2001-02

States	Area (m.ha)	Production (m. t)	Yield (kg/ha)
Andhra Pradesh	0.09	0.07	761
Gujarat	0.94	1.26	1344
Haryana	0.59	0.83	1423
Karnataka	0.21	0.11	531
Madhya Pradesh	0.16	0.21	1287
Maharashtra	1.40	0.83	594
Rajasthan	5.11	3.80	744
Tamil Nadu	0.18	0.26	1445
Uttar Pradesh	0.84	0.95	1136
Total	**9.55**	**8.35**	**875**

Source: Agricultural statistics at a glance-2003

Varietal Status

Pearlmillet as a plant does not resist the drought but cuts short its life cycle and comes to flowering early under such adverse condition and this can grow in areas that have extended dry periods. The adoption of high-yielding varieties has stabilized production even during the drought years. Hybrids have a higher yield potential than improved varieties. The hybrids and the improved varieties have given more than 2000 kg /ha grain in Gujarat, Haryana and Andhra Pradesh.

Varieties: CO 1, CO 2, CO 3, CO 4, CO 5, K 1, X 3, for Tamil Nadu, Bajra 207, Bajra 28-15, L-17, Baroda and Babapuri for Gujarat and Maharashtra, RSK and RSJ for Rajasthan, T-55, S 350, S-530 and S 28 for Punjab and Uttar Pradesh.

Hybrids: India has the privilege of being the first country in releasing hybrids in pearl millet. HB 3 is the most popular hybrid because of its shorter maturity, bold grains and adaptability to moisture stress conditions. Adoption of these hybrids led to 75-100% increase in yield over local varieties. Other hybrids are NHB 3, NHB 4, NHB 5, BK 560, MH 179, ICMH 451 and Pusa 23.

Composites: There are recurring problems of downy mildew in hybrids which has resulted in release of several composite varieties which yield as much as hybrids. They are adaptable to diverse environments and have more durable resistance to downy mildew than the genetically uniform hybrids. eg. WCC 75, ICTP 8203, Raj 171, ICMV 221, Pusa Bajra 266.

Downy mildew resistance types: Downy mildew (*Sclerospora graminicola*) is the most important biotic factor limiting pearl millet production. Some of the composites (WCC 75, MP 171) and hybrids (ICMS 451, Pusa 23) show resistance to downy mildew.

MINOR MILLETS

Small millets may be defined as millets cultivated for their small grains which are borne on short, slender, grassy plants. They are also known as minor millets. The list of minor millets is given in Table 1.24. Small millets are mainly grown in arid, semi-arid or mountain zones as rainfed crops in marginal and submarginal soils. They have the capacity of growing during adverse soil and climatic conditions and several of their varieties are of short duration (60-80 days) producing about 0.5 t/ha which is better than no crop. Some of the millets are ideal for contingency crop planning to take advantage of late receipt of rains, failure of the first crop due to unexpected long drought or even receding flood situations.

They are distributed in most of the Asian and African countries and parts of Europe. Finger millet is the principal small millet grown in South Asia. Foxtail millet and prosomillet are important in China and prosomillet is grown extensively in the South Western Russia. In Africa, finger millet is of local importance. Some of the small millets are grown in the United States and Europe on a very limited scale. The small millets contribute about 1 % of the world food production.

The small millets occupy about 3.0 %. of area and about 2.0 % to the total food grain production and contribute about 2 % of cereal grain production. Finger millet is cultivated in an area of 1.7 m. ha with the production of 2.3 m. t.

TABLE 1.24: List of minor millets

Name	Botanical name
1. Finger millet (Ragi)	*Eleursine coracana*
2. Proso millet (common millet)	*Panicum miliaceum*
5. Foxtail millet (Italian millet)	*Setaria italica*
6. Little millet	*Panicum sumatrense*
3. Banyard millet	*Echinochloa colona*
4. Kodo millet	*Paspalum scrobiculatum*

The productivity of finger millet is the highest (1.3 t/ha) among the millets. Other small millets are grown in 1.5 m.ha and total production is 0.66 m.t. The productivity of small millets is lowest (about 500 kg / ha) largely due to poor fertility of soils in which they are grown and non-adoption of improved package of practices. Small millets are predominantly grown in Karnataka, Tamil Nadu, Maharashtra, Andhra Pradesh, Uttar Pradesh, Bihar, Orissa and Madhya Pradesh. These states contribute about 90% of the area and production.

Varieties of minor millets

- ***Finger millet:*** Sharada, Godavari, Kalyani, Simhadri, BR 407, Gujarat Nagi, Indaf- I, 3,8, Dibyasingha, CO 12, Paiyur- 1, K 7, Nirmal
- ***Kodomillet:*** Jawahar, Kodo 1, Gujarat, Kodra 1, CO 2, CO 3
- ***Foxtail millet:*** Chitra, SIA 326, CO 2, CO 4
- ***Little millet:*** Gujarat, Vari 1, indori 2, CO 1, CO 2, K1
- ***Proso millet:*** Ramcheena, Shyamcheema, Varada, CO 2, CO 3, CO 4
- ***Barnyard millet:*** Anurag, RAU 3, Banti 1, K 2, CO1

PULSES

Pulses belong to the family *leguminaceae*. The grains are used for staple purpose and hence called as grain legumes. In the world, pulses are grown in an area of 69.8 m.ha with the production of 55.2 m.t. (2001-02). China, India and Russia are the important countries growing pulses. India accounts for about 32.8 % of the area and 25 % world production in 2002. Yield level in India is much lower (600 kg/ha) than the world average (790 kg/ha). The commonly grown pulse crops in India are given in Table 1.25.

In India, pulse area and production slowly increased from 19.1 m.ha in 1950 to 20.4 m.ha in 2000-01. The area and production have not increased; rather there was a reduction in the period, 1960-1980. There was also not appreciable increase in the yield level over the years. The yield level slightly increased from 441 to 544 kg/ha during 1950-2000. However, there were fluctuations over the years. Production of pulses fluctuates depending upon the monsoon behaviour. Pulses are largely grown on marginal lands, mostly under rainfed conditions. There was virtually no breakthrough in developing improved and high yielding varieties. (Table 1.26).

TABLE 1.25: Pulses grown in India

Crop	Botanical name
Chickpea or Bengal gram	*Cicer arietinum* (L.)
Pigeonpea or redgram or Arhar	*Cajanus cajan* (L.)
Blackgram or urd bean	*Phaseolus mungo* (L.)
Green gram or mungbean	*Phaseolus aureus (Roxb.)*
Cowpea	*Vigna unguiculata*
Lentil	*Lens culinaris*
Mothbean	*Vigna aconitifolia (Jaeq.)*

Crop	Botanical name
Horse gram	*Dolichos biflorus*
Lab – lab	*Dolichos lab lab*
Rajmash	*Phaseolus vulgaris* (L.)
Lathyrus	*Lathyrus sativus*
Pea	*Pisum sativum*

TABLE 1.26: Area, production and productivity of pulse in India

Year	Area (m.ha)	Production (m.t)	Yield (kg/ha)
1950-51	19.1	8.4	441
1960-61	23.6	12.7	539
1970-71	22.5	11.8	524
1980-81	22.5	10.6	473
1990-91	24.7	14.3	578
2000-01	20.4	11.1	544

Source: Agricultural statistics at a glance-2003

Among the pulses, chickpea and pigeonpea are the important crops accounting for 50 % of pulse area and 60 % of total production. Madhya Pradesh Uttar Pradesh, Maharashtra, Rajasthan, Andhra Pradesh, Karnataka, Bihar, Chattisgarh, Gujarat and Tamil Nadu, Orissa account for about 95 % of production. (Table 1.27). Pulses are grown in *kharif* and *rabi* seasons. Pigeonpea, greengram, blackgram, horsegram, mothbean, cowpea are known as *kharif* pulses. Chickpea, drypea, lentil, and lathyrus are known as *rabi* pulses. The *rabi* pulses contribute about 60% of the world pulse production. In India, out of total acreage, 45 % is *kharif* pulse which account for about 35 % of pulse production. *Rabi* pulses contribute 55 % of the total area and about 65 % of production.

Increasing pulse production

Pulses represent a group of crops and each crop has its own requirement for inputs and environment. Hence individual consideration is required for enhancing the production.

Production of french beans and mungbean with a growing export market should be stepped up by intensification of their cultivation. Cultivation of french beans during *rabi* season in non-traditional areas of northern plains and other suitable pockets should receive greater attention. There is ample scope of bringing more area under spring or summer cultivation of mungbean in northern India. High yielding and stress-resistant varieties should get top priority in the pulse-improvement programme.

There is a good scope of expansion of area under pulses in various inter, relay or sequential cropping systems to increase the productivity per unit area. Rice fallows should get maximum attention to grow pulse crops.

TABLE 1.27: Area, production and yield of pulses for important pulse growing states, 2001-02

States	Area (m. ha)	Production (m.t)	Yield (kg/ha)
Andhra Pradesh	1.91	1.14	596
Bihar	0.70	0.56	802
Chhattisgarh	0.82	0.42	514
Gujarat	0.73	0.38	525
Haryana	0.19	0.15	796
Jharkand	0.12	0.09	807
Karnataka	1.89	0.76	399
Madhya Pradesh	3.83	3.02	789
Maharashtra	3.39	1.88	555
Orissa	0.73	0.28	379
Rajasthan	3.6	1.43	425
Tamil Nadu	0.68	0.29	426
Uttar Pradesh	2.70	2.39	884
West Bengal	0.25	0.18	703
All India	**21.66**	**13.19**	**609**

Source: Agricultural statistics at a glance-2003

Economic importance of pulses

Pulses are unique as they have an in-built mechanism to fix atmospheric N in their root nodules. Pulses are important for maintaining soil health and sustainability of different cropping systems. Generally they are short duration crops and fit well in various cropping systems. Inclusion of pulses in cereal based cropping systems is considered as a component of integrated nutrient management. Their cultivation economises nitrogen to the tune of 30-40 kg/ha for succeeding cereal crop and also improve soil health.

Pulses have a unique position in dryland/rainfed agriculture. Pulses have an inherent quality to trap the moisture from lower strata of the soil and they are considerably moisture stress (drought) tolerant and fits well in rainfed environment. The heavy leaf drop increases the organic matter in the soil. Pulses are also used as valuable fodder for the cattle.

Pulses occupy an important place in meeting the protein needs of people in the developing countries. The protein content of various pulses ranges from 20-25 %. Pulses are not only rich in protein but also have essential amino acids compared to cereal protein (Table 1.28). They provide energy to the tune of 372 K.cal/100 g. They also contain other nutrients such as Ca, Fe and vitamins viz., ß-carotene, thiamine, riboflavin, niacine. In India, cereals and pulses generally account for about two-third of the dietary intake. For the vegetarian diet, pulses are the major source of nutrition. The Indian Council of Medical Research has recommended pulses intake of 50 g/capita/day.

TABLE 1.28: Amino acids composition (mg/100 g) of

Amino acid	Animal	Cereal	Pulses
Isoleucine	46.7	39.8	45.3
Leucine	79.6	86.3	78.9
Lysine	84.3	30.5	67.1
Methionine & Cystine	37.7	41.1	25.3
Tryptophan	11.4	12.1	12.3

Chickpea or Bengal gram

The crop probably originated from west Asia. This is an important pulse crop in India. About 70 % of world production of chickpea comes from Asia. Among the pulses, chickpea occupies about 30 % of area and 40 % of production in India. The crop is chiefly grown in cool, dry periods on receding soil moisture. About 55 % of the crop is cultivated as rainfed. Chickpea is predominantly grown in North India. Madhya Pradesh, Rajasthan, Uttar Pradesh, Rajasthan, Maharashtra, Karnataka, Haryana and Bihar contribute about 90 % of area and 95 % of the production. The average yield of the crop is about 865 kg/ha (Table 1.29)

TABLE 1.29: Important states growing chickpea in India, 2001-02

States	Area (m.ha)	Production (m.t)	Yield (kg/ha)
Bihar	0.07	0.07	987
Haryana	0.15	0.12	855
Karnataka	0.28	0.29	606
Madhya Pradesh	2.22	2.20	989
Maharashtra	0.76	0.45	595
Rajasthan	0.97	0.74	759
Uttar Pradesh	0.86	0.83	960
All India	**6.10**	**5.27**	**865**

***Source*:** Agricultural statistics at a glance-2003

There are two types of chickpea, 'desi' and 'kabuli' types. The former has small sized seeds with coloured seed coat. They are mainly cultivated in Eastern Africa. The 'kabuli' types have large sized seeds with white seed coat. The seeds are consumed whole after cooking or as dhal. Soaked grain and husk are fed to cattle.

Varieties for different situations

- *Important varieties:* Radhey, G-235, C-104, BR 78, R11, Gwalior-2, Vikas, Vishwas, Ujjain-21
- *Drought tolerant:* RS 10, G 24, T3, T87
- *Late sown situation:* JG 74, Strain 76, G 235, Pant G 114
- *Ascochyta blight resistant:* Gaurav, GNG 146, Pusa 261, PBG 1

- *Wilt Resistant:* Pusa 212, JG 315, BG 244, Phule G 81-1-1, ICCV 10, Pusa 10003 (Kabuli)

Pigeonpea, Redgram or Arhar

The origin of pigeonpea is now considered to be the peninsular India. About 90% of the world's pigeonpea is produced in India. It is a perennial shrub and a short day plant. The crop is grown as an annual crop in India and as a perennial in many other countries where the pods are harvested at regular interval. The crop has a deep root system and hence highly drought tolerant. In India, pigeonpea is the second important pulse crop occupying about 15 % of the area and total pulse production. It is predominantly cultivated in Maharashtra, Uttar Pradesh, Madhya Pradesh, Andhra Pradesh, Gujarat, Karnataka etc. These states contribute about 85% of the area and the production (Table 1.30).

TABLE 1.30: Important states growing pigeonpea in India, 2001-02

States	Area ('000)	Production ('000 t)	Yield (kg/ha)
Andhra Pradesh	0.42	0.19	449
Gujarat	0.33	0.19	449
Karnataka	0.48	0.15	303
Madhya Pradesh	0.33	0.28	837
Maharashtra	1.02	0.77	757
Orissa	0.14	0.08	555
Tamil Nadu	0.06	0.04	658
Uttar Pradesh	0.40	0.45	1142
All India	**3.38**	**2.30**	**681**

Source: Agricultural statistics at a glance-2003

Varieties of Pineonpea

- *Extra- early varieties (120-130 days):* Prabhat, Pant A1, Pant A 3
- *Early varieties (140-160 days):* T21, BS 1, Khargona 2, UPAS 120, Pusa Ageti, Pusa 74
- *Medium –maturing varieties (160-200 days):* Mukta, sharda, C-11, BDN 1, SA 1
- *Late-maturing type (230-260 days):* Gwalior 3, Sweta, NP (WR) 15
- *Mosaic resistant:* Bihar, DA 11
- *Hybrids:* ICPH 8, COPH1, COPH2, PPH 4
- *Wilt resistant:* NP (WR) 15, BDN 1, BDN 2, Mukta, Sharda

Green gram or Mungbean

Mungbean originated in India. The crop is widely cultivated throughout Southern Asia and to a smaller extent in parts of Africa. In India, it is the third important pulse crop and mostly cultivated in southern and eastern states in the rice fallow condition (January-April). It is quite versatile crop grown for seeds, green manure and forage as mixed or sole crop either on residual moisture of the previous crop or as a catch crop to make use of the land left idle between two main season crops. In north India, it is grown in summer season because of its shorter duration. The seeds are highly nutritious with protein content of 23-24%. The whole or split grains are used as a pulse. The straw and husks are fed to cattle.

Some of the promising early-maturing (60-65 days) high yielding varieties are PDM 11, PDM 54, Pusa 105. Varieties identified as resistant to yellow-mosaic virus are Pusa 101, Pusa 105, Hyb 12-4, Hyb 4-3, ML 131, Punt Mung-1.

Black gram or Urd bean

The primary centre of origin of this crop is India and its secondary origin is Central Asia. This is an important pulse crop in India, Pakistan, Myanmar and some parts of South East Asia, parts of Africa and America. It is a warm weather crop and cultivated in rainy, winter, spring and summer seasons in various parts of the country. The crop is predominantly grown in Andhra Pradesh, Madhya Pradesh, Orissa, Maharashtra, Karnataka, Uttar Pradesh and West Bengal. It is a highly prized pulse crop and rich in phosphoric acid The grains are used for various food preparations.

The variety 'T9' is early maturing (75-80 days) suitable for all seasons throughout the country. Powdery mildew resistant genotype, ' LBG 17' opened new vistas for its cultivation in the rice fallows of coastal Andhra Pradesh in *rabi*.

Other pulses

- **Cowpea** is a dual purpose crop used for fodder and grain. Green tender pods are used as a vegetable.
- **Lentil** is of two types: large seeded with yellow cotyledons and small seeded with pink cotyledons. The latter is mostly grown in India. Lentil is cooked whole or used as *dhal*.
- **Moth bean** is mostly grown as a dry crop and highly useful against wind-erosion. It is used as a green vegetable or whole grain as pulse.
- **Horse gram** is grown over a wide range of soils, mostly on poor or laterite soils of India. It is grown mainly as a rainfed crop. The grain is used as human food and also as a concentrate feed for cattle.
- **Lab-lab** is a perennial twining or creeping legume. There are two types: garden and field varieties and are used as grain, vegetable and fodder.
- **Rajmash** is cultivated in the sub-Himalayan 'terai' and partly in Satara district of Maharashtra.
- **Lathyrus** can withstand extreme moisture conditions. It is grown on the residual moisture under *'paira'* or *'utera'* cropping. The crop is mostly used as fodder. The grain is used as pulse by the poor people during scarcity period. When eaten in large quantity over a long

period, it initiates a physiological disease in human beings, lathyrism.

- **Peas** are one of the important pulses in the Indo- Gangetic plains. Unripe pods are used as a green vegetable. Broken parts of the pods are fed to cattle.

OILSEEDS

Oilseeds are grown widely in countries/regions such as India, China, Argentina, Canada, France, Nigeria, North Central America, USA and Western Europe. Soybean, groundnut, rapeseed and sunflower are the important oilseeds worldwide. Area, production and yield of different oilseeds are given in the Table 1.31.

In India, oilseeds are cultivated in an area of about 22.8 m. ha (2001-02). Compared to 10.7. m.ha in 1950-51, the area increased to 24.1 m.ha in 1990-91 and it declined to 22.8 m.ha in 2000-01. Production was 5.2 m.t. in 1950-51 and increased to 18.6 m.t in 1990-91 and it maintained in 2000-01.

TABLE 1.31: World production of major oilseeds, 2002

Oilseeds	Area (m.ha)	Production (m.t)	Yield (kg/ha)
Castor	1.1	1.1	1000
Groundnut	24.7	34.1	1381
Linseed	2.6	2.0	786
Rapeseed	22.3	33.2	1486
Safflower	0.8	0.6	796
Sesamum	7.3	2.8	388
Soybean	7.9	180.0	2266
Sunflower	18.9	23.9	1260

Source: FAO, 2003

Before 1985, the aggregate output of oilseeds did not cross 12-13 m.t. To bridge the gap between demand and supply and considering the mounting imports of vegetable oils, the Government of India set up a Technology mission on Oilseeds in 1986. The objective was to integrate all the facts and sectors of oilseeds under a common programme for breaking the stagnation in the oilseeds front. The current oilseed production in India is 20.8 m.t. The yield level has also increased substantially from 481 kg/ha in 1950 to 913 kg/ha in 2000-01 (Table 1.32).

TABLE 1.32: Area, production and productivity of oilseeds in India, 1950-96

Year	Area (m.ha)	Production (m.t.)	Yield (kg/ha)
1950-51	10.7	5.2	481
1960-61	13.8	7.0	507
1970-71	16.8	9.6	579
1980-81	17.6	9.4	532

Year	Area (m.ha)	Production (m.t.)	Yield (kg/ha)
1990-91	24.1	18.6	771
2000-01	22.8	15.8	913

Source: Agricultural statistics at a glance-2003
(1950-70: Oilseeds relate to groundnut, castor, sesamum, rapeseed, mustard and linseed only).

Important states growing oilseeds in India are Madhya Pradesh, Gujarat, Rajasthan, Maharashtra, Andra Pradesh, Tamil Nadu, Karnataka, Uttar Pradesh, Haryana and West Bengal. These states contribute 95% of the area and production in India (Table 1.33). The average yield of oilseeds in India is 913 kg/ha. However, compared to world average (1350 kg/ha), the country's average yield is very low. (about one-third only).

TABLE 1.33: Oilseed production in important states of India, 2001-02

States	Area ('000)	Production ('000)	Yield (kg/ha)
gAndhra Pradesh	2.44	1.61	661
Assam	0.31	0.16	506
Bihar	0.15	0.13	816
Gujarat	2.86	3.70	1294
Haryana	0.55	0.81	1477
Karnataka	1.74	1.06	612
Madhya Pradesh	5.47	4.44	812
Maharashtra	2.36	2.23	943
Orissa	0.31	0.14	453
Punjab	0.09	0.10	1058
Rajasthan	3.10	3.13	1008
Tamil Nadu	0.96	1.43	1496
Uttar Pradesh	1.24	1.05	842
West Bengal	0.60	0.49	816
All India	**22.78**	**20.80**	**913**

Source: Agricultural statistics at a glance-2003

Nine oilseed crops primarily grown in India are groundnut, rapeseed-mustard, soybean, sunflower, sesamum, castor, safflower, niger and linseed. Among them, groundnut and rapeseed-mustard are the two oilseeds that dominate the edible oil economy of the country, contributing about 66 % of production. The other oilseeds play a relatively lesser role. Currently soybean and sunflower have emerged as the major oilseeds with greater potential. Oilseeds are mainly cultivated during *kharif* season. However, important *rabi* season grown oilseeds are rapeseed-mustard, safflower and linseed.

Reasons for low productivity

About 90 % of the oilseed cultivation in India is under uncertain and abnormal weather conditions. Irregular rains and inadequate alternate irrigation sources at maturity largely affect the final yield. Unlike food crops, oilseed crops are grown under low management situations. Full package of practices is not followed since the major category of oilseed growers is small and marginal farmers. Poor plant population, inadequate plant protection, improper fertilizer application and poor adoption of post-harvest technology also contribute to low productivity.

Dietary need of fats and oils and use of oilseeds

Fats and oils are valuable food ingredients in human diet. They contain saturated and unsaturated fatty acids. Vegetable oils predominantly contain polyunsaturated fatty acids (PUFA). The two PUFA, linoleic and linolenic acids, cannot be synthesized by the body and hence must be supplied by the diet. They are called essential fatty acids. Vegetable oils of groundnut, sesamum and sunflower are rich in PUFA (Table 1.34). The country's per capita consumption of edible oils per annum is 7.5 kg which is far below the world's average of 15.3 kg.

TABLE 1.34: Fatty acid content and iodine value of oilseeds

Crops	Oil (%)	% Composition						
		Palmitic	Stearic	Oleic	Linoleic	Linolenic	Erucic	Iodine value
Groundnut (kernel)	44-50	6	5	61	22	-	-	101
Rapeseed	42-46	4	2	19	14	8	40	146
Soybean	17-22	12	2	24	54	8	-	134
Sunflower	36-38	8	5	21	66	11	-	134
Sesame	48-52	10	5	40	43	2	-	114
Safflower	30-32	8	3	13	75	1	-	146

Source: Weiss, 1983

Oilseeds are mainly used for extraction of edible oil. They also serve as an important raw material for the manufacture of soap, paint, varnish, hair oil, lubricants, etc. Commodities such as oilcakes, castor oil, high protein selects (HPS) groundnut, sesamum seed and extractions of rapeseed, sunflower and groundnut are the main export items. Oilmeal export during 2000-01 was 2.43 m. tonnes with a value of Rs. 2,044 crores.

Groundnut (*Arachis hypogaea* L.)

Groundnut is cultivated in tropical and sub-tropical countries. Brazil in South America is considered to be the country of its origin. Groundnut is primarily cultivated in USA, Nigeria, Senegal, Sudan, China, West Africa, Indonesia and India. It is grown in an area of 24.7 m.ha with an annual production of 34.1 m.t. in the world. India is the largest producer of groundnut. The crop was introduced to India during 16th century from one of the Pacific Islands of China. It ranks first both in respect of area and production contributing about 26 % of the area and 21 % of world production. Over the years, the area under groundnut has increased from 4.5 m.ha in 1950-51 to 8.3 m.ha in 1990-91. Similarly production has also doubled during this period from 3.5 m.t to 7.5 m.t. The increase in yield is due to adoption of high yielding varieties and improved production techniques. Average productivity of groundnut is about 977 kg/ha while the world average is 1100 kg/ha (Table 1.35).

Groundnut is predominantly grown in Saurashtra in Gujarat, parts of Tamil Nadu, Rayalseema area of Andhra Pradesh, Karnataka, Maharashtra, Rajasthan, Madhya Pradesh, Uttar Pradesh. These states contribute 95 % of total area and production (Table. 1.36). The crop is mainly grown in *kharif* under rainfed conditions. However, in Southern and Western India, cultivation of *rabi* groundnut is picking up. *Rabi* groundnut is usually raised with irrigation support. However, the season is not suitable for North Indian conditions due to cold temperature which adversely affects the crop growth.

In India, groundnut oil is popularly used for cooking. The HPS type of groundnut kernels are exported to foreign countries.

TABLE 1.35: Area, production and productivity of groundnut in India

Year	Area (m.ha)	Production ('000 ton)	Yield (kg/ha)
1950-51	4.5	3.5	775
1960-61	6.5	4.8	745
1970-71	7.3	6.1	834
1980-81	6.8	5.0	736
1990-91	8.3	7.5	904
2000-01	6.6	6.4	977

Source: Agricultural statistics at a glance-2003

TABLE 1.36: Groundnut production in important states of India, 2001-02

States	Area (m. ha)	Production (m.t)	Yield (kg/ha)
Andhra Pradesh	1.69	1.25	739
Gujarat	1.92	2.71	1412
Karnataka	0.86	0.60	702
Madhya Pradesh	0.24	0.26	1099
Maharashtra	0.43	0.49	1147
Rajasthan	0.24	0.30	1226
Tamil Nadu	0.77	1.33	1724
All India	**6.40**	**7.21**	**1125**

Source: Agricultural statistics at a glance-2003

Groundnut types and varieties

Groundnut is broadly grouped into two types: spreading (runner) and bunch varieties. The bunch type of groundnut has upright growth habit with long and erect main axis and the laterals are oblique to the main axis. The pods are clustered on the base of the plant. The spreading or runner types have very short and erect main stem and the laterals spread horizontally along the ground. In these types, the pods are scattered along the procumbent rooting stems.

Varieties

- ***Recently released varieties:*** BAU 13, Chitra, CSMG 84-1, DRG 12, GG 3, GG 20, IGGV 86325, IGGV 86 590, K 134, M 335, R 8804, TG 22, TAG 24, VRI 2, VRI 3, VRI 4
- ***Rainfed/ drought condition:*** AH 32, TMV 1, Spanish Improved, S-230, Jyoti, GAUG-1, DH 3-30, JL 24, Kadiri 71-1
- ***Export purpose (HPS):*** Polachi-1, BP-2
- ***Tikka resistant:*** TMV 9, C-501, DH 3-30
- ***Rust resistant:*** TMV 9
- ***Bud necrosis disease (PBND) resistant:*** Kadiri-3, ICGS 11, ICGS-14

Rapeseed-mustard

The crop requires cool temperature (18-25 °C) for satisfactory growth. Hence, it is mostly cultivated in the temperate and warm zones of Asia and Europe. The crop is predominantly cultivated in China, India and Pakistan and these countries contribute about 90 % of the world production. In India, the crop occupies a prestigious position accounting for 25.% of the total oilseed acreage and 30 % of total oil seed production. These crops are mainly grown in the northern part of India. About 60 % of the area and production is from Uttar Pradesh. Other states growing rapeseed-mustard are Rajasthan, Gujarat, Haryana, Madhya Pradesh, West Bengal, Assam and Punjab.

Cultivars and varieties

Rapeseed-mustard include the following groups:

1. Brown or Indian Mustard (rai or raya)	*Brassica juncea*
2. Sarson (Brown sarson)	*B. Campestris* var. brown sarson
Toria	*B. Campestris* var. *toria*
Yellow Sarson	*B. campestris* var. yellow sarson
3. Taramira or tara	*Eruca sativa*

About 70 % area is grown with brown or Indian mustard. *Sarson, toria and taramira* are commonly called as rapeseed. Yellow and brown *sarson* are widely grown in North and Central India. *Toria* is mostly cultivated as an irrigated crop. *Rai, sarson* and *tarmira* are usually cultivated under rainfed condition.

Varieties

- ***Indian mustard:*** Prakash, Varuna, Seetha, Kranti, *Krishna,* Vaibhav, Vardan, Rohini, 'Patan Mustard 67', Durgamani, Pusa Bold, Bhagirathi, RLM –619, RH 30, RH 81, RH 819, T 59
- ***Brown sarson:*** BSH1, Pusa Kalyani, KOS 1
- ***Toria:*** Agrani, Bhavani, Jowahar Toria 1, PT-30, PT-303, Sangam, TH 63, TL 15, RH 68, TCH 2
- ***Yellow sarson:*** Rajendra sarson 1, Subinoy, YS 92-3
- ***Taramira:*** RTM 314, T 27, TMC 1

The Indian mustard has a very high level of erucic acid in oil and glucosinolates in the meal. Erucic acid is to be removed before it can be used as edible oil for human consumption. Removal of glucosinolates in the meals has made it acceptable as cattle feed in the international markets. Some of the exotic varieties of rapeseed have low levels of erucic acid and glucosinolates ('0' or '00'varieties).

Soybean (*Glycine max*)

Soybean is predominantly cultivated in USA, Brazil and Argentina in South America. Soybean occupies an area of 79.4 m.ha with the production of 180 m.t. in 2002. In the Asia-pacific region, soybean is cultivated in China, Pakistan and India. The crop is cultivated in an area of 6.22 m.ha with the annual production of 5.86 m.t. in India. Among the major states, about 80 % of the area and production is from Madhya Pradesh; other states include Maharashtra, Rajasthan, These states together contribute about 98 % area and production (Table 1.37).

TABLE 1.37: Production of soybean in important states in India, 2001-02

States	Area (m.ha)	Production (m. tonnes)	Yield (kg/ha)
Madhya Pradesh	4.32	3.62	838
Maharashtra	1.10	1.39	1254
Rajasthan	0.66	0.72	1091
All India	**6.22**	**5.86**	**941**

Source: Agricultural statistics at a glance-2003

Growth of a large number of soybean processing industries in Madhya Pradesh is the primary reason for steep rise in soybean output in that state. Soybean is a short day plant and thrives best in varied climate and particularly in shaded environment. It is generally cultivated in *kharif* season.

Soybean contains about 38-42% protein and 17-22% oil. Soya-protein is a low cost protein and is highly nutritious. Soybean contains all essential amino acids and is rich in lysine. It can be used as a supplement to cereal diet. It is an important constituent in some of the infant foods and milk substitutes. Soya milk and *Tofu* (in Japan and Indonesia) are the important preparations from the soybean. It is utilized as a raw material for a number of protein and oil based industries. Soybean oil is rich in poly-unsaturated fatty acids and contains more of linoleic acid (54%). This results in rapid oxidation and deterioration of oil quality. The oil is extracted by solvent extraction and is used after refining for the production of hydrogenated fats, margarine and shortenings. The by-products are utilized in paint industry. The meal is an important source of vegetable protein and can be used for culinary purpose. The meal can also be used for the production of livestock concentrate.

Varieties: Ankur, Birsa Soy 1, Bragg, CO1, CO 2, Durga, Gaurav, Gujarat Soy1, Hardee, JS 2, JS 75-46, JS 79-81, JS 80-21, JS 355, KHBS 2, MACS 13, MACS 57, MACS 124, Monetta, NRC 2, PK 262, PK 308, J 27, J 362, J 416, J 471, J 472, J 564, J 1024, J 1029, Pusa 16, Pusa 20, Pusa 24, Pusa 27, Pusa 40, RIRC 7, RIRC 12, Shivalik, SL 4, SL 96, VL Soy 1, VL Soy 2.

Sunfllflower (*Helianthus annuus*)

Sunflower is an important oilseed crop after groundnut, rapeseed-mustard and soybean. The crop is grown in an area of 22.8 m.ha with the production of 25 m.t in the world. Sunflower is predominantly grown in Russian Fedration, Argentina India, Ukrain, USA, Romania. It was introduced in India during 1965 as an edible oilseed crop. Although commercial production of sunflower began in 1972, it had emerged as an important oilseed crop only in the 1980s. The crop was cultivated in an area of 0.1 m.ha with the annual production of 0.07 m. t in 1980-81. However, the area and production has increased significantly. The area increased to 1.3 m.ha and the production level to 1.3 m.t. The average yield is 600 kg /ha compared to global average of 1250 kg/ ha. Sunflower is mainly grown in the states of Karnataka, Maharashtra, Andhra Pradesh and Tamil Nadu. The crop has become an important one in Punjab, Haryana and U.P. The crop comes up well in any type of soil. Since it is not season-bound, it can be grown throughout the year. The crop generally requires 90- 100 days to mature but some new varieties come to harvest within 75 days.

Sunflower oil has an ideal combination of saturated and polyunsaturated fatty acids. The oil is rich in linoleic fatty acid (66.0%) and hence preferred for the reduction of high serum cholesterol levels. The oil is used for making margarine. The oil cake contains higher amount of protein (40-44%) and balanced amino acids and hence used as cattle and poultry feed.

- *Varieties:* Morden, EC 68415, CO 1, CO 2, CO 3, CO 4, GAU-SUF15.
- *Hybrids:* BSH 1, KBSH - 1, MSFH 8, MSFH- 17, Jwala Mukhi, DSH 1.
- *Hybrids for dryland:* BSH 1, KBSH 1, MSFH 8, MSFH 17.

Sesame (*Sesamum indicum*)

Sesame or sesamum is cultivated extensively in America, Asia, parts of

China and Latin America. It is cultivated in an area of 6.0 m. ha with a production of 2.4 m.t. Sesame is an important oilseed crop in India occupying about 1.6 m.ha with a production of 0.5 m tonnes. India is the largest producer of sesame in the world. Major sesame growing states in India are Gujrarat, Rajasthan, Tamil Nadu, Uttar Pradesh, Madhya Pradesh, Maharashtra, Karnataka, etc. Sesame can be cultivated on a wide range of soils. The crop thrives best in medium- textured soils with good drainage. Sesame is grown in all the three seasons viz., *Kharif, rabi* and summer. It is mainly grown in *kharif* as a rainfed crop. The seed contains all essential amino acids and fatty acids. It is a good source of vitamins (pantothenic acid and vitamin E). The seeds also contain important minerals such as calcium (1450 mg/ 100 g) and phosphorus (570 mg /100 g). Sesame oil is mainly used (about 80%) as cooking oil, particularly in South India. The oil cake is used as a valuable and nutritious feed for milch cattle.

Varieties: Pratap, Vinayak, Kanak, Kalika, T 13, T 22, TC 25, Madhuri, RT- 46, TM V 3, TMV 4, TMV 6, M-3-3, YLM 1, YLM 2.

Safflower (*Carthamus tinctorius*)

Safflower is grown both in tropical and temperate regions. The crop is cultivated to an extent of 0.80 m.ha with a production of 0.0.64 m.t. in the world. The average yield of safflower is 796 kg/ha. Safflower is grown in Ethiopia, Mexico, USA, Argentina, Australia, Russia and India. Safflower is a minor oilseed crop in India since its cultivation is restricted to Maharashtra, Karnataka, parts of Andhra Pradesh, Madhya Pradesh, Orissa and Tamil Nadu. India is the largest producer of safflower which is cultivated in an area of 0.44 m.ha with an annual production of 0.3-0.4 m.t. The average productivity is 0.6 t /ha. The crop possesses deep and efficient root system and hence utilizes the soil moisture efficiently. The crop is sown during *rabi* season and mostly cultivated as a rainfed crop. The crop, being spiny, does not require protection from the stray cattle and birds. The oil content of whole seed ranges from 28 to 32 %. Safflower oil is highly nutritious, rich in essential fatty acid (linoleic acid). The oil is used for edible purpose and highly useful in checking the cholesterol level. The oil is also used for various industrial purposes. A number of products could be developed from safflower such as carthamin pigments. This could be used as a food additive, for making a type of tea and extracting protein and amino acids.

Varieties: Annigeri-1, K-1, S-144, Nag –7, Tara, Manjira, CO 1, Sharda, Girna, Bhima.

Hybrids: DSH 129, MKH 11.

Castor (*Ricinus communis*)

Important countries where castor is cultivated are India, China, Brazil,

Paraguay, Latin America and the far East. Castor is cultivated in an area of 1.1 m.ha with an annual production of 1.2 m.t. in the world. In India, it is grown in Gujarat, Andhra Pradesh, Rajasthan, Tamil Nadu, Karnataka, Orissa, etc. accounting for about 90 % of the area and production. The crop is mainly cultivated as a rainfed annual crop. It is also raised in the bunds and irrigation channels.

The oil content in the seed varies from 35-58 % with the average of about 47 %. The oil is used for varied purposes such as lubricant in high speed engines and aeroplanes, manufacture of soaps, transparent paper, printing inks, varnishes, linoleum and plasticizers, etc. The cake is used as a manure. The leaves are fed to eri silk worms in the areas of eri silk production.

Varieties: TMV 3, TMV 5, Aruna, Bhagya, Sowbhagya, SA-1 GAUC -1, GAUC - H1, GCH-3, RC-8, SHB -18, HC 6, H-8.

Hybrids: GAUCH 1, GCU 4, GCH 5, DCH 30.

Linseed (*Linum usitatissimum*)

Linseed is moslty grown in the countries of temperate and tropical zones. It is cultivated in an area of 3.5 m. ha with the annual production of 2.9 m. t. The average yield of linseed is 858 kg/ha. Canada, China are the important countries growing linseed. Argentina, Russia, India, Bangladesh, etc. are the other major linseed growing countries in the world. India ranks first in the world acreage; however, the productivity is the lowest (300 kg / ha). The crop is extensively cultivated in Madhya Pradesh, Maharashtra, Bihar and Uttar Pradesh. About 60 % of the acreage is from Madhya Pradesh in sub-marginal rainfed lands. The crop is cultivated in *kharif* fallow as well as in a very large area as '*utera*' or '*paira*' in paddy fields.

The oil content is in the range of 40-45 %. The actual yield fluctuates 3-15 Q / ha. All parts of the crop are used for commercial purpose either directly or after processing. Oil is used for edible purpose and about 80 % of the linseed oil is utilized for industrial purposes such as in manufacturing of paints, varnish, oilcloth, linoleum, pad-ink, printing ink and medicinal purposes. The oil cake is a good cattle feed especially for the milch animals. The stem gives a good quality fibre.

Types of linseed

There are two main types of linseed namely peninsular varieties and alluvial varieties. The former has deep root system, bold seeds with a few branches. These types are highly suitable for the areas where the surface soil moisture dries up quickly. Rather the alluvial types have shallow root system having small seeds and many branches. They are best suited for the Gangetic alluvium where the upper layers of the soil are constantly moistened by the rise of underground water. These types give better seed production compared to the peninsular types. If these two types are grown at either condition, they fail to give better performance.

- ***Varieties:*** K2, Jawahar-7, Jawahar-17, Jawahar -552, Hira, Mukta, Neelum, BS 44, Gaurau (LCK 152), Jeewan (DPL 21), Kiran (RLC6)
- ***Seed and fibre types:*** Gaurav, Jeevan, LC 8528, Nagarkot, RL 993 (Meera)
- ***'Utera' (rice fallow):*** Jawahar 7, LC 185, Surabhi

Niger (*Guizotia abyssinica* L.)

The crop is grown in many parts of the tropical and temperate zones. India is the most important country in the world accounting for more than 50% of world niger area and production. Other important niger growing countries are East Africa, West Indies and Zimbabwe. In India, niger is cultivated in the states of Madhya Pradesh, Orissa, Maharashtra, Bihar, Karnataka and Andhra Pradesh. The crop occupies an area of about 0.5 m. ha with an annual production of 0.15 m. t. Average yield of the crop is 280 kg/ha. The crop is mainly gown in *kharif* season as a rainfed crop. It is also cultivated in *rabi* season. The oil content varies from 37- 43 %. The oil is used for edible purposes and for the manufacturing of paints, soft soaps, cosmetics, etc. The cake is a valuable feed for cattle.

Varieties: GA-10, IGP-72, IGP-76, Phulbani, No 71, Otacamand

Minor oilseed crops

The minor oilseeds of tree and forest origin are available in abundance and offer a good scope to be exploited commercially. It has been estimated that about 12 m.t. of minor oilseeds of identified plant species can be collected annually. This will result in the production of 1.7 m.t. of oil. As many as 100 different oil bearing plants have been identified in the forests of India, out of which only a dozen species have been exploited so far. They not only posses oil but also are well adapted to growing in varied types of wastelands. Important oil bearing tree species and their oil content in the kernel /seed are given in Table 1.38.

TABLE 1.38: Minor oil seeds and their oil content in the seed

Name	Oil content (%)
Kusum (*Scheleichera oleosa*)	57-60
Mahua (*Madhuca indica*)	33-43
Neem (*Azadiracta indica*)	40-50
Persian lilac (*Melia azedarach*)	25-30
Pongam or Karanj (*Pongamia glabra*)	27-30
Sal (*Shorea robusta*)	12-13

There are a number of other species that they also have good sources of oil. They are *Citrulus colosynthis, Jatropha curcas, Princepia utilis, Basia butrycea, Salvadora* spp, *Salicornia* spp, *Simmondria chinensis, Simarauba glauca, Cuphea* spp. and *Cucurbita foetidissima.*

FIBRE CROPS

Cotton (*Gossypium* spp.)

The important fibre crops are cotton, jute, mesta. Other fibre crops include sisal, hemp, flax, roselle. Cotton is the most important vegetable fibre cultivated in about sixty countries in the world. The countries such as India, USA, China, Pakistan, Turkey, Brazil, Turkmenistan, Greece, Australia, Uzbekistan, Argentina and Egypt, account for about 80- 85 % of the total area and cotton production. Cotton is cultivated in an area of 34 m.ha with the total production of 19 m.t. in the world. Cotton is one of the principal commercial crops in India. About 60 million people depend on cotton cultivation and allied enterprises. About 20% of the entire industrial output in the country is from the textile industry. Currently there are around 3.6 million handlooms and 1.1 million powerlooms that provide direct employment to about 14 million families. The organized textile industry with over 1500 mills is the second biggest in the world. The export materials from cotton include raw cotton, cotton yarn, textile finished products including garments and by-products of seed cotton. Foreign exchange worth of about Rs. 60 billion is earned annually, accounting for about 25 % of the countries' total exchange earnings.

India has the largest cotton area (8.5 m.ha) with about 25 % of world cotton acreage and 10 % of world cotton production. India is the third largest cotton producer, next to the USA and China. India consumes 14 % of world cotton output and is the second important consumer of cotton next to China. During the last 40 years, cotton area remained static; however, production has increased from 5.6 million bales to 9.5 million bales in 2000-01 (Table 1.39). The yield level also doubled but still the average productivity is the lowest among the major cotton-growing countries (world average is 580 kg/ha).

TABLE 1.39: Area, production and productivity of cotton in India

Year	Area (m.ha)	Lint Production (million bales)	Yield (kg/ha)
1950-50	5.9	3.0	88
1960-61	7.6	5.6	125
1970-71	7.6	4.8	106
1980-81	7.8	7.0	152
1990-91	7.4	9.8	225
2000-01	8.5	9.5	190

Source: Agricultural statistics at a glance-2003; (1 bale = 170 kg)

The major constraints in cotton production are the vagaries of monsoon battering major parts of the cotton growing area. Cotton is cultivated on marginal lands with low input use. The pest incidence is high; though cotton occupies only about 5% of total cropped area but it consumes nearly 55% of the pesticides used in our country. Adverse factors that affect cotton productivity in the Northern zone are rising water table, salinity, high temperature in the early phases, pest and disease problems like *Helicoverpa*. However, pink bollworm, white fly, root rot and the emerging problem of leaf- curl virus are also causing great concern. In the Southern zone, vagaries of monsoon and extensive damage due to pests are the real problems.

Out of the world extra long staple cotton (ELS) production of 5.8 lakh tonnes, India is ranked third important producer next to Egypt and the USA. But in the world ELS cotton export, the country shared very negligible quantity. Cotton is grown in different states and the major cotton growing states are Maharashtra, Andra Pradesh, Gujarat, Punjab, Haryana, Karnataka, Madhya Pradesh, Rajasthan and Tamil Nadu. These states contribute to about 99 % of area and production. Among the states, yield of cotton is the highest in Punjab (Table 1.40).

TABLE 1.40: Important states growing cotton in India, 2001-02

States	Area (m.ha)	Production (m.bales)	Yield (kg/ha)
Andhra Pradesh	1.10	1.87	289
Gujarat	1.75	1.70	165
Haryana	0.63	0.72	195
Karnataka	0.61	0.72	202
Madhya Pradesh	0.54	0.39	122
Maharashtra	3.10	2.69	147
Punjab	0.61	1.31	386
Rajasthan	0.51	0.28	94
Tamil Nadu	0.19	0.33	295
All India	**9.10**	**10.09**	**189**

Source: Agricultural statistics at a glance-2003

Production of quality cotton

There is urgent need to enhance cotton productivity and quality if demands for domestic and export market are to be met. The Central Government of India has sanctioned a special programme on technology mission on cotton with the object of improving production, productivity and quality of cotton. The raw material, seed cotton, is generally affected resulting in sub-standard quality of fibres. Sustainable increase in the production of quality raw cotton and its availability at reasonable prices would be vital for the viability of the textile mills. Cotton growers should also realize remunerative prices. Because of the stringent quality standards set by international buyers, the quality of raw cotton has assumed paramount importance.

Today, too many varieties of cotton are being grown in the country which has led to admixtures at various stages, creating problems of varietal impurity, difficulty in selecting appropriate variety and quality of cotton for the count spun. It had become a problem that cotton farmers were not able to realize stable and sustainable yield even under the best management practices.

Reduction in contamination of raw cotton by extraneous matters during the course of its harvest and transfer from the field to the mill are another priority area in view of the advent of modern automated, high speed spinning mills where manual cleaning of cotton is not possible. The issue of contamination - free cotton has also become crucial to cater to the international buyers in particular, who would not tolerate even a tiny spot on the yarn. Hence, there is a need for creating awareness among the farmers to keep cotton free from contamination and improve the systems of handling cotton at market yards, ginning and pressing factories, infrastructural facilities and transport to spinning mills. Grading-cum-price systems based on contamination of cotton should also enable the farmers to get premium price for their produce.

Types of cotton

There are four cultivable species in cotton. The primary distinction is based on chromosome number (Hutchinson, 1962). The species are *Gossypium hirsutum, G. barbadense, G. arboreum* and *G. herbaceum*. Among them, *G. herbaceum* and *G. arboreum* (n=13 chromosomes) are called the old world cotton and cultivated in tropical and sub-tropical regions. The other two species are with n=26 chromosomes and grown in the new world. The species, *G. hirsutum* (American upland types) is commercially grown throughout the world. The longer staple Egyptian and Sea Island cotton (*G. barbadense*) is cultivated to a much smaller extent. In India, all the four cultivable species are grown with the highest area under *G. hirsutum* (35.9%), followed by *G. arboreum* (17%) and *G. herbaceum* (11.0%). The remaining ones are with hybrids (36%).

Varieties:

- ***Rainfed:*** Khandwa-1, Khandwa-2, K 8, Mahalakshmi, GS 23s
- ***Rice fallow:*** Krishna, MCU 7, LRA 5166, SVPR-3
- ***Extra Long Staple:*** MCU 5, MCU 8

Pest and disease resistance:

- ***Verticillium wilt:*** MCU 5 VT, Savitha
- ***Whitefly:*** Kanchana
- ***Boll worm:*** Abhadita

Hybrid cotton

There is a phenomenal change in cotton improvement after the introduction of hybrid cotton in the 1970s. The major break-through in cotton production in India has come from the large-scale commercial cultivation of high yielding hybrid cultivars of long and extra long staple cotton. Over one fourth of the total cotton area in India is cultivated with hybrid cultivars. The spread of hybrid cotton has been mainly in Maharashtra, Gujarat, Karnataka, Madhya Pradesh, Andhra Pradesh and Tamil Nadu. Maharashtra has the distinction of growing the largest area of hybrid cotton, mostly under rainfed conditions.

Important Hybrids of cotton:

- *Superlong staple:* Hybrid –4, Varalaxmi, Suvin, DCH 32
- *Medium staple:* Dhanalaxmi, TSH 289, CDHB 1, DHB-105

JUTE AND ALLIED FIBRES

Jute and allied fibres consist of the crops like jute, kenaf, roselle, sunnhemp, sisal, and ramie and these are called natural bast fibres. Fibre is exctracted from the stem of jute, mesta (kenaf and roselle), sunnhemp and from the leaf of ramie, sisal. Except sisal and ramie, others are annual crops. Sisal and ramie are plantation crops of 6-10 years duration. Jute and mesta are extensively cultivated in India accounting for more than 53% world production.

Jute (*Corchorus spp*)

The world production of jute (nearly 95 %) is confined to India, Pakistan, Bangladesh, China, Indonesia, Thailand and Nepal. Pakistan and India are the most important producers of jute fibre in the world. Production of jute in India has increased tremendously from 3.3 million bales in 1950-51 to 10.6 million bales in 2000-01. However, the cultivated area has not increased much. The area under jute was 0.57 m. ha in 1950-51, which increased to 1.02 m. ha in 2000-01. The yield of jute has significantly increased over the period. It was only 1043 kg/ha in 1950-51 and increased to 1245 kg/ha in 1980-81. Current average productivity is 1996 kg/ha. The increase in yield is due to the development of high yielding varieties. In India, West Bengal has more than 70 % of area and 75% of jute production. Other states growing jute are Bihar, Assam (Table 1.41 and 1.42).

Quality of jute

The quality of jute is influenced by several factors such as variety, environmental conditions and method of processing. Among them, the method of retting is the most important factor that affects the quality. Retting is a microbial process that requires a large volume of water. Over-retting weakens the fibre and incomplete retting makes the fibre coarse. With perfect retting, the fibre gets fineness and strength. Recently advocated method of retting 'ribbon retting decortication' requires less water and the green ribbon rets faster than the whole plant.

Jute Products

Concerted efforts have been made by the government to promote the usage of jute fibre. Jute is now hailed as a "golden fibre", which would be the "fabric of the future". The demand for fine fibre has increased recently. The fine varieties having a denier of 10 or less are in great demand. Fine quality fibre is used for the manufacture of the value added products. The different value added products are household textiles, industrial textiles, re-inforced plastics, handicrafts, paper pulp and geotextiles. It has been proved that from jute fibre, fabrics of all designs and patterns could be woven on automatic looms and the products would be akin to those made of cotton. It may be highlighted that the export of only five major products (floor covering, hand and shopping bags, wall hangings, gift articles and decorative fabrics) fetched around 49 crores during 2000 which is about 10% of total jute goods export. At present 20% of the total jute goods belong to diversification sector. These products are emerging as major foreign exchange earners. Jute trade supports about 7 million small and marginal farm families, industrial employees and traders.

TABLE 1.41: Production of jute in India, 1950-96

Year	Area (m.ha)	Production (m.bales) *	Yield (kg/ha)
1950-51	0.57	3.31	1043
1960-61	0.90	5.26	1049
1970-71	1.08	6.19	1032
1980-81	1.30	8.16	1130
1990-91	1.02	9.23	1634
2000-01	1.02	10.56	1867

Source: Agricultural statistics at a glance-2003; (* bales of 180 kg each)

TABLE 1.42: Production of jute in different states of India, 2001-02

Countries	Area (m.ha)	Production (m.bales)	Yield (kg/ha)
Assam	0.07	0.71	1738
Bihar	0.16	1.05	1200
West Bengal	0.66	8.93	2426
All India	**1.05**	**11.64**	**1996**

Source: Agricultural statistics at a glance-2003; (* bales of 180 kg each)

Type of jute

Jute is a bast or phloem fibre obtained from the stems. There are two cultivated species, *Corchorus capsularis* (white jute) and *c. olitorius* (Tossa jute) (n=7). The former produces small, almost globular and wrinkled capsules. The fruits of *C. olitorius* are long, cylindrical and ridged capsules. About 75% of the jute area is with *C. capsularis*. This species is highly adaptable and cultivated both in lowlands and uplands. However, *C. olitorius* is basically an upland crop and cannot withstand flooded condition.

Popular Varieties of jute

- *Capsularis:* JRC-698 (Sharabanti white), D-110 (Bidhan Pat-3), Bidhan Pat-1, Bidhan Pat-2
- *Olitorius:* JRO 524, JRO 632, JRO8432 (Shakti), JRO 66 (Golden Jubilee Tossa)
- *Resistant to pests:* JRO 524, JRC 321, JRO 36 E

Mesta (*Hibiscus subdariffa / H. cannabinus*)

It is a fast growing fibrous bush, native to Africa. This fibre crop has been successfully introduced into many parts of Asia and now is widely cultivated in China, India, Pakistan, Russia and Thailand. A variety of kenaf known as mesta has been grown over large areas in many parts of the country. It is mainly cultivated in Andhra Pradesh, Bihar, Orissa and Maharashtra. These states contribute about 75 % of the area under this crop. Mesta is a hardy crop capable of growing under a wide range of climatic and soil conditions. It is wholly cultivated as a rainfed crop. High yielding varieties of mesta are HS 4288, HS 7910, HC 583, AMV-1, AMC 108.

In trade, jute and mesta are together categorized as raw jute. The fibre of mesta is called as kenaf, deccan hemp, mesta and Bimlipatam jute. The fibre is used principally for textiles, mainly for sacking and to manufacture of twine and rope. It is an excellent substitute for bamboo and wood pulp. It has been proved at the laboratory level that mesta is well suited for the production of newsprint. It has been estimated that about 10 tonnes of paper pulp can be produced from one ha of mesta. In India, the fibre is used on a fairly large scale in the jute mills in conjunction with jute. In other countries, the fibre is used for making ropes, twines and fishing nets. The seeds contain about 21 % of oil. The oil can be used for culinary purpose and also for soap making.

OTHER FIBRE CROPS

Agave (*Agave* sp.)

These are short-stemmed half woody plants bearing a rosette of long, erect, pointed, fleshy leaves. Six species of Agave were introduced in India during the 15th century by the Portuguese. They are A. anguistifolia, A. americana, A. lurida, A. cantala, A sisalana and A. vera –cruz. They are cultivated in the dry zones. Generally it is grown as a live fence. The widespread root system serves as a good soil erosion controller by planting across small gullies and slopes. Mature leaves can be harvested from 3-4 year old plants and from the fifth year onwards leaves can be harvested regularly and used for extracting fibre. The fibre is called to as "hard" fibre. Retting and mechanical methods are used for fibre extraction.

In Maharashtra, cantala fibre is extracted on a commerical scale by the retting process. The fibre is used for ropes, mats, cordage, twines and nets. Cantala fibre is pure white in colour, whereas sisal fibre is light yellow. Sisal (*Agave sisalana*) is cultivated in Andhra Pradesh, Assam, West Bengal, Bihar, Orissa, Tamil Nadu, Maharashtra and Karnataka.

Average annual production of sisal fibre in India is estimated at about 12,000 tonnes. The total demand of agave is about 50,000 tonnes. Annually India imports agave worth of Rs 2.0 crores from Tanzania, Kenya and other countries. However, India exports sisal ropes and twines to Nepal and Fiji Islands.

Hemp (*Cannabis sativa*)

The hemp fibre is a bast or phloem fibre. It is strong, durable and more rigid than flax. The fibre is used for the manufacture of ropes, twines, sacking, carpets, nets, tarpaulins and webbing.

Flax or Linseed (*Linum usitatissimum*)

Flax is meant both for fibre and oil. The fibre is soft, lustrous and flexible. The flax fibre is suitable for strong yarns such as are used for sewing thread.

Abaca or manila hemp (*Musa textilis*)

The fibre is obtained from the leaves of the plant which is a member of banana family. The Philippines is the chief producer of abaca. It is the strongest of the cordage fibres and is particularly used for marine cordage. The fibre is resistant to salt water and has low degree of swelling when wet.

SUGARS

Sugarcane (*Saccharum officinarum*)

Sugarcane is the native of India which is a major producer of sugarcane and sugar in the world next to Brazil. Other Important sugarcane producing countries include Cuba, China, Pakistan, Mexico, South Africa, Australia, Indonesia, etc. Sugarcane is cultivated in an area of 19 m.ha in the world with a production of 1250 m. t. In India, sugar industry is one of the largest processing industries, next only to cotton textiles. Production of cane has increased from a low level of 57.1 m.t. in 1950-51 to 241.0 m.t. in 1990-91 and to 296 m.t in 2000-01. Currently cane production is at 300 m.t. Between 1950-51 and 1994-95, the area under sugarcane recorded a compound growth rate of 1.8 %, yield by 1.2 % and production by 3. % per annum. The contribution of area in increasing the output was more than that of productivity. (Table 1.43)

Sugarcane area has spread to tropical and sub-tropical belts of India.

The area under sub-tropical belt is more than 70 %; however, productivity is less due to climatic disadvantage. Hence, the national average productivity is lowered to 68 t/ha that is only a fraction of the actual potential and it has to be raised to 82 t to meet the current requirement. In India, Uttar Pradesh is the major sugarcane growing state contributing about 48% of area and 40 % of total production. Other important states growing cane are Maharashtra, Tamil Nadu, Karnataka, Andhra Pradesh, and Gujarat (Table 1.44). In general, January to March is the period of planting and Dec- March is the period of harvesting. After the harvest, generally a ratoon crop is cultivated. In many countries, 2-6 ratoon crops are allowed.

In India sugarcane is mainly used for the production of sugar, gur and khandasari. About 50 % of cane production is used for production of white sugar, 40% for gur and 10% used for seed, feed and chewing purpose. Numerous producers of gur and khandasari are the main feature of the milling sector in India. Between white sugar and jaggery, the later contains more calcium and iron (Table 1.45). The by-products of sugarcane include molasses, bagasse, filter mud, sugarcane wax and cane trash. Molasses is used for alcohol production.

Varietal improvement

Flowering is essential for seed set. The natural climatic conditions at Coimbatore were found ideal for flowering and seed set and so Sugarcane Breeding Institute was started at Coimbatore in 1912 with the objective of evaluating suitable, improved varieties for sub-tropical India. The first hybrid variety 'CO 205' was successful in North India. The release of CO 312 for sub-tropical India and CO 419 for the tropical India were the major achievements in varietal improvement. Early ripening varieties had an appreciable impact on sugar production. Short duration varieties play an important role to enhance sugarcane productivity per unit time and inputs used.

Important varieties

- *Short duration varieties:* CO 997, CO 6808, CO 7704 CoS 510, CoC 671, BO 120, CoS 687, CoC 92061, CO 85004
- *Mid-late varieties:* CO 740, CO 1148, CoS 767, CO 86032
- *Red- rot resistant varieties:* CO 1148, CO 6907
- *For high sugar and tonnage:* CO 7201, CoC 671, CO 7634, CO 6304, CO 8153
- *Low water requirement:* CO 1158, BO 70, CO 997
- *Water logged area:* CO 1007, CO 1157, CoS 633, CO 975, CO 853
- *Ratooning ability:* CO1148, CO 419, CO 740, Co J 46
- *For jaggery manufacturing:* CoG 93076
- *Low temperature and stress conditions:* CO 1148, Co J 64
- *Saline or alkalinity:* CO 453

TABLE 1.43: Sugarcane production in India

Year	Area (m.ha)	Production (m.t.)	Cane yield (t/ha)
1950-51	1.7	57.1	33.4
1960-61	2.4	110.0	45.5
1970-71	2.6	126.4	48.3
1980-81	2.7	154.2	57.8
1990-91	3.7	241.0	65.4
2000-01	4.3	295.9	68.6

TABLE 1.44: Sugarcane production in different states of India, 2001-02

States	Area (m.ha)	Production (m.t)	Yield (t/ha)
Andhra Pradesh	0.21	17.61	82.8
Bihar	0.12	2.74	48.2
Gujarat	0.18	12.46	70.9
Haryana	0.16	9.33	57.6
Karnataka	0.41	33.75	82.5
Maharashtra	0.58	45.1	78.1
Punjab	0.14	8.82	61.7
Tamil Nadu	0.33	36.3	111.4
Uttar Pradesh	2.0	116.2	58.0
Total	**4.40**	**300.1**	**68.2**

Source: Agricultural statistics at a glance-2003

TABLE 1.45: Nutritive value of sugar (per 100 g)

Produce	Energy (k.cal)	CHO (g)	Ca (mg)	Fe (mg)
Sugar	398	99.4	12	0.15
Jaggery	383	95.0	80	2.64

Source: Srilakshmi, 1997

FORAGE CROPS

Forage refers to vegetative matter, fresh or preserved, utilized as feed for animals. These include grasses, legumes and other cultivated crops. They are used for hay, pasture, fodder, silage or soilage. Forages play an important role in the world food production, particularly in the production of milk and meat. In India about 5 % of the cultivated area is utilized for fodder cultivation. Important forage crops and their characteristic features are given in Table 1.46.

NARCOTICS

The products of these crops are used for stimulation. eg. tobacco.

Tobacco (*Nicotiana* sp.)

Tobacco is originated from America. India is the third largest tobacco producing country in the world, next only to USA and China. Tobacco is grown in an area of 0.46 m. ha with the production of leaf tobacco is 0.65 m. kg. The average yield is 1300 kg/ha. Tobacco is grown on a wide range of soils under different climatic conditions. Andhra Pradesh, Gujarat, Karnataka, Bihar, West Bengal, Maharashtra, Orissa, Tamil Nadu are the important states producing tobacco in India. There are two species of tobacco, *Nicotiana tabacum* and *N. rustica*. The former is grown in a large area all over the country.

TABLE 1.46: Forage crops and their features

Crop	Botanical name	Duration (days) or days for harvest	Green matter (t/ha)	Main features
Annual cereal forage crops				
Sorghum	*Sorghum bicolor*	55-65	40-60	Excellent for silage making
Sudan grass	*Sorghum sudanense*	45-50	30-40	Tolerance to extreme heat and drought
Maize	*Zea mays*	50-60	50	Ideal cereal forage and most useful for silage making
Teosinte	*Euchlaena maxicana* L.	7-10 days before tasseling	30-40	Useful for soiling, silage and hay making. Tolerance for flooding and excessive soil moisture
Deenanath Grass	*Pennisetum pedicellatum*	70-100	40-50	Most tolerant to soil acidity and salinity
Oats	*Avena sativa*	70-80	40-45	Winter cereal; highly nutritive fodder
Perennial Grass fodder				
Hybrid napier	Interspecific hybrid between napier grass and pearl millet (*Pannisetum purpureum*) and pearl millet (*P. americanum*)	9-10 weeks after planting; subsequent cuttings at 4-6 weeks	200	Fast growing and produce more herbage
Guinea grass	*Panicum maximum*	First cut 9-10 weeks after planting	150-200	High productive; palatable
Napier grass	*Pennisetum purpureum*	9-10 weeks after planting	150-200	Robust, perennial grass with high herbage yield

Crop	Botanical name	Duration (days) or days for harvest	Green matter (t/ ha)	Main features
Para grass / Buffalo grass/ water grass	*Brachiara mutica*	-	90-100	Tropical pasture grass; suitable for water logged condition
Rhodes grass	*Chloris guayana*	8-10 weeks after planting	50-60	Tolerant to salinity and alkalinity
Buffel grass	*Cenchrus ciliaris*	-	15-20	Suitable for pasture and range land; highly drought tolerant
Annual legume fodder				
Cowpea	*Vigna unguiculata*	60-70	30-40	Quick growing; tolerant for moderate shade; suitable for inter cropping
Mothbean	*Phaseolus aconitifolius*	120	20-25	Drought tolerant
Velvet bean	*Mucuna pruriens*	80-90	30-40	Grown for forage, green manure, cover crops
Guar	*Cyamopsis tetragonoloba*	60-80	20-25	Drought resistant; cannot withstand water logging and excessive moisture
Berseem (Egyptian clover)	*Trifolium alexandrium*	60-70	10-12	Highly nutritious, succulent winter legume fodder
Senji (Indian clover)	*Melilotus parviflora*	60-70	25-30	Tolerant to drought
Perennial legume				
Stylo	*Stylosanthes* spp	First cut at 90 days; subsequently 45-60 days	20	Perennial pasture or used as fodder legume. Best suited for rainfed mixed forage cropping
Alfalfa	*Medicago sativa*	First cut 120 days; subsequently 30-40 days	150	Wide adaptability; for dry and irrigated areas

N. rustica requires cooler climate and hence its cultivation is confined mainly to the northern and north- eastern regions of the country. The varieties of *N. tabacum* are called as 'desi' types.

The plants grow taller, produce broad leaves and the flowers are usually pink in colour. The *N. rustica* types are known as 'vilayati' and 'Calcutta' tobacco.

They are short plant types with round puckered leaf and yellow flowers. Specific varieties in *N. tabacum* arssssss for cigarette, cigar, cherrot, bidi, hookah and snuff tobacco. *N. rustica* varieties are used for chewing, hookah and snuff tobacco.

About one third of the country's total production of tobacco is used for the manufacture of cigarettes. The cigarette types comprise flue-cured virginia (f.c.v.), natu and Burley tobacco. The f.c.v. contributes approximately 95% of the total production of cigarette types. Because of the shift in the consumer's preference for cigarette smoking, the area under f.c.v. tobacco has shown considerable increase in recent times. Tobacco as an important commercial crop contributes the highest revenue of Rs. 2500-3000 crores to the government and a foreign exchange of Rs. 500 crores is earned annually. India exports tobacco mainly to Russia, the U.K., Belgium, Nepal, Germany, France, Czch Republic, Slovakia, Poland, the Netherlands and the U.S.

CHAPTER 2

Agro – Meteorology

Growth and development of crop plants depend on judicious management of intrinsic (genetic, hereditary) and extrinsic (environment) factors. Basically the environment in which the crops grow is represented by (i) the soil and (ii) the atmosphere. The interaction of these two natural entities acting in conjunction with the genetic make up of the plant and as compounded by man's interference in the form of various inputs supplied by him decides the pattern of growth of the plant concerned and its ultimate yield. The study of atmosphere involves greater understanding of behaviour of the weather elements. Study of the effect of weather elements on crop production may help the farmer to effectively plan for all his agricultural activities.

WEATHER

The physical state of the atmosphere at a given place and time is referred to as "weather". The study of weather is called "meteorology". It is often quoted as the "physics of atmosphere".

AGRO- METEOROLOGY

Agricultural meteorology or simply agro- meteorology is the science related to the atmosphere and its phenomena, especially to the weather and its effect on agriculture. Weather data are collected on actual observations of atmosphere at a given time on a particular day. Mean values of the weather data for a number of years (atleast 35 years) are denoted as climatic data.

- **Climate**: The word comes from the Greek word 'klima' which means the angle incidence of the sun's rays. Climate is the long term regime of the atmospheric variable or the composite of the day to day values of the weather elements for a given place or area for a given period.
- **Weather maps** represent the weather condition on a particular day. The average conditions of weather for a month, season or year are denoted as **climatic map.**

ELEMENTS OF CLIMATE

The characteristics of the atmosphere are called as the elements of climate. They include solar radiation, temperature, wind speed and direction, precipitation, humidity, cloudiness and evaporation. These elements are recorded daily at specified time using various instruments installed in an observatory.

Atmosphere

Earth is a unique planet of the solar system and has a suitable environment for living organisms such as plants, animals, and human beings. About 70 % of the earth is made up of water in the ocean, on land and in the atmosphere. The earth has a thick layer of air called as the atmosphere. The atmosphere is the most dynamic and changes take place not only seasonally but also over shorter periods of a few hours. Most of the atmospheric changes take place within a height of 32 km from the earth's surface. The atmosphere is held to the earth by the force of gravity. The density of the atmosphere is at its maximum near the earth's surface and decreases with height.

Composition of air

The air consists of N (78.084 %), Oxygen (20.946%). Orgon (0.934%) and CO_2 (0.033 %). Other gases are helium, krypton, xenon, hydrogen, methane, and nitrous oxide. The lower layer of the atmosphere also contains water vopour in variable quantities, usually less than 4 % of total volume of air. Apart from these gases, solid particles like dust, carbon, salt, pollen grains are also found. Nitrogen does not easily combine with other substances. Oxygen is highly active and combines readily with other elements due to oxidation. Oxygen is essential for all living beings. CO_2 plays an important role because of its ability to absorb heat and to facilitate the lower atmosphere to be warmed by heat radiation coming from the sun and from the earth's surface. Crop plants utilize CO_2 during the process of photosynthesis.

Structure of the atmosphere

Four distinct layers may be identified in the atmosphere. The lowest layer is called as **Troposphere.** It extends upto a height of 18 km along the equator and about 8 km along the poles. All phenomena of weather and climate take place within the troposphere. It also contains water vapour. Upper limit of the troposphere is called tropopause.

Above the troposphere there is another layer called the **stratosphere**. It extends upto a height of 50-55 km. The ozone layer is present in the upper portion of the stratosphere. This absorbs harmful ultra-violet radiation from the sun. The air temperature remains constant and then increases with height.

The **ionosphere** layer extends above the stratosphere. This layer contains electrically charged particles called ions. The upper most layer of the earth is called the **exosphere**.

The Troposphere and stratosphere are together known as homosphere because of its uniform layer. The overlying heterosphere is non-uniform in an arrangement of spherical shells.

Solar radiation

Sun is the earth's main source of energy. Sun emits energy in the form of electro-magnetic radiation. Sun is a hot gaseous body with a surface temperature of about 6000 °C and emits huge quantities of energy. The amount of energy radiated by the sun remains almost constant. Earth intercepts only a very minute part (1 in $2x10^9$) of the total energy. The radiant energy received by the earth at the outer limit of earth's atmosphere is about 2 calories per sq cm per minute. This is called as solar constant.

Insolation

The radiant energy received by the earth is called as the incoming solar radiation or insolation. They have a spectrum of waves of a wide range of length, mainly short waves. They travel at the uniform velocity of $3.0x10^5$ km/sec in straight lines radially outward from the sun. It takes about 9 1/3 minutes to reach the earth (150 million kilometers).

The solar radiation spectrum consists of a) x- rays, gamma rays and ultra violet rays (9 % of the total energy), (b) visible light rays (41 %) and (c) invisible infrared and heat rays (50%). The visible and ultraviolet portion of the spectrum is called as short waves ($<0.7\ \mu$)

Heat balance

As the insolation enters the atmosphere, a part of about 31 % is reflected by clouds or scattered back to space. About 4 % of insolation is lost by reflection from the earth. The ratio of the amount of radiation reflected to the amount received on a surface is termed as 'albedo'. The earth's mean albedo is about 35 %. The albedo of clouds varies widely with their thickness and composition.

The ozone present in the upper layer of the atmosphere absorbs the harmful ultraviolet radiation. The gases in the atmosphere and dust particles absorb only 14 % of the insolation. The remaining 51% [100- (35 + 14)] of the insolation reaches the earth's surface and heats it. The surface of the earth, in 'turn', radiates heat in the form of relatively long waves. This is called as 'terrestrial radiation'. Water vapour, CO_2 and other gases present in the atmosphere absorb 34 units (about 70%) of radiation. Remaining 17 units are radiated back to space without heating the atmosphere. Thus the earth's surface absorbs 51 units of insolation and radiates back the same amount. Hence, there is no net gain or loss between the earth and the atmosphere. The state of a balance or equilibrium between insolation reaching the earth surface and the terrestrial radiation from the earth is known as 'heat balance'.

Thus, the atmosphere receives heat by an indirect process which is permitted to pass through, but in its long waveform it is delayed in making its escape. Because of this reason, the lower atmosphere with its water vapour and CO_2 acts as a blanket which returns heat to the earth and helps to keep surface temperature from dropping excessively low during the night or winter at middle and high altitudes.

Variability of insolation

Because the earth is a sphere, the sun's rays do not fall vertically at every point on the earth at any given time. The quantities of insolation received in a day will depends on the angle at which the sun's rays strike the earth and the length of time of exposure to the rays. Intensity of insolation is greatest where the sun's rays strike vertically. With diminishing angle, the amount of solar energy spreads over a greater area of ground surface producing less heating per unit area. On an average, the Polar Regions receive the least heat per unit area compared to other regions. Because of these reasons, temperature is maximum in the low latitude and minimum near the two poles. There is also variation in daily intensity. The intensity is greatest in the noon but in the morning and evening it is small. The earth's inclination produces seasonal differences in insolation at any given latitude. There is also variation in the duration of daylight with the latitude and the season. At the season when the sun's path is highest in the sky, the length of day is also more. The day and night are equal at the equator. The day light period reaches a maximum of 24 hours in summer and a minimum of zero hours in winter in the Polar Regions.

Latitudinal zones

The sun's path, which determines the flow of solar energy, provides a basis for dividing the globe into latitudinal zones (Fig. 2.1). Though it is not absolute and binding the system be considered as a convenient terminology.

Tropical zone

The regions between the Tropics of Cancer (23 ½ °N) and the Tropics of Capricorn (23 ½ °S) is called as tropical zone. The sun's rays are vertically overhead during a part of the year. The seasonal contrasts are minimum in this zone.

Temperate zone

These regions lie between the Tropics of Cancer and the Arctic circle (23 ½° N to 66 ½ °N) and the Tropics of Capricorn and the Antarctic circle (23 ½ °S to 66 ½ °S). The sun's rays are never vertical during any part of the year. The angle of incidence and the duration of sunshine are greater in summer than in winter. The seasonal contrasts are much greater in the temperate zone than in the tropical zone.

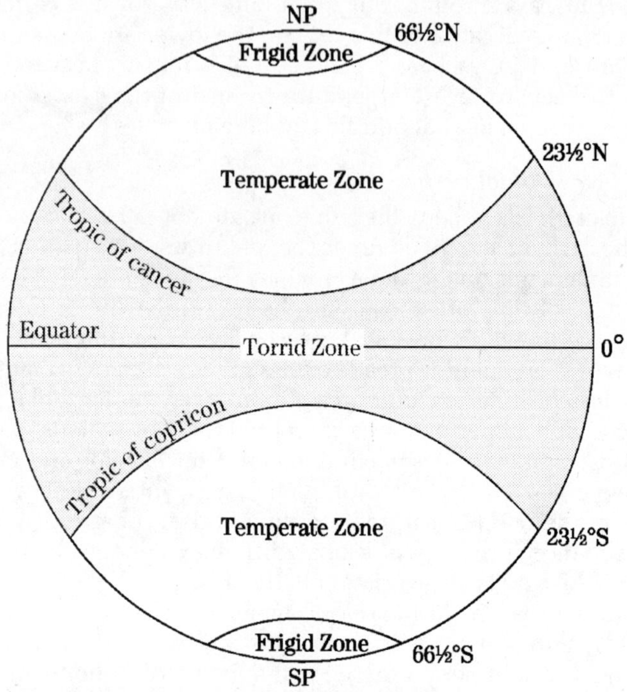

FIG. 2.1: Latitudinal Zones

The Polar zones (Frigid zones)

The regions around each pole extend up to the Arctic Circle in the Northern Hemisphere and the Antarctic Circle in the Southern Hemisphere. Sunray's are not received during the long winter in these regions and the sun may shine more than 20 hours during summer. Due to low angle of incidence of the sun's rays, temperature is quite low even in summer.

Atmospheric temperature

Daily cycle of air temperature

The earth rotates on an imaginary axis and takes nearly 24 hours to complete one rotation. This causes day and night and half the earth only receives insolation at any given time and the other half remains dark. The rotation of earth causes the changes in temperature between day and night. Temperature gradually increases from sunrise reaching maximum at about 2.00 p.m. It decreases gradually reaching a minimum before sunrise. 'The temperature difference between the maximum and minimum is called as diurnal range of temperature'. The diurnal or daily range of temperature is greater in the interior parts of continents than in those along the coast.

Seasonal differences in temperature

The seasonal differences in temperature are primarily due to the differences in the angle of incidence of the sun's rays and duration of sunlight. It takes one year for the earth to complete one revolution. On March 21st, the sun's rays fall vertically over the equator. There is an apparent movement of sun to the north of the equator from March 21st to June 21st. The sun's rays fall vertically over the Tropics of Cancer on June 21st. Since the northern hemisphere is inclined towards the sun, summer exists in the northern hemisphere and winter in the southern hemisphere.

After June 21st, there is apparent movement of the sun southwards and on Sep 23rd, the sun is again overhead at the equator. The movement of sun continues till December 22nd when the sun's rays are overhead at the Tropics of Capricorn (23 ½ °S). Hence, summer period prevails in the south and winter in the northern hemisphere. After December 22nd, there is an apparent movement of the sun northwards. On March 21st, the sun is overhead at the equator. This marks one complete revolution of the earth (Fig 2.2).

Normally temperature is maximum during the summer and minimum in the winter season. The angle of incidence of the sun's rays is greater and the duration of sunshine is longer during summer.

Generally maximum temperature is recorded in July and minimum in January in the Northern Hemisphere. The summer and winter seasons are reversed between the northern and southern hemispheres. The difference in mean temperature between the warmest month and the coldest month in a year at a station is called the "annual range of temperature". The annual range of temperature is the lowest in the equatorial region, as the amount of insolation received does not show much variation between summer and winter. Annual range of temperature is greater in the interior of continents in middle latitudes.

Air temperature maps

The distribution of air temperature over a large area is shown on a map composed of 'isotherms'. These are imaginary lines drawn on a map connecting all points having the same temperature. The map shows the world distribution of temperature in January and July. When the Northern Hemisphere experiences the winter season, extreme low temperature is reached in Northern Siberia in January, although the annual average temperature of Greenland and Antarctica are much lower. During July, the interior of landmasses in North America, North Africa and parts of South Asia experience high temperature and the southern hemisphere experiences winter in July.

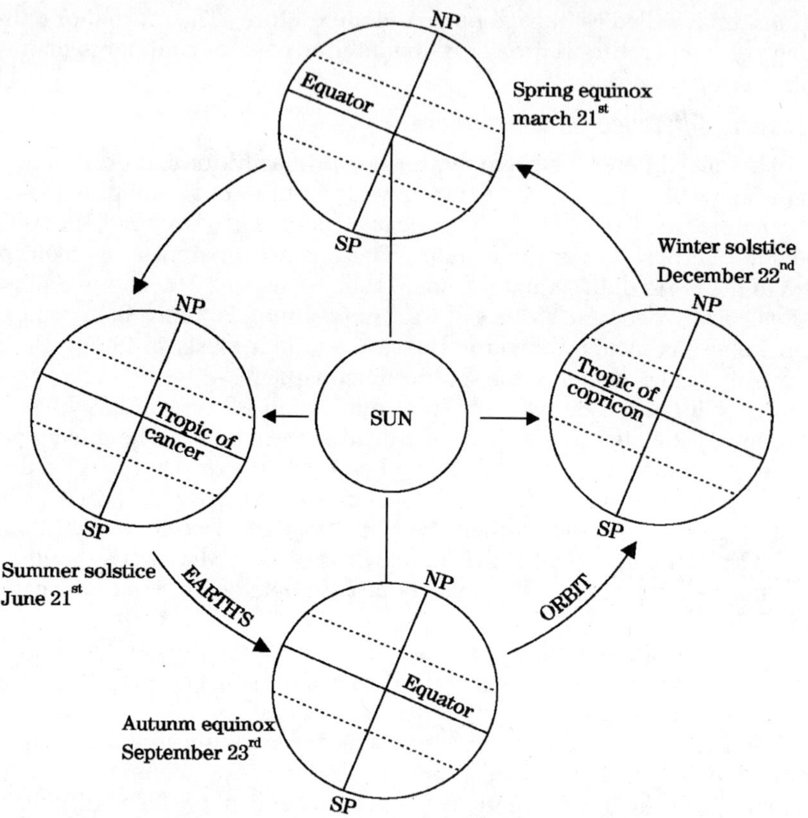

FIG. 2.2: Seasonal differences

Temperature inversion

Generally air temperature steadily falls with increasing altitude. The average decrease in temperature is approximately 6.4 °C per km. This rate of temperature drop is known as 'environmental lapse rate' or 'vertical temperature gradient'. However, the rate of decrease depends on the geographical location and season of the year. The lapse rate is approximately uniform at the troposphere.

Though the air temperature typically falls with increasing elevation, weather conditions at night in the lower air on land are typically such that, instead of the temperature falling, it first rises with increasing height above ground before beginning to drop off into the normal lapse rate. This condition is termed 'temperature inversion'. This signifies that cooler air lies below the warmer air.

Low-level temperature inversion or ground inversion commonly results at night due to rapid heat loss by radiation from the ground surface and basal air layer's upward movement into the space. Radiation loss from the earth is rapid due to clear skies or skies with high clouds. Inversion is particularly marked in snow-covered surfaces and on clear winter nights.

Atmospheric pressure and wind

The atmosphere exerts pressure on the surface of the earth owing to its weight. It is expressed in millibar (mb) equal to 100 N / m^2 or 1000 dynes/ cm^2. Pressure is also expressed in the units of height of mercury column. The average pressure at sea level is 1.034 g/cm^2. Unequal heating of the earth and its atmosphere by the sun and rotation of the earth bring about differences in atmospheric pressure. The distribution of pressure is represented on maps by 'isobars'. The imaginary lines drawn on a map to join places having the same atmospheric pressure is called as isobars.

Types of pressure system

Pressure systems vary both in size and duration. Pressure systems are of two types namely high and low pressure systems. The equatorial region (50°N and 5 °S) has a low-pressure belt called 'the belt of doldrums'. The low pressure is caused due to heating of the atmosphere and ascent of air. This zone has no strong pressure gradient to induce a persistent flow of wind. The Polar Regions are the centers of high pressure. This is due to low temperature and descent of cold air. Between the polar high-pressure belt and the equatorial low pressure belt lies a high pressure belt in the sub-tropical zone (30 °N and 30 °S) and a low pressure belt in polar regions (about 60 °N and 60 °S) latitude (Fig 2.3). Factors such as temperature, altitude, water vapour content and rotation of the earth affect the pressure of air.

Wind

Air in motion represents a form of kinetic energy. Wind also transfers energy to the surface of the sea as wind driven waves. Air circulation transports heat, both as sensible heat and latent heat present in water vapour. Wind blows in horizontal motion with respect to the earth's surface. It blows from the belts of high pressure to belts of low pressure. Wind is thus defined as the horizontal motion of air in response to pressure gradient force.

Air moving landward during the day in response to pressure gradient from higher (sea) to lower pressure (land) constitutes the 'sea breeze'. Air also moves from land to sea as a 'land breeze' during night. The earth's rotation produces another force called the 'coriolis' force which tends to turn the flow of air. Thus, the wind direction gets deflected to the right of their path in the northern hemisphere and to their left in the southern hemisphere.

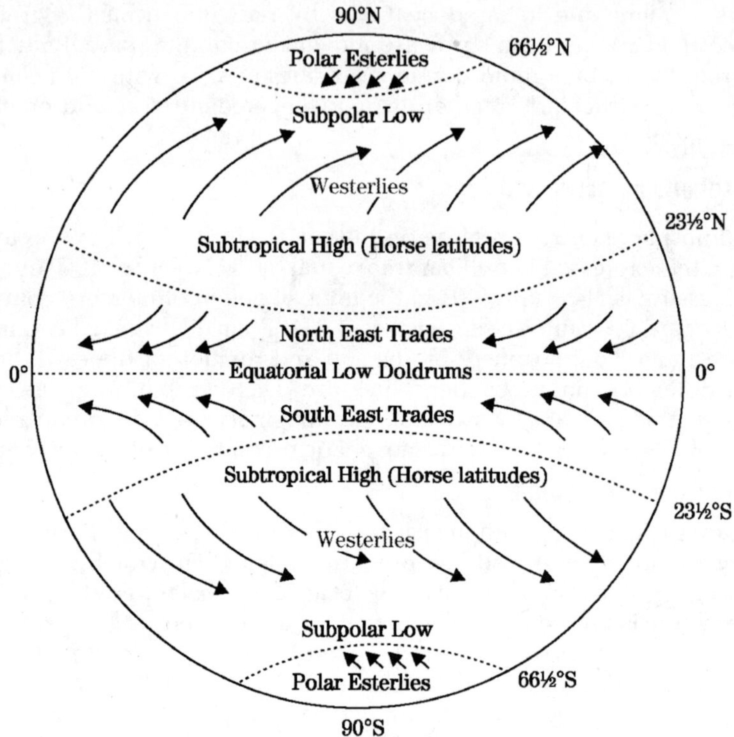

FIG. 2.3: Major pressure and wind belts of the world

Winds are given names by the direction from which they blow. Winds blowing from the major high-pressure belts to the adjoining low-pressure belts are called planetary winds or prevailing winds.

The major planetary winds are the Trade Winds, the Westerlies or prevailing westerly winds and the Polar Easterlies. The trade winds blow from the sub-tropical high-pressure belt to the equatorial low-pressure belt. These are northeasterly winds in the northern hemisphere and southeasterly winds in the southern hemisphere. The trade winds provide a splendid avenue for westward travel in the days of sailing vessels. The trade winds are noted for their steadiness and directional persistence. The westerlies blow from the sub-tropical high-pressure belts in each hemisphere to the adjoining sub-polar low-pressure belts. The winds may blow from any direction but the westerly components are definitely predominant. The polar easterlies blow from the polar high pressure centers to the sub-polar low-pressure belts in each hemisphere. The polar easterlies are variable in intensity and direction. These polar easterlies are described as characteristics of the arctic and polar zones.

Other wind systems

Besides major pressure and wind belts, other wind systems prevail caused by local pressure systems.

- **Monsoon winds:** "Monsoon" is the arabic word meaning seasons (*mausim*). Monsoons are seasonal winds that are characterised by reversals of wind direction. Monsoon winds are the most important as they affect a large area in Asia. These winds are primarily due to marked contrasts in seasonal conditions between the large continent of Asia and surrounding oceans. During summer, winds blow from the Indian and Pacific oceans towards the low-pressure centre located in the interior of Asia. This airflow constitutes the summer monsoon with heavy rainfall in Southeastern Asia. During the winter season, the interior of Asia cools down rapidly and the high pressure is formed. Cold dry winds blow from the high pressure towards the oceans. Blowing southward and southeastward towards the equatorial oceans, this winter monsoon brings dry, clear weather for a period of several months.
- **Cyclones and anticyclones:** The centre of low pressure is designated a cyclone and a centre of high pressure as anticyclone. As winds converge towards the low-pressure centre, passage of cyclone produces strong winds and heavy rainfall. Anticyclones have descending currents of air and are associated with fair weather and clear skies. Cyclones and anticyclones may be stationary or semi permanent type, or they may be rapidly moving pressure centres creating weather disturbances.
- **Local winds:** Sea and land breeze of coastal region are examples of local winds. The lands get heated more during the day than the sea and a low pressure is formed over the land. Sea breeze blows in the afternoon towards this low pressure. During the night, the air over sea is warmer than the air above the land. Hence, land breeze blows from high pressure over land to the relatively low pressure over the sea.
- **Southwest and northeast monsoons:** In summer, the plains of Northern India get very hot since the sun radiation falls at a high angle of incidence on the inland plains. Hence an intense low-pressure system develops over the northern plains. The strong winds from the nearby seas as well as from the Indian Ocean blows towards the plains. The planetary S.E. trade winds which blow south of the equator now cross it and change their direction in the northern hemisphere. The winds blow from the southwest direction instead of southeast. Hence they are called the southwest monsoon. This monsoonic winds cause heavy down pour in India as they carry a lot of moisture. They divide into two because of the peninsular of India and are called the Arabian Sea branch and the Bay of Bengal branch of the monsoon.

  In winter (Nov- Jan) the pressure conditions are reversed. The plains of northern India become very cold and have high pressure over the land. Dry light winds blow from land to low-pressure seas. These winds are in the northeasterly direction. Trade winds, which normally blow over India, are called the northeast monsoon.

Recent research evidences have shown that the process of monsoon rainfall is much more complicated. There are not only the surface air and winds involved, but also a complete replacement of hot dry tropical air by moist equatorial air up to a height of several kilometers of the atmosphere.

Atmospheric moisture

The atmosphere contains varying quantities of water vapour. The amount of water vapour that may be present in the air at a given time varies widely from place to place. Moisture present in the atmosphere plays a significant role in the weather and climate of a region. Three major components of the atmospheric moisture include humidity, precipitation and evaporation. The evaporation of water takes place due to heating of water bodies by the solar radiation. This causes addition of water vapour in the atmosphere. The process of evaporation cannot continue endlessly. There is an upper limit beyond which water vapour cannot be added to the atmosphere. For example, one cubic metre of air can hold 11.4 g of water vapour at 10 °C. This limit is known as the state of saturation. Normally warm air hold more water vapour than cool air.

Humidity

It refers to the degree to which water vapour is present in the air. It is indicated in terms of absolute humidity and relative humidity. Absolute humidity is the measure of the actual quantity of water vapour present in a given volume of air. It is expressed in g/m^3. The proportion of water vapour present relative to the maximum quantity is the relative humidity and is expressed as percentage. The changes in the atmospheric temperature cause change in the relative humidity. Relative humidity increases with decrease in temperature or by addition of water vapour. Relative humidity is a common parameter for expressing water vapour content of the air. Specific humidity is often used to describe the moisture characteristics of a large mass of air. It is defined as the moisture content of moist air as determined by the ratio of moist air in which the mass of water vapour is contained. Extremely cold dry air may have lowest specific humidity to extremely warm moist air.

Condensation

Condensation is the opposite of evaporation and it involves conversion of water vapour into droplets of water or crystallization of ice. Condensation starts only when the air is cooled beyond the dew point temperature. This occurs when the relative humidity exceeds 100 %. Condensation takes place around minute solid particles of dust, smoke, salt crystals and other materials. These droplets of water float in the air and form clouds. The materials are called 'Cloud Condensation Nucleus (CCN) '. Condensation takes place on objects on the earth surface and is called as 'dew'. It occurs as droplets of water on particles of rocks and leaves of plants near the ground. Fog and mist occur due to condensation of water vapour in the lower layer of the atmosphere near the earth's surface. Fog commonly occurs in the early morning hours during the winter season.

Classification of clouds

Clouds are classified into four families according to their height and appearance: (i) high clouds, (ii) middle clouds, (iii), low clouds and (iv) clouds with vertical development.

Each family is further divided into genera which are sub- divided into species and again species into varieties.

1. **Species:** This is described in different names based on the peculiarities in the shape of clouds and differences in the internal structure.
2. **Varieties:** Special features in appearance and degree of transparency of cloud have led to the concept of varieties.

Cloud classification and characteristic features are given in Table 2.1

TABLE 2.1: Cloud classification and characteristic features

Family	Genera	Features
Family A	High clouds (Mean lower level: 6.0 km)	
	Cirrus (Ci)	Nearly transparent, white and fibrous or silky. Systematically arranged as in bands and always composed of ice crystals.
	Cirrostratus (Cs)	Thin whitish sheet of cloud with milky appearance covering whole sky. Presence of celestrial ring called 'halo' around the sun and moon is the important character. The ring is red inside and white outside.
	Cirrocumulus (Cc)	Small white flakes or globular masses, usually without shade. They have the appearance of ripples similar to sand on a beach. They have flat bottom.
Family B	Middle clouds (Upper level 6 km and lower level 2 km)	

Family	Genera	Features
	Altostratus (A_s)	A uniform sheet cloud of grey or bluish colour, with fibrous structure; completely covers the sky.
	Altocumulus (A_c)	Arranged in lines or waves; contains layers of patches of globular clouds. Blue sky is seen in between the gaps. Formation of corona (a sphere surrounding the sun or moon) is seen.
Family C	Low clouds (upper level 2 km and lower close to the ground)	
	Stratocumulus (S_c)	Low, grey layer composed of globular masses or rolls arranged in groups, lines or waves.
	Stratus (S_t)	Low, uniform layer resembling fog, but not resting on the ground.
	Nimbo stratus (N_s)	The word 'Nimbo' in Greek means rainfall. Cloud layer lowers to become somewhat thicker and darker; continuous precipitation falls from its base; this may be called as rain bearing clouds.
Family D	Cumulus (C_u) Clouds with vertical development (mean upper level is that of the cirrus, mean lower level is 0.5 km).	Clouds are dense, dome -shaped, and have flat bases. Most cumulus are of the fair -weather type although towering cumulus may develop into cumulo- nimbus or thunder heads.
	Cumulonimbus (C_b)	They exhibit great vertical development, towering at times to 18 km or more. They are often accompanied by lightening and thunder storms. They are the chief sources of rainfall during summer.

- **Total cloud cover:** This is the fraction of the celestial dome covered by all the visible clouds. This gives an estimation how much of the total apparent area of the sky is covered with cloud. The international unit for reporting the cloud amount is the 'okta' or eighth of the sky.
- **Visibility:** Meteorological visibility is defined as the greatest distance at which a black object of suitable dimensions can be seen and recognized against the horizon sky.

Precipitation

Precipitation is the process by which condensed water vapour from the atmosphere falls to the earth's surface. It can also be defined as the water in liquid or solid forms, falling on the earth. The common forms of precipitation are rain, drizzle, snow and hail.

The most common form of precipitation is the rainfall. It is formed when cloud droplets in large numbers are caused to coalesce into drops too large to remain suspended in air. Droplets less than 0.5 mm in diameter make a 'drizzle'.

Water vapour condenses directly into tiny crystals of ice at temperature below freezing point through the process of sublimation. The ice crystals may fall down to the earth as powdery mass or flakes of snow. This form of precipitation is known as snowfall. Snowfall is a common occurrence in winter in the middle and high latitudes and high mountain regions.

Sleet is another form of precipitation in small particles or pellets of ice. They fall as rain drops through a cold layer of air near the earth's surface and frozen before reaching the earth (sleet means mixture of rain and snow).

Hail consists of large crystals of ice and is called as hail stones. They have an internal structure of concentric layers. Hailstones range from 0.5 to 5 cm in diameter and may be extremely destructive to crops.

Frost: When the dew point is below 0 °C, moisture passes directly from gaseous to solid state resulting in the formation of ice crystals called as frost. It mostly occurs in the valleys of the mountains.

Fog is simply a form of cloud lying very close to the ground. It is the microscope falling of small drops of water, condensed and suspended in the air at the surface of the earth. One type is known as radiation fog which is formed at night when temperature of the basal air falls below the dew point. Another type is called as advection fog resulting from the movements of warm, moist air over a cold or snow covered ground surface. Condensation sets in due to loss of heat to the ground and the air layer undergoes a drop of temperature below the dew point. The blend of smoke and fog is called smog.

Types of rainfall

Precipitation occurs due to cooling of air caused by ascent. Precipitation is of three principal types. They are: (I) convectional, (ii), orographic and (iii) cyclonic or frontal precipitation.

Convection types of rainfall: It mainly occurs in the equatorial regions. In these regions, the lower layer of the atmosphere gets heated up by the radiation from the earth's surface. This causes convectional ascent of air giving rise to heavy rainfall almost throughout the year. The convectional rainfall may also occur in the tropical and middle latitudes in summer.

The Orographic rainfall: It occurs resulting from raising and cooling of air masses when they are blocked by a topographical barrier (mountains). The rainfall is heavy on the slopes of the mountain regions located perpendicular to the path of winds. The highest annual rainfall of the world occurs in Cherrapunji (India) where the mountain barriers lie across the paths of moisture bearing winds. The West Coast of India and the Eastern Himalayan region get high rainfall from the south- west monsoon in summer. After passing over the mountain summit, the air will begin to descend the lee side of the range. The air has low moisture contents and warms up when it descends the slope. The leeward side is relatively dry. This is called the rain shadow region. The interior of the Deccan plateau gets low rainfall, as it is a rain shadow region.

Cyclonic rainfall: In the middle and high latitudes, much of the precipitation occurs in cyclonic storms or eastward-moving centres of low pressure into which air is converging and being forced to rise. Tropical cyclones are associated with strong winds and heavy rainfall.

FACTORS AFFECTING CLIMATE

Climatic conditions vary from place to place and between seasons at a given place. Distribution of each one of the elements such as temperature, pressure, winds and rainfall also affect the climate of an area. The climate of an area is mainly affected by the factors such as latitude, distribution of land and sea, topography and ocean currents.

Latitude

Latitude is the most important factor that influences the climatic condition. The amount of insolation received and its seasonal variation are related to latitude. The angle of incidence of sun's rays decreases gradually away from the equator. The temperature zones of the world are delineated according to the latitude.

The major pressure and wind belts of the world are affected by the latitude. At the equatorial region, low pressure exists and the Polar Regions have high-pressure belts. Wind belts move equator-ward or pole-ward and thus modify the temperature along their pathways. The rainfall pattern also varies with the latitude. The equatorial regions receive heavy rainfall due to warm moist winds. There is gradual decline in the annual rainfall towards the Polar Regions.

Distribution of land and sea

Daily and seasonal contrasts of temperature are greater on the continents than on the oceans. The interior parts of the continents experience a continental type of climate with high annual range of temperature. The coastal regions have maritime or marine type of climate with low annual range of temperature.

Distribution of pressure conditions is modified due to the contrast between land and sea. Normally low pressure exists during the summer in the interior landmasses. During winter, high pressure is formed in the interior landmasses. Variation is seen in the distribution of rainfall due to contrast between landmasses and oceans. The eastern regions of the sub-tropical zone receive more than 100 cm of rainfall because they are in the path of trade winds blowing from the oceans. The western margins of landmasses are tropical deserts, because hot dry winds blow offshore. Heavy rainfall is received in the western margin of the middle latitude because of the westerly winds. Rainfall decreases eastward towards the interior.

Topography

The nature of the surface of earth is known as topographic features. Increase in altitude is associated with decrease in temperature, increase in precipitation and wind velocity. High mountain regions have lower temperature. Rainfall is exceptionally high in places where the winds blow at right angle to the mountain ranges. This is due to orographic rainfall on the windward side. The leeward side gets low rainfall because of it is in rain shadow region. High mountain region acts as a barrier for movements of winds in the lower layer of the atmosphere. Northern plains of India experience mild winter due to arrest of cold winds from the Central Asia by the lofts of Himalayan ranges.

Ocean currents

Ocean currents transport large quantities of moisture over thousands of kilometers. There is increase in temperature and moisture content in the atmosphere resulting in high rainfall due to ocean currents. Temperature of the coastal region is reduced due to cool currents.

CLIMATE AND CROP PRODUCTION

The effects of weather elements on crop growth are described here. Daily, seasonal or annual variations in any or all the climatic elements are of importance in determining the efficiency of crop growth.

Temperature

The measure of intensity of heat energy is called as temperature. Plant growth is greatly influenced by the temperature. Extreme temperatures are destructive to plant growth. Plants are adapted to a wide range of temperature. Some species are capable of growing in extremely low or extremely high temperature conditions. Winter rye has relatively low temperature demands and can withstand freezing temperature. Tropical crops such as dates and cacao beans have high temperature requirements. Air temperature of above 90 °F (22°C) is most favorable for the tropical plants. Most of the temperate plants, however, grow well with a temperature of 15°-22 °F.

Temperature affects the physical and chemical processes within the plants. The diffusion rate of gases and liquids change with temperature. Solubility of different substances depends upon the temperature. The stability of the enzyme systems is affected by the temperature. Wide range of diurnal temperature variations may affect the grain production.

Except for the mountainous states of India, temperature does not act as a limiting factor to crop production. It is possible to raise crops throughout the year because the temperature is above the conventionally accepted threshold temperature (the point at which a stimulus begins to bring a response).

Cardinal temperature

Every plant community has its own minimum, optimum and maximum temperature known as their cardinal points or cardinal temperature (Table 2.2). These critical low and high temperatures are required for better growth and development of crops. They differ with the crop, variety, physiological stages of the crop plants, etc.

- **Optimum temperature:** The temperature at which a plant functions best is called as the optimum. The ideal temperature conditions for crop production are in the range of 18.3° to 23.9 °C.
- **Maximum temperature:** Maximum temperature is the one that can be tolerated without injury to crop plants. The maximum temperature tolerance varies greatly with the crop species. At about 40°C, changes begin to occur in the protoplasm that are detrimental to the life of the most plants which succumb at temperatures between 45° and 55°C.
- **Minimum Temperature:** Minimum temperature is the temperature at which any plant can continue its activity. It is approximately the freezing point of water. The growth of many of the tropical plants is retarded at 20 °C and is frequently killed at 10 °C.

TABLE 2.2: Cardinal points of some of the common crops

Crop	Temperature (°C)		
	Minimum	**Optimum**	**Maximum**
Wheat	3.0-4.5	25	30-32
Rice	10-12	30-32	36-38
Maize	8-10	32-35	40-44
Sorghum	8-10	32-35	40
Tobacco	13-14	28	35

Effect of abnormal temperature

- **Chilling injury:** Plants adopted for warm conditions, if exposed to prolonged chilling at temperature above freezing point are affected by retarded growth and killed. Transport of water from the roots is reduced and plants cannot regain transpiration loss. Crops such as rice and cotton are killed near freezing temperature if it prevails continuously for 2-3 days.
- **Freezing injury:** This generally occurs in the temperate regions. Water is frozen into ice crystals in the intercellular spaces at very

low temperature. Further fall in temperature results in withdrawal of water from the cells. The size of the ice crystals in the intercellular spaces increases. This results in dehydration in the protoplast resulting in killing of the cells and the plants die. Some of the plants have hardy underground portion, which remain alive even if the above ground parts die. A few other plants complete their life cycle within a short span of time and the hardy seeds remain dormant.

- **Heat injury:** High temperature facilitates high respiration rates and the plant faces incipient starvation. Plant growth is often stopped at very high temperature. Seedlings are highly susceptible to high temperature. Defoliation and premature dropping of fruits are the general effects of excessive heat.

Solar radiation

Solar radiation is the main source of heat energy in the biosphere. It is the primary source of energy for photosynthesis. Low light intensity reduces the rate of photosynthesis. The efficiency of photosynthesis depends partly on the interception of solar radiation by the crop canopy. Solar radiation at the reproductive phase of crop plant is very important for high crop yield. Very high light intensity is detrimental to plants in many ways. It increases the rate of respiration and disturbs photosynthesis-respiration balance. The most harmful effect of high light intensity is the phenomenon called as "solarization" in which all the cell contents are oxidized by the atmospheric oxygen.

Sunlight

Light intensity, quantity and duration are parameters that decide growth and development of crop plants. Light is the most important factor that influences the process of photosynthesis. Production of carbohydrate substances is controlled by the action of sunlight on green matter (chlorophyll) in leaves. This shows the dependence of crop plants on sunlight for the production of food and growth.

The length of the day or the duration of the light period is called the 'photoperiod'. Majority of the plants flower only when they are exposed to certain specific photoperiod. Based on the photoperiod response, the crops are classified as the short day, long day and day neutral plants.

A short day plant flowers when the day length is less than a certain critical length (<12 hours). Sunlight above this critical point will keep the short day plants vegetative. *e.g.* tobacco and soybean. Long day plants flower with increasing day length (> 12 hours) *e.g.* sugarbeet and spinach. Day-neutral plants flower after a period of vegetative growth regardless of the photoperiod. *e.g.* tomato and peas.

Quality of light

White light contains different colours with varying wave lengths (millimicrons-µm). Wave lengths of different colours are:

Violet	400-450 µm
Blue	435-490 µm
Green	490-574 µm
Yellow	574-595 µm
Orange	595-626 µm
Red	626- 750 µm

Green plants use a part of net solar radiation called 'Photosynthetically Active Radiation' (PAR) with wavelength from 400-700 µm for photosynthesis. Plants mostly use wavelength in the regions of violet-blue and orange -red for photosynthesis. The most favorable light for the growth is red followed by violet and blue. Short rays viz., x- rays and gamma rays and longer rays like infrared are detrimental for crop growth.

Precipitation

Rainfall is one of the important factors that influence the vegetation of a place. Most of the crops receive their water supply from rainfall. It is the main source of soil moisture in the tropical monsoon areas. About 75 % of the global area depends solely on rainfall for food production. In India, about 70 % of the cultivable area comes under rainfed agriculture which contributes about 42 % of total food production. Yearly precipitation, both in total amount and seasonal distribution greatly affects the choice of cultivated crop in a location. Low and ill -distributed rainfall are common features of dryland farming. Hence, drought tolerant crops like sorghum, pearl millet and other minor millets are predominantly grown in drylands. However, in places of heavy and regular rainfall areas, rice and sugarcane are grown in plains and tea, coffee and other plantation crops in the hill slopes. Heavy and torrential rainfall at early vegetative and crop maturity phases affects the crop stand and yield. However, optimum rainfall during the critical phases is useful, particularly for the dryland crops.

Relative humidity

Many of the plants grow well with high atmospheric humidity because very often-saturated air completely stops transpiration. High humidity at night is found beneficial to plants. The efficiency of water use would increase with more humidity in the air. Prevalence of high relative humidity favours spread of pest and diseases. Insect parasites such as aphids and jassids thrive under high humid situations.

Wind

Wind influences crop growth both physically and mechanically. Wind affects the plants directly by increasing transpiration and the intake of carbon di-oxide and also causes several types of mechanical damage. Moderate turbulence promotes the consumption of CO_2 for photosynthesis.

Wind helps in pollination and dispersal of seeds. Light and gentle winds are helpful for cleaning the agricultural produce. Hot dry winds frequently do much damage to vegetation in the growing crops by promoting excessive water loss. Wind has a powerful effect on humidity. Dry winds lower the amount of air moisture and favours increase in transpiration rate. Long, continued warm, dry winds injure blossoms by evaporating the secretion of the stigma. High wind velocity causes mechanical damage to plant structures, lodging of cereals and fruit drop from the trees.

AGROCLIMATIC NORMALS FOR THE FIELD CROPS

Different crops require varied optimal climatic conditions for better growth and development. It is important to select the crops according to the climatic suitability so that crop yields will be high.

Rice

Rice is indigenous to the humid regions of tropics and sub-tropics. The crop requires a relatively high temperature of 20°-40 °C for the optimum growth and development. A mean temperature of 22 °C is required during the growth period. Higher mean temperature may reduce the growth duration and accelerate flowering. Low temperature depresses the rate of germination, slows down the growth process and delays the maturity. Spikelet sterility is more if the temperature exceeds 35 °C at anthesis and lasts for more than one hour. If the night temperature falls below 15 °C during the vegetative phase, rice yield is significantly reduced due to formation of sterile spikelets. Optimum temperature requirements for the important growth stages are given in Table 2.3.

TABLE 2.3: Optimum temperature at different growth stages of rice

Growth stages	Optimum temperature (°C)
Germination	20-35
Seedling establishment	25-30
Tillering	31
Panicle initiation	33
Anthesis	30-32
Ripening	20-25

Solar radiation is another important parameter required for greater yield. The crop requires solar radiation of 300 cal/cm^2 per day at the reproductive stage. Low temperature coupled with bright sunshine during the ripening phase is highly conducive for the development of carbohydrates. Rice crop requires an optimum photoperiod of 10-10.5 hours per day for normal flowering, particularly for the season-bound rice varieties. The crop is sensitive to photoperiod only after the completion of its basic vegetative period.

Rice is a water-loving crop and is classified as hydrophyte. Under rainfed conditions, rice is cultivated in places receiving an annual rainfall of 1000 mm or more. Gentle winds are beneficial to rice plants. Heavy winds during cyclone may cause severe lodging and shattering. Wind damage may be of mechanical injury to leaves and panicles and also drying of leaves and earheads. Strong winds at the time of opening of flowers may induce sterility and increase the number of aborted endosperms. Heavy wind during ripening may lead to lodging.

Wheat

It requires relatively cool, moist growing season followed by dry, warm season for ripening. The crop is cultivated during the cool season with temperature of less than 25 °C. Wheat requires a minimum temperature of 3-4 °C, optimum of 25 °C and a maximum of about 30-32 °C. Prevalence of warm temperature during the early growth of wheat may retard heading. Temperature above 32 °C prevailing 3-4 weeks after flowering may ripen the grain prematurely. High temperature coupled with high humidity may encourage the spread of rusts causing reduction in yield. It requires approximately 100 frost-free days during the growing period.

The crop requires an average precipitation of 250-1750 mm. However, in most of the areas of wheat cultivation, the rainfall ranges from 375 to 825 mm. The optimum rainfall requirement is 625-825 mm. Moisture deficit at the time of heading stage results in shriveled grains and low yield.

Maize

Maize is a warm weather plant that requires high temperature during the growing period. The crop requires an average temperature of about 24 °C. Low temperature reduces growth and extremely high temperature may retard germination of seeds, particularly when it is combined with deficient moisture. High temperature above 35 °C is more injurious to plants at tasseling stage.

Maize is a short day plant and flowering is accelerated by shorter photoperiods. The average precipitation in the corn belts of the U.S. is 625-1250 mm. Maize is known to be relatively drought resistant and requires less soil moisture during the early phase of crop growth. Rainfall during 3-5 weeks before silking and from silking to 3 weeks afterwards is important. Hailstorms are most harmful during the stages of jointing and silking.

Sorghum

The crop is native of tropics and well adapted to temperate regions. It can grow better under dry, hot conditions. It requires a temperature range of 27-35 °C. Sorghum seeds require minimum temperature of 8-10 °C for germination. Sorghum is a short day plant. The varieties vary in their sensitivity to both temperature and photoperiod. The crop requires an average annual precipitation of 325-425 mm.

Groundnut

It is a sub-tropical crop that requires abundant sunshine and high temperature. The average temperature requirement is 25-30 °C during the cropping season. A temperature range of 14-16 °C is necessary for seed germination. The crop requires 30-33 °C during the vegetative stage and 27-30 °C during fruit setting. Groundnut is drought and high temperature tolerant and may tolerate a soil temperature of 60 °C for a very short period. It is basically a day neutral crop and is little affected by day length. Low light intensity during early growth and flowering stages and cloudy weather at flowering reduce fruit set. Total sunshine hours are in the range of 2300 to 2900/ha. Commercial groundnut production is taken up with the rainfall range of 500-1000 mm. However, the crop can be cultivated with a rainfall of 300-400 mm, seasonally distributed. Majority of groundnut are grown under rainfed conditions and hence time of sowing is important. Moist condition helps the pegs to penetrate the soil easily. Heavy rainfall at harvest causes germination of pods.

Rapeseed –mustard

This is basically a temperate crop and requires a moderate temperature below 25°-28 °C with optimum of 20 °C during the growth period. It requires a temperature of 20-30 °C for seed germination. The crop requires higher temperature for the completion of vegetative phase and cool temperature and clear sky during the reproductive phase for better development of seed and oil. Frost and cloudy weather during flowering is quite harmful; pest and disease incidence is more in such climate resulting in poor seed yield. Frost plays havoc, especially in brown sarson when it occurs at pod formation stage but raya has the recouping capacity and damage is very low compared to brown season. Mustard is a short day plant. The crop has a very wide photoperiodic range and the regional cultivars are locally adapted. A well-distributed rainfall of 700 mm is optimum with 450-500 mm rainfall during the vegetative and flowering period. The crop should be moisture stress free during flowering and pod filling stages.

Soybean

The crop is basically of temperate origin. Most of the varieties require a temperature range of 30-33 °C. A day temperature of 25 °C or less may delay the flowering and prolonged periods of cloudy weather may tend to extend the vegetative phase at the expense of seed yield. High temperature prevailing in the last 45 days of seed maturity adversely affects the seed viability and vigour. It is a short day plant and highly photoperiodic. A variation of 15 minutes in day length may be sufficient to inhibit flower development in a specific variety. Rainfall range of 500-750 mm is required for high seed yield. Adequate soil moisture is essential after flowering to pod filling. Strong winds at the time of pod filling may cause shattering when the pods are ripening. Yield reduction is greater when the moisture stress occurs during pod filling stage.

Sunflower

The crop is basically a temperate one; however, varieties which have adapted to a wide range of environments are available. It requires a temperature range of 20-25 °C but can tolerate 28-30 °C. Sunflower has a specific response to light. Because of the heliotropic response, heads with always face east. Photosynthesis is markedly affected due to low light intensity and hence seed yield is adversely affected. Sunflower is considered to be drought resistant. The crop requires a rainfall range of 550-1000 mm. However, moderate yield is achieved with the rainfall of less than 300 mm. Excessive soil moisture leads to vegetative growth affecting the seed yield. Water stress affects seed setting, yield and oil content. Sunflower is susceptible to damage by wind when it is half grown because of its height. There is possibility of lodging under irrigated condition where the soil support is less.

Sesamum

It is a tropical and sub- tropical crop and requires an optimum temperature of 25-27 °C. The crop is basically a short- day plant; but many varieties have become locally adapted to various light periods. The crop comes up well under long day periods. However, varieties grown during *kharif* season in India are day- neutral. Capsule setting is normally higher during summer. The crop is reasonably drought resistant and hence suitable for relatively arid zones and low rainfall areas. The rainfall requirement is 500-650 mm; however, the crop can be grown with rainfall of less than 300 mm and also upto 1000 mm. High rainfall at flowering drastically reduces the yield. Rainfall during maturity reduces the yield due to disease incidence and hampers handling and processing. The crop is extremely susceptible to water logging. The crop may be damaged due to wind after the main stem elongation. Heavy storms can virtually strip off leaves.

Cotton

Cotton is a heat-loving crop. During germination it requires 32-34 °C and 25-27 °C during the vegetative phase. Temperature range of 28-33 °C is most conducive for flower production. Average temperature of 21-22 °C is required for optimum growth. Sunshine is very important for proper development of cotton, particularly during the periods of early growth and fullbloom. It requires a minimum rainfall of 500-650 mm. Heavy rains during the seedling stage is very harmful. Drier period is required during the ripening period to hasten the boll maturity.

Jute

It is a sub-tropical crop and requires humid, tropical to warm sub-tropical climate. The crop is mainly grown in the regions having a temperature range of 15-38 °C. It requires high humidity (65-95 %). It is a short day plant and requires a critical photoperiod of about 12.5 hours. The olitorius type is more sensitive to short days than the capsularis. The crop requires high rainfall of about 150 cm distributed in such a way that most of the rainfall is received during the maturity phase. Jute is tolerant to water stagnation; however, it cannot withstand waterlogging at early stage of growth.

Sugarcane

Sugarcane is a tropical crop and requires an optimum temperature of 30-32 °C. The crop is mainly grown in the tropical and sub-tropical climate. The crop growth is better in places having mean monthly temperature range of 25-27 °C. Growth and yield are limited by the winter temperature having 5-6 °C during nights. Warm humid climate during the growth period is extremely suitable. The crop is grown in places receiving the rainfall of more than 1000 mm.

Forages

Berseem

It requires cool weather for better growth. However, excessive cold, hot and dry weather may retard the growth. The crop is adaptable to semi-arid regions. Freezing temperature of 4-5 °C may kill the plants. High temperature stimulates flowering and seed production. Longer period of cool temperature facilitates growth and yield of the crop.

Hybrid Napier

It grows well under tropical condition with the optimum temperature of 31 °C and the growth is reduced with the temperature of below 15 °C. Bright sunshine coupled with light showers are congenial for the crop growth.

Lucerne

It is adapted to warm temperature and cool sub-tropical regions. A hot dry climate is most suitable and the crop will not thrive in hot humid regions. Growth of seedling is higher with the temperature of 20-30 °C. The crop can tolerate a short spell of drought; water logging and high humidity in the rainy season are detrimental to crop growth.

Tobacco

Tobacco is grown under mild climate with the optimum temperature of 25-27 °C. Growth is rapid at the temperature of about 27 °C. The crop requires an annual rainfall of 1000 - 1125 mm.

WEATHER ABERRATIONS

Many types of weather aberrations occur which include tropical storms, tornadoes, dust storms, hail storms, etc. Agricultural production is affected due to prolonged dry spells, heat waves, cold waves and frost.

Tropical storms

The violent and destructive types of tropical cyclones originate over the tropical oceans. They are named differently according to the places of occurrence

(i) Hurricanes

They occur in the Caribbean and off the Pacific Coast of Mexico during late summer or early autumn. The important feature of the hurricane is its wind force. Winds are only moderate at the outer margins of the system, but velocities increase rapidly toward the centre, reaching a maximum along the outer edge of the central eye. Wind speed of 65 knots (118.8 km/hour) to 130 knots has been recorded. Heavy rainfall and flooding may cause extensive damage.

(ii) Typhoons

They occur in the sea off China, the Philippines, Japan and Islands of the Western Pacific; in the Indian Ocean, they are normally called cyclones. However, this should not be confused with cyclones in general.

Thunderstorms

Thunderstorms occur regularly in the tropics. Thunder and lightening accompany the typical mature thunderstorm. Intense precipitation occurs from the mature storm. Raindrops are large and it is literally a " cloud burst". They cause large proportion of rainfall and have considerable climatological importance. Thunderstorms are most common in summer due to surface heating of landmass.

Tornadoes

Tornadoes are the most violent storms of lower troposphere. They mostly occur during spring and early summer. They have been reported at widely scattered locations in the middle latitudes and tropics. Crop losses are heavy due to this event.

Dust storms

Dust storms take place during summer in the months of April, May and June. During this period, high temperature and low humidity prevail. Air gets heated, expands and blows with high velocity. It carries dust particles into the atmosphere. When it becomes violent, it acquires the form of dust storm. Dust and sand particles may deposit on the crops.

Frost

A single hardy frost may wipe out entire fruit orchards. The hazard is greatest during the critical stages of crop growth. Young seedlings are killed unless frost hardy varieties are chosen. Flowering stage is the critical period for most of the field crops.

Fog

The entire hilly region of North India is under the influence of foggy days throughout the year. Non-irrigated *rabi* crops get benefited from fog. The negative aspect of fog manifests itself when it persists for several consecutive days blocking the sunlight.

Weather related disasters

World Watch Institute (WWI) at Washington reported climatic changes and the latest dossier on weather-related disasters in 1998. Preliminary estimates of weather related economic losses worldwide during 1998 total $ 89 billion which is 48 % over the previous record of $ 60 billion in 1996 and far exceeds the $ 55 billion total for the entire decade of the 1980s. Among the most severe disasters of 1998 were the hurricane havoc in Central America and the floods in China and Bangladesh. Hurricane Mitch, the deadliest Atlantic storm in 200 years, caused an estimated 11,000 deaths in Central America. The flooding of China's Yangtze River resulted in 3700 deaths, displaced 223 million people, inundated 25 million ha of cropland and cost $ 30 billion. The Yangtze basin has lost 85 % of its forest cover to logging, agriculture and in recent years, wetlands have been drained and the river heavily dammed. As against flooding of the basin taking place once in 20 years in the previous centuries, the last few decades have seen flooding occurring in nine out of 10 years. Bangladesh suffered its most extensive flood of the century in the summer of 1998. Rice harvest was reduced by 2 million tonnes. Damage estimates exceed $ 4.3 billion. An ice storm in Canada and New England in the U.S. in January 1998 cost $ 2.5 billion. Floods in Turkey in June 1998 caused $ 2 billion in damages and floods in Argentine and Paraguay cost $ 2.5 billion.

Paddy cultivation has been hit in about 20 % of the total area in Punjab. In Andhra Pradesh, rain and flood have hit 8% of the area covered under groundnut, sunflower, pigeonpea and sorghum. In Rajasthan, about 20 % of the mustard cultivation area was hit by the rain.

MICROCLIMATE

Microclimate is the climate in which plants and animals live. It differs from the macroclimate which prevails above the first few meters over the ground. Temperature changes drastically in the first few centimeters from the surface into the soil or into the air. Changes in humidity with elevation are greatest near the surface. Very large quantities of energy are exchanged at the surface in the process of evaporation and condensation. Wind speed decreases markedly as the surface is approached. Micro- climate is largely a function of energy (heat and light) and moisture transfers within the plant environment.

Ameliorating microclimate

Soil

Agricultural practices are aimed at achieving the best possible arrangement of chemical, biochemical and physical factors in the microenvironment of plants. Considerable research efforts have been directed towards altering soil temperature under field conditions by cultural practices such as mulching, irrigation and tillage.

Opaque mulches act as thermal insulators and considerably damp the diurnal wave of soil temperature. Mulch material increases the minimum temperature. Lower temperature and high vapour pressure gradients in mulched crop result in restricted evapo-transpiration losses. In the early morning hours, the soil temperature is slightly higher than in non-mulched plots.

Successful production of winter wheat in Canadian pariries requires no-till seeding into standing stubble in order to trap snow. The snow cover acts as an insulating blanket that protects the wheat crowns from exposure to low temperature (-10°C or lower), thereby minimizing the risk of winter kill and/or low temperature injury.

Warm water may be useful for irrigation. Temperature changes in soil due to addition of warm (or cold) water are small and quite transitory. The effect may last for less than a day. Because of its great heat capacity, soil temperature will not markedly change by heat contained in water.

Canopy climate

Canopy temperature is altered by arrangement of rows. Air temperature patterns are relatively more in wide row arrangements. Horizontal temperature gradients are larger and more persistent in the wide row fields. Planting pattern also influences the distribution of radiation in the canopy as well as the total amount of incident radiation intercepted by the crop. East-west rows have higher net radiation than north-south rows. In arid areas with low relative humidity, a shade cloth windscreen would decrease the radiation load on crops. This helps in conserving water both by the decreased energy load and by functioning as a turbulent diffusion barrier and creating humidity blanket under the windscreen.

Wind breaks and shelter belts

Crop plants can be protected from excessively strong winds with the beneficial use of wind breaks and shelters belts. The use of windbreaks goes far back in the history of pastoral and agricultural civilization. Wind problems have been of major importance in determining the characteristic agriculture of the regions. Plants are subject to damage caused by excessive chilling, high temperature, desiccation or direct mechanical injury. Windbreaks and shelterbelts can reduce these stresses and have been found to be profoundly beneficial to the growth of plants.

In northern latitudes, a significant amount of the annual precipitation comes in the form of snow. The wind breaks help in snow trap and uniform distribution of snow and thus improves the soil moisture supply to the spring grown crops. Snow trapped and retained by the shelterbelts also provides an insulating layer to prevent winterkill of sensitive crops such as winter wheat.

The primary effect of any windbreak system is the reduction in wind velocity. Airflow modification depends upon the factors such as barrier height, porosity, physical characteristics of the barrier material (leafiness), barrier spacing, wind speed and wind direction. Protecting crops from excessive wind and from sand blasting can modify the crop yields. In arid regions, direct evaporation of moisture from the soil is reduced with the reduction of wind speed. Yield increase from the sheltered crops have been reported for both dryland (rainfed) and irrigated conditions.

CLIMATIC CLASSIFICATION

Approaches to climatic classification

Three broad approaches in classification of climate are (i) empirical, (ii) genetic and (iii) applied. Empirical classifications are based on the observable features of climate. This may be treated singly or in combination to establish criteria for climatic types. It is important to select criteria to suit the intended purpose. In the empirical classification, temperature and moisture are the important factors. Genetic classification is intended to organize climate according to their causes. Explanations are often theoritical, incomplete and difficult to quantify. Applied or functional classification of climate assists in the solution of specialized problems involving one or more climatic factors. Modern attempts of climatic classification provided a systematic relationship between climatic factors and the world pattern of vegetation. Relationship between temperature and moisture has also been established instead of simply taking rainfall or temperature. Precipitation- evaporation ratios and the concept of potential evapo-transpiration have been introduced indicating complex relationship and to establish criteria for climatic types. Variability of rainfall and seasonal distribution of rainfall and temperature are the additional factors that should also be taken into account for any classification. More widely used climatic classifications are described here.

Climate classification

Based on temperature

Ambient air temperature has been provided as the basis for climate classification. Mean monthly data on daily maximum and minimum temperature for many decades at thousands of observing stations the world over are taken into account. Based on this, three major climatic groups are identified.

I. Winterless climate of low latitudes
II. Climates of middle latitudes with both summer and winter seasons
III. Summerless climates of high latitudes.

The winterless climate has a monthly mean temperature of not less than 18°C during all the months. A summerless climate is the one in which no month has a monthly mean temperature higher 10°C. The climates of middle latitude exist between these two regions.

Air temperature is an important environmental factor for plant physiology and reproduction. However, air temperature alone does not provide meaningful climatic class since the ingredients of water availability is missing.

Based on precipitation

Seven precipitation regions are recognized in terms of annual precipitation with respect to particular location.

I. Wet equatorial belt of heavy rainfall: The annual rainfall is more than 200 cm. Thunderstorms are frequent in this region. This includes Amazon River basin in South America, the Congo River basin of equatorial Africa, African coast from Nigeria West to Guinea and the East Indies.
II. Narrow coastal belts of high rainfall: The annual rainfall range 150-200 cm. The area extends from near the equator to latitudes of about 25-30°N and S.
III. Tropical deserts: These are hot, barren deserts, with less than 25 cm of annual rainfall and in many places the rainfall is less than 5 cm. These lie upon the Tropics of Cancer and Capricorn. Sahara and Kalahari deserts in Africa, Californian and Mexican deserts in North America, Atacama desert in the South America and the Western Australian deserts are examples of hot deserts.
IV. Middle-latitude deserts: Annual rainfall ranges from less than 10 cm in the driest areas to 50 cm in the moist steppe. Interiors of Asia and North America lying between 30 and 50° latitude constitute this region. *e.g.* Tibet, Gobi and Mangolia.
V. Humid sub-tropical regions: The rainfall range is 100-150 cm. These areas receive heavy rainfall due to tropical cyclones.
VI. Middle latitude west coasts: The annual precipitation is more than 200

cm. These lie between 35° and 65°

VII. Arctic and polar deserts: Annual precipitation is about 30 cm. These regions have abundant moisture in the air and soil and are not considered as dry as those of the tropical deserts.

The Koeppen climate classification system

Wladimir Koeppen (1846-1940), a Russian-born biologist, attempted to relate climate to vegetation on numerical basis for defining climate types in terms of climatic elements. This system includes five major categories designated by capital letters.

This system is purely empirical based on temperature and precipitation computed according to the averages of the year or of individual months. It is possible to assign a particular climate sub-group to a given place based on temperature and precipitation of that place, provided that particular place has long term record of data. The climate can be delineated for large regions of the world. The system of classification has the important features of delineating major groups into sub-groups and further sub-division to differentiate particular seasonal characteristics of temperature and precipitation.

A. **Tropical forest climate:** The average monthly temperature is above 18°C. The annual rainfall is high and exceeds the annual evaporation.
B. **Dry climate:** The potential evapo-transpiration exceeds the average annual precipitation.
C. **Warm temperate rainy climate (mesothermal):** The coldest month has an average temperature of below 18°C but above -3°C. At least one month has an average temperature of above 10°C.
D. **Cold forest climate (Microthermal):** Mostly average temperature during the coldest months is –3°C. The average temperature of the warmest months is above 10°C.
E. **Polar climate:** Average temperature of warmest month is below 10°C.

Thornthwaite classification

Water balance is given greater attention for climatic classification because it represents the availability of water to plants as well as an assessment of the availability of surplus water to supply stream flow and groundwater. This approach has two variables: (i) precipitation and (ii) temperature. Temperature is taken into account for calculation of evapo-transpiration. Insolation is also used for calculating evapo-transpiration. Both precipitation and evaporation are measured as water depth or its equivalent per month or per year. An American Climatologist, C. Warren Thornthwaite (1899-1963) developed the concepts of the soil-moisture balance and devised a classification system using precipitation and evapo-transpiration. The climatic types have been designated with code letters. Two climatic classifications were introduced in 1931 and 1948.

- **Thornthwaites' 1931 classification:** This has two indices: 'precipitation effectiveness' index and ' temperature efficiency 'index. The former one relates precipitation to values of evaporation derived from temperature data. The temperature efficiency index is based on mean monthly temperatures.
- Thornthwaite established the fact that not only the amount of precipitation (P) but also the rate of evaporation (E) has significance for the growth of natural vegetation. This classification is almost similar to Koeppen's classification. However, interplay between the weather elements and other climatic factors are not clearly shown.
- **Thornthwaites' 1948 classification:** During 1948, Thornthwaite proposed the climate classification based on the concept of potential evapo-transpiration (PE). He regarded PE as a major climatic factor equal in importance to precipitation. PE is calculated from the mean monthly temperature with correction for day-length. Climate is considered as the existing balance between incoming and outgoing heat and moisture at the earth's surface.

The concept of evapo-transpiration can be applied to the practical studies on the water balance.

Trewarth's classification

Glenn T. Trewarth of the United States made modification of the Koeppen system in his book "An Introduction to Climate" (1980). He has simplified the world climatic map and redefined several climatic types. The classification combines the basic fundamentals of empirical as well as the genetic classification schemes. This classification favours empirical method of climatic classification. Two most important basic weather elements *i.e.* temperature and precipitation, are the basis for the classification. There are six great climatic groups (A, B, C, D, E and F). Except B, others are based on temperature criteria and B is the based on precipitation.

Based on temperature criteria

A. **Tropical humid climate:** It lies between 20 and 40°C and has uniform high temperature throughout the year with adequate annual rainfall. The sub-groups are Tropical wet climate (Ar) and Tropical wet and dry climate (Ar).
B. **Sub-tropical climate:** Temperature is 18°C for 8 months. These include sub-tropical humid (Cfw) and subtropical dry summer climate (Cs).
C. **Temperate climate:** It is also called as microthermal climate. This type of climate is found in middle latitudes between the sub-tropical and boreal climates. Temperate marine climate (Do) and Temperate continental climate (Dc) are the sub-groups.
D. **Boreal climate:** This type of climate is found in the higher middle latitudes. The summers are short and cool. The winters are long and very cold with a very short frost-free season. Rainfall occurs during

the warmer months when the water vapour content is highest. Boreal climate has the sub-group of Tundra climate (Pt).

E. **Polar climates:** This is found in the high latitudes. These climates are confined to the northern hemisphere only. The average temperature never exceeds 10°C and there is no summer season. Two climatic types are tundra climate and iceap climate.

Based on Precipitation criteria

A. **Dry climate:** The main characteristic feature of dry climate is that loss of moisture through evapo-transpiration is in excess of the annual receipt of water gain from the precipitation.

Based on the average precipitation, the dry climate is classified into two climatic types;

1. BW – the arid or desert type and 2. BS-the semi-arid or steppe type. These two types have been divided into four sub-divisions based on temperature. They are (i) Tropical-subtropical hot deserts (BWh), (ii) Temperature-boreal cold deserts (BWk), (iii) Tropical-sub-tropical steppes (BSh) and (iv) Temperate-boreal steppes (BSk).

Agro-Ecological regions of India

An agro-climatic zone is a land unit in terms of major climate and growing period which is climatically suitable for a certain range of crops and cultivars. An ecological region is characterized by distinct ecological responses to macroclimate as expressed in vegetation and reflected in soils, fauna and aquatic systems. Therefore, an agro-ecological region is the land unit on the earth's surface carved out of agro-climatic region when it is super imposed on land form and the kinds of soils and soil conditions that act as modifiers of climate and length of growing period (LGP). Several approaches have been made in the past to delineate the land area into climatic regions for purpose of agricultural planning. These approaches have the major limitation of non-uniform application of the criteria used. The Planning Commission, as a result of mid-term appraisal of the planning targets of VII Plan (1985-1990), divided the country into 15 broad agro-climatic zones based on the physiography and climate (Fig. 2.4). The emphasis was on the development of resources and their optimum utilization in a sustainable manner within the framework of resource constraints and potentials of each region. These zones were further divided into 120 sub zones under National Agricultural Research Project (NARP).

Western Himalayan Region

This region comprises Jammu and Kashmir, Himachal Pradesh and the hills of U.P. Shallow skeletal soils of cold region, mountain meadow and hilly brown soils are predominant. The soil belongs to the textural group of silty loam. The productivity of this region is lower than the all India level.

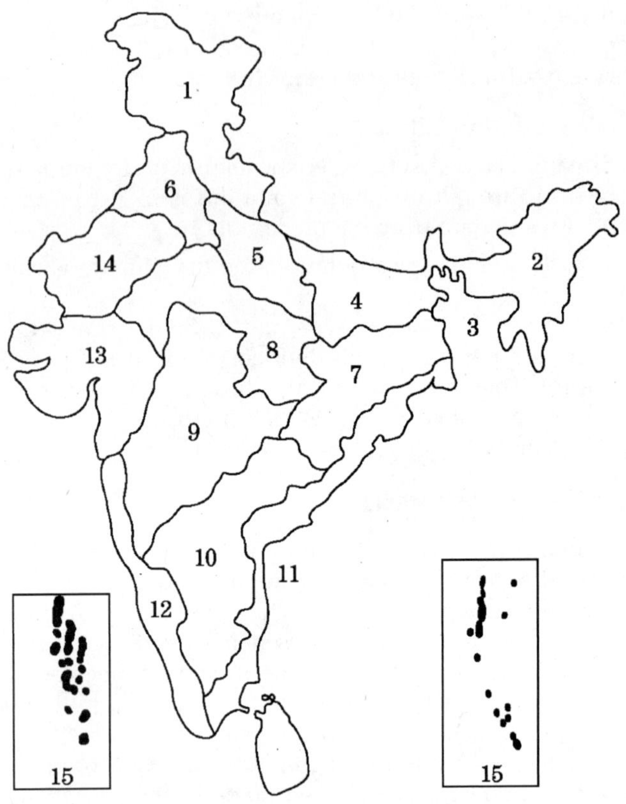

FIG. 2.4: Agro-climatic zones of India. (1) Western Himalayan Zone, (2) Eastern Himalayan Zone, (3) Lower Gangetic Plains, (4) Middle Gangetic Plains, (5) Upper Gangetic Plains, (6) Trans–Gangetic Plains, (7) Eastern Plateu & Hills, (8) Central Plateau & Hills, (9) Western Plateau & Hills, (10) Southern Plateau & Hills, (11) Eastern Coast Plains & Hills, (12) West Coast Plains & Hills, (13) Gujarat Plains & Hills, (14) Western Dry Region and (15) Island Zones.

Eastern Himalayan Region

This comprises Sikkim and Darjeeling hills, Arunachal Pradesh, Meghalaya, Nagaland, Manipur, Tripura, Mizoram, Assam and Jalpaiguri and Coochbehar districts of West Bengal. The rainfall is high with thick forest cover. High rainfall causes severe erosion and degradation of soil. This region is having a high potential for agriculture, forestry and horticulture.

Lower Gangetic Plains Region

This constitutes four regions in West Bengal viz., basin plains, central alluvial plains, alluvial coastal plains and Rark plains. Rice cultivation is predominant and this region accounts for 12 % of rice production in India. The crop damage occurs due to frequent floods.

Middle Gangetic Plains Region

This region comprises 12 districts of eastern UP and 27 districts in Bihar. About 61 % of the area falls under rainfed farming. The cropping intensity is 142 %. Rice productivity is the lowest in this zone.

Upper Gangetic Plains Region

This zone is spread in 32 districts and is divided into 3 sub-zones. Problem soils constitute for about 9 lakh ha. The cropping intensity is 144 %. Productivity of rice and wheat is fairly high. This zone has 131 % irrigation intensity with good potential of groundwater.

Trans-Gangetic Plains Regions

Punjab, Haryana, Union territories of Delhi and Chandigarh and SriGanganagar in Rajasthan constitute this region. There are some special features such as highest net area sown, irrigated area and cropping intensity. There is scope for further increasing the productivity level.

Eastern Plateau and Hills Region

The sub-zones in the region are: (i) Madhya Pradesh eastern hills and Orissa inlands, (ii) Northern Orissa and Madhya Pradesh eastern hills and plateau, (iii) Chotanagpur North and eastern hills, (iv) Chotanagpur South and West Bengal hills, and (v) Chathisgarh and South Western Orissa hills. The soils are shallow to medium in depth. The topography is undulating with a slope of 1-10 %. Crop productivity is low due to low rainfall.

Central Plateau and Hills

This region comprises of Madhya Pradesh (46 districts), Uttar Pradesh and Rajasthan. The topography of the land is highly variable and about 30 % of land is not available for cultivation. About 75 % of the area comes under rainfed cultivation.

Western Plateau and Hills

This zone spreads to the major part of Maharashtra, parts of Madhya Pradesh and one district in Rajasthan. Major parts of Peninsular India come under this region. Irrigated area is hardly 12 % only. Sorghum and cotton are the predominant crops in this region.

Southern Plateau and Hills

This is a typical semi-arid zone comprising 35 districts of Andhra Pradesh,

Karnataka and Tamil Nadu. About 80 % of the area falls under rainfed farming and hence the cropping intensity is very low.

East Coast Plains and Hills Region

There are five sub-zones: (I) Orissa coast, (ii) North coastal Andhra Pradesh, (iii) North coastal Tamil Nadu, (iv) Thanjavur, and (v) South coastal Tamil Nadu. The soil is deep, loamy, coastal and deltaic alluvial type. This region contributes about 20 % rice production of India. About 70 % of the area comes under rainfed agriculture.

West Coast Plains and Hills Region

The west coastal plain covers parts of Tamil Nadu, Kerala, Karanataka, Maharashtra and Goa. The soils are shallow and medium, loamy, red and lateritic. Rice, tapioca, coconut and millets are the important crops.

Gujarat Plains and Hills Region

This zone comes under arid climate and covers 19 districts in Gujarat. This is an important zone of oil seed production. About 78 % of area comes under rainfed agriculture with low rainfall.

Western Dry Region

This region is characterized by hot sandy desert spread in nine districts of Rajasthan. Rainfall is erratic with high evaporative demand. The climate is characterized by extreme temperatures, 0 °C in winter to 45 °C in summer. Vegetation is scanty. Drought and famine are very common features. Rainfall is only 400 mm. About 80 % of rainfall occurs from July to September. The cultivable wastes occupy about 42%. Pasture development for livestock has a very important role to play.

Island Region

Island territories of Andaman, Nicobar and Lakshadweep come under this region. Soils are medium to deep, red loamy and sandy. Annual rainfall is more than 3000 mm spread over 8-9 months. Forest, coconut and rice are important.

The agro- climatic classification of planning commission has been further modified and a new map depicting 21 agro-ecological regions was prepared (Sehgal *et al.*, 1990). The basic emphasis was: (i) growing period was given precedence over rainfall, (ii) the soil groups were considered more relevant than physiography; and (iii) geographic boundaries were adjusted to district boundaries for better utilization by user agencies. These 21 regions have been further condensed to six groups viz., arid, semi-arid, sub-humid, humid to per humid, coastal and island agro- ecosystems.

AGRO-METEOROLOGICAL OBSERVATORY

In an observatory several instruments are installed to observe various weather elements. The observations are recorded at stipulated time. Study of these instruments will help to handle them effectively and record the data accurately.

Agro-meteorological observatory can be classified into three groups viz., principal, ordinary and auxiliary types, depending on the instruments (essential and optional) equipped in the observatory.

Instruments equipped in the observatory

Principal observatory

a) Essential instruments	b) Optional instruments
• Maximum, minimum Thermometer • Wet and dry bulb thermometer • Soil thermometers • Grass minimum thermometer • Rain gauge (ordinary and self recording) • Wind vane and Anemometer • U.S.W. B. open pan evaporimeter • Sunshine recorder • Assmann Psychrometer • Dew gauge • Thermohygrograph • Soil moisture equipments • Solar radiation instruments	• Lysmeters • Thermopile sensing element for short and long wave net radiation • Potentiometer • Microvoltmeter

Ordinary observatory

a) Essential instruments	b) Optional instruments
1. Maximum, minimum thermometer	1. Sunshine recorder
2. Wet and dry bulb thermometer	2. Dew gauge
3. Soil thermometers	3. Self recording rain gauge
4. Grass minimum thermometers	4. Thermohygrograph
5. Rain gauge (ordinary and self recording)	
6. Wind vane and anemometer	
7. U.S.W.B. Open pan evaporimeter	
8. Assmann Psychrometer	

Auxiliary observatory

a) Essential instruments	b) Optional instruments
1. Maximum, minimum thermometer	1. Wind wane and anemometer
2. Dry and wet bulb thermometer	2. Dew gauge
3. Ordinary rain gauge	

Selection of site for observatory

The following basic requirements should be met out in the selection of site for installation of an observatory. Proper site selection will ensure that the observations are representative of the place and sufficiently comparable with those made at other stations.

1. The site should be representative of the surrounding area and the soil type.
2. It should be located in the center of farm.
3. It should be free from waterlogging / stagnation.
4. It should have easy accessibility during the rainy season.
5. The site should be away from any permanent irrigation sources and tall structures like buildings, hillocks and trees.
6. The site should not have extreme topography and it should be well exposed and leveled.

Recommended layout

The minimum dimensions for an observatory are a length of 25-30 m and width of 15 m and the longer side running South-North. The ground plan for an agromet observatory is given in Fig. 2.5

Measurement of weather elements

Temperature

Temperature is a relative term implying a degree of molecular activity or heat of a substance. Mean daily temperature is an average of the highest and the lowest temperature recorded during the 24-hour period. It is usually computed by the formula:

$$\text{Mean temperature} = \frac{\text{Maximum temperature} + \text{Minimum temperature}}{2}$$

Unit of temperature

Scales used for the quantitative measurements of temperature are based on the reference or fixed point.

Name of the inventors	Name of the scale	Symbol	Lowest (Freezing point)	Reference Point Highest (Boiling point)
G.D. Fahrenheit (1714)	Fahrenheit	°F	32°	212°
Anders Celsius (1942)	Celsius or centigrade	°C	0°	100°
Kelvin	Kelvin or absolute	°K °A	273°	373 °C

Conversion of the scales

°F = C x 9/5 +32
°C = (F-32) x 5/9
°C = °K-273
°K = °C+273.

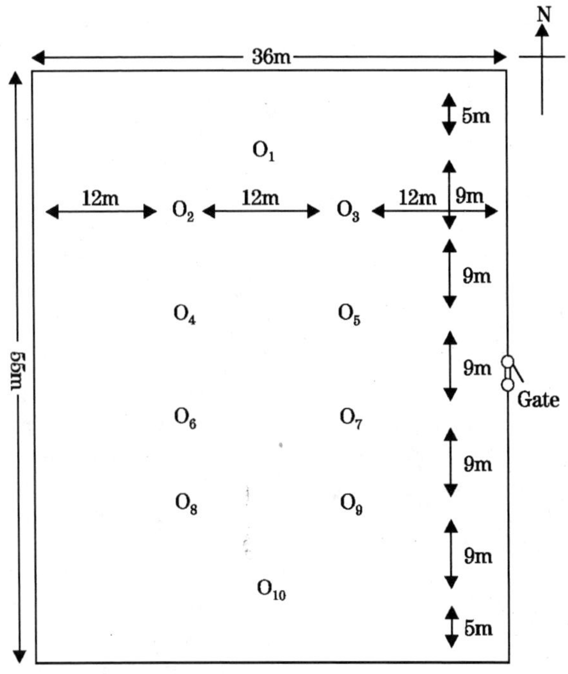

FIG. 2.5: Layout plan – Agro-meteorological observatory (1. Sunshine recorder; 2. Wind wave; 3. Anemometer; 4. Single Stevenson screen; 5. Double Stevenson screen; 6. Ordinary rain gauge; 7. Self recording rain gauge; 8. Soil thermometers; 9. Grass minimum thermometer; 10. Evaporimeter)

Note: The entire periphery should be fenced with barbed wires to prevent cattle trespass. All the tall instruments should be installed at the northern side of the observatory to avoid shade effect.

Thermometers

Thermometers are used to measure the air temperature. They are classified based on: 1. The physical effect of differential expansion: (i) Liquid in glass thermometers; (ii) Bimetal strip; 2. The electrical flow and resistance: (i) Thermocouples; (ii) Thermistors.

Liquid in glass thermometers

Most commonly used thermometers are the liquid-in glass types having mercury or alcohol. Changes in temperature produce expansion or contraction of the liquid which is recorded in the graduated scale. The accuracy of the measurement depends on the care with which the thermometer is constructed and calibrated as well as on its exposure to the air.

Maximum thermometer

It is a mercury thermometer. It has a constriction near the point where the capillary joins the bulb. The size of the constriction is such that when the temperature rises, the mercury will pass through. When the temperature drops, the mercury column will break at the constriction. The mercury in the bulb then contracts while the mercury above the constriction remains as such. As a result, the top of the mercury registers the highest temperature since last set. The thermometer can be reset in the morning hours by whirling it rapidly. The centrifugal force due to whirling drives the mercury pass the constriction. The maximum temperature is recorded in the afternoon.

Minimum thermometer

A colorless fluid, alcohol is used in this thermometer. The use of liquid alcohol facilitates to measure the temperature even below freezing point of mercury and also to get the visibility of the index immersed. In the capillary inside the alcohol column, a tiny dark index is held by surface tension. The thermometer is mounted horizontally. With the decreasing temperature, the alcohol column diminishes in length and pulls the index down. With the increasing temperature, the alcohol moves freely in the capillary, leaving the index in the lowest position reached since the last setting. The minimum temperature can be recorded by noting the scale reading opposite to the end of the index farthest from the bulb. Resetting can be accomplished by turning the bulb end up until the index slides down to the end of the alcohol column. The minimum thermometer is read in the morning and set in the afternoon.

Grass minimum thermometer

It is another type of minimum thermometer with the stem completely sheathed. This is used to measure the grass minimum temperature (reduced temperature just above the ground level during night). Measurement of this temperature provides information about the occurrence of ground frost. This is also called as terrestrial radiation thermometer.

Soil thermometer

It is a mercury glass thermometer used to measure the soil temperature. Different thermometers are used to measure temperature at different depths of 5, 15 and 30 cm. These thermometers have a bulb bent at an angle of 30° attached to the stem. A graduated portion is left protruding above the ground from which temperature is recorded. The stem above the ground is supported by steel angle bracket set in the ground.

Bimetal strips

This indicates temperature differences since the shape of a bimetallic element is affected by temperature. A bimetallic bar is formed by welding together of two strips of different metals. Increase in temperature causes the bar to expand. Since two metals expand at different rates, that causes the unit to bend. The curve thus formed is translated into temperature values on a calibrated dial.

Thermograph

Continuous recording of temperature is made by using the thermograph. It consists of an element responsive to temperature changes. A lever system is provided to translate these changes to a pen arm. A calibrated chart is mounted around a cylindrical clock drum. The chart provides a continuous ink trace of temperature for seven days. Thermograph readings are not as accurate as that of a mercury thermometer. Hence, frequent checking of these readings with mercury thermometers is needed. The thermograph sheet should be replaced once in a week, usually on every Monday. The sheet is perfectly fixed with the help of a clip. The pointer and the ink are to be cleaned. The instrument should be kept neat and dust- free.

Electrical flow and resistance thermocouples and thermistors

Accurate and rapid readings of temperature can be made by using these thermometers. Hence they are suitable for microclimatic observations in air, soil, plant tissues, clothing and other special exposures.

Thermocouples

These consist of a pair of junctions of two unlike metals. One junction is kept at a constant temperature and the other is exposed to a different temperature. The electromotive force generated in the circuit is measured using a potentiometer calibrated in degrees.

Thermistor

This contains of a ceramic element which is a semiconductor. It offers less resistance to the flow of current as its temperature increases. The temperature thus indicated is a function of flow of current.

Shelter for the thermometers

Stevenson's screen

Certain instruments like thermometer are kept in a wooden box with louvered sides. This type of shelter is called 'Stevenson's screen'. It provides a standard uniform exposure to the instruments placed inside. Over exposure of the instruments to direct atmosphere or protection from shade are avoided by this arrangement. Thus measurement of readings is reliable. The shelter should face the northern side of the observatory. The height is 1.2 m from the ground level.

Time of observation

The longitudinal position of a place decides the time of observation. To determine the time of observation of a local place, it is important to note the reference longitude (82 ½ °E. for India) for which the standard time is known. The earth rotates eastwardly at a speed of 15° longitude each hour (1° every four minutes). Hence the sunrise is delayed by 4 minutes for every 1° rotation of E longitude of the earth. If the local place is east of the reference longitude, subtract and if it is west add 4 minute for every 1°.

For example, the reference longitude for India is 82 ½ °E. The Indian Standard Time at which the observations are recorded at this reference place is 7 a.m. and 2. p. m. For example, Coimbatore is positioned at 77°E (West to the reference longitude). The difference is 5 ½ (82 ½ -77°). Delay in sunrise is 5 ½ x 4 = 22 minutes. Hence, the time of observations is 7.00 + 22= 0.22 or 0722 hrs and 2+22 = 2.22 p.m. or 1422 hrs.

Measurement of rainfall

It is measured in terms of depth of rainwater in millimeter. The instrument used for measuring the rainfall is called rain gauge. There are two types of rain gauges:

- Non- recording or ordinary type
- Self- recording type

Ordinary rain gauge

It is to be installed in a fairly open ground away from the trees and buildings. The standard dimension of the rain gauge being used is 200 cm. It consists of a (i) base, (ii) body, (iii) receiver and (iv) funnel. The amount of rainwater collected by the gauge is measured with the aid of a graduated measuring cylinder known as rain measuring cylinder. Rainfall is measured at 0830 hours IST representing the past 24 hours and the entry is made in the register on the date of measurement (Fig. 2.6).

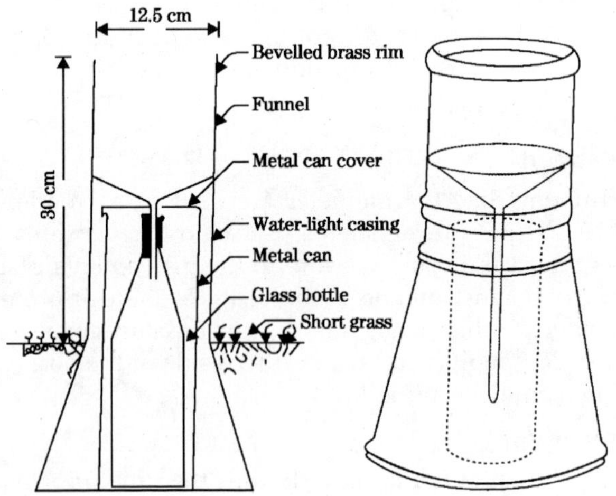

FIG. 2.6: Ordinary rain gauge

Maintenance and care

1. Whether there is rain or not, the rain gauge should be attended to every day.
2. In the case of heavy rainfall, measurements can be taken as many times required in a day. Normally recording is done at 0830 hours.
3. The receiver and the body should be examined carefully for leakage.
4. The water collected in the container only should be measured.

Self recording rain gauge

The natural siphon rain gauge is designed to give a continuous recording of the rainfall. The rainwater falling over the funnel is directed to flow down gently to the receiver. It is provided with a float and a siphon tube. A pen is mounted on the rod of the float.

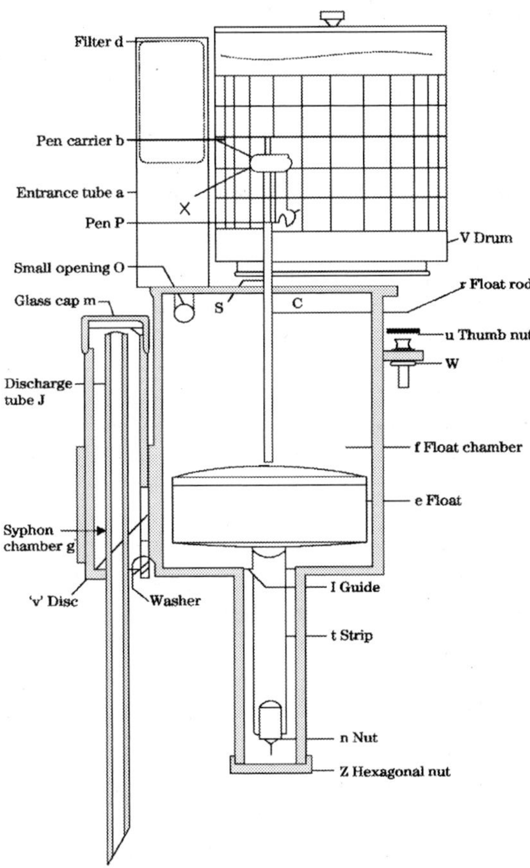

FIG. 2.7: Self recording rain gauge

When water level rises due to rainfall, the pen records on a graph chart wound over the rotating drum. Siphoning occurs automatically when the pen reaches the top of the chart marking 10 mm of rainfall. Later pen comes to zero point of the chart. The pen traces a horizontal line at the zero level when there is no rain. From the graph chart, the intensity of rainfall and the time of rainfall received could be noted (Fig 2.7).

Maintenance and care

1. The graph chart has to be changed every day at 0830 hours with date written on the chart.
2. The pointer (pen) has to be cleaned periodically and inked every day.
3. The timepiece should be wound once in two days/ a week according to the type.
4. At the time of initial setting, the working of the float should be checked by pouring rainwater.
5. Instrument should be cleaned off the dust every day and the hole in the stem of the funnel should be checked.

Wind

Wind velocity is measured with anemometer that gives the movement and a wind vane, the direction. These are often combined to one unit.

Cup anemometers

The most common way of measuring the wind movement/ speed is by using the rotating cup anemometer (Robinson's cup anemometer). It is the simplest form that measures the movement of the wind. Each rotation of the cup wheel corresponds to a definite distance traveled by the wind. Therefore, the number of turns the cup wheel makes in a given time interval corresponds to the distance traveled by the wind in that interval. By dividing the distance traveled by the time taken, the wind speed can be determined.

Cup anemometers are with varying sizes and styles but usually have three or four cups, either hemispherical or conical in shape. By means of counting dials equipped in the cup anemometers, the wind movement and/or speed may be determined by observing the anemometer itself. The cup anemometer can be fixed at a height of 60, 120, 180, 240 and 300 cm.

Measurement

To determine the wind speed at the time of observation, two successive readings at an interval of 3 minutes are recorded and the wind speed is calculated. The wind speed per day is taken from the difference between two successive readings at an interval of 24 hours taken at a fixed time. The wind speed per hour is obtained by dividing this reading by 24.

Units of expression

Wind speed may be noted with any one of the units such as Knots (or nautical miles per hour), Metres per second (mps), Kilometres per hour (kmph) and Miles per hour (mph)

1 knot = 0.5148 metres / second or 1.836 kmph or 1.147 mph

1 mph = 0.8684 knot or 1.6093 kmph or 0.4470 mps

1 mps = 2.234 mph or 1.942 knots

Measuring atmospheric pressure

Instrument used for measuring atmospheric pressure is the barometer. Basically there are two types of barometers, mercury and aneroid. Mercury barometers are characterized by a high degree of accuracy, permanence and fragility as compared to aneroids. The latter are small, light, highly portable and relatively rugged. Accurate measurements of atmospheric pressure can be made without any reference to any standard by using mercury barometer. But aneroids must be compared with a standard to establish calibration.

Mercury barometers

Mercury barometer is operated with the principal of balancing the column of air against a column of mercury in a sealed glass tube. A vertical column of mercury 75 cm long exerts approximately the same pressure per unit area as the atmosphere at sea level. The height of the mercury column is proportional to the pressure. Fluctuation in air pressure produces corresponding difference in the height of the mercury and a graduated vernier is mounted along the tube to facilitate accurate reading.

Maintenance and care: A thermometer is mounted on a mercury barometer with its bulb exposed so as to indicate the temperature as representative as possible to that of the entire barometer. The barometer should be mounted on a solid support. It should not be exposed to direct sunlight. It must hang vertically and be kept at a height convenient to read. Mercury barometers are fragile and must be carefully handled.

Aneroid barometers

For certain purposes, the mercury barometer is too expensive or cumbersome to move; so, a type of barometer known as 'aneroid' was developed. The aneroid barometer indicates pressure using the principle of the sylphon cell, which is a partially evacuated metal wafer. With the increase in pressure outside, the cell tends to collapse and it expands when pressure decreases. This fluctuation with pressure changes is mechanically linked to an indicator on a calibrated dial. These barometers are easily portable and convenient to use. An adjustment is provided for setting an aneroid to indicate the correct position.

This is a direct reading barometer, which is commonly used as an altimeter. Inside the barometer there is a small meter box, which is particularly evacuated. The top of this box is made of thin corrugated metal and is easily compressed by atmospheric pressure. Small changes in atmospheric pressure cause varying compression to occur. These movements are magnified by a system of levers, which cause the points to move over a calibrated dial. The atmospheric pressure decreases fairly uniformly with increasing altitude. The barometer may also be used to find the altitude of a place. An altitude scale enables to read the height directly.

Barograph

It is a self- recording instrument. This has a pressure sensitive element, sylphon bellows with an interval spring. Through a suitable lever system, this element moves the pen arm and the change in pressure are recorded automatically. The chart cylinder for recording is driven by a jeweled clock movement mounted inside the cylinder. Weekly charts are generally used. The chart contains horizontal and vertical lines representing the pressure in millibars and the time of the day in hours.

Maintenance and care: Chart drive clocks require the same care and attention normally given to high-grade clocks. They should be cleaned, oiled and repair, if any, should be attended to by competent clock repairmen.

Measuring humidity

Relative humidity is measured by using either wet and dry bulb thermometer or psychrometers (Assmann, whirling or Sling Psychrometer)

Wet and dry bulb thermometers

The two thermometers are alike except that in the wet bulb thermometer, the bulb is kept moist by means of a muslin cloth and a wick. Due to evaporation from the wick, the temperature of the wet bulb drops and this is called 'wet bulb depression'. The depression is directly proportional to the dryness of the air. The difference in temperature between wet and dry bulb can be translated into relative humidity with the help of hygrometric table.

Measurement and care: Measurements are to be taken at a fixed time for the locality in the morning and afternoon. The wet bulb should be kept moist. The wick should be examined every time and distilled water alone should be added to the container from which the wick draws water.

Assmann's psychrometer

This instrument contains two thermometers mounted on the same packing. One is mounted a little lower than the other. The lowered thermometer bulb is covered with a piece of muslin cloth or wick. This can be wetted for observation and is known as wet bulb thermometer. The other one is the dry bulb thermometer. The psychrometer is swung freely in the air or is aerated by a fan. The loss of heat required to evaporate water from the wet bulb will read a lower temperature. The difference between the readings of dry and wet bulb is called as the wet bulb depression. Relative humidity can be determined from the psychrometric tables. It is computed by the use of formulae based on mathematical relationship. If there is no depression of the wet bulb, the air is saturated and relative humidity is 100 %.

Precautions: The two thermometers are well matched, since in many cases, the difference between the wet and dry bulb temperature is very small and must be known accurately. The wick must be cleaned and kept free from any deposit. It must be completely saturated prior to use with water at the prevailing air temperature.

Hair hygrometer

Direct measurement of relative humidity is possible by using the hair hygrometer. The principle of the operation is that human hair lengthens as relative humidity increases and contracts while it decreases. The instrument has strands of human hair, which changes its length in proportion to the changes in relative humidity. The changes are indicated by a pointer or hand over the calibrated circular scale.

Hydrograph

This instrument has a clock drum and pen arrangement as in the case of thermograph. The pen moves over the graph chart wound over the clock drum and makes continuous record of relative humidity. Often the activating elements of the thermograph and the hygrograph are combined. In such cases, the pens trace their respective records on the same chart. This combination is called as the hygrothermograph.

Whirling hygrometer

This is a portable instrument consisting of two identical thermometers fixed on a wooden frame. One of them is converted to wet bulb thermometer with a piece of muslin cloth. The instrument is rotated 20-30 times and the temperature is recorded in both the thermometers. The relative humidity is noted using a hygrometric table.

Dew

Dew is recorded using a "dew gauge" which is a rectangular wooden block of 32 x 5 x 2.5 cm size coated with red oxide. The blocks are exposed to the atmosphere at about sunset. The size of the drops deposited on the block is compared with a set of ready photographs. The photographs bear the dew scales 1 to 8, each number bearing its equivalent in mm of dew.

Sunshine recorder (Heliograph)

This instrument is used to record the duration of bright sunshine during a day. A glass sphere is used to focus the sun's rays on a paper card strip, which is graduated in terms of hours. As the sun moves across the sky, its image burns the paper card strip and from the length of strip burnt, the hours of sunshine are calculated. Three types of cards are used according to the season. The position, season, and types of cards to be used are as follows:

Position of the card	Season	Type of the card	Period of use
Bottom	Summer	Long curved card	12th April to 31st August
Top slot	Winter	Short curved card	13th October to end of February
Middle slot	Equinoxes	Straight card	1st March to 11th April 1st September to 12th October

The respective cards are inserted in the appropriate slots before the sunrise and removed after the sunset. A transparent 'sunshine scale' is used to calculate the duration of sunshine. One graduation in the scale is equal to 6 minutes. The length of the burnt portion is measured for each hour and is totaled to get sunshine hours for a day. Example for calculating hours of bright sunshine is illustrated below:

Time	Hours of bright sunshine
6-7	0.50
7-8	0.90
8-9	0.40
9-10	1.00
10-11	0.80
11-12	1.00
12-1	1.00
1-2	1.00
2-3	0.80
3-4	0.90
4-5	0.40
5-6	0.50
Total	**9.20**

The date of observation and total hours of bright sunshine are written on the back side of the card for easy reference.

Bellani's pyranometer (Lucimeter)

Solar radiation on a particular day is measured with the use of Bellani pyranometer. The instrument consists of a glass sphere containing alcohol and is coated with a fine metallic layer to receive solar radiation. The energy received by the sphere warms the alcohol, which vaporizes and distills into a graduated tube below. The amount of alcohol collected in the tube is proportional to the solar radiation received from the sky. At 6.00 p.m. the instrument is set by tilting the stem for a couple of minutes and the set reading is noted. Next day morning at 6.30 a.m. reading is again noted down. At 2.00 p.m. reading is taken and the instrument is set by tilting the stem. At 6.00 p.m. reading is again recorded.

Example:

Set reading at	0630 hours	2.0
	1400 hours	32.0
	Actual value	30.0
Set reading at	1400 hours	2.5
Reading at	1800 hours	28.5
	Actual value	26.0
	Total	**30 + 26 = 56**

In the stem of the meter, one graduation is equal to 8 cal/cm^2/day. Hence radiation on a particular day is 56 x 8= 448 cal/ cm^2 /day.

Evaporimeter

It is known as U.S.W.B. class A open pan evaporimeter. It consists a pan made of copper with 122 cm diameter and a height of 25.5 cm. A still well is found inside the drum with a point gauge. It serves as a reference point for the level of the free water surface in the pan. The amount of water lost by evaporation from the pan in any given interval of time is measured by adding known quantities of water to the pan from a graduated cylinder till the water level touches the reference point. The opening portion of the drum is covered with wire gauge to protect the water from birds. The still well is made of brass and three performations are found at the base. The pan is placed on a wooden plank coated with white paint. (Fig. 2.8).

Every day the water level is adjusted till it touches the tip of the point gauge. On the normal days, water added to bring the level to the tip of the point gauge is measured using a graduated cylinder. During rainy days, if the water level is above the tip, excess water is lifted out till the level reaches the point. This value is substracted from the rainfall and gives the evaporation loss. In heavy rainy days, if overflow occurs, the evaporation is taken as zero. When the water level is less than 12 cm from the rim of the drum, evaporation is denoted 'zero'. Observation with the evaporimeter is a made daily at 0830 hours IST.

Synoptic chart

The weather elements collected from different observations are charted on outline maps using the international code signals and observations. Such charts are called 'synoptic charts' or 'weather charts'. Simplified synoptic charts appear in some newspapers (Fig. 2.9). Observations consist of air temperature, atmospheric pressure, wind, humidity, precipitation, etc. In addition, visible evaluation of clouds, visibility, present weather, etc. are also recorded. Surface observations are made every 3 hours and upper air observations every 6 hours (full hours GMT). These observations are referred to as "synoptic observation" and the time as 'synoptic hour'.

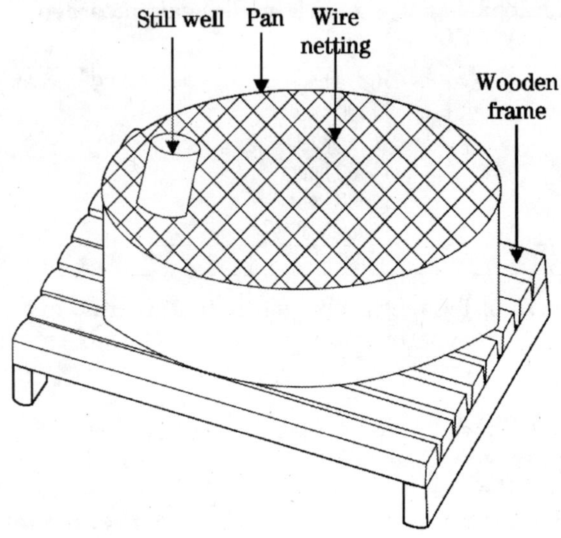

FIG. 2.8: USWB Open pan evaporimeter

Synoptic observations are taken simultaneously at Greenwich Time (0000, 0600, 1200 and 1800 hours). In India, the main surface synoptic hours are 0300 and 1200 hours GMT equivalent to 0830 and 1730 hours IST. Other important synoptic hours are 00,06 and 18 GMT.

The report for each station is plotted in and around the circle, which represents the observing station. Some elements like temperature and pressure are entered in plain figures. Other elements such as rain, snow, fog and cloud, which could not be easily expressed in figures, are plotted in internationally agreed symbols. Some of the symbols used for the synoptic chart are shown in Fig 2.10.

The meaning to be attached to the figures and symbols depend upon where they are placed in relation to the circle. The amount of shading in the circle is an indicator of the proportion of sky covered by clouds. Temperature (in whole degree) is written to upper left of the circle, the sea- level pressure in millibar and tenths to the upper right.

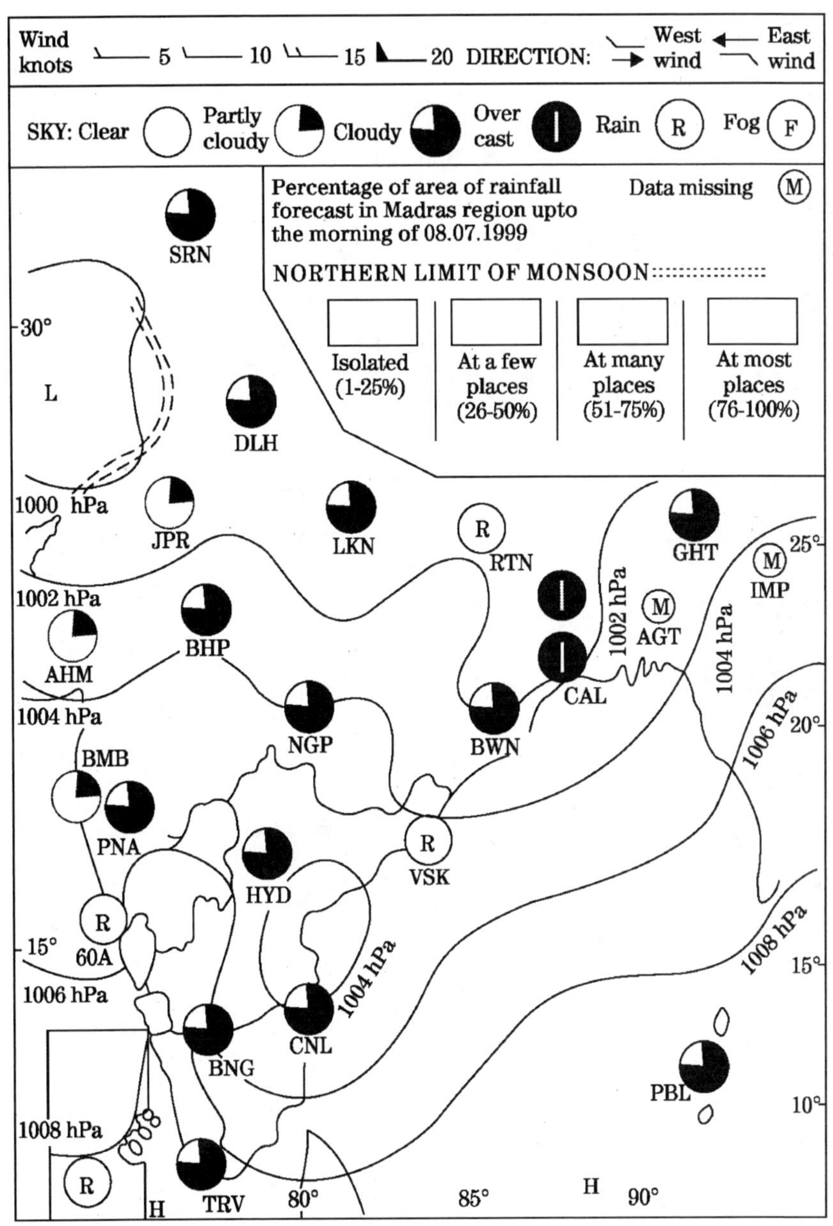

FIG. 2.9: Synoptic chart

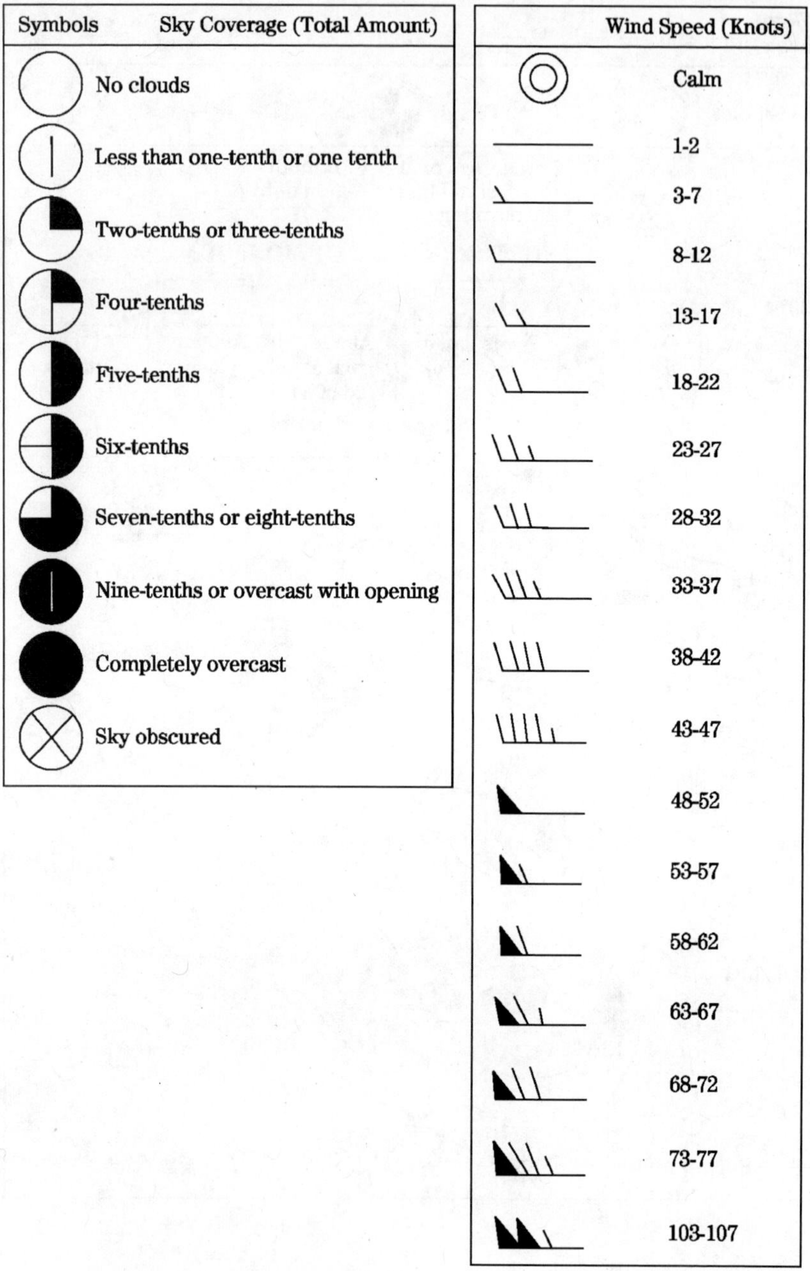

Symbols	Sky Coverage (Total Amount)
	No clouds
	Less than one-tenth or one tenth
	Two-tenths or three-tenths
	Four-tenths
	Five-tenths
	Six-tenths
	Seven-tenths or eight-tenths
	Nine-tenths or overcast with opening
	Completely overcast
	Sky obscured

	Wind Speed (Knots)
	Calm
	1-2
	3-7
	8-12
	13-17
	18-22
	23-27
	28-32
	33-37
	38-42
	43-47
	48-52
	53-57
	58-62
	63-67
	68-72
	73-77
	103-107

FIG. 2.10: Symbols used for the synoptic chart

WEATHER FORECASTING

In an agricultural country like India, where 70% of the agriculture depends on rainfall, correct weather forecast should be made available to the farmers well in time to minimize crop losses. Early forecast of the likely trend of the monsoon rain would be of paramount importance in increasing the individual and societal capacity to deal with the weather aberrations in a pragmatic way.

Types of forecast

Broadly there are three types of weather forecast based on the validity of the forecast:

Short range forecast	:	valid for 3 days
Medium range forecast	:	valid for 3-10 days
Long range forecast	:	beyond 10 days upto a season or a year beyond

Short range forecast

The short range forecast is based on synoptic considerations and operational numerical weather predictions. Synoptic consideration involves a subjective assessment of the evolution of weather system. The surface and upper air charts are studied. The forecast is mainly based on empirical 'thumb rule'. The accuracy depends on the experience of the forecasters and the knowledge of the local climatology.

In the recent years, operational numerical weather prediction methods have been introduced by the Indian Meteorological Department (IMD) with the installation of computers and speedy telecommunication system. It takes into account of the current state of weather in a fairly large number of synoptic stations of a given region.

Medium range forecast

The validity of the forecast ranges 3-10 days. This type of forecast is helpful to the farmers to plan for various cultural operations. Forecasting of rainfall over different parts of India for periods ranging from 3 to 10 days is very useful for agricultural operations.

Long term forecast

Long term forecast for a generalized behavior of the monsoon over the country is issued annually. Variability of 15 independent parameters is studied for such forecasting. The forecast is qualitative and can be important for the management of agricultural resources and for economic planning in general.

Weather forecasting organization

Many organizations have been set up all over the world for forecasting weather. All the participating countries adopt internationally accepted methods of measuring weather elements, assigning values and representing them in international codes. About 300 meteorological observation stations of different types are distributed all over India to aid in forecasting weather as the accuracy of weather forecasts depend on the availability of detailed weather data.

Crop weather calendar

This is the pictorial form of chart containing different stages of crops, optimum and unfavourable weather conditions for different stages of crops. This chart helps the weather forecaster to look at a glance and issue warning to a particular area at a given weather situation and during a particular phase of crop. This calendar has three parts (i) bottom, (ii) middle and (iii) top.

(i) Bottom part

This provides the activities related to crop or information related to phenological stages of the crops and about the months.

(ii) Middle part

This gives information regarding normal weather condition required for active crop growth. It is divided into different sections according to rainfall, rainy days, minimum temperature, maximum temperature, pan evaporation and sunshine hours.

(iii) Top part

This gives information related to the weather abnormalities or to take precautionary measures. Top part is divided into different sections according to dry spell length, high wind, heavy rainfall and cloudy weather.

Use of satellite data in Agro-meteorology

The primary application of meteorological satellites is to observe the earth's cloud cover. Since 1982, the multi- purpose geostationary Indian National Satellite System (INSAT) has been providing meteorological coverage for India. The INSAT-ID space craft is the last of the INSAT-I series. This will be succeeded by the indigenously fabricated satellite of the INSAT-II series. Satellite observations can supplement surface information to make the weather forecasts more accurate. The onset of the south west monsoon could be predicted with the use of satellite information. The INSAT pictures help the meteorologists by providing information about the conditions over the equatorial zone, Arabian sea and Bay of Bengal. The *in situ* formation of monsoon depression can be noticed in the satellite pictures in the very early stage. Development and movement of the depressions can also be followed using satellite pictures.

For detecting tropical cyclones and predicting their intensification and movement over the Bay of Bengal and Arabian Sea, INSAT is a very powerful tool. Satellite pictures can be used for giving precise advance warning of thunderstorms and hailstorms in the pre and post monsoon seasons. Cold waves generated due to western disturbances could be very easily tracked with the aid of INSAT. Their movement can be predicted upto 2-3 days in advance. Farmers can take measures against possible cold waves and occurrence of frost. Persistent cloudiness can be observed from satellite pictures and the farmers in such areas can be alerted. Persistent cloudiness is harmful to crops during flowering and generally conducive to pest and disease incidence.

REMOTE SENSING

This is the art or science of collecting data about an object or area at distance without having any contact with it. The source of remote sensing is Electromagnetic Radiation (EMR). The sources of EMR are (i) natural source and (ii) man made source. The natural source of EMR is the sun and emitted and reflected energy from the earth's surface. The artificial source of EMR is the radar systems, which operate in the microwave band of the electromagnetic spectrum. Reflectance emittance of objects at different wavelengths constitutes spectral signature of that object. Spectral signature helps in identification and discrimination of the objects.

Photography from the ground or from aerial platforms is a familiar and conventional form of remote sensing that has been extensively used since 1930. Laser profilometer has been introduced later. This enabled to measure very small distance relationship of a highly focused light pulse. This method could replace extensive ground surveying for vertical control of topographic maps. Airborne sensors have been later introduced due to advancement in military and space research. The sensors capture energy from various portions of the spectrum and therefore, have greatly increased the information gathering potential of aerial over flights. The use of electronic systems enables to analyze and display the data in pictorial format or on tape for input to a computer. Recent development on thermally sensitive photoconductors now permits to discriminate very minute temperature differences of 0.01 °C.

The development of the Multi Spectral Scanner (MSS) has given a new dimension in air-borne and space-borne surveys. In this method there is simultaneous registry of several spectral bands in the visible and in the infra-red (IR) regions. The data are stored on a magnetic tape and by using electronic data processing techniques, large volume of data are analyzed.

Remote sensing satellites have placed the present day agriculture in an enviable position. Space based earth observation systems (remote sensing satellites) have a lot of application in agriculture and environment monitoring. The satellites send precise information on earth's resources in the shortest possible time establishing superiority over ground and aerial (air craft) surveys. The satellites rely on sunlight, its spectral band, bouncing off the earth's elements and features. The information is sent to ground stations as electronic digits and stored in magnetic tapes. The digital information is then processed by the computers.

Application

Remote sensing plays a pivotal role in assessing the land and water resources. The forest cover estimation is best done with remote sensing. Soil maps are prepared with the use of remote sensing and satellite data. Remote sensing can help in finding out target areas where ground water exists. The information can be correlated with the geophysical survey for actual drilling in the area. In large-scale monocropped area, remote sensing will help in assessing crop yields. Agricultural estimates with the use of remote sensing began in 1978 with the launching of the Large Area Cropping Experiments (LACE) in USA. This was done to make an estimate of wheat production on the world. Correct estimates could be made for large area. However, in fragmented holdings as in India, it was not successful.

Remote sensing will be of immense value in monitoring the outbreak and spread of crop pests and diseases, particularly for monitoring locust swarms. The flood-prone areas and crop damage due to floods are determined using satellite imagery. Satellite imageries are used to design irrigation projects, regulate snowmelt run- off. It is also possible to delineate irrigated croplands as single cropped and multi cropped fields.

GLOBAL WARMING

Atmosphere acts similar to a glass house or green house. It allows solar radiation to pass through but does not allow escaping of terrestrial radiation immediately. This is simply known as the green house effect of the atmosphere.

Carbondioxide, methane, nitrous oxide, ozone, chlorofluorocarbons and other trace gases in the atmosphere are the greenhouse gases. These gases allow sunlight to reach the earth, but trap heat which would, otherwise, radiate back into the space. Excessive use of oil, gas and coal and destruction of tropical rain forests release enormous quantity of CO_2 into the atmosphere. Methane, a product of fossil fuel extraction, also forms from nature and rubbish. Nitrous oxide is produced as a result of the denitrification process from nitrogenous fertilizers and burning of fossil fuel. This also contributes to the global warming. Chloroflourocarbons (or CFC's) are extensively used in refrigeration and aviation industries. These substances react with ozone and reduce the amount of ozone creating a 'hole' through which ultraviolet radiation can pass through.

Among the different gases, CO_2 is chiefly responsible for the green house effect (Table 2.4). It is possible and necessary to stabilize the concentration of CO_2 at <450 ppm. This would limit global temperature increase to 1.5 - 2.0°F over the next 100 years according to a study by the Environmental Defense Fund.

TABLE 2.4: Contribution of greenhouse gases to global warming

Gases	Amount (%)
Carbon -di-oxide	49
Methane	18
Chlorofluorocarbons	14
Nitrous oxide	6
Others	13

Global summit

Developed countries account for the largest contribution (over 80 %) to green house gases. The Rio Earth summit urged all nations to maintain the green house emissions at the 1990 level. The most influential individual national entities to global warming are the U.S., China, Brazil, Germany, Japan, India, Indonesia and Russia. They are loosely referred to as the E-8. According to Dr. Lester Brown of Word Watch Institute, these eight countries collectively constitute about 58 % of carbon emissions associated with global warming.

Impact of global warming

Studies have shown that an increase in atmospheric CO_2 could lead to increased summer dryness with serious consequence on agriculture. Storms, powered by increasing ocean temperatures, could cause greater havoc. The observed records reveal a global warming of about 0.5 °C from 1860 to 1985. It has been forecast that the rise in atmospheric CO_2 from 350 to 700 ppm would increase the temperature on earth by 3-5 °C. According to one wheat model study, a 0.5 degree Celsius increase in temperature could decrease yield in North India by 10 %. The decreasing ozone concentration will raise the level of ultra violet radiation coming to the earth-creating problem for agriculture and animal and human health. Trees can absorb a large volume of carbondioxide and store the carbon part of the gas releasing the rest as oxygen in the atmosphere. Hence tree planting (greening) is an effective way of reducing the effect of green house gases.

CHAPTER 3

Tillage and Tillage Operations

TILLAGE

Tillage refers to mechanical manipulations of the soil that are used to provide necessary soil conditions favourable for the growth of crops. Tillage includes all operations and practices that are used for the purpose of modifying the physical character of the soil. Tilling the soil is the most difficult and time consuming operation in field crop production. About 30 % of the total cost of cultivation is for tillage operations. Jethro Tull, who lived in the 18th century, is considered the father of tillage. He emphasized the need of tillage to improve the productivity of the soil as it causes breaking large sized soil particles into finer ones. Soil surface area is thus increased from which the plant roots obtain their food. He had introduced "Horse-hoeing husbandry" in which crops are planted in rows and "horse-hoeing" is done in between.

Tillage was considered as an 'art' and in the recent years, research evidences has focussed tillage as "science". From time immemorial, various methods of ploughing have been tried by trial and error, based on the lobour availability and economic status of the farmer. Cultural practices have also undergone quite a lot of changes due to shortage of labour and /or increased cost of labour and availability of machinery. A lot of cultural operations are needed to prepare the virgin soil into a good seedbed. Tillage operations and methods of land preparation vary from place to place and even in the same place, depending upon the climate and crops cultivated.

Objectives of tillage

1. To prepare the seedbed to a satisfactory level which promotes good germination and establishment of the seedlings.
2. To control weeds and improve close plant-soil interaction in the rooting zone.
3. To manage the plant residues by incorporating into the soil or to retain on the top layer to reduce erosion.
4. To improve the physical conditions of the soil so that rainwater could be absorbed easily and soil erosion can be minimised.

5. To establish specific surface configurations for sowing, irrigation, drainage, etc.
6. To incorporate and mix applied fertilizers into the soil.
7. To destroy the eggs and larvae of insects and their breeding places.
8. Tilth

Tilth is the term used to express the physical condition of soil resulting from tillage. The physical condition is related to the soil-structural changes, which promote good seed germination and crop establishment. Tillage operations are aimed at producing and maintaining good tilth. A soil with good tilth will be mellow, friable and adequately aerated. Such soils will have high retentive capacity of rainwater and good aeration with adequate infiltration. Soil tilth is not static but varies with time. The capillary and non-capillary pores are about equal when the soil is in good tilth. Soil aeration, activity of microorganisms and chemical reactions in the soil increase with the increase in non-capillary pores. Total porosity and pore size distribution are important to improve moisture retention and availability of oxygen in the rooting zone. Soils having crumb structure of 1-5 mm size are considered favourable for crop growth. Powdery soil encourages surface crusting when the soil dries after wetting. Soil aggregate should be stable enough to withstand water and wind erosion. There may be deterioration in tilth when the land is continuously cropped by using heavy machinery like tractor drawn implements. Factors such as heavy rainfall and erosion by water and wind may destroy the tilth. The action of wetting and drying or freezing and thawing often regenerates desirable soil tilth.

TILLAGE AND CROP PRODUCTION

Tillage favours break up of clods, incorporates the organic matter into the soil and kills the weeds to create more favourable seed bed conditions. Physical condition of the soil significantly influences its moisture retention, root spread and penetration. It also influences the supply and uptake of nutrients by the crop plants. Soil aggregation depends on the clay and the humus contents in the soil. Soil porosity considerably influences root penetration. Exchange of CO_2 from the soil and oxygen from the atmosphere is essential for normal root development and microbial activity. Tillage ensures good soil aeration on heavy clay soils. The critical level of oxygen for better root growth is about 1-2%. The oxygen supply normally determines the rate of root growth. Due to restricted oxygen supply, the root hair growth is much restricted. High concentration of CO_2 in the soil is toxic to the roots. The critical limit of CO_2 for most species is between 10 to 20%.

Tillage results in better aeration and hence increases the activity of microorganisms. Because of the increased activity of microorganisms, the rate of decomposition of organic matter is rapid, thus enabling the release and availability of plant nutrients.

Weeds are burried into the soil with tillage operations. Weed seeds go deep into the soil and hence their germination is arrested. Deep tillage is always preferred as one of the measures to control the perennial weeds.

Tillage also helps in reducing the insect pest population in certain situations. Insects (pupae) are exposed to the sun's heat and to the attack of birds and are eliminated. The places for living and feeding of the insects are also destroyed. Clean cultivation is generally advocated as one of the methods of controlling insects and diseases. Tillage helps to destroy some of the fungi causing plant diseases. *e.g.* scab disease causing organism of Gibbrella.

Limitations

Tractors and heavy equipments are used for the land preparation. Hence there is a possibility of wind and water erosion as the land is left barren after the conventional tillage. There is also soil compaction due to repeated usage of heavy equipments and possibility of development of a dense zone (plough pan) below the plough layer.

Tillage operations

Seed germination and seedling growth are greatly affected by the fineness of the soil clods. The degree of soil pulverization differs with the type of machine used, tilling method and operating condition of machine. Pulverization also differs with soil conditions such as water content or particle distribution and ground cover like straw or grass. Some soils are compact and do not allow the entry of plant roots into the soil. Ploughing improves the physical conditions of the soil and enables the farmer to grow a good crop. Soil furnishes anchorage for plant roots. Soil must be sufficiently open so that roots can penetrate easily. Ploughing means stirring the soil rather deeply. It involves complete or partial turning of the soil. The soil is being constantly and uniformly moved in a forward and upward direction as the plough advances and hence pulverization takes place.

Climate and ploughing

Under semi-arid regions, it is better to leave crop residues mixed with surface soil than to turn them under. The crop residues prevent erosion and destruction of soil structure by beating raindrops and reduce surface run-off. However, under the temperate humid regions like the USA, ploughing with mould board plough gives better yield of maize as compared to other methods of cultivation. Wherever the field is infested with weeds and poorly drained, ploughing improves the crop yield.

Time of ploughing

Early ploughing has a distinct advantage over late ploughing because it gives more opportunity to kill weeds. Early ploughing may help in getting the soil granulated at the time of sowing. In intensive cultivation, the field is to be prepared without any time lapse for raising the next crop. In western countries, fall season ploughing before the onset of snow is preferred than the spring ploughing. Ploughing is to be done immediately after the harvest of the crops like sugarcane and crops that leave heavy stubbles or sod. Ploughing is also needed after the harvest of crops which have thick stand. *e.g.* sorghum and maize.

Ploughing operations should be carried out at appropriate soil moisture conditions to improve the physical condition of the soil. Ploughing dry soils with a hard consistency may lead to form numerous clods; at plastic consistency, it may cause puddling. There is an optimum moisture range for each soil for the most effective ploughing. This moisture range is called as 'friable consistence'. It is important to plough the field within the moisture range of friable consistence. This will help in achieving maximum granulation with minimum energy input.

Depth and intensity of ploughing

The purpose of cultivation is to control weeds and conservation of soil moisture. Deep ploughing gives better response in fields infested with weeds. This is also practised to incorporate the residues, particularly in sandy soils. Incorporation of residues in the deep layer having fine texture may improve the chemical properties of the soil. Under dryland conditions, deep ploughing improves soil moisture content. However, yield advantage due to deep ploughing depends on rainfall and the type of crop. Normally yield advantage is reported during normal and above normal rainfall years. It is important to practice deep ploughing for long duration, deep-rooted crops. Root crops generally respond better to deep tillage than shallow rooted crops like cereals. Potato generally responds better to deep tillage, particularly in clayey and loamy soils. Sugarbeet also shows positive response to deep ploughing. In black cotton soil, deep ploughing gives higher yield in flue-cured cigarette tobacco. Deep tillage is normally practised for crops like sugarcane. Small grain crops such as millets, sesame and flax do as well with shallow ploughing as with deep ploughing.

Deep cultivation is important to break the compact layers. The compacted layer at the bottom of the zone of ploughing is known as plough soil compaction. Compaction occurs due to use of tractors in wet soil condition. Chiseling upto 75 cm helps to break the subsoil compaction. Sub-soiling or deep ploughing helps to break the soil compaction and increase water absorption and root penetration, resulting in improved plant growth.

The tendency of the farmers is to plough the field frequently so that fine seedbed could be prepared. However, a large number of studies clearly indicate that increasing the number of ploughings does not help much. Ploughing at optimum soil moisture is important to prepare the seed bed with restricted ploughing.

Seed bed preparation

A good seed bed preparation enables the seed to come in close contact with moist soil and to begin its growth under favourable conditions. Weeds are removed, which otherwise compete with the crop and limit its growth. Seedbed preparation needs adequate care so as to provide early seed germination and better crop stand. Seedbed preparation varies with the crops to be grown, soil type, prevailing climate and type of farming. The fineness of the seedbed is determined by the seed size. Small seeded crops need a finer seedbed than the large-seeded crops. It is also important to make the fine seed bed fairly firm. Small seeded crops like finger millet, sesame and lucerne require a fine seedbed. However, crops like sorghum do well in moderately compact, coarse seedbed. Maize, chickpea and cotton require a coarsely prepared soil.

Coarse textured soils like sandy soils and red soils can be easily brought to a powdery condition with the receipt of rainfall. However, heavy clay soils like black cotton soils are to be ploughed and left in cloddy condition to facilitate the rains being retained on the surface. If such soils are repeatedly ploughed and kept in powdery condition for a long period before sowing, they get caked when dried after a rain. Then the soil is unable to absorb more water and there is loss of rainwater due to run-off.

Preparatory cultivation

Cultural operations carried out after the harvest of the previous crop and before sowing and/or planting of succeeding crop are known as preparatory cultivation. Preparatory cultivation includes primary tillage and secondary tillage. Primary tillage is followed by a number of secondary tillage operations such as harrowing. These operations kill the weeds and break up the clods to provide a good seed bed.

Off-season tillage

Preparatory tillage operations that are carried out during the off-season, before the main crop is cultivated, are known as off-season tillage. These include post harvest tillage and summer ploughing. Soil is tilled immediately after the harvest of the crop under adequate soil moisture. This is mostly practised after the harvest of the long duration crops like sugarcane ratoon, sod or turf crop. This operation helps in controlling weeds and the soils are receptive to rain water. Tillage operations done during the summer using the rainfall are known as summer ploughing. This helps in preparing the main field well in advance.

Primary tillage or ploughing

Ploughing is initially done to open the compact or hard soil. During the primary tillage, the soil is inverted, weeds are uprooted and stubbles incorporated into the soil. The depth of the tillage varies from 10 to 30 cm. A number of primary tillage implements are used to invert the soil and bury the surface vegetation and weed seeds. During this operation, soil is cut, lifted, shattered, twisted, inverted and sheared for further ploughing. The implements used for this purpose are called "primary tillage implements". These implements may be bullock or tractor drawn. Bullock drawn implements may be indigenous (desi) plough and mould board plough. The tractor drawn implements include mould board plough, disc plough, sub- soil plough and chisel plough.

Secondary tillage

Tillage operations that are carried out after the primary tillage are called secondary tillage operations. The main objective is to prepare a good seed bed. Soil is stirred and the clods are broken, weeds are removed and a fine seedbed is prepared. Secondary tillage normally includes harrowing, pulverizing, raking and leveling. Various types of implements are used for this operation. *e.g.* cultivators, harrows, clod crushers and leveling implements. They are both bullock drawn and tractor drawn.

Intercultural operations

Tillage operations that are carried out for manipulating the soil after the seed is planted or young plant has emerged are known as intercultural operations. The objective is to control weeds and to have dust mulch in the soil surface. Large area can be easily weeded with the use of intercultural implements. Intercultural operation decreases the bulk density of the soil and increases the total porosity. Dust mulch reduces the evaporation losses. Loosening the surface soil due to intercultivation enables to maintain high porosity at the soil surface. There is rapid increase in the initial rate of infiltration. The run-off loss is reduced and there is rapid intake of water in the beginning of the rainy season. Intercultural operation provides aeration in the root zone. Depth of intercultural operation depends on the condition and the type of crop. Shallow or deep cultivation may be advantageous for certain specific cases. Intercultural operations using cultivators are normally followed for wide spaced crops like cotton, particularly under dryland conditions.

Tillage of wetland soils (Puddling)

The traditional method of tillage for transplanted paddy is ploughing and puddling. The world 'puddle' means a soil layer that can be worked to a water-impermeable stage. Puddling is an essential practice for transplanted rice culture and is widely practiced although it is high-energy consuming.

Puddling is mixing soil with water to render it impervious. The soil structure is destroyed; aggregates lose their identity and soil is converted into a structurally homogenous mass of fine aggregates and textural separates. There are two phases in the puddling operation: increase in the soil moisture content and the mechanical operation. When moisture content increases, there is decrease in cohesion within the aggregates resulting the clay to swell and become soft. The degree of puddling depends on the cultural practices and the nature of the soil. High clay content facilitates puddling and high organic matter content increases the soil's resistance to puddling. An important difference between the dryland and puddled soil is the presence of oxidized and reduced soil layer in the puddled soil system. Energy requirement experiments at Pantnagar, U.P., show that tractor puddling requires 300 hp of energy/ha and bullock power may require 100 hp/ha.

Advantages of puddling

Puddling reduces the non-capillary pore space and a close packing of soil particles is obtained which, in turn, decreases hydraulic conductivity and free percolation of water. Due to reduction in hydraulic conductivity, drainage from a puddled soil may be 1000 times slower than from a granulated soil. Puddling enables improved weed control and provides congenial soil condition for easy transplanting. Reduced soil condition due to puddling provides the required physical, chemical and biological conditions for the growth of the rice plant. Rice grown on puddled soil may be less affected by drought because of higher moisture retention than in a non-puddled soil. Puddled soil has 2.5 % higher efficiency in water use than a non-puddled soil.

Limitations

Water requirement for land preparation with puddling is high (150 mm). A shift from a wetland puddled soil to dryland soil requires major alteration in the physical condition of the soil. Conversion from puddled to well-granulated soil conditions requires that the moisture content fall below the lower limit of plasticity.

Soil compaction

Soil compaction is the simple tillage practice adopted to meet the physical requirements of the soil for rice growth (Ghildyal, 1969). In this system, the soil is first ploughed and harrowed, fertilized and brought to optimum moisture content. Heavy rollers or tractors with loaded wheels are passed repeatedly over the soil until the desired density is achieved. The soil is then flooded and crop transplanted. Rice seeds can also be drilled directly into the compacted soil with a suitable drill. Such a system of cultivation is especially useful for dryland rice where nutrient and water conservation are important. During compaction, soil particles move to a closer state of contact and there is change in the bulk density. Plant available water in the soil increases since water is retained at high suction. Compaction may alter the gas composition of soil if pore spaces are reduced sufficiently. Compaction affects the thermal characteristics of the soil and there is increase in thermal conductivity. Soil strength increases with increasing compaction. Soil compaction facilitates mobility of nutrient ions to roots by both diffusion and mass flow.

MODERN CONCEPTS OF TILLAGE

Conventionally it is thought that land should be prepared thoroughly with repeated ploughings. However, modern concepts of tillage emphasize minimal cultivation. Considering the time loss for tillage operations, minimum and zero tillage have been advocated and this concept is together known as 'conservation tillage'. The objective of this type of tillage is to reduce loss of soil and water compared to conventional tillage. This concept is generally followed in western countries where a large amount of plant residues are left in the soil surface. The plant residues protect the soil against the beating action of rain drops, keep the surface of the soil open and increase the infiltration of water compared to a bare soil. Soil structure and organic matter content in the soil are improved and the productivity level is maintained. Under these conditions, sowing operations are carried out with little disturbance to the crop residues. The system is frequently referred to as stubble mulching, eco-fallow, limited tillage, reduced tillage, minimum tillage, no tillage and direct drill. These systems of tillage are widely adopted in the United States.

Minimum tillage

In this system, tillage operations are considerably reduced to the minimum required for good seed bed preparation. In situations where crop residues are left *in situ* in the field for decomposition, this method of minimum tillage is normally followed. Minimum tillage is comparatively easy to adopt in coarse and medium textured soils and is practised for a period of 2-3 years. Minimum tillage practices have the advantages of cost effectiveness and time saving in field preparation. A saving of about 50-58 % of fuel can be made in minimum tillage compared to conventional tillage. This system is particularly advantageous in heavy clay and clay loam soils where it is often difficult to create optimum conditions in the seed zone. However, weeds may become over-abundant and reduce the yield levels in the course of time.

Types of minimum tillage

Combined tillage and planting: Land is ploughed early and additional tillage is provided during planting/sowing with cultivator or disk. The operation at the time of sowing enables to kill the weeds and firm the soil lightly before planting. This type of tillage operations is followed in large farms where early ploughing is normally adopted.

Plough-plant system: Tillage and planting are done in one operation. Using a planter trailing behind the plough or with a planter mounted in the plough itself, crop is sown simultaneously. This method is most suitable on sandy loam soils.

Till- plant system: Tillage and planting are done in one operation. Wide sweeps are operated 5-8 cm deep on the ridge top made during the previous year cultivation. The old stalks and root clumps are moved into the areas between the rows and thus a trash-free zone is formed for sowing. Ridges may be re-formed annually using heavy disk to cut the residue and level the old ridges.

Zero tillage: The extreme form of minimum tillage is known as ' zero tillage'. This method of tillage is gaining momentum in the developed countries like the United States and Western Europe. The concept has been developed with the availability of herbicides for weed control, which is one of the objectives of tillage operations. Some of the soils retain desirable physical properties and such situations warrant minimum primary tillage. Zero tillage method is highly effective under slopy lands where soil and water erosion are heavy. Wherever natural drainage is good, this method shows favourable results. In no tillage system, herbicide application, planting and harvesting are the only cultural operations that are followed during crop cultivation. No tillage method has been successfully adopted for planting grasses and legumes. Tilling and seeding are done in one operation. Non-selective broad-spectrum herbicides are used to kill a sod (grass, grass legume) or residue from previous crop. The usage of machinery completes all the operations at a time.

The extreme example of zero tillage is sod seeding, a technique widely used by rice farmers in southern Australia. Sod seeding involves sowing of rice directly on a well-grazed pasture sward with a sod-seeder and with minimum disturbance of the soil. The pasture is heavily grazed by sheep before sowing. Field is irrigated before sowing, if the soil is too hard for sod seeding. After sowing, the field is irrigated, flushed or grazed. The sheep may graze some rice tops but those soon recover. Advantages of this system are reduced cost of production, improved utilization of pastures and less soil disturbance. Non-specific herbicides like paraquat is used to control weeds. This technique is called as ' chemical sod seeding'.

Minimum tillage under Indian conditions: Minimum tillage practice is generally adopted under intensive cropping. Groundnut- groundnut-sesame cropping system is predominantly followed in North-Eastern Zone of Tamil Nadu, India. After the harvest of second crop of groundnut, sesame seeds are broadcast sown. Harvest of groundnut at optimum moisture condition is almost equal to a ploughing operation. After sowing of sesame, one ploughing is done to cover the seeds and provide a firm seed bed. In Cauvery Delta Zone, Tamil Nadu, India, pulse seeds are sown when the soil is in waxy condition 7-10 days prior to harvest of rice.

The rice fallow pulse is thus cultivated fully under zero tillage situations without any land preparation. Similarly linseed is cultivated in Eastern part of India under 'paira' condition (rice fallow) with minimum tillage.

IMPLEMENTS AND THEIR USAGE

A large number of implements are used for different tillage operations. Based on the operations for which they are designed, implements are classified into different groups.

1. Implements used for ploughing
   a) Country plough
   b) Mould board plough
   c) Disc plough
2. Cultivators and harrows
   a) Junior hoe
   b) Disc harrow
   c) Spring harrow
   d) Spike tooth harrow
   e) Indigenous blade harrows
3. Implements for wetland operations
   a) Wetland puddler
   b) Helical blade puddler
   c) Green manure trampler
   d) Cage wheel
4. Leveling implements
   a) Wooden leveling board
   b) Buck scraper
   c) A-frame ridger
   d) Ditcher
   e) Float
5. Implements used for soil compaction and breaking clods
   a) Iron roller
   b) Wooden or stoneroller
6. Implements for special operations
   a) Bund former
   b) Ridge plough
   c) Bed furrow former
   d) Rotovator
   e) Chisel plough
   f) Sub-soiler
7. Sowing/planting implements
   a) Seed drills
   b) Paddy Transplanter
8. Weeders
   a) Dryland weeders

b) Rotary weeders

Implements for ploughing

In the early stage of civilization, primitive man would have first developed a plough just to stir the soil. Modern ploughs are used to open the soil and pulverize it. Ploughs are also used to incorporate the crop residues and manures. Ploughing is done at varied depth depending on the type of crops grown and the condition of the filed. Implements may be of animal drawn or power operated.

Desi or country plough

The most important tillage implement used all over India is the country plough or 'desi' plough. The shape of the plough is more or less similar throughout the country. However, the size varies depending upon the soil type in which the plough is operated. According to the size of the cattle engaged in a particular region, the plough size varies. Most of the 'desi' ploughs are light in weight and can be easily carried on the shoulders. In the regions of black cotton soils (vertisols), heavier ploughs are normally used.

Parts of country plough

The plough consists of a wooden body to which a handle and a shaft pole are attached. The body is made with a bent piece of hard wood, like babul or neem with arms making an abtuse angle of about 120° to 135°. A small piece of bar share made of mild steel is fixed at the plough bottom. It actually penetrates the soil and protects the wooden wedge against wear and tear. The length of shaft pole varies from 2.5 to 3.5 m. One end of the shaft pole is fixed to the body and the other end is free to be secured with yoke during working. The handle is fixed to the back of the body. (Fig. 3.1)

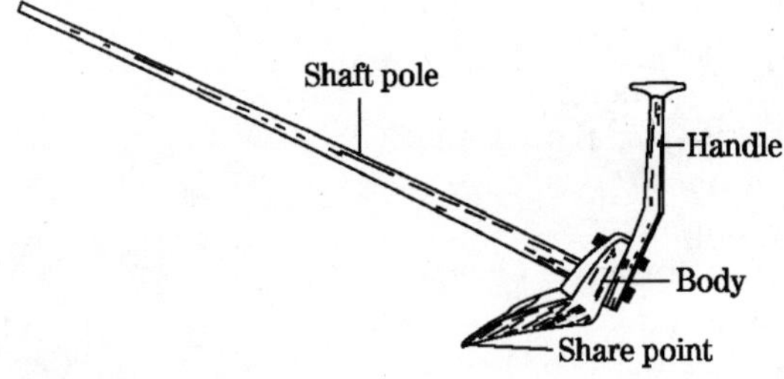

FIG. 3.1: Desi or country plough

Operation with the country plough

Adjustments: While operating the plough, a 'V' shaped furrow is formed. The depth of the furrow is usually 10-20 cm and the width varies between

13 and 18 cm. The depth of the furrow can be easily adjusted by varying the distance between the yoke and the body. If the shaft pole is pulled behind, the distance between the plough bottom and the yoke is increased and a deep furrow is formed. Similarly, if the shaft pole is tied under the yoke, the depth of the furrow is increased. Rather if the shaft pole is tied above the yoke and pulled forward, distance between the yoke and body is reduced and shallow furrow is formed.

Ploughing: Field is covered in strips at the time of ploughing. The ploughing is always started from the right side of the field and the animals are turned towards their left side. First furrow is opened parallel to the end of the field and taken to the headl and and turned at a distance of about six meters, which is convenient for the animals to turn. The plough is taken along the headlands and the second furrow is opened close to the previous furrow. The plough is worked round and round repeatedly turning always to the left, till nearly half the area of the strip is completed. Thus half of the area is left unploughed in the middle. At this stage, a new strip of similar width is taken and ploughing is proceeded. The field is covered fully in this manner. First ploughing is usually taken along the length of the field. This may reduce the number of turnings at the headlands. Subsequently ploughing is taken cross-wise in order to have thorough coverage of the field. Normally ploughing should be done across the slope to reduce loss of top soil.

Mould board plough

The mould board plough is an improved tillage implement over the country plough. This is probably one of the first implements to be introduced from abroad to India. The advantage of using the mould board is that a layer of soil is separated from the underlying sub-soil and is inverted. Thus, any vegetation or manure present on the surface is buried under. A soil layer is brought to the surface, where it is exposed to the action of weathering agents and other implements. As a result, the soil gets pulverized. Heavier mould board ploughs can work even in very hard soils.

Plough components: The components of the mould-board plough are the plough bottom, handle, beam (Fig. 3.2.). Some of the ploughs may also have clevis or bridle, wheel and coulter.

Plough bottom: This part actually contacts with the soil and contains main working parts. The plough bottom consists of (i) the share, (ii) the mould board, (iii) the land side (iv) frog and (v) coulter.

i) **The share:** It has a sharp cutting edge, which sinks into the soil making passage for the plough bottom. The share is made up of a flat piece of steel or cast iron. Steel shares have the advantage of being less liable to damage from stones than the shares of cast iron and also they may be built up and 'hard surfaced' when worn.
ii) **The mould board:** It is also called as the 'breast' or 'wing'. The mould

boards are made up of cast iron, steel and soft centre steel. This part helps in inverting the furrow slice. Because of the twisting and inverting action, the furrow slice is broken and pulverized depending on the shape and curvature of the mould board. With the use of mould board of gentle curvature, furrow slice is left unbroken. While furrow slice is more or less pulverized when a short and broad mould board with an abrupt curvature is used.

iii) **The landside:** The other names of the landside are 'slad' or 'heel'. It is positioned on the side opposite to the mould board. It is made up of cast iron or steel and usually rectangular in shape. It helps to resist the side pressure exerted by the furrow slice and helps in stabilizing the plough during the operation.

iv) **The frog:** The parts like share, mould board and landside are attached rigidly to the frog. It is an irregular piece of metal made of cast iron or welded steel.

v) **The coulter:** A knife or disc like attachment is fixed to the beam. The coulter helps in separating the furrow slice from the unploughed land. The 'knife coulter' is used in grasslands and the 'disc coulter' in the fields infested with weeds. The coulter cuts the weeds and enables easy penetration of share point.

Other parts

i) **Handle:** It helps in guiding the plough; the handles are usually provided with wooden gripes. Most of the mould boards have two handles while light ploughs have single handle.

ii) **Beam:** Beam is fixed to the plough bottom, which extends forward and is connected to the yoke by means of chains or ropes.

iii) **Clevis or bridle:** Some type of arrangements is provided at the end of the beam to regulate the width and depth of the furrow. It is also called as 'clevis' or 'hake'. There are provisions for horizontal or vertical adjustments. Some of the ploughs may have either or both the adjustments. A number of holes are provided to facilitate hitching at a desired point. In the horizontal bridle, if the hitching is done to the hole nearest to the mould board, widest furrow is formed. Hitching in the farthest hole from the mould board results in narrowest furrow. In the vertical bridle, if the draught chain is fixed at the top most holes, furrow will be deeper. Hitching at the lowest hole results in shallow furrow.

iv) **Wheels:** One end of the beam of heavy ploughs is fitted with wheels. The wheels assist the ploughman while steadying them; thereby ploughing is rendered easier and less tiring.

Types of mould board plough

Mould board ploughs are of five types: general purpose, stubble type, sod or breaker type, slat type and high-speed type.

General-purpose ploughs are used for shallow ploughing (20-25 cm), grasslands and clay soils. Stubble types are engaged for deep ploughing (25-30 cm) and for root crops. Sod or breaker types are preferred for complete inversion of the furrow slice. Slat types are made of slats with gaps between the slats. These types are preferred to plough the sticky soils. Simple size ploughs are used with animal power. Most of the tractor drawn mould board ploughs are high-speed type and are used for deep ploughing (30 cm).

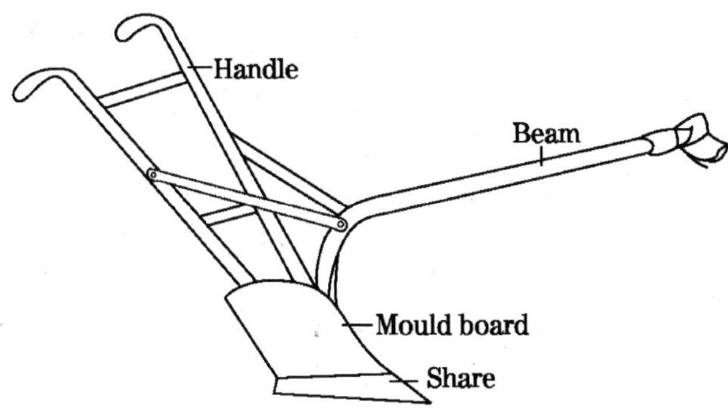

FIG. 3.2: Mould board plough

Ploughing with mould board plough: The field is marked into plots of convenient sizes so that work animals could turn easily. The plots should not be too big which may have empty turnings in the headlands. This type of marking is known as 'feering'. The field is then ploughed either by 'gathering' or 'splitting' method. In 'gathering' method, ploughing is started from the centre of the plot and is turned round and round always towards the mould board side. Lastly a ridge is left in the centre of each plot. In splitting method, ploughing is started at the two opposite edges of the plot. Ploughing is continued inward and completed with a furrow in the centre. Plough is turned always towards the 'landside'.

Disc plough

Disc ploughs have steel discs of 50-90 cm diameter. The discs are made of hard high carbon steel and have sharp cutting edge. The discs are set at an angle to the direction of travel. Each disc revolves on a stub axle. The angle of the disc is adjustable. The discs are mounted on a frame, which is supported by wheels. Lever arrangements are provided for lifting the disc and clear off the ground. Depth of penetration of the disc can also be changed by using the lever arrangements. While working, the discs rotate, scoop out furrows, invert the furrow slice and pulverize them thoroughly. The disc ploughs are particularly suitable for soils having hard plough pans. It works well in conditions where mould board plough does not work satisfactorily, particularly in sticky soils. It can be operated for incorporation of stubbles and green manures. Disc ploughs are basically tractor drawn because of their weight and size (Fig. 3.3).

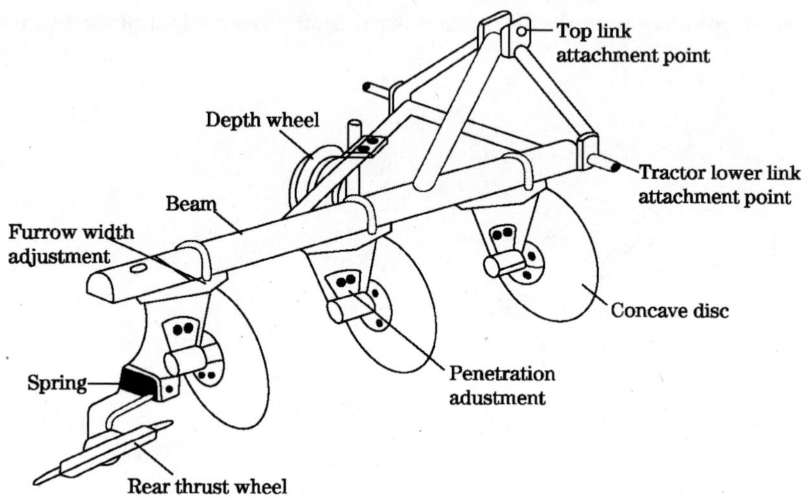

FIG. 3.3: Disc plough

Cultivators and harrows

These are the secondary tillage implements used after initial ploughing of the soil. With the use of the primary tillage implements, the furrow slice and clods are left unbroken. Cultivators and harrows are used for pulverization and to bring the soil to desired tilth. These implements help in destroying the weeds and to mix manures and fertilizers with the soil.

Cultivators

Cultivators are commonly called tillers in India. A number of tynes are attached for easy penetration into the soil and break the clods. Cultivators usually have two or three rows of tynes at specified space. Tynes are mounted in such a way that they provide clearance between adjacent tynes through which clods and rubbish can pass freely. Cultivators are of different sizes. The large models are designed for tractor mounting. Small models are walking types drawn by animals. Tractor drawn cultivators are of two types: (i) cultivator with spring-loaded tynes and (ii) cultivator with rigid tynes.

Junior hoe

It is a cultivator of walking type drawn by animals. Junior hoe is normally used as an intercultural implement for wide row crops like sugarcane, cotton, etc. It has a light frame which is approximately triangular in shape in which the tynes are attached. A wheel is provided in the front to regulate the depth of penetration. The handle provision is useful in guiding the implement. To adjust the frame width according to the inter-row spacing, lever arrangement is provided. (Fig. 3.4). Three-tyned cultivator with seeding attachment is very common in most parts of the country.

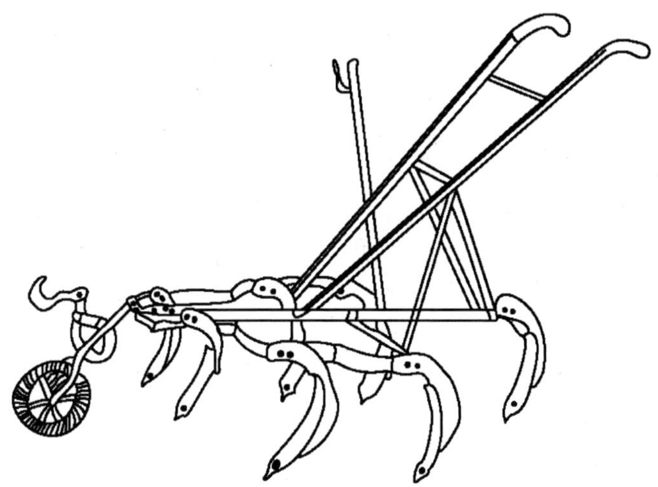

FIG. 3.4: Junior hoe

Harrows

Disc harrow

Disc harrows (Fig. 3.5) are suitable for hard ground with grassy weed infestation. It consists of number of concave disc sets or gangs, positioned to move angularly with the direction of travel. The concave discs are mounted on a common shaft or bolt, called 'gang bolt' and spaced by using spacer spools. Scrapers are suspended close to the concave surfaces from the frame. The discs may have plain or serrated edge or both in one gang. The implement is useful in the preparation of land after ploughing, particularly grasslands and virgin lands and also for incorporation of manures. Disc harrows are of three types depending on the arrangements of discs: single action, double action (tandem) and offset harrows.

Spring harrow

Spring tooth harrow is fitted with springs having loops of elliptical shape. These are suitable for hard and stony field. The tynes pulverize the soil and help in killing weeds.

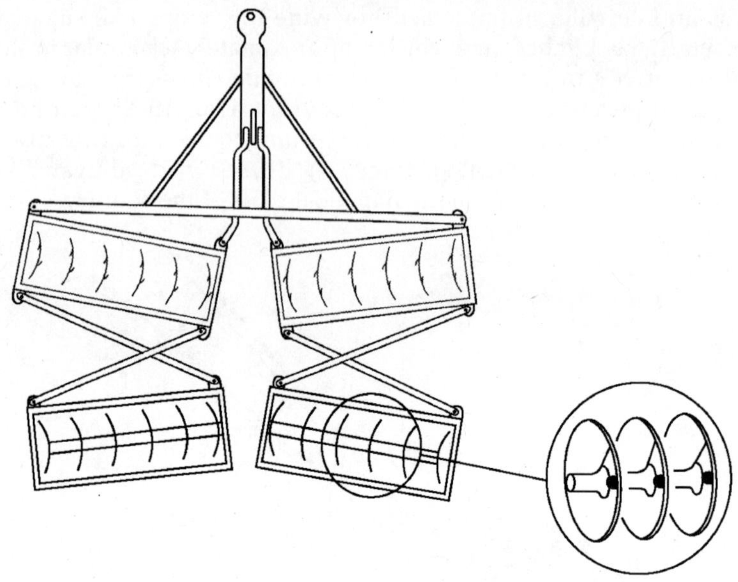

FIG. 3.5: Disc harrow

Spike tooth harrow

In this type, teeth are fixed to a frame. The teeth vary in length from 12.5 to 25.0 cm according to the heaviness of the implement. The teeth are of different shapes such as round, square, rectangular, triangular, etc. They are mounted rigidly or on a flexible frame in a zigzag manner. The tynes (teeth) are staggered in such a way that those in the rear do not follow the track of the front ones. The implement is used for sowing or drilling and also for covering the seeds after sowing.

Spike tooth harrow, disc harrow and spring harrow are mainly tractor drawn.

Indigenous blade harrows

Some of the implements used for inter- cultivation are 'danti' and 'Guntaka'.

Danti

It is an indigenous blade harrow used for inter-cultivation in row crops spaced 30-40 cm apart. 'Danti' consists of a horizontal beam of about 15 cm diameter and 45 cm long to which the handle, shaft pole and a harrow blade are attached. The blade is fixed to the beam near the ends of two standards. Five or six danties are attached to a common yoke for inter-cultivation. The area covered by a single danti (30 cm width) is about 0.4

to 0.6 ha in a day of eight hours. (Fig. 3.6).

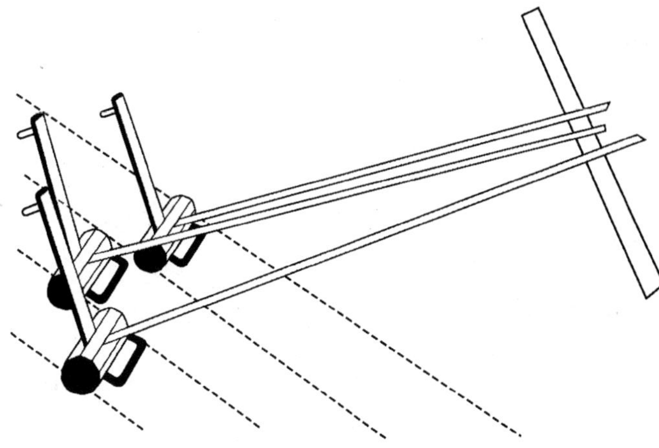

FIG. 3.6: Danties

Guntaka

It is a comparatively larger indigenous blade harrow mainly intended for stirring the soil and to cover the seeds (without blade). It has a horizontal beam of 1.5 to 2.0 m to which an iron blade is attached by means of two standards, one at either end and a handle on the other end. The implement with blade is used for harrowing the land. Without blade and standards it is used for covering the seeds (Fig 3.7).

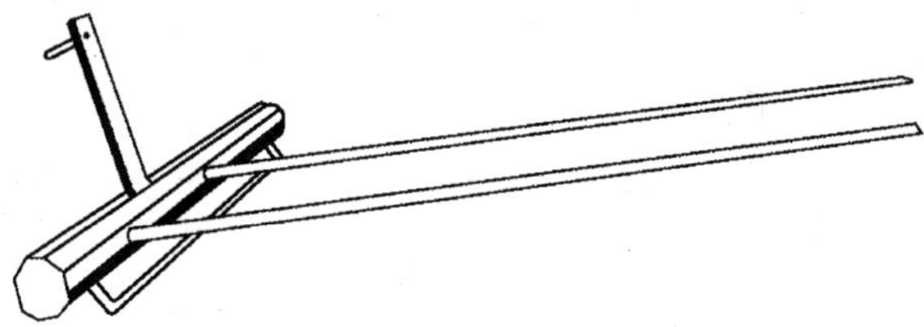

FIG. 3.7: Guntaka or blade harrow

Guntakas- types

Guntakas are named locally. Large sized guntakas of 2.0 m wide are called as 'Bara' Guntakas which are mainly used for the primary tillage. Small sized guntakas are designed for inter-cultural operations. They are: (i) 'Meesalu' Guntaka, (ii) 'Reggala' Guntaka, (iii), 'Metla' Guntaka and (iv) R-E. Guntaka. (Fig. 3.8).

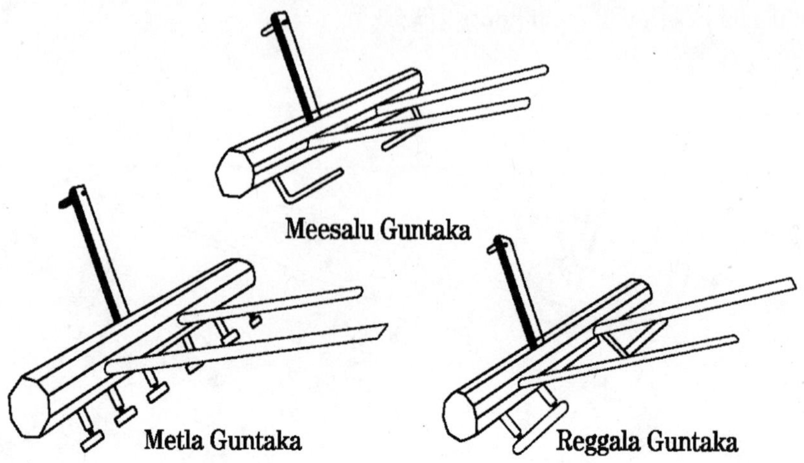

FIG. 3.8: Types of Guntakas

i) *Meesalu Guntaka*: The blade is not continuous as in ordinary guntakas. The blade has an opening through which the cropped line passes. Two arms of the guntaka help in stirring the soil and uproot the weeds in the interspaces of the crop.
ii) *Reggala Guntaka:* Instead of one continuous blade, two short blades each about 40 cm apart are fixed to the beams each with two standards. While working in the field, the individual blade passes through one interspace between two rows. In each blade, there is a projection towards the crop line to work to the root zone.
iii) *Metla Guntaka:* Six numbers of small blades are fixed to the beam at about 30 cm apart by means of a standard. A blade of about 15 cm length passes through the inter- space and the field is intercultivated.
iv) *R. E. Guntaka:* These are used for multipurpose operations like harvesting groundnut and intercultivation operations. Guntakas are fitted with 90 cm curved or straight blade with standard of 60 cm. Some are fitted with iron spikes for easy penetration. The curved type is used for harvesting spreading type of groundnut.

Implements used in wetlands

Ploughing in the wetlands is done with stagnation of water in the field. This operation is called as puddling, which facilitates destruction of soil structure and causes water stagnation in the field. The condition of the soil obtained due to puddling is called as "puddle". A semi-pervious hard pan is covered approximately with 10 to 15 cm dense mud and very little free water on the surface. Considerable human energy is utilized in the wetland preparation. Use of implements eases the operation of puddling.

Wetland puddler

It is a labour saving implement used for puddling the wetlands. This implement consists of three angular bladed cast iron buds rigidly fixed to a hallow horizontal pipe and is rotated when dragged by a pair of bullocks. The blades work into the puddle, break up lumps and leave the field in a fine condition. This implement is also used for trampling the green manure in the puddled field. When used for trampling, the vegetative matter is cut and buried into the soil. For satisfactory working of the puddler, a preliminary ploughing of the land is important. Puddler is operated keeping standing water of 5.0 – 7.5 cm in the field. An area of about 0.80 ha can be covered in a day of 8 hours of puddling.

Helical blade puddler

Six to eight blades of 5 cm width are helically bent and fixed in the radial arms by welding. These are mounted on a wooden frame having wooden bearings, such that the blades can rotate freely. A handle and a shaft are also provided. Helical shape of the blade gives continuous contact between the blades and the soil. While operating the implement the soil is continuously sliced and weeds are cut and buried into the soil. On an average, an area of 0.5-0.6 ha per day can be covered. (Fig. 3.9)

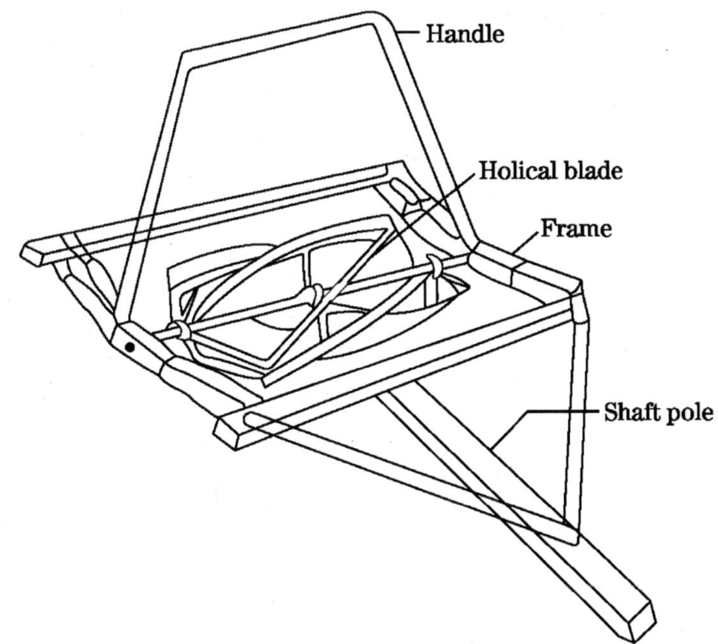

FIG. 3.9: Helical blade puddler

Green manure trampler

It is a labour saving implement used for trampling green manure in the rice fields. The implement consists of 3-4 steel discs of 25 cm diameter of cast iron hubs rigidly mounted on a pipe shaft 22.5 cm apart, rotating in wooden block bearings. There are steel blades fixed across the discs. The implement cuts green manure spread over the field and enables to bury into the puddle to a depth of 5-cm.

Leveling implements

The choice of the implement used for land leveling depends on the quantity of earthwork involved, type of power available, economic feasibility and farm size. Among the different implements available, animal drawn implements such as leveling board and buck scrapper are normally used.

The wooden leveling board

It is made of wood and extensively used for leveling the paddy field after puddling. Leveling board has a wooden plank of about 2.0 -m long and 0.30 -m wide with a handle. Two hooks are provided at the end of the plank for hitching. When the operator stands over the board, it sinks lightly into the loose mud; excess soil is collected and released to the depressions when he gets down. The implement is also used to a limited extent in the uplands for leveling the field after ploughing. Under such conditions, iron levelers are preferred to wooden planks.

Buck scrapper

This implement is made up of thick mild steel plate lapped and revetted at the corners to form a rectangular box with the front-end open. At the bottom, two flat steel plates or runners are provided. These arrangements protect the base and prevent the sheet from being worn out due to dragging over the land. Two handles are provided at the sides to assist in filling the box with earth and emptying the contents. The land is ploughed first to loosen the soil so that leveling is easy. Buck scrapers of different sizes are available and approximately 0.20 to 0.40 ha can be covered in a day depending on the evenness of the filed.

A-frame ridger

It is a wooden implement used for land leveling and forming ridges. The operation principle is simple as that of the bund former. The operator rides on the ridger applying his weight to get more effective job.

V-ditcher

This implement is used for leveling and construction of field channels. The operation of this implement is much similar to that of an over-sized mould board plough.

Wooden float

The implement is used for land smoothening with animal power. It is desirable to operate the implement three or more times by going across the field lengthwise, crosswise and diagonally for better smoothening before taking up sowing.

Implements for soil compaction and breaking clods

Rollers made up of wood, stone or iron, are used to consolidate the soil, crush the clods and smoothen the surface. The general principle involved is the rotation of massive material round the axle.

Iron rollers

There are two types of iron rollers, 'flat roller' consisting of steel or cast iron cylinders made in two or three sections to facilitate turnings and ' Ring or Cambridge' rollers effective in crushing the clods. Number of ribbed cast iron segments is mounted loose on an axle. The implement is also used for breaking the surface crust.

Wooden and stone rollers

Wooden rollers are occasionally used in the fieldwork. The stonerollers are meant for clod crushing and soil compaction. However, they are mostly used for threshing the millets.

Implements for special operations

Bund former

The implement consists of two divergent gathering steel blades fixed to a framework with a long wooden shaft pole. Different sizes of bund formers are available. The steel blade gathers loose soil from the surface and forms bunds. Adjustments are provided for increasing or decreasing the size of the bund. The implement is worked along and across the field at suitable intervals so as to form required sizes of beds. Irrigation channels can also be formed by making narrow spaced bunds. The bund former is also used for soil conservation work. Temporary bunds across the field can be formed to conserve moisture and prevent run-off water (Fig. 3.10).

Ridge plough

This is a double mould board plough having adjustable wings with which the width can be suitably altered at the rear. While working, the implement lays earth on both sides equally and an open furrow is formed in the middle. The vertical bridle provision in the implement is useful in forming deeper or shallow furrows by adjusting it according to the needs. An area of about 0.8 to 1.0 ha can be covered in a day (Fig. 3.11).

The bund former/ridge plough may be animal drawn or tractor drawn.

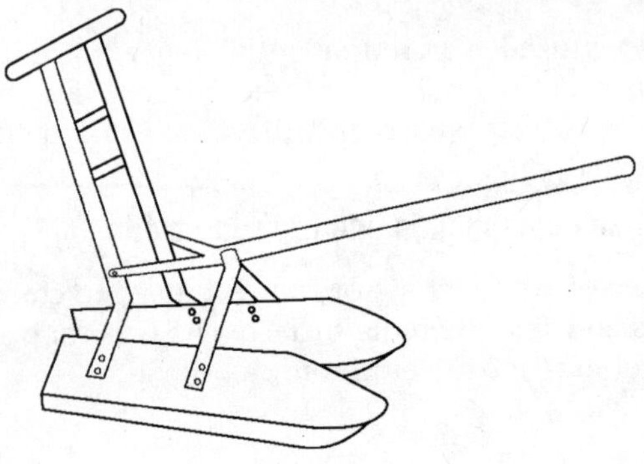

FIG. 3.10: Bund former

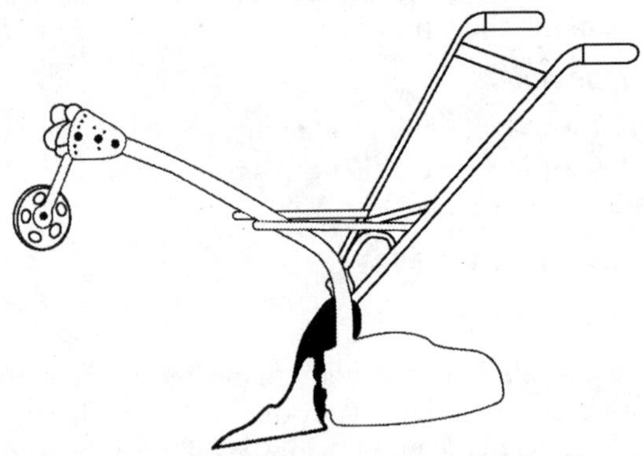

FIG. 3.11: Ridge plough

Bed – Furrow Former

It is a tractor drawn implement capable of forming alternate beds and channels simultaneously in one pass. The unit is made of 8 SWG M-S sheet welded together in the same profile as the beds are required to be formed. It is provided with suitable brackets for hitching it to the three-point linkage of the tractor for easy and efficient operation. It is possible to cover 3 ha / day of operation.

Rotovator

This is also called as rotary plough or rotary cultivator. This is a tractor mounted or power tiller drawn implement. This performs the primary and secondary tillage operations simultaneously so as to prepare a fine seed bed in a single pass. The drive sprockets transmit the rotary power to the rotor axis through a chain drive. As the machine is drawn along the tyne the soil is broken. The implement can also be effectively utilized for stubble mulching. In each implement, there may be two or three blades. Depending upon the soil type, soil moisture and the positioning of the trailing board, tilth is obtained. The depth of ploughing is controlled by positioning the depth skids.

Chisel ploughs

Chisel ploughing is not a method of ploughing but is a heavy cultivating operation. Chisel ploughs are used to break the hard pan or plough sole, improve the moisture holding capacity and pull out deep rooted weeds. This implement is useful in hard conditions and in reclaiming rough lands and orchards. The implement is heavily structured and has a heavy job to do. It requires considerable power to pull it. The chisel plough developed at Tamil Nadu Agricultural University, Coimbatore has a sturdy tyne which is hinged in the main frame and locked with the main frame by using bolt. This shearing off is to safeguard the tractor when the draft required exceeds the predetermined limit. The locking arrangement may help in easy transport of the implement without causing damage to the trailer or to keep the tyne in position.

Sub- soiler

Sub soiler is used to penetrate the soil deeper than with conventional cultivation machinery. This helps to break up the layers of soil which have become compacted due to the movement of heavy machinery or as a result of ploughing. Sub-soilers may have one or more heavy tynes which break through the impervious layer, causing a shatter. Normal depth of work is approximately 50-cm. The operation of sub-soiler should be carried out under very dry condition to get maximum fissuring of the soil.

Sowing/planting implements

Seed drills

Simple designed indigenous seed drill is called " gorru" This is operated using animal power. It consists of a tube or tubes on to which a seeding bowl is fixed. The bowl has a number of holes in it. The construction of the holes is ingenious and hence seed is dropped fairly even into the tubes. The seeds go down to the tynes fixed at suitable distance in a horizontal beam. Gorrus are of different sizes suitable for sowing of field crops. A pair of bullocks is used to drag the gorrus. A small quantity of seeds is dropped at a time into the bowl. The seeds are sown at a uniform depth and space. (Fig. 3.12)

A number of mechanical seed drills are now available. These are power operated. There are provisions for sowing and fertilizer application simultaneously. A mechanical seed drill consists of (i) frame, (ii) seed box, (iii) seed dropping mechanism, (iv) furrow opener, (v) covering device and (vi) transport wheels. Seed drills having automatic drilling of seeds are also available.

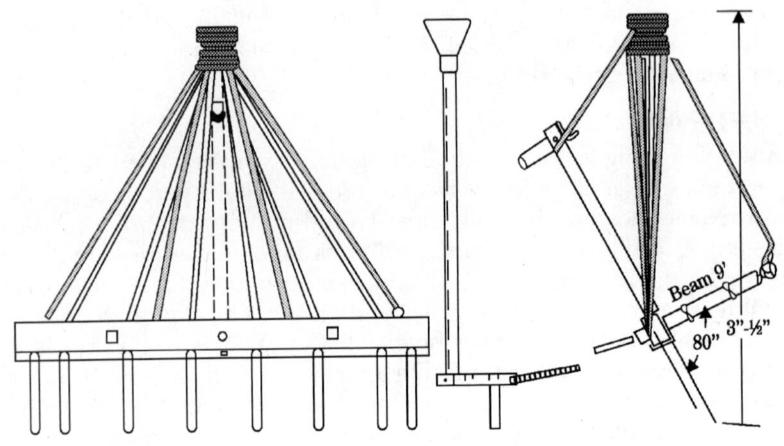

FIG. 3.12: Indigenous seed drill

Seed planter

The planter is normally used for seeds of larger size. Row to row spacing and intra-row spacing are fixed. The main functions of the planters are: (i) to open the furrow, (ii) meter the seed, (iii) deposit the seed in the furrow, (iv) cover the seed and (v) compact the soil. A planter normally consists of (i) hopper, (ii) seed metering device, (iii) knock-out arrangement, (iv) cut off mechanism, (v) furrow opener and (vi) other accessories.

Tractor drawn seed planter

The TNAU model seed planter consists of seed boxes along with cup feed type seed metering mechanisms. These are mounted on the cultivator frame and seeds are dropped in the furrows opened by the cultivator shovels. Detachable side wings are fixed to the existing shovel type furrow opener of the cultivator which helps in placing the seed at the required depth. To operate the seed-metering disc, power is taken from the ground drive through a clutch. A square bar is provided at the back of the unit to close the furrows. This implement is quite suitable for drylands and to sow crops like groundnut, maize, sorghum and pulses. Average area coverage is 4 ha/day.

Till planter for cotton

This has been designed and developed by TNAU as an attachment to tractors of 35 hp range. This unit consists of a tilling mechanism, a ridge forming mechanism and a planter to plough, form ridges and furrows and plant on one side of the ridges in one pass. In order to suit sowing different varieties of cotton, provisions are made for altering the row spacing, plant spacing and depth of seed placement. The capacity of the unit is 0.80 ha/hour.

IRRI Model Paddy Transplanter

The International Rice Research Institute, Philippines, has developed a manually operated paddy-transplanting machine. The mat type paddy nursery grown in compartments is required for transplanting. The machine consists of seedling tray, tray movement mechanism, frame with skid, seedling pickers and a handle. Seedlings are picked from the tray by the seedling picker when the handle is pushed forward. The seedlings are planted in the puddle when the handle is further pushed down. The seedling tray moves sideways positioning the next batch of seedlings to be picked up by the pickers. The machine is pulled to the next station to repeat the cycle. At a time, 4-8 rows can be transplanted depending on the model of the machine. It is possible to cover 0.15 - 0.25 ha in a day of 8 hours with the help of 4-5 labourers.

Weeders

Dryland weeders

These weeders are manually operated and used for removing weeds in line-sown crops under dryland conditions. The weeders are star and peg types depending on the shape of the roller attached at the foot of the long handle. Peg types are used for black, clay and clay loam soils and star types for loam and sandy loam soils. (Fig. 3.13)

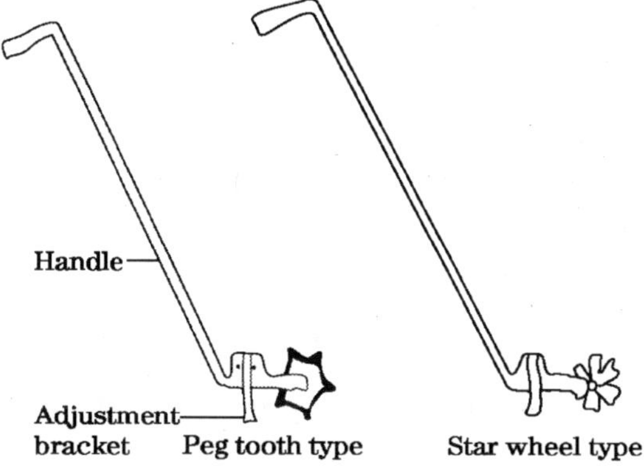

FIG. 3.13: Dryland weeders

Rotary weeders

This is a hand-operated implement used for weeding in planted rice fields. There are two small-toothed conical rollers or drums mounted on a frame provided with a handle. Each roller consists of about 5-toothed blades. At the time of working, it is pushed and pulled alternatively by the operator in between rows. A float provided at the anterior part guides the implement smoothly at the time of working and prevent it sinking into the puddle. An area of about 0.2 ha can be covered in a day. Weeds in the intra-row spacing between the rice plants can be removed by hand.

CHAPTER 4

Crop Establishment and after Cultivation

Plant growth is affected by the biological (biotic) and physical (abiotic) factors. The physical factors mainly consist of climate which accounts for greater variation in crop yields. Hence, it is important to remove all the physical factors limiting plant growth resulting in substantial increase in the yield of crops per unit area per unit time. The crop growth generally lies in the range of 15-20 g/m^2/day for crops without stress. Photosynthetic efficiency of crop plants should be stimulated for full utilization of all biological and physiological reserves in the plants. Higher crop production is possible by increasing the biological solar energy conversion.

CROP GROWTH

Growth in general may be defined as a vital process which brings about a permanent change in any plant or its part in respect to its size, form, weight and volume. Growth occurs in meristematic region, the activity of each meristem influences the activity of other meristems. The main apical shoot meristem is active and it retards the activity of more recently initiated lateral bud meristem. This phenomenon is usually referred to as 'apical dominance'.

In higher plants, growth includes cell division, enlargement and cell differentiation. Cell differentiation is the transformation of genetically identical cells of common origin (*e.g.* zygote) into different tissues. This is accomplished by various structural, functional and physiological specialization. Growth and differentiation results in development leading to characteristic form and chemical composition of plants.

The growth may be grouped into two types in higher plants: (i) limited and (ii) unlimited. In the limited type (*e.g.* annual plant), the plant grows upto a predetermined size and stops growing any further. On the otherhand, woody perennials exhibit a pattern of unlimited growth where the plant adds to its mass by growth every growing season of the year.

Growth curve

Under favourable conditions, there is characteristic course of increase in the plant growth. If a graph is drawn (growth rate vs time), it results in a sigmoidal or S shaped curve. There are three well-marked regions in a standard growth curve. (i) The initial slow growing phase called the lag phase. (ii) A rapid growing phase called log phase; the growth is in logarithmic phase. (iii) The third phase is the period of declining growth and the organism maintains the size it has already achieved. This is called as steady state phase (Fig 4.1).

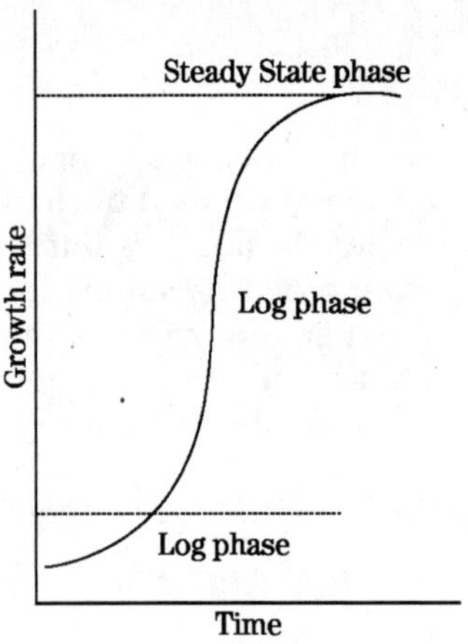

FIG. 4.1: Sigmoid curve

YIELD MAXIMIZATION

With the best management practices under less limited environment, it is possible to achieve the highest crop yield. Maximum yield achievable under a production system includes the best of all controllable factors needed to produce, the highest possible yield. The yield maximum generally varies with climate, soils and growing season. In a place where all the parameters are optimum during a perfect growing season, maximum yield should be approximate to the maximum potential yield. In this situation, all the production factors will be interrelated.

Research in U.K. has shown that yields of 12-15 tonnes of wheat and barley, 85-100 tonnes of potatoes and 75-85 tonnes of sugarbeet per ha are possible when all the growth factors are optimized. Johnson (1982) estimated the theoretical maximum yield of maize and soybean in the United States at over 30 and 11 t/ha respectively. However, the maximum yield that is achievable is much less than the theoretical maximum. The potential of a crop can frequently be increased by changes in management practices which may involve the change of a single or multiple interaction.

All the vegetation depends on solar energy, CO_2, water and nutrients and solar energy is considered as the basis for determining productivity potential. If all the factors are non-limiting, the radiation use efficiency determines the photosynthetic rate, dry matter production and yield. The highest crop yields reported in most of the field experiments in India are given in Table 4.1. However, the national average yield is much lower than the potential and the highest experimental yield.

TABLE 4.1: Highest yield of crops in India

Crop	Yield (t/ha)
Rice	14.0
Wheat	10.0
Maize	11.5
Sorghum	8.5
Pigeonpea	3.5
Bengalgram	4.5
Mustard	3.8

Source: Sinha, 1989

Maximum Economic Yield (MEY)

Maximum Economic Yield is the yield level where net profits are maximized in response to increasing use of inputs and management. Maximum Economic Yield is slightly lower than the maximum yield and is the point where the last increment of an input just pays for itself. Maximum Economic Yield also varies with the location, economic and soil conditions. This also represents the farmer's greater potential for economic survival. It is possible to get maximum net profit by selecting cost-effective inputs and management practices to produce MEY. Each must be cost-effective when used singly but may provide the most profit from an interaction effect. The interaction should occur without limitations; changes in fertility and cultural practices play an important part.

An integrated multiple production strategy should be worked out to achieve MEY. Choice of crop cultivars, timeliness of planting or sowing, treatment of seeds, maintenance of adequate plant population, amount and method of application of manures and fertilizers, optimum irrigation and appropriate plant protection measures are important to reap the maximum yield potential.

PLANT POPULATION AND GEOMETRY

It would be useful to know optimum or critical population densities to exclude population as limiting factor for crop yields.

Plant population is defined as the number of plants per unit area.

Geometry is the pattern of distribution of plants over the ground or the shape of the area available to the individual plants. When plants are widely spaced, dry matter production may first tend to increase linearly with increase in plant density due to no or minimum competition between the adjoining plants. Further increase in density may reduce the dry matter production probably due to competition between plants and the yield of the individual plants may be reduced. However, this is compensated by the increase in the number of plants per unit area. Any further increase in plant density results in a plateau of practically constant dry matter production. This indicates that equilibrium has been reached at which the increase in production due to increased plant number compensates the reduction in the production of the individual plants.

Optimum number of plants is required per unit area to utilize efficiently the available production factors such as water, nutrients, light and CO_2. Maximum exploitation of these factors is achieved when the plant population putsforth maximum pressure on all the factors of production. As a result, individual plants are put under severe stress because of inter-plant competition. Normally maximum yields are obtained from plant population which do not allow plants to achieve their individual maximum potential. Thus, the entire community of plants is considered for higher production rather than the individual plant performance.

Response of crop plants to population and geometry

Modern varieties are much more responsive to closer plant spacing than traditional varieties. Though the yield per plant is lower at closer spacings, greater number of plants per ha compensates the loss in yield of individual plants (Table 4.2).

TABLE 4.2: Grain yield of modern and traditional varieties of rice

Spacing (cm)	Grain yield (t/ha)		
	Modern varieties		Traditional tall varieties
	Low tillering	High tillering	
15 x 15	6.2	7.6	4.1
25 x 25	5.7	8.2	4.5
35 x 35	5.3	7.4	4.4
45 x 45	4.2	6.9	4.3

Source: De Datta, 1981

Maize hybrids grown under irrigated condition require 8.0 – 10.0 x 10^4 plants per ha for higher production. Flannery and Woodard (1981) designed an experiment to measure the effects of maize hybrids, plant population, irrigation, macro and micro- nutrients application and their interaction on maize silage and grain yield on sandy loam soils. The maize hybrid produced 19.6 t grains/ha and 100 t silage when grown at 10 x 10^4

plants/ha. At Coimbatore, a population of 11.0 x 10^4 plants/ha produced the highest yield of 10.3 t/ha during *kharif* season and further increase in population did not give any beneficial yield increment.

There is also negative effect of very high population density, particularly in branching crops. In soybean, there is elongation of internodes and plant height due to competition for sunlight under dense situation, because of the etiolation. There is also lodging with increased plant density in soybean, particularly in indeterminate types. Increase in plant population also results in decrease in side branches and number of pods in soybean. There has also been yield reduction per plant from 1.2 g to 8.2 g when plant density increased from 8 plants to 40 plants/m^2 and this is mainly due to reduction in pod number. To maximize seed yield in determinate type of soybean varieties, 5 x 10^5 plants/ha is found optimum.

Maintenance of optimum plant population is the biggest contributor to narrow down the yield gap in high value crops like cotton. An extra yield of 5 q/ha could be achieved with the adoption of closer spacing of 75 x 60 cm in Varalaxmi hybrid cotton. However, cotton cultivars like MCU 5 and MCU 7 registered highest yield (24 and 25 q/ha respectively) when grown at a spacing of 75 x 30 cm. The wider spacings have decreased the plant population per ha to the extent that it adversely affected the yield

Under dryland conditions, maintenance of adequate plant population enables insurance against yield reduction. Farmers from vertisol areas generally adopt low seed rates and plant population primarily as an insurance against rainfall failure. While such practice is well suited to non-responsive traditional varieties, it results in below-optimum yields in the case of newly available improved crop varieties, particularly at high levels of inputs and stored moisture. Highest yields with improved *rabi* sorghum genotype was obtained at 1.35 lakh plants/ha under favorable moisture conditions in Bijaphur. In the years of low rainfall and poor soil moisture, however, plant stands higher than 50,000 or 60,0000/ha exerted negative influence on sorghum yield even in the case of improved genotypes. In contrast to sorghum, safflower showed no response to plant density over a range of 3 to 5 plants/m^2 owing to its multiple branching habit.

Calculation of plant population

Plant population can be easily calculated for a given crop if the spacing is known. For *e.g.*, maize is planted with a spacing of 60 x 20 cm. The population is calculated as follows:

Area occupied by a single plant = 0.60 x 0.20 m = 0.12 m^2

Population for 0.12 m^2 = 1 plant

For one ha or 10000 m^2 = 10000/0.12 = 83333 plants/ha

SEASONS FOR CROPPING

Crop seasons in India may be broadly grouped into three: *kharif*, *rabi* and *zaid* or summer seasons. The *kharif* or southwest monsoon season is the important season in India. Crops are sown during June-July and harvested in September-October. All warm weather crops and crops having shorter-day length are grown during this season. *e.g.* rice, maize, millets groundnut, etc. The *rabi* or winter season crops are sown during October-November and harvested during February-March. Peninsular India gets Northeast monsoon during this period. The crops requiring cold-dry weather and having longer day length are particularly cultivated during this season. *e.g.* wheat, barley, oats, chickpea, peas, mustard, linseed, lentil, berseem etc. *Zaid* or summer crops are grown during February-March to May-June. Since warm dry weather prevails during this season normally short-duration crops like pulses, sesame, etc. are preferred.

Rice growing seasons

Rice growing seasons are almost similar to the three seasons mentioned already, but it is predominantly grown during *kharif*. The name of the season varies from place to place. Rice growing seasons are called as 'aus', 'aman' and 'boro'. The 'aus' season means early ('ashu', a Sanskrit word for quick or early) wherein direct seeded rice is cultivated during March-April to July-August. This crop is also called as autumn rice with respect to time of harvest. The transplanted rainfed crop of rice during *kharif* is known as 'aman' (an Arabic word for 'safety' or 'stability') in North Eastern India (West Bengal, Assam and Orissa). 'Boro' is irrigated winter rice grown during January-February to April-May. It is also known as summer rice.

In Tamil Nadu, there are three specific rice-growing seasons. Double crop seasons are *'Kuruvai'* (June-July to September-October) and *'Thaladi'* (October-November to January –February). Single season crop is called as *'Samba'* (August –September to December –January).

Other cropping seasons

There are also overlap seasons for crops like jute sown during February-March and harvested during July-August. Sesame is adaptable both in kharif and rabi/summer in the South; however, it is grown during kharif season in the North. The crop is adaptable during the summer in the southern plains of West Bengal. Long duration crops like sugarcane do not follow specific season. Sugarcane is normally planted from December to March. The planting of *'adsali'* crop of sugarcane (1 ½ years duration) is taken up in June-August and harvested next year in the winter season (December-January) in parts of Maharashtra, Andhra Pradesh and Karnataka. Planting of sugarcane from September to November in sub-tropical India (Bihar, Uttar Pradesh) is designated as 'autumn planting'.

TIME OF SOWING

Sowing or planting the crops at right time is quite important. Early sowing may be one of the most cost effective ways of increasing crop yields. Since it costs no more to plant early than late, yields can be increased significantly by earlier planting without incurring any additional cost of production. Under Indian conditions, time of sowing of crops varies with the choice of the crop, availability of soil moisture and irrigation facility. However, there are specific seasons for achieving high crop yields.

Timely sowing and its importance: In the river basin areas of Tamil Nadu where rice is the major crop, sowing time depends on the availability of irrigation water in the canal. Due to shortage of water in the dam, water may not be released in time. Hence sowing is not taken up in time (June). This causes delay in harvest and many times the harvest coincides with the peak Northeast monsoon rain (October). Delayed planting of first crop causes delay in the second crop cultivation. On many occasions, water may not be available for one or two irrigation during the maturity phase of the second crop. In the eastern states and coastal belts of India, rice planting is delayed due to floods or cyclones leading to drastic fall in the productivity.

Under irrigated conditions (gardenlands), since water is available throughout the year, crops are grown according to the season throughout the year. Even under this situation, time of sowing is utmost important to get higher yield. Optimum time of sowing of wheat in India is during the second fortnight of October to the first fortnight of November. In the hill regions, sowing begins early during the middle of September. Late sowing of wheat reduces the yield due to rust damage as well as premature drying of crops. Yield declines at the rate of 100 kg/day due to sowing beyond 15 December. Sowing later than mid-December drastically decreases the yield.

Time of sowing makes a big difference in pulse production. Pulses are generally sown after the completion of planting of other crops and they get the last priority in sowing schedules. Late sowing not only results in poor growth but also makes them prone to pests and disease incidence at the ripening stage.

There is significant reduction in yield of mustard to the tune of 7-8 q/ha when sowing is delayed for a month from October 1st to 31st in Hissar. The delayed sown crop of brown sarson is affected due to frost at the pod formation stage. Pest and disease incidence is also more with delayed sowing.

Sugarcane planted after wheat harvest in north-western India suffers from hot weather and desiccated seed material for planting, shorter tillering or growth span which affect the population of millable canes and average cane weight vis-à-vis cane and sugar yields.

Under dryland conditions, sowing of crops depends on the receipt of rainfall and availability of soil moisture. Early sowing utilizes the soil moisture more effectively. The crop puts forth early vigour, growth and development resulting in higher production. Normally *kharif* sowing is taken up with the onset of Southwest monsoon during June- July. The *rabi* season crops are sown in the residual soil moisture from October to early November. Pearl millet is sown in the first fortnight of July. The maximum temperature range of 28-32 °C prevailing during this period is optimum for plant growth in the initial stages. Sowing during this period gives maximum grain yield and net profit. Due to delayed sowing the rate of decline in yield varies from 4 to 80 kg / day/ha. *Rabi* sorghum is generally sown during October- November. Delayed sowing leads to lower yield because of the prevalence of low temperature and severe terminal drought.

DEPTH OF SOWING

One of the most important agronomic practices that costs nothing but gives greater benefit is the depth of sowing. Optimum depth of sowing is needed for better availability of moisture, avoidance of bird damage and quick and uniform germination of seeds. Depth of sowing varies from shallow (2-3 cm) to deep (10-12.0 cm) depending on the soil type and moisture condition. Generally, optimum depth of sowing of most field crops is 3-5 cm. Deeper sowing is advantageous in sandy soils while in heavy soils shallow sowing is beneficial. Under dryland conditions, crop sown in deeper layers utilizes the moisture and germinates better. Very shallow sowing promotes quick germination of seeds but later the seedlings cannot withstand surface drying. Good soil contact is very important with surface or shallow sowing to ensure efficient water uptake. This is generally improved by raking the soil after seed sowing. Bold seeded crops such as maize, chickpea and groundnut can be sown deep (up to 10 cm). However, small seeded crops like mustard, sesame and pearl millet should be sown at a shallow depth of 3-5 cm. Seeds mainly depend on the reserve food for growth until it becomes photosynthetically self-sufficient. Larger sized seeds contain considerable energy store and can grow for a longer time without becoming photosynthetically dependent. Hence, larger sized seeds are sown deeper than the small sized seeds with a limited energy store.

Sowing depth is also determined based on the mode of seed germination (hypogeal and epigeal). In the hypogeal mode of germination, the cotyledons remain in the soil. *e.g.* chickpea, pea, etc. Such seeds, if sown deep, neither delays nor retards germination. With the seeds of epigeal mode of germination, cotyledons emerge out of the soil. *e.g.* mungbean (Fig. 4.2). Such seeds, if sown deep, will fail to germinate. There is difference in coleoptile length between the varieties of the same crop. Mexican wheat possesses short coleoptile than the traditional wheat varieties. Hence, the former types of wheat give higher yield when sown at a shallow depth of 4-5 cm.

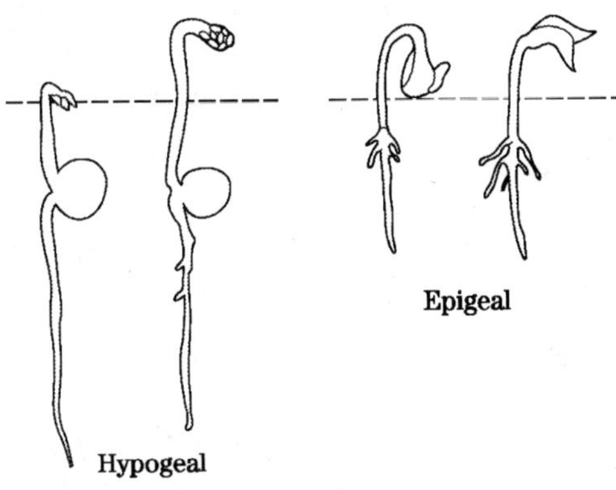

FIG. 4.2: Mode of germination

SEEDS AND SOWING

Botanically seed is a fruit which is a mature, ripened ovary containing one or more ovules that develop into seeds. The seed possesses an embryo, a nutritive tissue and protective cover. Embryo consists of a plumule, hypocotyl and a radicle in the form of an embryo bud. The embryo upon germination develops into seedling. The large part of the seed consists of the nutritive tissue and in most of the seeds, it may be seen as the cotyledons. The storage tissue provides nutritive support to the young germinating seedling till it supports itself. The seed coat provides protection to the embryo and has a structure, which helps in dispersal and survival of seeds.

Seed is a basic tool and is the principal means to get higher crop yields. Seed should be distinctly superior in quality, varietal purity, freedom from admixtures and having high germination and vigour. They should be healthy without infection and with optimum moisture content. It is always important to use fresh, quality seeds that facilitate higher germination and early establishment. Seeds, tubers, bulbs and vegetatively propagated materials (*e.g.* sugarcane setts) are used as seed material.

Seed germination

Germination is the transformation of an embryo into a seedling. During the process of germination, the metabolism and growth, which were suppressed or suspended, are resumed. Seedling develops from the seed from its quiescent state. Water is the basic requirement for initiating the chemical reactions. Optimum temperature is essential for good germination. Individual species has its own temperature requirement which occurs within a limited range. Normally the temperature range for germination is 15- 40 °C. Seed germination is also affected by oxygen supply since it is required for respiration. The primary role of oxygen is electron acceptor in catabolism. Many of the seeds are markedly light sensitive for germination, primarily due to the activity of the phytochrome system.

A good medium is required for better germination of seeds. The medium should have high infiltration, adequate aeration, high water holding capacity and be free from toxic substances. Seed germination and establishment are a problem in arid regions where the soil moisture availability is not adequate and there is high evaporative demand. Stress during germination and seedling establishment directly affects the crop stand and often is a major constraint, especially in small millets with limited seed reserves. Soil containing more of Fe and Al has the problem of surface crusting. In such soils seed germination may not be proper, as the tender seedlings are unable to emerge through the crust. Proper seedbed preparation and compaction also enable better seed germination.

Seed vigour

Vigour of seed is defined as the condition of the seed that permits germination to proceed rapidly and uniformly and allows production of uniform seedling stand. Seed vigour is a pre-requisite for rapid and uniform germination and fast growth of seedlings under field conditions. Vigourous seeds produce seedlings that will have good health and natural robustness. The vigour of the seeds depends on the genome, history of the individual seed and the environment in which it is sown. Seed vigour is normally determined by germination, growth and development, resistance to variations in environmental conditions and the presence or absence of abnormal seedlings.

Hybrid seeds normally posses greater vigour due to inherent genetic make up. High vigour of hybrid seeds has been associated with super efficient mitochondria and extra active enzyme systems for assimilation, growth and development. Fully mature seeds possess complete physical and physiological development needed for maximum expression of vigour. Prevalence of high humidity and high temperature during seed storage affect the seed vigour and cause loss of viability. Other factors such as mechanical damage attack by pathogens and passage of time also affect the seed vigour. Mechanically affected seeds are prone to infestation by fungi and other microorganisms. Insect incidence, particularly of seed borer (Bruchus), causes damage to the stored seeds which lose their vigour. Vigourous seeds are disease-free, physically sound, germinate quickly and produce rapidly developing seedlings.

Seed viability

Seed viability is defined as the degree to which a seed is metabolically active and capable of germinating under favourable condition. Seed viability is the highest at the time of physiological maturity. Seeds with high moisture content deteriorate quickly due to energy expenditure and accumulation of breakdown process. Ageing is one of the reasons that affect the seed viability. As the age of seed increases, the semi-permeable membrane of the cell organelles loses their selective permeability and allows the metabolites to leach out. One of the important changes that take place due to ageing is the degradation of mitochondria which permanently lose their ability of swelling and contraction. Normally the viable seeds of many of the field crops germinate within seven days. It is important to maintain the viability of seeds during germination.

Longevity

It means the duration of the viability of seeds. Normally the seeds possess maximum germination potential during the physiological maturity and the deterioration of seed quality occurs from this point of maturation onwards. The rate of deterioration increases due to mechanical injury at the time of harvesting and processing. Higher moisture content in the seed also causes deterioration of seed quality and longevity. Stored seeds exposed to microorganisms and insects cause reduction in longevity. Seeds stored in low moisture, cool temperature and low oxygen tension enable increase in longevity. However, due to aging, there is break down of compounds that are essential for germination and accumulation of toxic by-products. Lipid auto-oxidation is one of processes that destroy seed viability due to ageing, particularly in oilseeds. Small millets retain their viability for a long period. The seeds of tobacco remain viable for 10-15 years, if properly stored.

Seed dormancy

Seed dormancy is any condition of prefect and viable seeds which makes them resistant to germination under environmental conditions that are ordinarily favourable for quick germination (Evenari, 1957). A dormant seed will not germinate even under conditions which are normally favourable for growth. Many seeds possess dormancy mechanisms which prevent germination until the internal and external conditions for growth are suitable. Seed dormancy is an important adaptive property that promotes the survival of plants under adverse environmental conditions. Many seed species show variability in depth of dormancy. Dormancy assumes significance in some of the situations in relation to the prevention of vivipary and precocious germination. In the later situation, seeds germinate even while they are still on the mother plant. Sufficient dormancy is always required to prevent pre-harvest sprouting but not to interfere with the rapid establishment of a new crop.

Crop species of *Phaseolus* possess little or no dormancy and the germination occurs readily after sowing at a suitable temperature. The seeds of cereals viz., wheat, rice, oats and barley possess dormancy to some degree for a few weeks or months. In some conditions, there have been deliberate attempts to introduce dormancy. For example, "dormoat" is a cross between cultivated oats (*Avena sativa*) which has little dormancy and wild oats (*A. fatua*) having very deep dormancy. The purpose of introducing dormancy is to overcome winter when the seeds are sown during autumn season. This is done with the aim that autumn sown seeds germinate and establish early during spring and give higher yield.

Types of dormancy

Dormancy are of two types: (i) physical dormancy and (ii) physiological dormancy

Physical dormancy

Physical dormancy may be due to the presence of impermeable or mechanically resistant seed coat. Hard and impermeable seed coat interferes with water uptake and gaseous exchange. Impermeability is due to the presence of cuticle and the extensively developed layer of palisade cells. Seed coat also acts as physical barrier and thereby restraints the expansion of embryo. Several woody species have seed coat imposed dormancy.

Many of the plants of leguminosae family produce seeds having hard seed coat with external waxy covering. This hardness in seed coat is primarily an inherited trait. Some of the seeds are permeable to water but are impermeable to gases *e.g.* Xanthium. The seed coat of the upper seed limits the supply of oxygen to the embryo. In some situations, the seed coat may be freely permeable to both water and oxygen; however, they resist embryo expansion *e.g.* pigweed (*Amaranthus retroflexus*). These seeds remain dormant and viable for many years. Such type of seed dormancy can be broken by scarification.

Physiological dormancy

Physiological dormancy may be due to the presence of immature embryo, need for after-ripening, specific light and temperature requirement or the presence of a substance inhibiting germination.

Germination of seeds is possible only when the embryo is fully mature. Seeds with immature embryos remain dormant until the embryo develops completely within the seed. A number of crops produce seeds that do not germinate immediately after harvest but takes some more time under normal conditions for proper germination. This pre-requisite to germination of this type of seed is a period of 'after-ripening'.

Many of the seeds are markedly light sensitive for germination. This is primarily due to the activity of the phytochrome system. Studies in some of the crops showed the requirement of red light as promotive (near 660 m μ) and far-red radiation as inhibitory (maximum near 735 m μ) for seed germination. Temperature also plays greater role in promoting germination. A period of pre-chilling is required for many seeds to germinate properly.

In potato, newly formed potato tuber will not sprout when placed under favorable environments. This is due to the persistence of the dormant state in the individual buds (eyes). The bud dormancy can be eliminated by dry storage at 35°C or moist storage at 20°C. Presence of inhibitory substances in different parts of a seed also promotes dormancy.

Abscissic acid (ABA) is an effective growth inhibitor responsible for dormancy control in seeds. It inhibits the synthesis of specific enzyme necessary for the initiation of germination.

Seed treatment

Seeds are chemically treated with fungicides or biocontrol agents to destroy seed borne diseases. Seed treatment is also done to break the dormancy and to harden the seeds to withstand drought. Seed treatment is practiced in cotton to remove the fuzz. Seed treatment is also practiced for inoculating the biofertilizers.

Seed treatment with fungicides

Seed treatment with fungicides is necessary to destroy seed borne infection and protect the germinating seeds from soil inhabiting microorganisms. Seed treatment is done at least 24 hours prior to sowing. Seed treating drum is mostly used for this purpose.

Chemicals used for seed treatment

There are several types of chemicals used for seed treatment. They are disinfectant, seed disinfestants and seed protectants.

Seed disinfestants kill or inactivate the pathogen present in the seed. They do not remain active for a long time. Seed disinfectants act as eradicants. They help in destroying the pathogens present deep in the tissue or embryo. Seed protectants destroy the pathogen present on the seed surface., The compound usually stays for sufficiently long time on the seed surface.

Different formulations are available for seed treatment. Powder formulations are predominantly used for dry seed treatment because it ensures uniform coating. The fungicides normally used for seed treatment are captan or thiram @ 4 g / kilo of seed; carbendazim is used at 2 g/ kilo of seeds

Seed treating drums

Seed treating drums are used for treating seeds with fungicides. The seed-treating drum consists of a small opening in one end and two handles on either side. One rests over the stand and the other is used to rotate the drum kept at an angle. Seeds along with the fungicides are fed into the drum through the lid and rotated rapidly with the handle. The tilted angle of the drum helps thorough mixing of seeds and chemicals. Seed treatment with fungicides should be done at least 24 hours prior to sowing.

Seed pelleting

This is another method of treating seeds with fungicides. If the dry seed treatment is not given, seed pelleting with fungicides is recommended. Fungicides are dissolved in water and gum is added as adhesive (1 g / 100 ml of water). Seeds are put in the solution and mixed thoroughly to ensure uniform coating of fungicidal slurry over the seeds. The seeds are shade-dried and used for sowing. Seed pelleting is particularly suitable for dryland sowing.

Seed treatment with bio-control agents

Instead of the fungicide, a biocontrol agent can be used for seed treatment. The fungal bio-control agent, *Trichoderma viride* is widely used for seed treatment. It is used at 4 g / kg of seed and the treatment is done at the time of sowing. The treatment reduces the seed infestation of seed borne pathogens and increases the percentage of germination and seedling vigour.

Seed treatment with biofertilizers (bacterial culture)

Biofertilizers such as Rhizobium and Azospirillum are used for seed treatment. Rhizobium culture is used for the pulse seeds and Azospirillum is used for treating the seeds of cereals, millets, cotton sesame, etc. Specific bacterial culture is required for greater efficiency. Three packets (200 gx 3 =600 g) of the culture are recommended for seed treatment in one hectare. The bacterial culture slurry may be prepared with rice gruel or jaggery solution. Seeds should be thoroughly mixed with the bacterial culture slurry and shade-dried for 15 minutes before sowing. Fungicide treated seeds can be used for bacterial culture treatment.

Seed treatment for breaking dormancy

Scarification of seeds

Some of the seeds have hard seed coat. Such seeds take more time for germination. To quicken the germination, scarification is done. Seeds are mixed with sand and hand pounded. This operation helps to smoothen the seed coat and facilitate rapid germination. While doing this operation, care should be taken that the endosperm is not damaged. Scarification is normally done for the seeds of wild indigo (*Tephrosia purpurea*) which has waxy impermeable hard seed coat.

Soaking seeds in hot water

Another way of improving the germination of the seeds with hard seed coat is by soaking them in hot water. Steeping the seeds of wild indigo in boiling water for 2-3 minutes facilitates easy germination.

Delinting of cotton seeds

In cotton, fuzz remains on the seed coat after ginning. Separation of individual seeds with fuzz becomes difficult at the time of sowing. The fuzz may sometimes also harbor pathogens. Hence, removal of fuzz is important for easy sowing and to reduce seed borne pathogen. The fuzz is removed from the seed coat using acid and is known as delinting of cottonseeds.

Commercial sulphuric acid @ 100 ml is used for one kilo of fuzzy seeds. Required quantity of seeds is taken in a plastic bucket and acid is added to the seeds. The seeds are stirred vigourously and continuously using a wooden stick for about 2-3 minutes till the fuzz is completely digested and the seed coat turns dark brown in colour. At this stage, water is added and the seeds are washed repeatedly four to five times to remove any trace of acid. The ill-filled and damaged seeds floating on the water are discarded. Good seeds remaining at the bottom of the bucket are collected, shade-dried and used for sowing. Acid delinting could be done well in advance before sowing.

Precaution

Earthwares, metal vessels or wooden drum should not be used for acid delinting since concentrated sulphuric acid may corrode these materials.

CROP ESTABLISHMENT TECHNIQUES

Establishment of field crops may be grouped into direct sowing and transplanting. Many of the field crops are sown directly in the well-prepared field. However, some of the crops like rice, tobacco, etc. are first sown in the small seed bed (nursery) and then the seedlings are transplanted in the field. Transplanting of rice seedlings in the puddled field is followed in the South East Asia mainly for better weed control. The seedlings are large enough to compete with weeds that emerge later. Rather, weeds emerge about the same time as the seedlings from direct sowing and thus compete with the crop during the growing season. Tobacco seeds are small 0.08-0.09 mg) and the emerging seedlings are tiny and delicate. Hence, the seeds are unsuitable for sowing directly in the field and are sown in the nursery and tended carefully until the seedlings attain a particular size before transplanting in the main field.

Nursery techniques

Adequate care is required for successful raising of nursery. Choice of nursery field, land preparation, manuring, adequate facilities for irrigation and timely control of pest and diseases are required for the production of healthy seedlings.

Nursery site

Nursery area should be a good fertile piece of land nearer to the water source. It should have good drainage facility and located at an elevated place. The field should be fully exposed to sunlight. It should be devoid of any perennial weed infestation. Nursery site may be regularly changed to minimize the incidence of pest and diseases and weed infestation. This will also eliminate contamination of other varieties.

Nursery methods

Depending upon the method of preparation of land, nursery can be grouped as 'wet' or 'dry' nursery. In the wet nursery, land is puddled, leveled and pre-germinated seeds are sown. *e.g.* rice. Dry nursery is prepared for crops like finger millet, tobacco, etc. Land is ploughed to fine tilth and raised nursery beds are formed under dry condition. Dry nursery is also followed for rice in some of the situations.

Ideal seedling

An ideal seedling should be healthy and free from pest and diseases. It should be robust and sturdy having shallow root system. Seedlings should be dark green in colour with high content of carbon and nitrogen.

Nursery for rice

Rice nursery preparation may be categorized as wet nursery, dapog nursery, modified dapog nursery and dry nursery. Among them, wet nursery is commonly practiced for rice.

Wet nursery

Usually nursery area for rice is about one tenth of the main field area. About 800-1000 m^2 area of nursery is sufficient to transplant one hectare. The land is puddled well and properly leveled and converted into nursery beds of 40 m^2 (one cent) area. Hence, it is called as 'cent' nursery. Each bed may have a breath of 1.5-2.0 m and with convenient length. In between the beds, a drainage channel of about 30 cm width is provided. The surface of the bed is smoothened with gradual inclination towards both sides to facilitate easy drainage of water.

Seeds and sowing

Seed rate depends on test grain weight, germination percentageage, spacing to be adopted and number of seedlings to be planted. Seed rate for rice can be calculated using the following formula:

$$\text{Seed rate (kg/ha)} = \frac{\text{1000 grain weight (g)} \times \text{Number of seedlings per hill}}{\text{Spacing (cm}^2\text{)}} \times 100$$

Corrections are made for germination percentageage and another 20% seed rate is added to cover the risk.

Example: Calculate the seed rate for one ha for rice variety, IR 20. Recommended spacing is 20 x 10 cm and planting is done with three seedlings/hill. (Germination percentage is 80).

Seed rate (kg/ha) = 20 x 3 x 100/ (20 x 10)
= 30

Seed rate after correction for germination

= 30x 100/80 = 37.5 kg.

Seed rate after allowance for risk (20 % extra)

= 37.5 + (37.5 x 1/5) =37.5 + 7.5
= 45 kg

Seeds treated with fungicides are soaked in water for about 18-24 hours and kept in a dark room for incubation. After 24 hours of incubation, the sprouted seeds are sown in the nursery. The pre-germinated seeds are sown evenly on the nursery beds keeping a thin film of water. The seeds are sown @ 2-3 kg/40 m^2 nursery area.

After care: Irrigation is regulated until proper germination and establishment of the seedlings. The beds are allowed to saturate until the sprouts are about 5 cm in height and thereafter, a constant level of 2.5 cm of water may be maintained. Pre-emergence herbicide, butachlor or thiobencarb @ 1.0 kg a.i/ha is applied 8 days after sowing to control weeds in the nursery. A thin film of water is maintained at the time of herbicide application and then allowed to disappear. Adequate plant protection measures are required to guard against pests.

Nursery is manured with organic manure, FYM or compost @ one ton per 1000 m^2. At the time of nursery preparation, diammonium phosphate (DAP) @ 2 kg /40 m^2 is applied. If the seedlings show symptoms of N deficiency and the growth is not satisfactory, urea is top dressed at the rate of 500 g per 40 m^2, 7-10 days prior to uprooting seedlings.

Optimum age and pulling out of seedlings: Optimum age of seedlings is important, especially for the short duration rice varieties having a very short vegetative period. Seedlings are ready for transplanting at four-leaf stage. Normally one-week period of nursery for one-month rice duration is the thumb rule. The duration of nursery is 21-25 days for short duration, 25-30 days for medium and 35-40 days for long duration varieties.

Water is ponded to a depth of about 10 cm before pulling out of seedlings. Seedlings are pulled out carefully to avoid root snapping. They are made into bundles of convenient sizes (5-8 cm in diameter). If planting is done immediately, the seedlings are distributed throughout the main field. If not, the seedlings are protected from drying by keeping the roots submerged in water until transplanting is taken up. Pulled out seedlings should be transplanted within a day for better establishment.

Dapog nursery

The dapog method of raising seedlings was developed in the Philippines. This involves growing seedlings on a concrete floor or on a raised bed of soil covered with polythene sheets. A small nursery area of 30-40 m^2 is required for one ha of main field. Raised seedbeds are prepared after final land leveling and are covered with polythene sheets. Banana leaves with the midribs removed can also be used instead of polythene sheets. The polythene sheets prevent entry of roots into the soil. The dapog beds should be about 1.5 m wide and its length depends on the area to be planted. Pre- germinated seeds are sown on the top of the sheets at the rate of 2.0 kg/m^2 of nursery. Water is sprinkled and the seeds are pressed gently with hand or with a wooden flat board twice a day for the first 3-6 days. This helps the roots to remain in contact with water retained on the surface and prevents drying. After six days, the seedbeds are watered up to a depth of 1-2 cm. In about 14 days, seedlings are ready for transplanting. By this time, the roots are well developed and interwine with one another so that the nursery can be cut into stripes, rolled and transported easily to the planting site. One m^2 of dapog nursery can be used to transplant about 200 m^2.

Modified Dapog nursery

Modified dapog or 'sathupai' nursery is a combination of 'dapog' and 'field nursery' developed at Tamil Nadu Rice Research Institute (TRRI), Aduthurai. In canal irrigated areas, when the water receipt is delayed, a short period of about 10 days could be easily managed by raising 'dapog' nursery without any land preparation. Water requirement and care are minimum at this stage. When water is received in the canal, the first stage nursery can be planted in a relatively smaller area. At this stage water requirement is very much limited water and hence seedlings can be retained for about 15-20 days before planting in the main fields.

I. **Stage nursery (Dapog nursery):** Ordinary dapog nursery is raised with slight modification having soil medium. Any hard surface or threshing floor can be selected. Beds of one square meter area are prepared with thick mud wall of about 6.0 cm height all around. Twisted straw can also be used instead of mud wall. Thick 300-gauge polythene sheet is spread and by turning their edges over the bunds, a basin can be formed. The soil medium is prepared using the field soil. The medium is treated with carbofuran 3 G (1 g / 1 m^2). The mud slurry is poured on the sheet and spread to form a thin layer of about 5 mm. The mud is allowed to settle and sprouted seeds are uniformly sown @ 1 kg/m^2 area. The area required for raising the nursery depends on the quantity of seeds to be used. The nursery is covered with rice straw for a day. Diammonium phosphate 3% or urea 1% may be sprinkled over the sprouts to turn them green. Usual care of pressing and adequate moistening the beds is needed for the development of root mat. The duration of this nursery should not exceed 10-15 days.

II. **Stage nursery (field nursery):** Nursery area for this stage is four times that of the first stage nursery. For example, if the nursery area of first stage is 10 m^2, an area of 40 m^2 is needed for the field nursery. The nursery is prepared in the conventional manner. A mixture of 200 g urea, 100 g carbofuran 3G and 80 g zinc sulphate is applied to 40 m^2 area. Seedlings of first stage nursery are planted thickly in this nursery. After one week, another 100 g urea and 50 g corbofuran are top dressed in the 40 m^2 area. Seedlings can be pulled out on 15th day and used for planting.

Dry nursery

In places of water scarcity, raising of dry rice nursery is practiced. The nursery area is ploughed under dry condition and the field is brought to fine tilth. Light soils are preferred for dry nursery bed preparation. Farmyard manure or compost @ 12.5 t/ha is spread uniformly and incorporated into the soil, 2-3 weeks before sowing. Long beds of convenient length and 1.0-1.5 m width are formed. Channels of 30 cm width between the beds are formed for irrigation.

The seeds are sown dry, either broadcast or in lines and covered with a thin layer of soil or compost. In some places, water is impounded into the bed and soil is stirred to form mud. After the clay particles settle, sprouted seeds are broadcast sown. Nursery beds are irrigated periodically. In dry areas and in calcareous and saline alkaline soils, chlorosis is the major problem in dry nurseries. Seed treatment with $FeSO_4$ and flooding the soil may give some relief. The seedlings obtained from the dry nurseries are generally hardy and establish very fast in the main field.

Nursery for finger millet

Nursery preparation: An area of 500 m^2 is selected nearer to the water source to prepare nursery for one ha of main field. The land is ploughed well and about one ton of well decomposed FYM or compost is incorporated. About 37.5 kg of superphosphate is added and mixed well with the soil. Units of 6 plots each of size 3.0 m x 1.5 m are marked. Channels of 30 cm width are provided between the plots for irrigation.

Sowing and after care: Shallow rills are formed on the beds and the fungicide treated seeds are broadcast evenly on the beds and then covered by light hand leveling over the soil. Powdered FYM is sprinkled over the beds to cover the seeds. Sevin dust is mixed with sand and applied all around and on the beds to prevent ants carrying the seeds. Immediately after sowing, irrigation is given followed by irrigation on 3rd day and subsequently irrigation is given at an interval of 5-7 days. Nursery duration is 17-20 days.

Nursery for tobacco

Nursery Preparation: Sandy or sandy loam soils are preferable for raising nursery. Seedlings raised in heavy soils with poor drainage are predisposed for damping- off disease. Raised beds are prepared with one m width and convenient length, not exceeding 10 m. All around the beds, channels are formed to a width of 50 cm and depth of 10 cm. The soil is removed from the channel and evenly spread over the bed and leveled. In heavy soils, sand is mixed in the bed to improve drainage.

Manuring: Proper manuring is important to obtain healthy and sturdy seedlings in a short time. Nitrogen, phosphorus and potash are essential. In sandy soils, magnesium should also be added. Nitrogen deficiency causes stunting and yellowing of seedlings resulting in poor growth. Excess nitrogen produces seedlings which are lanky and succulent and interferes with proper establishment in the main field. High dose of organic manures gives better results. However, under unfavorable seasonal conditions, it pre-disposes the seedlings to damping- off disease which is difficult to control. A combination of organic and inorganic manuring is normally practiced.

Seeds and sowing: Tobacco seeds are tiny. One g of seed contains about 10,000 seeds and hence a low seed rate of 3 kg/ha of nursery is sufficient. Normally 40-60 m^2 nursery area is required to plant one ha of main field. Seeds are broadcast- sown over the beds. Since the quantity is very low, the seeds are normally mixed with sand and sown in the beds. After sowing, the beds are raked with fingers to ensure proper covering of seeds with the soil. Shallow sowing to a depth of about 0.25-0.50 cm is practiced.

Care of nursery: It is necessary to keep the surface of the bed moist till germination is completed. For the first ten days after sowing the bed is kept moist. Especially in the hot moons, even missing one watering can cause severe damage to the germinating seeds. Provision of covers and mulches over the seedbeds is beneficial as they conserve moisture during germination. They also protect the tender seedlings from strong sunlight and beating rains. When the seedlings emerge, the cover can be removed. Otherwise, the seedlings may become etiolated and lanky for want of adequate sunlight. It is also necessary to harden the seedlings by withholding water a week to ten days before planting. This practice helps the seedlings to withstand the shock of transplanting.

Age of nursery: Normally seedlings of pencil thickness and with 10-15 cm height are preferred. Short seedlings may establish well under optimum conditions in heavy soils. However, in light soils lengthy seedlings are preferred. The seedlings are ready for planting in 7-8 weeks after sowing.

Sugarcane nursery (short crop)

The present system of sugarcane planting consists of using one third top portion of fully matured canes as seed material. Setts are also obtained from ratoon crops and arrowed canes which results in poor germination (25-30%) due to the presence of high sucrose and low reducing sugars. Setts selected from poorly maintained field will lead to less seedling vigour, transmit pest and disease through setts, ultimately affect the cane yield drastically. Large-scale multiplication of seed cane (short crop) can provide nearly 6-8 times seed materials from well-managed nursery. The management of seed crop (nursery) plays a major role in deciding cane yield out put. Planting of short crop seed material recorded better juice quality as well as increased sugar yield than using top seed material from the cane. A good seed should be free from pests and diseases, high in moisture content, rich in reducing sugars and soluble N compounds. The seed crop should be well manured and properly irrigated. Combined application of groundnut cake and green manure may increase germination percentage of the seed material. Many of the experimental results have shown that setts obtained from canes applied with high dose of N not only give better germination but also higher sugar yield than setts obtained from low N application. An additional dose of 35-50 kg N and 25-30 kg P_2O_5 / ha is recommended for seed crop. The cane setts obtained from the crop with higher dose of N with more splits upto later stages of cane growth recorded better germination due to increased leaf nitrogen and reducing sugar contents. The requirement of optimum dose of N differs from region to region due to soil and agroclimatic conditions. Favourable response to N was obtained with the application of N ranging 225-300 kg/ha. Most of the N should be applied at the start of the crop as the luxury feeding is in the first few weeks of young crop. It can be applied in equal splits at 30,60 and 90 days after planting. Potash @ 112.5 kg/ha is recommended to be split-applied along with N. Production techniques are almost similar to that of plant crop. However, detrashing and propping are not adopted. The short crop can be harvested at 6-8 months of age.

Planting techniques

Planting of rice

Rice seedlings are transplanted in the puddled field. Proper puddling and leveling are needed for easy transplanting. Rice planting is normally done manually in line or randomly. Machine planting can also be adopted.

Line planting

Rice seedlings are planted in line to maintain plant population and easy management. Ropes are stretched along the field and planting is carried out keeping the rope as base line. The spacing between the rows varies from 15-30 cm. The intra-row spacing of 10-15 cm is normally adopted. A rogue spacing of about 30 cm is left for every 10-15 lines to facilitate after cultivation practices.

Random or bulk planting

Farmers normally adopt random planting. In this method of planting, entire field is demarked into a number of strips having a width of 1.5- 2.0 m and convenient length. A rogue spacing of 30 cm is allowed between the strips. The borders of the strips are first planted. Seedlings are then spread in each strip and planting is carried out. In most situations, seedlings are planted covering entire field without leaving the rogue space. In this type of random planting, optimum plant population and spacing between the hills cannot be maintained. However, maintenance of adequate population depends on the skill of the labourers.

Planting under irrigated condition (Gardenland)

Crops such as finger millet and tobacco are transplanted under irrigated condition. The field is prepared with repeated ploughings and flat beds of convenient sizes are formed. Normally beds of 10-20 m^2 are prepared and irrigation channels are provided. Water is let into the plots and with the saturated moisture, seedlings are planted. Finger millet is planted at 15 x 15 cm spacing. Tobacco seedlings are planted with a spacing of 80x 80 cm for cigarette, bidi, chewing or snuff types. For cheroot and cigar types, 75 x 60 cm spacing is adopted.

Sowing Techniques

Field crops are established by sowing seeds in the field. Proper tilth is important for better germination and establishment of the seedlings. The field is ploughed repeatedly and brought to a fine tilth. Organic manures such as well decomposed FYM or compost are added and incorporated into the soil at the time of ploughing. The method of seedbed preparation and sowing differ with the crops. Fine seedbed preparation is very much required for sowing of small seeded crops like sesame. After ploughing, the field is converted into flat beds or ridges and furrows. Most of the field crops are sown in the beds. The size of the beds varies with the soil type and irrigation availability. Normally a bed size of 20 m^2 is preferred. After the beds are formed, they are leveled uniformly. Irrigation channels are provided around the beds. For crops like maize, cotton, sugarcane, etc., ridges are formed. Under this condition, irrigation channels are normally formed across the furrows at convenient length.

Method of sowing

Broadcasting

Generally, the seeds are broadcast-sown and later planked. This method of sowing is easier and area coverage is quick. However, uniform population cannot be maintained since the seeds are not placed in uniform depth and germination may not be uniform. The skill of the labour is important to sow the seeds evenly covering the entire field. Broadcast sowing is normally practiced under dryland condition. Seed requirement is generally higher for broadcast sowing.

Sowing behind the country plough

In this method, sowing is taken up behind the country plough operation. Seeds are dropped in the furrow opened during ploughing and subsequently covered while the next adjoining furrow is formed. Bold seeded crops like groundnut are sown by this method in drylands. It is important to take up sowing at the appropriate soil moisture so that the depth of sowing is uniformly maintained.

Drill sowing or drilling

Drill sowing is one of the best methods that provide uniform plant population since seeds are uniformly dropped in the furrows. Animal drawn or power operated seed drills are used for this purposes; seed-cum-fertilizer drill can also be used. By this way, depth of sowing can be maintained; fertilizer can also be applied simultaneously. Pelleting of small sized seeds may reduce the risk of irregular dropping. Since sowing is taken up in lines, intercultural operations can be easily practiced. It is possible to take up sowing of intercrops also.

Dibbling

In the method, a seed or few seeds are put in a hole and covered. Under irrigated condition, seeds are dibbled in lines or on the sides of the ridges maintaining optimum intra-row spacing. *e.g.* maize and cotton. Though this method is laborious and time consuming, it gives rapid and uniform germination and the requirement of seed is less than in broadcasting.

The seeds rate and the row spacing recommended for different field crops are given in Table 4.3.

TABLE 4.3: Seed rate and spacing for important field crops

Crops	Seed rate (kg/ha)	Spacing (cm)
Wheat	100-125	25-30 x 5-6
Maize	15-20	60 x 20
Barley	75-80	20 cm between rows
Sorghum	8-10	45 x 12
Pearl millet	4-5	45 x 15
Pulses (General)	20	30 x 10
Pigeon pea	15-20	45 x 30 or 90 x 30
Chickpea -*Desi*	60-75	30 x 10

Crops	Seed rate (kg/ha)	Spacing (cm)
Chickpea -*Kabuli*	80-100	45 x 10
Groundnut (kernels)	125	30 x 10
Rapeseed- mustard	5-7	30 x 10 or 45 x 15
Soybean	60-70	30 x 5
Sunflower	10	45 x 30
Sesame	5-7	30 x10
Castor	8-10	60 x 30 or 90 x 30
Safflower	8-12	45 x 15
Niger	4-6	30 x 10
Linseed	20-30	30 x 10
Cotton –Variety	8-10	60 x 30 or 60 x 45
Cotton-Hybrids	4-5	90 x 60 or 120 x 60
Jute	8-10	30 x 5
Mesta	10-15	30 x 10

Planting of sugarcane setts

Sugarcane is vegetatively propagated and the seed material is called as 'setts'. Normally 2-3 budded setts are used for planting sugarcane. Top one-third portion of the cane is normally used for the seed purpose. It contains high amount of reducing sugar (glucose) and the soluble nitrogenous substances. However, if the seed crop is exclusively used, entire cane can be used for preparing the setts. The cane that is used for seed material should be free from pests and diseases. The cane is detrashed and cut into pieces (setts) using sharp knife. The setts having damaged and sprouted buds should be discarded. To plant one hectare, 75,000 two budded setts or 50,000 three budded setts are required. Ridges and furrows are formed at a spacing of 80-100 cm. At the time of planting, the furrows are irrigated to form slurry. Setts are placed end to end in the centre of the furrow. The buds are kept in the lateral position and pressed just below the ground level. Exposure of setts to the sun should be avoided.

AFTER CULTIVATION PRACTICES

Once the crop is established, proper care is required to control weeds. Soil around the plant is to be stirred to control weeds and to provide aeration. Adequate measures are taken to avoid lodging of tall growing crops. Special operations are undertaken to induce the crop growth and to get large harvest of economic produce. All the practices that are carried out after the establishment of the crop are to be called "after-cultivation practices". General after-cultural operations include: hand weeding, hand hoeing, working junior hoe, earthing up, detrashing and propping, topping and desuckering and quartering.

Other practices such as irrigation, manuring and plant protection are also known as after-cultivation or after care measures. Hand hoeing or weeding and earthing up operations that are carried out in the standing crop are called as 'intercultural practices'.

Hand Weeding

Hand weeding is normally practiced in wetland rice where the standing water in the field hinders the use of tools such as hand hoe for weeding. Hence weeds are uprooted by hand, gathered and carried away from the rice fields. Timely weeding is important to reduce crop-weed competition and expenditure on labour. Normally weeding is done twice, 15-20 and 30-40 days after planting of rice. At the time of weeding, shallow water level should be maintained so that weeds can be completely uprooted. Too much of standing water in the field may hinder to locate the weeds and hence weeding may not be proper.

Hand hoeing

Under upland situations (irrigated and drylands), weeds are removed using hand hoe. During this operation, soil is just stirred and soil mulch is formed. Weeding at appropriate soil moisture helps to remove the weeds completely. Otherwise, roots may remain in the soil and regenerate immediately after irrigation. Weeds are allowed to dry and later collected and removed. Implements such as weeders (peg/ star type) can be used, particularly under drylands. In wide row spaced crops like cotton, sugarcane, etc, junior hoe can be operated between the rows. By this operation, land area in the inter-row space is completely stirred and weed population is totally removed.

Blind hoeing

It is practiced in most of the coastal districts of Andhra Pradesh. Hand hoeing is done in the newly planted sugarcane fields with the optimum soil moisture. This operation is termed as blind hoeing since none of the setts would have germinated by that time. This practice is desirable in areas where irrigation water supply is scarce and where the soil is likely to cake up and prevent easy sprouting of sugarcane setts.

Earthing up

This operation is done to provide anchorage to the crops and to facilitate drainage during the rainy period. Earthing up helps in better tuber development. With the use of a spade, soil is dug and mounted on both sides of the crop. Thus, a ridge is formed in the cropped row. Ridge plough can also be used for this purpose. Earthing up operation is usually practiced for crops like maize, cotton, sugarcane and tuber crops. Earthing up is normally done around 45 days after sowing. For crops like sugarcane, partial earthing up is given at 45 days. Ridges are formed at 90 days and spade work is again given at 150 days when 2-3 internodes are visible. Earthing up is practiced for groundnut after gypsum application at the time of peg formation at about 45 days after sowing. This practice helps easy penetration of pegs into the soil and better pod formation.

Detrashing and propping

In sugarcane, dried leaves (trashes) are removed at 150 and 210 days after planting. This practice is called as detrashing. The cane stalks are exposed and hence the rind hardness increases. Detrashing also prevents water drops adhering to the bud region which will induce sprouting of buds in the standing crop. Propping is a simple operation done by tying the cane clumps together by wires or by trash twists to prevent lodging of cane. This operation is done at the age of 240 days.

Topping and desuckering

The practice of topping and desuckering is commonly followed in tobacco. The operation of topping consists of removal of the terminal bud with or without some of the small top leaves just before or after emergence of the flower head (inflorescence). Since the terminal growth is arrested, the auxiliary buds become active and put forth shoots known as 'suckers'. These side shoots are also removed as and when they arise and this operation is known as desuckering. Desuckering is done 2-3 times as and when the suckers reach convenient size for handling. The objective of topping and desuckering is to divert the energy and nutrient of the plant from flower heads to the leaves, which are the economic parts. Thus the leaves grow in size and gain in body and there is increase in yield and quality of tobacco. Topping increases the size of individual cells like epidermal, palisade, parenchyma and spongy parenchyma. If the suckers are not removed, they will grow at the expense of the leaves. Consequently the effect of topping on the development of leaf may be completely lost. Desuckering is also practiced with the use of oils. A drop of coconut oil is applied with a brush to the top five or six leaf axis of the plant. This not only aids in killing the bud but also suppresses the development of buds in the lower leaf axis. It is also recommended to apply neem oil at 35 % concentration immediately after topping to completely suppress the growth of the suckers (neem oil 1.75 litres+ sandovit 0.5 litre + water 2.75 litre for 1000 plants).

CHAPTER 5

Nutrient Management

Adequate supply of plant nutrients is important to ensure efficient crop production. Adding animal and vegetable manure to the soil to restore fertility is the practice from time immemorial. As the use of the chemical fertilizers increased due to their large availability and easy-to-adopt technique, organic manure application slowly declined. Since the nutrient turn-over in soil plant system is considerably high under intensive farming, neither the chemical fertilizers nor the organic or biological sources alone can achieve a sustainable production. Choice of manures and fertilizers and their application at right quantity and time are important to get higher production.

PLANT NUTRIENTS

Criteria for essentiality

Arnon (1954) has laid down the criteria to distinguish the essential elements. They are:

1. Plant must be unable to grow normally or complete its life cycle in the absence of the element;
2. The element is specific and cannot be replaced by another element and
3. The element plays a direct role in metabolism.

ESSENTIAL PLANT NUTRIENTS

Sixteen plant elements have been recognized as being essential to all plants for their normal growth and development. Carbon (C), hydrogen (H) and oxygen (O) are derived from the air and water.

Nitrogen (N), phosphorus (P) and potassium (K) are used in large quantities by the plants and are called as major or "primary nutrients".

Calcium, (Ca), magnesium (Mg) and sulphur (S) are required in relatively smaller but in appreciable quantities and hence named as "secondary nutrients".

Iron (Fe), zinc, (Zn), manganese (Mn), copper (Cu), boron (B), molybdenum (Mo) and chlorine (Cl) are needed in small quantities and are called as "micronutrients" or trace elements.

In addition to the above, some elements are required by a particular group or species of plants. They are vanadium (V), silicon (Si), iodine (I), selenium (Se), gallium (Ga) and aluminum (Al). Apart from these elements other elements like rubidium (Rb), strontium (Sr), nickel (Ni), chromium (Cr) and arsenic (As) may be required at very low concentrations by some plants. These are often referred as beneficial elements or "micro-elements".

ROLE OF ESSENTIAL NUTRIENTS

Carbon, hydrogen and oxygen are the most abundant elements in plants. Carbon and hydrogen are absorbed in a combined form and oxygen is partly taken up in the molecular form. These three elements are essential for all life forms. By utilizing C, H and O_2 the plants synthesize carbohydrates and sugars on which all life forms ultimately depend. These elements are, however, not considered mineral nutrients. They provide a key role in providing energy required for the growth and metabolism of plants.

Nitrogen

Nitrogen plays a vital role in all living plant tissues and constitutes about 1-4 % of the dry weight. It is absorbed as nitrate (NO_3^-) and ammonium (NH_4^+) ions. Nitrogen is an integral part of chlorophyll and enzymes essential for plant growth processes. It plays an important role in plant metabolism because it is an essential constituent of different types of metabolically active compounds like amino acids and proteins. These are important not only as building blocks for plant tissues but also in the cell nuclei and protoplasm, controlling heredity.

Adequate supply of N promotes higher photosynthetic activity and vigorous vegetative growth and as a result, the plants turn into dark green color. A high N supply favours the conversion of carbohydrate into protein which, in turn, promotes the formation of protoplasm. Protoplasm, being highly hydrated, is conducive for the succulent plant growth. An excessive dose of N in relation to other nutrients such as P and K may delay the crop maturity.

The plants deficient in N become stunted and yellow in appearance. The loss of protein N from chloroplasts produce yellowing or chlorosis. Lower leaves are first affected since N is a mobile nutrient. Under severe deficiency the lower leaves may turn brown and die. Most common deficiency symptoms of N are the accumulation of anthocyanin pigments in the epidermal and sub-epidermal cells of the leaves and stems. Flowering and fruit setting are adversely affected due to N deficiency. Flower buds often turn pale and are shed prematurely. The size and quality of fruits are poor.

Excessive dose of N produces succulence in plants and enhances the plant's sensitivity to water and temperature stress. Plants also become susceptible to lodging and pest and disease incidence. In the case of sugar crops, sugar content is reduced and impedes sugar crystallization.

Phosphorus

The concentration of phosphorus (P) in most of the plants varies from 0.1 to 0.4%. Plants mostly absorb P as primary orthophosphate anion ($H_2PO_4^-$) and to a lesser degree secondary orthophosphate (HPO_4^{2-}). The uptake of $H_2PO_4^-$ is high at low pH whereas the uptake of HPO_4^{2-} is more at higher soil pH.

Phosphorus is an essential constituent of nucleic acid of phytin and phospholipids. It is a constituent of the sugar phosphates and adenosine di and triphosphates (ADP and ATP) which act as "energy currency" within plants. Phosphorus is required for the synthesis of ATP which is important for both photosynthesis and respiration.

Phosphorus plays an important role in donation or transfer of the energy-rich phosphate molecules from ATP to energy requiring substances in the plants. This process is known as phosphorylation.

Phosphorus is involved in the metabolic processes of plants and activation of a number of enzymes participating in the dark reactions in photosynthesis.

Deficiency causes overall growth retardation and the symptoms appear in the lower leaves. Adequate supply of P is essential at the early stage of crop growth when the limited root system is not yet capable of absorbing the P reserves of the soil. Adequate supply of P at a later stage cannot remedy the adverse effects of deficiency at the critical earlier stage. Deficiency at the early phase of crop growth affects the production of primordia for the reproductive phase.

Deficiency results in disturbing the nitrogen metabolism and reduces total N content of the plants. Phosphorus deficiency also results in an increased accumulation of free reducing sugars.

Potassium

Potassium is absorbed as ionic (K^+) form from soil solution by plant roots. Potassium content in the plant tissue usually ranges from 1 to 4% on dry weight basis. The most important function of K is to stabilize various enzyme systems. It plays an important role in osmotic regulation and helps in maintaining the plant turgor. Potassium is needed to regulate stomatal opening and hence affects the rate of transpiration and uptake of water. Potassium is important for the synthesis of high–energy phosphate molecules (ATP), which are required in both photosynthesis and respiration for the translocation of sugars. Potassium is known to increase the resistance of plants to the stress of moisture, heat and diseases caused by fungi, nematodes and other microorganisms. Potassium improves the development of mechanical tissues in the stalks of cereals and makes them less susceptible to lodging.

Deficiency of K prevents normal ripening of cereals and results in shriveled grains. The deficiency also results in the decrease of the total and reducing sugars. Accumulation of the diamine putriscine is a characteristic feature of potassium deficient plants. Mottled chlorosis of leaves and necrosis at tips and margins of leaves are common symptoms of potassium deficiency

Calcium

Calcium (Ca) is absorbed as Ca^{++} and its concentration in the plants ranges from 0.2 to 1.0 %. Calcium is a part of the structure of cell walls (calcium pectate) and membrane structure. Calcium is involved in the maintenance of cellular organization by regulating the permeability of cellular membranes. Calcium provides inter and intra molecular linkages giving stability to a variety of cytoplasmic structures and enzymes. It is involved in root elongation, cell division, growth and activation/inhibition of enzymes. It also plays an important role in neutralizing the charges on the acidic molecules of phosphoric and organic acids which may be injurious to plants. High supply of calcium is a pre-requisite for making the symbiotic leguminous plants susceptible to infection by rhizobium.

Calcium deficiency is first observed on the growing tips and the youngest leaves. They become small, distorted, cup-shaped, crinkled and dark green in color. Root growth is impaired in the Ca deficient plants.

Magnesium

Magnesium (Mg) is absorbed as Mg^{++} ions and the concentration in crops varies from 0.2 to 0.4%. It is required in the formation of chlorophyll as it is the only mineral constituent of chlorophyll. Hence it is indispensable for photosynthesis by plants. Much of Mg^{++} is probably bound to polyphosphates (Mg-ATP). It plays greater role in transferring phosphate nucleotides and carboxyl groups. Magnesium is known to play a catalytic role as an activator of a number of enzymes concerned with carbohydrate metabolism, phosphate transfer and decarboxylations. It is also an essential constituent of polyribozomes, the key organelle concerned in protein synthesis.

Typical symptom of Mg deficiency is the inter-veinal chlorosis of older leaves in which the veins remain green but the inter-veinal areas turn yellow and the leaves may remain small or brittle. Crops such as jute, sugar beet and potato are the most sensitive to Mg deficiency.

Sulphur

Sulphur (S) is absorbed by plants as sulphate ion (SO_4^{2-}). Concentration of S in plants ranges from 0.1 to 0.4%. Sulphur requirement is high for the crops of families of *Gramineae*, *Leguminosae* and *Cruciferae*. Sulphur is involved as a ligand in a number of enzymes and metallo-proteins, most conspicuously in the iron-sulphur proteins and copper proteins. It is an integral part of some of the essential amino acids viz., cysteine, cystine and methionine. It is also a constituent of glutathione, a compound that plays a part in plant respiration and synthesis of essential oils. The biologically active sulphate-3 phosphoadenosine-5 phosphosulphate is an important sulphate donor involved in the synthesis of glucosides to get higher yield of oil seeds. Sulphur is also involved in carbohydrate metabolism of the crop plants. The characteristic taste and smell of plants in mustard and onion families is due volatile compounds containing S.

The deficiency of S results in increase in nitrate, soluble organic nitrogenous compounds, amides and ammonia and a decrease in insoluble (protein) nitrogen. Sulphur deficiency symptoms mostly resemble that of N deficiency. Leaves become pale yellow or light green and the symptoms will persist even after N application. Plants become small and spindly with short and slender stalks and crop growth is retarded. In sulphur deficient plants, the stem becomes hard and woody.

Iron

Iron (Fe) is absorbed by plants as Fe^{2+} or Fe^{3+} and also organically complexed or chelated Fe. Fe^{2+} ion is the active form, used in plant metabolism. Iron plays a direct role in the primary process of photosynthesis. Though iron is not a constituent in chlorophyll, it is involved in the synthesis of chlorophyll. Iron has an important catalytic role in enzyme activity. It is directly or indirectly involved in all the major metabolic processes of plants such as synthesis of carbohydrates, organic acids and vitamins. Being a constituent of ferredoxin, iron is involved in N fixation. The leghaemoglobin of root nodules contains iron as an essential constituent.

Iron deficiency has been shown to result in decreased levels of photosynthesis due to reduction in chlorophyll production. The deficiency results in iron- chlorosis in which the inter-veinal area of leaves turns yellow. The leaves may turn into almost pale white with severe deficiency. Crops such as maize, sorghum, groundnut and soybean are considered sensitive to Fe deficiency.

Manganese

Manganese is absorbed in its biologically active form of Mn^{2+}. It is important for nitrogen assimilation because Mn is known to be a constituent of nitrate reductase involved in the activation of a number of enzymes participating in the Calvin cycle. Hence it is important for photosynthesis, particularly in the evolution of O_2.

Manganese deficiency is characterized by "gray speck" in oats wherein grey lesions develop in the leaves but the tip remains green. Chlorotic patches develop between the veins in the younger leaves of dicots. Deficiency symptoms are usually observed in the older leaves.

Copper

Copper (Cu) is absorbed by plants as cupric ion (Cu^{2+}). It is a constituent part of several enzymes participating in the cellular oxidation-reduction. It is also involved in carbon assimilation. Copper deficient plants are known to accumulate amino nitrogen. The crops most susceptible to Cu deficiency are alfalfa, wheat, barley and oats. The younger leaves of maize become yellow and turn pale while the older leaves die back.

Zinc

Plants absorb Zinc as Zn^{2+} and it is a constituent of several dehydrogenase, proteinase and peptidase enzymes. Zinc is believed to promote RNA synthesis which, in turn, is needed for protein synthesis. It plays an important role in the formation of some growth hormones and starch formulation. It also promotes seed maturation and production. Crops such as rice, soybean, maize and linseed are classified as very sensitive to Zn deficiency. Zn deficiency causes decrease in the level of photosynthesis. Flower and fruit setting are considerably reduced and delayed. Plant growth is stunted and tillering is poor. Characteristic brown rusty spots occur on rice leaves called as '*khaira*'. In maize and sorghum, the deficiency is known as 'white bud' and in cotton it is called 'little leaf '.

Molybdenum

It is absorbed by plants as molybdate (MoO_4^{2-}). Molybdenum is a constituent part of the enzyme nitrate reductase which is responsible for the reduction of nitrates in soils and plants. It is a component of enzyme, nitrogenase essential for nitrogen fixation and assimilation. It is known to be a specific inhibitor of acid phosphatase. The nutrient plays a more fundamental role in protein synthesis, carbohydrate and protein metabolism. It plays an essential role in iron absorption and translocation in plants.

The deficiency can cause marginal scorching and rolling or cupping of leaves. Crops such as legumes, maize and cotton are considered sensitive to Mo.

Boron

Boron is mostly absorbed as boric acid (H_3BO_3). Boron is essential for cell division and development, particularly of vascular elements. It is important for cell maturation by regulating the formation and lignification of the cell wall. It is involved in the translocation of sugars, synthesis of nucleic acids and plant hormones.

Deficient plants exhibit necrosis and disorganization of tissues. Boron deficiency is normally detected in the growing points of roots, shoots and youngest leaves and results in the death of growing points. Some of the specific symptoms of boron deficiency are barren ears in maize and hollow heart in ground nut.

Chloride

Chloride is absorbed as the Cl^- ion and is involved in the oxygen evolution in the primary photosynthetic reactions. It also contributes to turgor in leaves and other plant parts. Coconut and oil palm are considered sensitive to chloride deficiency. However, crops like tobacco, potato and beans are sensitive to high level of chloride. Chlorosis in younger leaves and an overall wilting of the plants are the two common symptoms associated with Cl deficiency.

ABSORPTION OF PLANT MINERAL NUTRIENTS

The mechanism of plant nutrient mineral absorption may be grouped into passive and active absorption.

Passive absorption

The mass flow

It has been assumed that ions are taken up by the roots along with mass flow of water under the influence of transpiration pull. Generally the salt content of the plants differs from that of solution in which roots grow and hence this concept was discorded.

Diffusion

Mulder (1851) hypothesized that difference in concentration results in net movement of particles by diffusion. When a small quantity of a solute is added to water, there is a diffusion of particles of the solute from the region of high concentration to low concentration and the concentration of the solute in solution becomes equal.

Ion exchange

Ions can move across permeable membranes if there is no disturbance in the balance of the electrical charges on the two sides of a membrane. This process occurs just like ion exchange between soil colloids and soil solution. For example the cation, K^+ of the external solution exchange with a hydrogen ion, H^+, adsorbed to the surface of the cell membrane. Brook's hypothesis is essentially based on ion exchange. According to him, plant membranes have some areas which are permeable to cations and others permeable only to anions. Due to respiration, the membrane becomes alternatively permeable to cations and anions. It has been viewed that CO_2 produced during respiration dissolve in the water and by dissociation H^+ and HCO_3 resulted in the absorption of cations and that of HCO_3 in the uptake of anions.

Donnan Equilibrium

The Donnan equilibrium theory takes into account the effect of fixed or indiffusable ions. Plant systems are known to have sites where indiffusable anions or cations may be present and at such sites there may be accumulation of either cations or anions. A membrane may be permeable to some ions and not to others and which separates the cell from the external medium. The inner side of this membrane may have concentration of anions to which membrane is impermeable (fixed anions). In case, the above membrane is freely permeable to the cations and anions in the external solution, equal numbers of cations and anions from the external solution will diffuse across the membrane until an equilibrium is established. This equilibrium would be in general electrically balanced.

Active absorption

The transport of ions with the aid of metabolic energy has been termed active absorption. Several theories of the uptake of ions involving metabolism have been proposed. The general acceptance is that the active transport of an ion across an impermeable membrane is accomplished through the mediation of a carrier compound present in the membrane.

The carrier concept theory

This theory has been formulated by van den Honert in 1937. According to this concept, the ion transport process from one side of the membrane to the other is carried out by means of carriers which may be organic molecules or vesicles. A carrier meets the particular ion for which it has affinity, forms a carrier-ion complex and moves across the membrane. The direction of the movement of ion carrier complexes is from outer space to inner space only. Ions released in the space are accumulated because they take up ions only in the phosphorylated form. The presence of enzyme, phosphate, at the inner membrane boundary, releases the ion after splits off the phosphate group from the carrier complex. The involvement of adenosine triphosphate (ATP) provides energy to this process of transport.

SOURCES OF PLANT NUTRIENTS

Plant nutrients are essentially supplied through manures and fertilizers. Manures are organic in nature and applied in large quantities. They are also called as organics or organic manures. They are of animal or plant origin and contain more than one nutrient element. Nutrient content in the organic manures is low. Fertilizers are inorganic or synthetic and the nutrient content is higher than in manures. Fertilizers are available for a particular nutrient or combination of nutrients.

Organic manures

Organic manures are the valuable by-products of farming and allied industries derived from plant and animal sources. Organic manures are broadly classified as bulky organic manures and concentrated organic manures. Bulky organic manures are applied in large quantities and contain low amount of plant nutrients. *e.g.* farm yard manure, compost, night soil, etc. Concentrated organic manures contain higher percentage of major plant nutrients. *e.g.* various oil cakes and waste products of animal origin like dried blood, bone meal, fish manure, etc.

Farm Yard Manure (FYM)

The manure is produced in the farm chiefly with animal excreta. It is also called as stable manure, barn manure, dung and cattle manure. The manure consists of a mixture of cow dung, the liquid excreta or urine, the bedding material used in the stable and any remnants of straw and plant stalks fed to cattle. The quantity of dung excreted by an animal depends on several factors such as age, breed and condition of the animal and the nature of food eaten by it. The average excretion of urine per cattle per day is 7-8 litres. Average daily dung excretion pattern is give in Table 5.1. On an average well rotten FYM contains 0.5% N, 0.2%, P_2O_5 and 0.5% K_2O.

TABLE 5.1: Daily excretion by animals

Animal	Dung (kg/ha)
Cattle	
Young stock	4.90
Adult female	11.30
Adult male	15.60
Buffaloes	
Young stock	5.70
Adult female	14.80
Adult male	14.90

Manure preparation

Trenches of 6 m long, 2 m wide and 1 m deep are dug. The material consisting of dung and urine soaked in it is collected daily and placed in these trenches. Additions are normally applied in sections of one meter length. When each section is filled up to a height of about 0.5 m above the ground level, the top of the heap is rounded off to the shape of a dome and plastered with slurry of cow dung and earth. Before plastering, it is important to apply 4-5 buckets of water in the pit. Plastering conserves moisture and nitrogen and also prevents housefly nuisance. The manure pit should be protected from sun and rain. The manure becomes ready for use in about 4-5 months after plastering. It is possible to obtain 5-6 tonnes of good quality manure per year per head of cattle. Normally 10-

25 cartloads of manure are applied per hectare. A cartload of manure measuring 9 cubic meters weighs about 0.5 tonnes.

Compost

Decomposed plant residues/farm wastes are known as farm compost. The waste materials that are available in urban areas can be made into compost called urban compost. The processes of composting facilitate narrowing down the C: N ratio of the material to 10 or 12:1. The nutrient content of compost is 1.01% N, 0.5% P_2O_5 and 0.8-0.9% K_2O. Applications of partially or fully decomposed materials quicken the nutrient release to the crops.

Methods of composting

There are two methods of compost making: aerobic and anaerobic.

Aerobic method

A pit of one m deep, 2 m width and of convenient length is prepared. Organic wastes consisting of a mixture of crop wastes, weeds, leaves etc., that are collected in the farm are spread to a layer of 0.2 to 0.3 m deep. Cow dung solution is uniformly sprinkled to the top of the refuse. If the refuse is too dry, water is sprinkled over the material equal in weight of the refuse. Urine, earth ashes and bone meal may also be spread in a thin layer. This process is continued till the heap rises to about 0.5 m over the ground. After a month, the heap is turned over, mixed well and refilled adding water if necessary. Two more turnings are given, one at the end of the second month and the other after the third month. Sufficient water should be added in each turning over. Decomposition is ordinarily completed within 4-5 months. In places of heavy rainfall or where the water table is high the compost heaps may be prepared above ground level instead of pits.

Anaerobic method

A pit of convenient size (4.5 x 1.5 x 1.0 m) is prepared. Every day collections of mixed farm residues are spread in the pit to a thin layer. A mixture of fresh cow dung, ash and water is sprinkled and compacted. The pit is filled till the raw material stands about 0.5 m above the ground. Later it is plastered to a thickness of 2.5 cm with mud and cow dung. Plastering helps to prevent housefly nuisance. Decomposition is completed within 4-5 months.

Enrichment of manure and compost

The importance of organic manure is very well established, however, the non-availability of these materials in adequate quantities restricts the farmers to apply the manure at its recommended dose. An alternate method has been developed to reduce the quantity, at the same time maintaining its manurial value. The method is known as enrichment of

FYM/compost. By this technique, the nutrient availability of compost can be enhanced by addition of inorganic fertilizers while composting.

Enriched farmyard manure

Well-decomposed and finely sieved FYM is required at 750 kg/ha. Along with this, super phosphate (at the recommended dose of P_2O_5 for each crop) is thoroughly mixed. The heap is plastered with red earth-cow dung paste. Adequate care is required to seal the cracks whenever they appear. After about a month, the manure is ready for application. At the time of application, recommended dose of N and K as urea and muriate of potash respectively are added and mixed thoroughly. The enriched manure should be applied in the seed furrow. This is particularly recommended for the drylands.

Enrichment of compost with microbial inoculants

Compost prepared by traditional method is usually low in nutrients and there is need to improve its quality. Enrichment of compost using low cost N fixing and phosphate solubilising microbes is one of the possible ways of improving nutrient status of the product. It could be achieved by introducing microbial inoculants which are more efficient than the native strains associated with substrate materials. Both the nitrogen fixing and phosphate solubilising microbes are more exacting in their physiological and ecological requirements and it is difficult to meet these requirements under natural conditions. The only alternative is to enhance their inoculum potential in the composting mass. Studies conducted at IARI, New Delhi, showed that inoculation with Azotobacter/Azospirillum and phosphate solubilising culture in the presence of 1 % rock phosphate is a beneficial input to obtain good quality compost rich in nitrogen (1.8 %). The humus content was also higher in materials treated with microbial inoculants.

Super digested compost

Application of super phosphate at 5 % over the raw waste materials during composting improves the manurial value of compost. Application of this compost to acidic, calcareous and heavy soils increases the P availability.

Sheep and goat manure

The droppings of sheep and goat provide valuable manure. Penning of sheep and goat in the fallow field is the common practice in India. It has been estimated that by stocking 1000 sheep for a night will add about 2 tonnes of droppings. The manure contains 3 % N, 1 % P_2O_5 and 2 % K_2O.

Poultry manure

The excretion of birds contains both solid and liquid parts and hence there is no urine loss. The decomposition rate of the poultry manure is very quick. The manure should not be exposed to sun since there is 50 % N loss within a month. The fresh droppings contain 75 % moisture, 1.5 % N, 1.2

% P_2O_5 and 0.5 % K_2O.

Sewage and sludge

Sewage has two components, the solid portion called sludge and the liquid part called sewage water. Major portion of the suspended solids and effluents (99%) in the sewage is removed by settling. The sludge is collected separately, dried and used as manure. Under Indian conditions, the sludge on an average contains 1.5 - 3.5 % N, 0.8-4 % P_2O_5 and 0.3 - 0.6 % K_2O.

Once the solid portion or sludge is removed, sewage water is known as treated effluent. This can be used for irrigation. Since the sewage water is in concentrated form, it is important to dilute it with water in the ratio of 1: 1. It has been reported that irrigation with sewage effluent may result in improved soil structure and water holding capacity by decreasing the bulk density and hydraulic conductivity. Though there are many beneficial effects of sewage effluent, it may also contain harmful bacteria. The municipal sewage, particularly, may contain high amount of heavy metals.

Night soil poudrettes

Night soil contains appreciable amount of N. It can be profitably converted into useful manure known as " POUDRETTE". Dehydration of night soil can be done as such, or admixture of absorbing materials like soil, ash, charcoal and saw dust. Among the materials, saw dust is the most effective one which can be very well used. Saw dust has high dehydrating capacity as well as the property of absorbing foul smell. About 40-50 % of sawdust could be added with the night soil. By this way, it is possible to get a dry, acidic poudrette which may contain 2-3 % N. Odourless manure can also be obtained by admixing night soil with equal volume of ash and 10 % of powdered charcoal. The poudrette produced by this way contains 1.3 % N, 2.8 % P_2O_5, 4.1 % K_2O and 24.2 % lime.

Oil cakes

After extraction of oil from the oilseeds, the residues are called as oil cakes. The edible oil cakes from groundnut and sesame are mainly used as cattle feed. The non-edible oil cakes viz., neem, karanj, mahua, etc. are used as organic manures. The powdered oil cakes should be incorporated into the soil before planting for quick decomposition. Effect of oil cake is improved when applied afresh compared to dry form. It has been shown that neem cake application reduces the pest incidence. Oil cakes contain high amount of N and small quantities of P and K (Table 5.2) they have low C: N ratio (3-15) which helps in releasing the nutrients quickly. Unlike bulky organic manures, they have no residual effect. Oil cakes are sometimes adulterated with earth, sand, hulls or husks and the manurial value is lowered.

TABLE 5.2: Nutrient content of important oil cakes

Dung (kg/ha)	Nutrient content (%)		
	N	P	K
Karanj (*Pongamia glabra*)	4.0	1.0	1.3
Mahua (*Bassia latifolia*)	2.5	0.8	1.8
Neem (*Azadirachta indica*)	5.2	1.0	1.4

Meal group of manures

Bone meal, horn and hoof meal and blood meals are examples for meal group of manures. These are quick acting and can be used in a wide range of soils and crops.

Bone meal is obtained by crushing the bones of animals. When treated with steam, it is known as " steamed bone meal". This is a good source of phosphorus. It contains about 1-2 % N and 25-30 % P_2O_5. Bone meal is best suited for acidic soils.

Hoof and horn-meals are obtained by grinding hoof and horns of dead animals. They contain 10-15 % N, 1.0 % P_2O_5 and 2.5 % lime.

Blood meal has high N content (10-12 %) and is obtained from the slaughterhouses. Since the C-N ratio is very narrow (1: 3-4), it decomposes and supplies nutrient rapidly for crops.

Crop residues

Residues left out after the harvest of the economic portions are called crop residues/straw. In the developing countries like India, they are mostly used as cattle feed. In the developed countries, harvesting is done using combine harvester and hence the straw cannot be used as cattle feed. They are generally burnt in the field itself. Straw has good manurial value since it contains appreciable amount of plant nutrients. On an average, cereal straw and residues contain about 0.5 % N, 0.6 % P_2O_5 and 1.5 % K_2O. The crop residues can be recycled by way of incorporation, compost making or mulch material.

Agro-industrial wastes

Agro-industrial wastes are available in substantial quantities at processing sites and can be effectively utilized as manure.

Rice husk

It is the major by-product of the rice milling industry. Unhulled paddy grain constitutes 20-25 % of husk. It is a poor source of manure and the nutrient content is very low (0.3–0.4% N, 0.2-0.3% P_2O_5 and 0.3–0.5% K_2O). Rice husk should be incorporated into the wet soil and can be used in saline and alkaline soils to improve the physical conditions. It can also be used as a bedding material for animals.

Bagasse

The most important by-product of sugar industry is bagasse. It is mainly used as fuel in boilers of sugar factories. It can be used as manure raw or after composting. It contains 0.25 % N and 0.12 % P_2O_5.

Pressmud

It is a by-product obtained during the process of sugar manufacturing. It contains about 1.25 % N, 2.0 % P_2O_5 and 20-25 % organic matter. Addition of pressmud is highly useful to acidic soils since it contains high amount of lime (up to 45 %)

Tea wastes

In the tea industry, tea wastes are available during the course of tea production, processing and storage. Tea wastes are used for extraction of caffeine. The decaffeinated tea wastes can be used as manure. Nutrient content of the spent tea waste is 0.3-0.35 % N, 0.4 % P_2O_5 and 1.5 % K_2O.

Coir waste

It is a waste product from the coir industry and mostly dumped near the roadsides. Coirpith contains high amount of lignin (30 %), cellulose (26 %) and wide C:N ratio (112:1). To reduce the bulk and C:N ratio, composting is recommended. The composted coirpith contains 1.26 % N, 0.06 % P, 1.20 % K with C/N ratio 24:1. The lignin content is reduced to 4.8 % due to composting.

GREEN MANURING

Green manuring is a practice of ploughing or turning into the soil undecomposed green plant material for improving the physical conditions of the soil or for adding nutrients. Any crop or plant (generally leguminous) grown and ploughed *in situ* is called a 'green manure'. *E.g.* dhaincha, sesbania, sunnhemp, wild indigo and pillipesara. A leguminous crop producing 10-25 tonnes of green matter per ha will add about 60 to 90 kg N. 'Green leaf manure' refers to turning under of green leaves and tender green twigs collected from shrubs and trees grown on the bunds, wastelands and nearby forest areas. Common shrubs and trees useful for this purpose are karanj, glyricidia, neem, subabul, etc. The nutrient content of green manure and green leaf manure crops are given in the Table 5.3.

TABLE 5.3: Nutrient content of important green manure and green leaf manure crops

Crop	Nutrient content (% on dry weight basis)		
	N	P	K
Green manure			
Sesbania aculeata	3.3	0.7	1.3
Crotalaria juncea	2.6	0.6	2.0
Sesbania speciosa	2.7	0.5	2.2
Tephrosia purpurea	2.4	0.3	0.8
Phaseolus trilobus	2.1	0.5	-
Green leaf manure			
Pongamia glabra	3.2	0.3	1.3
Glyricidia maculeata	2.9	0.5	2.8
Azadirachta indica	2.8	0.3	0.4
Calatropis gigantea	2.1	0.7	3.6

Promising green manure crops

Dhaincha (Sesbania aculeata)

It is suitable for loamy and clayey soils. Dhaincha is an ideal green-manure crop for rice based cropping system. It is fairly resistant to drought as well as stagnation of water. The green manure grows well even in alkaline soils and corrects alkalinity if grown repeatedly for 4-5 years. The roots have plenty of nodules. It yields about 10-15 tonnes of green manure per ha and requires a seed rate of 30-40 kg/ha.

Sesbania speciosa

It is a valuable green manure for wetlands and can be grown in a wide range of soils. Seed production is prolific; however, pods are frequently attacked by insects. The green manure can be raised on the field borders along the bunds. Sesbania seedling (21 days) can be planted in a single line at 5-10 cm apart in the borders of the fields close to the bunds. In about 90 days it produces about 2-4 tonnes of green manure per ha. It does not affect the rice yield by shading or root effect. If second rice crop is planted immediately after the first crop, the manure can be incorporated into the field. About 300-400 g of seeds are sufficient to raise nursery and plant the seedlings along the bunds of one hectare.

Sesbania rostrata

One of the important features of this green manure is that in addition to the root nodules, it produces nodules in the stem. The stem nodulation is an adaptation for waterlogged situation since flooding limits growth of green manures and may reduce root nodulation. Under normal condition, both root and stem nodules are effective in N fixation. It can produce about 40-50 tonnes of fresh biomass from one ha in about 50-60 days. It has higher N content of 3.56 % on dry weight basis. Biomass production is higher during summer (April - June) than in winter (Dec-Jan) season. This green manure can also be produced by raising seedlings (30 days old) and planted in the paddy field along the bunds or as intercrop with rice.

Sunnhemp (Crotalaria juncea)

It is a quick growing green manure crop and gets ready for incorporation in about 45 days after sowing. It does not withstand heavy irrigation leading to flooding. The crop is at times subject to complete damage by leaf eating caterpillars. The crop can produce about 8-12 tonnes of green biomass per ha. The seed requirement is 30 kg/ha.

Wild indigo (Tephrosia purpurea)

This is a slow growing green manure crop and cattle do not prefer to graze it. The green manure is suitable for light textured soils, particularly in single crop wetlands. It establishes itself as a self sown crop and the seeds remain viable till the harvest of rice. On an average about 3-4 tonnes of green manure is obtained in one ha. The seed rate is 30 kg/ha. The seeds have a waxy impermeable seed coat and hence scarification is required to induce germination. Soaking seeds in boiling water for 2-3 minutes is also equally effective in promoting germination.

Indigo (Indigofera tinctoria)

It resembles wild indigo and is a long duration crop with more leafy growth. It comes up well in clayey soils with one or two irrigations.

Pillipesara (Pheseolus trilobus)

This is a dual purpose crop yielding good fodder for the cattle and green manure. Pillipesara comes up well in hot season with sufficient soil moisture. Loamy or clayey soils are best suited. After taking one or two cuttings for fodder or light grazing by animals, the crop can be incorporated into the soil. About 5-8 tonnes of manure can be obtained from one ha.

Green leaf manure crops

A number of leguminous and non-leguminous plants are grown on bunds or wastelands with the prime objective of utilizing their foliage as green manure.

Glyricidia (Glyricidia maculeata)

This is a shrubby plant that comes up well in moist situations. Under favourable conditions, it grows well like a tree. It can be easily grown in waste lands, farm road sides, field bunds, etc. The crop can be established by stem cuttings or seedlings planted in the field borders. It can be pruned for its tender loppings and compound leaves for green leaf manuring at the time of puddling rice. On an average, a well-established plant yields 12-15 kg green matter. About 400 plants on the peripheral bunds yield 5-6 tonnes green manure/ha.

Karanj (Pongamia glabra)

It is a leguminous tree grown in wastelands. On an average, a tree can yield 100-120 kg of green matter. The leaves contain about 3.7 % N (on dry weight basis).

Neem (Azadirachta indica)

It is an indigenous tree with wide range of adaptability. Almost all parts of the tree have been used for several millennia for preparation of medicine and its leaves and leaf–extracts to repeal insect pests of crops and stored grains. The leaves are pruned at the time of planting rice and incorporated as green leaf manure.

Calatropis (Calotropis gigantea)

On roadsides and fallow lands, the plant grows wild under different soil and climatic conditions. Leaves are more succulent and a plant can produce about 4-5 kg of green matter.

MANAGEMENT OF GREEN MANURING

Time of sowing and seed rate

March is the best-suited period for raising green manure. Studies at coimbatore, Tamil Nadu reveal that summer season is ideal for seed production of *S. rostrata*. Pre-season showers can be very well used to raise a green manure crop in single crop wetlands (August-January).

A seed rate of 40-50 kg/ha is required to get higher biomass of green manure. If the population is dense, the stem will be very thin and the crop will not seed early (eg. dhaincha).

Seed treatment

Germination is a problem for the green manure seeds like *Tephrosia purpurea* because of their hard seed coat. Scarification of the seeds with sand and pre-soaking in hot water (50 °C) for 5-minutes are found to improve seed germination upto 98%. Acid seed treatment is also found effective.

The seeds can be treated with concentrated commercial grade sulphuric acid (400 ml/kg of seed) for 30 minutes. The seeds are washed thoroughly with water, shade-dried and used for sowing.

Stem cuttings

Glyricidia is one of the green leaf manure tree crops propagated through seedlings and stem cuttings. A large percentage of the cuttings fail to root readily. The cut ends have been kept immersed in 0.005% IAA and 0.1% seradix A for one day and planted in small beds and irrigated for six days.

The hormonal treatment aided root formation to a remarkable degree (90%).

The green manure crops can be established using cutting of soft wood (from freshly formed branches) and hard wood (leaving top and bottom 30 cm in the stem and older branches). Soft woodcuttings of *S. aculeata* and hard wood cuttings of *S. rostrata* are superior. The establishment of the cuttings can be improved by dipping in fresh cowdung (10% suspension).

Mixed cropping

It has been found feasible to cultivate green manure mixed with rice fallow pulses. Green manure crops like indigo and pulses (black gram) can be mixed with the ratio of 1:3. pillipesara can also be sown in the same proportion. By adopting such practice in rice fallow pulses, no yield reduction has been noticed. Growth of green manure crop is also not spoiled. By the time pulse is harvested, the green manure putforth growth only to a few cm. After the harvest of pulses, the green manure put on growth.

Intercropping

Field investigations at Coimbatore reveal the possibility of intercropping green manure in transplanted rice. Seedlings of *S. rostrata* were planted at an interval of 1.5 m. On 30 days after planting, the green manure is cut at a height of 15 cm from the ground level and incorporated as manure. The ratoon is allowed and the reflesh incorporated while planting second crop of rice.

Border planting

Border planting of green manure, particularly *Sesbania speciosa* in the rice field bunds was advocated even during 1950s in Thanjavur, Tamil Nadu. The seedlings of the green manure were planted at 60-90 cm apart on the bunds at the time of planting *kuruvai* crop during June. About 70% of the crop was used as green manure for the *thaladi* crop planted in October. About 1.5-2.0 tonnes of green leaf was obtained from the bund crops and incorporated. The remainings left standing for producing seeds. It was also possible to produce in one ha, the seeds sufficient to raise green manure for 2.5 ha.

Phosphorus response

Incorporation of green manure with single superphosphate or rock phosphate facilitates higher response to added phosphorus. Recommended dose of phosphorus for rice can be very well applied to green manure crop and incorporated for greater efficiency.

BIOFERTILIZERS

The term " biofertilizers" includes selective microorganisms like bacteria, fungi, and algae which are capable of fixing atmospheric N or convert insoluble phosphate in the soil into forms available to plants. Biofertilizers are cost effective, eco-friendly and renewable sources of plant nutrients to supplement chemical fertilizers. Biofertilizers also play a vital role in maintaining long term soil fertility and sustainability.

Groups of biofertilizers

Nitrogen fixing organisms are either free living or having symbiotic association with plants. They directly or indirectly contribute N nutrition to crop plants.

Free living

This group includes numerous species of blue green algae and certain bacteria such as Azotobacter.

Symbiotic association

The bacteria, Rhizobium, live symbiotically on the roots of legumes. Azolla, a water fern, fixes atmospheric N in symbiotic association with blue-green algae (BGA), *Anabaena azollae* in rice ecosystem.

Associative symbiotic

One of the species of Azospirillum, *A. lipoferum* has associative symbiosis with higher plant systems.

Based on the type of microorganisms, the biofertilizers can also be classified as follows:

1. **Bacterial biofertilizers:** *e.g. Rhizobium, Azospirillum, Azotobacter, Phosphobacteria.*
2. **Fungal biofertilizers:** *e.g. Mycorrhiza.*
3. **Algal biofertilizers:** *e.g.* Blue Green Algae (BGA) and Azolla.
4. **Actinomycetes biofertilizers:** *e.g.* Frankia.

Biofertilizers are mostly cultured and multiplied in the laboratory. However, bluegreen algae and azolla can be mass-multiplied in the field.

CHARACTERISTIC FEATURES OF BIOFERTILIZERS

Rhizobium

Rhizobium is relatively more effective and widely used. Rhizobium, in association with legumes, fixes atmospheric N. The legumes and their symbiotic association with the rhizobium bacterium result in the formation of root nodules that fix atmospheric N. Successful nodulation of leguminous crop by rhizobium largely depends on the availability of a compatible strain for a particular legume. Rhizobium population in the soil depends on the presence of legume crops in the field.

In the absence of legumes, the population of rhizobium in the soil diminishes. Most strains of rhizobia native to the soil are effective in N fixation. Some of them may be ineffective and produce ineffective nodules. These nodules are smaller in size, soft and whitish in color. Their N fixing capability is much low. The effective strains produce large, pink and firm nodules. Their N fixing capacity is far greater. Artificial seed inoculation is often needed to restore population of effective strains of rhizobium near the root zone to ensure high yields. Each legume requires a specific species of rhizobium to form effective nodules (Table 5.4).

TABLE 5.4: Cross inoculation group of Rhizobium

Rhizobium species	Cross inoculation group	Legume types
R. leguminosarum	Peas	Pisum, Vicia
R. phaseoli	Beans	Phaseolus
R. trifolii	Clover	Trifolium
R. meliloti	Alfalfa	Melilotus, Medicago, Trigonella
R. lupini	Lupini	Lupinus, Orinthopus
R. japonicum	Soybean	Glycine
R. sp.	Cowpea	Vigna, Arachis

Azospirillum

Azospirillum is known to have a close associative symbiosis with the higher plant system. These bacteria have association with cereals like sorghum, maize, pearl millet, finger millet, foxtail millet and other minor millets and also fodder grasses. Bacteria colonizing the roots not only remain on the root surface but also a sizable proportion of them penetrates into the root tissues and lives in harmony with the plant. They dot not, however, produce any visible nodule or outgrowth on the root tissue.

Azotobacter

It is a common soil bacterium and the species *A. chrococcum* is present widely in Indian soils. Soil organic matter is the important factor that decides the growth of these bacteria. Poor organic matter content in the Indian soil is a limiting factor that not only affects the proliferation of Azotobacter in soil but also limits its N fixing capacity.

Blue Green Algae (BGA)

Blue green algae are referred to as paddy organisms because of their abundance in the paddy fields. Many species belonging to the genera, *Tolypothrix, Nostoc, Schizothrix, Calothrix, Anoboenopsis* and *Plectonema* are abundant in tropical conditions. Most of N fixing BGA are filamenters, consisting of chain of vegetative cells including specialized cells called heterocyst which function as a micronodule for synthesis and N fixing machinery. BGA, *Anabaena azollae*, also occurs in symbiotic relation with the aquatic fern, Azolla.

In addition to N fixation, BGA also synthesis and liberate growth promoting substances such as auxin and amino compounds which stimulate the growth of rice.

Multiplication of BGA

Algae may be multiplied in troughs or cement tanks for small quantity and in the field for large-scale production.

Trough method

Shallow trays of 2 x 0.2 m of galvanized iron sheet or permanent tanks are constructed. They are kept in the open air and exposed to the sun. The size may vary according to the quantity of algae material to be produced. About 10 kg of soil is taken and mixed well with 200 g of super phosphate. Water is stagnated to a depth of 5-15 cm in the trays depending on the local conditions to meet the evaporative demand. The soil should be neutral in pH and if it is acidic, lime should be added. To prevent predators, carbofuran 3 G is to be applied @ 25 g/tray. About 250 g of algal culture is sprinkled on the surface of the standing water.

Growth of algae is rapid during hot summer months (April - June). In about 7-10 days, a thick mat of algae is formed. If the daily evaporation loss is high, water is added intermittently. When the algal growth becomes sufficiently thick, watering is to be stopped. Water is allowed to evaporate completely. The dry algae crack into flakes which are collected and stored for further use. About 1.5 to 2.0 kg of algae material can be collected from each trough of 0.4 m^2 area.

The troughs are again filled with water and a small amount of dry algal flakes are added as inoculum. Multiplication can be continued in this manner. Once the soil in the trough is exhausted (usually after three or four harvests) it can be replaced with fresh soil mixed with super phosphate and continued as above.

Mass multiplication of BGA in the field

Field production of algae is adopted for multiplication of the material on a commercial scale. In the wetland, about 40 m^2 area is demarked and puddled to facilitate water stagnation. The area is encircled with strong earthen bunds of about 15 cm height. Super phosphate is applied at 2 kg for 40 m^2 area. About 5 kg of composite algal culture is required for 40 m^2 area. To control predators like daphnids, snails, and mosquitoes, carbofuran 3 G is applied at 200 g. In about 7-10 days period, a thick mat of algae develops in clay soils. In loamy soils, about 3-4 weeks are required for full growth of algae. Once the algae have attained full growth with complete coverage, algal flakes are collected and stored in sacks for further use.

During summer months, the average yield of algae ranges from 20 to 30 kg/40 m^2. Continuous harvest of algae may be made from the same area by reflooding the plot and applying super phosphate and pesticides. Addition of further inoculum is not necessary for subsequent production.

Azolla

Azolla is a free floating aquatic fern. Azolla in symbiotic association with blue green algae (*Anabaena azolla*) assimilates atmospheric N and enrich rice field. Azolla contains 4-5% N on dry weight basis and 0.2-0.4% on wet weight basis. The freshly harvested plants contain about 80-90 % water. Azolla is widely distributed in the rice growing tracts of tropics and temperate zones and grows on the irrigated rice fields. There are six species of Azolla: *A. caroliana, A. nilotica, A. filiculoides, A. mexicana, A. microphylla and A. pinnata*. The common species occurring in India is *A. pinnata.* A heat tolerant species, *A. microphylla* is introduced to India from the Latin America. *A. filiculoides* is a temperate species got from Europe. New crosses between *A. microphylla* and *A. filiculoides* are also available. Several of hybrids have high nutritive value (4.0 – 4.5 % N on dry weight basis) and grow fast. The hybrids can also withstand both heat and cold.

Azolla mutants with a high degree of tolerance to salinity have been developed at International Energy Agencies, Vienna. Scientists in China and U.S. are now working on introducing a *Bacillus thuringiensis* (Bt) toxin in Azolla to fight against insect pests.

The water fern is mainly propagated by vegetative means. It may yield on an average about 1.5 kg per square meter in a week. Under normal conditions, the fern doubles itself in three days. Multiplying Azolla through sporocarp technique have also been developed in many research institutions in the world.

Multiplication of Azolla

Azolla can be multiplied in small cement cisterns or galvanized iron trays of convenient size. Azolla can also be multiplied in the field nursery.

Cement cisterns

Azolla can be multiplied in cement cisterns of 2 x 1 x 0.3 m. A layer of 7.5-10.0 cm soil is provided at the bottom of the cisterns. About 5.0 – 7.5 cm depth of water is maintained in the cisterns. Super phosphate @ 8-12 g and carbofuran at 2.0 g are applied. About 200 g of fresh azolla is inoculated to each cistern. In about 12-15 days, about 2.0 –2.2 kg of azolla can be harvested. After each harvest, super phosphate is applied to facilitate fast multiplication. Every time, 200 g of azolla is inoculated for further multiplication.

Mass multiplication in nursery plots

The field selected for azolla nursery should be nearer to shade, thoroughly ploughed and inoculated. The field is divided into plots of 40 m^2 area

(20 x 2 m) by providing suitable bunds and irrigation channels. Water is maintained to a depth of 10 cm. About 10 kg of fresh cattle dung is mixed with 20 litres of water and sprinkled uniformly throughout the plots. Fresh azolla is inoculated at 8 kg/plot and super phosphate (100 g) is applied twice at an interval of 4 days. Carbofuran is added at 100 g per plot, 7 days after inoculation to control insect pests. About 50-75 kg of fresh azolla can be harvested 15 days after inoculation. Azolla can be again inoculated with the addition of cattle dung, super phosphate and carbofuran granules.

P-solubilising microorganisms

A group of heterotropic microorganisms are known to have the ability to solubilize P from insoluble sources. The organisms include bacteria: *Bacillus megatherium, B. circulans* and *B. subtilis;* and, fungi: *Aspergillus awamori, Penicillium digitum* and *Trichoderma spp.* These organisms secrete various organic and inorganic acids. They act on insoluble phosphates and convert them into soluble phosphates in the rhizosphere. Among the microorganisms, bacteria are found to be more efficient in the secretion of organic acids. They are generally called 'phosphobacteria'. Addition of organic manures helps in increasing the solubilising power of the microorganisms.

Vesicular Arbuscular Mycorrhiza (VAM)

Many of the graminaceous and legumenous plants harbour VAM. These plants contain special structures which help in the transfer of nutrients from soil into the root system. The VAM fungi are intercellular and obligate endosymbionts. Most of the economically important crops, particularly perennials such as apple, rubber, coffee, tea and oil palm are infected by VAM. The fungi are mass-produced only in the presence of living roots. The production of inoculum needs a host plant and a growth medium, usually soil, which provides congenial conditions for growth and reproduction of fungi.

Frankia

Some of the actinorrhizal plants like Casuarina and Alnus are found to have nodules infected by Frankia. In has been reported that N fixed by Frankia in Alnus ranges from 50 to 150 kg/ha/year. The potentiality of these microorganisms has been demonstrated in increasing the biomass yield of Casuarina and Alnus.

Biofertilizers and their usage in field crops

Biofertilizers are used in different ways in the field crop production:

- Seed treatment or seed inoculation
- Seedling root dip

- Soil application.

Seed treatment or seed inoculation: Each packet (200 g) of inoculant is mixed with 200 ml of rice gruel or jaggery solution. The seeds required for one ha are mixed in the slurry so as to have uniform coating of the inoculant over the seeds and then shade-dried for 30 minutes. The treated seeds should be used within 24 hours. One packet of inoculant is sufficient to treat 10 kg seeds. Rhizobium, Azospirillum, Azotobacter and Phosphobacteria are applied as seed treatment.

Seedling root dip: This method is used for transplanted crops. Five packets (1.0 kg) of the inoculant are required for one ha and mixed with 40 litres of water. The root portion of the seedlings is dipped in the solution for 5 to 10 minutes and then transplanted. Azospirillum is used for seedling root dip particularly for rice.

Soil application: Ten packets (2.0 kg) of the inoculant are required for one ha of main field. The inoculant is mixed with 20 kg of well dried, powdered FYM and broadcast in the field just before transplanting / sowing.

Use of VAM biofertilizer

The inoculum should be applied 2-3 cm below the soil at the time of sowing. The seeds are sown or cuttings planted just above the VAM inoculum so that the roots may come in contact with the inoculum and cause infection. Bulk inoculum of 100 g is sufficient for one meter square area.

Seedlings raised in the polythene bags need 5-10 g of bulk inoculum for each bag. For large scale usage, 10 kg of the inoculum can be mixed with one tonne of potting mixture. This can be packed in polythene bags before sowing. At the time of planting of the saplings, VAM inoculum is to be applied @ 20 g/seedling in each spot. In the existing tree, inoculum of 200 g is required for each tree. The inoculum is to be applied near the root surface.

Use of blue green algae

Algal culture is applied as dried flakes at 10 kg/ha over the standing water in the rice fields. This is done two days after transplanting in loamy soils and six days after planting in clayey soils. Addition of excess quantity of algae is not harmful; instead it may accelerate the build up of population. The field is kept water logged for atleast a couple of days immediately after algal application. The biofertilizer is to be applied for 3-4 consecutive seasons in the same field. Further application may not be required once soil build up the inoculum is achieved.

Use of azolla

Green manure: Azolla is applied at the rate of 0.6–1.0 kg/m^2 (6.25-10.0 t/ha) and incorporated before transplanting of rice.

Dual crop: Azolla is applied at the rate of 100 g / m^2 (1.25 t/ha), one to three days after transplanting of rice and allowed to multiply for 25-30 days. Azolla fronds can be incorporated into the soil at the time of first weeding.

FERTILIZERS

Fertilizers are inorganic/synthetic substances containing one or more plant nutrients in easily soluble and quickly available form. Because of their availability in concentrated form they have the advantage of being small for bulk storage and transport and handling are easier. In addition, crops may be supplied with exact quantity of nutrient required for their growth and development in soils of varying fertility levels.

Groups of fertilizers

Fertilizers are grouped according to the nutrients they contain. They are:

1. Nitrogenous fertilizers
2. Phosphatic fertilizers
3. Potassic fertilizers
4. Complex or mixed fertilizers
5. Micronutrients.

NITROGENOUS FERTILIZERS

Nitrogenous fertilizers may contain N in NH_4^+ or NO_3-N forms or both. Some of the fertilizers contain N in amide form. These fertilizers, when applied to the soil, are rapidly converted into ammoniacal form. Commonly used N fertilizers are grouped as follows:

1. **Ammoniacal fertilizers:** Ammonium sulphate, ammonium chloride, ammonium phosphate and anhydrous ammonia
2. **Nitrate fertilizers:** Calcium nitrate, sodium nitrate and nitrophosphate
3. **Fertilizers containing ammonium and nitrate:** Ammonium nitrate, calcium ammonium nitrate and ammonium sulphate nitrate
4. **Amide:** Urea, urea phosphate
5. **Nitrogen solutions:** Anhydrous ammonia, aqueous ammonia and solutions containing urea, nitrate, ammonia of their combinations
6. **Slowly available N fertilizers:**
   a) Chemicals having inherent capacity of slow release: Ureaform, IBDU, CDU, Oxamide, etc.
   b) Coated urea fertilizers: Sulphur coated urea
   c) Modified urea forms: Urea super granules, nitrification inhibitor (N serve, AM, thiourea) treated urea

Properties of important N fertilizers

1. **Ammonium sulphate:** It is one of the most important and oldest N fertilizers. It is a white crystalline salt containing 20-21 % ammoniacal

N and 24.2% S. It is readily soluble in water. The main advantage of this fertilizer is low hygroscopicity and chemical stability. This fertilizer is particularly suitable for wet land crops like rice since the ammonium ion is retained by the clay particles. Since the fertilizer is of acidifying in nature, it is advantageous to apply it to soils having alkaline pH and for acid requiring crops. Ammonium sulphate is recommended for tobacco and potato to improve the quality of the produce. Ammonium sulphate can be used as a part of the basal dressing and also for top dressing.

2. **Ammonium chloride:** It is a white crystalline compound containing 26% ammoniacal N and is acid forming. Like ammonium sulphate it can be applied to rice crop. It is also suitable for other crops viz., barley, wheat, corn, sorghum, fibre crops and sugarcane. Since the fertilizer contains both N and Cl it can be recommended for crops that love chloride *e.g.* coconut, oil palm and kiwi fruit. It is generally not recommended for tobacco and potato as the added Cl may affect the burning quality of tobacco and keeping quality of potato.
3. **Ammonium nitrate:** It is a white crystalline salt, containing 33-35 % N with equal proportion of nitrate and ammoniacal N. This is a quick acting fertilizer. It is highly hygroscopic and hence adequate care is required to prevent caking and physical deterioration while storing and handling. It is prone to leaching and denitrification losses than other ammonia products.
4. **Calcium ammonium nitrate (CAN):** It is also called nitro-lime or nitrochalk and consists of a mixture of ammonium nitrate and powdered chalk made into granules coated with soapstone. Nutrient content is 25.0 % N. It is hygroscopic and hence adequate care is required while handling. As half of N is present in nitrate form, it is a quick acting fertilizer.
5. **Ammonium sulphate nitrate (ASN):** It is a double salt made from a combination of ammonium nitrate and ammonium sulphate containing 26% N and 12% S. Nitrogen is both in ammoniacal (19.5%) and nitrate form (6.5%). This fertilizer is recommended for basal application prior to sowing or as top dressing. However, it should not be applied along with the seeds.
6. **Urea:** Urea was the first organic compound to be synthesized from inorganic substances (ammonium cyanate) by the German Chemist, Wohler in 1828. It is white, crystalline in appearance containing 46% N, all in amide form. In India, it is the most popular nitrogenous fertilizer. Urea is completely soluble in water. In the wetland condition it is subjected to loss through leaching and in dry condition by volatilization. It has been reported that a loss of 16-25% could occur from the surface application of prilled urea in wetland. Urea should, therefore, be worked into the soil under moderate moist conditions. Because of the incorporation, it is quickly converted into ammonia.

It is retained by the soil colloids and does not get leached out or volatilized.

Urea is applied basally or as top dressing and is suitable for most of the crops and soil types. Application of urea in combination with the seed resulted in a poor germination of wheat and barley. Hence, it is advisable to apply the fertilizer as side- dressing. Biuret (NH_2-CO-NH-CO-NH_2) content of urea is an important factor to be considered because of its phytotoxicity. When urea is applied as foliar nutrition the biuret content should not exceed 1 %, preferably lower than 0.5 %. Otherwise, scorching may occur on the leaves. It has been reported that injury to citrus occurred even when the biuret content was as low as 0.25 %. Citrus and other crops including pineapple are sensitive to biuret in urea when applied as foliar spray. Soil-applied urea does not cause any deleterious effect to citrus even when the biuret content is 2.5 %.

7. **Anhydrous ammonia:** The highest N containing fertilizer is the anhydrous ammonia (82 % N). It is a colourless gas at normal pressure and temperature and easily liquified under pressure. To avoid ammonia losses, it should be applied at some depth (10-20 cm) depending on soil conditions. It has been observed that losses are much less when ammonia is applied below 7.5 cm. The moisture content of the soil is also important. Losses are minimum when the soil is worked slightly below the field capacity. The fertilizer can also be applied through irrigation water. Application of ammonia in sprinkler irrigation may result in greater losses of ammonia. Considerable care is required while handling this material as it gives irritation.
8. **Liquid nitrogenous fertilizers:** Principal nitrogenous solutions are produced from urea and NH_4NO_3 in water and they are known as UAN solutions. A mixture of ammonium nitrate and urea is much more soluble in water than either of them alone. The liquid nitrogenous fertilizers have certain advantages over the conventional solid fertilizers. Solution form can be easily handled and applied more uniformly and accurately. They are suitable for various types of irrigation systems. Many pesticides are compatible with N solutions and can be applied together. Unit cost of N is usually less and handling is much easier. But they require special application equipment and storage containers since they are corrosive. The equipment made of aluminium or certain stainless metals is recommended for solutions containing dissolved nitrogen.
9. **Slow release N fertilizers:** Fertilizers which slowly release N have been developed to supply N continuously over an extended period. An ideal source of slow release fertilizer is the one that will release nutrients, at the rate approximately equal to the crop removal.

Nitrogenous fertilizers having slow availability

Slow rate of release of N is achieved by the use of substances having low solubility or due to a physical barrier formed by coating an insoluble material or modifying the size of urea.

1. **Low solubility N fertilizers:** Low solubility materials are developed by condensation products of urea with formaldehyde, crotonylidene diurea and isobutylidene diurea and urea - Z. (Table 5.5). Among them, urea-formaldehydes (ureaform) are most widely used in USA.
2. **Coated urea materials:** Nitrogenous fertilizers are coated with substances that reduce their rate of solubility. Sulphur coating of prilled urea reduces the dissolution rate. It also minimizes the toxicity arising due to heavy application of urea. Sulphur-coated urea (SCU) is a controlled- release N fertilizer (36-38% N) consisting of S shell around each urea granule. The advantage of this fertilizer is that in addition to N, it also contains S.
3. **Urea super granules (USG):** Urea in the bigger size granular form is called urea super granule. The size of the urea granule varies from 1-3 g. Because of the bigger size, it is slowly soluble. Deep placement of these granules in puddled soil enables higher use efficiency. Machines have also been developed for placement of granules in the reduced zone of puddled soils for rice cultivation.

TABLE 5.5: N content of slow release fertilizers

Fertilizers	N content (%)
Ureaform (urea–formaldehyde)	35.0
Crotonylidene diurea (CDU)	30.0
Isobutylidene diurea (IBDU)	30.0
Urea –z (UZ)	35.0
Sulphur coated urea (SCU)	36-37

Nitrification inhibitors

Nitrogen loss from the applied fertilizers takes place mainly after conversion to nitrate form by the activity of the bacteria, *Nitrosomonas* and *Nitrobacter*, together known as nitrobacteria. Losses can be reduced by inhibiting the growth or activity of these bacteria and thereby reducing conversion of ammonium to nitrate.

Several chemicals have been found to be toxic to the nitrifying bacteria. When these chemicals are added to the soil, they temporarily inhibit nitrification. *e.g.* N- serve (2- chloro- 6 (trichloromethyl) pyridine) referred as nitrapyrin and AM (2- amino- 4- chloro –6 methylpyrimidine). These materials are, however, expensive and not cost- effective. Hence some of the indigenous materials like neem (*Azadirachta indica*) and karanj (*Pongamia glabra)* oil cakes have been tested and found to reduce the bacterial activity. Coating or mixing of urea with powered neem cake has been found to give better response.

1. **Neem coated urea (NCU):** To prepare neem coated urea, the required materials are urea 100 kg, powdered neem cake 20 kg, coal tar 1 kg and kerosene 1.5 litres. First tar is melted in an iron pan. After a slight cooling, kerosene is added. This solution is poured in the heaped urea and powdered neem cake mixture. It is then thoroughly mixed well. The coated urea is shade-dried and used for basal application in rice.
2. **Neem blended urea (NBU):** For the preparation of neem blended urea, 100 kg urea and 20 kg neem cake (5:1) are required. The finely powdered neem cake is thoroughly mixed with urea and kept overnight. This can be used for top dressing rice at tillering stage.

PHOSPHATIC FERTILIZERS

Phosphatic fertilizers are classified into three groups depending on the form in which phosphoric acid is combined with calcium and their solubility.

1. Water soluble phosphoric acid or monocalcium phosphate [$Ca(H_2PO_4)_2$]: These fertilizers contain P in the available form of phosphoric acid. *e.g.* super phosphate, triple super phosphate and ammonium phosphate.
2. Citric acid soluble phosphoric acid or dicalcium phosphate ($CaHPO_4$): Fertilizers of this group are particularly soluble in citric acid. *e.g.* basic slag and dicalcium phosphate.
3. Insoluble phosphoric acid or tricalcium phosphate [$Ca_3(PO_4)_2$]: Rock phosphate, raw bone meal and steamed bone meal.

Properties of important P fertilizers

1. **Super phosphate:** Super phosphate is the oldest commercially available fertilizer and it is manufactured in three grades: single super phosphate (16-20% P_2O_5), dicalcium phosphate (35-38 % P_2O_5) and triple super phosphate (44-49%P_2O_5). Single super phosphate (SSP) is the most commonly used phosphatic fertilizer in India. It also contains sulphur (12%). It is available in the form of grey to brownish powder as well as in granulated form. Granulated SSP is the most suitable for application by machine, but is somewhat costlier than powdered SSP. The fertilizer is suitable for a wide range of soils and crops. It should be applied before or at the time of sowing/planting as basal application. To increase the efficiency of applied fertilizer in acid soils, it should be used with organic manures.
2. **Ammonium phosphates:** The available fertilizers in this group are monoammonium phosphate (MAP) containing 11% N and 52 % P_2O_5 and diammonium phosphate (DAP) containing 18% N and 46 % P_2O_5. Use of DAP is now gaining momentum. These fertilizers can be used

for direct application to the soil. DAP is recommended for rice nursery and foliar spray for pulses.

3. **Rock phosphate (RP):** In India, rock phosphate deposits are found in different parts of the country. Mussorie deposit, found in Uttar Pradesh, is exclusive of sedimentary origin and has relatively high reactivity. The calcium phosphate present in phosphate rocks is less stable and gets easily acidulated by the soil acidity and organic acids present in the soil organic matter. Thus its direct application to acid soils is a cheaper and efficient alternative to application of water-soluble forms.

   The particle size plays a vital role in the effectiveness of phosphate rock for direct application. Finer the particle, more effective is the rock phosphate for direct application. Agronomic evaluation of indigenous rock phosphate has been done for mussorie rock phosphate (MRP) containing 20-21% P_2O_5 for different crops all over the country. Available experimental evidences indicate the economic importance of MRP in the intensive agriculture.
4. **Basic slag:** It is obtained as a bye-product from steel industry. The high grade European slag (15-18 % P_2O_5) is widely used as a phosphatic fertilizer in Central Europe. But the product obtained from Indian steel plants has a low content of phosphorus (3-8 %) and is not used as a fertilizer. It contains considerable quantity of CaO and hence it is suitable for acidic soils.

POTASSIC FERTILIZERS

Commercially available potassic fertilizers are salts of potassium. They are completely soluble in water and contain nutrients in readily available form. Commonly used potassic fertilizers are: (1) muriate of potash (potassium chloride) and (2) sulphate of potash (potassium sulphate).

1. **Potassium chloride or muriate of potash (MOP):** The principal fertilizer source of potassium is potassium chloride or muriate of potash. It is a low cost and high analysis (60-63% K_2O) K fertilizer. It also contains 45-47% chloride, depending on the original rock composition. It is white to slight red in colour depend on the impurities present in the potash minerals and the method of refining. The salt is neutral in reaction and can be applied to all soils and crops. However, for tobacco and potato this fertilizer should not be used since the quality is affected due to the presence of chloride. Muriate of potash is generally applied basally. But in light textured soils, where the loss due to leaching is more, it is recommended for top dressing also.
2. **Potassium sulphate or sulphate of potash (SOP):** It is a white crystalline salt containing 50-53 % K_2O and 17% S. It can be used for all soils and crops as basal as well as top dressing. This fertilizer is costlier than muriate of potash. It is generally used in crops like potato

and tobacco which are sensitive to high amount of chloride.

In addition to these two fertilizers, soluble potassium nitrate (13–0-46) is marketed by some companies. This is specially suited for foliar application and fertigation (application through drip irrigation system), as the fertilizer dissolves completely in water without leaving any residues. As it is very costly, it is recommended only for high value crops.

COMPLEX FERTILIZERS

These fertilizers contain two or more plant nutrients (of which two are major nutrients) in chemical combination. They are generally granular in form and can be uniformly applied to the field. Unit nutrient cost of complex fertilizer is lower than that of the conventional fertilizers. Complex fertilizers produced in India can be broadly grouped as (i) ammonium phosphates, (ii) nitrophosphates and (iii) NPK complex fertilizers.

1. **Ammonium phosphates:** These fertilizer materials contain ammonium and phosphate radicals in varying proportion: (a) Ammonium phosphate sulphate (18-9-0, 16-20-0, 19.5- 19.5-0, 20-20-0); (b) urea ammonium phosphate (24-24-0, 28-28-0); (c) Ammonium phosphate sulphate nitrate (20-20-0); and (d) Diammonium phosphate (18-46-0).
2. **Nitrophosphates:** These fertilizers are prepared by acidulation of rock phosphate and ammoniation of the resultant slurry. If needed, slurry is combined with potassium salt. The final product is made up of ammonium nitrate, dicalcium phosphate, mono- ammonium phosphate, etc.
3. **NPK Complex fertilizers:** Several grades of these fertilizers are being produced in India. NPK composition varies with the fertilizers: *e.g.* 10-26- 26, 12-32-16, 14-35-14, 14-28-14, 17-17-17, 19-19-19 and 22-22-11. These fertilizers possess good physical properties.

In addition to these complex fertilizers, new speciality fertilizers with varying compositions of NPK and micronutrients, specially designed for specific crops, are produced and marketed by many companies in the last few years. These are completely soluble in water and are suitable for foliar application and fertigation. As the cost of these fertilizers is very high, they are recommended only for high value crops.

MIXED FERTILIZERS

Fertilizer materials containing two or more plant nutrients are physically mixed manually or mechanically. There is no chemical combination of nutrients. Special mixtures are prepared for specific crops. The mixture can be prepared in the farm itself. Preparation of such mixtures requires great care and adequate knowledge about the chemistry of the ingredients used. This will avoid uneven mixing of incompatible fertilizers causing nutrient loss in the form of gases, conversion of soluble nutrients into insoluble forms and caking of materials. The following materials should not be mixed and used for making mixed fertilizers:

1. Ammonium sulphate, ammonium chloride, other ammonium fertilizer and nitrogenous organic manures with lime.
2. Sodium nitrate or potassium nitrate with super phosphate
3. Ammonium- sulphate- nitrate with lime.
4. Urea with super phosphate
5. Super phosphate with lime or calcium carbonate or wood ashes.

Bone meal, sulphate of potash and muriate of potash can be mixed with all the fertilizers.

MICRONUTRIENT SOURCES

There are four main classes of micronutrient sources: inorganic, synthetic chelates, natural organic complexes and fritted glass products (frits). Inorganic sources are usually the least expensive but are not always the most effective sources for crops. The inorganic sources include oxides and metallic salts such as sulphates, chlorides and nitrates. Sulphates are the most common of the metallic salts. Oxides of Zn and Mn are also widely used.

Synthetic chelates are formed by combining a chelating agent with a metal through co-ordinate bonding. They are generally the most effective micronutrient sources, but are also the most expensive. *e.g.* Zn EDTA (Na_2 Zn–ethylenediamine tetra-acetic acid) and Fe EDDHA (Fe-ethylenediamine di-orthrohydorxy phenyl acetate).

Natural organic complexes are made by reacting metallic salts with some organic by–products of the wood-pulp industry. Several classes of these complexes are the lignosulphonates, phenols and polyflavonoids. These complexes cost less per unit of micronutrient but they are usually less effective than synthetic chelates.

Fritted micronutrients are glassy products and are generally used only on sandy soils in regions of high rainfall where the leaching loss of nutrient is more. Frits have only a small share of the micronutrients market.

The common micro nutrient fertilizers and their nutrient contents are given in Table 5.6.

TABLE 5.6: Micronutrient fertilizers and their nutrient content

Fertilizers	Element /form	Content (%)
Zinc sulphate (heptahydrate)	Zn	21.0
Manganese sulphate	Mn	30.5
Ammonium molybdate	Mo	52.0
Borax	B	10.5

Fertilizers	Element /form	Content (%)
Solubor	B	19.0
Copper sulphate	Cu	24.0
Ferrous sulphate	Total Fe	19.5
	Ferrous	19.0
	Ferric	0.5
Chelated Zn (EDTA form)	Zn	12.0
Chelated Fe (EDTA form)	Fe	12.0
Zinc sulphate (monohydrate)	Zn	33.0

SOIL AMENDMENTS

Soil amendments are substances that influence plant growth favourably by changing the soil pH, increasing the nutrient availability, improving the physical condition of the soil and counteracting the effects of injurious substances. There are three types of soil amendments.

i) Materials used for amending acidic soils: *e.g.* lime
ii) Materials used for ameliorating alkali soils: *e.g.* gypsum and phosphogypsum
iii) Soil aggregating agents or soil conditioners to stabilize soil aggregates and to form granular structures: *e.g.* poly-electrolytes including polyvinytites, polyacrylates, cellulose gums, lignin derivatives and silicates.

1. **Gypsum:** Gypsum is dihydrate calcium sulphate ($CaSO_4.2H_2O$) and used as a popular amendment for the reclamation of alkali soils. Pure gypsum contains 18.6% S and 23.2% Ca. Commercial agricultural grades (70-80% purity) contain 13-15% S and 16-19% Ca. The S in gypsum is in plant-available sulphate form and its solubility is comparable to that of SSP. Most of the gypsum mines are located in Rajasthan.
2. **Phosphogypsum:** Phosphogypsum is obtained as by-product in the wet process of phosphoric acid production. The $CaSO_4$ in phosphogypsum is available as dihydrate ($CaSO_4$. $2H_2O$), hemihydrate ($CaSO_4$ ½ H_2O) and anhydrate ($CaSO_4$) or in combination of dihydrate and hemihydrate. Phosphogypsum is high-grade gypsum with 80-90% purity. It may also contain traces of iron, manganese, zinc and copper. This fertilizer is of great importance in alkali soils and as a source of S.
3. **Lime and liming materials:** Calcium oxide (CaO) is the only material to which the term lime may be correctly applied. It is also called as unslaked lime, burned lime or quicklime. It is most effective with high neutralizing value or calcium carbonate equivalent (CCE) of 179 % compared to pure $CaCO_3$. Complete mixing of this material into the soil is very difficult. Calcium hydroxide ($Ca(OH)_2$) is a white powder and called slaked lime or hydrate lime. The neutralizing value is 136.

The other common liming materials are calcium carbonate ($CaCO_3$), calcite or calcium-magnesium carbonate ($CaMg(CO_3)_2$) or dolomite. Limestone is mined by open pit method. Most of the agricultural limestones have the CCE value of 90-98 % because of impurities present.

STATUS OF FERTILIZER USAGE IN INDIA

Fertilizer usage in India has steeply increased during the past 50 years. In 1951-52, total NPK consumption was just 0.55 kg/ha. It has increased to about 70 kg/ha in 1991-92. In 1999-2000 it has further increased to 95 kg/ha. During this period, the percentage of irrigated area has also increased substantially. Out of the total nutrients used, N fertilizers shared the maximum (64%) followed by phosphatic (27%) and potassic fertilizers (9 %) (Table 5.7).

TABLE 5.7: Consumption of plant nutrients in India

Year	% irrigated area	Nutrient consumption (kg/ha)			Total (kg/ha)
		N	P_2O_5	K_2O	
1951-52	17.4	0.44	0.05	0.06	0.55
1961-62	18.2	1.60	0.39	0.18	2.17
1971-72	23.3	10.88	3.38	1.82	16.08
1981-82	29.1	23.02	7.48	3.83	34.33
1991-92	33.6	44.03	18.18	7.45	69.66
1999-00	76.3	61.16	25.31	8.86	95.33

Source: Agricultural Statistics at a Glance, 2003

The total consumption of N was nearly 59 thousand tonnes in 1951-52 and in 1991-92 it has tremendously increased to 8.0 million tonnes. About 92% of this is produced in India. Consumption of N in 1999-2000 was 11.6 m. t. Consumption of P from 7.0 thousand tonnes in 1951-52 to 4.8 m. t in 1999-2000. Potash fertilizer consumption raised to 1.6 mt. in 1999-2000 compared to almost none in 1951-52. Almost all the requirement of K fertilizers is imported (to the tune of 1.6 m. t. in 1999-00). Table 5.8.

TABLE 5.8: All India Production, imports and consumption of fertilizers ('000 tonnes)

Year	N			P_2O_5			K_2O	
	P	I	C	P	I	C	I	C
1951-52	28	28	58	9	15	6	7	-
1961-62	154	307	249	65	-	63	75	28
1971-72	949	481	1798	290	247	558	268	300
1981-82	3144	1054	4069	949	343	1322	644	673
1991-92	7301	566	8046	2562	967	3321	1236	1361
1999-2000	10890	833	11596	3398	1503	4798	1648	1679

P – Production; I – Import; C – Consumption.

FERTILIZER MANAGEMENT IN CROP PRODUCTION

About 40 % of the current food grain production can be attributed to fertilizer use. The recovery of applied nutrients by crop is generally poor. It is less than 50 % for N, about 15 % for P and upto 80 % for K depending upon soil characteristics. Most soils are only able to supply a fraction of thes nutrients needed to achieve high yields of arable crops. Even the nutrients available in the soil are rarely present in a balanced condition to meet the nutrient requirement of different crops. Fertilizer recommendation aims at providing balanced nutrition to crops. Addition of fertilizer nutrients should be such that they are available in adequate quantities and in ratios found in the plant for achieving desired yield target. The approaches that are being extensively used in India are described below.

Approaches for fertilizer recommendation

1. **Generalized or blanket recommendation:** This is based on the field experiments conducted with fertilizer rates for different crops and varieties in different regions. From these results, optimum dose of fertilizer is recommended for a particular crop for a given agro climatic region. *e.g.* general recommendation for high yielding rice varieties is 120,60 and 40 kg N, P_2O_5 and K_2O/ha. In this approach variation in soil fertility is not taken into account. Uniform adoption of a fertilizer dose may not be economical and efficient. There is a possibility of wastage of fertilizers in some cases and under-usage in other situations. However, this is the mostly adopted method.
2. **Fertilizer recommendation based on soil fertility categories:** Soils are calibrated into different fertility categories based on soil testing. Representative soil sampling is the first step in soil testing. Soil samples are collected from the plough-zone from where more than 50% of the plant nutrients are absorbed. The depth of sampling varies from 10 to 30 cm depending upon the crops. Soil testing is to be done atleast once after three crops. Based on the soil test data, ratings are given as very low, low, medium, high and very high. Generally there are three classes of soil fertility ratings: low, medium and high (Table 5.9). The general recommendation is equated to the soils rated as medium. For soils testing low or high, the general recommendation is increased or decreased by 30-50 % of the general recommendation.

TABLE 5.9: Soil test ratings

Nutrient /method	Low	Medium	High
Organic carbon (%) (Walkley and Black method)	< 0.5	0.5-0.75	>0.75
Available N (kg/ha) (Aklaline permanganate method)	<280	280-560	>560
Available P (kg/ha) (Olsen's method)	<10	10-24.6	>24.6
Available K (kg/ha) (Ammonium acetate method)	<108	108-280	>280

Source: Muhr et al., 1965

3. **Soil test based fertilizer recommendation for a certain percentage of yield maximum:** This is based on Mitscherlich and Bray approach. In this approach, an empirical relationship is developed between percentage yield and soil and fertilizer nutrients so that fertilizer doses can be recommended for various percentages of maximum yields. The soil-testing laboratory of the Department of Agriculture, Tamil Nadu, presently uses the modified form of this approach. Mitscherlich–Bray equation is:

$$\text{Log}\,(A\text{-}Y) = \text{Log}\,A\text{-}cb\text{-}c_1\,x$$

Wherein A is the calculated maximum yield, Y is the percentage of maximum yield, b is the soil test value, x is the fertilizer nutrient to be added, c is the proportionality factor for soil nutrient and c_1 is the proportionality factor for added nutrient. Value of A is fixed based on the yield potential of the crop in a given agro-ecological situation; b is obtained by soil testing; c and c_1 are calculated from the data generated from a series of fertilizer experiments conducted for the purpose; and x is calculated from the equation.

4. **Fertilizer recommendations based on critical limits:** Soil test values are calibrated from the data of multi-location fertilizer rate trials to deduce critical limits for the nutrients tested. For the value below critical limit, there will be positive or economic response to added fertilizer and above the limit, the response either diminishes at a faster rate or it is nil (Cate and Nelson, 1965). Soil critical limits for many elements, especially for phosphorus and potassium, have been determined by several workers. A critical level of 35-40 kg available P_2O_5 (Olsen's method) is used for all the field crops. The critical limit concept is very much useful in recommending micronutrients for the soils deficient or sufficient with respect to a particular nutrient. Critical limit for zinc for some soils and crops are presented in Table 5.10.

TABLE 5.10: Critical limit for soil available zinc for some field crops (EDTA extractable)

Crop	Soil order	Critical limit (ppm)	Remarks
Rice	Vertisols	1.00	Black clay soils
	Alfisol	0.70	Red soils
	Mollisols	0.80	Tarai soils
	Inceptisols/ Alfisols	0.70	Mixed red and black soils
	Entisols	0.50	Alluvial (noncalcareous)
	Entisol	0.70	Alluvial (Calcareous)
Wheat	Alfisols	0.60	Red soils
	Inceptisols/ Alfisols	0.60	Mixed red and black soils
	Entisols	0.50	Alluvial

Crop	Soil order	Critical limit (ppm)	Remarks
Maize	Alfisols	0.50	Red soils
	Entisols/ Inceptisols	0.75	Alluvial
Sorghum	Vertisols	1.00	Black clay soils
Pearl millet	Inceptisols/ Entisols	0.60	Alluvial
Chickpea	Inceptisols/ Alfisols	0.35	Mixed red and Black soils
Pigeonpea	Inceptisols/ Entisols	0.45	Alluvial
Groundnut	Alfisols	0.50	Red soils
Mustard	Inceptisols/ Entisols	0.50	Alluvial

Source: Katyal, 1985

5. **Soil test based fertilizer recommendation for maximum profit:** Optimum dose of fertilizer is the amount of fertilizer that produces the greatest profit per hectare (Cooke, 1972). Ramamoorthy (1974) established a significant relationship between soil tests, the added fertilizers and crop yields by fitting a multiple regression equation of the quadratic form as given below:

$$Y = A + b_1 SN + b_2 SN_2 + b_3 SP + b_4 SP_2 + b_5 SK + b_6 SK_2 + b_7 FN + b_8 FN_2 + b_9 FP + b_{10} FP_2 + b_{11} FK + b_{12} FK_2 + b_{13} SNFN + b_{14} SPFP + b_{15} SKFK$$

   Where: Y= crop yield (kg/ha), A= intercept (kg/ha), bi= regression co efficient and SN, SP and SK= soil available N, P and K (kg/ha) respectively and FN, FP and FK= fertilizer N, P and K (kg/ha) respectively.

   Adopting this equation, it is possible to obtain fertilizer calibrations for varying soil test values for obtaining maximum profit per hectare.

6. **Soil test crop response approach (STCR):** Ramamoorthy *et al.* (1967) established a critical basis and experimental proof for the fact that Liebig's law of minimum operates equally well for N, P and K. This forms the basis for fertilizer application for targeted yield, first advocated by Troug (1960). In this approach the crop needs and the nutrient present in the soil are taken into account to recommend fertilizer dose to achieve targeted yield. The underlying principle is to obtain as large a variation as possible in soil fertility in one and the same field to evaluate the real relationship between the yield and the soil fertility level without interference from other factors affecting the yield. This also helps to extrapolate the results to any soil type.

There is a significant linear relationship between the yield of grain and uptake of nutrients. This implies that for obtaining a specific yield (grain or economic produce), a definite quantity of nutrient must be taken up. This value can be determined by the magnitude of the expected yield (T) and the nutrient required to produce unit quantity of that yield (NR in kg/ha).

The fertilizer dose (FD in kg/ha) can be estimated taking into account of the efficiency of soil contribution (CS in %) from the soil available nutrients (STV in kg/ha) and the efficiency of fertilizer contribution (CF in %) from the fertilizer nutrients (FD in kg/ha) towards the total uptake. Using these parameters, fertilizer adjustment equations are derived for obtaining fertilizer dose for a desired yield.

Fertilizer dose (kg/ha) = NR/CFx 100T - CS/CF x Soil test value.

The response ratio of a crop in kg/ha of nutrients is calculated as follows:

Response ratio = 100/ A+B+C

Where: A = NR of N/ CF of N;
B = NR of P/ CF of P and
C = NR of K/ CF of K.

As an example, soil test-based fertilizer prescription for yield targeting in rice grown in an alfisol is given in Table 5.11.

TABLE 5.11: Soil test-based fertilizer prescription (kg/ha) for yield targeting in rice (Kranti) grown in Alfisols of Chhatisgarh region

Soil test values (kg/ha) *	**Yield Target (Q/ha)**		
	40	**50**	**60**
Available N (kg/ha)		Fertilizer N	
200	60	99	137
220	51	89	127
240	42	80	118
260	33	71	109
280	24	62	100
300	14	53	91
320	5	43	81
340	-	34	72
Available P (Olsen's P)		Fertilizer– P_2O_5	
13	86	116	147
16	77	108	138
19	69	99	130
22	60	91	121
25	52	82	113
28	43	74	104
32	35	65	96
35	26	57	87

Source: All India Co-ordinated Soil-Test Response Correlation Project Co- ordinator's Report VIII-XIII (1975-85); * Available K in soil is adequate for the indicated yields

Targeted yield equation used:

$$FN = 3.81\,T - 0.64\,KMnO_4\text{-}N\;F\,P_2O_5$$
$$= 3.06\,T - 2.83\text{ Olsen's P;}$$

Where: T is targeted yield (q/ha).

Nutrient requirements and their ratios

Nutrient requirement of crops vary with the soil types. For good yields to be achieved, crops must contain nutrients ($N+P_2O_5+K_2O$) in the order of 123, 43, 164 kg for 50 q/ha yield of wheat, 101, 56, 150 kg for a 50 q/ha yield of rice, 132, 70, 179 kg for a 50 q/ha yield of maize, 90, 53, 136 kg for a 40 q/ha yield of sorghum and 134, 35, 89 kg for a 20 q/ha yield of soybean (Velayutham, 1986). The results of long-term fertilizer experiments indicate that most soils in India could supply about 78 kg/ha of N, 14 kg of P and 76 kg/ha of K when continuously cropped without external addition of plant nutrients. Hence it is important to apply the limiting nutrients through fertilizers in quantities to ensure balanced nutrition for a given yield of the crop. The nutrients should be added in adequate quantities and in ratios found in the plant for achieving a desired yield target. Such balanced fertilization ensures efficiency and economy in fertilizer use.

Crop yields are highly correlated with the levels of fertilizer application. The role of chemical fertilizers has become obvious with the introduction of high yielding, non- lodging and fertilizer responsive varieties. Higher nutrient removal from soil over the years has resulted in widespread deficiency of secondary (particularly S) and micro- nutrients (mostly Zn) in addition to NPK. Increasing multi-nutrient deficiency is posing serious problem to the maintenance of soil fertility and sustaining agriculture. Efficient fertilizer management not only increases the fertilizer use efficiency but also reduces the potential pollution hazard.

To increase the efficiency of the applied nutrients, it is important to apply (i) correct quantity to meet the needs of soil and crop, (ii) at right time and (iii) with right method.

Optimum Dose of fertilizers

Nutrient requirement varies according to the crops grown. Since the nutrient supplying capacity of the soil varies, it is necessary to adopt soil test based fertilizer recommendation. Wherever it is not possible to adopt this method, blanket recommendation is followed (Table 5.12). It is easy to calculate the actual requirement of fertilizer to be used to meet the recommended dose by using the conversion factor for each nutrient as given in Table 5.13. Examples calculation are also given for easy understanding.

TABLE 5.12: General fertilizer recommendation for important crops

Crop	Fertilizer dose (kg/ha)		
	N	P_2O_5	K_2O
Rice	100-150	50-60	50-60
Wheat	80-120	40-60	40
Maize	100-125	60	40
Barley	40-60	20	-
Sorghum	100-120	50	40
Pearl millet	100-120	40-60	30-40
Finger millet	50-60	30-40	20-30
Pulses	25	50	-
Groundnut	20-40	40-80	20-40
Rape seed-mustard	60-90	60	40
Sesame	25-30	20-30	0-20
Linseed	50	40	-
Castor	40	40	20
Safflower	20-45	-	-
Sunflower	60-80	60	40
Niger	20	20	-
Sugarcane	125-250	120-150	100-150
Sugarbeet	120	80	100
Jute	40-80	20-40	40-80
Cotton	100-120	60	60
Tabacco	100	100	100

TABLE 5.13: Conversion factors to work out quantity of fertilizer from nutrient

Nutrient	Multiplication factor	Fertilizer
Nitrogen	4.9	Ammonium sulphate
Nitrogen	2.2	Urea
Nitrogen	4.0	Ammonium chloride
Nitrogen	3.0	Ammonium nitrate
Phosphoric acid (P_2O_5)	6.3	Super phosphate
Potash (K_2O)	1.7	Muriate of potash
Potash (K_2O)	2.0	Sulphate of potash

Example

1. Calculate the quantity of urea, super phosphate and muriate of potash required for one hectare of rice with the N, P_2O_5 and K_2O 100-50-50 kg/ha.

Urea = 100/46 x 100=217.4 kg
Super phosphate = 100/16 x 50= 312. 5 kg
Muriate of potash = 100/60 x 50= 83.3 kg.

Requirements of fertilizer can be calculated using the conversion factor. (Urea: 2.2; super phosphate: 6.3; Muriate of potash: 1.67.

Urea: 100x 2.2 = 220 kg
Super phosphate: 50x6.3 = 315 kg.
Muriate of potash: 50x 1.7 = 85 kg.

2. Calculate the quantity of DAP, urea and muriate of potash required for one ha of rice to meet the nutrient requirement of N, P_2O_5 and K_2O at 100-50-50 kg.

DAP to met 50 kg P_2O_5 = 100/46 x 50 = 108.7 kg

Quantity of N present in 108.7 kg of

DAP = 18/100 x 108.7
= 19.6 or 20 kg.

Quantity of N to be supplemented with

Urea = 100 – 20 = 80 kg
Requirement of urea = 100/46 x 80 = 173.9 kg
Muriate of potash = 100/60 x 50 = 83.3 kg.

(*Note*: Whenever complex fertilizer is involved, calculate first for the contribution of that fertilizer for the nutrient that is present in higher quantity. For example, in the case of DAP, first calculate for P as DAP contains higher quantity of P. Then calculate the quantity of the next highest quantity of nutrient (in this case N) contributed by that quantity of the fertilizer.

3. Work out the quantity of complex (17:17:17) and urea required to meet the nutrient requirement of 100:50:50 kg N, P_2O_5 and K_2O/ha.

Quantity of complex fertilizer = 100/17 x 50 = 294 kg.

This will supply 50 kg each of N, P_2O_5 and K_2O. Remaining 50 kg N is to be supplemented with urea.

Quantity of urea = 100/46 x 50 = 108.7 kg.

Time of fertilizer application

Time of fertilizer application depends on the type of crop cultivated, its growth stage, nutrient requirement, soil conditions and nature of fertilizer. Fertilizers are applied (i) prior to sowing, (ii) at sowing and (iii) after sowing the crop.

1. **Application before sowing:** Amendments should be applied well in advance to sowing. Some of the water insoluble P fertilizers such as rock phosphate and basic slag should be applied about 2-4 weeks before sowing. This enables conversion of water insoluble form of P to soluble form for efficient crop utilization.
2. **Application at sowing:** Application of fertilizers at the time of sowing

or just before sowing is called 'basal application'. Mostly phosphatic and potash fertilizers are basally applied. A part of recommended N is also applied as basal dose. Micronutrient fertilizers should be applied at the time of sowing on the soil and should not be incorporated into the soil.

3. **Application after sowing:** Application of fertilizers after the crop establishment is called top dressing. Usually a portion of N is applied as top dressing depending on the stage of crop. In light textured soils, potash is also recommended for top dressing.
4. **Split application of N:** Split application increases the nitrogen use efficiency by supplying N at the critical stages when the crop requirement is high. This also avoids large amounts of basally applied N being subjected to various losses. It is the most convenient and easily adaptable technique. Factors such as total amount of N to be applied, soil texture, crop duration, critical stages of growth, crop season and water management practices largely govern the number of splits. In irrigated crops N is generally applied in 2-3 splits. In dryland condition, the entire N is applied at sowing as it is difficult to apply N at later stages in the absence of adequate soil moisture. Nitrogen application is recommended at tillering and panicle initiation stages for rice. Basal application is sufficient for pulses. Split application of N at 30, 60 and 90 days after planting are recommended for sugarcane.

Method of fertilizer application

1. **Broadcasting:** Fertilizers are applied on the open field at the time of sowing or spread in the standing crop. Broadcasting is mostly done manually in India and with fertilizer spreaders in other countries. Broadcast fertilizers should be incorporated into the soil. Fertilizers that are applied in large quantities are normally broadcast applied.
2. **Placement:** Whenever a small quantity fertilizer is applied, placement is practiced. This method of fertilization is generally practiced in wide-spaced crops and the soils having low fertility. Placement of fertilizer is done in different ways: drilling, band application and spot placement.

Drilling is one of the methods to place fertilizers simultaneously at the time of sowing by the use of seed- cum- fertilizer drill.

Band application is generally practiced in the standing crops. If the fertilizer is placed in bands to one or either sides of crop rows, it is called "side dressing". Fertilizer application to fruit trees is adopted by 'circular band' (ring placement) away from the base of plants.

Application of fertilizer nearer to each plant is called as 'spot placement'. This method of fertilizer application is generally practiced for vegetable crops. Urea super granules (USG) are deep-placed in lowland rice.

Advantages of placement: Surface broadcasting of nitrogen is the commonly used practice. It results in higher ammonia volatilization losses. These losses can be considerably reduced by deep placement. The efficiency of the fertilizer phosphorus depends on the method of application. Except in the case of lowland rice, placement of water soluble phosphates increases its effectiveness. The localized placement of water soluble P fertilizer helps in minimizing soil fixation. Placement of P gives additional yield advantage of 6-7 Q/ha over broadcasting in wheat.

- **Foliar application:** Fertilizer nutrients that are soluble in water are applied on the foliage as a solution or suspension. Low concentration solutions (less than 1 to 2 %) are prepared to supply one plant nutrient or combination of nutrients. In general, nitrogen and micro- nutrients are applied as foliar sprays. Among the N fertilizers, urea is quite suitable for foliar application. DAP spraying is recommended for pulses and cotton. Of late, water-soluble speciality fertilizers have come into the market. These are highly suitable for foliar application since they do not leave any residues on dissolution. Compatible insecticides can also be mixed with the fertilizers and applied as foliar spray. Micronutrients are applied in small quantities and hence foliar spray is an effective method. Soluble inorganic salts are used for foliar spray. Generally high volume sprayers are used for foliar application.
- **Aerial application:** Large contiguous areas could be fertilized aerially with solid fertilizers or fertilizer solutions by aircrafts. This method is practiced widely in USA, Australia, New Zealand, Holland and Canada. Aerial fertilization is most practicable in hilly regions and grasslands.
- **Injection into soil:** Fertilizers such as anhydrous ammonia and N solutions are injected directly into the soil with the help of special equipments. This method is most popular in USA.
- **Application through irrigation systems or fertigation:** Fertilizer nutrients are applied through irrigation water in either open or closed systems. Open systems include sprinkler and trickle systems. Principal nutrients that are applied by fertilization are N and S. By adoption of fertigation it is possible to apply nutrients at the time of the crop need. For the crops like sugarcane it is difficult to enter into the field to apply fertilizers. In such situation, fertigation comes in handy to apply fertilizers easily. Fertigation may also be adopted to correct mid-season deficiencies. Uniform distribution of fertilizer is important under fertigation and hence different metering devices are employed.

INTEGRATED NUTRIENT MANAGEMENT

Integrated nutrient management (INM) aims at efficient and judicious use of all the major sources of plant nutrients in an integrated manner so as to get maximum economic yield without any deleterious effect on physico-chemical and biological properties of the soil. The basic concept underlying INM is maintenance and possible improvement in soil fertility for sustained productivity on a long-term basis. Major sources of plant nutrients are fertilizers, FYM/composts, green manures, biofertilizers and crop residues /recyclable waste. Proper integration of one or more sources will ensure optimum nutrient supply.

Fertilizer is the most important component in integrated nutrient supply system under intensive cropping. Use of balanced fertilization is required to boost the crop productivity. Chemical fertilizers are to be properly integrated with other sources.

Integration of fertilizers with bulky organics: Farmyard manure and compost are the traditional organic sources that have been used in crop production. About 50 % of the manurial potential of the livestock population is only utilized for crop production. Sizable amount of plant nutrients are lost because of improper storage, handling and incorporation techniques. Results of various field experiments have clearly indicated the importance of integrated use of FYM and fertilizers for overall improvement in soil fertility. Results also indicate that a part of fertilizer requirement of rainy season (*kharif*) crop can be met with the use of FYM in different cropping systems without any adverse effect on the total productivity. Based on a number of experiments on rice, it is concluded that 1 tonne of FYM supplying 12 kg nutrients ($N+P_2O_5 + K_2O$) produces as much grain as 3.6 kg fertilizer nutrients (Singh and Dwivedi, 1996). In addition to supplying plant nutrients to the current crop, FYM leaves substantial residual effect on succeeding crops in the system. Meelu and Morris (1984) reported that 12 t FYM and 80 kg N/ha gave residual effect on the succeeding wheat equivalent to 30 kg/ha each of N and P_2O_5. There was also a build up in soil fertility with FYM application. Kulkarni *et al.* (1983) on the basis of 240 trials conducted in cultivators' fields in rice growing regions of the country concluded that application of 12 tonnes of FYM along with 90 kg N/ha to the *kharif* crop followed by 60 kg N/ha to *rabi* crop could produce an yield comparable to 120 kg N, 60 kg P_2O_5 and 60 kg K_2O/ha in *kharif* and 60 kg N/ha to *rabi* crop in rice-rice cropping system.

Besides supplying plant nutrients, FYM application also improves the physico - chemical and biological properties of the soil. Application of FYM along with recommended level of fertilizers enables to maintain the organic matter in the soil compared to fertilizer application alone.

Green manuring with inorganic fertilizers: Before the introduction of inorganic fertilizers, green manuring was invariably practiced for crops like rice, wheat, sugarcane, etc. With the easy availability of fertilizers and adoption of highly intensive cropping, the practice was almost given up. In the recent years, there is a renewed interest on green manuring. Sunnhemp and dhaincha are the most common green manure crops in India. Green manures produce large amount of green biomass of narrow

C: N ratio. When incorporated into the soil, green manures contribute sizable amount of plant nutrients, particularly N and also improve the soil physical conditions. Experiments carried out at several locations have distinctly established the advantage of introducing green manure crop as a supplement to fertilizers in cereal crop rotations. Green manuring along with the recommended level of fertilizers benefits the crops in the rotation and increase the total productivity of the system to the tune of 10-20 %. Incorporation of 10 tonnes / ha of green manure through Sesbania or Crotolaria supplement fertilizer N equivalent to 40-45 kg/ha. Integrating P with green manure in the first crop of rice produces higher yields of second season rice.

Green manuring in drylands is rare, but is practiced in small pockets in India. On vertisols receiving more than 1000 mm of rainfall in Khammam district of Andhra Pradesh, green manure is grown during the South-West monsoon season in June followed by its incorporation before sowing sorghum in September. Depending on sowing of green gram, it is either incorporated as green fodder or harvested as pods. This practice has been observed to supplement 50 % N (Venkateswaralu, 1987). Inclusion of a grain legume has been found to be advantageous for sustained yields under rainfed situations. *e.g.* cowpea–fingermillet (Bangalore), green gram-finger millet (Bhubaneswar), sunnhemp-wheat (Hoshiarpur) and black gram-wheat (Rewa). The benefit of green manuring is felt only after continued applications for 3-5 years (Singh and Venkateswaralu, 1985).

Wherever it is not possible to include green manure in the multiple cropping system, there is a possibility of inclusion of legume in the system. Because of their shorter duration, small stature and erect growth habit, legumes could be easily accommodated as intercrops. Legumes of short (Vigna group) or long (pigeonpea) duration group offer greater advantage as intercrops in cereals by providing additional profit to the farmers. The Vigna group is harvested earlier and provides some nitrogen to the longer duration companion crop. Pigeonpea is of longer duration. It is least competitive during the early growth phase and starts using the space effectively by putting up additional growth after harvest of the early duration companion crop. These pulses provide N upto 50 kg/ha to the associated crops in vertisols. Higher benefits have been reported for crop combinations of cowpea (fodder) + sorghum, green gram/black gram + sunflower and pigeonpea + groundnut.

Green manure crops can be very well accommodated as intercrops in wide-spaced crops like sugarcane and maize. Since initial crop growth up to 100 days after planting of sugarcane is very slow, this period can be utilized for growing legumes in inter-row spaces as intercrops for grain or fodder purposes. Summer legume crops like black gram and green gram intercropped with spring planted sugarcane increased the cane yield markedly besides producing 0.4 – 0.5 tonne of pulse grain/ha (Yadav, 1980).

In addition to their capacity to fix atmospheric N, the legumes are capable of extracting less soluble form of P from the soil. They also extract the higher valency nutrient cations better.

Biofertilizers with inorganics: Various biofertilizers can be used according to needs of the crops. Biofertilizers act as complimentary and supplementary sources of plant nutrients. Biofertilizers help in increasing the biologically fixed atmospheric N and enhancing native P availability to the crops. Among the biofertilizers for increasing N supply, N- fixing bacteria (Rhizobium, Azotobacter and Azospirillum), blue green algae (BGA) and Azolla are important. The availability of P is improved by P solubilizing microorganisms (PSM) and mycorrhizae.

Rhizobium is of vital importance to various pulses and some of the oilseeds and fodder legumes as 80 to 90 % of their N requirement are met through biological nitrogen fixation (BNF). Inoculation of legumes with specific species of Rhizobium is widely used and is a successful practice throughout the world. Responses to Rhizobium under field conditions have been quite variable and depend on soil conditions, quality of inoculum and effectiveness of native Rhizobium. It fixes atmospheric N ranging from 50 to 60 kg/ha in groundnut and 100-300 kg/ha in alfalfa. Pulse crops fix 50-110 kg N/ha under optimum conditions. It is generally accepted that the fixation is about 50 kg/ha in a season. Field studies have indicated an increase in pulse yields by 14-53% due to Rhizobium inoculation.

Azospirillum and Azotobacter are the other important groups of bacteria. Azospirillum fixes N in associative symbiosis with the plant roots and Azotobacter is a free-living N fixer. On an average, they contribute 15-20 kg N/ha to different crops when inoculated with efficient strains. Application of organic manure along with Azospirillum enhances N fixation to the tune of 20-40 kg/ha. Promising results have been obtained with the use of Azospirillum in crops like wheat, rice, maize, barley, sorghum and millets. Azotobacter has given promising results in rice, sugarcane, wheat and pearl millet. Response to the bacterial inoculant appears to be enhanced when applied along with N and P in rice and cotton and with P in sugarcane (Gaur, 1982).

Blue green algae and Azolla are very well suited for rice ecosystems. In lowland rice, the average N contribution by these N fixers is equivalent to 25-40 kg/ha. Various field studies have shown positive influence of BGA on rice plants under different agro-climatic conditions. If this technology is popularized, nitrogen equivalent of 1.5-1.7 m.t. urea could be supplied to rice through BGA (Venkataraman and Tilak, 1990). Besides supplying N, BGA also synthesizes and liberates growth-promoting substances such as auxin and amino compounds which stimulate the growth of rice plant. It also supplies additional humus to the soil. Results of the studies conducted by the International Network on Soil Fertility and Fertilizer Evaluation for Rice (INSFFER) have shown that incorporation of 10 tonnes of fresh azolla before or after transplanting is equivalent to split application of 30 kg fertilizer N/ha. It can be applied along with fertilizer N to step up rice yields. Based on field trials, an increase in rice yield by 13-54 % has been reported, besides building up organic carbon, total N and availability of P in the soil (Satapathy and Singh, 1980).

In recent years several strains of P solubilizing bacteria and fungi have been isolated. Phosphobacteria solubilize the residual and insoluble phosphates available in the soil-water solution very near to root surfaces. The phosphate solubilizing power is further enhanced by addition of organic matter. Studies reveal that integrated use of P solubilising cultures with low-grade rock phosphate can add 30-35 kg P_2O_5/ha in neutral to mildly alkaline soils. Vesicular-arbuscular mycorrhizae (VAM) exploit the soil phosphate better, leading to more efficient use of added fertilizers, particularly of slowly mobile ions like NH_4^+, Cu^{2+} and Zn^{2+}. VAM infected sorghum had significantly high P in roots and shoots and increased the dry matter production. Because of problems in isolation and multiplication of pure strains of VAM fungi, large-scale use on commercial basis is yet to be established.

ORGANIC FARMING

Organic farming is the backbone of sustainable agriculture. The U.S.D.A. report (1980) defined it as " organic farming is a production system, which avoids or largely excludes the use of synthetically compounded fertilizers, pesticides, growth regulators, and livestock feed additives. To the maximum extent feasible, farming systems rely upon crop rotations, crop residues, animal manures, off-farm organic wastes, mechanical cultivation, mineral-bearing rocks, and aspects of biological pest control to maintain soil productivity and tilth, to supply plant nutrients, and to control insects, weeds, and other pests". The approach is based on the perception that tomorrow's ecology is more important than today's economy. According to the definition of FAO, organic farming should involve successful management of resources for agriculture to satisfy changing human needs while maintaining or enhancing the quality of the environment and consuming natural resources. Organic farming may result in comparable performance as conventional agriculture and crops grown with high organic manure application could tolerate the pest and disease attack better. It is an ecologically sound and sustainable way of growing more food.

Organic agriculture aims at to utilize local resources, maintain the long- term fertility of the soil, avoid all forms of pollution, provide foodstuffs of highly nutritional quality, to reduce fossil energy in agricultural practices, to maintain rural environment and also preserve non- agricultural ecological habitats.

Waste recycling

Organic farming mainly depends on organic recycling. Harnessing the nutrient energy from biological and industrial wastes is of prime importance for maximizing production. When these wastes are recycled as manure for crop production and are subjected to the degradation and assimilative capacity of soil, pollution of streams and/or rivers receiving these wastes is reduced to a large extent as compared to their direct disposal in water bodies. Organic recyclable wastes include crop residues, animal wastes, farm/industrial wastes, municipal and sewage wastes. They are valuable sources of plant nutrients and humus. In tropical and sub-tropical soils found in India, there is a general deficiency of organic carbon and plant nutrients due to rapid loss of these components by biodegradation. To make up for these losses, extensive utilization of organic residues in agriculture is essential. In addition, they also protect the soil from erosion. The manurial value and quality of these wastes could be improved by composting and enriching these organic sources along with inexpensive materials such as rock phosphate.

In India, there is a great potential for utilization of crop residues/ straw of some of the major cereals and pulses. Approximate availability of straw is to the tune of 141.2 m.t. which contribute about 0.7, 0.84 and 2.1 m. of N, P_2O_5 and K_2O respectively. Considering that about 50 % of these residues are utilized as animal feed, the rest could be very well utilized for recycling of nutrients. Crop residues have wide C: N ratio and when applied directly, nutrients may get immobilized leading to initial adverse effect on crop growth. Hence, adequate care is required to use the residues after proper composting with efficient microbial inoculants. Inoculation of these wastes with efficient cellulotic microorganisms produces enough simple sugars for growth and multiplication of beneficial microflora like free living N fixers and phosphate solubilizers in the soil which ultimately increases crop yields.

While the incorporation of crop residues *e.g.* wheat and rice straw, as such or inoculated with fungal species had beneficial effects on crop yields and improvement in physico-chemical properties of soils. Incorporation of legume residues viz., green gram or soybean stalks in rice, cowpea stalks in pearl millet or wheat saves energy input besides improving the soil physical and chemical properties.

Sugarcane trash compost: Sugarcane trash left out after harvest is about 19-38 m. t. It is either burnt *in situ* or used as domestic fuel. It can be recycled after composting suitably. Technology has been developed for production of enriched compost from sugarcane trash at Pune (Bhavanase *et al.*, 1995). In the compost pit of 1x1x1 m^3, chopped sugarcane trash is filled in layers. In the bottom of the pit, trash is filled to 30 cm thickness. A mixture of cellolytic fungi @ 500 g/tonne of sugarcane trash and Azotobacter are added. These biofertilizers are mixed with cow dung. Sufficient quantity of water is applied on the surface of trash. A mixture of cellulolytic fungi is inoculated: *Trichoderma viride, Trichurus spiralis, Aspergillus awamori, Pencillium spp* and *Paecilomyces fusiparus*. These inoculants improve the rate of decomposition and mineralization of nutrients. Another layer of sugarcane trash is then added. Above this layer, urea (to supply 8.33 kg N / ha) and rock phosphate (5% of trash) are applied dissolving in sufficient quantity of water. Cow dung with biofertilizer mixture should not be applied simultaneously with the fertilizers. Thus the pit is filled with trash in layers. Water is regularly added on alternate days to maintain 60% moisture in the compost pit. Adequate moisture is important for proper activities of the microbes. Turning of the material is to be done at regular intervals (at least once in a month) to improve aeration and maintain temperature at 50-60 °C which is optimum for composting.

Fresh sugarcane trash contains 0.36% N with a wide C: N ratio of 122:1 Small bits of trash decompose earlier than big size trash. Addition of rock phosphate, urea, biofertilizer and moisture play significant role in early composting. The composted trash contains higher content of N (1.09%) with reduced C:N ratio (20:1).

Biogas slurry: Organic manures from animal wastes are very important nutrient sources in building up the soil fertility. In India, the estimated production of dung and urine from bovine population works out to 1002 and 658 million tonnes respectively. They contribute about 5.71 m. tonnes of N, P and K. Proper method of collection and preservation is required to fully utilize the manurial value of these materials. Cow dung is an input in biogas plants. The biogas route has the dual advantage of providing both fuel (gas) and fertilizer (slurry).

The residual slurry that comes out of the digestion tank has a manurial value superior to that of FYM. The wet slurry should not be used as such. it should be dried for usage as manure. While drying, there is some loss of N and the dry manure contains about 1.8 %N, 1.10 % P_2O_5 and 1.50 % K_2O.

Industrial wastes: Among the industrial by products, spent wash from distilleries and molasses and pressmud from sugar industry have good manurial value. It is important to use only well- decomposed pressmud at 10 tonnes per ha. Addition of pressmud improves the soil fertility and enhances the activity of microbes. It is also used as an ameliorating agent in saline and sodic soils.

Coir waste is the byproduct from coir industry. Its production is about 1 million tonne in India. Coir waste can be used as manure after proper decomposition. Composted coir wastes (inoculated with *Pleurotus spp*. and 5 kg urea/tonne) is recommended for irrigated and dry crops. It has been reported that addition of 12.5 t/ha of composted coir waste with recommended fertilizers increased the yield of groundnut and maize.

Municipal and sewage wastes: Municipal and sewage wastes form an important component of organic wastes. In India, the total municipal refuse is about 12 m.t. per annum containing about 0.5 %N, 0.3% P and 0.3

%K. Sewage sludge is available to an extent of 4 million tonne per annum containing 3% N, 2% P and 0.3% K (Bharadwaj and Gaur, 1985). Sewage sludge, particularly from industrialized cities, is contaminated with heavy metals and thus pose hazard to plants, animals and human beings. Segregation of toxic wastes at the source will minimize the concentration of such elements in the sludge. High N input through excessive hydraulic loading of sewage can lead to ground water contamination. Further, survival of pathogens in soil and on crops causes health risk. This can be minimized by proper treatment, design of hydraulic loading, selection of suitable crops and adoption of modified irrigation system.

Vermicomposting

Vermicompost is organic manure produced by the activity of earthworms. Vermicompost is a mixture of worm casts which are rich in macro and micronutrients, vitamins, growth hormones and immobilized microflora. The average nutrient content of vermicompost is much higher than that of FYM. Vermicompost contains 1.60% N, 5.04% P_2O_5 and 0.80% K_2O with small quantities of micronutrients. The C: N ratio of vermicompost is much lower (1:16) than that of FYM (1:30). Application of vermicompost facilitates easy availability of essential plant nutrients to crops. The activity of earthworms is recognized as beneficial for the improvement of soil physical condition and plant growth.

Numerous species of worms have been identified for vermicomposting. The worm species more commonly used are *Eudrilus eugeniae, Lumbricus rubellus, Eisenia foetida, Perionyx excavatus* and *P. arboricola*. Wide varieties of wastes and byproducts which cannot be directly applied to soil as a source of nutrient can be composted by this method. Vermicompost can be used for different crops.

Horticultural crops/ Forest trees .... 100-200 g / tree
Potted plants .... 50 g / pot
Field crops .... 5 t/ha

Preparation of vermicompost: Method of preparation of vermicompost has been described by Purakayastha and Bhatnagar (1997). A tank of 2x1x1 m is constructed with brick lime in a shaded place. The bottom of the tank (about 5.0 cm) is made up of pieces of brick, stone chips and sand. This will facilitate easy drainage of water. Loamy soil is spread over this to a thickness of 15 cm. About 4-5 kg of diluted dung may also be applied. About 100 number of locally available worm species are placed over the soil bed. Dried leaves or hay may be put to 5 cm thickness on the vermibed. It should be moistened without flooding. A layer (about 10 cm) of straw, leaves of plants, kitchen wastes, etc. are spread over this layer. This can be continued till the bed is completely filled. Liquid cow dung suspension is then applied and waste paper and bigger leaves are used to cover the contents in the tank and finally the tank is fully covered with a gunny cloth.

Watering the tank is very important to keep the contents sufficiently moist (50-60%). After a month time, the contents are turned up and down and covered with gunny cloth. Watering is continued for another month. At maturation, watering is stopped to ensure drying of compost and for inducing the worms to migrate to the vermibed.

Vermicompost can also be prepared in pots and unused packing boxes of 45 x 60x 25 cm, provided with drainage holes at the bottom. The mature compost is a grey to brown coloured loose granular mass. After removal from the pit, it is sieved, dried and packed. The nature and quality of vermicompost vary with types of waste material and worm culture used.

CHAPTER 6

Water Management

History of the development of civilization clearly indicates that water had always been a fundamental building block for the growth of a health economy. With the growth of economy and improvement in the living standards, there is an ever-increasing demand for water from different sectors of the society. Availability of 1000 cubic metres of water per head is considered essential for a good living with assured food supply, adequate water for hygiene and for all the well-articulated commercial and industrial activities. Per capita water availability was more than 5300 m^3 in 1951 had decreased to 1905 m^3 in 1999 and is likely to be less than 1500 m^3 by 2025. Per capita availability of water less than 1700 m^3 is considered 'stress' level beyond which water availability gets classified as 'scanty' level. Below this level, availability of water is considered a severe constraint on socio- economic development and environmental quality. The UN General Assembly passed a resolution in February, 1993 calling upon the member countries to organize a World Water Day every year on March 22 for generating public awareness about the water related issues.

India depends heavily on the southwest and northeast monsoons, both for the surface and groundwater resources. Conservation, sustainable and equitable use of rainwater is of paramount importance. For successful crop production, adequate water is a pre-requisite. This water may come directly from rains or through water stored above and below ground. The available water should be efficiently utilized for better crop production.

PHYSICAL PROPERTIES OF SOIL

Soil is a complex, polyphasic system comprising solid, liquid and gaseous phases. Soil solids consist of organic and inorganic fractions forming the framework, the air and the water filling the intervening space. The solid phase is frequently referred to as mechanical composition. Different phases of the system cannot be separated easily as they interact strongly with one another. Soil holds water to be used by plants through the roots present in the same medium. The entry of water into the soil and its retention, movement and availability to plant roots are all physical phenomena related to the soil. Understanding the physical characteristics of the soil in relation to water is important for efficient management of irrigation for field crops.

Soil texture

Soil texture refers to the relative proportion of various sized mineral particles in a given soil. The size of particles in the soil is not easily altered. Since the proportion of each size group in a given soil (the texture) cannot be easily altered, it is considered a basic property of a soil. The mineral particle of a soil can be separated into groups according to the size and are referred to as soil separates. The analytical procedure by which the particles are separated is called particle size analysis. The principle of Stock's law is used for determination of particle size. According to this law, the velocity of settling (v) of soil particles is proportional to the square of the radius (r) of each particle ($v=kr^2$, k is constant).

Physical nature of soil separates

Soil particles are usually divided into three size groups called textural fractions or separates. They are sand, silt and clay. The classification is based on particle diameter ranges. The most commonly used classifications are those suggested by the USDA and International Soil Science Society (ISSS) (Table 6.1).

TABLE 6.1: Classification of textural fractions

Soil Separates	U.S.D.A.	I.S.S.S.
Gravel	>2 mm	>2 mm
Vary coarse sand	1-2 mm	-
Coarse sand	0.5-1 mm	0.2-2 mm
Medium sand	0.25-0.5 mm	-
Fine sand	0.1-0.25 mm	0.02-0.2 mm
Very fine sand	0.05-0.1 mm	-
Silt	0.002-0.05 mm	0.002-0.02 mm
Clay	<0.002 mm	<0.002 mm

Sand and gravel

The water holding capacity of sand grains is low and the water and air pass through the large spaces between the separate particles. Hence soils dominated by sand or gravel possess good drainage and aeration.

Silt

It is intermediate in size and has properties between sand and clay particles. They possess plasticity, cohesion (stickiness) and adsorptive capacity but much less than the clay separates.

Clay

Because of their small size, the surface area per unit mass of clay is very high. The soils having the clay fraction are fine textured and the movement of water and air are slow. The water holding capacity is high. They are sticky on wetting and hard and cloddy on drying.

Soils predominant in large sized particles are commonly referred to as coarse textured or light soil. Soils with high percentage of fine particles are called as fine textured or heavy soils.

Soil textural classification

Soil texture is designated based on the proportion of soil separates present in the soil. The field soil sample is analyzed to find out the relative proportion of these particles and the textural classification is made. The textural classification chart (Fig. 6.1) is used to designate the texture of a soil.

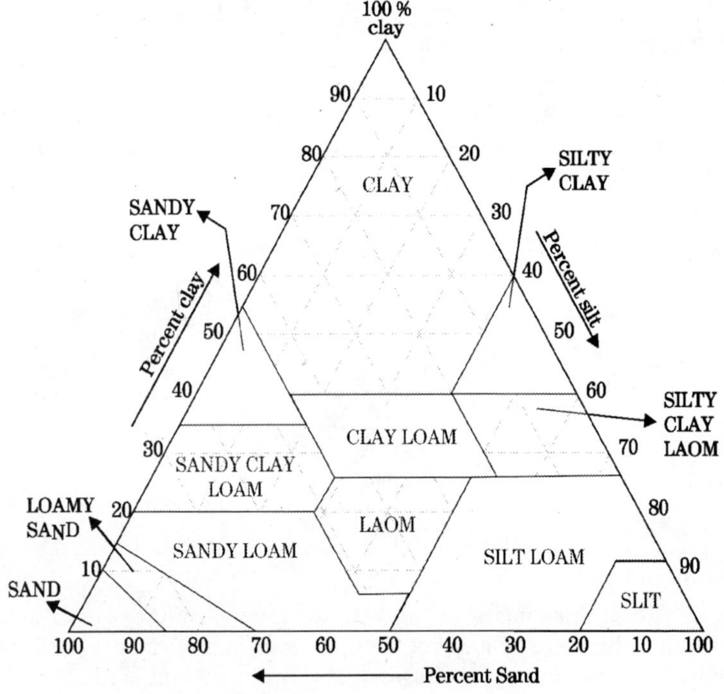

FIG. 6.1: Textural classification of soils

Sandy soil

The soil must contain sand separates atleast to an extent of 70% and the clay separates 15% or less. The properties of the soil are almost same as that sand separate. Sand, loamy sand, loamy fine sand and loamy very fine sand groups are included in this type.

Silt

This soil group possesses atleast 80% silt and 12% or less clay. The soil has only one textural class silt.

Clayey soil

The soil must contain atleast 35% of the clay separate and in most cases, not less than 40%. This includes clay, sandy clay and silty clay.

Loamy soil

It is a mixture of sand, silt and clay separates in more or less equal proportion. Hence, these soils have the properties of these separates. These include sandy loam, silty loam, silty clay loam, sandy clay loam and clay loam.

Among the different textural classes, loamy soil is best suited for cultivation of most of the field crops.

Soil structure

The term soil structure relates to the grouping or arrangement of soil particles. The primary particles are bound together to varying degrees into larger units termed as secondary particles or crumbs. The soil particles are bound to form temporary or stable aggregates. Aggregate formation in the soil depends on (i) silt and clay content, (ii) organic compounds present in the soil, (iii) the microbial activity and (iv) presence of iron and aluminium oxides. There are three main types of soil structure: single grained, massive and aggregated. On the basis of the shape, soil structure is classified as columnar, platy, prismatic, blocky, etc. Soil structure affects the water movement, heat transfer, aeration and porosity. Proper management of soil is important for the formation of structure, which influences the distribution of solid-void proportion.

Density of soil

The density of the soil solid is defined as the mass of the soil to its volume.

- **Particle density (Dp):** It is usually defined as the mass of a unit volume of soil solids. It is expressed as megagrams per cubic meter (Mg/m^3) or g/cm^3. For most of the mineral soils, the particle density ranges from 2.60 to 2.75 Mg/m^3 (g/cm^3).
- **Bulk density (Db):** This is the mass of a unit volume of dry soil (including particles and pores). The dry bulk density depends on the soil texture and structure. The bulk density of sandy soil is high (1.6 g/cm^3) and that of the fine textured soils is low (1.1 g/cm^3). Bulk density is generally higher in lower layers of the soil profile.
- **Porosity:** Porosity is defined as the ratio of pores (voids) to the total soil volume. Porosity is the index of the relative volume of pores. Coarse textured soils have less porosity as compared fine textured

soils. Porosity generally varies from 0.3 to 0.6 or 30-60%. The porosity of organic soil and well-aggregated clay soil may exceed 0.6. A well-aggregated soil facilitates easy percolation and penetration of rainwater. A sufficiently large pore volume is available for gaseous exchange. Soil air moves through these pores, which form a continuous system throughout the depth of a well-drained soil.

SOIL -WATER RELATIONSHIP

When water is added to a dry soil either by rainfall or irrigation, it is distributed around the soil particles where it is held by the forces of adhesion and cohesion. When all pores are filled with water, the soil is said to be saturated. Adhesion is the attraction of water molecules towards solid particles. Cohesion is the attraction of water molecules towards each other.

There are three main classes of soil water:

1. **Hygroscopic water:** Water is held tightly to the surface of soil particles by adsorption forces. The tension with which water is held in soil surface is from 10000 to 31 atmospheres.
2. **Capillary water:** Water is held by forces of surface tension as continuous film around soil particles and in capillary spaces. Capillary water is held between tension of 31 and 1/3 atmosphere.
3. **Gravitational water:** Water moves freely in response to gravitational force and drains out of the soil. This state of water will appear when the soil is saturated.

Movement of water in the soil

Movement of water from the surface into the soil is called infiltration. The rate of infiltration into a soil is an extremely important factor in soil moisture recharge by rain and irrigation. Maximum rate at which water can enter the soil under specific conditions is called infiltration rate. The infiltration rate usually decreases with time, following irrigation. For practical purposes, infiltration data are often presented in units such as cm per hour. The actual rate at which water is entering the soil at any given time is termed as infiltration velocity.

Factors affecting infiltration: The major factors that affect infiltration of water into soil are the initial water content, surface permeability, internal characteristics of the soil (such as pore space), degree of swelling of soil colloids and organic matter, duration of rainfall and temperature of the soil and water.

As the initial water content increases, the initial infiltration rate is reduced, but the effect is less pronounced with increasing time. Infiltration rate decreases due to some of the impedance's such as surface crust, clay pan and hardpan zones, surface compaction caused by farm implements and also by dispersed clay structure caused by an excess of alkali. Infiltration rates are also affected by the porosity of the soil, which is changed by cultivation or compaction. Infiltration rates are generally lower in soils of heavy texture than in soils of light texture. Addition of organic residues often improves the surface permeability and increases infiltration rate substantially. The rate of infiltration is normally high with the start of rainfall. The infiltration rate is high in the tropics due to viscosity of warm water.

Movement of water within soil

Water movement occurs as saturated conductivity in saturated soils and unsaturated flow or saturated flow or capillary conductivity in soils, which are unsaturated. The term hydraulic conductivity is also used for water flow. In saturated soils, gravity controls the water potential gradient, while in drained soils it is controlled by the matrix potential.

Saturated flow

Saturated flow in soils occurs when the water is not under tension. Pore spaces are filled with water. The theory of movement of water is based on a generalized form of Darcy's law. It states that the quantity of water passing a unit cross-section of soil is proportional to the gradient of hydraulic head.

$$q = kia$$

Where, q = volume of flow per unit time in cm^3/sec., i = hydraulic gradient, dimensionless and a = cross-section of flow area in cm^2, k = hydraulic conductivity in cm/sec.

Darcy's law can also be of the form

$$q/a = ki = v,$$

Where, v is the velocity of flow (cm/sec), q/a is also called the velocity flux and v is flow per unit area.

Unsaturated flow

As drainage proceeds in a soil and the larger pores are emptied of water, the contribution of hydraulic head or gravitational component of total potential becomes progressively less important and the contribution of the matric potential (ψ_m) becomes more important. The effect of pressure is generally negligible because of the continuous nature of air Space. The solute potential (ψ_s) does not affect the potential unless these are unusual concentration of salts at some point in the soil.

In moisture movement under unsaturated conditions, the potential (ψ) is the sum of the matric potential (ψ_m) and gravitational potential (ψ_g) to some extent. Darcy's law is still applicable under unsaturated flow. As the soil water content and water potential decreases, the hydraulic conductivity decreases very rapidly. The unsaturated soil moisture movement is often termed as capillary conductivity, though the term hydraulic conductivity is also frequently used.

Water vapour movement

Movement of soil water in unsaturated soils involves both liquid and vapour phases. At soil moisture potential of about 15 bars, water moves only in the form of vapour. Diffusion of water vapour is caused by a vapour pressure gradient as the driving force. Movement of water vapour is maximum in the fine textured soils. Maximum water vapour movement in soils occurs just before permanent-wilting point is reached.

Soil moisture characteristics

Release of water from the soil is directly related to the size and volume of water filled pores. The amount of water present in the soil at equilibrium is a function of the size and volumes of water filled pores. The graphical presentation of the relationship between matric suction and moisture contents is termed as soil- moisture characteristic curve (Fig. 6.2).

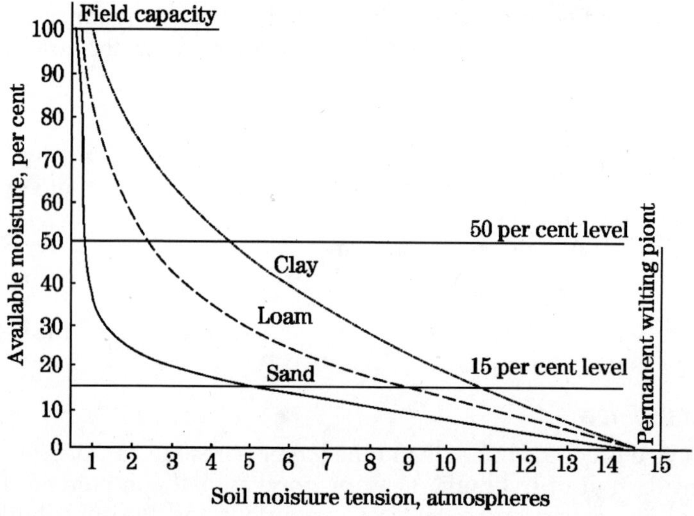

FIG. 6.2: Soil moisture characteristic curve

The typical curve shows the relationship in clay loam and sandy soils. This characteristic curve differs with different basic properties. With the increasing tension from 0 to 1/3 atm, water release is more than 75 % in a light textured soil but it is about 50 % only in a heavy textured soil (Rao and Ramacharlu, 1959).

SOIL MOISTURE MEASUREMENT

Plants utilize the soil moisture available in the root zone for growth and development. As the plants continue to utilize the soil moisture, available moisture supply diminishes. Unless otherwise more water is added, plant growth is arrested and finally the plant dies. Hence, it is important to irrigate the field at the appropriate time. Measurement of soil moisture helps to know the water status of the soil. It is also useful to schedule irrigation and compute water requirement of crops. Various methods are available for the measurement of soil moisture. They may be grouped into direct and indirect methods.

Direct methods of soil moisture determination

Gravimetric method

It is the most commonly used method of soil moisture measurement wherein loss of moisture is determined. Weight of wet samples and oven-dried samples are recorded. This gives the weight of moisture in the soil and expressed as a percentage on dry soil.

Procedure

A leveled spot is selected in the middle of the field. In the cropped field, sampling should be done in between two plants in a row. The screw auger is driven to the desired depth and the soil sample is drawn. A composite sample of not less than 100 g is taken in a moisture box. The lid is covered immediately to avoid moisture loss. The sample is weighed with an accuracy of two decimals (Ww). The sample is dried in an oven at a constant temperature of 105 °C for about 48-72 hours to get a constant dry weight. After drying, the samples are weighed (Wd).

Soil moisture content is calculated by using the formula,

Soil moisture content on dry weight basis (%) =

$$= \frac{\text{weight of moist sample (Ww) - weight of oven dry sample (Wd)}}{\text{Weight of oven dry sample (Wd)}} \times 100$$

Example: A fresh soil sample weighs 100 g and after oven drying, it weighs 80 g. Calculate the moisture content of the soil?

$$\text{Moisture content } (\%) = \frac{\text{Ww-Wd}}{\text{Wd}} \times 100 = \frac{100\text{-}80}{80} \times 100 = 25\%$$

Volumetric basis

It is convenient to express the soil moisture on volumetric basis by multiplying the soil moisture content with bulk density.

Soil moisture (%) on volumetric basis = Soil moisture content (%) on dry weight basis x bulk density

Moisture content on volumetric method can also be obtained by taking core sample. In this method, soil sample is drawn using a core sampler or a tube auger whose volume is known (v_t). The soil sample is transferred to an aluminium moisture cane and the weight is recorded (Ww). Oven-dry weight of the soil sample is again recorded (Wd). The soil moisture percentage is calculated by the relationship as given below:

$$\text{Volumetric moisture percentage (Pv)} = \frac{Ww - Wd}{\rho_w \times V_t} \times 100$$

Where, Ww- wet weight of soil sample (g), Wd- dry weight of soil sample (g), ρ_w-density of water (g/cc), and V_t- volume of soil including pores (cc).

Example: Soil sample is drawn with a core sampler having the dimension of 2.0 cm radius and 15 cm height. The fresh and oven-dry weights of the soil are 591.8 and 539.6 g respectively. Calculate the moisture percentage on volume basis.

$$\text{Volume of the core} = \pi r^2 h = \frac{22}{7} \times (2.0)^2 \times 15 = 188.6 \text{ cm}^3$$

$$\rho_V = \frac{Ww - Wd}{\rho_w \times v_t} \times 100 = \frac{591.8\text{-}539.6}{1 \times 188.6} \times 100 = 27.7\%$$

Indirect methods of soil moisture determination

Tensiometer

Basic principle of this method is that the capillary tension increases with decrease in moisture content. Tensiometers or irrometers consist of a porous cup made of ceramic material. It is connected through a tube to a pressure-measuring device or manometer (Fig. 6.3). At the time of installation, the tube is filled with water through the opening at the top and tightly corked. The porous cup is buried to the desired depth. Equilibrium is established through the porous material of the cup between the water in the apparatus and that in the soil. As the soil moisture depletes, water moves to the soil creating a vacuum in the tube, which is measured in the manometer. By calibration, the tension units are converted into soil moisture percentage. Tensiometer works well within a narrow moisture range up to 0.8 bar. At low moisture content, tension increases and air may enter the system through the pores of the cup, affecting perfect functioning of the instrument.

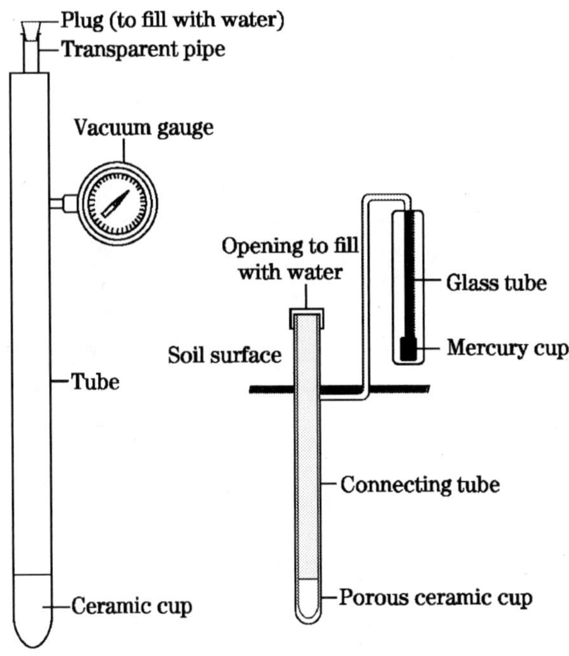

FIG. 6.3: Tensiometer

Electrical resistance method

It works on the principle based on the linear relationship between the electrical resistance and moisture content of the soil. Electrical resistance increases with decrease in moisture content. The resistance blocks are made of different materials and gypsum blocks are most widely used. The electrodes in the blocks are attached by wires to a resistance or conductance meter that measures the electrical resistance or conductance.

Electrodes embedded with gypsum blocks are buried at an appropriate depth in the root zone at a certain distance. (Fig. 6.4). After being in the soil for sometime, equilibrium is reached between the water content of the porous block and that of the surrounding soil. As the soil moisture increases or decreases, the water content of the block also increases or decreases correspondingly. The resistance offered to the flow of electricity depends on the wetness of the block. Higher the water content, higher is the conductivity or lowers the electrical resistance and vice versa. By passing an electrical current through the electrodes, resistance can be measured and the soil moisture is estimated. The relationship between the electrical resistance and soil moisture is expressed quantitatively by calibration. This method is not suitable for soils at freezing temperature as it causes a marked increase in resistance. This method cannot be used for soils having high salinity as resistance drops with increase in salinity.

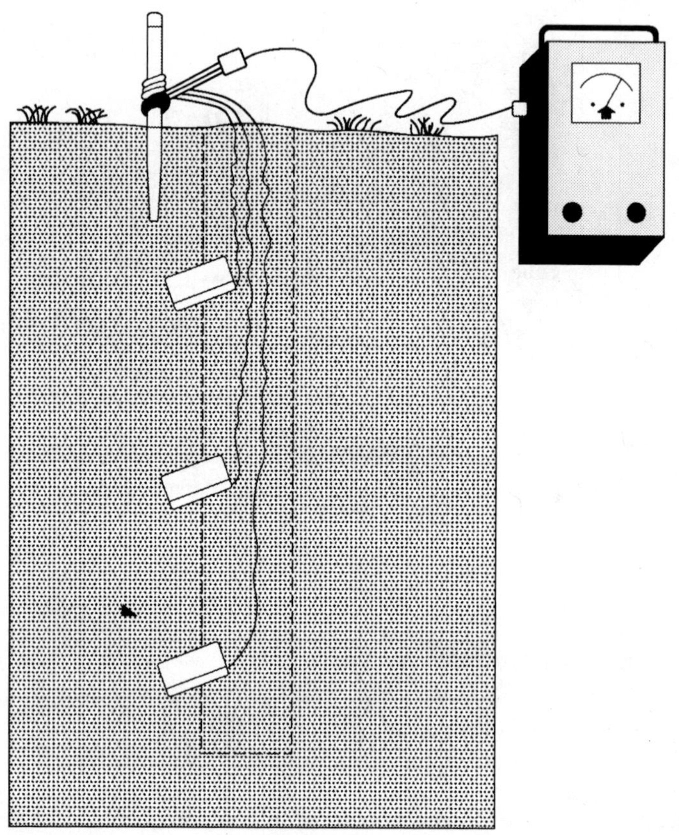

FIG. 6.4: Gypsum block and conductance meter

Neutron probe method

A rapid means of making *in situ* measurement of soil moisture is the neutron scattering method. In this method, radioactive materials are used to measure the soil moisture. The basic principle of moisture measurement is that when fast moving neutrons collide with the nuclei of hydrogen atoms in the soil, they are transformed into slow neutrons. Water is the main source of hydrogen atoms in the soil and the number of collisions depends on the moisture content of the soil. The number of slow neutron counts at various depths is used to estimate the amount of soil moisture content.

The neutron probe consists of two main parts (i) probe unit and (ii) counting unit. (Fig. 6.5)

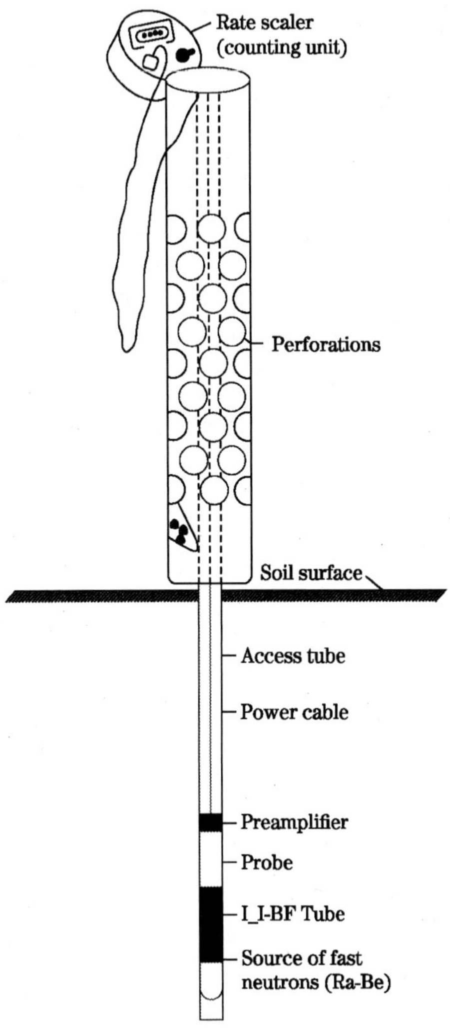

FIG. 6.5: Diagram showing neutron probe

Probe

The probe contains a radioactive source for fast neutrons and a detector for slow neutrons. The source of fast neutrons is Americium- Beryllium (Americium- 241 and Beryllium-9). The detector has boron trifluoride. The neutron probe is inserted into the access tube by carefully lowering down the cable to the desired depth. Slow neutrons produced due to collision with hydrogen nuclei will move to the detector tube and be captured. This results in transient break down of the gas in the tube. Short pulses are produced and amplified which are recorded on the counting unit (Scalar).

Calibration: Calibration is important for each soil before using the neutron probe. The count rate of the probe is proportional to the volumetric water content of the soil. Hence field calibration is done by comparing neutron count rate (cps) with volumetric water content. The volumetric water content is assessed by taking soil samples on the periphery of about 30-50 cm radius from the access tube at different depths. It is advisable to take the reading at the depths of 15, 30, 45 and 60 cm.

SOIL MOISTURE CONSTANTS

The status of soil mass or changes occurring in the soil mass after the irrigation or rainfall is called the soil moisture constant. The moisture constants are:

1. Water holding capacity or saturation
2. Field capacity
3. Permanent wilting point
4. Available soil moisture
5. Moisture equivalent

Field capacity and permanent wilting point are commonly used soil moisture constants. These represent the upper and lower limit of available soil moisture respectively.

1. ***Water holding capacity (WHC):*** It is the moisture content of the soil when all the pores are filled with water. This condition is also called as saturation point. The water is held without any force or tension at this condition. The gravitational force may pull down a part of water and is called as gravitational water or free water.
2. ***Field capacity (FC):*** Field capacity is the moisture content of the soil attained after drainage of gravitational water. The moisture content at this point is relatively stable. This situation usually exists for two or three days after rain or field irrigation. Sandy soils reach the field capacity earlier than clay soils. The force with which water is held is measured in terms of moisture tension. The moisture tension at field capacity is 1/3 atmosphere.
3. ***Permanent wilting point (PWP):*** Permanent wilting point or wilting coefficient is the moisture content at which the plants can no longer get enough moisture to meet the transpiration requirements and remain wilted even if water is added to the soil. At this point soil moisture tension will reach very high level and the moisture is retained at 15

atm. Wilting and drooping of leaves are the most common symptoms at this level.

4. ***Available soil moisture (ASM):*** Moisture that lies between field capacity and wilting point (permanent wilting point) is called available soil moisture. Field crops may be able to utilize 50 % depletion of this range. In some cases, it may be upto 75 %. It is expressed in terms of depth dimension of particular root zone. The approximate available moisture holding capacity for different soil textures are given in Table 6.2.

TABLE 6.2: Approximate available moisture holding capacity of different soil texture classes

Soil texture	Available moisture holding capacity (cm/m)
Coarse, fine and loamy sands	6-10
Sandy and fine sandy loam	10-14
Very fine sandy and silt loam	12-19
Clay and silty clay loam	14-20
Sandy and silty clays and clays	13-20

***Source*:** Sivanappan and Karai Gowder, 1977

1. ***Moisture equivalent:*** It is defined as the amount of water retained by a sample of initially saturated soil after being centrifuged for 1000 times that of the gravitational force for a definite period of time, usually half an hour. Moisture equivalent is the laboratory analogue of field capacity and may be used in the place of field capacity. Moisture equivalent also represents the moisture content in the inner capillary or microcapillary pores. In medium textured soils, the values of field capacity and moisture equivalent are almost the same. In sandy and clayey soils, the values may slightly vary.

Determination of soil moisture constants

Field method

Field capacity

A representative spot is selected in the field where the water table should be within two meters. An area of 2.5 m^2 is marked forming bunds all around. Weeds are removed to avoid transpiration losses. The area is ponded with water till the desired layer gets sufficiently wet. Paddy straw or black polythene sheet is spread over the area to prevent evaporation. After 48 hours, soil samples are drawn from the desired layer. Moisture content is determined at every 12 to 24 hours interval till the values of two successive samples are nearly equal. Readings are marked on a graph having time interval and moisture content. The lowest reading can be taken as the field capacity. Field capacity may be attained after 72 hours of saturation for clay loam soil.

Permanent wilting point (Sunflower method)

Five containers are taken and a hole is made at the bottom of each container to facilitate drainage. The containers are uniformly filled with about 500 g dry soil. Four seeds of sunflower are sown and allowed to germinate. After the emergence, only two seedlings are retained. In the lid of the container, two holes are made and the seedlings are allowed to pass through the holes and the lid is placed. The plants are watered as and when required for about 40 days till 3 pairs of leaves develop. A glass tube is inserted in the soil for aeration and is plucked with cotton wool. Plants are watered when the soil surface is sealed with wax and the drainage hole is also closed and then allowed to wilt. When the plants show sign of loosing turgor, the container with plants is transferred to a dark humid chamber or kept into a small water tray and covered with a bell jar or wire net cabinet to create high humidity. The bell jar or cabinet is covered with a black polythene sheet so as to reduce transpiration. The plants are allowed to extract moisture from the soil. If the plants gain turgidity, they are exposed to atmosphere for about two hours and again transferred to the humid chamber. This process is repeated till the plants fail to recover in the dark humid chamber. At this stage, the lid is open and the plants are cut. After removal of roots, soil samples are taken in duplicate and the moisture content is determined. The moisture content of the soil represents the permanent wilting point.

Laboratory methods

Pressure plate membrane apparatus method

The moisture content of soils for field capacity and permanent wilting point can be measured in the laboratory using an instrument called pressure plate membrane apparatus. The porous plates are saturated and the soil samples are placed in these plates and are also saturated. The plates are then transferred to the metallic chambers. The outlet tubes of the plate are connected to the chamber outlets. The chamber is closed with special wrenches and tightened. By using compression, pressure is applied at desired level. It is important to check any leakage of moisture from the chamber. With the application of pressure, water starts to flow out from the saturated soil samples until equilibrium against the applied pressure is achieved. Soil samples are then taken out and moisture content (%) is determined on oven dry basis. Soil moisture content for various pressure levels can be determined by similar procedure. Soil moisture characteristic curve can be drawn by using this method of moisture estimation.

PLANT-WATER RELATIONSHIP

Most of the herbaceous plant parts constitute about 80 to 90% of water (Table 6.3.) Almost every plant process is affected directly or indirectly by the water supply. An important function of water in plants is to act as a solvent entering plant cells and moving from cell to cell and organ to organ. The metabolic activity of cells and plants is closely related to their water content.

TABLE 6.3: Water content of plant parts

Plant parts	Water content (%)
Apical portion	90-93
Stem, leaves	70-90
Woods	50-60
Freshly harvested grains	15-20

Plant growth is affected due to water deficits since the cell enlargement is particularly dependent on atleast a minimum degree of cell turgor. Turgor is also important in the opening of stomata and the movement of leaves, flower petals and various specialized plant structures. Rate of photosynthesis and respiration are reduced due to decrease in water content. Continued dehydration causes disorganization of the protoplasm and death of most organisms. Water has a high specific heat, which permits the living tissue to undergo considerable heat absorption or loss with only small changes in temperature. The heat of vaporization is highest (540 cal/ g at 100 °C) that favours evaporation of water, which has a pronounced cooling, effect.

Plants absorb water chiefly through the roots and the loss occurs mainly from the leaves. The direction in which water flows from one part of plant to another or even from one cell to another cell depends on the water potential in the two regions. This is otherwise known as water potential gradient. Water moves from a region of high water potential to that of lower water potential. The water potential is denoted by ψ (psi) and usually measured in bars. The amount of solutes present in the water and external pressure affects the water potential. Pure water at atmospheric pressure has zero water potential (ψ=0 bar). Addition of solutes lowers the water potential.

Cell water terminology

Osmosis

Movement of water across a membrane in response to the presence of solutes is known as osmosis. This occurs from a region of low solute concentration to a region of high solute concentration.

Osmotic pressure or Osmotic potential

It is the pressure needed to prevent the passage of pure water into an aqueous solution through a differentially permeable membrane, thereby preventing an increase in the volume of solution. Osmotic pressure and osmotic potential are numerically equal; however, the two terms differ in sign. Osmotic pressure is designated positive and Osmatic potential as negative.

Turgor pressure

Plant cell, when placed in pure water, swells only to a small extent and does not burst. Due to high osmotic pressure of the cell contents, water moves into the cell. This results in pressing the cell membrane against the cell wall. The actual pressure that develops, or the pressure responsible for pushing the cell membrane against the cell wall is called turgor pressure. The opposite pressure exerted by the cell wall is known as wall pressure. The turgid cells provide mechanical support necessary for the non-woody tissues. Loss of turgidity leads to wilting and drooping of leaves. Opening and closing of stomata are regulated by the turgidity of the guard cells.

Diffusion pressure deficit (DPD)

DPD of water in a cell or solution is defined as the amount by which its diffusion pressure is lower than that of pure water at the same temperature and atmospheric pressure.

$$\text{DPD} = \text{OP-TP}$$

Where OP is the osmotic pressure of the cell content and TP is the turgor pressure within the cell.

Cell water potential

The tendency of water to move in any system is best expressed in terms of water potential. It is a measure of the free energy status of water and can be expressed by the equation,

$$\psi\ \text{cell} = \psi_s + \psi_p + \psi_m$$

where ψ cell is the potential of the water in the cell and the other terms express the contributions to ψ cell by solutes (ψ_s), pressure (ψ_p) and the matric forces (ψ_m). (ψ_s) and ψ_m are negative and ψ_p is positive. ψ_s expresses the effect of solutes in the cell solution and ψ_m the effect of water binding colloids and surfaces in the cell. The sum of the three terms is a negative number, except in fully turgid cells when it becomes zero. The DPD is numerically equal to ψ cell but opposite in sign. *i.e.* ψ cell = – DPD (Kramer, 1969).

Water uptake and movement

There is continuous movement of water within the cells, from cell to cell and from tissue to tissue. Different mechanisms and factors are involved in the movements of water. These can be classified into (i) passive movement and (ii) active transport.

Passive movement of water occurs along gradients of decreasing free energy or potential. If the gradients of pressure potential constitute the driving force, the movement is generally termed as mass flow. If gradients of total potential are involved, the movement is generally denoted as diffusional.

Active absorption occurs by a non-osmotic mechanism dependent on the expenditure of metabolic energy. Normally active mechanisms do not account for any appreciable amount of water adsorption.

Water can enter the plants through its entire surface (leaves, stems and roots). However, bulk of the water is absorbed by the plants through the roots, especially the root hairs. Absorption of water occurs when there is a decreasing gradient in water potential from the soil or solution surrounding the root to the root xylem. Movement of water from soil into the root hairs and from there to cells of the xylem with lower water potential results in root pressure which pushes the water up the xylem vessels. Root pressure can account for transport of water to tips of herbaceous plants to a few metres. In rapidly transpiring plants, the pressure in the xylem sap is often below the atmospheric pressure and water is pulled in through the roots, which act as passive absorbing surfaces. This is termed as passive absorption.

In slowly transpiring plants grown in a medium of high water potential, loss of some quantity of liquid water occurs in the form of drops from the margins or tips of leaves. This process is called as guttation. This can be frequently seen at night under conditions of high soil moisture and atmospheric humidity. Guttation occurs through specialized pores called hydathodes situated near a vein ending. This type is termed as active absorption, although it does not involve active transport of water.

Water is drawn continuously from the tip of the tree along the xylem of the stem and the root tips in contact with the soil that creates transpiration pull. A negative pressure or tension is generated in the xylem which is transmitted down to the roots. Water absorption occurs by moderately and rapidly transpiring plants.

Factors affecting absorption of water

There are several factors that affect the absorption of water by roots. Most important factors are soil temperature, osmotic potential of the soil solution, aeration and the availability of water. Though the atmospheric conditions also affect absorption, soil factors are generally limiting the absorption of water by roots.

Soil temperature

Soil temperature influences the water absorption and transpiration to a considerable extent. Water absorption is sharply reduced when soil temperature drops below 10 °C and uptake steeps upto 25 °C. Above this limit, the uptake is again slowed down. Temperature above 40 °C in the rhizosphere does not support water absorption and the plant shows sign of wilting. Low temperature causes reduction in water absorption. This is mainly due to decrease in root growth, increased viscosity of water, increased resistance to movements of water into roots and decreased metabolic activity of root cells.

Osmotic potential of soil solution

It is known that water is absorbed due to water potential gradient between the soil solution and the cell sap of the interior root cells. The osmotic potential of the soil solution is often more negative than that of the cell sap of the root cells, causing reduction in water absorption. However, some of the plants (halophytes) have a greater tolerance for salt concentration in the soil solution.

Soil aeration and flooding

Most of the plants do not withstand waterlogging and show wilting after continuous rainfall *e.g.* cowpea, greengram, maize, etc. In tobacco, this wilting is often termed as 'flopping'. The crops which are grown under marshy condition (*e.g.* rice) are little affected by waterlogging. Rice can withstand waterlogging because of large inter-cellular spaces in leaves and stem which maintain continuity with roots. Poor aeration, depletion of oxygen and accumulation of carbon-di-oxide occur due to water logging. Partial water logging alters the form of the root system which becomes shorter, shallow, less branched and often lacking root hairs.

Root systems

The root system of crops and varieties differ and there is variation in absorption of water by roots. Root growth is very much influenced by the soil. Root structure has greater significance under dryland conditions where moisture is limiting. When irrigation is available, the depth of root system may not have any significant effect. The spread of root system in the soil depth of 15-30 cm zone plays a greater role in water absorption.

Effective root zone

Effective root zone is the depth from which the roots of an average mature plant are capable of reducing soil moisture to the extent that it should be replaced by irrigation. The approximate values of effective root zone depth of some of the crops grown in deep well-drained soils are given in Table 6.4.

TABLE 6.4: Effective root zone depth of some crops

Shallow rooted (60 cm)	Moderately deep rooted (90 cm)	Deep rooted (120 cm)	Very deep rooted (180 cm)
Rice	wheat	Maize	Safflower
Potato	Tobacco	Cotton	
Onion	Castor	Sorghum	Lucerne
	Groundnut	Pearl millet	
	Pea	Soybean	
	Beans		

Shallow rooted (60 cm)	**Moderately deep rooted (90 cm)**	**Deep rooted (120 cm)**	**Very deep rooted (180 cm)**
	Chillies		

Moisture extraction pattern within root zone

The moisture extraction pattern indicates the relative amount of moisture extracted from different depths within the crop root zone. The moisture extraction pattern of a crop plant grown in deep uniform soils is shown in Fig. 6.6. Generally about 40 % of the total moisture absorbed by the plants is extracted from the first quarter of root zone, 30 % from the second, 20 % from the third and only 10 % from the last quarter.

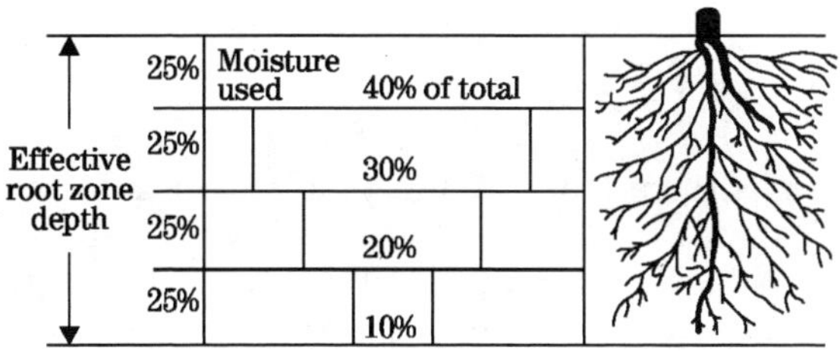

FIG. 6.6: Moisture extraction pattern in the root zone

Transpiration

Plants give off water vapour continuously from all of their above ground parts, particularly through leaves. The process of evaporation of water from the aerial parts of plants is termed "transpiration". About 98 % of water absorbed by crops evaporate from the aerial parts of the plant and diffuse into the atmosphere. Only 2% or less of water absorbed is used for building up the plant and maintaining the plant metabolism. There are three kinds of transpiration. (a) cuticular (b) lenticular and (c) stomatal. Culticular transpiration takes place through the cuticle. Lenticular transpiration involves loss of water through the lenticules. Transpiration through lenticules is slight and probably not significant except during cold spells in winter when it accounts for water loss by deciduous trees. Most crop plants of temperate climate lose approximately 10% of their water by cuticular transpiration. Transpiration mostly occurs through the stomata. About 90-97% of transpiration takes place through the stomata.

The size and shape of guard cells, resulting from the changes of their turgor control opening and closing of the stomata. When water supply in the plant is adequate, the guard cells taking in water become turgid and there is free exchange of gases and escape of water vapour. However, water shortage results in loss of water from the guard cells and stopping gas exchange and stomatal transpiration. Water stress causes a reduction in turgidity of the guard cells leading to closure of stomata. Severe drought or intense solar radiation causes the production of a plant hormone, abscissic acid (ABA) which signals the closure of stomata.

Effect of transpiration

Transpiration helps in keeping the leaves cool and this is indeed an important function of transpiration in many broad-leaved species. Transpiration is a necessary evil and helps in the movement of water and minerals within the plant body. The cells of plant body are able to remain turgid. Transpiration causes the ascent of sap.

Factors affecting transpiration

Plant structure and environmental conditions affect the rate of transpiration.

Plant structure

The leaf area and structure of leaf affect the rate of transpiration. Plants having larger leaf area have higher transpiration. Transpiration rate also differs with morphology and anatomy of the leaves. Plants grown in arid regions bear small leaves with thick cuticle, sunken stomata, epidermal hairs and well-developed palisade parenchyma. Leaves are also absent in some of the plants. The succulent stems take up the photosynthetic function and contain mucilage or latex in their tissues. These features help in reducing the water loss from plants. Transpiration rate also depends on the root and shoot growth. The increase in shoot–root ratio increases the rate of transpiration.

Environmental factors

The environmental factors such as solar radiation, temperature, relative humidity, wind velocity affect transpiration.

Solar radiation tends to raise the leaf temperature which, in turn, raises the energy of movement of water molecules in the mesophyll and hence the rate of evaporation from the cell surface. The rate of evaporation of water is generally doubled with about every 10 °C rise in temperature. Relative humidity has its effect on transpiration modified by the response of the stomata. Stomata of most species tend to close when relative humidity is low and open when it is high. If the moisture content of the atmosphere is high, the rate of transpiration is relatively low and it increases as the moisture in the air decreases.

Movement of air removes accumulated water vapour near leaf surfaces and increases the transpiration. High wind velocities often induce stomatal closure due to rapid water loss from the guard cells causing a decrease in transpiration. Moderate wind reduces leaf temperature which, in turn, decreases the rate of transpiration. This occurs on a sunny day when the leaf temperature is higher than that of the surrounding atmosphere.

WATER REQUIREMENT OF CROPS

Water requirement (WR) may be defined as the quantity of water, regardless of its source, required by a crop or diversified pattern of crops in a given period of time of its normal growth under field conditions at a given place. Water is required to meet the demands of evapotranspiration (ET) and the metabolic activities of the plants. These two demands are together known as consumptive use (Cu or U). Normally the water required for the metabolic activities is negligible and hence water requirement is usually equal to evapotranspiration. In addition to ET demands, water requirement also includes losses during the application of irrigation water (unavoidable losses) and the quantity of water required for special operations such as land preparation, transplanting, leaching, etc.

WR = ET or Cu + application losses + special needs

Water requirement can also be described with the formula,

$$WR = IR + ER + S$$

Where IR- Irrigation requirement of water, ER-Effective rainfall and S- Soil profile contribution

Water requirement for special needs include land preparation, nursery requirement including water for puddling and nursery growth, deep percolation including seepage and percolation and leaching requirement if the soil is saline.

Irrigation requirement (IR): Field irrigation requirement of a crop refers to the water requirement of crops exclusive of effective rainfall and soil profile contribution.

$$IR = WR - (ER+S)$$

Evapotranspiration (ET): In the field condition, it is difficult to separate the losses of evaporation and transpiration and hence the combined effect is called evapotranspiration (ET).

Potential evapotranspiration (PET): PET is the evapotranspiration that occurs when the ground is fully covered by actively growing vegetation and there is no limitation of soil moisture. It is taken as the upper limit of evapotranspiration for a crop in a given climate.

Consumptive use (Cu): The term consumptive use is to designate the losses due to evapotranspiration and the water used for the metabolic activities of the plants. Since the water used in the actual metabolic process is insignificant (about 1 %), consumptive use is generally taken equivalent to evapotranspiration (ET).

Determination of water requirement

The techniques employed in determination of water requirement of crops are grouped into the following:

1. Transpiration ratio approach
2. Depth-interval yield approach
3. Soil moisture depletion
4. Water balance method
5. Climatological approach - use of empirical and semi-empirical formula, pan evaporation and lysimeters
6. Drum culture techniques for rice

Transpiration ratio approach

Water requirement of crop is taken as transpiration ratio *i.e.,* the total quantity of water transpired by a crop to produce a unit amount of dry matter. Plants are grown in a pot culture house. Evaporation is minimized by sealing the soil surface. Water is added at intervals on the basis of periodic weighing of the pots. Detailed records are maintained on the quantity of water added and dry matter produced.

Limitations

In such trials, the values of transpiration ratio vary from place to place. It is observed that addition of manures and fertilizers reduces the transpiration ratio. For the 'dry matter', some workers use shoot weight while the others the economic produce of the crop. In the case of tuber and bulb crops, fresh weight is considered. Transpiration and dry matter produced by a plant are not related in a simple manner as in the transpiration ratio. Under field conditions, dry matter production is affected by several factors while the water use of plants by certain other factors. Thus, knowledge of transpiration ratio is of little value in planning irrigation practices in the field and working out water needs of crops.

Depth- interval–yield approach

Experiments are conducted with variation in depth of irrigation (5-10 cm) and intervals (5-15 days) of application. The depths and intervals are fixed arbitrarily taking into account of soil characteristics and weather conditions. The treatment which gives the minimum requirement of water for higher crop yield is taken as the optimum water requirement for a particular crop. In India, bulk of the work conducted in the field irrigation falls in this category.

Limitations

i) The arbitrarily fixed depth of irrigation causes either under-irrigation or over- irrigation.
ii) The intervals fixed arbitrarily result in pre-mature or delayed irrigations, thus affecting the crop by excess water at one stage or lack of water at the other.
iii) In some trials, irrigation is not actually measured in the field.
iv) Data on effective rainfall, water table depths and their contributions, irrigation efficiencies, soil types and general crop stand are not

recorded.

Soil moisture depletion approach

This method is usually employed to determine the consumptive use of field crops grown under irrigation on a fairly uniform soil. The depth of the ground water is such that it will not influence the soil moisture fluctuation within the root zone. In this method, soil moisture is measured at various depths a number of times throughout the crop growth period. Consumptive use (Cu) is calculated from the change in soil moisture content in the successive samples.

$$u = \sum_{i=1}^{n} = \frac{M_{1i} - M_{2i}}{100} \times A_i \times D_i$$

Where, u = water use from the root zone for a successive sampling periods or within one irrigation cycle, mm; n = number of soil layers sampled in the root zone depth, D; M_{1i} = soil moisture percentage at the time of first sampling in the $_i$th layer; M_{2i} = soil moisture percentage at the time of second sampling in the $_i$th layer; A_i = apparent specific gravity of the $_i$th layer; and D_i = depth of the $_i$th layer of the soil, mm.

The consumptive use values of each sampling interval are summed up for calculating seasonal consumptive use (Cu = Σu). A correlation is made by adding PET value (s) for accelerated water loss for the interval (s) 2 to 3 days just after irrigation and before soil moisture sampling.

Water balance method

This method is also called the inflow-outflow method. This method is suitable for large areas over longer periods. Gain of water in the field is generally due to precipitation and irrigation and occasionally due to run off collection from higher tracts and shallow ground water table. Losses of water include ET; surface run off, sub-surface changes and changes in soil water content. Gain minus loss gives the change in storage.

Climatological approach

It is difficult to obtain accurate direct measurement of pan evaporation under field conditions. Instead, evapotranspiration can be predicted based on climatological data. The magnitude and variation of evapotranspiration are related to one or more of the climatic factors such as temperature, day length, humidity, wind, sunshine, etc. Many empirical formulae have been developed for estimating evapo-transpiration. Most commonly used approaches in estimating ET are described here.

Blaney-Criddle method

Blaney and Criddle (1950) observed a close relationship between consumptive use of water with mean monthly temperature and day length.

$$U = K.F = S.k.f = Su = \sum \frac{k.t.p.}{100}$$

Where, U = seasonal consumptive use of water by the crop for a given period (inches) K = empirical seasonal consumptive use crop co-efficient for the growing period; F = sum of monthly consumptive use factors (f) for the growing season which is a function of temperature and day light hours; f= $\left(\frac{t \times p}{100}\right)$; t = mean monthly temperature (°F); p = monthly day light hours expressed as % day light hours of the year; k = empirical consumptive use crop co-efficient for the month; and, u = kf = monthly consumptive use (inches)

This method is relatively easy to use and required data are readily available. This method is extensively used and has practical applications.

Thornthwaite formula

Thornthwaite (1948) assumed an exponential relationship between mean monthly temperature and mean monthly consumptive use. The formula for estimating potential evapotranspiration uses lysimeter and watershed observations of water losses in the Central and Eastern US.

$$e = 1.6 \, (10\,t / I)^{a}$$

Where, e = potential evapotranspiration, unadjusted (cm/ month); t = mean temperature (°C); I = annual or seasonal heat index, the summation of 12 values of monthly heat indices; and, a= an empirical exponent.

To evaluate a, the following equation is used:

$$a = 6.75 \times 10^{-7} \times I^3 - 7.71 \times 10^{-5} \times I^2 + 1.792 \times 10^{-2} \times I + 0.49239.$$

This method requires only monthly mean temperature and hence is most extensively used to compute potential evapotranspiration for many regions.

Penman equation

The Penman method for estimating PE combines the turbulent transfer and the energy balance approaches. This method was first suggested to calculate ETo from open water surface. This method has been found to be satisfactory in both humid and arid regions under calm weather conditions. The equation is derived for calm radiation where day and night ratio ranges 1.5 – 2.0 and the relative humidity maximum upto 70%.

Modified Penman method

Doorenbos and Prutt (1977) proposed modified Penman method to compute potential evapotranspiration, also called as reference evapotranspiration (ETo). The Pan factor changes according to crop, wind speed and windward side. The radiation terms and aerodynamic terms are taken equally important.

$$ETo = (w \times Rn) + (1\text{-}W).\ f(u).\ (e_a - e_d)$$
$$= \text{radiation term} + \text{aerodynamic term}$$

Where, ETo = reference crop evapotranspiration (mm/day); W = temperature & elevation related weighing factor; Rn = net radiation in equivalent evaporation (mm/day); f (u) = wind related function = 0.27 [1+ (u/100)]; u = wind speed (km/ day) at 2 m height; and, $(e_a - e_d)$ = difference between the saturation vapour pressure at mean air temperature and the mean actual pressure of the air, both in millibar.

Pan evaporation

A close relationship exists between the consumptive use of crop and the evaporation rates from a well-located evaporation pan. Evaporimeters provide accurate estimation of short-term fluctuations in ET. Since the pan evaporation is normally higher than in the large free water surface, a factor of about 0.7 is usually recommended for converting the observed evaporation rate to those of large water surface areas.

Crop water requirement (ET) using pan evaporation

Data required: Daily evaporation (mm/day); mean RH (%) and mean wind velocity (km/day) at 2 m height.

$$ETo = E\ pan \times K\ pan.$$

Where, E pan = evaporation (mm/day); K pan = pan co-efficient which can be obtained by referring the Table. 6.5

E.g. If the wind velocity of a particular place is 175 km/day, RH 65% and the green crop coverage is 1000 m, the k pan for that place will be 0.85.

$$ET = ETo \times Kc$$

Where, ET= evapotranspiration, ETo = reference evapo-transpiration and Kc- crop co- efficient.

Crop co-efficient (K_c): To find out the K_c value, information on the length of growing period is required. The growing period may be divided into four stages:

1. Initial stage (germination to 10% ground coverage)
2. Crop development stage (10% to 80% ground coverage)
3. Mid- season stage (80% ground coverage to start of ripening)
4. Late season stage (start of ripening to harvest).

The Kc values for important crops are given in Table 6.6.

TABLE 6.5: Pan co- efficient (K pan) for class A pan evaporimeter at different levels of RH and wind velocity

RH mean%				
Wind speed (km/day)	**Wind ward side distance of green crop (m)**	**Low 40**	**Medium 40-70**	**High 70**
Light 175	1	0.55	0.65	0.75
	10	0.65	0.75	0.85
	100	0.70	0.80	0.85
	1000	0.75	0.85	0.85
Moderate 175-425	1	0.50	0.60	0.65
	10	0.60	0.70	0.75
	100	0.65	0.75	0.80
	1000	0.70	0.80	0.80
Strong 423 -700	1	0.45	0.50	0.60
	10	0.55	0.60	0.65
	100	0.60	0.65	0.65
	1000	0.65	0.70	0.75

Example: Total crop water requirement of sorghum is calculated for the crop cultivated during June- August with the following data:

	June	July	August
E pan (mm/day)	10.6	10.2	9.3
K pan	0.75	0.75	0.85
Kc	0.35	1.0	0.5
E pan (mm/ month)	(10.6x30) 318	(10.2x31) 316.2	(9.3x31) 288.3
k pan	0.75	0.75	0.85
ETo (E pan x K/pan)	238.5	237.2	245.1
Kc	0.35	1.0	0.50
ET (mm/month) (ETo x Kc)	83.5	237.2	122.6

Value of ET during crop growth = 83.5 + 237.2 + 122.6 = 443.3 mm.

TABLE 6.6: Kc value for important field crops

Crop	Crop development stage					
	Initial	**Develop-ment**	**Mid**	**Late**	**Harvest**	**Total growing period**
Rice	1.1-1.5	1.1-1.5	1.1-1.3	0.05-1.05	0.95-1.05	1.05-1.20
Wheat	0.3-0.4	0.7-0.8	1.05-1.2	0.65-0.75	0.2-0.25	0.80-0.90
Maize	0.3-0.5	0.7-0.85	1.05-1.2	0.80-0.95	0.55-0.60	0.75-0.90
Sorghum	0.3-0.4	0.7-0.75	1.0-1.15	0.75-0.80	0.5-0.55	0.75-0.85
Groundnut	0.4-0.5	0.7-0.8	0.95-1.10	0.75-0.85	0.55-0.60	0.75-0.80
Sunflower	0.3-0.4	0.7-0.8	1.05-1.2	0.7-0.8	0.35-0.45	0.70-0.85

Crop	Crop development stage					
	Initial	Develop-ment	Mid	Late	Harvest	Total growing period
Cotton	0.4-0.5	0.7-0.8	1.05-1.25	0.80-0.90	0.65-0.70	0.80-0.90
Sugarcane	0.4-0.5	0.7-1.0	1.0-1.3	0.75-0.80	0.5-0.6	0.85-1.05
Tobacco	0.3-0.4	0.7-0.8	1.0-1.2	0.9-1.0	0.75-0.85	0.85-0.95

Lysimeters

Lysimeter studies involve growing of crops in large containers (lysimeter) installed in cropped fields. Conditions that exist in the lysimeter should be as close to the surrounding field condition as possible. Water loss and gain are measured periodically and irrigation is monitored. It is possible to measure the water balance, *i.e.*, water added, water retained by soil and water lost through evaporation, transpiration and deep percolation. These measurements involve weighing with the use of scale balances.

There are two types of lysimeters: non-weighing and weighing types. Weighing type of lysimeters give accurate measurements than non-weighing types. The volume of lysimeters should be atleast one cubic metre for short statured crops and four cubic metres for tall growing crops like sugarcane. Fairly a large guard area of the same crop with similar moisture conditions should surround the lysimeter. This will minimize the clothesline effect and also the data recorded will bear a close relationship to the crop water losses in the surrounding field.

Whenever surrounding crops are irrigated, water is applied in measured quantity to the lysimeter. The over flow and deep percolation are measured. Water used by the crop through evapotranspiration constitutes the water received either through irrigation or precipitation, excluding over flow and deep percolation.

Lysimeters provide precise and direct measurement of the amount of water supplied to and lost by the crop. Some of the limitations encountered with the lysimeters are that reproduction of physical conditions such as temperature, water table, soil texture and density, etc. within the lysimeter to those outside the field is difficult to achieve. To ensure proper drainage, the bottom of an isolated soil column requires artificial application of moisture suction equivalent to that present at the same depth in the natural soil. Soil temperature in lysimeter sometimes rises to such an extent that air conditioning of the entire system becomes a necessity.

Drum culture technique

Drum culture technique is used to estimate the crop water requirement by assessing the evaporation, evapotranspiration, percolation and effective rainfall in the rice fields. In this technique, three containers (drums) are used; of which, bottom of drum A is closed and those of the other two (B &C) are opened. The drum capacity is 100-120 litres with the height of 50-

60 cm. The drums are installed in the rice field in such a way that top 20-25 cm is protruding above the soil level.

Drums A and B are planted with the rice seedlings and drum C is kept vacant without the crop. The water level and irrigation regime are maintained in all the containers as in the main field. Quantity of water applied and daily water loss are recorded.

Drum	Description	Component of water loss
A	Bottom closed Rice planted	Evaporation/Transpiration
B	Bottom opened Rice planted	Evaporation/Transpiration Percolation
C	Bottom opened Without rice crop	Evaporation/Percolation

From the readings recorded, the following components are assessed:

Percolation loss : Difference between A and B
Transpiration : Difference between B and C
Evaporation : Difference between C and (B – A)

SCHEDULING OF IRRIGATION

Absorption of water from the soil, its translocation through plants and loss as water vapour during transpiration to the atmosphere is a continuous process. Hence water use by crops is influenced by atmospheric demand, plant characteristics and soil factors. Various soil, plant and evaporative measurements have been considered for scheduling irrigation. Most important approaches in scheduling irrigation are: (i) based on soil moisture status, (ii) according to phenological stages of crop plants, (iii) based on meteorological approach and (iv) micro-plot technique.

Scheduling of irrigation based on soil moisture status

The soil in the crop root zone profile acts as a water reservoir for crop use. The moisture content in the soil changes with its withdrawal by plant roots and surface evaporation in the field or with the addition of water either by rain or irrigation. The change in the moisture content is monitored for scheduling irrigation to crops and it also provides information about the quantum of water to be added. Plants are able to use soil moisture within the range of plant available moisture. On an average crop plants utilize about 30-60% of stored available water in the root zone soil profile.

Soil moisture content in the rooting depth is determined at frequent intervals. Whenever, the soil moisture availability reaches some minimum value below which yield will be reduced, the crop is irrigated. Scheduling of irrigation to crops based on soil moisture potential changes is very reliable. Soil moisture sensors are widely used in advanced countries in automatic irrigation systems. Irrigation scheduling for important crops based on soil moisture depletion and moisture tension is given in Table 6.7. Irrigation should be given when the soil moisture depletion reaches that particular level.

TABLE 6.7: Soil moisture depletion and suction at active root zone (0-30 cm) of important crops

Crops	Depletion of available soil moisture (%)	Soil moisture tension (bar)
Wheat	50	0.5
Maize	50	0.5
Sorghum	75	1.0
Soybean	60	0.6
Cotton	50	0.5
Sugarcane	65	0.7
Sugarbeet	50	0.5
Tobacco	25	0.3

Scheduling irrigation based on the physiological stages of crops

Soil moisture status in a particular area is an ever-changing phenomenon and plants are generally not supplied with adequate quantity of water throughout their growth period. Plant systems also try to adjust to the moisture variations to some extent without substantial reduction in growth and yield. Irrigation may be scheduled according to the physiological stages. Generally there are four broad growth stages in crop plants. They are:

(i) Initial growth stage — Sowing to 10% ground cover
(ii) Crop development stage — 10-70% ground cover
(iii) Mid-season stage — Flowering to grain setting
(iv) Late season stage — Ripening to harvest

Certain physiological stages (phenophases) are critical at which there should not be any moisture stress. These stages are called the critical growth stages. Water supply is to be ensured at these stages to get a fairly high yield. In general, the mid-season stage (flowering to grain formation) is the most sensitive stage for soil moisture. The critical stages of important crops for irrigation are given in Table 6.8.

TABLE 6.8: Critical stages for irrigation of field crops

Crop	Critical stages
Rice	Early tillering, flowering
Wheat	Crown root initiation, flowering
Maize	Tasseling and silking
Barley	Pre-flowering
Sorghum	Flowering
Pearl millet	Flowering

Crop	Critical stages
Groundnut	Pegging, flowering, pod development
Mustard	Flowering, siliqua formation
Soybean	Pre-flowering, pod development
Cotton	Pre-flowering, boll formation
Sugarcane	Sprouting, maximum vegetative stage

Meteorological approach for scheduling irrigation

The atmospheric dryness or evaporative demand of a place will actually determine the amount of water transpired from a cropped field. Atmospheric evaporative demand can be estimated using various methods (Penman's formula, Blanney and Criddle) and correlated with the actual crop water use. Prihar *et al.*, (1974) suggested the use of ratio (s) between irrigation water applied (IW) and the cumulative pan evaporation (CPE) to schedule irrigation to crops under specific soil and climatic conditions. The quantity of water to be applied at each irrigation will depend upon soil and crop characteristics. Due corrections are to be made for effective rainfall received during the irrigation interval.

Example: Irrigation is scheduled at IW/CPE ratio of 0.8 and the crop is irrigated to a depth of 6.0 cm. Cumulative pan evaporation (CPE) at which irrigation is to be scheduled can be calculated as follows:

$$\text{Depth of irrigation (IW)} = 6.0 \text{ cm}$$
$$\text{CPE} = x \text{ cm}$$
$$\text{IW/CPE} = 0.8$$

$$\text{so, } \frac{60}{x} = 0.8.$$

Then crop is irrigated when CPE is 75 mm.

Micro-plot technique for scheduling irrigation

This technique is inexpensive and is a rough method of scheduling irrigation. In this method, a representative plot of one cubic metre is dug in the main field. The physical condition of the soil is altered by mixing with sand at either 1:1 or 1:2 ratios and filled in the plots. Seeds are sown in the main field as well as in the micro-plot. Since the infiltration rate is faster and retentivity of moisture is less in the micro-plot owing to its lighter texture than the main field, the plants in the microplots show wilting symptoms earlier than the plants in the main field. Irrigation is given to the main crop when the plants in the micro-plot show water stress symptoms.

MEASUREMENT OF IRRIGATION WATER

Water is measured in two stages:

1. **When the water is at rest:** *e.g.* dams, reservoirs, tanks, wells, etc. It is measured in units of volumes such as litre, cubic metre, hectare-centimetre, hectare metre or TMC.
2. **When the water is in motion:** *e.g.* water flowing in rivers, canals, pipe lines, field channels, etc. It is expressed in rate of flow units such as litre/second (lps), litre/hour (lph), cubic metre/sec (Cumec), hectare-centimetre/hour, hectare-metre/day, cusec (cubic foot / second).

Units of water measurement

- **Litre:** It is the volume equal to one cubic decimetre or 1/1000 cubic metre.
- **Cubic metre:** A volume equal to that of a cube having one metre each of length, width and depth (1 cubic metre = 1000 litres).
- **Hectare-centimetre** (1 ha cm): A volume required to cover an area of one hectare of land to a depth of one centimetre (1 ha cm = 1,00,000 litres or 100 m^3).
- **Hectare-metre** (1 ha m): A volume of water required to cover an area of one hectare of land to a depth of one metre (1 ha m = 10,000 cubic metre).
- **Thousand million cubic foot** (TMC) or (10^9 cubic feet): This unit is most widely adopted in India since the reservoir regulators were designed in cusec (fps) units during the British rule. This volumetric unit is used to quantify volumetric scheme of water to different states in large basins like the river Cauvery.
- **Cusec** (fps): This unit is still in use because the existing regulators were designed in fps system. The rate of flow is equal to one cubic foot of water crossing a given cross section in one second.
- **Cubic meter per second** (cumec): A flow of water equivalent to a rectangular stream of one metre wide, one metre deep flowing at a velocity of one metre per second.

Methods of water measurement

Methods of measuring irrigation water may be grouped into:

1. Volume method
2. Velocity-area method and
3. Measuring structures

Volume method

It is a simple method of measuring water in small irrigation streams. A graduated bucket or barrel with known volume is placed near to the down stream end. Time taken to fill the bucket is recorded using a stopwatch and the rate of flow of the stream is measured.

$$\text{Discharge rate (l/s)} = \frac{\text{Volume of bucket (l)}}{\text{Time taken to fill the bucket(s)}}$$

Velocity-area method

This method is used to determine the discharge rate in a pipe or open channel. The rate of flow is calculated by multiplying the cross-sectional area of flow at right angle to the direction of flow by the average velocity of water.

$$Q = A \times V$$

Where, Q – discharge rate (m^3/s), A – cross sectional area of a channel or pipe (m^2), and V-velocity of flow, (m/s)

Cross sectional area can be determined by direct measurement and velocity is measured by 'float method' or by using current meters.

Float method

In this method a float material is used to cross a known distance of water flow. The distance traveled is divided by the time taken to cross the distance. The velocity is determined by the following relationship:

$$\text{Surface velocity} = \frac{\text{Length of channel (metre)}}{\text{Average time taken by float (seconds)}}$$

$$\text{Average velocity } V = 0.85 \times \text{surface velocity}$$

$$\text{Rate of flow } Q = 0.85 \times A \times V$$

Where, Q= average rate of flow (m^3/s); A = cross sectional area (m^2); V = average velocity (m/s).

Current meters

The velocity of water in a stream or river may be measured directly by using current meters. It consists of a small wheel with cups at the periphery or propeller blades rotated by the force of flowing water and a tail or fins to keep the instrument aligned in the direction of flow. The current meter is mounted on rod and moved vertically to measure the velocity at different points. The number of revolutions of the wheel in a given time is noted and corresponding velocity is reckoned from a calibrated table or graph.

Water measuring devices

The most commonly used devices for measuring water are weirs, parshall flumes, orifices and metergates. Using these instruments makes direct measurement of rate of flow. The discharge rate can also be obtained from the standard tables or calibration curves prepared specially for the instruments.

Weirs

It is an over flow structure built across an open channel, usually to measure the rate of flow. Depending upon the shape of the opening, weirs may be termed as triangular, rectangular and trapezoidal.

Triangular weir (90° V- notch)

The weir is an accurate flow-measuring device particularly suited for small flows. The crest of the standard 90°V- notch weir consists of a thin plate, the sides of the notch being inclined at 45° from the vertical plane (Fig. 6.7). The discharge through a 90° V notch may be computed by the formula,

$$Q = 0.0138\ H^{5/2}$$

Where, Q = discharge rate (l/s) and H = head (cm)

The discharge rate can also be referred from Table 6.9.

TABLE 6.9: Discharge rate through 90° V notch

Height of water over V notch (cm)	Discharge (l/s)	Height of water over V-notch (cm)	Discharge (l/s)
5.0	0.8	18.0	19.3
6.0	1.2	19.0	22.4
7.0	1.8	20.0	25.5
8.0	2.5	21.0	28.3
9.0	3.4	22.0	31.0
10.0	4.5	23.0	35.7
11.0	5.7	24.0	40.0
12.0	7.1	25.0	44.5
13.0	8.6	26.0	48.8
14.0	10.5	27.0	53.8
15.0	12.3	28.0	58.7
16.0	14.5	29.0	64.5
17.0	16.7	30.0	69.4

Calculation: From a source of irrigation, water flows through a 90° V notch at a height of 10 cm for a period of 12 min. 45 sec. Calculate the quantity of water passed through the weir.

$$Q = 0.0138H^{5/2}$$
$$Q = 0.0138 \times 10^{5/2}$$
$$= 0.0138 \times 316.2 = 4.4 \text{ lps.}$$

Total quantity of water passed in 12 min. 45 sec or 765 sec.

$$= 4.4 \times 765 = 3366 \text{ litres or } 3.4 \text{ m}^3$$

Rectangular weir

Rectangular weirs are used to measure comparatively large discharges. It has horizontal crest and vertical sides. The weirs may be of two types: (i) contracted rectangular weirs or (ii) suppressed rectangular weirs.

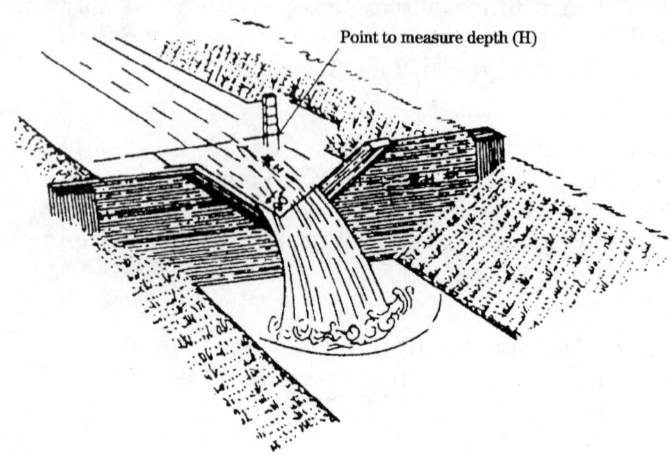

FIG. 6.7: 90° V-notch

The discharge through rectangular weirs may be computed by the formula,

For suppressed rectangular weir $Q = 0.0184\ LH^{3/2}$

For contracted rectangular weir $Q = 0.0184\ (L - 0.2H)^{3/2}$

Where, Q = discharge (l/s); L- length of crest (cm), H- head over weir (cm).

Trapezoidal weir

This was invented by an Italian Engineer, Cipoletti. Hence, it is also called Cipoletti weir. Each side of the weir has a slope of one horizontal to 4 vertical to eliminate the effect of end contraction in rectangular weir. It is used to measure medium discharges. Discharge through Cipoletti weir is computed by the following formula,

$$Q = 0.0186\ LH^{3/2}$$

Where, Q = discharge (l/s), L = length of crest (cm), and H = head over crest (cm).

Parshall flume

This has been designed by Mr. Ralph L. Parshall and hence named after him. A parshall flume is especially shaped for open channel flow section which may be installed in a canal, lateral or ditch to measure the rate of flow of water. It can operate with relatively small head loss. It is a self-cleaning device and sand or silt in the flowing water does not affect its operation or accuracy. It gives reasonably accurate measurement even when partially submerged. (Fig. 6.8)

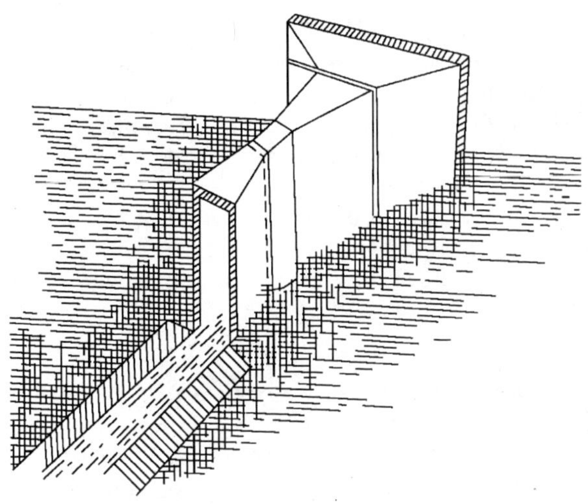

FIG. 6.8: Parshall flume

Small flumes are made of sheet metal and large ones made of concrete. The size of the flume is determined by the width of its throat. The flumes of 7.5, 15, 23 and 30-cm sizes are generally used. Table 6.10 gives the discharge rate (litres/second) at different heads of water flowing through various sizes of flumes.

TABLE 6.10: Free - flow discharge values for parshall flumes

Head (cm)	Discharge (l/s)			
	7.5 cm	15.0 cm	23.0 cm	30.0 cm
5	1.7	3.3	5.5	7.0
6	2.3	4.4	7.2	9.6
7	2.7	5.4	8.5	11.4
8	3.5	7.2	11.1	14.4
9	4.3	8.5	13.5	17.7
10	5.0	10.2	15.9	21.1
11	5.8	11.6	18.1	23.8
12	6.7	13.5	21.1	27.8
13	7.5	15.0	23.3	31.0
14	8.5	17.3	26.7	35.0
15	9.4	19.2	29.5	38.7
16	10.4	21.2	32.5	42.7
17	11.4	23.2	35.6	46.7
18	12.4	25.3	39.0	51.2
19	13.6	26.8	42.5	55.0
20	14.3	30.0	45.0	59.7

Cut–throat flume

This flume is an improvement in construction details over the parshall flume. The flume has a flat bottom, vertical walls and zero length throat section *i.e.* it has no throat section. The flume length may vary from 45 cm to 3.0 m and the width ranges between 2.5 cm to 1.8 m. Cutthroat flume may be used either in free flow or in submerged condition. It should be installed in a straight section of the channel and not near a gate because of instability and surging effects which might result from the gate operation. However, it is better to have flow-measuring device operated under free flow condition.

Orifice

An orifice is sometimes used as a water-measuring device. It is a well-defined sharp- edged opening in a well or bulkhead through which flow may occur. Usually the orifice should have a specific and standard size and shape and a means of measuring the head acting upon it. Orifices may be used to measure rates of flow when the size and shape of the orifices and the heads acting upon them are known and when there is knowledge of whether the jet issuing from the orifice is discharging freely into the air or under water in submerged condition.

The discharge (free flow) through an orifice is calculated by the formula:

$$Q = 0.61 \times 10^{-3}\ a\ \sqrt{2gh}$$

Where, Q = discharge, (l/s); a = area of cross-section of orifice (cm^2); g = acceleration due to gravity (981 cm/s^2); and h = depth of water over centre of orifice (cm)

Discharge rate (litres per second) can also be found out from the table for different diameters of orifice (Table 6.11).

Example: Calculate the total quantity of water discharged with following data: diameter of orifice -5.0 cm; height of water over centre of orifice - 4.0 cm; time of water delivery - 8 min. 45 sec.

$$Q = 0.61 \times 10^{-3}\ a \sqrt{2gh}$$

$$= 0.61 \times 10^{-3} a \frac{1}{1000} \times \frac{22}{7} \times 2.5^2 \times \sqrt{2 \times 981 \times 4}$$

$$= 0.012 \times 88.59$$

$$= 1.06 \text{ lps.}$$

Discharge for the given time (8 minute 45 sec or 525 sec) = 1.06 × 525 = 556. 5 litres

TABLE 6.11: Discharge through circular orifice

Height of water over centre of orifice (cm)	Discharge rate, litre/second		
	Diameter of orifice (cm)		
	2.5	5.0	7.5
2.5	0.21	0.81	1.8
3.0	0.23	0.91	2.1
4.0	0.26	1.15	2.4
5.0	0.30	1.21	2.7
6.0	0.32	1.30	2.9
7.0	0.35	1.39	3.1
8.0	0.38	1.50	3.4
9.0	0.40	1.60	3.6
10.0	0.42	1.70	3.8
11.0	0.44	1.75	3.9
12.0	0.46	1.83	4.1
13.0	0.48	1.90	4.3
14.0	0.50	1.96	4.5
15.0	0.51	2.50	4.6
16.0	0.53	2.10	4.8
17.0	0.54	2.20	4.97
18.0	0.56	2.25	5.13
19.0	0.58	2.31	5.20
20.0	0.59	2.37	5.32
21.0	0.60	2.42	5.17
22.0	0.62	2.50	5.60
23.0	0.63	2.53	5.70

Meter gate

It is basically a modified submerged orifice arranged in such a way that the orifice is adjustable in area. It is used to control the water flowing from one channel to another and may serve to measure the rate of flow. Meter gates are commonly used by canal irrigation agencies in USA and some other countries at the outlet of canals where irrigation water is charged on volumetric basis.

IRRIGATION METHODS

Irrigation method refers to the manner in which water is applied to the field. Various methods of irrigation to be adopted depend on the soil type, climate, crop and its physiological nature, the source and head of available water resources, land terrain, etc. The objective of selecting a particular irrigation method is to use minimum water and to get optimum yield.

Various methods of irrigation are:

1. Surface method
2. Sub- surface method

3. Sprinkler method
4. Drip method

Surface method: In the surface system, water flows by gravity either through furrows, basins or borders. In this type, water loss by conveyance and deep percolation is heavy and the efficiency of irrigation is only 40 to 50% at field level. Efficiency can be improved by lining the canal and by proper leveling of the field.

Sub- surface method: The method is suitable for specific types of soils. Evaporation and other losses are reduced considerably since water is applied below the surface through porous pipes.

Sprinkler method: Water is applied in the form of rain. Water is conveyed through pipes and sprayed through sprinklers. This method is most suited for steep sloppy and sandy soils.

Drip irrigation: Drip irrigation is adopted in water scarce areas for conserving water. In this method, water is applied in drops around the root zone through a pipeline with appropriate drippers.

Surface method of irrigation

Surface method of irrigation is followed from time immemorial. Several improvements and modifications have been made in improving the efficiency.

Flooding the field

This method is practiced where water is in abundance and inexpensive. It is followed in smooth and even lands. There is no control over the rate of flow or distribution and the wastage of water is more. Uncontrolled or wild flooding is followed in river basins for rice crop.

Water flow is evenly guided by means of bunds or furrows and hence is called as controlled flooding. Different controlled flooding methods are (i) check basin (ii) border (iii) furrow (iv) corrugation and (v) surge.

Check basin method

In this method, the field is divided into a number of plots and leveled. It is also known as bed method. This method is most suitable for leveled fields with low permeability and where water is not a constraint. The size of the beds may vary from 1.5 m x 1.5 m to 6.0 m x 4.5 m depending upon the topography of the land. Checks are formed to have rectangular plots. The field channels conveying water are laid for every two lines of check plots. In this method, water does not stand at a uniform depth over the entire check resulting in uneven distribution of water within the plot. Normally the field channels and bunds occupy about 30 % of the area. The cross ridges or bunds interfere with the use of animal drawn or tractor drawn implements. (Fig. 6.9).

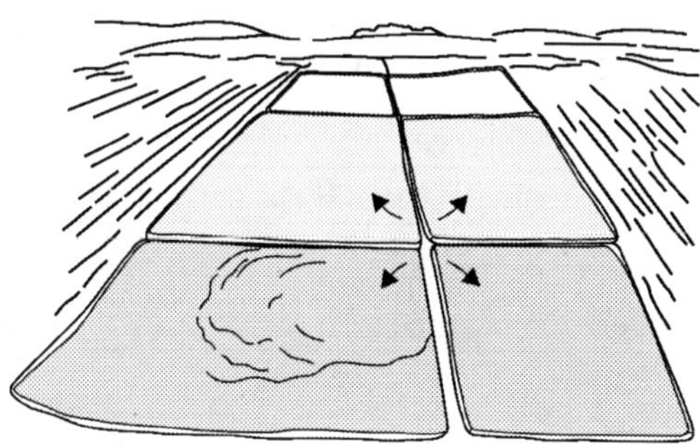

FIG. 6.9: Check basin method

Basin method

It is a modified check method adopted particularly in orchards. Round basins for small trees and square basins for bigger trees are formed. Basin is formed for each plant or for a number of plants and connected by ditches. Basins allow more water to be impounded as the root zone of orchard crops is very deep. The size of the basin is adjusted to soil permeability and size of streams. Each basin is flooded in turn and water is allowed to soak into the soil. Depending upon the soil type and crop, about 5-10 cm depth of water may be required for each irrigation. The ridges are built wide enough to guard against under-mining by irrigation water. They are usually constructed with rounded top to a height of 30-35 cm and a bottom width of 90-120 cm. Basin method has the advantage that unskilled labour can be used as there is no danger of erosion. However, it has the disadvantage of high labour requirement and restriction in the use of modern machinery in the field.

Border strip method

In this method, the field is divided into narrow strips by small parallel ridges on the sides. The border strip is formed by leveling and grading the land between the ridges. Cross slope is completely removed and a gentle longitudinal gradient (0.05 to 0.5 %) is provided in each border strip. Width of the border strip varies from 3 to 15 m depending on the slope of the land and size of irrigation stream. The length of a strip ranges between 50 and 300 m depending on the type of soil, longitudinal slope and the size of the irrigation stream. Some specifications for border strips are given in Table 6.12.

Each border is irrigated by allowing the water to flow from the upper end of the border in a thin sheet. Water moves towards the lower end at non-erosive velocities covering the entire width of the border. As a result, sufficient moisture is provided to the soil profile to the entire length of the border. This method can be used on all types of soils but it is best suited to soils having moderately low to moderately high infiltration rates. However, it is not suited to coarse sandy soils and clay type of soils.

TABLE 6.12: Specifications for border strips

Soil type	Admissible border length (m)	Safe limit of land slope (%)
Sandy and sandy loam	60 to 120	0.25 to 0.60
Medium loam	100 to 180	0.20 to 0.40
Clay loam and clay	150 to 300	0.50 to 0.20

Furrow method

In furrow irrigation, water is applied in small streams between the rows of crops, grown on ridges or furrow sides (Fig. 6.10). The size and shape of the furrows depend upon the soil, crop spacing and the equipment used for furrow forming. Water is applied in small stream into the furrow. It infiltrates into the soil and spreads laterally to wet the area between the furrows. The size of the furrow streams usually varies from 0.5 to 2.5 l/s. The purpose of the optimum stream size is to wet the entire furrow length uniformly as quickly as possible without causing soil erosion. This method of irrigation is generally used to irrigate row crops and vegetables. It is most suited for soils having infiltration rate of 0.5 and 2.5 cm per hour. Water use efficiency is high and the furrows also function as drains. It is possible to irrigate alternate furrows in times of water scarcity. Furrow method is not recommended for very light soils with high infiltration capacity as water is wasted on the upper end of the furrow due to deep percolation.

FIG. 6.10: Furrow method of irrigation

Alternate furrow irrigation: In this method, a particular set of furrows is irrigated during any one run of irrigation. During the next run, the left over furrows is irrigated. The interval of irrigation is normally shortened compared to the conventional furrow method.

Skip furrow irrigation: This method is best suited to heavy soils like clay and loams. Alternate furrows are skipped and converted to ridges of wide bed. To avoid crop congestion, the furrow width can be widened compared to the original width.

Both alternate and skip furrow irrigation methods are recommended during the period of water scarcity for crops like cotton.

Corrugation method

This method can be placed between border and furrow irrigation methods. It is a partial flooding method, as water may not cover the entire field surface. Corrugations are V- shaped or U- shaped channels of about 10 cm deep, 40-75 cm spaced apart. The slope should be just enough not to permit soil erosion. Corrugations are usually made after the crops are sown and a simple implement called 'corrugator' is used for this purpose. This method is recommended for medium type of soils and close growing crops.

Surge irrigation

In surge irrigation, water is applied to the surface furrows intermittently in a series of relatively short 'ON' and 'OFF' periods. The 'ON', 'OFF' cycle produces 'surges' during the ON period and influences the soil intake rate during the OFF period. This reduces soil infiltration rates during the subsequent surge (ON period) and an increase in the rate of water- front advance. Thus the difference in intake opportunity time between the upper and lower ends of the furrow becomes less and it results in uniform soil moisture storage and distribution along the furrow after irrigation. The surge effect depends on soil texture and consolidation, antecedent moisture content, number and duration of ON-OFF cycles.

Studies were conducted at Tamil Nadu Agricultural University, Coimbatore on surge irrigation for the crops like maize and sunflower. Paired rows were followed in which two rows of crops were sown in a pair. There was a saving of 30-50 % of irrigation water. Surge irrigation in maize resulted in reaching of waterfront in 50 % opportunity time. Labour for irrigation is reduced to 50 %. Surge irrigation is highly useful wherever lift irrigation method is followed.

Sub-surface irrigation

In this method of irrigation, water is applied below the ground surface by maintaining an artificial water table at a depth of 0.3 to 1.0 m depending upon the soil texture and rooting depths of crops. This system of irrigation is not widely followed in India. It may be seen in cultivation of vegetable crops around 'Dal' lake area in Kashmir. This method is also followed for irrigating coconut palms in the organic soils of Kuttanad area in Kerala.

Sprinkler or overhead method of irrigation

In this method, water is applied to the crop above the ground surface in the form of spray developed by orifices or nozzles. The advantage of this system is uniform and efficient distribution of water at a rate less than the infiltration rate of the soil. This method is highly suitable for the areas with rolling or rough topography where leveling the land is not economical. Water can be uniformly applied without much wastage. Sprinkler irrigation can be used for almost all crops except rice and jute. This method is not suitable during the periods of wind velocity of more than 24 km per hour. Wind distorts sprinkler patterns and causes uneven distribution of water. Sprinkler irrigation is not suitable where water contains large amount of dissolved salts. High initial investment and operating cost are the limitations for its wide scale adoption.

Methods of sprinkling

Two principal methods of sprinkling are rotating head sprinklers and perforated pipes.

Rotating head sprinkler

It consists of a head provided with a single or two nozzles. The heads are placed on riser pipes fixed at uniform intervals along the length of pipes. The heads are always provided above the crop height. Water under pressure strikes against the swing arm that is provided in the head that creates thrust for rotation. According to the pressure range, rotating head sprinklers are classified as low pressure, moderate pressure, intermediate pressure, and high-pressure types. Moderate to intermediate pressure sprinklers (1.05 – 4.20 kg /cm^2) are suitable for orchard crops. High-pressure sprinklers (3.5 – 7.0 kg/cm^2) are used for all field crops and in most of the soils.

Perforated pipe sprinklers

They have lateral pipes with lines of small perforations in the upper third of pipe diameter. This system works under low pressure (0.8 – 1.4 kg/cm^2) and hence needs no pumping unit. These types are suitable for short statured crops (40-60 cm) and for lawns, gardens and vegetables.

Sprinkler system

A sprinkler irrigation system consists of a 'pump' to develop desired operating pressure; 'mainlines', 'laterals' and 'risers' are used to convey water. 'Sprinkler head' or 'nozzle' discharges the water in the form of spray. The selection of sprinkler head is the key for the efficient operation of the entire system. (Fig. 6.11)

Selection of a sprinkler system depends on topography, water source, head and climatic conditions. Based on the portability of different parts, sprinkler systems are classified into (i) portable system, (ii) semi-portable system, (iii) semi- permanent system, (iv) solid set system and (v) permanent system. Portable systems are widely used and the entire unit of the system can be portable from field to field. The rate of water application through sprinkler system should be in such a way that the infiltration rates are less than water application rate. In slopy topography, the discharge rate is reduced to prevent run off. Maximum rate of water application for different soil types is given in Table 6.13.

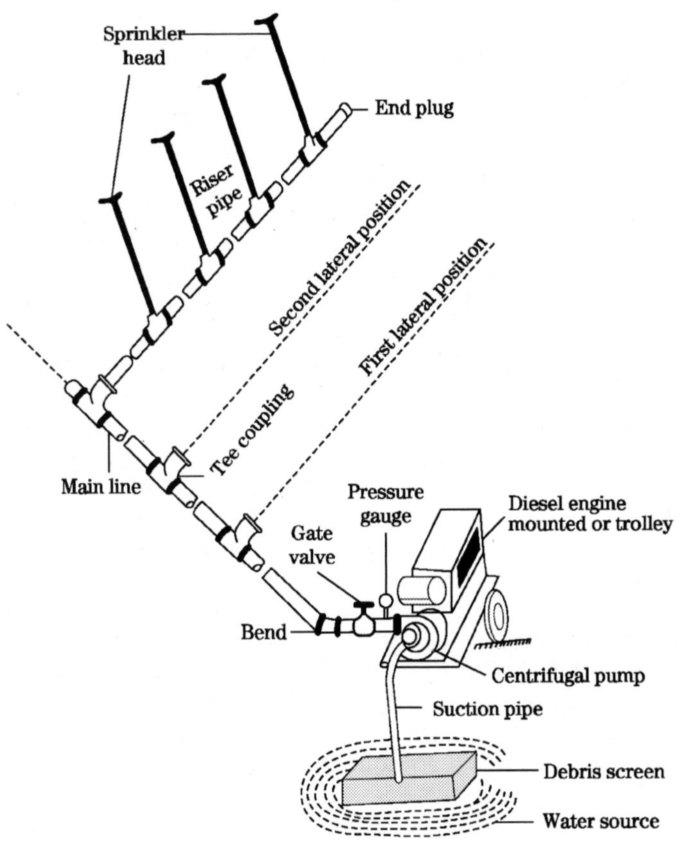

FIG. 6.11: Layout of sprinkler irrigation

TABLE 6.13: Discharge rate (cm/hour) of sprinkler system for different soil types and topography

Soil texture	Slope (%)			
	0-5	**5-8**	**8-12**	**12-16**
Coarse sandy soil	4.0	2.5	2.0	1.0
Light sandy loam	2.5	2.0	1.5	1.0
Silt loam	1.3	1.3	0.8	0.5
Clay loam	0.4	0.3	0.2	0.1

Drip or trickle irrigation

Drip irrigation is termed as 'micro-irrigation' as the approach involves controlled supply of water in small amounts. It is a simple method to discharge water at the root zone of a plant in small, measured quantities. An Israeli Engineer, Simcha Blass, accidentally stumbled upon the drip irrigation concept by discovering abnormal growth of a tree near a leaking pipe.

The drip unit consists of a 'head' which includes a pumping unit to create a pressure of about 2.5 kg/cm^2, a 'filter' unit to remove the suspended impurities of water and a 'fertilizer tank' to dissolve nitrogenous and other soluble fertilizers and a meter. (Fig. 6.12)

The 'mainlines' are of PVC tubing which convey water from the head to the trickle lines or 'laterals'. The laterals are of plastic tubing with 'nozzles/ drippers / emitters' to drop water in small quantities.

In the drip irrigation, water is supplied only to the roots with the help of pipes and emitters. There is little water loss due to distribution and evaporation. It is most suitable for arid and semi-arid regions where the limited availability of water and high evaporative demands are the constraints. This method of irrigation is very effective where only saline water is available for irrigation. Drip irrigation with saline water helps to maintain a zone of low salt concentration and high moisture content resulting in a favourable condition for plant growth. This method is best suited for wide spaced and perennial crops such as grapes, banana, coconut, mango, pomegranate, citrus, sapota and vegetables. It can also be used for crops such as sugarcane, cotton, etc.

Precautions: Water supply should be adjusted according to the crop growth and fertilizer application at appropriate intervals. Proper maintenance of the system and periodical inspection of drip holes is important. Any clogging of holes by dirt or salt deposits should be rectified. For long life and economy of the system it is important to use good quality materials.

Limitations: Although drip irrigation has many economic and resource related advantages over the surface method of irrigation, its growth in terms of area is not appreciable barring a few states in India. High fixed initial investment, regular maintenance, high replacement and repair cost and clogging are some of the problems encountered with this system.

Fixed investment is not very high when compared to the long-term benefits realized. The cost of the system depends on the nature of crops, its spacing, amount of water required, condition of the terrain, discharge capacity of the emitters and distance from the source of water.

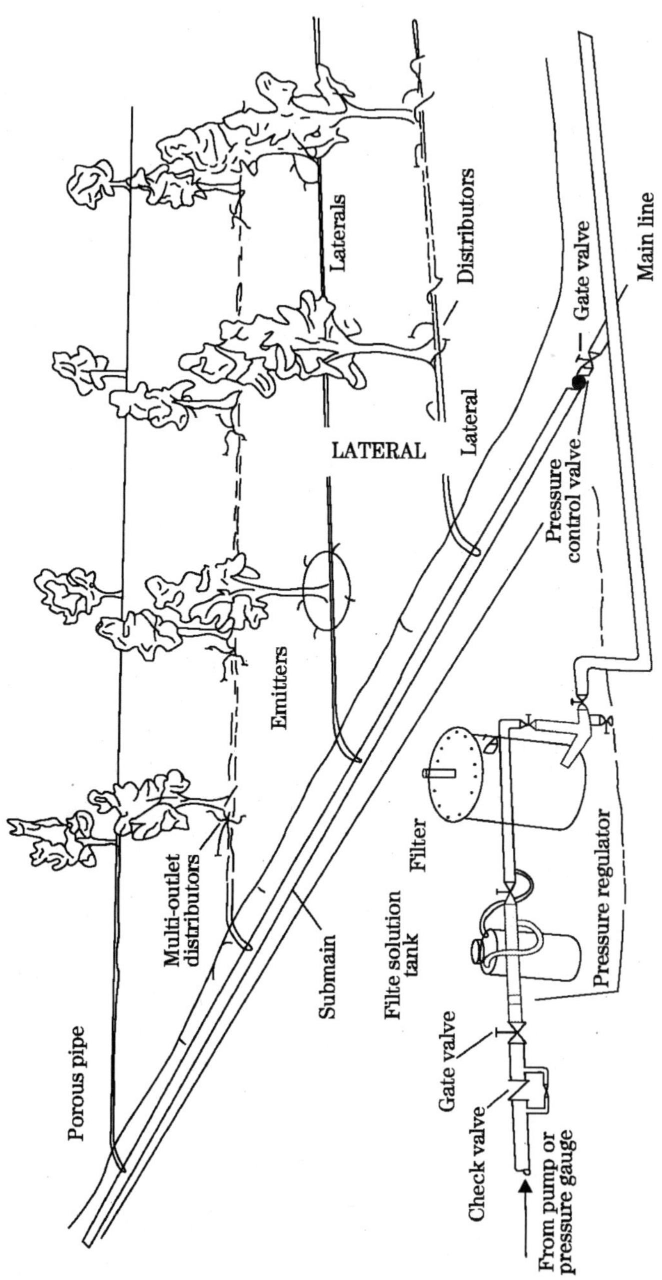

FIG. 6.12: Layout of drip system

Realizing the importance of drip irrigation, Govt. of India has implemented a systematic subsidy scheme. This has created much awareness among the farmers and many State Governments encourage the drip irrigation technology.

WATER MANAGEMENT FOR IMPORTANT FIELD CROPS

Rice

Rice is a semi-aquatic plant and requires large quantity of water for its cultivation. Water requirement of rice under lowland condition is 1110-1250 mm. Water requirement for land preparation varies from 200 to 400 mm depending upon the soil type. Nursery requires about 50 mm and about 1000 mm of water is required during the crop growth period.

There are four critical stages at which water supply is very much important. The critical stages are seedling, tillering, panicle initiation to flowering and milk dough grain stage. Water supply during seedling stage provides early rooting and at tillering promotes more tiller production. Watering during panicle initiation to flowering facilitates development of fertile grain and at milk-dough stage for filling of grains. The most sensitive stage to moisture stress is flowering. Stress at this stage results in sterile spikelets.

It is important to maintain optimum depth of water in the field. As the depth of water increases, the plant height increases; resulting in decreased culm strength and crop tends to lodge. Tiller production is also greatly affected by prolonged stagnation of water. The field should be irrigated to a depth of 5 cm when the ponded water disappears. By adopting this method, there is water saving to the tune of 30 – 50% compared to continuous submergence wherein water is always stagnated in the field. Water must be withheld two weeks before harvest of crop to hasten ripening of grains and to promote favourable condition for harvesting.

When continuous submergence is followed, it is important to adopt drainage once or twice during the growth period, particularly in poorly drained clay soils. Drainage at maximum tillering stage stimulates vigorous growth of roots and checks the development of ineffective tillers. The drainage period could last for 4-8 days depending upon the type of soil.

Wheat

The irrigation water requirement varies from 180 to 420 mm. About 4-6 irrigations are required to maintain the moisture availability in the soil. The actual number of irrigations depends on the occurrence of winter rains. In soils having shallow water table, number of irrigations is reduced substantially. Scheduling of irrigation is generally adopted based on the physiological growth stages which are critical for demand of water. Different growth stages in wheat are crown root initiation (CRI) (20-25 DAS), tillering (40-45 DAS), jointing (55-60 DAS), flowering (85-90 DAS), milk (100-105 DAS) and dough grain (115-120 DAS) stages. Most of the experimental results indicate the need for irrigation at crown root initiation stage for maximum production in dwarf varieties of wheat. The second important stage is flowering. Based on the moisture demand, the critical stages are arranged as crown root initiation, flowering, jointing and milking followed by tillering and dough grain stages. Based on the pan evaporation, the crop may be given irrigation at IW/CPE ratio of 0.75-0.9.

Maize

Maize is highly sensitive to water stress and water logging. Submergence of soil for 3-5 days during seedling to flowering stages reduces the yield considerably. Water requirement of the crop is about 450-mm. Optimum depletion of soil moisture for scheduling irrigation is 50 % depletion of available soil moisture from the surface of soil (30-60 cm) on sandy loam to clay loam soils. Irrigation requirement varies with the type of soil and the season in which the crop is grown. The critical stages for water demand are the early vegetative stage (20-40 DAS), tasselling and silking (45-60 DAS). Maximum yield reduction is recorded when moisture stress occurs at tasseling (51%) and silking (48%) followed by active vegetative (30%) and milky stage (22%). Water stress at seedling, knee- high or dough stage has little effect. Irrigation scheduling at IW/CPE ratio of 0.8 to 1.0 is recommended for higher grain yield.

Sorghum

It is considered as the most drought resistant crop, which utilizes the moisture efficiently and produces more dry matter. However, high yielding varieties are responsive to good irrigation practices. Water requirement of sorghum is about 450-500 mm and it varies with the climate and soil. The crop can be irrigated at 25 % soil moisture availability during *kharif* season on heavy clay soils. During the summer, the crop is to be irrigated at 50 % soil moisture availability and may need about 10 irrigations. The critical period for irrigation is seedling, pre-flowering and grain formation stages. The crop may be irrigated at the IW/CPE ratio of 0.4-0.6.

Pulses

Pulses have deep root system and utilize soil moisture very efficiently and hence require less number of irrigations compared to cereals. During the *kharif* season, pulses are grown without irrigation and during *rabi* and summer seasons, limited irrigation is needed. At the early vegetative stage, legumes do not require irrigation as it may do more harms than good by interfering with the nodulation and oxygen requirement. Irrigation is beneficial at flowering and pod formation stages.

Gram

It is a *rabi* pulse and gives good response to irrigation in the absence of winter rain, especially on the lighter soils of northern India. Although water requirement of the crop is relatively low, it suffers from periodic water deficits due to low and uncertain rains during *rabi* season. One irrigation either at pre-flowering (45 DAS) or at flowering stage (70 DAS) gives better response. The crop can be given irrigation at IW/CPE ratio of 0.4. Water requirement of the crop is 250-400 mm.

Pigeonpea

The crop gives better response to irrigation if dry spells prevail for longer periods. Two irrigations, one at flower–initiation and the other at pod-filling stage are recommended. Water requirement is 70-140 mm.

Oil seeds

Groundnut

The critical period for groundnut is the pegging stage (45 DAS) and care must be taken to meet the irrigation needs during this period. Generally the crop is irrigated once in 10 days. The number of irrigations vary from 9 to 13 with water requirement of 500-700 mm. Depending upon the soil type, the crop may be irrigated at 25-50% soil moisture availability. Based on the pan evaporation, irrigation may be given at IW/CPE of 0.6. However, during summer season irrigation is required at the ratio of 0.9.

Rapeseed–mustard

Early irrigation at the vegetative stage (21-28 DAS) encourages deep rooting and increases the use of stored moisture. One irrigation at flowering (85 DAS) or pod- development stage is important. Irrigation may be given at 25 % soil moisture availability. Based on the IW/ CPE ratio, irrigation may be scheduled at 0.8. Water requirement of the crop varies from 200 to 300 mm.

Sunflower

Irrigation is required at 40-60 % available soil moisture or at IW/CPE ratio of 0.75. The crop may be irrigated once in 10 days with the total water requirement of 400-550 mm. Important critical stages are pre-flowering (20 DAS), flowering /bud development (30-40 DAS) and seed development stages (50-60 DAS). Among these stages, flowering is the most important one and there should not be any moisture stress to have proper head development.

Cotton

A planned moisture regime during the crop growth period promotes efficient root system, optimum vegetative growth, reduced boll shedding and uniform bursting in short period. Cotton is sensitive to excess moisture, especially during the grand growth and reproductive phases. Flowering and boll formation stages are critical for soil moisture stress. Lack of adequate moisture at these stages may result in premature flower drop, boll shedding and poor development of bolls. The total water requirement is 400-700 mm. Water requirement of cotton increases rapidly from 3-5 mm per day during pre-flowering stage to 8-10 mm per day from the commencement of flowering to peak flowering stage. During boll development stage, optimum moisture conditions would result in increased boll retention. Water requirement at boll bursting stage is limited to 4-5 mm per day.

Sugarcane

The vegetative part is of economic importance in sugarcane and hence the crop should not suffer moisture stress during any stage of its growth. However, just prior to harvest, irrigation may be delayed since this practice result in the accumulation of sucrose in the cane. It is observed that optimum yields are obtained by maintaining a very high moisture level in the root zone during the entire growing season. It is necessary to keep the soil moisture at 65% of available moisture. Irrigation is most important during tillering phase. Light irrigation is necessary to get optimum germination if soil moisture is inadequate. Irrigation at 10-15 days interval is required upto tillering phase. Irrigation may be given at an interval of 7-10 days during the growth phase. At maturity phase, irrigation may be scheduled once in 15 days. In light soils, more frequent but light irrigations are required. Total water requirement of sugarcane is 1800-2200 mm.

Forages

Forage crops normally have longer active growth stage and hence need more frequent irrigation. This will ensure fast vegetative growth and result in high biomass yield. Water requirement of winter grown forages like berseem is about 800 mm. It requires about 20 irrigations during November-April, with an interval of about 15 days. Lucerne needs about 1800-2000 mm of water in a year. Summer grown forages (teosinte) require 12 irrigations in summer at an interval of 7-12 days. Water requirement is 640 mm. Perennial forages like napier grass need 22-24 irrigations in addition to rainfall. Highest foliage production could be obtained by irrigating the crop at an IW/CPE ratio of 0.75. Forage maize can be irrigated at 50 % soil moisture availability for higher production.

Tobacco

Tobacco can tolerate drought than excess of moisture as it has fairly deep and vigorous root system. When the moisture stress is once relieved there should be ample supply of water till growth is completed. It requires about 450-500 mm of water. About 10 irrigation is needed in addition to irrigation for the land preparation. Furrow irrigation practice economizes irrigation water compared to check basin. Higher chloride content in irrigation water may affect the burning quality adversely.

QUALITY OF IRRIGATION WATER

Use of inferior irrigation water with high sodium or total salt or both may cause deterioration to the physical properties of the soil. Plants are adversely affected by high concentration of salts in the soil solution and by poor physical condition of the soil. Further salts formed *in situ* by weathering of soil minerals or by salt deposition from applied water tend to accumulate in the soil profile. Hence appropriate techniques are required for proper management of poor quality water.

The quality of irrigation water is determined by the following chemical characteristics.

1. Total concentration of soluble salts or salinity
2. Concentration of sodium relative to other cations or sodicity
3. Anionic composition of water, particularly concentration of bicarbonate and carbonate
4. Concentration of boron, fluorine or other elements that may be toxic to plant growth.

Total concentration of soluble salts

The effect of salt on crop growth is believed to be mainly osmotic in nature and hence related to the total concentration rather than the concentration of individual ionic species. Two methods are commonly used for determination of salt concentration: total dissolved solids (TDS) and electrical conductivity (EC.). The former method is accurate in the case of water free of bicarbonate. In the electrical method, EC of the water sample is determined which is approximately proportional to the amount of salts present in the water. The quality characterization of irrigation water based on electrical conductivity is given in Table 6.14.

TABLE 6.14: Quality characterization of irrigation water based on EC

Class	EC (dsm^{-1})	Quality characterization
1	1.5	Extra fresh, normal, excellent, very sweet, non-saline, very high quality
2	1.5-3.0	Fresh, slightly saline, good, sweet, low salinity, high quality
3	3.0-5.0	Brackish, moderately saline, fair, medium salinity, marginal quality
4	5.0-10.0	Saline, bad, low (poor) quality
5	10.0-15.0	Highly saline, very bad, very low quality
6	15.0	Excessively saline, highly bad, extremely low (poor) quality

Concentration of sodium

Sodium adsorption ratio (SAR)

This ratio gives an idea about the relative proportion of Na to that of other cations like Ca^{2+} and Mg^{2+}. Increase in the ratio depends on the ratio of soluble sodium to the divalent cations in the solution.

$$SAR = \frac{(Na^+)}{\sqrt{\frac{Ca^{2+} + Mg^{2+}}{2}}}$$

(Na) and (Ca+Mg) are the concentrations of the soluble ions in meq/ litre

Soluble sodium percentage (SSP)

It is expressed in terms of meq / litre and serves the same purpose as that of SAR.

$$SSP = \frac{Na^{2+}}{(Ca^{2+} + Mg^{2+} + Na^+ + K^+)} \times 100$$

Concentration of carbonate and bicarbonate

Relative sodium carbonate (RSC)

Among the anions, $CO_3^{\ 2-}$ and HCO_3^- are found to affect the crop growth adversely. The adverse effect would be reduced if Ca and Mg were present in sufficient amounts. Eaton (1950) proposed the concept of relative sodium carbonate for evaluating high carbonate water and this be expressed as meq/litre.

$$RSC = (CO_3^{\ 2-} + HCO_3^-) - (Ca^{2+} + Mg^{2+})$$

Table 6.15 gives the relationship among the above three parameters on the basis of which water quality can be characterized.

TABLE 6.15: Quality parameters for irrigation water

Class	EC (dsm^{-1})	SAR	RSC (meq/l)
A - Good	< 2.0	<10.0	<2.5
B - Normal	2-4	<10	<2.5
C - Sodic	<4	>10	>2.5
D - Marginally saline	4-8	<10	0
E - Poor	>4	>10	>2.5

Boron content

Boron is essential for plant growth; however, it becomes toxic at concentrations slightly above optimum. If the boron content is more than 0.75 ppm, it may cause some toxicity and at more than 2 ppm, the toxicity will be severe.

Management of saline water for irrigation

Factors such as soil characteristics, plant types, climatic parameters and management practices are to be considered while using the saline water for irrigation.

Soil texture is one of the most important factors, which influences the salt tolerance of crops. Lighter the texture, greater is the tolerance to saline water. Water with SAR value upto 25 to 30 can be used successfully in arid and semi-arid zones of India. In heavy textured soils, only water with low salinity is used. Higher organic matter content of the soil enhances the tolerance of crops to saline water used for irrigation.

The suitability of crops to saline water is based on the tolerance of specific crop/crops to the total ionic concentration. Some varieties of a particular crop may also show tolerance to saline water. Critical levels of EC at which yield reduction take place is important in selecting crops or varieties for cultivation. Many crops show a progressive decrease in yields with increasing salinity.

Climatic factors also play a greater role in tolerance to poor water quality. Rain leaches down the salts from the root zone, which might, otherwise, have accumulated due to saline water irrigation. Tolerance to saline water is greater in winter than in summer.

Furrow irrigation is best suited for saline water usage. In this method, the salts move away from the furrow and deposit on the top of ridges. Adopting broad bed furrow system and sowing on the slope of the bed near the irrigated furrow may avoid the zones of high salt accumulation. Providing field drains in sandy loam soils having high water table of poor quality ground water may reduce salt deposit and increase the crop yield. Adequate irrigation is necessary to leach out salts away from the root zone. Sprinkler irrigation can be adopted to maintain the soil surface wet and to lower the salt environment for better crop growth. Dilution of saline water with good water quality may also reduce salt injury.

FIELD DRAINAGE METHODS

Drainage is the provision of a suitable method for the removal of excess irrigation or rainfall from the field to facilitate favourable moisture conditions for the growth of plants. Proper drainage will prevent salt accumulation and deterioration of irrigated lands. Ground water table is lowered facilitating increased root zone depth. Soil aeration is improved and there will be increase in soil temperature due to drainage. Microbial activity is induced as a result of accelerated organic matter decomposition.

Drainage methods

Drainage methods can be grouped into surface and sub surface drainage.

Surface drainage

This is the most economical method of drainage commonly adopted in India. In this method, large outlet channels or field ditches are formed on the surface to remove the excess water due to heavy rainfall, over irrigation, seepage from water source or from overlying areas. Irrigation channels also serve for drainage purpose. Though the surface method of drainage is cheaper, it has some disadvantages. Valuable cropland is used for drainage purpose. Open ditches may cause hindrance to the use of implements and intercultural operations. They are subjected to silting and growth of weeds which are to be removed regularly. Animals and rodents may damage the surface drains.

Systems of surface drainage

Adoption of a particular method of surface drainage depends on the topography of land, soil characteristics and crops to be grown. Topography is the main consideration for economical planning of the surface drainage. Different systems of surface drainage are used. They are: (i) random field ditches, (ii) land smoothing, (iii) bedding, (iv) parallel field ditches and (v) cross slope ditch system.

Random field ditches

Field ditches of shallow depth are formed at random connecting local depressions or ponds scattered over the field. All the ditches are converged to a common natural outlet. Otherwise the drained water may be allowed to spread over the land just below the tail end. This method of drainage is most suited for uneven land with a number of local depressions.

Land smoothing

In this method, the elevated areas are cut off and the excess soil is spread over low areas so that the surface will be even with a uniform grade or slope. All tillage operations are carried out parallel to slope. Field ditches are provided at the lower end to collect excess runoff from the smoothed slope. This method is suitable for flat lands with low depressions and for areas with less percentage of slopes.

Bedding

In this system, dead furrows are formed at known intervals parallel to the greatest slope of the land. Sufficient widths of land surface (bed) are left between furrows. Either side of the bed will have a gradual slope. Excess surface run off moves laterally to the dead furrows and conveyed to the collection ditches placed at regular intervals across the slope of the land. This system is suitable for flat lands or lands having a slope upto 1.5%.

Parallel field ditch system

It is almost similar to bedding system but the parallel ditches of greater capacity are formed instead of dead furrows. Ditches are formed at unequal distances. This system is suitable for flat lands with a number of small depressions.

Cross slope ditch system

This method of drainage is suitable for the fields having greater slope. Cross slope ditches are shallow drains constructed at flat slopes and low ridges are left between the drains.

Sub-surface drainage

The purpose of sub-surface drainage is to lower the ground water level below the root zone of the crop. Drainage systems like open trenches, tile drains, mole drains and perforated pipe drains are used. Sub-surface drainage facilitates aeration to the root zone and promotes better crop growth. Unlike surface drainage, valuable cropland is not wasted and there may not be any interference to farming operations. Some of the disadvantages in this system are high initial investment, regular maintenance of inlet and outlet and difficulty in diagnosing any failure in the system.

CHAPTER 7

Weed Management

Weeds are often called as plants out of place. They are unwanted, useless, prolific, competitive and often harmful to the total environment. They interfere with agricultural operations and reduce the production potential of crop plants. The problem of weeds has been observed in cropped and non-cropped areas. It has accentuated under intensive farming, with the heavy use of inputs like fertilizers and irrigation, and adoption of multiple cropping. These inputs also help in better growth of weeds, thereby causing severe competition between crop and weeds resulting in poor yield. In non-cropped situations, the problem of weeds has been observed in various types of aquatic environment, forests, railways, highways, airports, industrial sites and places of aesthetic value.

DAMAGE CAUSED BY WEEDS

Weeds are competitive and adaptable to all adverse environments. It has been estimated that in general weeds cause 5% loss in agricultural production in most developed countries, 10% loss in less developed countries and 25% loss in least developed countries.

In India, yield losses due to weeds are more than those from pest and diseases. Yield losses due to weeds vary with the crops. In wheat, direct yield losses due to weeds have been estimated to range from 10 to 82%. This depends on the cultivar, weed species and density, cropping season, plant spacing, fertility and moisture status of the soil and climatic and environmental conditions. Estimated yield losses due to weeds in different crops are given in Table 7.1.

Besides reduction in yield, weeds remove large amount of plant nutrients from the soil. An estimate shows that weeds can deprive the crops 47% N, 42% P, 50% K, 39% Ca and 24% Mg of their nutrient uptake. Weeds indirectly reduce the yield potential by serving as alternate host to a number of crop pests.

Aquatic weeds reduce the flow of water in irrigation and drainage channels, canals and streams. They indirectly increase water levels in the system which results in seepage, breakage of canal banks, flooding and siltation besides reducing aesthetic value of water bodies and inadequate delivery of irrigation water to farms.

TABLE 7.1: Yield losses due to weeds

Crops	Yield reduction (%)
Rice (Transplanted)	30-40
Rice (drilled)	70-80
Maize	50-70
Sorghum	50-70
Pulses (*Kharif*)	40-60
Pulses (*rabi*)	20-30
Groundnut	40-50
Mustard	10-15
Soybean	40-60
Cotton	40-50
Sugarcane	20-30

Source: Bhan (1994)

WEED CLASSIFICATION AND CHARACTERISTICS

Weeds are classified into different groups based on various criteria. Broad classification of weeds is based on plant morphology, life span and habitat. Other classifications include the season of the year when they appear, the crops they affect and parasitic or poisonous nature.

Plant morphology

Classification of weeds based on morphology is very important and useful in weed control. Based on morphology, weeds are generally divided into three main groups (types):

Grasses

Grasses are monocots and propagate by seeds, rhizomes, stolens and stem cuttings. e.g. *Echinochloa crusgalli, Cynodon dactylon, Phalaris minor, Sorghum halepense, Dactyloctenium aegyptium, Digitaria* sp. *Imperata cylindrica, Avena fatua*, etc. *E. crusgalli* and *E. colonum* are almost certainly the most ubiquitous weeds of rice (Fig. 7.1.)

Sedges

Sedges are also monocots and the stems are solid and triangular in cross-section. Propagation is through modified rhizomes. *e.g. Cyperus iria, Cyperus* difformis and *Fimbristylis miliace. Cyperus iria* is a typical sedge (Fig. 7.2.).

Broad leaved weeds

These weed species are mostly dicotyledenous plants. The leaves are usually broad with netted veination *e.g. Amaranthus spp., Chenopodium album, Convolvulus arvensis, Phyllanthus niruri*. An example of broad weed, *Amaranthus viridis*, is shown in the Fig. 7.3.

FIG. 7.1: *Echinochloa colonum*

FIG. 7.2: *Cyperus iria*

FIG. 7.3: *Amaranthus viridis*

Life span

Annuals

The weed species complete their life cycle in one year or less. They usually produce large quantity of seeds, grow fast and are shallow-rooted. Propagation is through seeds which are produced in a single growing season. Most of the common weeds are annuals. *e.g., Boerhaavia diffusa, Commelina benghalensis, Chenopodium album, etc.*

Biennials

These weed species complete their life cycle in two seasons. Vegetative stage is completed in the first season followed by the reproductive phase during the second season. *e.g., Alternanthera echinata.*

Perennials

There are a large number of weeds which are perennial in nature and live for more than a year. These weed species infest both cropped and non-cropped areas. They are well adopted to withstand adverse conditions. Propagation is not only through seeds but also by underground bulbs, stolons, rhizomes and tubers. The food material is stored in the subterranean parts which putforth new shoots wherever conditions are favourable. Perennial weeds are very difficult to control by common method of weed control. *e.g., Cyperus rotundus, Convolvulus arvensis, Aristolochia bracteata, etc.*

Perennial weeds are classified according to their mode of reproduction in two groups: (i) simple perennials and (ii) creeping perennials.

Simple perennials

Propagation is through seeds. Vegetative propagation also occurs when roots and stems are cut mechanically. Each piece of the cut portion gives out roots and become a plant, *e.g. Sonchus arvensis.*

Creeping perennials

They reproduce through seeds as well as by other modes viz., rhizome (*Sorghum halepense, Agropyron repens),* stolen (*Cynodon dactylon*), roots (*Convolvulus arvensis)* and tubers (*Cyperus sp.*)

Occurrence

Based on the occurrence of weed species, they may be classified as weeds of croplands, pasturelands, wastelands, playgrounds and roadsides.

Weeds of croplands

Majority of the weeds occur in the croplands and are detrimental to crop growth.

Weeds of pasturelands

The common weeds occurring in the pasturelands are *Tephrosia procumbens and Boerhaavia diffusa.*

Weeds of wastelands

Weeds occur in wastelands like the corner of fields, margin of channels and hedges. They are the actual sources of contamination of the cultivated fields. *e.g., Gynandropsis pentaphylla, Tribulus terrestris, Calotropis gigantea.*

Weeds of playgrounds and roadsides

The weed species are hardy, prostrate perennials and are capable of withstanding trampling. They are dispersed by man and animals. *e.g., Alternanthera echinata, Euphorbia prostrata,* etc.

Ecological affinities

Weeds of drylands

They are hardy in nature and thrive in moisture scarce situations. They possess drought adaptation through mucilaginous nature of the stems and hairiness. *e.g., Trianthema triquetra, Digetaria arvensis.*

Weeds of wetlands

The plants are tender annuals with semi-aquatic habit. They thrive under waterlogged condition. Propagation is mainly through seeds. *e.g., Moniera cuneifolia, Echinochloa colonum.,* etc.

Weeds of irrigated uplands (Gardenlands)

They are intermediate between dryland and wetland weeds with respect to their water requirement. They neither withstand waterlogged situation nor the extreme drought. *e.g., Trianthema portulacastrum, Corchorus trilocularis.*

Edaphic factors

Some of the weed species are closely associated with a particular type of soil though not in a strict sense. Sometimes, the same species may also occur in other soil types.

Black cotton soils

The weed species are mainly associated with dry conditions. e.g., Aristolochia bracteata, Alysicarpus rugosus, Hibiscus vitifolius etc.

Red soils

The weeds predominantly occur in the irrigated uplands. *e.g., Commelina benghalensis, Leucas urticaefolia.*

Light sandy or loamy soils

Weeds such as Mollugo oppositifolia, Oldenlandia umbellata and Leucas aspera occur in soils having good drainage.

Laterite soils

Some of the weeds are specific to laterite soils. e.g., Bidens pilosa, Lantana camara, Spargula arvensis.

Habitat

Depending on the habitat, weeds are broadly grouped into terrestrial and aquatic weeds.

Terrestrial weeds

These are the weeds of economic importance, found in cultivated and uncultivated fields where the soils are not waterlogged, *e.g., Sorghum halepense, Amaranthus spp.,* etc.

Aquatic weeds

Weeds of this group grow and complete a part of their life cycle in water. The plants are well adopted to thrive under aquatic conditions because of the possession of special tissues. They commonly propagate vegetatively. The aquatic weeds are grouped into submerged, emerged and floating weeds.

Submerged weeds

They are mostly vascular plants and produce most of their vegetative growth beneath the water surface. They have true roots, stems and leaves. *e.g., Hydrilla verticillata, Najar sp, Utricularia stellaris, Myriophyllum sp., Ceratophyllum demersum, Lemna polyrrhiza.*

Emerged weeds

The plants put forth roots in the bottom mud while their aerial stems and leaves are protruding at or above the water surface. *e.g., Typha sp., Nelumbium speciosum.*

Floating weeds

The leaves of these weeds are floating on the water surface. Some of the weeds are free floating while some others root in the mud and the leaves rise or fall according to the water level. Under favourable conditions, they rapidly spread and cover the entire water body. *e.g., Eichhornia crassipes, Pistia stratiotes, Salvinia, Nymphaea pubescens.*

Algae

They are primitive forms of plants and their body consists of long, slender, filamentous structures. Commonly seen algae are *Spirogyra* and *Oscillatoria*. The former is green in colour and occurs in masses. The latter is dark or bluish green normally attached to the soil.

Special weeds

There are few other types of special weeds: (i) poisonous weeds, (ii) parasitic weeds and (iii) problem weeds.

Poisonous weeds

The weeds of such type cause ailment to livestock. The weeds are harvested inadvertently along with fodder or grass and fed to cattle. Sometimes, the cattle may graze the weed species and become weak and not capable for heavy work. The milk yield may get reduced in milch animals. In some instances, abortion is inevitable. There may be causality to children eating the berries. *e.g.,*: *Datura fastuosa, D. stramonium, D. metel* - poisonous to both animals and human beings. All parts of the plants are toxic but the seeds are the most virulent.

1. *Abrus precatorius:* Seeds are poisonous.
2. *Withania somnifera:* Berries are poisonous.
3. *Solanum nigrum*: Poisonous to children in rare occasions.

Parasitic weeds

Parasitic weeds may be classified into total or partial parasites based on their dependence on crop plants. *e.g., Orobanche* is a total parasite; *Striga* is partial or semi-parasite. The parasites may also be termed as stem or shoot parasite (*e.g., Striga, Cuscuta, Loranthus*) and root parasite (*e.g., Orobanche*) depending on their attack on the host.

Problem or noxious weeds

The problem or noxious weeds are very difficult to control because of their high competitive nature. The weeds persist in adverse conditions and reduce the yield of crops even at very low density. The following are considered as the worst problem weeds of the world.

1. *Cyperus rotundus*- Purple nutsedge
2. *Cynodon dactylon*- Bermuda grass
3. *Echinochloa sp.* - Jungle rice
4. *Sorghum halapense*- Johnson grass
5. *Eichornia crassipes*- water hyacinth
6. *Imperata cylindrica* - Quack grass
7. *Lantana camera*- Lantana
8. *Parthenium hysterophorus* - wild carrot

WEED SAMPLING TECHNIQUES

The sampling techniques of weeds may be broadly grouped into (i) destructive and (ii) non-destructive methods. In the destructive method, the weed species are pulled out and fresh or dry weights are recorded. Dry weight of the weed species is more appropriate since the fresh weight may vary depending on the moisture content of the plant. In the non-destructive method, minimal damage is caused to the vegetation. In both the methods of sampling, quadrats are used as sampling unit. Three methods are used for weed sampling.

i) Quadrat methods which include list or census quadrat and clip quadrat method
ii) Point intercept method
iii) Line intercept method

1. **Quadrat methods:** The quadrat is a square area of varying sizes. Since the sample unit is a quadrat, it is popularly known as the quadrat method. In this method, sample area is marked off in the field for the purpose of detailed weed study.

   List or census quadrat: In this method, individual weed species are listed and the actual number of species per unit area is counted. It is easier to account the number of annual weed species having a single stem. But it is difficult to count the species which propagate vegetatively. To overcome this problem, the rooted sprouts of individuals can be considered as individual number. While counting the species, care should be taken to count the species which fall within the quadrat only. The species which are lying or just overlapping the quadrat but not have sprouted from the sampling unit should be omitted. This method gives accurate assessment of abundance of a species. However, this method is tedious and time consuming. The accuracy depends on the size and the number of quadrats used.

   Clip quadrat: In this method, each species in a quadrat is clipped off at the soil surface and the oven dry weight is recorded. Relative dry weight of a particular species can also be worked out.

2. **Point intercept method:** This method of sampling is followed in the pastures where the vegetation is dense or matted and difficult to determine where one individual species starts and the another one ends. A sample unit is a frame having vertical row of slender pins equally spaced at 5 or 10 cm apart. When placed over the vegetation, only the stems of the species which have first touched by each pin point is recorded. Instead of a frame, a measuring length tape can also be used. It is stretched out for any desired length over the area to be sampled and is taken as the sample plot. The length should be constant for each sampled plot. Sampling pins are pushed vertically into the ground at any desired but constant interval along the tape. The weed species touched by the pins are recorded. If no species are contacted, that should also be noted.

3. **Line intercept method:** In dense stands of tufted plants where plant outlines are clear, this method of sampling can be used. In this method, a measuring tape is stretched out for any required length over the area to be sampled. This represents the sample plot. Length should be constant for each plot sampled. The intersect line is then subdivided into intervals of any desired length. The species which have touched

the intersect line should be recorded.

Weed vegetation analysis

Some of the indices are used to assess the weed vegetation quantitatively in a particular place.

$$\text{Relative density (RD)} = \frac{\text{Absolute density for a given species}}{\text{Total absolute density for all species}} \text{x100}$$

Absolute frequency (Af) =

$$= \frac{\text{Number of sample unit in which a given species occur}}{\text{Total number of sample units}} \times 100$$

$$\text{Relative frequency (Rf)} = \frac{\text{Absolute frequency value for a species}}{\text{Total absolute frequency for all species}} \text{x100}$$

Importance value (I.V.) = Relative density (RD) + Relative frequency (Rf)

Summed dominance ratio (SDR)= I.V. / 2

Weed community

Another part of vegetation study deals with the techniques to compare the areas of different weed communities, relate vegetation variation to environmental factors and to identify the controlling factors. The parameters used for these aspects are:

Co-efficient of community

Two communities or the vegetation stands of two regions can be compared by using mathematical expression of the similarities of the lists of species. If community X is compared to Y, the number of species common to both is accounted and expressed as a percentage to the total number of X plus Y (Pablico and Moody, 1983).

Co-efficient of similarity (c)

By using quantitative data such as I.V. and SDR for various species, pairs of communities may be compared by calculating co-efficient of similarity (C).

$$C = \frac{2W}{a+b} X100$$

Where, C = co-efficient of similarity; W = sum of the lower I.V. or SDR of species shared by two communities; a = sum of I.V. or SDR of all species of first community and b= sum of I.V. or SDR of all species of second community.

The values (C) are calculated based on the absolute and relative values of vegetation parameters. They may not be identical but are comparable. The community similarity co-efficient can be converted to a dissimilarity co-efficient (D) by the equation:

$$D = 100\text{-}C.$$

Simpson's index (S)

This index is used to measure the concentration of dominance and to determine the degree of diversity in a given community type.

$$S = \sum \left(\frac{Y}{N} \right)^2$$

Where, Y = I.V. of a given species; N = Sum of I.V. for all species in the sample (100).

Weed sample collection and preservation

Weeds that have been collected should be preserved properly. This will serve as a ready and reliable reference at a later period. A collection of plants in preserved form is technically known as herbarium.

Collection and preservation

Individual weed specimens in good condition with flowers and / or fruits are collected. It is necessary to collect 2-3 specimens per species. Growth habit and other important characteristics are recorded. The specimen is to be properly pressed. It is essential to see that the specimen should not get wilted before pressing. Vegetative and reproductive parts should be clearly shown by proper arrangement while pressing. Pile the specimens on top of each other, being separated by absorbent boards. Apply gentle pressure to the pile kept between a pair of wooden presses. The specimen can be dried properly either in sunlight or artificial heat. The former provides better colour retention though it may take longer time. Under artificial heating, proper ventilation is necessary for retention of colour. The presses can be kept inside a drying cabinet at 45-60 °C temperature. Drying time depends on the moisture content of the specimen. Over-drying of the specimen should be avoided. If needed the absorbent boards may be changed. The dried specimen may be dipped in a poisonous solution (12-15 g of mercuric chloride and 5-10 g of phenol crystals dissolved in one litre of denatured alcohol). Adequate precaution is required while handling the solution since it is poisonous. After dipping the specimens, they may be redried for 3-5 hours at room temperature.

Mounting

The specimen is affixed on a sheet of heavy paper for permanent filing. Dried and poisoned specimens are mounted by means of glue or tape on herbarium sheet. Attach label containing scientific name, family, collector's name, date of collection, etc. If a particular species is not identifiable, it could be referred to Botanical Survey of India.

CROP-WEED COMPETITION

Crops and weeds compete for light, water and nutrients. Weeds benefit from crop management practices such as irrigation, fertilization and pest control that are intended to benefit the crops. Competition begins when crops and weeds grow in close proximity and the supply of any necessary growth factor falls below the demand of both. Competitiveness in both crops and weeds is related to their ability to exploit and sequester the environmental resources upon which plant growth depends. Competition is important only during the crop-growing season. Therefore, relative crop /weed competitiveness generally depends on plant performances during only a part of each year.

Critical period of weed competition

The critical period of crop-weed competition is the period from the time of sowing to the time to which the crop is to be maintained in a weed-free environment to get the highest yield. Many studies have shown that the critical period for crop-weed competition occurs only during the early part of the growing season. Generally early one-third of crop period should be maintained weed-free. In a crop of 100 days duration, the first 35 days are considered critical period for weed control. The critical period of weed competition varies with crop, cultivars and growing conditions. Vigorously growing plants with rapidly expanding leaf canopies and root systems are more efficient in utilizing the resources that are essential for plant growth. Weeds occupy the ecological vacuum which is created in a crop as part of cultural practices. Crops like maize grow fast and cover the field quickly and smother the weeds early. However, crops like cotton and sugarcane have slow initial growth and are wide spaced. Hence they take comparatively longer time to cover the field and the critical period of weed competition is also longer. The critical period also differs with the cultivars used. For examples, 20 days of weed-free growth appears best in short- stature plant like of rice. For an intermediate stature variety, the weed-free period should be extended to the first 30 days after planting of rice. Generally weed competition is less under flooded condition where rice is transplanted, compared to upland situations.

Components of competition

The factors that affect the crop competition from weeds are conditions in which the crop is grown, its density, stage of the crop, weeds and their density, stage of growth of weeds and the management practices adopted by the farmers. Normally competition is the greatest when plants have similar growth habits.

Light

The presence of a weeds or crop canopy alters the quality or wavelength distribution as well as the quality of the light energy passing through it. Competition for light occurs when one plant shades another to the point that the intensity and quality of light received by the shaded plant are less than necessary for optimum growth. Any decrease in incident light from canopy shading by weed or crop will decrease the rate of growth.

Water

Competition for water and nutrients is usually more important because it begins before the competition for light. Competition for water is greater since the roots of the crop and weed are closely intermingled and both take up moisture from the same volume of soil. The transpiration ratio of weeds is generally higher than that of the crops. Weeds compete with crops for often-limited soil water resource and further reduce the availability of water to the crop. Reduced soil water availability increases the level of moisture stress experienced by the crops. Weed competition for water is more serious for upland and rainfed rice than for irrigated rice because moisture is often limiting in the former case. In the drylands, soil moisture storage is greatly reduced due to weed infestation in the previous season. Weeds native to arid regions are more competitive when soil moisture is limited. At high moisture levels, weeds of humid regions or those normally present in irrigated crops are more competitive.

Nutrients

Weeds absorb more of nutrients than the crop plants. Since the weeds have a competitive advantage in water uptake, they also have competitive advantage in nutrient uptake. Weeds accumulate more of nutrients than the associated crop plants. Among the major nutrients, N is the one for which competition is most severe. Crops show the deficiency symptoms for N in heavily weed infested fields. Unchecked weed growth in wheat fields removed about 20 kg N/ha and reduced the grain yield to the tune of 12 q/ha. When supplemental N is applied to fields of upland rice infested with *Cyperus rotundus*. L., weeds benefited more than rice. This is because the weeds compete more effectively for soil moisture under high N condition. However, addition of higher N level to cotton in competition with annual weeds resulted in a substantial increase in the height of the cotton plants. This gave cotton an advantage in competition for light not realized at low N level.

Allelopathy

Allelopathy is any direct or indirect harmful effect by one plant on another through the production of chemical compounds or the antagonistic interaction of phytochemicals on the growth of other plants. Allelopathic effect may occur with weeds on crops and vice versa. Allelopathy may be one mechanism through which aggressive weed species gain dominance on agricultural sites. Numerous weed species have alleged alleopathic potential. The important weed species that show allelopathic effect are *Agropyron repens, Ambrosia psitostachya, Cyperus rotundus, Euphorbia maculata, Lantana camara, Sorghum halepense,* etc.

Quackgrass (*Agropyron repens)* is a rhizomatous perennial weed which causes severe crop losses in temperate regions of the Northern Hemisphere. Addition of dead quackgrass rhizomes to soils reduces the emergence and growth of alfalfa. Crops such as oats and alfalfa become chlorotic and stunted when grown in the presence of quackgrass shoot residues. The residues of the grass also reduce nodulation by rhizobium in several legume species. The seed exudates of wild oat (*Avena fatua*) affect the germination and early seedling growth of wheat. The inhibitory substances produced by the leaves of flax weed (*Camelina alyssum)* greatly reduce the yield of flax.

There are reports to show that some of the crop plants show allelopathy on weeds. Root exudation of maize inhibits the growth of *Chenopodium album* and *Amaranthus retroflexus.*

METHODS OF WEED CONTROL

Weed control and weed management are the two terms often used in weed science. Weed control is the process of limiting infestations so that crops can be grown profitably or other operations can be carried out efficiently. The primary objective of weed management is to maintain an environment that is as detrimental to weeds as possible.

Weed management methods can be broadly grouped into preventive and curative and can be further broadly categorized into mechanical, agronomical, biological and chemical methods. Any one or combination of methods can be employed for effective weed management.

Preventive methods

It comprises all measures taken to hinder the introduction and spread of weeds. It includes clean cultivation, use of clean seeds, keeping seed bed free from weeds, keeping bunds and irrigation channels free of weeds, keeping tools and machinery clean and control of weeds before they attain reproductive stage or setting seeds.

The number of viable weed seeds that remain in the soil reduces to the tune of 25-50% each year provided the soil is cultivated several times and no more weed seeds are allowed to enter it. Clean farming for several years significantly reduces the amount of weed seeds and vegetative propagules which are stored in the soil.

Control measures

Mechanical methods

Mechanical control involves the usage of different types of tools, implements and machinery for better weed control.

Tillage

In the non-disturbed soil, deeply buried dormant seeds retain their viability for many years. When the soil is disturbed the seed dormancy is broken, stimulating the weeds to emerge. Number of weed seeds in the ploughed layer can be reduced by repeated tillage that stimulates emergence. Under optimal rainfall, 50% of weed seeds in the plough layer germinate within 5-6 weeks of cultivation.

Depth and frequency of tillage operations affect the weed growth. Deep tillage has a favourable impact on weed growth. Sub-soiling results in better crop growth and hence enables suppression of growth of weeds. Frequent tillage operations provide opportunity for the weed seeds to germinate. Repeated harrowing during hot weather period before the onset of monsoon reduces the weed intensity. Tillage also disturbs the root system. By the usage of shallow tillage implements such as harrows and rotary hoes, the soil is loosened and the root system is cut off. This facilitates the weeds to die by desiccation before it can reestablish its roots. The principal tillage machinery are ploughs, harrows and cultivators.

Blind tillage

This method is extensively used to combat weeds in row crops. Various types of harrows are used as soon as the weeds appear even before the crops establish fully.

Post- plant tillage

Various types of implements are used to control weeds after the crop is grown.

Spike-tooth harrow is employed in row crops like maize, cotton, soybean, groundnut and grain sorghum. It can be used when the crop is about 7-10 cm high. Spring type harrow is used as that of spike tooth harrow but may stir the soil upto 7.5 cm depth. Rotary hoe cultivator destroys the sprouting weeds and grasses in the rows close to the young plants. Wheel hoe is the manually operated weeding tool. It is suitable for weeding in small vegetable gardens and some flowerbeds. Blade harrows are the animal drawn row cultivation implements commonly used on heavy black soils.

Many cultivator designs are widely used for inter-row weeding in wide row crops. Rice rotary weeder is a specific tool for weeding in rice fields. Single or double row weeders are also available. They are worked manually with back and forth movement in between rice rows of wetlands.

This rotary weeder is less strenuous than hand weeding. At the time of weeding, it is essential to retain 1.5 -2.0 cm depth of water. With the single row rice weeder, one labour can cover about 0.5 ha/day.

Dryland weeders: Two types of weeders, star and peg types, are used for weeding under dryland situations. (Also refer page 154).

Solarization

Solarization is a method of heating the surface soil by using plastic sheets placed on moist soil to trap the solar radiation. Soil acts as a resevoir of weed seeds and therefore, the importance of soil solarization in destroying the seed reserve are being well recognized. By covering soil with polythene sheet, the soil temperature is increased to the lethal level for weeds. The possible mechanisms of weed control by soil solarization is direct killing of germinating weed seeds whose dormancy is broken due to rise in soil temperature. The success of soil solarization largely depends on the availability of intense summer with bright sunshine at least for one or two months. Being in the tropical regions, many parts of India experience extreme summer during which period soil solarization can be effectively practiced.

The effect of solarization varies with weed species. In perennials, with an established underground system of deep roots, rhizomes or tubers, solarization may not be effective. Solarization is found effective against imbibed but dormant seeds. The obligate parasite, broom rape, could be controlled by solarization. Mulching by polythene sheets for 32 days decreased the emergence of *Dactyloctenium aegyptium, Acrachne racemosa, Trianthema portulacastrum* and *Cyperus rotundus* by more than 90% and the main solarization effect is restricted to the 0-5 cm layer of soil. Besides controlling weeds, soil solarization has other benefits such as control of pathogens and increased availability of plant nutrients

Cultural measures

Various cultural measures such as choice of crop varieties, planting density, geometry, intercropping, crop rotation and fertilizer and irrigation practices have profound effect on weed management.

Crop varieties

Some of the crops grow quickly and produce canopy early resulting in shading and thus suppress weed growth. Crops vary in their capacity of suppressing the weed growth. Maize has the highest weed suppressing ability (92%) compared to other crops (pearl millet -88%, cowpea-88%, sorghum -81%, groundnut -62%, pigeonpea- 54%, castor -51%). To control weeds like *E. Colonum,* which are morphologically similar to rice, a pigmented variety 'Kalashri' (R 260-292) grown in Orissa State, India, may be useful in distinguishing weeds from rice in early growth stage. Semi-tall rice variety 'Kalinga-3' is superior to smoother weeds than dwarf cultivars.

Plant population

Plant population and row arrangement also affect the weed growth. Higher plant population and narrow row spacing can put pressure on the availability of space for weed growth. A narrow (15 cm) spacing was found superior to wide (30 and 45 cm) spacing in minimizing weed competition and increasing productive tillers and yield in upland rice. Higher density of plant population in transplanted rice and wheat had lower dry weight of weeds.

Intercropping

Intercropping suppresses weeds better than sole cropping and thus provides an opportunity to utilize crops themselves as tools for weed management. In intercropping, more complete crop coverage and high population density cause severe competition to weeds and thus reduce the weed growth. Results of a large number of experiments have indicated that short duration pulses like greengram, cowpea (fodder) and soybean as intercrops effectively smother weeds. Horsegram also combines well as intercrop and suppresses weeds. Intercropping not only suppresses weeds but also reduces weeding cost and gives bonus yield of intercrop. Inclusion of cowpea or greengram as an intercrop in sorghum virtually replaces weeding without reducing sorghum yield.

Crop rotation

In monoculature, a number of weed species persist and expand rapidly while crop rotation helps to interrupt the life cycle of weeds and prevent any weed species to become dominant. In continuously transplanted rice fields under irrigated condition, *Scirpus maritimus* persists. When dryland crops are rotated with rice, the population of this weed has been reduced drastically even without adoption of weed control measures. In maize, Johnson grass (*Sorghum halepense*) becomes dominant which can be controlled by rotating with cotton. In winter season crops, weeds are a major problem in the North Indian belt where considerable areas follow rice - wheat cropping sequence. These areas have been found heavily infested with the *Phalaris minor*. It has been found through experimental evidences that introducing a crop of sugarcane in the rotation helps in minimising the population of this weed by 60-70% without any chemical application.

Crop rotation plays a significant role in the management of parasitic weeds. Different trap crops have been identified in controlling *Striga* and *Orobanche*. The trap crops induce germination of the parasitic weeds but are not parasitised. *e.g.*, cotton, sunflower and cowpea are trap crops for *Striga*. Linseed, sunnhemp, sorghum, groundnut and chilli for *Orobanche*.

Other management practices

Other management practices like irrigation and fertilization also affect weed growth. Under upland conditions, frequent irrigation facilitates weed growth. In wetlands, whenever rotational water supply is followed in command areas, the field often dries up. Hence intermittent wetting and drying promote weed growth. However, continuous flooding suppresses the weed growth.

Fertilizer management practices also affect weed growth. Whenever heavy dose of fertilizers is applied under upland situations, weeds take up more of nutrients and put forth vigorous growth. Single time application of fertilizers also gives room for weed problem.

Biological method of weed control

Biological management is a broad term for the exploitation of living organisms or their products to reduce or prevent the growth and reproduction of weeds. A large number of biocontrol agents such as insects, mites, pathogens, animals, fish, birds and their toxic products have been identified for weed control. Among them, insects are one of the important groups. Biological control is widely accepted as an important method of weed control and is considered an option in the control and management of most weeds.

Use of insects

Certain species of insects have been introduced in the regions where some weeds such as cactus, klamath weed, lantana, water hyacinth and parthenium have become a serious nuisance. During 1860s, a cochineal insect, *Dactylopius ceylonicus* was used in South India to control prickly pear cactus, *Optuntia vulgaris.*

Lantana camera, L. is the perennial shrub which is used as an ornamental plant throughout the world. This species became a menace in coconut plantations, rangelands and hindered reforestation. A seedfly (*Ophimoyia lantanae*), a lacebug (*Teleonania scrupulose*) and butterfly (*Theola spp.)* have been used to control this weed.

The Klamath weed (*Hypericum perforatum,* L.) is considered as a noxious weed in the rangelands of Australia, New Zealand, Canada and USA. Two species of the leaf feeding beetle, *Chrysolina hyperici, C. gamellata* and a root borer, *Agrilus hyperici* have been used against this weed.

Water hyacinth is a major aquatic weed causing problem in many parts of India. Two species of weevils of the genus, Neochetina *viz., N. bruchi* and *N. eichhorniae* are specific and feed on this weed. The dry weight of the weed declined from 2.5 to 1.5 kg/m^2 after the use of this insect.

The mexican beetle (*Zygogramma bicolorata)* is found to have great potential to bring about permanent reduction in the density of *Parthenium hysterophorus* in the parts of India experiencing moderate weather conditions.

Use of pathogens for weed control

There are three ways of using pathogens for weed control. They are classical, augmentative and mycoherbicidal methods.

Classical strategy

A fungus is introduced or released in a place where it did not previously exist. The control agent once released reproduces and disperses on its own. This method is most suitable to areas of low economic return per unit area such as range areas. In Australia, fungi *Puccinia chondrilla* was released for the control of skeleton weed, *Chonadrilla juncea.* In Hawaii, *Entyloma compositarum* was introduced from Jamaica to control *Ageratina riparia.*

Augmentation strategy

It requires an annual introduction or release of an organism to raise the level of primary inoculum or population to levels sufficient to cause epidemics. This method has the advantage of controlling the weed only in the area of application. The cost depends on the area treated and the duration of the treatment. *e.g.,* release of *Puccinia canaliculata* to control *Cyperus esculentus* and *P. lagenophorae* for the control of *Senecio vulgaris* in USA.

Bioherbicide

Bioherbicides are the biological control agents applied in similar way as that of chemical herbicides to control weeds. The active ingredient in a bioherbicide is a living organism or its metabolite and is applied in moderate doses. Fungi, bacteria and viruses offer greater promise for use as bioherbicide. Most commonly used microorganisms is fungus and hence the bioherbicide is sometimes called mycoherbicide. Fungal pathogens that are virulent, host-specific and genetically stable but constrained naturally by low inoculum production and poor dissemination are good candidates for development as mycoherbicides.

The inoculum is prepared from axenic culture of the pathogen and disseminated by artificial means. Pathogens are applied to specific areas in pre-determined volumes and dosages to achieve control of target weed within the specific period and before economic losses are incurred. The fungus is not expected to survive or provide control beyond the growing season in which it is applied. This approach is receiving greater attention from industry because of its potential commercial values. *e.g.* a fungal pathogen, *Colletotrichum gleosporodies f.* sp. *aeschynomene* was used to control Northern Joint Vetch weed in USA where the achievement was 92% in rice and 98% in soybean. This fungus is commercially sold under the trade name "COLLEGO". Another important mycoherbicide "Devine" is a liquid formulation of *Phytophthora palmivora.* Some of the mycoherbicides under commercial use are given in the Table 7.2.

TABLE 7.2: Commercial mycoherbicides

Name of pathogen	Trade name	Weeds controlled
Colletotrichum coccodes	VELGO	*Abutilon theopharsti*
Colletotrichum gloeosporioides f. sp. aeschynomene	COLLEGO	*Aeschynomene virginica*
Cercospora rodmanii	ABG 5003	*Eichhorinia crassipes.*
Colletotrichum gloesoporioides f.sp. malvae	BIOMAL	*Malva pustilla*
Phytophythora palmivora	DEVINE	*Morrenia odorata*
Alternaria cassiae	CASST	*Cassia obtusifolia*

Bio-herbicides, when used in conjunction with chemical herbicides, can increase the range of weeds controlled and may enhance control of a particular problem weed. *e.g.* Some control was achieved of the weed, *Cyperus esculentus* by spray of rust fungi, *Luccinia canaliculata* when infested plants were sprayed with post-emergent herbicides.

Insecticides such as carbofuran, benomyl and triphenyltin hydroxide can be effectively integrated with the mycoherbicides.

Utilization of plant and microbial phytotoxins

Several plant secondary metabolites (allelo-chemicals) as well as fungal and microbial toxins possess good herbicidal activity. Some of the naturally occurring compounds that exhibit promizing herbicidal activity are given in Table 7.3.

Only biolophos is currently marketed under the trade name "Herbiaceae" as a commercially developed herbicide in Japan. It exhibits strong herbicidal activity against a wide spectrum of grasses and broad-leaved weeds as foliar application.

TABLE 7.3: Plant metabolites used for herbicidal activity

Natural phytotoxin	Plant or microbial source
Anisomycin	*Streptomyces* sp.
Biolophos	Streptomyces hygrocopicus, S. viridachromogenes
Cercosporin	*Cercospora* sp. *Pseudocercosporilla capsulla*
Coffeine	Coffee plants
Dhussion	Sorghum plants
Tab toxin	*Pseudomonas tobaci*
Teu toxin	*Alternaria alternata*

Synthetic derivatives of naturally occurring compounds as herbicides

Methoxyphenone is the herbicide developed as a synthetic analog of the microbial toxin, anisomycin by employing bio-rational chemical synthesis of a herbicide based on a natural chemistry. In Japan, this herbicide is marketed as a selective herbicide for the control of barnyard grass (*Echinochloa crusgalli*) in rice and is easily degraded in soil. Fusaric acid is a marasmin produced by many species of *Fusarium* fungi and has been detected in infested tomato plants and wilted cotton. Pichoram, a chlorinated anologue of fusaric acid, has been marketed as an herbicide.

The structures of naturally occurring phytotoxins serve as a lead for the synthesis of new herbicides. Biorational design is used for the discovery of new herbicides, in isolation and characterization of additional microbial toxins and allelochemicals from higher plants.

Use of fish

Several species of herbivorous fish feed on aquatic weeds. The most important fish are *Tilapia melanopleura, T. zillii, T. nilotica* and *Puntiux gonianatus*. Grass carp feeds voraciously on Hydrilla, Nechamandra and *Lemna spp*. Ponds chocked with Hydrilla can be cleared within a month by stocking 300 to 375 grass carps.

CHEMICAL METHOD OF WEED CONTROL (USE OF HERBICIDES)

Use of herbicides is widespread worldwide. In the recent decades, growth of herbicides took place principally at the expense of fungicides which declined from a market share of 40 % in 1960 to 25 % in 1995. About 72 % of the herbicide consumption took place in the developed countries like USA, Western Europe and Japan. The usage of chemicals for weed control in India started with the introduction of 2,4-D in the late forties. Commercial use of herbicides, however, began in 1980s. From a mere 2 % share of the total pesticide consumption in the seventies, herbicides now account for about 11 % of the pesticide market in India. Punjab and Haryana are leading in herbicides use. Herbicide usage has been largely limited to a few crops: wheat (42%), rice (30%) and tea plantation (23%). Its usage is increasing due to higher cost of labour.

Classification of herbicides

Herbicides are classified based on time and method of application, mode of action and their chemical nature.

Time of application

Based on time of application, herbicides are classified into three groups: (i) pre-planting, (ii) pre-emergence and (iii) post- emergence herbicides.

Pre-planting

Herbicides are applied before the cultivation of crop plants. Normally the herbicides having greater toxicity on the emerging seedlings are applied before sowing or planting. For example, glyphosate or paraquat is applied to rice fallow fields.

TABLE 7.4: Classification of herbicide based on chemical nature

Group	Common herbicides	Time of application	Rate	Crops / weed species
Acetamides	Acetochlor	PPI or PRE	1.5-3.0 kg/ha	Soybean, maize
	Alachlor	PPI, PRE, or E.Post	2.0-4.0 kg/ha	Maize, sorghum, groundnut, soybean, cotton
	Butachlor	PRE	1.0-3.0 kg/ha	Rice, groundnut, soybean
	Metolachlor	E –PPS, PPI, PRE, or E-Post	1.5-4.0 kg/ha	Maize, cotton, groundnut
	Propanil	POST	3.0-5.0 kg/ha	Rice, wheat
Aliphatics	Aerolein	-	15 g /100 li	Floating weeds
Arsenicals	DSMA	POST	2.5-5.0 kg/ha	Cotton, non-crop areas
	MSMA	POST	2.5 kg/ha	Cotton, non-crop areas
Benzamides	Isoxaben	PRE, POST or PPI	1.5-2.0 kg/ha	Tobacco
Benzoics	Dicamba	PPS, PRE or POST	0.25-0.50	Maize, sorghum, wheat
Bipyridiliums	Diquat	POST	2-0.4 kg/ha	Aquatic weeds and desiccant in cotton
	Paraquat	POST	0.25-1.0 kg/ha	Non crop areas and plantation crops
Carbamates	Asulam	POST	1.0-3.0 kg/ha	Sugarcane, non-crop areas
	Desmedipham	POST	0.8-1.5 kg/ha	Sugarbeet
Cineoles	Cinmethylin	PPI or PRE	0.5-1.5kg/ha	Soybean, cotton, groundnut
Cyclohexanediones (Cyclohexenones)	Sethoxydim	POST	0.10-0.5 kg/ha	Cotton, sunflower
Dinitroanilines	Fluchloralin	PRE	1.0-4.0 kg/ha	Groundnut, pulse crops
	Pendimethalin	PRE or E-POST	0.5-2.0 kg/ha	Maize, sorghum, wheat, sunflower, cotton, sugarcane
	Trifluralin	PPI	0.5-1.0 kg/ha	Maize, soybean, sunflower, castor, safflower

Group	Common herbicides	Time of application	Rate	Crops / weed species
Diphenylethers	Oxyfluorfen	POST	0.25-2.0 kg/ha	Soybean, groundnut
Imidazolidinones	Buthidazole	PRE or POST	-	Maize, wheat
Imidazolinones	Imazethaphyr	POST	50-70 g /ha	Soybean
	Imazamethabenz	POST	20-40 g /ha	Sunflower
I mines	CGA – 248757	POST	3-15 g /ha	Maize, soybean
Isoxazolidinones	Clomazone	PPI or PRE	0.56-1.7 kg/ha	Soybean
Nitriles	Bromoxynil	POST	0.20-0.56 kg/ha	Wheat, barley, oats, maize, sorghum
	Dichlobenil	POST	4.0-8.0 kg/ha	Forest nurseries
	Ioxynil	POST	0.5-1.0 kg/ha	Wheat, barley
Oxadiazoles	Oxadiazon	PRE	0.5-4.0 kg/ha	Rice, soybean, groundnut, cotton, sugarcane
Oxadiazolidines	Methazole	PPL, PRE or POST	0.5-1.5 kg/ha	Sorghum, maize, wheat, soybean, cotton
Phenols	Dinoseb	POST	0.75-1.2 kg/ha	Cereal crops, potato
Phenoxyalkanoic acids				
Phenoxyacetics	2,4-D	POST	0.26-2.24 kg/ha	Cereal crops, sugarcane, non-crop areas
	MCPA	POST	0.25-1.5 kg/ha	Cereal crops, legumes
Phenoxybutyrics	2,4-DB	POST	0.20-0.45 kg/ha	Forage legume crops
Aryloxyphenoxy propionics	Fluazifop-P	POST	50-200 g /ha	Wheat, soybean, cotton
N–phenylphth-alimides	Flumiclorac	POST	30-60 g /ha	Maize, soybean
Phenylpyridazines	Sulfentrazone	PPI or PRE	60-90 g /ha	Soybean
Phthalamates	Naptalam	PRE or POST	2.0-4.0 kg/ha	Groundnut, soybean
Pyrazoliums	Difenzoquat	POST	0.7-1.0 kg/ha	Wild oats
Pyridazinones	Picloram	POST	0.15-1.0 kg/ha	Non-crop area
Pyridines	Dithiopyr	PRE	0.25-0.5 kg/ha	Rice
Pyridinones	Fluridone	-	0.06-0.09 mg /litre	Aquatic weeds

Group	Common herbicides	Time of application	Rate	Crops / weed species
Pyrimidinylthio-benzoates	Pyrithiobac	POST	0.07 kg/ha	Cotton
Quinolinecarxoxylic acids	Quinclorac	PRE, late – PRE or early – POST	0.25-0.50 kg/ha	Rice
Sulfonylureas	Chlorsulfuron	PRE or POST	10-20 g /ha	Wheat
	Sulfometuron	PRE or POST	50-200 g /ha	Non-crop areas
Thiocarbamates	Butylate	PPI	3.0-6.0 kg /ha	Maize
	Diallate	PPI	2.0-5.0 kg/ha	Wheat, maize, soybean, oilseed crops
	EPTC	PPI	2.0-5.0 kg/ha	Maize, sunflower, cotton
	Thiobencarb	PRE	1.0-1.5 kg/ha	Irrigated rice
Triazines	Ametryn	POST	0.5-2.0 kg/ha	Sugarcane
	Atrazin	PRE	1.0-2.0 kg/ha	Maize, sorghum, sugarcane
	Prometryn	PPI or PRE	0.5-3.0 kg/ha	Cotton, soybean, non-crop areas
	Simazine	PRE	1.0-4.0 kg/ha	Maize, sugarcane
Triazinones	Metribuzin	PPI, PRE or POST	0.25-0.80 kg/ha	Maize, soybean, sugarcane
Triazoles	Amitrole	POST	2.0-10.0 kg/ha	Non-crop areas
Trizolopyrimidine				
Sulfonanilides	Flumetsulam	PRE, PPI or PPS	50-75 g /ha	Maize, soybean
Uracils	Bromacil	PRE	1.5-5.0 kg/ha	Non-crop areas
Ureas	Diuron	POST	0.2-0.4 kg/ha	Maize, sorghum
	Fluometuron	PPI or PRE	1.0-1.5 kg/ha	Sorghum, cotton, sugarcane
Unclassified	Bensulide	PPI or PRE	5.6-6.7 kg/ha	Vegetable crops
	Glyphosate	POST	0.5-4.0 kg/ha	Perennial weeds

(PPL – preplanting; PPS – Pre planting surface; E – PPS – Early pre planting surface; PPI – Pre planting incorporated; PRE – pre emergence; late - PRE – late pre emergence; POST – Post emergence; E – POST – Early post emergence)

Source: Rao, 2000

Some of the herbicides which need proper incorporation in the soil are applied before planting. *e.g.*, bensulide is incorporated into the soil before planting chillies.

Pre-emergence

Herbicides are applied before the emergence of crop or weed. In annual crops, it is referred as pre-emergence to the crop and in the perennial crops, pre-emergence to weeds. Examples of pre-emergence herbicides are butachlor to rice, isoproturon to wheat and atrazine to sugarcane, maize, sorghum.

Post-emergence

Herbicide treatment enforced after the emergence of crop or weed is referred to as post- emergence application. *e.g.* propanil to rice and 2, 4-D to rice or wheat.

Method of application

Herbicides are applied on the soil or on the foliage. Herbicides which are used as pre-planting or pre-emergence are generally applied to the soil. Placement of soil-applied herbicides is important to enhance the weed control efficiency.

Post-emergence herbicides are sprayed on the plant parts. Foliage is the main source of entrance and the herbicide molecules are absorbed by the foliage. In addition, trichomes and stems are also involved in the absorption of herbicides.

Chemical nature

Herbicides are classified as inorganic and organic compounds and the latter are widely used. Inorganic compounds are $CuSO_4$, H_2SO_4, etc.

Classification of herbicides (organic compounds) based on the chemical nature is given in the Table 7.4.

Herbicide formulations

Formulations refer to the way in which the basic weed killing chemicals are prepared for practical use as herbicides. The most important types of formulations are:

1. Solution or soluable concentrates
2. Emulsion or emulsifiable concentrates
3. Wettable powders
4. Soluble powders
5. Granules
6. Fumigants

Solutions or solution concentrates (SC)

Herbicides of this group are dissolved in a solvent system to provide a concentrate that is soluble in the carrier. Most common herbicides are water-soluble and can be dissolved in water and sprayed. *e.g.* 2, 4-D, 2,4-5-T, MCPA, amine salts of DNBP, sodium salt of pentachloro phenol, isopropylamine salt of glyphosate. Some types of solution concentrates have 'parent acid' formulations and are soluble in oil. *e.g.* 2,4-D EE.

Emulsion or emulsifiable concentrates (EC)

An emulsion is one liquid dispered in another liquid, each maintaining its original identity. *e.g.* oil in water. An emulsifying agent is added which, on mixing with water, forms solution. Herbicides belonging to haloalkanoic acids, anilides, pyridines, carbamates, thiocarbamates and nitriles are usually available as emulsifiable concentrates.

Wettable powder (WP)

Wettable powder formulations contain finely divided solid particles (size less than 3 microns) and readily form a suspension. A wetting agent is included to form easy suspension and to increase the retention of the preparation on plants or other surfaces. Usage of WP provides a high degree of dispension of the active ingredients of the preparation. Most widely used wettable powders contain 50 to 80% active ingredient. While spraying it requires constant agitation in the spray tank to prevent settling of the solid particles. While storing and packing, these herbicides are to be properly guarded against absorption of moisture. Most of the commonly available herbicides are in wettable powder formulation. Examples of wettable powder formulation are triazines and ureas.

Soluble powders (SP)

Soluble powders are similar to wettable powders, except that the ingredients used completely dissolve in water. *e.g.* sodium salt of 2,4-D, TCA, dalapon.

Granules (G)

The technical active ingredient is mixed with, or coated on, inert carrier material such as sand, saw dust or crop wastes to form granules of appropriate size. The granules contain 1-20% a.i. and are most suited for direct field application. Uniform particle size of granules helps to apply the herbicides properly in the field. The advantage of using granular herbicides is to avoid the drift problem and foliage injury when they are applied in the soil surface. However, production, package and transport are costlier than for EC or WP forms. Some herbicides have low mobility in soil. Hence performance of these herbicides in granular formulation is less than that in liquid concentrate and powder formulations. *e.g.* butachlor, alachlor.

Fumigants

Some of the volatile chemicals are used as herbicides which are applied to confined spaces or into the soil. They produce gas to destroy weed seeds and act as a soil sterilant. Fumigants are injected as pressurized liquid to the required depth below the soil surface. The vapour penetrates into the soil zone and acts as a soil sterilant. Fumigants are effective to control deep rooted perennial weeds and for eliminating weed seeds from the soil. *e.g.* methyl bromide, allyl alcohol, carbon disulphide, chloropicrin and tetrachloroethane.

Calculation of herbicide dosage

Herbicides are usually applied in the form of solution or granules. Solution formulations are applied using sprayers. Granular forms are sand mixed and applied manually or with the use of applicator. Correct dose of herbicide application is important for effective weed control.

To calculate the herbicide dose, first, account for the dosage (kg a.i./ha) of the chemical required for the crop and active ingredient of the herbicide to be used. The quantity of herbicide requirement may be computed by using the formula,

Quantity of commercial formulation (kg or li / ha) =

$$\frac{Dosage\,(kg\,a.i./\,ha)}{a.i.} x100$$

Example 1. A farmer wants to apply butachlor (50 %EC) to rice at 1.5 kg a.i/ha. Calculate the quantity of the herbicide required for one hectare?

- Recommended dosage of the herbicides for rice = 1.5 kg a.i. / ha
- a.i. of the commercial formulation = 50%
- Quantity of commercial formulation for one ha = $\frac{1.5}{50}$ X 100
- = 3 litres

Example 2. A farmer wants to apply atrazine to maize @ 0.5 kg/ha in the form of Atratraf 50% WP. Calculate the quantity of the herbicide required for one hectare?

- Recommended dosage of the herbicide = 0.5 kg a.i.
- a.i. of the commercial formulation = 50%
- Quantity of commercial formulation for one ha = $\frac{0.5}{50}$ X 100
- = 1 kg

Spraying equipments

Sprayers are used to apply herbicide formulations of wettable powder, soluble powder, emulsifiable and solution concentrates. Two types of sprayers are in use for herbicide application. They are hand operated and power driven. Among them, hand operated hydraulic knapsack sprayers are mostly used for herbicide application in India. It is a high volume sprayer with the tank capacity of 15-20 litres. The spray drop size will be around 400 microns and the droplet density is 200/cm^2. Depending upon the volume of spray fluid required to cover a unit area, sprayers are classified into:

1. High volume (> 400 litres/ ha)
2. Low volume (5-100 litres/ha)
3. Ultra low volume (< one litre/ha)

Components of sprayer

The components of a sprayer are tank, nozzle, pump, filter, pressure regulators, spray boom and lance.

Tank

It is used to hold the spray solution and the capacity of the tank varies with the sprayer. The hand operated knapsack sprayers have a capacity of 5 to 15 litres. Tanks are made up of materials resistant to corrosion of the chemicals. Sprayers have mechanical and hydraulic types of agitators to prevent separation and settling of emulsions and suspensions. Mechanical agitation is more efficient for uniformity in dispersion.

Nozzle

Nozzle is considered as the heart of the equipment as the main function of a nozzle is to obtain uniform distribution of the herbicide. The ability of a nozzle is to produce spray of desired droplet size. A nozzle consists of body, cap, lip or disc and core. To prevent blocking of the nozzle orifice, a filter is provided. Different types of nozzles are available. They are fan, solid cone and flooding or deflector nozzles. (Fig. 7.4)

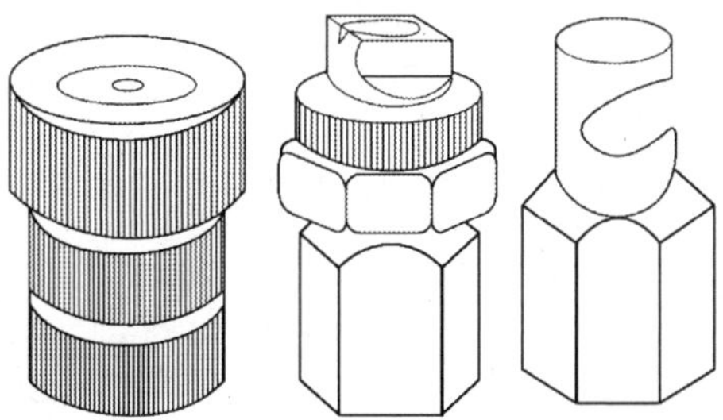

FIG. 7.4: Nozzle types

Fan nozzles

Fan nozzles put out a flat spray which strikes the surface being sprayed in a straight line. It is particularly good to apply an even coating on a flat surface.

Cone type nozzles

Two types of cone nozzles are available: (i) hollow cone and (ii) solid cone nozzles. They are generally used for spraying of insecticides and fungicides. They are also used for the spot application of post-emergence herbicides.

Pumps

To deliver the liquid under pressure, pumps are used. They are operated by gas, air or liquid pressure. Among different types, piston pumps are most widely used.

Filters

Generally filters are built as a part of the nozzle and placed on the inlet of the spray tank or installed as a line filter.

Pressure regulators

To maintain a constant desired pressure, regulators are used. A pressure gauge is placed on the outlet side of the regulator to indicate the nozzle pressure.

Spray boom

A boom is a horizontal pipe with the length of 1-10 m depending on the sprayer. The boom helps to cover more area in one trip because of the wider swath.

Hoses

They are generally made up of chemical or oil resistant synthetic rubber and plastics to withstand the chemicals particularly the petroleum solvents.

Spray lance (Extension spray tube)

The lance is made up of brass and fitted to the hose in one end and with the nozzle in the other. A trigger mechanism is fitted at the joint of hose and lance. This enables to shut off the flow of the liquid.

Spraying

Spraying should not be taken up when the wind is too strong. When spraying is unavoidable, hold the nozzle close to the ground (within 50 cm) to prevent the droplets from being blown away. It is important to always walk downwind; to necessitate the spray blown off the crop is carried away from the person involved in spraying. Soil applied with herbicide should not be trampled. Maintain a constant walking speed and always walk backward while spraying. Soft materials should be used to clean the blocked nozzle. A nozzle height of about 50 cm from the target to the ground is ideal. Missing strips or overlapping spray swath should be avoided.

Herbicide drift

Herbicide drift occurs when the smaller drops in the spray are carried away from the target by wind. Vapour from the volatile herbicide is carried away during or after spraying. The drift damage is more whenever growth regulator herbicides such as 2,4-D or MCPA are sprayed. Crops like tomato and cotton are particularly sensitive to these herbicides.

Drift damage can be avoided by a) spraying at the time of light wind; b) use of large nozzle tips so that droplets size will be larger and hence spray volume is increased; c) using minimum pressure required for the nozzles to operate properly; d) lowering the spray height from the ground; and, e) leaving a wide strip of about 10 m between the crop and other fields where sensitive crops are grown.

Decontamination of sprayers

Separate sprayers are to be used for spraying herbicides. However, farmers normally use the same sprayer for insecticide, fungicide as well as herbicide. In such cases, extra care is required to avoid any possible damage to the crop. The procedure listed below should be adhered to for safer use of the sprayer for herbicide application.

- Rinse the sprayer with fresh water.
- Wash with detergent and then rinse again with water.
- When sprayed with oil-based herbicides, wash with kerosene or acetone after the wash with detergent.
- If 2,4-D salt is used, rinse for two minutes with 1% activated charcoal.
- If 2,4-D herbicide is sprayed, fill the sprayer with half cup of ammonia solution dissolved in 12-15 litres of water and allow it to remain for 18-24 hours.

Calibration of sprayer

Calibration is an important aspect in herbicide application. This is done to apply correct dose of herbicide over a given area under a given set of condition. The best way to calibrate is to spray a known area and measure the volume of the spray fluid required to cover that area. A simple formula is given below for calibration:

$$Q = \frac{V_1 - V_2}{a} x A$$

Where, Q = Quantity of water required (litre/ha); V_1 = Volume of water (litre) in the sprayer before spray; V_2 = Volume of water (litre) in the sprayer after spray; a= Measured area of spray (m^2), A= One hectare (10000 m^2)

Example: Quantity of water taken in a hand operated knapsack sprayer is 10 litres. After spraying an area of 40 m^2, the remaining water in the tank is 8 litres. Find out the quantity of water solution required to cover one hectare of field?

Quantity of spray solution required (li/ha) = $\frac{V_1 - V_2}{a} xA = \frac{10-8}{40} x10000$

$= \frac{2}{40} x10000 = 500$ litres

Area coverage

Area covered per unit hour can be calculated using the formula given below:

$$\text{Area (ha) / hour} = \frac{\text{Walking speed (metre/hour)} \times \text{Spray width (cm)}}{10000}$$

Example: A person walks with a speed of one kilometer per hour covering a swath of 0.5 m wide. How much area will he cover in one hour? Calculate the time required to spray an area of one hectare?

Area (ha) to be covered in one hour=

$$\frac{\text{walking speed (metre/hour) X spray width (cm)}}{10000}$$

$$= \frac{1 \text{ X } 1000 \text{ X } 0.5}{10000}$$

$$= 0.05 \text{ ha/hr} = 500 \text{ m}^2\text{/ hour}$$

Time required to cover one hectare $= \frac{1X\,1}{0.05} = \frac{1}{0.05}$ hour or 20 hours

ABSORPTION AND TRANSLOCATION OF HERBICIDES

The herbicide applied must be absorbed and translocated in adequate quantity to the site (s) of action.

Absorption of herbicides

The process of penetration of herbicides into the plant tissue is called as absorption. Absorption of herbicides depends on the method of application (soil or foliage applied) and the plant part with which the chemical comes into contact.

Soil applied herbicides

Absorption of herbicides from soils is usually associated with roots of plants. The primary absorbing region of a root lies between 5 and 50 cm behind the root tip. Water soluble herbicides are also absorbed by rhizomes, stolons and tubers of perennial plants. From root hairs and cortex, ascend of herbicides takes place via transpiration stream.

Herbicides are absorbed both by passive and active mechanisms. Passive absorption involves the diffusion of substances through the plasma membranes and is controlled by the electrochemical potential gradient across plasmalemma and tonoplast membranes of cytoplasm. The active absorption is energy requiring mechanism. Depending upon the chemical and physical nature of the herbicides, they are absorbed by one or both these mechanisms.

Foliage applied herbicides

Post-emergence herbicides are applied on the foliage. The amount of herbicide reaching the plant surface and then adhering on the foliage depends on the leaf orientation, density of plant canopy, leaf pubescence, surface waxiness and surface tension of the spray solution. The cuticle covers the surfaces of all epidermal cells of the above ground shoot systems. Cuticle is the most significant barrier to herbicide absorption into shoot tissue. The cuticle composition, structure and development affect the herbicide penetration movement through plant cuticle.

Trichomes or leaf hairs present on the plant surfaces are also involved in foliar absorption of herbicides. They provide a microclimate which can alter the drying time of aqueous sprays and thus the pattern of absorption.

Herbicide entry also takes place through stomata opened at the time of application. Stomata are more on the lower surface of leaves and hence stomatal absorption is greater in the lower surface. The cuticle over the guard cell appears thinner and more permeable. The spray solution conceivably moves through the pore of open stomata. Aquous solutions do not penetrate stomata and hence addition of wetting agent is required to lower the surface tension and improve spreading of herbicide solution on the leaf surface. Under favourable conditions, herbicide entry through stomata is comparable with uptake through cuticle.

Stems of plants also play a useful role in absorbing herbicides. The degree of absorption depends on the growth and stage of development of the plant. Penetration through young and immature stem is more rapid than through the mature stem. Entry of herbicides through the bark of woody plant is very difficult. Oily herbicides permeate through the bark rapidly and reach the site of action but aqueous herbicides fail to absorb through the brown bark. Hence herbicide entry is made in woody plants by mechanical cuts or by injection.

Translocation of herbicides

Once the herbicide is absorbed into root or shoot tissue, further movement must occur before reaching the site of action. Movement of herbicides may occur either through apoplast or through symplast. Apoplast is the interconnecting cell walls and intercellular spaces. Symplast is the system of interconnected protoplasm excluding vacuoles. Herbicide movement in cell walls can be by diffusion or with mass flow of water. Once absorbed into the cell, the herbicides move into appropriate conducting tissues for their translocation to distinct plant parts. Apoplastic movement takes place predominantly through the xylem and intercellular spaces. The symplast includes the phloem transportation mechanisms. The soil-applied herbicides are absorbed by the root or shoot and penetrate into the xylem. The root mobile herbicides translocate acropetally along the transpiration stream, reaching all live leaves, both mature and immature above the point of application. The phloem mobile herbicides move along with photosynthates in phloem tubes. Along with food material, the herbicides are translocated in plants from source to sink such as growing points, young leaves, fruits, roots and rhizomes.

Factors affecting herbicide absorption and translocation

The degree of absorption and translocation can govern the efficiency of weed control. Only a small portion of the applied herbicide reaches the site of action. A number of factors affect and modify the absorption and translocation of herbicides. They are plant, soil, climatic and chemical factors.

Plant factors

Plant factors such as branching habit, plant surface, stage of maturity and type of crop and cultivar used influence the absorption and translocation. Most of the broadleaved species have open or horizontal branching habit. This helps in retention of spray droplets and easy surface coverage. Grass species have minutely ridged surface on the leaves and the growing regions are covered with sheath. Hence, non-polar herbicides are most effective against grasses. Most of the leaf surfaces and stems are covered with waxy and fatty substances and restrict the entry of herbicides. Addition of wetting agents in the sprays may result in lowering surface tension and better spread of the chemical.

Absorption and translocation of herbicide depend on the maturity of plants. Uptake is greater in the actively growing meristematic tissues. Rapid growth of shoot and root also favour absorption.

There is difference in absorption and translocation between crops and cultivars used. For example, cotton is moderately tolerant to prometryn while soybean is sensitive. This is because of uniform distribution of the chemical in the entire plant of soybean compared to cotton.

Climatic conditions

The climatic condition during and after the herbicide application has greater influence on the absorption and translocation of herbicides. Higher temperature results in adverse effect on the metabolic and physiological activities of the plants affecting absorption and translocation of herbicides. Higher relative humidity improves the leaf water content and facilitates free movement of the herbicides. Generally increase in temperature from 22 °C to 32 °C results in higher uptake and translocation of herbicides. Rainfall has greater effect on the effectiveness of applied herbicides. Rainfall immediately after herbicide application may wash off the spray deposits. Polar herbicides such as dalapon, 2,4-D salts and maleic hydrazide are highly soluble in water and penetrate very slowly with the receipt of rainfall within 4-6 hours of spraying. However, herbicides like paraquat and 2,4-D ester penetrate rapidly and are not much affected due to rainfall even within one hour of application. Oil emulsions or herbicides formulated in oil are less affected by rainfall. Wind can accentuate the action of contact herbicides like paraquat whenever high temperature and low humidity prevail. Wind also causes reduction in absorption due to rapid drying of spray solution on the foliage.

Soil factors

Movement of soil-applied herbicides is affected by roots and shoots. Soil moisture stress and temperature affect the permeability of roots to water and herbicide solution. High moisture stress coupled with high temperature greatly reduces the rate of penetration of herbicides molecules. Soil moisture stress also reduces the entry and translocation of foliage applied herbicides due to increased thickness of cuticle. Most of the herbicides remain in the ionic form in the soil between pH 4.3 and 7.5. The increase in pH increases the concentration of ionic forms of herbicides. Soil organic matter and type of clay mineral influence the movement, availability and absorption of herbicides in the soil.

Chemical nature

Herbicide concentration, pH of herbicide solution and chemical structure affects the herbicide absorption by the plant tissues. Use of surfactants (adjuvants) enhances the absorption of aqueous solutions of polar herbicides. Several surfactants can be used in the herbicide spray to enhance foliage retention, penetration, absorption and translocation of post emergence herbicides.

Adjuvants

Adjuvants are materials that facilitate action of a herbicide or that facilitate or modify characteristics of herbicide formulation or spray solution. One or more adjuvants may be included in the herbicide formulations and also in the spray mixture.

Adjuvants are classified into different groups: (i) activator adjuvants: surfactants, wetting agents, penetrants and oil; (ii) spray-modifier adjuvants: stickers, film formers, spreaders, spreader-stickers, deposit builders, thickening agents and foams; (iii) utility moidifiers: emulsifiers, dispersants, stabilizing agents, coupling agents, co-solvents, compatibility agents, buffering agents and anti- form agents.

The surfactant (adjuvant) molecules have the components of (i) polar hydrophilic segment which is readily soluble in water and (ii) lipophilic portion which is water insoluble and comparatively non-polar.

Hydrophobic - lipophobic balance (HLB): These numbers are an index used to suggest the applicability of surfactants as emulsifiers, detergents and increasingly as activator adjuvants. HLB values are used in a practical manner to match compatible oil phases and surfactants of mixtures by selecting components with the same HLB number for trial emulsions. (Table 7.5) Surfactants used as activator are marketed as liquids and they usually contains 50-90% active ingredient with HLB values of 10-13.

TABLE 7.5: Hydrophobic- lipophobic balance range

HLB range	Dispersibility or soluability of surfactant in water
1-3	No dispersibility in water
3-6	Poor dispersion
6-8	Milky dispersion after vigorous agitation
8-10	Stable milky dispersion
10-13	Translucent to clear dispersion
>13	Clear solution

***Source*:** Duke (1987)

An important property of surfactants in herbicide spray is that they retain water and act as humectants. Surfactant concentration applied with herbicides would normally be less than 0.5% and almost certainly only minute amounts of this would be translocated within the plant.

Wetting and spreading agents: Wetting agents are the substances which make the herbicide to get contact with the waxy leaf surfaces. Most of the wetting agents are also spreading agents and help in uniform spreading and easy penetration. Spreading agents reduce the angle of contact between the liquid drop and leaf surface.

Emulsifiers: They are also known as stabilising agents and help in maintaining the stability of an emulsion. Most of the herbicides in liquid formulations are emulsions of oil-in-water type.

Thickening and sticking agents: These improve the viscosity of the spray film and increase spray adherence on the leaves and thus reduce run off from spray. Many thickening agents are also sticking agents (stickers).

Penetrants: They improve the absorption and penetration of herbicides by solubilizing the waxy culticular cell wall.

Humectants: These chemicals prevent the rapid drying of herbicides by raising the humidity between the herbicide and leaf surface.

Dispersing agents: They tend to reduce cohesion between like particles and promote easy separation of like particles, causing deflocculation.

Fertilizer additives: Small quantities of fertilizer materials are added with herbicides to enhance absorption of aqueous herbicides.

e.g. ammonium sulphate and dihydrogen phosphate. Addition of small quantity of ammonium sulphate with glyphosate enhances its activity against *Cyperus* sp.

BIOCHEMICAL PROCESSES OF HERBICIDES IN PLANT TISSUES

Herbicides have effect on various biochemical processes in the plants. These processes depend on particular herbicides, plant species, formulation, method of application and climatic conditions like temperature, humidity, etc. The major biochemical responses to herbicides are: (i) respiration and mitochondrial electron transport, (ii) photosynthesis and Hill reaction, (iii) nucleic acid metabolism and protein synthesis and (iv) lipid metabolism to a lesser extent.

Respiration and mitochondrial electron transport

Mitochondria are the cellular organelles in which respiration takes place. Plant cells typically contain 500 to 1000 mitochondria. Electron transport and phosphorylation pathways occur in mitochondria. Most of the herbicides interfere with mitochondrial activity. Some herbicides completely inhibit ATP synthesis without interfering with electron transport. *e.g.* dinitrophenol (DNP), dinosam, dinoseb, PCP. Some other herbicides are inhibitors of energy transfer reactions which interfere in phosphorylating electron transport in the energy coupling chain and thus inhibit the phosphorylation process. Electron transport inhibition is yet another form of affecting the respiratory process by some other herbicides. They characteristically interrupt electron flow along the electron transport chain. *e.g.* pyrichlor and diphenyl ethers. Apart from the effects associated with electron transport and ATP synthesis, effects on glycolysis and pentose phosphate pathway have also been observed.

Photosynthesis

Photosynthesis inhibitors are widely employed as herbicides today. Herbicides inhibit photosynthetic process in different ways: (i) interference with the reproduction development, structure and integrity of chloroplasts, (ii) interference in the light reactions involved in the conversion of light energy into chemical energy and (iii) inhibition of biosynthetic pathways concerned with the production of photosynthetic products.

Most of the herbicides show high affinity for chloroplasts and carotenoid synthesis is a favorite herbicide target. This results in leaf chlorosis as a result of chlorophyll degradation in the light when carotenoid synthesis is blocked. Some of the herbicides modify the chloroplast structure by direct or indirect biochemical mechanisms.

Herbicides act as inhibitors of light reactions through their effects as (a) electron transport inhibitors, (b) uncouplers, (c) energy transfer inhibitors (d) inhibitory uncouplers and (e) electron acceptors. Electron transport inhibitors act by removal or inactivation of one or more of the intermediate electron transport carriers. Examples are chlorinated phenyl ureas, bicarbanates, chlorinated triazines and substituted uracils. These compounds act at a single site on the photochemical pathway. The uncouplers dissociate electron transport from ATP formation and inhibit phosphorylation. The energy transfer inhibitors act on phosphorylation process by inhibiting both electron transport and ATP synthesis in coupled system. The inhibitory uncouplers act on more than one site as they inhibit electron transport or act as uncouplers. Examples are N-phenylcarbamates, nitriles, etc. Electron acceptors are compounds which compete with some components of the electron transport pathway. Examples of electron acceptors are diquat, paraquat.

Nucleic acid and protein metabolism

Cell division, nucleic acid metabolism and protein synthesis are essential for plant growth and development. Herbicides may act directly or indirectly on these reactions by inhibiting ATP synthesis and neucleic acid or protein synthesis. Cell division is affected by a number of herbicides. They act on spindle formation and inhibit cell wall formation. Examples are N- phenyl carbonate, dinitroaniline, diallate and CDAA. Haloalkanoic acids interfere with the meristematic activity of root tips and apical meristems, modify protein structure, enzyme and membrane permeability. Secondary effects include change in carbohydrate, lipid and nitrogen metabolism. Application of dalapon reduces the content of amino acid in *Cynodon dactylon*.

Lipid metabolism

Lipids occur in plants in the form of true fat, phospholipids and waxes. Herbicide affects lipid biosynthesis and physicochemical properties of the epicuticular or cuticular waxes, permeability of cell or organelle membrane and storage of fat. Herbicides such as TCA and dalapon may affect the lipid metabolism and cuticle wax deposition on peas and maize and render the leaves more wettable to subsequent sprays.

TRANSFORMATION OF HERBICIDES IN PLANTS

Once the herbicide molecule finds its place in the living tissue of a plant like phlasmolemma, a number of biochemical changes take place. Herbicide molecule alters the metabolism of plant and the plant itself degrades the structure and activity of the herbicide molecules. Both these changes are utmost important since the herbicide molecule either becomes phytotoxic or non-toxic indicating selectivity. A wide variety of chemical reactions take place and most of them are considered to be catalyzed by specific enzymes. However, non- enzyme changes have also been reported.

Non enzymatic chemical reactions

Degradation of herbicide molecule in plant is mostly brought about by enzymatic reactions. There are stray instances of non-enzymatic reactions also. The classic example is the transformation of simazine and similar halogenated triazines into inactive hydroxy compounds. The non-enzymatic reactions may completely convert the herbicide molecule into a non-toxic metabolite. Then the herbicide molecule may accumulate or get converted. Depending upon the accumulation and disappearance, tolerance or susceptibility results in.

Enzymatic reactions

The type of enzymatic reactions involved in herbicide degradation in plant are oxidation, decarboxylation, deamination, dehalogenation, dethioation, dealkalylation, hydrolysis, hydroxylation and conjugation. Any one or more of the reactions act at the same time on the herbicides to bring about degradation.

Oxidation

Phenoxy herbicides offer an example of oxidation reactions.

Decarboxylation

A number of herbicides including phenoxy, benzoic and urea derivatives undergo decarboxylation. This reaction requires a molecule of water.

Hydroxylation

The herbicides involved in this reaction are the derivatives of phenoxy, benzoic and triazine groups. In phenoxy herbicides, ring hydroxylation occurs accompanied by a shift in the position of a chlorine atom on the ring. Ring hydroxylation of triazine herbicides may involve dechlorination demetoxylation.

Hydrolysis

This is a common mechanism of degradation in higher plants. This involves a major split in the compound to form two relatively large fragments which are non- phytotoxic. These may further break down into simpler substances. Herbicides that are degraded by this way include phenoxy alkanoic acids, carbamates, thiocarbamates, ureas and triazines.

Dealkylation

Substitution of alkyl (or alkyloxy) group in the herbicide molecule is an important mechanism of detoxification and acts as a basis for selectivity. Dealkylation and dealkyl- oxylation reactions have been found to occur in a number of herbicide groups which include dinitroaniline, carbamates, thiocarbamates, ureas and triazines.

Conjugation

The conjugation of a herbicide into degradation products with the endogenous plant constituents have been reported. The commonly involved conjugates are sugars, aminoacids, protein and lignin. Simple conjugates of herbicides with sugars or amino acids are generally soluble in the extracting solvent and readily detected.

Ring cleavage

Generally, the ring structure of many herbicides of both aromatic and heterocyclic structure split following their entry into the plant. This takes place very slowly. Though various substitutions on the ring are broken off, the ring itself may persist as a non-toxic compound throughout the life of plant.

FATE OF SOIL APPLIED HERBICIDES

Herbicides applied to the soil are dissipated or removed in different ways:

1. Uptake and metabolism
2. Volatilization
3. Photodecomposition
4. Chemical decomposition
5. Absorption by the soil colloids
6. Leaching
7. Degradation by soil microorganisms

Uptake and metabolism

Only a small portion of the applied herbicides is absorbed and retained by the plants. The germinating weeds and seedlings absorb the chemical and are killed. A part of the herbicide absorbed by crop plant is retained in the edible parts of the plant such as grains. The rest is returned to the soil through crop residues. The residues of herbicides in harvested produce are in very low undetectable quantity of less than one ppm.

Volatilization

A number of herbicides volatilize readily from soil surface and lost to the atmosphere as volatile gases. The ester form of 2,4-D is volatile and the vapours or fumes frequently cause injury to susceptible crops like tomato or cotton. The herbicide may move into the porous soil as a volatile gas. Example is EPTC which volatilize from a free liquid surface at the rate of 57 μg per sq.cm of surface area per hour at 30 °C. Herbicides like trifluralin and fluchloralin are lost by volatilization. About 90 % of the trifluralin applied to the soil surface is lost within 2-3 days after application during summer. Herbicides with very low vapour pressure may be lost from a surface over an extended period of time especially if exposed to high temperature. The loss of herbicides as volatilization is reduced once it is adsorbed by the soil. Hence it is important to incorporate the herbicides into the soil immediately after application.

Photodecomposition

Photodecomposition or decomposition by light is reported by some herbicides. Herbicides such as trifluralin, monuron, chloramben and PCP are prone to photodecomposition and hence can be applied in the evening or incorporated into the soil.

Chemical decomposition

It includes oxidation, reduction, hydrolysis and hydration. Chemical decomposition destroys some of the herbicides and activates others. Sesone (Sodium 2,4-dichlorophenoxy ethyl sulphate) is quickly hydrolysed to 2,4-dichlorophenoxy ethanol when applied to moist soil. Potassium cyanate and dalapon are slowly hydrolized in the presence of water.

Adsorption by soil colloids

Soil clay colloids have unusual adsorptive capacity. Many clay particles resemble the negative radical of an acid such as SO_4^{--} and attract the positive ions (cations). Organic colloids have a very high adsorptive capacity. Soils containing high organic matter require relatively large amounts of pre-emergence herbicides and soil sterilants for effective weed control. High organic matter content in the soil tends to hold the herbicides for a longer period of time than sand. Soils having high clay content also require more herbicide.

Leaching

Some of the herbicides may be removed from the soil by leaching. The extent of herbicide that is leached is determined by the solubility of the herbicide in water, amount of water passing downward through the soil and adsorptive capacity of soil for the herbicide. Leaching losses are more in light soils. Herbicides such as 2,4-D sodium salt, dalapon, TCA, etc., are highly soluble and have to be avoided in coarse textured soils.

Microbial degradation

Some of the herbicides are easily decomposed and utilized by the microorganisms. The soil microorganisms have the capacity to detoxify and inactivate the herbicides present in the soil. Soil-applied herbicides tend to lose their activity fastest in a neutral soil where the microbial activity is the greatest. Among the microorganisms, bacteria predominate in detoxification of herbicides. The microbes use carbonaceous organic matter for their energy requirement for degradation. This results in the release of CO_2 during microbial degradation of herbicides.

HERBICIDE RESIDUES

A number of herbicides are recommended for field crops. Continuous application of herbicides to each crop in the intensive cropping system may lead to residue accumulation in soil and crop. This causes considerable health hazards and environmental pollution. Residue studies are essential to determine the duration of herbicidal efficacy and effect on follow up crop. Such studies have to be conducted in different soil and agro-climatic conditions. It is always advisable to study the residue at optimum and higher dosage of herbicide application.

Preliminary investigation is required in green house using an indicator plant. However, it is important to analyse the soil sample chemically using sensitive instrumentation techniques. The analysis should be carried out at regular intervals till harvest to get an idea about the rate of degradation of herbicides. The study should also include the fate of the parent molecule in the soil.

Collection of soil sample for residue studies should be done in such a way that atleast 5% of the surface area is covered. Though the depth of sampling is confined to top 15 cm, soil collected from different depths should also be analysed. Adsorption and leaching behaviour of herbicide in soil are the important aspects that should also be studied.

Bioassay technique

Bioassay is a major tool for qualitative and quantitative determination of herbicide residual effect. In this method, the property of a chemical is measured in terms of some biological responses. Sensitive plant species called as indicator/ test species are used for conducting bioassay.

The major advantage of this technique is that the procedure followed is generally more economical and easy to perform. Costly equipment is not required.

Indicator plants: Bioassay is conducted following various procedures such as root and shoot bioassay, cotyledon disc bioassay, etc. Bioassay using sensitive plant species is common in determining the herbicide residues. The test plants used for some of the common herbicides are given in the Table 7.6.

TABLE 7.6: Indicator plants commonly used for bioassay techniques

Herbicide	Indicator plants
Atrazine	Soybean, oats, cucumber
2,4-D	Mustard, cucumber
Oxadiazon	Sorghum
Fluchloralin	Minor millets
Pendimethalin	Minor millets
Simazine	Oats, mustard

The indicator/ sensitive plant is grown in a field or extracts of soil and is compared with that of similar plant grown in untreated soil/ extract. A response curve is drawn between inhibition/ injury/kill vs dosage. To get an idea about leaching/movement, soil samples collected from different depths of the field (0-5, 5-10, 10-15 cm) are used for pot studies using the plant species.

Instrumentation techniques in estimation of herbicide residue

Different instrumentation techniques are used in determining herbicide residues. They are: (i) spectrophotometry, (ii) thin layer chromatography (TLC), (iii) gas chromatography (GC) or gas liquid chromatography (GLC), (iv) high performance liquid chromatography (HPLC).

Spectrophotometry

The principle involved in this technique is the interaction of electromagnetic radiation with the matter. Spectrophotometers are widely used for the radiant spectrum of 340 to 625 µm, while UV spectrophotometers are used for the spectrum range of 165 and 205 µm. Due to the advent of improved instrumentation techniques, this method is not widely used in herbicide residue estimation.

Thin layer chromatography (TLC)

This technique was originally profounded by Izmailov and Straiber (1938) and was later perfected by Stahl (1958). It is a simple, rapid technique with less cost involvement. The sensitivity range is about 5-500 µg. This technique is mainly used for comparison of residues following initial screening and quantification by GC. This method is more applicable for polar herbicides which are not suitable to be analysed with GC derivative formation. Isolation of molecular species is the main function of TLC and hence is an important supplement to GLC in the identification of natural products and related compounds. This technique involves the use of glass plate coated with absorbents (silica gel, alumina, etc) as stationary phase and solvents as mobile phase. Solvent system is useful for separation of a wide range of pesticides. Benzene mixed with varying amounts of ethanol is used for polar compounds; hexene for non-polar compounds. Chromatogram is carried out in a development chamber, saturated with solvent vapours. Deduction is achieved by spraying suitable chromogenic reagent. Rapid semi-quantitative estimation can be achieved by visual comparison of sample and standard spot size and / or intensities.

Gas chromatography (GC) or gas liquid chromatography (GLC)

This technique provides quantitative identification, isolation and separation of organic herbicide residue. Structure of the chemical compounds, mechanism and minetics of chemical reactions can be studied. It is possible to determine the physico-chemical measurement (isotherms, heat of solution), specific surface of solids and elementary analysis of organic substances. In multi-residue analysis, GLC is the only method of choice. The basic modules in a modern GLC are gas assembly, sample injector, chromatographic columns, deductors and recorder and integrators.

Gas assembly

Cylinders are fitted with a double stage pressure regulator from which the carrier gas (mobile phase) is supplied. Most commonly used carrier gases are nitrogen, argon, helium, neon and carbon-di-oxide. Uses of the gases enable non-interference either with the stationary phase or with the components of the sample.

Sample injector

It is used to inject the sample very rapidly and in a reproducible manner into the column. Normally one microlitre syringe is used.

Column

The best column material is silanzied glass. This avoids adsorption and thermal decomposition of the sample. Columns are with dimension of 1-2 m in length and 1-2 mm in width. Materials such as Methyl silicone coated on inert absorbents are packed in the column. They separate the compounds according to their molecular configuration.

Detectors

The prime task of the detector is to sense the components which appear in the carrier gas as it emerges from the column. The detector should be so sensitive to trace very meagre content (μg to ρg) of the pesticide. The detector senses the changes in certain physical or chemical property of the effluent gas stream on the appearance of the components. Specific detectors are used to improve the quality of experimental results and to minimize sample clean up. Some of the common detectors in use are:

i) Thermal conductivity detector (TCD)
ii) Flame ionization detector (FID)
iii) Electron capture detector (ECD)
iv) Flame photometric detector (FPD)

Recorders and integrators

A single pen ink potentiometric recorder furnishes chromatogram as the result of the analysis. Currently computerized integrators are used which help to improve the speed and accuracy of the results.

High performance liquid chromatography (HPLC)

The use of liquid chromatography dates back to 1903, when Michael Iswell, a Russian chemist, presented the results on the separation of chlorophyll pigments using a chalk column. Martin and Synge (1941) later profounded the theoritical basis for the separation mechanism.

Classical liquid chromatography consists basically of a high pressure pumping system, narrow bore short columns packed with stationary phase and an on-line highly sensitive detector system.

Many of the newer classes of pesticides are inherently difficult to be quantitated by GC due to their thermal instability, involatality or lack of sensitivity when element specific detectors are used. These problems can frequently be overcome by a judicious use of derivatisation procedures. Derivatisation is a standard practice for acidic herbicides which are considered as the prime candidates for HPLC analysis.

ASSESSING THE EFFICACY OF HERBICIDES

Herbicides may be assessed both for its effectiveness and phytotoxicity as described below:

Effectiveness

For assessing the effectiveness of a herbicide, observation on weed population and dry matter accumulation should be recorded at specified intervals (weekly, fortnightly or monthly). This should be done atleast from two quadrates in each sampling plot.

Indices for the efficacy of herbicides: Some of the indices worked out to find out the efficacies of a particular method of weed control are:

Weed control efficiency (WCE)

This gives the efficiency of a particular method of weed control.

$$\text{WCE} = \frac{Wpc - Wpt}{Wpc} \times 100$$

Where, Wpc = Weed population in unweeded control plot and Wpt = Weed population in treated plot.

Weed index (WI)

This gives the impact of weed control method on crop yield.

$$\text{WI} = \frac{X - Y}{X} \times 100$$

Where, X = Yield from weed free plot and Y = Yield from treated plot.

Weed smothering efficiency (WSE)

This is worked out to find out the effect of intercrops on the smothering of weeds.

$$WSE = \frac{WDS - WDI}{WDS}$$

Where, WDS = Weed dry matter in sole crop and WDI = Weed dry matter in the intercrop.

Phytotoxicity

Phytotoxicity of a particular herbicide could be assessed by taking observations on seed germination (in the case of pre- emergence herbicides), plant height, number of tillers (in tillering crops), dry matter production and final grain and straw yield. Phytotoxicity of herbicides may also be assessed by visual observations, particularly for post-emergence herbicides. These observations may be taken by more than 3 persons and the average is arrived for proper assessment. Scoring may be done from 1-10 for making comparative assessment (Table 7.7).

In addition to assessing the damage to the foliage, it is also important to note down the time required for recovery.

TABLE 7.7: Rating scale

Injury (%)	Rating
1-10	1
11-20	2
21-30	3
31-40	4
41-50	5
51-60	6
61-70	7
71-80	8
81-90	9
91-100	10

HERBICIDE RECOMMENDATION FOR FIELD CROPS

The choice of the herbicides differs with the crops. Herbicides should be used at the correct dosage to get the maximum effect. The herbicides recommended for important field crops are given in the Table 7.8.

TABLE 7.8: Herbicide recommendation for the field crops

Crops	Herbicide Recommendation (kg a.i./ha)
Rice (Rainfed/upland)	Oxadiazon/nitrofen/thiobencarb 1.0 kg/ha; Propanil 2-3 kg/ha -20 DAS.

Crops	Herbicide Recommendation (kg a.i./ha)
Transplanted	Anilophos 0.4 kg/ha
	Thiobencarb/butachlor 1.0 kg/ha
	Fluchloralin 1.0 kg/ha + 2,4-D -0.5 kg/ha
Wheat	Pendimethalin 0.75-2.0 kg/ha
	Oxyflourfen 0.30 kg/ha
	Isoproturon 0.75- 1.25 kg/ha- post emergence
Maize	Atrazin 0.5 kg /ha/ thiobencarb/ alachlor/ prometryn/ isoproturon / pendimethalin - 1.0 to 1.5 kg/ha
Sorghum	Metribuzin 0.25 kg/ha; atrazin 0.25-0.5 kg/ha
	Thiobencarb/ pendimethalin / alachlor -1.0 kg/ha
Redgram	Metribuzin 0.25 kg/ha, fluchloralin 0.5 kg/ha
	Alachlor / nitrofen at 1.0 kg/ha
Blackgram	Thiobencarb 1.0 kg/ha
Greengram	Thiobencarb 1.0 kg/ha
	Pendimethalin 0.75 kg/ha
Gram	Fluchloralin 1.5 kg/ha
	Oxyfluorfen 0.15 kg/ha
	Terbutryn 0.75 kg/ha
	Metalachlor 1.0 kg/ha
Soybean	Fluchloralin 1.0 kg/ha
	Alachlor/ metribuzin/oxyfluorfen 1.0 kg/ha
Groundnut	Pre-plant
	Fluchloralin 1.5 kg/ha
	Trifluralin 0.75 kg
	Pre- emergence
	Pendimethalin 0.5-1.5 kg/ha
	Alachlor 1.0-1.5 kg
	Oxadiazon 1.0 kg
	Butachlor 2.0 kg
Sunflower	Pre-emergence
	Pendimethalin 1.0 kg
	Oxadiazon 0.5 kg
	Thiobencarb 1.5 kg/ha
	Pre-plant
	Fluchloralin 0.5 kg/ha
Sesame	Alachlor 1.0 kg /ha
	Thiobencarb 2.0 kg/ha
Rapeseed- Mustard	Pendimethalin or butachlor 1.0 kg/ha
Cotton	Diuron 0.5-1.5 kg/ha
	Fluchloralin 1 kg /ha
	Pendimethalin 0.75 kg/ha
	Alachlor 1.2-3.0 kg/ha

Crops	Herbicide Recommendation (kg a.i./ha)
Sugarcane	Atrazine 1.0 kg/ha
	Atrazine 1.0 kg/ha + paraquat 0.50 kg/ha
Jute and Mesta	Fluchloralin 1.0 kg/ha
	Dalapon 3 kg / ha + MSMA 2.25 kg/ha
Hybrid napier	2,4-D at 1 kg/ha as post -emergence
Berseem	Isoproturon 1.0 kg/ha as post- emergence
Lucerne	Trifluraline/ EPTC / dalapan 4 kg/ha

INTEGRATED WEED MANAGEMENT

Integrated weed management involves the utilization of a combination of physical, chemical and cultural methods of weed control in a well-planned sequence so designed as not to affect the ecosystem. The best-integrated weed management practices are those that take into account the crop grown, weed infestation and the farmers' socio-economic environment. Appropriate weed control methods are some of the potential considerations that determine the successful exploitation of the integrated weed control approach. Integrated weed management has the following advantages: (i) shifts of crop-weed competition in favour of crops, (ii) preventing weed shift towards perennial nature, (iii) no danger of herbicide residue, (iv) avoiding environmental pollution and (v) realising higher net return. Integrated approach for weed control using chemical and mechanical methods has been in practice for several crops to achieve better weed control efficiency.

Most problematic weeds require judicious amalgamation of the maximum components of management (mechanical, biological and chemical integration) simultaneously or at different times. Different cultural practices involved in a cropping system strongly influence the composition of weed flora. For example changing from rice-wheat sequence to any other sequence not involving rice in rainy season tends to reduce the population of *Phalaris minor* in wheat.

MANAGEMENT OF PARASITIC AND PROBLEM WEEDS

Striga (witch weed)

This root parasite infests a number of crops of *Gramineae* family particularly sorghum, maize and sugarcane. When the weed population is high, they completely suppress the crop growth, causing heavy yield loss. This parasitic weed gives a serious problem in the whole of Asia and Africa. The yield loss ranges from 15 to 75% depending on the severity of infestation. In India, five species of Striga are known to occur (Hosamani,1978). They are *S. lutea, S. angustifolia, S. densiflora, S. gesnerioides, and S. sulphurea.* Among them, *S. lutea* (Fig. 7.5) causes economic loss in agriculture, particularly in crops like sorghum and millets.

FIG. 7.5: *Striga lutea*

Striga control can be achieved by adopting different measures such as inducing the germination of the seeds, by rotating with trap crops, destroying the emerged weeds by tillage and with herbicides. Trap crops produce chemical stimulants to induce the germination of the weed seeds. Trap crops such as soybean, cotton, cowpea, groundnut, chickpea and pigeopea can be used in rotation with sorghum, maize or millets. Post-emergence herbicides such as 2,4-D, MCPA or paraquat can be used to kill the emerged weeds. Pre-emergence application of simazine or atrazine effectively controls the parasitic weed in maize, sorghum and sugarcane.

Cuscutta (*Cuscuta campestiris* c. *trifolii*)

It is an annual stem parasite. The shoots of the parasite, coming into contact with suitable host species, establish connection with it by producing numerous sucking organs called 'haustoria'. These organs extract water and nutrients from the host plant. If the parasite establishes a strong hold on the host, the latter is almost smothered and dies with the depletion of food. This parasitic weed affects legumes (lucerne,) niger and forest trees.

Cuscuta does not parasitize any crop of grass family and hence they may be used in rotation. Use of pre-emergence (chlorpropham at 4 kg /ha) or post- emergence (pronamide at 1.5 kg/ha) herbicides will also control the parasite.

Loranthus (Bird vine) (*Loranthus longiflorus*)

It is a stem parasite on mango and other trees. It occurs on a variety of hosts such as Albizzia, Acacia and Melia. Occasionally, it causes considerable damage to pomegranate. Because of its dense presence on the trees, control is difficult. Hand picking the parasite in the early stage of its growth is the most common method of control. Spraying of 30-40% diesel oil emulsion in soap water has also been found effective in eradicating the parasite.

Orobanche (Broom rape) (*Orobanche cernua)*

It is brown or yellowish herb, without green leaves (Fig. 7.6). This root parasitic weed entirely depends on the host plant (tobacco) for its growth and development. Its infestation results in stunted crop growth and very poor yield. It is endemic every year, but in certain years it attains epidemic proportion. Orobanche occurs at an intensity of 4.3 to 7.3 shoots per diseased plants. Growth inhibition and yield loss in tobacco is to the tune of 50% with an infestation of 7.3 shoots per host plant.

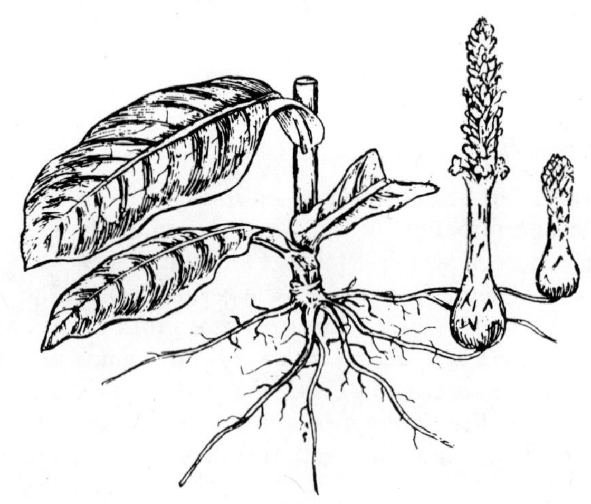

FIG. 7.6: *Orobanche cernua*

Hand removal is the quick method of control of orobanche but is very laborious and expensive. Trap crop can be very well used in rotation to control the weed. The trap crops are sunflower, sesame, cotton, soybean and finger millet. These crops stimulate germination of the parasitic weed. But the infected weed dies either during the filamentous stage or during the subterranean button sized growth stage without any subsequent emergence into flowering shoot. Application of kerosene at the tip of emerging orobanche arrests its growth. Though chemical weed control is not very effective, application of post-emergence herbicides 2,4-D sodium ethyl sulphate or alleyl alcohol at 0.1 to 0.2 % has given high percentage of control.

Nutsedge (*Cyperus rotundus*, L.)

It is an obnoxious weed distributed throughout the tropical and temperate zones of the world. It is found in almost all types of soils under adequate moisture condition. The growth is congenial with the atmospheric temperature of 26-30 °C and at 70-90 %. RH. Ample moisture in the soil is conductive for the spread of the weed. Weed growth is suppressed at low temperature during winter. The weed competes with the field crops for various environmental resources. It secretes toxic substances which affect the crop growth adversely.

Deep ploughing and exposure of the underground tubers and rhizomes to sun, removal of weeds through manual labourers is required. The tubers and rhizomes exposed to the solar heat may result in moisture depletion below the critical limit and they die ultimately. Nutsedge is sensitive to light and could be suppressed in shade. A quick growing crop which will cover the canopy may minimize the infestation satisfactorily. It has been noticed that by growing a green manure crop, dhaincha continuously for three years under dhaincha- potato - wheat sequence, the aerial shoots and tubers of this grass declined by 41.9 and 53.1 % respectively.

Glyphosate, a non-selective herbicide @ 1 kg/ha either with 0.05% 2,4-D sodium salt or with 1% ammonium sulphate is more effective in the suppression of this weed.

Bermuda grass (*Cynodon dactylon*)

This perennial grass occurs throughout the tropical, sub-tropical and semi-arid regions of the world. It reproduces by creeping rootstock and seeds. Rooting occurs at the prostrate nodes. The decayed residues of the weed inhibit seed germination, root and top growth of crops (*e.g.* barley). In addition to the depletion of nutrients, moisture, soil aeration, light and space, it also becomes alternate host for many pest and diseases.

Cultural methods such as summer ploughing, digging, flooding, etc. keep the weed infestation under control. Most suited herbicides for the control of the weed are: dalapon or TCA (2-4 kg/ha); Fluazi-fop-butyl or glyphosphate (1.0 kg/ha)

Parthenium (*Parthenium hysterophorus*)

This is commonly known as congress weed or wild carrot weed. It is an annual weed and reproduces through seeds and grows throughout the year. A single plant is capable of producing more than 10,000 seeds. The seeds do not have dormancy but remain viable for a long period. The plants have remarkable adaptability to environmental extremes. The herbicides/chemical that can be used as post-emergence application are atrazine 0.25 kg/ha + 2,4-D-1.25 kg/ha, paraquat-1 kg/ha, 2,4-D-1 kg/ha or 20% common salt spray.

CHAPTER 8

Dryland Agriculture and Watershed Management

In India, about 70% of arable land depends entirely on rainfall for crop production and the practice of agriculture here is called dryland farming. Drylands constitute the land both on steep slope and flat valley plains where water resources (surface and ground water) are not suffice and hence, agriculture depends on rainfall. As per the Encyclopedia Britannica, "Dryland farming consists of making the best use of a limited water supply by storing in the soil as much of the rainfall as possible and by growing suitable crop plants by methods that make the best use of this moisture".

The Fourth Five Year Plan document of India defines dry farming areas as those, which receive an annual rainfall ranging from 375 to 1125 mm and with very limited irrigation facilities. Areas, which receive less than 375 mm of average rainfall, are considered as absolutely arid or desert areas, which require special treatment.

Dryland agriculture is a system of crop farming under situations where water becomes a major limiting factor for production with no provision of any planned irrigation. Crop production is solely dependent on rainfall.

Rainfed farming is the practice of growing crops, entirely depending on rainfall as source of moisture where the mean annual rainfall is around 750 mm. The quantity of rainfall should be adequate/sufficient to meet the crop demand.

Dryland farming technology refers to cropping pattern/rotation, varieties and agronomic practices adjusted and adopted to the moisture regime of the region.

DRY FARMING - CONSTRAINTS

Rainfall is the primary and most important factor affecting productivity in drylands and the occurrence of rainfall is mostly uncertain and erratic. About 40% of cereals, 70% of finger millet and cotton, 90% pulses and oil seeds and almost 100% of millets are grown on rainfed lands. Drylands are generally poor in productivity. Most of the crops and varieties grown in drylands are subsistence oriented with low yields. The cultivars are of longer duration, photosensitive and have a low harvest index with low response to inputs such as fertilizers. Deforestation, overgrazing and unlimited cultivation on sloping lands have increased the run-off, reduced the recharge of the soil profile and ground water and caused severe soil erosion. Crop production in such area is highly marginal.

The major constraints of dry farming may be classified as follows:

- Basic resource constraints
- Socio-economic constraints
- Technological constraints

Basic resource constraints: Dryland farms have, for centuries, been the scene of frequent drought, floods and other forms of human tragedy due to erratic rainfall pattern and other natural hazards. More than 80% of the dryland farmers own less than 2 ha of land per capita. The drylands are characterized by uncertain and aberrant weather. Uncertainty and variability of rains, of both space and time, is the biggest constraint affecting agricultural production in rainfed farming. Drylands are generally low in soil fertility. The soils are universally deficient in nitrogen and frequently in phosphorus. Potash is adequate in many cases except in light textured soils or in soils under continual high production. Problems such as soil salinity or alkalinity further aggravate the situation. The average consumption of fertilizers in cropped area of drylands is less than 10 kg/ha in the 114 predominantly non-irrigated semi-arid tropical districts. In rainfed agriculture, drought stress can occur at any time during crop growth.

Socio- economic constraints: Most of the dryland farmers are poor and have very little cash reserve available. The total operation is of the subsistence type and the farmer's concern is to grow staple crops for home consumption. Dryland farmers are not able to utilize the credit facilities provided by the co-operatives and banks in areas where they exist because of their ignorance/low literacy rates.

Technological constraints: Lack of suitable genotypes capable of giving high and stable yields under rainfed conditions is a major constraint. Many farmers are unable to use inputs like fertilizers, herbicides and pesticides due to lack of adequate moisture.

Dry farming techniques

Dry farming technology is highly site-specific and will vary from region to region, depending on the type of soil and rainfall pattern in the area. The following approaches and practices may help in boosting crop production in drylands:

1. Determination of the effective growing season

2. Selection of suitable genotypes to match the rainfall pattern
3. Selecting an intercropping system to ensure sustainability of production and income
4. Creation of a local, cheap water source like a farm pond or a dug well
5. Using improved agricultural implements for timeliness and precision of operations
6. Use of moderate amounts of nutrients to starve off nutrient stress
7. Harvesting water and recycling it in the event of drought.
8. Maintaining a vigil on yield reducers like diseases, pests and weeds and controlling them effectively
9. Harvesting the crop at physiological maturity stage

SOIL CHARACTERISTICS IN DRYLANDS

Drylands occur in almost all the states in India. The major soil orders to which the soils belong to are alfisol, aridisol, inceptisol and vertisol.

Alfisols (Red soils): Alfisols are agriculturally important soils found in drylands. They are generally low in organic matter, available N and P and in a number of places, available Zn also. Available potash is usually adequate and pH of the soils ranges from 5.8 to 6.7. Rooting depth of crops is limited by the presence of compact argillic horizon. Many crops are susceptible to even moderate droughts. These soils have the characteristics of rapidly sealing the surfaces after the rainfall. Water supply in the soil is reduced by impaired infiltration due to lower conductivity. Problem of crusting affects the crop establishment.

Vertisols (Black soils): Black soils in India cover an area of about 72.9 m ha which accounts for 22.2% of the total geographical area of the country. These are generally rainfed and experience considerable fluctuations in crop production. The clay content of the soil ranges from 40 to 60%, occasionally going to as high as 80%. Organic carbon content remains low ranging from 0.3 to 0.7%. pH of the soil normally ranges from 7.5 to 8.6. Cation exchange capacity is 35-50 meq/100 g. Inversion takes place in the soil because of the cracking that is a unique feature of the vertisols or deep black soils. Vertisols are necessarily deep. The soils invariably have wide and deep shrinkage cracks and gilgai microrelief on the surface that changes with variation in the soil moisture region. The cracks remain open depending on the accretion and reduction of soil moisture by evapotranspiration. The deep black soils, because of their high clay content, expanding nature of clay and depth, have a very high water holding capacity enabling crops to withstand drought.

Laterite soils: The texture of the topsoil is loamy or clayey with many concretions. Laterite soils are generally associated wit undulating topography in regions with a relatively high annual rainfall. These soils cover 13 m.ha in India.

Alluvial soils: They are generally loamy sands or sandy loams, very deep with low clay, low water - holding capacity and also low nutrient holding capacity. The moisture and drainage characteristics of the soils are highly variable.

Sierozemic soils: These soils are sand, loamy sand and sandy loam in texture. Soil erosion through winds is common. Since these soils are light textured, water and nutrient holding capacity is less. Sub-soil salinity is common due to extreme aridity. *Kharif or rabi* cropping is possible in deep soils. But in loamy sands and sand, only the *Kharif* crops can be raised.

Submontane soils: The soils are silty loam to loam in texture and are medium to deep. Landslides and soil erosion are common.

RAINFALL CHARACTERISTICS IN DRYLAND FARMING

Rainfall is the primary and most important factor affecting productivity of drylands. Occurrence of rainfall is uncertain and erratic in nature. Rainfall in dry regions varies from 500 to 1200 mm/year. Rainfall pattern is highly erratic and undependable with frequent rainless periods, even in the rainy season. Rainfall is highly variable in space and time, especially in low rainfall years.

Variability of rainfall

The co-efficient of variation of annual rainfall is 20-30%. The distribution within the year is highly variable and cannot be predicted with any reasonable degree of confidence. Variability is also high with respect to onset and cessation of rainfall, with dry spells occurring at the vegetative and grain formation stages of crop. In places receiving average rainfall of 700 to 1000 mm, two out of 5 years have aberrant weather. This leads to variations in normal cropped area or serious failures of crops. In regions receiving a rainfall between 500 and 700 mm, nearly four out of five years have weather which is unfavourable for any type of agriculture.

Short-term rainfall probability studies may help in assessment of rainfall variability. Variability can be quantified by assessing the probability of receiving a certain amount of rainfall during a given week. This is termed as initial probability (p/w). Conditional probability provides data on the amount of rain expected to be received next week if the current week is wet {p (W/w) } or dry {P (W/d) }. There are four important variations in the behaviour of the southwest monsoon in India.

1. Commencement of rains may be quite early or considerably delayed: Normal onset of monsoon is towards the end of May over Kerala coast and by 15th July in the extreme north west part of Rajasthan. There is variability in the dates of onset of the monsoon from year to year.
2. There may be prolonged 'breaks': There will be break in the monsoon associated either with weak monsoon current or with the temporary withdrawal of the monsoon. Breaks of more than 2-3 weeks can affect the crop to varying degrees.

3. The rains may terminate considerately earlier or persist longer than usual: Withdrawal of the monsoon begins in the beginning of September in north western Rajasthan and disappears over Kerala towards the end of October. The dates of withdrawal of the monsoon vary from year to year.
4. Uneven distribution of monsoon in space and time: Monsoon may be excessive in one part of the country and deficient in another, and /or excessive during one part of the season and deficient during another.

Analysis of long term rainfall data

Long term rainfall data (more than 10 years) of the given region may be analyzed which will help in planning in dry farming agriculture. The different types of rainfall analysis are:

1. Mean standard weekly rainfall
2. Mean monthly rainfall
3. Seasonal rainfall
4. Mean annual rainfall
5. Number of rainy days (Monthly and annual)
6. Variability of rainfall
7. Rainfall probability analysis.

Mean weekly rainfall: The rainfall for each standard week over the years is worked out and the mean is arrived.

Mean monthly rainfall: Total rainfall for each month over certain number of years is calculated and mean is worked out.

Seasonal rainfall: This type of analysis will greatly help in selecting crops for each season and planning for cropping pattern in a particular place/ region. There are four predominant seasons: winter (January and February), summer (March - May), south -west monsoon (June- September) and northeast monsoon (October -December). The total rainfall for each season is separately worked out over years and the mean is arrived.

Mean annual rainfall: Mean annual rainfall is worked out as the average over the years (25 or 50 years). This will give an idea about whether the particular year has received normal or deficit rainfall based on the deviation, as given in Table 8.1.

TABLE 8.1: Deviation range of rainfall

Category	Deviation range
Excess	>19%
Normal	19% to -19%
Deficit	-19% to -59%
Scanty	<-59%

Number of rainy days: Rainfall of 2.5 mm and above received in a day is taken as one rainy day. Number of rainy days gives an idea about the distribution of rainfall in a month, season or year. More number of rainy days is an indication of better distribution of rainfall. However, this may not reflect on the distribution over a period.

In all the cases, mean is arrived over a period. Analysis of data for more number of years (25 and above) will help in drawing valid conclusions. However, if data for such a long period are not available, at least 10 years data may be taken for calculation.

Variability of rainfall

Variability of rainfall is an indication of the dependability or reliability. If variability is more, dependability is less and vice-versa. Working out the co-efficient of variation (cv) is one of the ways to find out the dependability. If the cv (%) is more, dependability is less. The cv should be within 20% and for all practical purpose, values within this limit is assumed as normal.

$$CV\% = \frac{SD}{\bar{x}} \times 100$$

Probability Analysis

Probability is the chance of occurrence of rainfall in a particular place. At least 30 years of rainfall data is required to work out the probability.

Initial probability (I.P.): This type of analysis will give an idea about the quantity of rainfall that will be received at certain probability. Normally 75% probability is taken for agricultural purpose.

$$I.P. = n \times p/100$$

Where, n = number of years of rainfall and p = probability level (75%).

Rainfall data is arranged in descending order and using the formula given above, the corresponding rainfall will be taken as I.P. For example, for 30 years of rainfall, 23 serial number of rainfall (30 x 0.75) can be taken as 75% probable rainfall.

Conditional probability: It is defined as a chance of getting a fixed quantity of rainfall in an event.

$$\text{Conditional probability} = \bar{x} - x / SD$$

Where, X = Mean rainfall for a particular standard week and X = conditional quantification of rainfall (20 or 30 mm).

This type of rainfall analysis helps in predicting the time of sowing under dryland condition. Weeks having higher percentage of probability indicate the greater chance of getting the specified quantity of rainfall.

Seasons of dry farming

The seasons in dry farming regions depend on the rainfall pattern and evaporation. There are three prominent seasons in drylands.

Humid or monsoon season: This period has the duration of 100-110 days during which period rainfall exceeds evaporation. Rainfall during this season ranges from 600 to 1000 mm/year with about 85% occurring during the monsoon period. This period has highly potential for crop production.

Cool, dry, post- harvest period: This period is about 140- 150 days and there is little or no rain. Stored soil moisture helps crop production, particularly in deep vertisols because of their high moisture-retention capacity. Crops can also be cultivated on alfisols and shallow vertisols by adopting supplemental irrigation (5-15 cm).

Hot dry season: This period extends to 100-130 days. The season is not suitable for cultivating any crop. However, land preparation can be done with one or two good rains received during this season.

Drought

Failure or occurrence or low rainfall is responsible for droughts and famines. The word 'drought' generally denotes scarcity of water in a region, whether for drinking, agriculture, or industry. The severity of drought depends on (i) intensity of aridity or degree of moisture deficiency, (ii) duration of dry spell and (iii) extent of affected area. Thornthwaite (1947) considered drought as a period of dryness *i.e.*, want of rain or water, especially such dryness of water or climate as affecting the earth and preventing the growth of plants. Based on the water budget approach, drought is defined as a condition when the amount of water needed for transpiration and direct evaporation exceeds the amount available in the soil.

CLASSIFICATION OF DROUGHT

Based on the relevance to the user, droughts are classified as: (i) meteorological drought, (ii) hydrological drought, and (iii) agricultural drought.

Meteorological drought: This classification is mainly based on rainfall. It indicates the deficiency compared to normal rainfall in a given region. The time scale may be a month, season or year. The Indian Meteorological Department defines an area as affected by drought if the meteorological division receives less than 75% of the total normal southwest monsoon. During the crop-growing season, there would be a deficiency of water to meet the demands of evapotranspiration.

Hydrological drought: A hydrological drought is due to below average rainfall and low water content in streams, reservoirs, ground water, aquifers, lakes and soils. The flow may be either superficial or underground. A hydrological drought is normally said to exist if there is a deficiency in water for hydrological purposes such as power generation, irrigation or for an industry which uses a large volume of water.

Agricultural drought: Agricultural drought is a situation when the rainfall and soil moisture are inadequate to meet the water requirement of crop for their healthy growth and maturity. Prolonged and abnormal soil moisture deficiency leads to an imbalance in crop water requirement affecting the crop growth. The extent to which a growing plant has suffered moisture deficiency or stress indicates the severity of drought. The National Commission on Agriculture (1976) considered agricultural drought to occur when soil moisture and rainfall are inadequate during the growing season to support healthy crop growth to maturity and cause crop stresses and wilting.

Drought under dry farming situation can be classified into:

1. Early season droughts associated with late commencement of sowing rains
2. Mid-season droughts associated with the failure of rains during the growing season
3. Late season droughts due to early cessation of rainy season
4. Permanent drought as a result of mismatches of the rainfall and water availability to the crops.

SOIL MOISTURE CONSERVATION TECHNIQUES

Lower rainfall in semi-arid areas compared to that in humid areas does not mean low level of soil erosion. In fact, erosion can be higher in semi-arid regions than in other regions. This is because the rainfall in semi-arid areas often has a high proportion of convective thunderstorm rain of high intensity and high erosive power. There is little protective vegetative cover, especially at the beginning of the rainy season. Soils in semi-arid areas are often vulnerable and poorly resistant to erosion because of their physical and chemical properties. There are always strong links between measures for soil conservation and measures for water conservation. Reduction of surface run off by structures or by changes in land management will also help to reduce erosion. Reducing erosion may involve preventing splash erosion and formation of crusts or breakdown of structures. All such practices will increase infiltration and help in water conservation. Soil and moisture conservation can be approached through engineering (mechanical) and agronomic measures.

Soil and moisture conservation - Mechanical measures

Contour bunding: Bunding is the most effective and widely practiced field measure for controlling or preventing erosion. Contour bunding is defined as series of mechanical barriers across the land slope to break the slope of the land on a contour. By adopting this type of contour bunds, the length of the slope and the slope degree may be reduced wherever necessary. Small bunds are constructed across the slope and cut into a series of small ones. Each contour bund acts as a barrier to the flow of water. Thus the water flow is restricted and there is possibility of impounding water, which enables increase in storage of soil moisture. This type of bunding is recommended for rolling lands with the slope of less than 6% and flat land with scanty or erratic rainfall. Medium deep black soils are quite suitable for bunding. In deep black soil, contour bunds are not recommended. Research studies at Bellary showed that contour bunds are highly unsuitable for black soils because of water stagnation and loss of area and breaches of bunds resulting in formation of fresh gullies. In soils of very shallow depth (< 7.5 cm), contour bunding is not suitable.

Graded bunds: Graded bunds or channel terraces are laid along a pre-determined longitudinal grade instead of laying along contour. The bunds are laid along the longitudinal grades and provided with a channel if necessary and hence graded bunds are also called channel terracing. The purpose of graded bunding is to make run off water to trickle rather than to rush out. Graded bunds consist of constructing wide and relatively shallow channels across the slope very near the contour ridges and at critical intervals. Bunds of 0.8 m^2 cross-section at a vertical interval of 0.7 m with a channel (grade of 0.1 to 0.25%) on the upstream side connected to a grass water way is advocated. Graded bunds generally have a grade of 0.1 to 0.5% for diverting excess water along the grade. This method of moisture conservation is highly suitable for areas with the annual rainfall of more than 800 mm. It is also quite suitable for areas of less rainfall under clay soil condition. Graded bunds are ideally suitable for most of the red soils where run-off loss is high. This practice is restricted to 6% slope and in specific cases; it may be extended to a slope of 10%.

Graded- border strips: Graded border strips are formed in between the contour bunds or graded bunds. It is a small section bund having a cross section of 0.2 m^2. The interval of bunds varies from 10-15 m with the length of 100-200 m. It is useful for deep red soils areas where the land slope is 2-3%. Graded border strips are suitable both for high and low rainfall areas.

Bench terracing: This is one of the most widely adopted mechanical measures of soil moisture conservation suitable for hilly areas with a slope of 6-33%. In this method original slope is converted into level fields and thus all hazards of erosion are eliminated. It consists of construction of step like fields along contours by half cutting and filling. Cultivation is carried out in these leveled fields.

Types of bench terracing

a) **Leveled bench terrace or tabletop:** This is suitable for areas having medium rainfall with uniform distribution and soils having high permeability rates. Normally paddy cultivation in the bench terraces require uniform leveling for impounding water. In such situations, leveled terraces are quite useful.

b) **Inward sloping bench terraces:** This type of bench terraces are most effective for high rainfall areas. Inward slope helps to drain excess water as quickly as possible. They have a drain on inner side, which has a grade along its length to convey the excess water to one side from where it is disposed-off by well-stabilized vegetated waterway. The bench terraces are widely used in Nilgiri hills of Tamil Nadu as well as steep Himalayan slope in Hamachal Pradesh and North-Eastern Hill regions. Bench terracing in the Nilgiris was observed to reduce run off by 50 % and soil loss by 98 % in the fields under potato cultivation in up and down slope. This method had provided good moisture condition throughout the year. The chances of crop failure are reduced in the bench terracing.

c) **Outward slopping bench terraces:** These types are suitable for soils having medium depth with good permeability rate. In places of low rainfall or shallow soils, outwardly sloping bench terraces are used to reduce the existing steep slope to mild slope (from 8% to 4%).

d) **Puertorican or California type of terraces:** The soil is excavated little by little during every ploughing and gradually developing benches by pushing the soil down hill against a vegetative or mechanical barrier laid along the contour.

Compartmental bunding: This method is one of the cheapest and easily manipulable soil moisture conservation techniques suitable for rainfed vertisols having slope of less than 1 %. Compartmental bunds are formed in a field with a size of 40 m^2 with the dimensions of 8x 5 m. The longest bund is usually formed across the slope while shorter bunds along the slope. By this method, the entire field is divided into small sections, which helps in storing the initial rainfall and permitting increased infiltration rate. This method ensures better germination of seeds, maintaining optimum plant stand. Compartmental bunding is suitable for short duration crops like millets, sunflower and pulses.

SOIL AND MOISTURE CONSERVATION - AGRONOMIC MEASURES

Agronomic measures of soil and moisture conservation include contour farming, dense growing crops, strip cropping, mixed cropping and vegetative barriers. These measures help in greater intake rate of water by the soil due to improve in organic matter and soil structure. There is better interception of rainwater and hence reduction in splash erosion.

Contour farming

It is a simple practice in which farming is practiced across the slope, keeping the same level, as far as possible. Planting is done across the slope and this acts as miniature barrier to the water moving over the soil surface. It has been proved that contour farming reduces run off and prevents soil erosion as compared with the up-and-down cultivation in the slope. Contour farming also conserves soil fertility and increases crop yields. Contour farming requires less power exerted by man, animals and machines.

Normally bunding is done on long slopes to reduce its length of the slope. All the cultural practices are carried out parallel to these bunds, which are laid on contour (the line passing through the points having the same level).

Close growing crops

Cultivation of close growing crops is one of the agronomic measures to reduce erosion and improve moisture conservation. Among the field crops, legumes, in general, provide better cover and hence give protection to land against erosion. Among the legumes, cowpea and mungbean give a good cover for the land during the rainy season.

Strip- cropping

In this method crops are grown in strips. Strip cropping is of different types:

1. Contour strip cropping
2. Field strip cropping
3. Wind strip cropping
4. Permanent or temporary buffer strip-cropping

a) **Contour strip cropping:** In this method, soil-exposing and erosion permitting crops are grown in strips at suitable width across the slopes on contour, alternating with strip of soil-protecting and soil resisting crops. By adopting this method of cropping the length of the slope is shortened.

This method helps in checking the movement of run-off water and increasing the absorption of rainwater by the soil. In addition, the dense foliage of the erosion-resistant crops prevents the rain from beating the soil surface directly. It is found that crops such as groundnut, mothbean and horsegram are the most efficient and suitable crops for checking erosion. These crops can be alternated with erosion permitting crops like sorghum and pearl millet. The strip width according to the slope is given in Table 8.2.

TABLE 8.2: Strip width on slope.

Slope (%)	Width of erosion permitting crop (m)	Width of erosion-resistant crops (m)
0.5 and below	45	9
1-2	24	6
2-3	13.5	4.5

b) **Field strip-cropping:** The field crops are planted in more or less suitable strips across fairly uniform slope, but not on exact contour.

c) **Wind strip- cropping:** This type of strip cropping consists of planting tall growing crops alternated with low-growing crops arranged in straight and long, but relatively narrow, parallel strips laid out right across the direction of the prevailing wind, regardless of the contour.

d) **Permanent or temporary buffer strip cropping:** The strips are established particularly in steep or highly eroded slopes in the fields. The strips are generally planted with perennial legumes, grasses or shrubs on a permanent or temporary basis. The strips do not form part of the rotation practiced in normal strip cropping.

Mixed cropping

This type of cropping is extensively followed in India. The important objectives of mixed cropping are a better and continuous cover of the land, protection against the beating action of the rain, a complete protection against soil erosion and assurance against crop failure. The roots of various species in a mixed cropping harness nutrients at different depths. Mixed cropping of wheat + gram is one of the examples which give a consistently higher yield than either of the pure crops.

Vegetative barrier

Dense vegetation is raised across the slope for making the live bunds. The vegetative barrier helps to reduce the length of field slope, check the run off velocity, improve the soil moisture, control the soil erosion and trap the silt up to some extent. Vegetative hedge is a cheaper and more permanent soil and water conservation measure than engineering measures. The vegetative hedge, *Sachharum munja* used as live bund is found to perform better under Bundelkhand condition of Uttar Pradesh, India. During the summer season, it grows well and made compact hedge for reducing the run off velocity from the initial stage of monsoon. In the experimental fields of watershed, the yield of blackgram and sorghum increased by 27 % 33 % respectively due to vegetative bunding. Experiments conducted at Regional Research Station, Aruppukottai, Tamil Nadu revealed that vegetative bunding with vetiver (*vertiveria zizanoides*) not only conserved soil moisture but also increased the yield of cotton, maize, sorghum. Similarly vegetative bunding using (*Cenchrus glaucus*) is also found to effectively control soil erosion, conserve soil moisture and increase the yield of annual crops.

The field bunds can be protected from frequent breaches by planting bhabbhar grass (*Eulaliopsis binata*) on the top and sides of field bunds. *Imperata cylindrica* is very effective in checking soil erosion. These vegetative barriers establish fast and have strong deep root system. Over a period of time, such barriers help in automatic leveling. To avoid shade effect of these vegetative barriers on the cultivated crops and to promote tillering, these must be pruned annually up to a height of about 0.5 m.

In- situ soil moisture conservation

The most efficient and cheapest method of conserving rainfall is to hold water '*in situ*'. In most of the semi-arid tropics, the rainfall is erratic and falls within a short time. "*In situ*" moisture conservation can help in retaining soil moisture for a longer period. Evaporation losses can also be greatly reduced if rainfall is stored in the soil rather than in a structure with a free water surface. There are many location-specific moisture conservation techniques that must be chosen appropriately. These measures include forming dead furrows, ridging, graded furrows, broad beds and furrows and tie ridging. For tree crops, micro-catchments, saucer basins, semi-circular bunds, crescent bunds and catch pits can be introduced.

It is important to adopt '*in situ*' moisture conservation techniques, in addition to large-scale soil and moisture conservation and water harvesting scheme in the catchment. Before initiating '*in situ*' moisture conservation measures, the land should be treated with vegetative barriers or bunds followed by cultivation and planting on contours.

By adopting these measures it is possible to increase crop yields by 15-20% in alfisols and 30-50% in vertisols. The survival rate of the crops may reach 90-95% if suitable methods are implemented. In addition, contour stones and vegetative barriers across slope may also increase water/moisture availability to the crops or trees.

Broad-bed furrow system (BBF)

The broad bed and furrow system is one of the most efficient land management practices evolved by ICRISAT for *in situ* moisture conservation in deep black soils. By adopting this method, it is possible to store the moisture from early precipitation in the surface layers without disappearing in deep cracks. The beds and furrows provide considerable protection against soil erosion throughout the year as they form permanent land feature. As per the reports of ICRISAT, this system controls run off and erosion and facilitates infiltration of water into the soil uniformly over the watershed areas. Primary tillage operations are carried out immediately after the harvest of the previous crop. The secondary tillage is completed with the help of summer and pre-monsoon showers. Results at ICRISAT indicate that the optimum slope for the bed and furrow system is 0.3 to 0.6% on alfisols (red soils) and 0.4 to 0.8% on vertisols (black cotton soils).

Broad bed system consists of broad raised beds with furrows of 30 cm wide and 15 cm deep on either side of each bed. The width of the bed is 120 cm from centre of one furrow to the adjacent furrow. The beds are maintained permanently. The beds function as minibunds at a grade and help in reducing the velocity of surface run off and increase infiltration opportunity time. The excess water is removed through the furrows.

Permanent bed and furrow system thus provides *''in situ''* soil and water conservation. (Fig. 8.1).

Tractor drawn multi-purpose broad bed furrow former cum seeder is used to form wide beds separated by furrows and to take up sowing simultaneously. Crops like maize, sorghum, cotton, pigeonpea, blackgram, redgram and bengalgram can be sown using this implement. While operating this equipment, care should be taken to maintain uniform seed depth throughout the sowing.

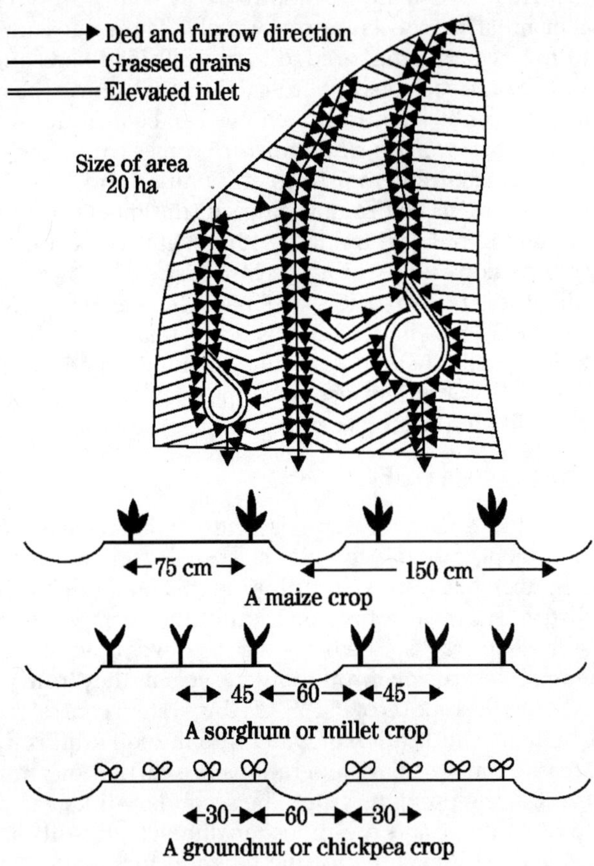

FIG. 8.1: Broad Bed furrow system

Other *'in situ'* soil moisture conservation technique suitable for different situations are given in Table 8.3.

TABLE 8.3: Soil moisture conservation measures for different soil types

Soil type	Rainfall	Practices
Red soil	Low	Dead furrow at 3-6 cm interval
(Alfisol)	Medium	Sowing in flat and ridging later with eventual cultivation
	High	Graded border strips
Black soil	Low	Contour cultivation compartmental bunding
(Vertisol)	Medium	Dead furrow 3-6 m interval
	High	Graded open furrow (0.2 to 0.3 cm^2) at 10 m interval across the slope.

WATER HARVESTING AND RECYCLING

'Water harvesting' is generally used as an umbrella term covering a range of methods of collecting and conserving various forms of runoff from different sources. Water harvesting can be done both *'in situ'* and dugouts /ponds depending upon the situation as well as socio-economic status/ capabilities of the farmer. In dryland agriculture, water harvesting usually denotes the collection of excess run off in a storage tank and using it for the betterment of crop production in the collected or other areas. There are three types of collector tanks, namely farm ponds, percolation ponds and silt detention tanks. The water collection in the farm pond is directly used for protective irrigation. The water stored in other structures will recharge the groundwater and used for protective or supplementary irrigation by digging wells.

Water harvesting *'in situ'*

Water harvesting techniques adopted *'in situ'* are inexpensive to augment rainwater use efficiency in drylands. Any process of reducing the run off volume will increase moisture infiltration in the soil leading to increased moisture volume. However, there should not be any water stagnation in the field. Contour ploughing or ploughing against the slope will ensure *'in situ'* water harvesting. Soil clods and plough furrows resist water flow from the land surface. In light textured soils, shallow preparatory tillage is adequate for better moisture conservation.

'In situ' water harvesting and run off recycling are the potent measures of crop life saving during periods of moisture stress.

Appropriate land configurations for *'in situ'* moisture conservation are broad-beds and furrows, graded border, strips, inter-row and inter-plot water harvesting systems. For shallow alfisols and related soils even dead furrows serve this purpose very well.

Inter-row and intra-row water harvesting

Under this system, furrows of about 30-40 cm diameter alternated by ridges of 60-70 cm are formed at right angle to the field slope. This practice reduces run-off and at the same time water is concentrated in furrows causing better availability. The crops are planted in furrows in lighter soils while in heavy soils on the side of ridges to eliminate the problem of water logging. This system of moisture conservation can be adopted for soils having the depth of 60 cm or so.

The method of rainwater harvesting on inter-row basis also helps in improving the crop stand, especially on small seeded crops like pearl millet by mitigating the adverse crust effects on germination and seedling burying problems due to rain during germination. This practice also helps in safe disposal of excess rainwater in high rainfall areas.

Micro-catchment

Micro catchment water harvesting is a method of collecting surface run off from a small run off area and storing it in the root zone of an adjacent infiltration basin to cover crop water requirements. The aim of micro-catchment water harvesting is to store enough run off water in the soil profile below the basin during the rainy season, to cover the water requirement of the crop or tree during the growing season.

Micro-catchments are formed on one or both the sides of cropped area. The crop strips are alternated by micro-catchments. This system is particularly suitable for horticultural crops and may be practiced in all types of soils. This system helps to increase the moisture storage in deeper layer which is less prone for evaporation.

Various micro-catchment methods are used *viz.,* compartmental bunding, basin, circular basin and crescent methods. The basins should be formed in such a way that gentle slope is given towards the base of stem of orchard trees so that the harvested rain water could be gathered to the maximum level. During summer, dried leaves from the trees should be spread as mulch over the basin to control evaporation.

Run- off harvesting

In rainfed areas, one or two occasional heavy rainfall occurs which creates run off. In vertisols, the run off is about 60 % and in alfisols it is about 40 %. Hence, efforts should be made for proper utilization of the run off after taking measures for '*in situ*' soil moisture conservation.

Methods of run-off harvesting

1. Water harvesting structures, such as farm ponds, check dams and *nalla* bunds are constructed wherein water can be stored and used for supplemental irrigation.
2. Traditional tanks where large amount of water is collected from big catchment areas. The tanks should be desilted once in three years and path way leading to the command area should also be cleared. The water is irrigated to lands situated in the lower reaches.
3. Percolation tanks are used for saving the land overflow and to

recharge the water table.

'Nalla' bunding

Bunds with suitable dimensions are constructed across the *nalla* or gullies to hold maximum run off water to create flooding of the upstream area temporarily for some days or weeks, with surplusing arrangement at suitable intervals to drain the water. This method helps in impounding water mostly in the *'nalla'* and thereby recharging underground acquifer. Thus water yields of the structures located down stream of *nalla* bund are increased.

Nalla bunds prevent free flow of water, allow water to percolate, check the soil erosion and run off and saturate the substrata. *Nalla* plugs also serve as silt trap dam. *Nalla* bunds help in increasing the water level in the wells located at the watershed areas.

Farm ponds

'In situ' moisture conservation is preferable on light soils while in heavier soils, drainage of excess water is desired to maintain the crop health. In spite of these measures, run off is bound to occur. A part of this run off can be intercepted and stored in farm ponds. Run off in tropical and subtropical climate varies from 10-40% of total rainfall. Of this, about 30% can be harvested for recycling to the donor areas. The water, thus, stored can be utilized for critical life saving irrigation/supplemental irrigation and/or increasing cropping intensity in rainy season. In post-rainy season, this water can be used for pre-sowing irrigation or for minimal irrigation at critical stages. Ponds are the bodies of water made either by constructing a dam or an embankment across a watercourse or by excavating a pit or dug out. The former type of farm ponds is constructed on hill slopes. Dugout farm ponds are a common feature on relatively flat terrains.

Catchment area is selected on the basis of its potentiality for yielding sizable run off. Higher the rainfall intensity in excess of infiltration rate of the soil surface more will be the surface run off. Rainfall received in small, localized part of the catchment will promote the surface collection. Increase in rainfall duration may decrease the infiltration rate and hence more water will be available for farm pond collection.

Soil type in the catchment area may greatly influence the surface runoff because of the difference in the infiltration capacity. Alfisols have less water holding capacity and produce more runoff in the monsoon season. In vertisols, run off will be more towards the latter part of the monsoon when the soil is already fully recharged or nearly saturated. If the moisture content of the soil is high, the infiltration capacity will be low and as a result, the catchment will be capable of yielding higher runoff. A rain occurring shortly after the previous rain may produce a sizable runoff.

SITE SELECTION FOR FARM POND

The basic objective in selecting the site for a farm pond is to irrigate certain fields below it by natural flow and the upland field by forcing the water by pumps. The pond should be located in such a way that it has the maximum run off flowing into it. A pond should be located where the largest storage volume can be obtained with least amount of earthwork. The pond should be constructed to a sufficient depth as compatible with local conditions.

Farm pond size is decided considering the total requirement of water for irrigation, livestock and domestic use. The size of the ponds vary from 250 to 300 m^3/ ha of catchment based on the runoff volume and the criterion is that atleast one irrigation of 1.0 to 1.5 cm is to be given to the cropped area. The excavated dug out ponds may be constructed to almost any shape desired. A square or rectangular shape is most common and convenient for excavating equipment.

A large quantity of water is lost from the unlined or untreated ponds due to seepage and percolation losses. Lining the pond is important to reduce the seepage losses. The choice of the material for lining depends on the availability, durability and cost. The materials generally used for lining of the ponds are (i) natural clay soil of low permeability, (ii) bituminous materials, (iii) soil cement mixture, (iv) stone or brick lining, (v) cement concrete., (vi) chemical additives and sealants and (vii) asphalt compounds, (viii) polythene, rubber, plastics, etc.

In red soils (Alfisols), seepage and percolation losses are more and the use of 'sealants' is suggested to prevent these losses. A mixture of soil and cement (8:1) 2.5 cm thick, coal tar (bitumen) and thick plastic sheets are suggested as sealants. Work at Hyderabad suggested that asphalt sprays of 0.25 cm thickness or 10 cm plastering with the mixture of sieved surface soil, cow dung and straw (10:1:1) appeared promising or preferably with a 10 cm think plastering of saline sodic soils.

Run off recycling

The harvested water needs to be judiciously used for crop life saving/ supplemental irrigation to increase and stabilize crop yield and to increase cropping intensity. The quantity of water to be applied as irrigation should be just enough to take care of the critical period and to cover as large an area as possible. Since the amount of water is sufficient for only one or two irrigations, it is essential to decide the time of irrigation. For crops like sorghum, flowering seems to be most critical stage. In tobacco, irrigation 3 weeks before topping has given maximum benefit. A study conducted in Punjab has shown that average response to one supplementary irrigation in maize and wheat at their most critical stages increased the grain yield by 0.4 t/ha in maize and 0.77 t/ha in wheat. The yield increase due to life saving irrigation varied depending upon the crop and the region (Table 8.4).

TABLE 8.4: Yield increase in field crops due to one critical irrigation of 5 cm.

Region	Crop	Yield increase (%)
Anand	Bidi tobacco	49.6
Agra	Wheat	25.4
Bangalore	Finger millet	158.4
Bangalore	Maize	79.4
Bangalore	Cowpea	166.6
Bellary	Sorghum	218.6
Bijapur	Sorghum	43.3
Dehradun	Wheat	65.9
Lundhiana	Wheat	114.1
Rewa	Upland rice	71.6
Rewa	Wheat	229.8
Solapur	Sorghum	85.7
Varanasi	barley	29.2

***Source*:** All India co-ordinated Research Project for Dryland Agriculture, Annual reports, ICAR New Delhi.

Pre-monsoon dry seeding

In dry regions, seeds are generally sown just prior to monsoon to ensure early establishment. Pre-monsoon dry seeding is a common practice in the rainfed areas which ensures timely and early sowing. Early sowing enables full utilization of pre-monsoon showers for better germination, optimum crop stand and growth. Early sowing avoids pressure on bullock and human labour for field preparation and sowing. It also ensures the crop against pest and disease incidence. Pre-monsoon sown sorghum escapes shootfly incidence as well as midge incidence. Pre-monsoon dry seeding is in vogue in some of the pockets of dry farming areas having clay soils.

Crops suitable for dry seeding

Cotton is extensively sown under pre-monsoon dry seeding condition. Sorghum is the next important crop suitable for pre-monsoon sowing. These crops can be sown either as pure stand or with intercrops of pulses like greengram, blackgram, cowpea and redgram. Rice under semi-dry condition is sown as dry seeding in anticipation of rainfall.

The success of the pre- monsoon dry seeding depends on the following components:

- Prediction of on set of monsoon
- Seed hardening
- Depth of sowing.

Prediction of onset of monsoon

By way of analyzing the long-term rainfall using the conditional probability, the probability of occurrence of rainfall can be predicted. The predicted time of dry seeding for various districts of Tamil Nadu, India is given in Table 8.5.

TABLE 8.5: Period of dry seeding for different districts of Tamil Nadu based on rainfall probability analysis.

Districts	Predicted standard week for pre-monsoon sowing	Relevant months / week.
Coimbatore	37-38	September II- III week
Dharmapuri	38-39	September III to IV week
Ramanathapuram	40-41	October I week
Tuticorin	39-40	September IV week
Virudhunagar	36-37	September I week

Seed hardening for drought tolerance

Pre-sowing treatment is important to induce drought tolerance and this method is called seed hardening. In this process, seed are subjected to alternate hydration and desiccation. The pre-seed treatment involves repeated soaking and drying of seeds. The seeds are soaked in water, nutrient solution or growth regulators for 6-18 hours depending on the nature of seed coat. The soaked seeds are then dried under atmospheric condition to bring them to the original moisture content.

The seed is allowed to absorb about 30-40% moisture as that of its dry weight. The amount of water absorbed varies with crop and variety. During the process of soaking, care should be taken that the embryonic tissue absorbs just sufficient quantity of water to satisfy cell elongation, cell division and set in germination process but not to induce emergence of radicle.

Beneficial effects of seed hardening

1. Seed viability is improved by preventing catabolic activities under stress.
2. It improves water absorption of seeds by greater membrane permeability.
3. It facilitates translocation of sugars from seeds to young growing points, *viz.*, radicle and plumule and hence vigorous seedlings are obtained.
4. It helps in better development of root system which helps in more absorption of water and nutrients at deeper layer.
5. Relative water content in the leaves is improved during the moisture stress conditions.

Adopting seed hardening technique has recorded yield increase recorded to the tune of 15-40 %. The cost involved for pre-sowing seed treatment is negligible and does not require sophisticated equipments.

The chemicals used for seed hardening are given in Table 8.6.

TABLE 8.6: Seed hardening chemical for field crops

Crops	Chemical	Concentration	Period of soaking (hours)
Sorghum/ Pearl millet	Potassium dihydrogen phosphate (KH_2PO_4)	10 %	6
Maize	KCl	2 %	5
Cotton	Succinic acid	1-2 %	6
	Cycocel (CCC)	1000 ppm	5
	KCl	2 %	5

Seed pelleting

Seed pelleting is the process of enclosing a seed into a small quantity of inert material to produce a globular unit of standard size to facilitate precision sowing /planting. The inert material creates natural water holding capacity and provides nutrients to seedlings.

Pelleting can be done by wetting the seeds with adhesives (1 ml per 10 g seed) with gum arabica, gelatin, casein and fevicol. They are then rolled in a powder (charcoal 150 g/ kg of seed) and each seed is dried. Fungicides, herbicides, nutrients and biofertilizers can be used either singly or in different combinations as coating material. Pelleted seeds should be dried under shade and can be stored for about a month. Hand driven seed pelleters are available for seed pelleting.

Advantages of pelleting

1. It is easy to incorporate nutrients which nourish the seedlings.
2. Seedlings are protected against fungi or insect pests.
3. Pelleted seeds ensure uniform seed shape. This helps while handling the seeds in seed box of mechanical seed drill. Pelleted seeds ensure maintaining optimum metering mechanism and thereby sowing uniform number of seeds per hill.

Depth of sowing

Optimum depth of sowing prevents inducement of seed germination under inadequate rainfall. The seeds placed at shallow depth quickly germinate with the receipt of meagre rainfall. However, moisture may not be sufficient for later establishment. But seeds sown deeper take more time for emergence and the crop stand may get affected. Generally seeds are sown at optimum depth of 5-7 cm. To achieve uniform depth of sowing, seed drill could be used.

TABLE 8.7: Alternate crop strategies for dry regions of India.

Zone/ Region	June to mid- July	Mid-August	Mid-September	Mid-October	Mid- November
SOUTHERN REGION					
Red soils Hyderabad	Sorghum Castor Pearl millet Pigeonpea	Finger millet	Cowpea Foxtail millet Horse gram	Horsegram	-
Anantapur	Sorghum Pigeonpea Castor, Cowpea Groundnut	Pearlmillet Foxtailmillet Sunflower Cowpea	Pearlmillet Horse gram	-	-
Bangalore	Groundnut Maize Fingermillet Sunflower Pigeonpea	Finger millet	Cowpea Foxtailmillet Horsegram Safflower Direct seeding of fingermillet Sunflower	-	-
Black soil Bellary	-	-	Sorghum Fieldbean Safflower Coriander	Sorghum Chickpea Sunflower Safflower Limabean	Sorghum Coriander Chickpea
Bijapur	Green gram Blackgram Pigeonpea Pearlmillet	Foxtailmillet Cotton	Sorghum	Sorghum Safflower Chickpea	-

Zone/ Region	June to mid- July	Mid-August	Mid-September	Mid-October	Mid- November
Kovilpatti	-	-	Sorghum Pearlmillet Foxtailmillet Cotton Pigeonpea Pulse	Cotton Sorghum Foxtailmillet Chillies Greengram Blackgram Cowpea	Coriander Sesame
CENTRAL REGION					
Alluvial soils					
Varanasi	Upland rice Maize Pearlmillet Blackgram Greengram Sesame Pigeonpea	Short duration rice Pearlmillet Blackgram Greengram Fodder crops of sorghum/ Pearlmillet/ maize	-	Chickpea Barley wheat Lentil Mustard Linseed Safflower	Wheat Mustard
Rewa	Rice, Greengram Pigeonpea Groundnut Sesame Blackgram Soybean	Early variety of rice Pigeonpea Groundnut	Minormillet	Wheat Safflower Barley Linseed Chickpea Lentil	Wheat Barley
Agra	Pearlmillet Blackgram Greengram Pigeonpea Groundnut Clusterbean Cowpea	Pearlmillet Greengram	-	Mustard Barley Chickpea Safflower Lentil	-
Black soil					

Zone/ Region	June to mid- July	Mid-August	Mid-September	Mid-October	Mid- November
Indore	Maize Sorghum Groundnut Soybean Pigeonpea	Sunflower	Safflower	Chickpea	Wheat
Jhansi	Sorghum Pigeonpea Soybean Groundnut Maize	Soybean Blackgram Pearlmillet Fodder Sorghum Cowpea	-	Chickpea Safflower Mustard	-
Submontane soil Dehradun	Maize, Rice Soybean	Rice	Maize Toria	Wheat Barley Chickpea	Chickpea
NORTHERN REGION					
Submontane soils Hoshiarpur region	Maize Pearlmillet Groundnut Soybean Blackgram	Fodder crops of maize and cowpea	-	Wheat Barley Mustard Chickpea	Wheat
Rakh Dhiansar region	Maize, Sorghum Pearlmillet Greengram Blackgram Cowpea, Sesame Castor	Greengram Blackgram Cowpea Sunflower	-	Wheat Barley Rapeseed Linseed Chickpea Lentil	Wheat

Zone/ Region	June to mid- July	Mid-August	Mid-September	Mid-October	Mid- November
Desert soils Hisar	Pearlmillet Clusterbean Greengram Monthbean	Transplanted Pearlmillet Clusterbean Cowpea, Greengram	Clusterbean Cowpea	Chickpea Taramira Rapeseed Safflower	Mustard Taramira
EASTERN REGION					
Red soils Ranchi.	Mesta, Fingermillet Sorghum, Maize Groundnut Greengram Blackgram Soybean Soybean, Rice *Kharif* potato	Transplanted Fingermillet	Toria	Safflower Linseed Lentil	Wheat
Bhubaneshwar region	Pigeonpea Mesta	Transplanted Fingermillet	Pigeonpea Horsegram	Horsegram	-
WESTERN REGION					
Black soil Solapur	Pearlmillet Pigeonpea Greengram Blackgram Cowpea Kidneybean Horsegram Groundnut Sesame	Foxtailmillet Pigeonpea Kidneybean Horsegram Castor	Sunflower Sorghum Foxtailmillet Greengram Blackgram	Sorghum Safflower Chickpea	Sorghum (fodder) Chickpea Safflower

Zone/ Region	June to mid- July	Mid-August	Mid-September	Mid-October	Mid- November
Akola	Pearlmillet Greengram Blackgram Cowpea, Sorghum Cotton, Groundnut Pigeonpea Sunflower Pigeonpea Sunflower	Cowpea Sorghum	Safflower	Safflower Chickpea	-
Rajkot	Sorghum Pearlmillet Groundnut Castor, Cotton Sesame Greengram Blackgram Clusterbean	Cotton Castor Sesame	-	-	-
Udaipur	Sorghum Maize, Pigeonpea Cowpea	Greengram Blackgram Cowpea	Greengram Blackgram Cowpea	Chickpea Safflower Mustard Barley, Wheat	--
Desert soils	Pearlmillet Sorghum Fingermillet Pigeonpea Castor Clusterbean Greengram	Transplanted pearlmillet Fingermillet Castor Sunflower	Tobacco	Tobacco	

Zone/ Region	June to mid- July	Mid-August	Mid-September	Mid-October	Mid- November
Jodhpur	Pearl millet Greengram Cowpea Clusterbean Mothbean Castor Sesame	Greengram Cowpea Sunflower Castor, Clusterbean Mothbean Transplanted pearlmillet	-	-	-

Contingency crop planning for aberrant weather

In semi-arid Tropics of India, rain is the only source of irrigation for sustaining crops grown under rainfed conditions. Rainfall in its quantity and distribution is highly unpredictable. Aberrant weather appear in any one of the ways:

1. Delayed onset of monsoon
2. Short or long dry spell during the growing season either in mid season or late season
3. Withdrawal of rainfall before the crop completes its life cycle.

According to the type of aberrations, crops and varieties should be chosen and contingent plan is drawn to meet the arising situation. The following strategy measures can be adopted:

a) Choice of alternate crops
b) Mid-term correction including ratooning, thinning, and emergency nursery for upland rice
c) Providing life saving irrigation to prevent moisture stress.

Choice of alternate crops

It is important to choose appropriate crops/ cropping system to suit aberrant weather. Crops such as pulses and oil seeds are preferred over cereals in the event of delayed *kharif* sowing. For example, sesame may be chosen in the place of upland rice. Pearl millet could be transplanted if the season is delayed. Minor millet, Setatria, is most suited for late sown condition without any serious adverse effect on productivity. Alternate cropping strategies for dry regions in India are given in the Table 8.7.

MID-TERM CORRECTION

Mid-season correction is a contingent management practice to overcome unexpected and/or unfavourable weather condition. The weather abnormalities (unfavourable weather conditions) are such as early cessation of monsoon rains or a long spell of drought in between two rains. The drought may extend over a period of three to six weeks. Several practices have been developed to mitigate the damaging effects of dry spells.

1. If dry spell leading to moisture stress occurs within a week to 10 days of sowing, germination of the crop may be severely affected. Under this situation, resowing is a better option to maintain adequate plant stand.
2. If the moisture stress occurs at about blooming, crops like sorghum and pearl millet can be cut and ratooned.
3. Thinning of the plant stand is recommended to lessen the severity of moisture stress of about 35-50 days. Thinning of alternate plants in the rows in the event of mild stress and every third row under severe

moisture stress condition is recommended. Thinning is resorted particularly to the more sensitive component for soil moisture such as sorghum, in sorghum + redgram inter- cropping.

4. If the break of monsoon is very brief, cultural practices like shallow interculture is adopted to eradicate weeds and to maintain soil mulch. Soil mulching can be effectively practiced by working dantis. Mulching is advantageous during *rabi* than in rainy season. Under drought conditions, organic mulches, particularly under receding moisture conditions favour crop growth and increase yield in many situations.

Mulching

Mulches have a definite controlling effect on the evaporation of soil moisture and hence play an important role in dryland agriculture. Under field conditions, surface soil is just stirred and the soil becomes air-dry. By adopting this practice, some amount of moisture is lost from the upper layer. After the preliminary loss of moisture, the soil mulch effectively controls further evaporation from deeper layers by breaking the capillary continuity. This system is highly suitable for medium to heavy textured soils.

Crop residues as mulch

Locally available materials like straw, stalks and coir pith can be very well used as mulch material. Crop yield increase has been noticed in the mulched field due to better water use and reduction of soil loss by run-off. It has been reported that use of straw mulch minimizes evaporation. Straw mulch acts as a barrier between the incident radiation and soil surface leading to reduction in evaporation losses.

Vertical mulching

In heavy black soils, where infiltration is a great problem, vertical mulching may be practiced. Keeping sorghum stubbles as vertical mulch in trenches of 40 cm deep, 15 cm wide and protruding 10 cm above the ground level enhances available soil moisture by 4 to 5 cm. There was improvement in grain yield by as much as 400 to 500% in drought years and 40 - 50% in normal years over unmulched plots in Bellary, Andhra Pradesh.

Spraying of nutrient solution

Nutrient solution spray is recommended in the event of revival of rain and release of moisture stress. Urea or DAP spray (2% solution) is useful for quicker regeneration of crops like legumes and castor after rain.

Use of anti-transpirants

The possibilities of reducing transpiration are of greatest importance in dry farming. Any material that is applied to transpiring plant surfaces for reducing water loss from the plant is called "anti-transpirant". Many herbicides, fungicides and growth harmones possess anti-transpirant characteristics. Anti-transpirants may be of a) stomatal closing type, (b) film forming types, (c) reflectant type or (d) growth retardant.

Some of the fungicides like Phenyl Mercuric Acetate (PMA) and herbicides like atrazine in low concentrations serve as anti-transpirants by inducing stomatal close. The plastic and waxy materials which form a thin film on the leaf surface retard the escape of water due to formation of a physical barrier, *e.g.*, Mobileaf, hexadeconol, silicone. The success of these chemicals is limited since they also reduce photosynthesis.

Some of the white materials form a coating on the leaves and increase the leaf reflectance (albedo). Transpiration loss is reduced by reflecting the radiation, reducing leaf temperature and vapour pressure gradient. Spraying of kaolin (5 %) forms thin layer on the leaf surface and reduces transpiration. Some of the growth retardants (cycocel) induce stomatal closure and thus reduce transpiration losses.

Crop life saving irrigation

The water stored in the farm pond may be recycled to the donor area during the critical periods of crop growth under conditions of either prolonged drought spell or early withdrawal of monsoon.

WATERSHED MANAGEMENT

A watershed is the land area from which surface water drains into a single outlet. Watershed units provide a logical framework for the management and control of water, which is a severely limiting natural factor to crop production in the semi -arid- Tropics.

Watershed management involves conservation, development and management of water. Since water is the most important commodity for sustainable production in rainfed areas, watershed management envisages a systematic and scientific approach towards conservation, harvesting, proper utilization and safe disposal of flowing water from the moment it strikes the land surface as a tiny drop till it joins the ocean for optimum production on sustained basis. The basic approaches in watershed management is an integrated effort on land development for effective soil and water conservation with a view to *'in situ'* utilization of rain water for crop production and animal husbandry.

Objectives of watershed management

1. To protect, conserve and improve the land resources for efficient and sustained production
2. To protect and enhance water resources, moderate floods and reduce silting up of tanks, increase irrigation and conserve rain water for

crops and thus mitigate droughts

3. To utilize the natural local resources for improving agriculture and allied occupation or industries (small and cottage) so as to improve socio-economic conditions of the local residents.

The size of the watershed may vary from a few hectares to thousands of hectares depending upon the size of the river or stream passing through it and the location of the outlet. For providing conditions for optimum utilization of land, water, plant and animal resources and for protecting the environment, it is necessary to treat the land from top to bottom or ridge to valley as a natural unit. Watershed reflects the interaction of soil, geology, water and vegetation by providing a common end product, runoff or stream flow, whereby the net effects of these interactions on that product can be measured and appraised. The size of the model watersheds varies from 200 to 2000 ha.

Benefits of the watershed management

The watershed approach benefits the farmer through improved soil health, better drainage and more efficient use of rainwater with the possibility of excess water being stored in suitable structures for use during scarcity periods. With voluntary farmers participation, sustainable improvement in crop and animal production is possible. The society benefits from floods to downstream farmlands and human habitation, reduced siltation of expensive irrigation structures and protection to natural resources.

Technological options for watershed management

Technological options available for different landforms can be categorized as under:

Near flat or valley lands: To collect excess rainwater from mini-watersheds, broad bed and furrow system with grassed waterways is relevant for black soils. This system can be adopted for community participation on a whole village basis or those inhabiting the undulating position. Off-season tillage, dry seeding and fertilizer placement are accomplished by animal drawn farm implements. Double cropping becomes possible in most years by utilizing water stored in small reservoirs. For flat lands in black soil regions, with less than 0.5% slope and where water stagnation during monsoon months is a problem, drainage can be practiced through narrow ridge and furrow and raised beds during rainy months. Crops can be raised in the furrows with stored moisture during the post-monsoon season.

Foot hills: In the sub-Montane tracts with light textured soils, contour farming and bench terracing at suitable intervals supplemented with organic mulching and *'in situ'* water harvesting in run-off reservoirs reduce the erosion losses. Horticultural and silvi-pastoral systems are recommended for higher sections. Gully plugging or putting across check dams in the upper parts of seasonal cracks increases the recharge of ground water in the downstream basin.

Steep slopes: Contour bunding, bench terracing or a combination of both may help in retaining 90 to 100% rainfall in the treated area of steeper slopes. Vertical intervals between contour bunds or bench terraces are kept within 0.5 and 1 m for operational convenience. Contour branches along the bunds or terraces carry excess flow through grassed waterways into a common pond.

A live hedge planted just above the bench acts as a soil filter preventing soil erosion and with time makes the terraced bed less sloppy.

For still steeper slopes with soil depth not less than a metre, horticulture is the most appropriate form of agricultural activity. Hilltops are to be used only for forestry purposes. Such a system allows retention of almost 90% of rain water within the watershed reducing soil loss to less than one t/ha/ year.

Watershed development methods

Watershed management essentially consists of three elements of operation:

1. Basic land treatment to conserve soil moisture, control land erosion and harvest run-off.
2. Application of crop and animal management practices, and
3. Alternate land use such as agro-forestory, social or silvi-pastoral system.

Basic land treatment

This is needed to conserve moisture, control erosion and harvest run-off water into farm ponds, small tanks or small dams for recycling or to recharge ground water down stream. Actually these are soil-engineering measures for water disposal through diversion channels and water ways. Contour bunds, graded bunds, submergence bundhies, terracing and land leveling form part of these measures. These measures help in increasing the opportunity time for infiltration of rainwater into the soil and decreasing soil erosion. In the gully with less than 1 m in depth, earthen or stone structures fortified with vegetative cover are good enough for safe disposal of run off water and control erosion. Storage of water in run-off harvest tanks serves the purpose of providing irrigation to crops when needed.

Crop and animal husbandry practices

These practices comprise contour tillage and selection of crops with quick growing nature. This helps in preventing erosion loss from the bare ground surface and *'in situ'* moisture conservation. Intercropping of taller crop plants (maize, sorghum, cotton, pigeonpea) with short statured legume is advisable. Flat sowing followed by ridging up is an appropriate technique to prevent soil erosion during in-season rainstorms. Bed and furrow system of planting is more appropriate for black soils. Use of organic mulches in wide spaced crops is often desirable.

Sustainability of agricultural enterprise cannot be ensured unless pragmatic animal husbandry practices are encouraged concurrently. Cattle or ruminant rearing are to be advocated. Fisheries in water reservoirs, wherever feasible, provide buffer during the lean season.

Alternate land use system

It aims at land utilization according to its capability. About 10-30% area in any of the watershed is found unfit for raising conventional crops due to soil degradation. Agro-forestry, instead of arable crop production, is a preposition to prevent soil erosion and for getting higher income from the land. Silvi-pastoral systems can be developed with grasses and fodder legumes between tree rows.

Water shed development experiences

Government of India launched National Watershed Development programme for Rainfed Areas (NWDPRA) in 1991. Watershed development programmes require involvement of several development departments dealing with agriculture, soil conservation, horticulture, forestry, fisheries, sericulture, etc. The geographical area of the watersheds varies from 146 ha to 3490 ha located in different soil and rainfall situations. Soil and water conservation are effected through contour bunds in low rainfall areas and graded bunds or bench terraces in high rainfall areas. Water harvesting structures, small farm ponds or community large ponds has been constructed. Gully plugging is also resorted to wherever needed. Lands not suitable for arable crop production are put to agro-forestry use or planting of horticultural crops or seeded with grasses or grass legume mixtures. Animal husbandry and fisheries are encouraged wherever feasible to supplement farmer's income.

As a result of the development activities, the cropped area increase in the water sheds ranges between 12 and 53% with the augmentation of sub-surface water storage. The raise in water level in dug wells ranges between 1.0 and 7.0 m.

1. There is increase in cropping intensity as a result of exploitation of stored sub-surface water ranging from 115 to 157 %.
2. Consumption of NPK fertilizers in most of the areas has gone up substantially (almost 290% averaged over the 47 watersheds) after 4-5 years of sustained efforts.
3. Crop yield increase in the watersheds ranges from 51% for mustard to 91% for pearl millet and to a maximum of 206% in sorghum.
4. There has been enhanced employment generation by 13 to 100% depending upon the stage of development. The increase in per capita

income is 16 to 649% as a result of the development activities.

Participatory Watershed Management

Watershed management emerged as a new paradigm of planning, development and management of land, water and vegetation resources with a focus on social and institutional aspects apart from bio-physical aspects following a participatory 'bottom up' approach. Sustainability and replicability of the watershed management programmes call upon peoples' participation in the planning, implementation and equitable share of benefits and responsibilities. The experience of participatory watershed management showed resource conservation and productivity and income generation.

CHAPTER 9

Agroforestry and Wasteland Development

Agroforestry is an age old practice of integrating farming with forestry practices, preferably on the same unit of land on a sustainable basis. Agroforestry systems have received increasing emphasis in the recent years because of their potential to yield fodder, fuel wood and small timber in addition to food. The country is losing about 1.3 million ha of forest cover every year due to deforestation. Both rural and tribal populations depend on the forests for meeting their daily needs of fuel wood. Shortage of fuel wood has increased the pressure on forests. Besides, there is a phenominal increase in the use of wood for construction and commercial purposes. Implementation of developmental activities like mining, quarrying and river valley projects are the other reasons for deforestation. Shifting cultivation which is practiced in the Northeastern zone of India has also affected forest acreage. Hence, it is felt important that afforestation should be encouraged through agroforestry and social forestry programmes. Agroforestry plays a vital role in the development of wastelands. Agroforestry is considered as an alternate land use system for the wasteland development.

IMPORTANCE OF AGROFORESTRY

Meeting the needs of the farmer

Agroforestry is primarily aimed at fulfilling the basic needs of food, fuel, fodder and timber besides helping the farmer in increasing productivity, profitability and sustainability of production, particularly from marginal agricultural land. Leaf fodder from trees constitutes an important source of fodder in many parts of the country and particularly in hilly, semi-arid and arid regions. The estimated fodder requirement of the country is 882 million tonnes; however, availability is only 434 million tonnes. There is a global crisis for energy and agroforestry provides an alternate source of energy. Trees supply cheap source of fuel wood. The estimated domestic consumption is 235 million m^3 of which only 40 million m^3

come from forest sources. Fruits and timber yielding trees would help in enriching the diet of rural people and in meeting the demand for timber. About 10 million ha of forests are estimated to harbour bamboo with an annual production of about 2 million tonnes. The canes are commercially important for making a variety of baskets, handicraft and utility furniture for domestic use and export.

Conserving soil and water

Agroforestry offers an answer to the problem of soil and water conservation. It has been estimated that the annual loss of soil due to erosion is equivalent to 16.4 t/ha/year as against the permissible limit of 4-5 t/ha / year. Two means of achieving erosion control are the barrier approach and the cover approach. The former refers to the use of physical barriers to check run-off and down slope soil movements. The latter measure is adopted for checking erosion by maintenance of ground cover surface throughout the period of erosive rains. Tree species reduce wind velocity and prevent the soil being blown away. Tree species act as a barrier or cover and check run-off water and suspended sediments. Species composition of grasses plays an important role in controlling run-off, soil loss and water infiltration. Integrating tree species with grasses, thus, reduces soil and water loss. Deep-rooted trees planted along the contours and hedges with cover crops help in soil stabilization and reduction of land slide problems.

Maintenance of soil fertility

Appropriate agroforestry system benefits maintaining soil organic matter and physical properties, augment N fixation and promote efficient nutrient cycling. Tree foliage is used as mulch, green leaf manure, etc. It has been reported that growing *Leucaena* for three years on a sandy soil improved the soil fertility considerably. Agroforestry can also be used to break the impermeable layers in certain soils.

Controlling salinization and waterlogging

Strongly rooted tree species may assist in reclamation of alkaline, flooded soils by penetrating buried 'caliche' layers created by improper irrigation. The shade of the vegetative cover retards evaporation and reduces upward movement of ground water to the soil surface. Some of the tree (*Prosopis juliflora)* and grass species (*Diplachne fusca)* are found to be tolerant to saline and alkaline conditions.

Positive environmental impact

Agroforestry may help in moderation of microclimate in the vicinity of trees. Planting rows of trees on the field boundaries has beneficial influence as wind breaks in protecting the crops. Agroforestry may also help in maintaining balance in oxygen-carbondioxide, atmospheric temperature and relative humidity.

Alternate land use for marginal and degraded lands

Agroforestry systems offer considerable scope of harnessing advantages of forest by growing trees on the marginal lands. In semi-arid and arid regions of India, arable farming has dominated which is not a stable enterprise due to poor yields and frequent crop failures because of low and unreliable rainfall. Hence alternate land use system like agroforestry is gaining attention in marginal lands. These systems provide stability to the resource-poor, small and marginal dryland farmers. Trees and grasses use the off-season precipitation gainfully and at the same time soil is also protected.

MULTI-PURPOSE TREE SPECIES (MPTS)

Crop production from the rainfed areas is not stable and hence these lands can be effectively utilized for multipurpose tree production system. The land is utilized for planting various types of trees which provide multi-purpose uses such as wood, leaves, fruits, pods, fodder, etc. These products are very valuable and provide more income to farmers as compared with the income obtained from arable farming. The tree species should have the following characteristic features:

1. High survival %age and easy establishment
2. Fast growing
3. Ability to fix atmospheric N
4. Multiple uses such as firewood, timber, green manure, fodder and raw material for local industry
5. Wide acceptability by local people
6. Produce nutritious and palatable foliage
7. High coppicing and pollarding capacity

Important multi-purpose tree species

1. *Albizia amara*
2. *Hardwickia binata*
3. *Leucaena latisiliqua*
4. *Albizia lebbeck*
5. *Albizia procera*
6. *Caillica glomerata*
7. *Dichrostachys nutans*
8. *Azadirachta indica*

i) Trees for fuel wood

The species chosen for fuel plantation should have the capacity to survive, grow fast and produce large volumes of fuel wood. They are amenable for easy management with minimal skill. *e.g., Albizia lebbeck, Acacia albida,*

A. nilotica, A. senegal, A. tortilis, A. holosericeae, Emblica officinalis, Prosopis juliflora.

ii) Fodder trees

Various indigenous trees and shrubs have been identified suitable for fodder based on the palatability rating. *e.g.*, Hardwickia binata, Prosopis cineraria, Ziziphus nummularis, Acacia nilotica, Acacia senegal, Albizia lebbeck, Azadirachta indica, Grewia tanax.

iii) Green manure value

The foliage of some of the species can be pruned and used as green leaf manure. *e.g.*,

Pungamia glabra, Glyricidia cebium, Azadirachta indica, Erythrina indica, Leucaena leucocephala, Sesbania grandiflora, Thespesia populnea, Parkia sp.

iv) Nitrogen fixing tree species (NFTs)

The N fixing trees (NFTs) are getting attention in agroforestry and silvipastoral systems. They are the source of N and organic matter to improve the soil fertility. These trees grow rapidly on poor soils because of their ability to fix the atmospheric N. The leaves of these trees are used as a source of nutrients, particularly N. The trees should have the capacity to give more leaf which will improve the organic status of the soil. *e.g. Leucaena leucocephala, Sesbania spp., Gliricidia. Leucaena* is a very fast growing tree species and is known to fix about 200 kg N/ha.

(v) Woodlots

Woodlots are adapted on lands which are too poor or not suitable for profitable agriculture. It is now being practiced even on good agricultural lands in association with agricultural crops because of attractive returns. The tree species, *Casuarina equisetifolia* is planted in large woodlots in the states of Andhra Pradesh, Tamil Nadu, Karnataka, and Orissa. Growing of woodlots of *Eucalyptus sp.* and Populars on farmlands is profitable in Punjab, Haryana, Gujarat and U.P. in India.

AGROFORESTRY SYSTEMS

A number of location-specific agroforestry systems have been evolved due to diverse biophysical, ecological and socio-economic factors. Classifications of agroforestry systems based on various approaches are described below:

1. **Based on structure (Composition and dimension of crop)**
   a) Agri-silviculture: The land is used to produce both forest trees and agricultural crops either simultaneously or alternately.
   b) Silvi-pastural system: In this system, trees are managed to produce wood and fodder grasses and for rearing of domestic animals.

c) Agri-silvipastural system: This system combines agri-silviculture and silvi- pasture.
d) Multipurpose forestry production system: Forest is managed to yield multiple products in addition to wood. They are grown to yield fruits, flower, leaves, honey, gum and medicine. This system is best suited for hill tribals.

2. **Based on the dominance of components**

a) **Silvo-agriculture:** The trees are the major component of land use and the agricultural crops are integrated with them. *e.g.,* shifting cultivation, Taungya cultivation.
b) **Agro-silviculture:** Agricultural component is the major one and trees are the secondary. *e.g.,* hedge cropping, alley cropping.
c) **Silvo-pastural system:** Tree is the major component and pasture is secondary to allow the animals for grazing.
d) **Pastoral silviculture:** Pasture is the major component and trees are secondary, sometimes allowing over grazing of forest beyond its carrying capacity.
e) **Agro-silvipastural system:** Combination of crops, trees and pastures. *e.g.,* home gardens, wherein trees, herbs, shrubs, climbers and grasses are grown on the same land.
f) **Silvo-agri-pasture:** Silviculture is the dominant component. Agriculture and pasture are secondary.

3. **Based on temporal arrangement of components**

a) **Coincident:** Different crops occupy the land together, *e.g.,* coffee under shade trees, pasture under trees.
b) **Concomitant:** The components stay together for some part of life, *e.g.,* agricultural crops are grown for only a few years.
c) **Intermittent:** Space is dominated; the annual crops are grown with perennial crops.
d) **Interpolated:** Space and time are dominated. Different components occupy the space during different times as in home garden.

4. **Based on allied component**

a) Agroforestry-cum-sericulture
b) Agroforestry-cum-apiculture
c) Agroforestry-cum-pisciculture
d) Agroforestry-cum-lac culture

There are three basic sets of components in all agroforestry systems, woody perennials, herbaceous plants and animals.

The common agroforestry systems in India can be classified as follows:

1. Agri-silviculture (crops+trees)
2. Silvi-pastoral (trees + pasture + animal)

3. Agri-horticulture (crops + fruit trees)
4. Agri-silvipastoral (crops + trees + pasture + animals)
5. Agri-horti-silviculture (crops + fruit trees + multipurpose tree species)
6. Homestead agroforestry (multiple combination of various components)

Agri- Silviculture

This system emphasizes raising of trees and cultivation of food crops and/ or fodder crops in the available space between the trees. Compatibility between different components of agroforestry depends on the growth stage due to varying shade effect and root competition. In the plantation of *Leucaena,* field crops such as pigeonpea + blackgram can be grown successfully with least reduction in fodder yield of tree component. In West Bengal, cultivation of direct seeded rice in *kharif* and greengram in *autumn* gave better performance. Sorghum is found to be more compatible in *kharif* and taramira in *rabi* with *Eucalyptus tereticornis.* Cowpea could be intercropped with eucalyptus. The wood yield of eucalyptus was found to increase in association with the intercrops of cassava + groundnut in Kerala in sloping laterite soils.

Sesbania sesban can be grown successfully under dryland conditions, especially in medium textured soil of good depth. Intercropping sorghum has recorded maximum green fodder and dry matter production. *Acacia tortilis* can be grown in combination with the fodder crops like cowpea, clusterbean or pearl millet with remunerative returns. *Acacia nilotica* is raised on the bunds of rice fields and has high tolerance to waterlogging. It grows rapidly getting benefits from irrigation and fertilizer given to rice crop. *Dalbergia sissoo* grown with rice+ pigeonpea was found to be the best under rainfed condition of Orissa. It has been reported that grain production of greengram and clusterbean was not affected when grown with *Prosopis cineraria.* Based on 5 years of study at Jhansi, wheat and gram were found to perform better with multi-purpose tree species, *Hardwickia binata.* Yield reduction in tree component was only 9 and 12% with wheat and gram respectively compared to sole cropping.

In the hilly region, tree species such as *Grevillea robusta, Albizia lebbeck, Ailanthes excelsa, Populus sp.* and *Eucalyptus globus* are grown in association with wheat, pea, potato, cauliflower, mustard, etc. It has been indicated that potato can be grown as intercrop in the first two years after the establishment of tree plantation of blue gum (*Eucalyptus globulus)* and black wattle (*Acacia mearnsii)* planted at 2 metres apart in the Nilgiris.

Silvi- Pasture

In the silvipastural system, improved pasture species are introduced with tree species. In this system, grass or grass-legume mixture is grown along with the woody perennial simultaneously on the same unit of land. This is the best management system for the wastelands with marginal fertility. Much higher forage yield (8-11 t/ha) is possible through silvipasture system. This system also has an additional advantage of providing green fodder through tree loppings. Trees provide fuel and timber in the extreme dry season and lean periods; animals graze on the pasture and feed on the leaves of nutritious trees and shrubs. Silvipasture system facilitates improvement in soil fertility status through litter fall and root biomass. There is increase in soil organic carbon and N, P contents. Multi-layered vegetation covers are very effective in controlling run-off and soil loss from erosion-prone areas. This system not only reduces surface run off but also facilitates infiltration and storage of rainwater in the soil profile.

Choice of components

The tree component should have deep root system with minimum superficial roots. It should be fast growing, hardy with light crown and preferably multipurpose. Tree species with good coppicing and tolerant to lopping are preferable. They should have complementary effect on pasture species. The tree foliage should be highly palatable and nutritious with minimum toxic effect. The important tree species of fodder value for different regions of India are given below:

1. **Arid and Semi-Arid Tropics:** *Acacia albida, A. nilotica, A. tortilis, Albizia lebbeck, A. amara, Leucaena leucocephala, Prosophis cineraria, Sesbania aegyptica, Hardwickia binata, Dalbergia sissoo, Melia azadirach, Azadirachta indica.*
2. **Humid tropics:** *Gliricidia sepium, L. leucocephala, Sesbania grandiflora, Acacia mangium, Albizia falcataria, A. lebbeck, A. procera, Calliandra calothyrsus.*
3. **Highland tropics:** *Acacia famesiana, A. mearnsii, Leucaena diversifolia, A. facataria.*
4. **Temperate region:** *Robina pseudoacacia, Alnus glutinosa, A. nepalensis, A. acuminata, A. rubra, Grewia optiva.*
5. **Grass species:** The grass species should be palatable, high yielding and should have the ability to sustain more than one cut and self seeding characteristic. They should have tolerance to shade and with good competing ability. Rotational grazing is effective in increasing the grazing potential and efficiency. Some suitable grasses are: *Pennisetum pedicellatum, Cenchrus ciliaris, C. setigerus, Sehima narvosum, Chrysopogon fulvus, Dicanthium annulatum.*
6. **Legumes:** *Stylosanthes humilies, S. quianesis, S. scabra, S. hamata, Macroptilim atropurpureum cv. siratro.*

Silvi-pastoral combinations

Fodder trees such as Leucaena, Gliricidia, Acacia and neem can be planted along the border. *Cenchrus ciliaris* is found to be the best grass that could be grown with *Acacia nilotica* in black soils of Bellary (Karnataka). *Acacia leucocepholea and A. planiformis* are the tress species that occur extensively in the coastal parts of Tirunelveli and localized pockets of Ramanathapuram and Coimbatore districts in Tamil Nadu. The grass species, *Cenchrus ciliaris,* is grown along with these trees species.

Leucaena can be planted in association with hybrid napier and is found to be highly profitable in Jhansi region of U.P. *Dalbergia sissoo* with *Chrysopogon fulvus* is the ideal tree- grass combination at Dehradun (U.P.). In the arid regions of Rajasthan, *Sesbania grandiflora* or *S. sesban is* grown with *Cenchrus ciliaris, Setaria anceps, Desmanthus, etc.* It has also been reported that for the arid region of Rajasthan, multi-layered plantations comprising tall and medium trees like *Eucalyptus commandulensis, E. terminalis, E. tortilis, Prosopis juliflora, P. cineraria* and shrubs like *Dichr ostachys cinerea* with grass (*Lasiums and Cenchrus*) would be highly suitable. *Acacia tortilis* in association with *Cenchrus* species has given higher return as compared to pure tree or grass cultivation.

Agri-Horti system

Agricultural crops are normally grown in the interspace of fruit trees planted at a spacing of 5-7 m apart. The fruit trees are managed for 30-35 years and they give regular income. In addition, they also provide fuel wood and fodder. Intercultivated agricultural crops provide seasonal returns. Several kinds of crops are suitable. However, shade is not always desirable for crops like maize, sorghum and groundnut. Under dryland conditions, the amount of rainfall and its distribution decide the types of fruit trees that can be grown. Fruit trees such as guava, custard apple, ber, phalsa, jamun, bael, wood-apple and pomegranate are found promising under dryland situations. On marginal and wastelands, ber, anona and citrus show good promise. Crop production can be maintained by proper management practices and right choice of crops in the interspaces of the fruit trees. Millets, pulses or oil seeds can be grown as intercrops under fruit trees in the Semi- Arid Tropics.

In Gujarat ravines, crops such as pearlmillet, groundnut, cowpea, greengram, blackgram, barley, maize, chillies and coriander are grown as intercrops with papaya, kazzi lime, sapota, pomegranate, guava and mango.

In the North-Eastern Hill regions of Sikkim and Nagaland, mandarin (*Citrus reticulata)* is an important commercial fruit tree. Mandarin orchards are intensively intercropped with a number of field crops *viz.,* cereals, pulses and vegetables. Ginger is the most important remunerative intercrop in the mandarin orchards.

In high hills of temperate zone, apple is intercropped with potato, barley, radish, cabbage and turnip. In Jammu and Kashmir, in some of the established orchards of apple, peach and almond, cultivation of pulses and vegetables is becoming very popular for generating more income from smallholdings. Peach can be intercropped with both *rabi* and *kharif* crops in the Doon valley of Uttar Pradesh. Due to its deciduous nature, the tree does not provide shade effect on the crop during *rabi*.

In the temperate zone of Himalayas, plum with potato/cabbage gives high returns. In the Eastern parts of Himalayas, guava is grown with ginger. The fruit trees having thin canopy and high bearing are most preferred.

Agri-Silvipasture

It is the combination of agri-silviculture and silvi-pastoral system. Under this system, farmers in dryland grow field crops and forest trees together up to a particular stage but in a later stage, the grasses are raised in place of field crops in the vacant space between the forest trees. Thus, the resource-poor farmers are assured of wood, agricultural products and grasses. Woody hedges such as *Delonix alata, Erythrina spp* and *Lannea coromendelica* are common features along the inland and coastal areas and *Thespesia populnea* in paddy field bunds. These species provide green leaf manure for the paddy field, fuel wood and fodder for cattle.

Components suitable for mild- tropical climate

1. **Tree species:** *Eucalyptus, Robinia pseudoacacia, Erythrina suberosa, Morus leaevigata, Putranjiva roxburghii.*
2. **Crops:** Rice, maize.
3. **Fodder grass:** *Teosinte, Spilanthus, Vetiveria zizanoides, Cymbopogon citratus, Medicago sativa.*

Agri-Horti-Silviculture

In this system, fruit trees are grown along with crops and multipurpose tree species (MPTs). Agri-Horti-Silviculture is highly diverse in vegetation with highest productivity upto 25.8 t /ha/ year. Studies at Jhansi revealed that the tree species, *Leucaena,* can be planted in lines between the fruit trees such as ber, pomegranate, citrus, guava, etc. Crops like wheat and sorghum are sown as intercrops during *rabi* and *kharif* seasons respectively. *Leucaena* is harvested a year before sowing of *rabi* and *kharif* crops. By adopting this system, it is possible to obtain green leaf fodder yield of about 2.5-7.5 t/ha and dry fuel wood of 2.3 - 4.7 t/ha. The MPTs also provide green fodder and fuel wood in addition to protecting the fruit trees from hot wind in the summer and cold wind during winter. Besides, the trees also help in improving the soil by virtue of its N fixing ability. It is important to manipulate the canopy of the tree for minimizing light competition. There is also scope for minimizing root competition by regular ploughing during which the superficial roots are cut.

In Manipur valley, agri-horti-silvi system is highly remunerative. Crops like rice, mustard, soybean, beans and vegetables (mainly pumpkin/ potato) are grown in between walnut, cherry, banana, guava, etc. In this region, forest tree species are grown to produce wood and leaves for fodder.

Homestead agroforestry

Farmers generally plant trees in and around their habitations, courtyard, threshing floor and in the field. These home gardens are aimed to satisfy the family needs of fuel, fodder and small timbers. They also fulfill the needs of fruits, vegetables, spices, etc. The trees are normally grown for fruits, wood and shade. Along with the trees, vegetables, spices and agricultural crops are also grown. Fruit trees such as mango, jack, citrus, guava, sapota and anona are normally planted. The other trees commonly preferred for homestead garden include tamarind, bamboo, neem, teak, coconut and arecanut. Spices (garlic and ginger) and vegetables (beans and cucumbers) are also commonly cultivated in the home gardens. Some of the root crops such as arrow root and cassava are also included in these gardens. The system of home garden is more prevalent in high rainfall areas of Kerala and Tamil Nadu. In these regions, coconut and arecanut are the main crops. A variety of animals are supported in most of the home gardens. The foliage from the trees is used as fodder.

Ley farming

Ley farming or ley rotation is one of the alternate land use systems aimed to increase the food and fodder production and to enhance soil fertility concurrently. In this system, grasses and/or legumes are grown in rotation with arable crops. The objectives of this system are tonnage production of fodder and enriching soil fertility. Ley farming is more productive as well as sustainable against climate and economic risks than cropping alone. Productivity of drylands can be improved by incorporating leguminous pastures/crop rotation. The soil fertility is increased when a ley is sown for 3 years or more. Considerable amount of organic matter is added through roots and above ground biomass and legumes. There is reduction in weeds, pest and diseases since ley provides a break in the crop sequence. There is improvement of nutritious leguminous fodder crops in drylands. Yield of grain and stover of sorghum increased when it is grown after four years of continuous cultivation of *Stylosanthes hamata.*

Alley cropping

Alley cropping is an agroforestry system in which fast growing N fixing shrubs are planted as hedgerows. Food crops are grown in alleys formed by hedgerow of trees and shrubs. It is also known as hedgerow cropping or hedgerow intercropping system. Alley cropping is an important step in meeting the fodder, fuel and food requirements of the farmer. This system is most suitable for marginal and sub-marginal lands. Scientists at International Institute for Tropical Agriculture (IITA), Nigeria, have developed this system of agroforestry in the 1970s.

In this system, trees or shrubs, preferably legumes are planted in rows along the contour. The hedgerows are periodically pruned to prevent shading and to reduce competition with the associated food crops. In the summer after the harvest of food crops, the hedgerows are allowed to grow freely to cover the land. Agronomic management of both the hedgerows and alley crops is very important to optimize the production.

Advantages: Alley cropping is more remunerative under rainfed conditions. The trees are often pruned and lopped. The foliage obtained from these trees is either used as green manure or mulch in the field or as fodder for animal during lean period. In the semi-arid regions, where organic matter and nutrients are deficient, alley cropping has high potential for improving the soil fertility and increasing the biomass production. It has been reported that growing *Leucaena* enabled improvement in the soil fertility. On an average, there was increase in organic carbon from 0.37 to 0.43%, available N from 163 to 190, P from 8.2 to 14.9 and K from 460 to 500 kg/ha with decrease in soil pH.

In the hilly areas, alley cropping has specific role of protecting the soil from erosion. The tree hedge and alternate strips of erosion permitting and resisting crops reduce water and soil loss and increase the productivity of land.

Classification of alley cropping

According to the purpose for which the alleys are raised, alley cropping may be grouped into:

- Forage alley cropping
- Green manure -cum-mulch alley cropping
- Forage- cum-mulch alley cropping
- Forage-cum-green manure alley cropping.

Among them, forage alley cropping is recommended as an alternate land use system for semi-arid regions with main benefit of green fodder production during the dry season.

Management of alley cropping

Several tree species are used as hedge species. They should have the ability of easy establishment, fast growing nature and high foliage productivity. They should be tolerant to pruning and ability to coppice vigorously. Trees such as *Leucaena leucocephala, Sesbania grandiflora, Giliricidia sepium and Cassia siamea* are used in this system. Among these species, *Leuceana* is preferred due to its easy management on heavy soils with less than 800 mm of rainfall. *Leucaena* performs better than any other perennial herbaceous legume.

Arable crops are grown in the interspaces between the rows of trees or woody shrubs. Crops such as maize, sorghum, pulses and oilseeds (particularly safflower and groundnut) are grown as alley crops. Based on the classical work at IITA, Wilson and Kang (1981) reported that the alley cropping system based on *Leucaena*-maize was promising because, *Leucaena* tops maintained maize grain yield at reasonable levels with no additional N input on a sandy soil. Under Semi-Arid Tropics with vertisols, maximum production was obtained from the alley cropping system of *Leucaena* and sorghum. *Leucaena* can be grown with sorghum + pigeonpea (1:1) for higher biomass and net returns. In entisols with 3% slope under rainfed condition, *Brassica campestris var.* yellow sarson grown during winter season within the alleys of Eucalyptus hybrids and *D. sissoo* gave fairly good yield. Under Jhansi (U.P.) conditions, *Leucaena leucocephala* and *Sesbania sesban* as hedge crops and pearlmillet as alley crop provided higher LER.

Alley width

Proper maintenance of alley width is important to get fairly high yield of alley crops. Alley width may vary from 4.5 to 6.0 m for vegetative cover and higher fodder yield. Wider alleys of 10-15 m may serve as vegetative barriers in conjunction with terrace level structures. Studies at Jhansi have emphasized the need to maintain 6-8 m alley width so as to minimize yield reduction of alley crops. In *Leucaena* + maize, wheat and greengram system, fodder and wood yields were higher in the narrow alleys while grain production was higher in the wide alleys. Growth and yield of the crops are suppressed when grown close to tree rows. As the distance between the field crops and hedge plants increased growth and yield performance of the crops have also increased. Poor performance of intercrops nearer to the hedgerows is mainly attributed to competition between field crops and tree species for light and water. However, hedge plants did not have any adverse effect on the yield of crops during the initial period of establishment.

Hedge management

The perennial vegetation is managed in such a way as to keep the competition between the hedge species and field crops at a minimum. To reduce shading effect of the hedgerows on companion crops, frequent pruning should be adopted. Height of the hedge and intensity of pruning affect the biomass production of hedge species. The cutting height varies from 0.5-0.75 m and approximately 4 cuttings can be adopted in a year at every three months interval. It has also been reported that fairly good yield of arable crop could be obtained with the alleys of eucalyptus hybrid, and *D. sissoo* when pruned twice (May and October), a year before sowing of crops. Several cereal fodder crops like sorghum, pearl millet, maize and teosinte were grown along with *Leucaena* both under managed canopy at a height of 50-100 cm and also as a full grown tree. Under managed canopy, the productivity of the associated crops were generally reduced by 15-20%, whereas under non-managed canopy the yield reduction of associated fodder crops was 40-60% during rainy season and 30% during summer season.

Windbreaks and shelterbelts

Any barrier erected to break or slow down the effect of wind is known as windbreak. A belt of trees or shrubs maintained for the purpose of shelter from wind, sun or snowdrift is called a shelterbelt. The area coverage under shelterbelt is more extensive than under windbreaks.

In India the mean daily wind speed is 10-15 kmph. However, during the cyclonic storm, wind speed is very high (>50-60 kmph). In arid and semi-arid regions, where the soil has loose sand, soil particles are disturbed and shifting sand dunes are formed. The salt laden wind causes serious damage to the vegetation if saltish water is laid on leaves. In North India, strong cold winds during January-February cause extensive crop damage. Strong winds cause uprooting and lodging of crops.

Windbreaks divert the whole force of the wind over their top. Generally the windbreaks and shelterbelts are planted in parallel line one after another so that the direction of wind would necessarily reduce the wind velocity. The climatic factors such as temperature, precipitation, humidity, wind velocity, snow, evapotranspiration and frost are influenced to some extent by windbreaks and shelterbelts.

Windbreaks and shelterbelts have beneficial effect of conserving the soil and moisture in the sheltered areas. Wind in carrying the soil particles is obstructed by windbreaks and shelterbelts and hence minimize deposition of soil particles.

Designing windbreaks and shelterbelts

Maximum protection is obtained when windbreaks are planted in right angle to the direction of wind. In areas with 5% slope, windbreaks should be planted along the contours. Windbreaks should be continuous and any a passage or road through windbreaks should be avoided. The width of the windbreaks decides the degree of density required at different levels. Moderately dense barriers are considered best as they filter the wind and do not allow dogging. The density of 50-60% is considered best. Tall trees with cylindrical or conical shape are preferable. The trees should have wind firmness, moderate to dense crown, strong stem, uniform fast growth and good height.

SOCIAL FORESTRY

Social forestry is a programme of forestry development and conservation under various agro-climatic and soil conditions through (i) mixed plantation on wastelands and panchayat lands and (ii) reafforestation of degraded forests and raising shelter belts.

The objective of social forestry is to meet the basic needs of rural community aiming at bettering the conditions of living through (i) meeting the fuel wood, fodder and small timber requirement, (ii) protecting agricultural fields against wind, (iii) meeting the recreational need (iv) maximizing production and increasing farm returns.

There are three component in social forestry programmes, (i) farm forestry (ii) community forestry and (iii) rehabilitation of degraded land.

In the farm forestry, tree plantation and management is purely on private lands. In community forestry, afforestation is practiced in the lands outside the conventional forest area for the benefit of the local population. This is practiced on community lands, village panchayat lands and government wastelands and managed by the community. In rehabilitation of degraded forest area, afforestation practices are in the degraded forests mainly to meet the fuel wood and fodder requirement of the local population. Rehabilitation of degraded forest is usually managed by the forest department.

The National Commission on Agriculture (NCA, 1976) recommended the programme of raising trees, grasses and fodder in the farmers' own land, village commons, wastelands and degraded forests close to habitations to meet the requirement of fuel wood, fodder, small timber for small housing and agricultural implements and thorns for fencing. The programme of 'Van Mahotsav' was proposed to motivate the farmers to take up tree planting with the creation of a National Wasteland Development Board (NWDB) during 1985 and special emphasis was given on social forestry.

The social forestry programmes are strengthened with aid from different international donor agencies *viz.,* World Bank, Swedish International Development Agencies (SIDA), United States Agency for International Development (USAID) and Canadian International Development Agency (CIDA).

Management of tree species

Raising quality seedlings is an important activity that decides the early vigour and establishment. Choice of good seeds ensures better germination and vigour. Good quality seeds should be collected and used to produce quality seedlings. The seeds should be collected from tall, straight and best shaped, middle aged to mature trees. Young and over matured trees should be avoided since the seeds from these trees may have low viability. Fully ripened seeds/pods without any pest incidence should be collected and large, plump and well-filled seeds to be used for better germination. It is also important to find out the germination %age of the specific seed lot. The collected seeds should be dried and stored in airtight containers to maintain viability. There are two classes of seeds based on the nature of longevity:

Orthodox seeds: The seeds can be dried at low moisture (5%) and stored successfully at low or sub-normal temperature for a long period.

Recalcitrant seeds: Seeds cannot survive drying below a relatively high moisture content (20-50%) and cannot be stored successfully for a long period. The viability of seeds varies with the species from 2 weeks to 2 years and more. Seeds of species of Acacia, Albizia, Cassia, Leucaena and Prosopis can be stored successfully for more than 20 years. However, the seeds of Azadirachta, Hevea and Shorea cannot be stored for more than two weeks.

Nursery management

Seed treatment

Seeds of many tree species show some degree of dormancy. These seeds require a period of storage referred to as post-harvest dormancy. The seeds of some tree species, particularly those with hard seed coat, should be subjected to scarification. The seeds are also treated with hot or cold water as well as chemicals (*e.g. Acacia sp., Albizia sp).* Mechanical scarification is required for the seeds of *Cassia sp., Delonix sp. and Terminalia arjuna.*

Seeds of oaks and chestnut respond well to immersion in boiling water for 30 seconds. Alternate soaking and drying in the sun is a recognized method of treating the seeds of teak. Various chemical solutions may prove effective in softening the hard seed coats and rendering them permeable to water. The chemicals which have been used with success are lime water, dilute acid and dilute alkali solution with 5-15% concentration. The seeds may be soaked for 1 to 24 hours. The most commonly used chemical for various tree species is concentrated sulphuric acid.

Biofertilizers such as Rhizobium and Franckia are commonly used for supplying N to the tree species. Rhizobium can be used for legume seeds as seed treatment or to the seedling with FYM. Franckia can be used for the seedlings of species such as Alnus, Eleagnus and Casuarina. Azospirillum can be used as seed treatment and seedling dip for tree species of non-legumes. e. g. neem. Ectomycorrhizal fungi (VAM) are used for temperate forest species, particularly for Pines and Eucalyptus.

Fertilizer application

Proper manuring is important to boost the growth of the seedlings. Organic manures *viz.,* dried cow dung, sheep and goat manure, oil cakes, etc. can be applied. Fertilizers such as urea, ammonium sulphate and ammonium nitrate can also be used.

Sowing

Seeds are sown in the containers or in the nursery bed from where they are taken to the main field for planting. *e.g. Acacia, Cassia.* All large sized seeds are sown by this method. However, small sized seeds and those with poor germination are first sown in the mother bed. After a specific duration they are pricked out. *e.g. Eucalyptus, Casuarina.* Raising seedlings in the containers is a common practice.

The nursery bed is prepared by mixing soil, sand and farmyard manure in the ratio of 3:1:1. The surface of the seedbed is smoothed and moderately watered. Seeds are sown broadcast on the surface and lightly covered with a layer of fine earth. It is preferable to take up line sowing. Seeds are sown at proper depth; shallow sowing is preferable to deep sowing. After sowing, watering is important and this can be done using rose can. The seedlings should be protected from hot sunshine by providing shade with thatch, grass, palm leaf mattings, etc.

Pricking out

Moving of plants from one nursery bed to another or into a pot for better root and shoot growth is called as pricking out. This is commonly done for coniferous species like Pinus. This method has been found advantageous for Eucalyptus and Casuarina. Greater care is required while pricking out and planting the naked seedlings in the container. The age of the seedling for pricking out varies from species to species normally one week to 4 months. While pulling out, healthy and vigorous seedlings alone are chosen. Less healthy and poor grown seedlings are allowed to remain in the mother bed. The container should be moistened and a hole is made by inserting a wooden stick of small diameter. The depth of the hole should be more than the length of taproot. Seedlings should be planted in the hole carefully without any bending of the taproot. The hole must be filled with soil and pressed firmly on all sides. This operation should be done preferably on a humid day.

Stump or root shoot cutting

Cutting root and shoot is known as stump. Plants with a collar diameter of 1.5 -2.0 cm and taproot with a length of not less than 30 cm are selected. Shoots are cut off at 3 cm and all the lateral roots are pruned. The taproot should be cut at a distance of 20-30 cm from the collar region. The cutting should be done with a very sharp knife or scissors. The stump planting has been found to give better results in *Tectona grandis*.

Nursery care

Watering, weeding, culling out and pest and disease control are important for raising quality seedlings. At the initial stage, watering should be done twice a day for 15 days; after that once a day for a month. Finally the watering may be restricted to once in 4 days based on the evaporation demand. It is necessary that watering be always done with rose cans. The quantity of water is calculated as 200 ml per plant per watering. The quality of water is also utmost important.

Weak seedlings with lesser growth should be culled out periodically. Weeding is necessary as soon as the seedlings are established. It is important to keep the seedlings free from root competition. Container plants should be shifted periodically to avoid roots striking the ground. This can be carried out after 45 days and subsequently at an interval of one month. At the time of shifting, the plants should be graded according to height. The seedlings should be protected from insect attack with the application of sevin, monocrotophos, etc. Appropriate disease control measures should be also be taken.

Planting

Time of planting plays a vital role in survival and growth of tree plants. The most opportune time for planting tree seedlings is at the start of monsoon rains. Planting should be done in such a way that the collar of the plant should be at or near ground level and neither buried nor raised. Soil around the plant should be packed well after planting and a convex mound is formed around the plant with a circular depression around for rainwater to collect. Apart from planting in ordinary pits some of the special techniques such as saucer pits, crescent pits and trenches may be followed during monsoon or pre-monsoon seasons for moisture conservation. Normally seedlings are planted in square, rectangular, triangular or quinquennial espacement.

After care

After planting, weeding and soil working at the end of the rainy season are needed for better growth. Weeding should be done when the soil is dry enough to completely uproot the weeds. To provide better aeration, digging the soil around the plant is important. It also helps in preventing aeration and facilitates easy absorption of rainwater. In summer, mulching around the tree seedlings helps in checking evaporation losses. Leaf litter or some organic matter is used as mulch.

In case, seedling mortality is high, the plants are replaced with healthy seedlings. This operation is known as replacement of casualty and is also called 'beating up' or 're-filling'. Healthy, vigorous, robust and tall seedlings should be used for beating up. This operation should be done within a month of planting so that the planted seedlings could use the rainfall for their establishment and better growth.

The plants should be protected from illicit felling and browsing. Under agroforestry system, trees are protected as long as the annual crop is not harvested. After the harvest of crops, trees are left to face the fallow period during summer against hordes of cattle. Creation of biofence is the only practical alternative to protect the plants. Biofence can be raised through seeds and seedlings of *Acacia farnesiana, A. melligera, Albizia amara* and *Prosopis juliflora.* Stem cutting and vegetative propagules can be used for raising biofence such as *Agave americana, A. sisalana and Aloe barbadense.*

Survival %age of seedlings in spite of best efforts normally may not exceed about 40-50% due to subsequent hot summer. Watering atleast for the first summer after planting has given very good results. Wherever watering is done carefully and systematically the seedling survival is more than 90-95%. Approximately 5-7.5 litres of water is required per seedling at an interval of 7-12 days depending on the area and water availability. Pitcher pot technique can also be adopted with restricted water availability.

Tree management

Proper management of tree is very important in agroforestry. Otherwise, the crown may produce a striking shade effect which, in turn, may affect the productivity of the system. Tree canopy or tree cover has enormous effect on the under storey grown crops. The tree having dense canopy permits very little solar radiation to fall on the underneath crop to meet its light requirement. There are several management options available *viz.*, coppicing, pollarding, lopping and pruning.

Coppicing: The word 'coppice' means the ability to regenerate by shoot or root suckers of an established forest tree. This practice involves regular harvesting of trees which produce numerous shoots from the stump after cutting. Coppice sprouts usually grow vigorously because they are served by roots big enough to feed the former tree.

Pollarding: In this practice, the branches are removed usually at a height of about 1-3 m at periodical intervals. This practice is mostly adopted for live fence and alley cropping.

Lopping: During the lean period, major branches are removed to obtain fresh fodder. The fodder material obtained due to this practice depends on the species, its age, moisture level, soil fertility, season, severity of lopping and weather conditions. Lopping is a powerful management tool for controlling crown spread in the agroforestry systems.

Pruning: Small branches and twigs are removed one or two times during a year. The biomass/foliage obtained due to this operation is used as fodder. Such a practice is mostly adopted for maintaining trees/ shrubs especially in live fence and alley cropping systems.

WASTELAND DEVELOPMENT

Soil is the basic resource for all agricultural activities. However, over time as biotic pressure is built up beyond the carrying capacity of this resource, there is misuse or overuse of cropland. On account of disturbed hormony of natural environment, there are increasing instances of soil degradation. The reasons for land degradation may be due to inherent or imposed disabilities or both such as location, environment, chemical and biological properties and even suffer from management conditions. The explosive increase of population, increasing desire of man to exploit marginal and sub-marginal lands, pressure from industry for its raw material needs, defective land use and improper irrigation management emerged as the main factors causing land degradation. At some places, degradation has reached disastrous proportions and if not corrected in time, will have a devastating effect on our future population.

Failure in the restoration of degraded areas and increase in the population may reduce the available land area for productive use. Due to environmental destruction, the weaker section, particularly the rural poor and tribes, are affected mostly because their life revolves around constant search for food, fodder, fuel and water. As ecological conditions worsen, their survival becomes increasingly difficult.

Late Prime Minister of India, Shri Rajiv Gandhi, in his broadcast address to the nation on 5th January 1985 said "continuing deforestation has brought us face to face with a major ecological and socio-economic crisis. The trend must be halted. I propose immediately to set up a National Wasteland Development Board with the objective of bringing 5.0 million ha of land every year under fuel wood and fodder plantations". A technical Task Group was constituted by the Planning Commission and National Wasteland Development Board. The primary task was comprehensive estimation of wastelands in the country and to propose standardized definitions for various category of wastelands.

According to dictionary meaning, wasteland is the land area which is unfit for use. The lands, which are unproductive and least utilized, are termed as wastelands. This does not mean that they are unfit for use. Due to neglect or degradation, these lands are not utilized to their full potential. The Wasteland Survey and Reclamation Committee (1961) defined wastelands as those lands which are either not available for cultivation or left out as fallows and cultivable wastes.

According to the National Wasteland Development Board, wastelands are defined as the lands which are currently lying unutilized due to different constraints. These include culturable and unculturable wastelands. The wastelands are also termed as degraded lands.

Classification of wastelands

Out of 329 million ha of total geographical area in India, about 158 million ha comes under different kinds of land degradation. Wastelands are broadly grouped into culturable and unculturable wastelands.

Culturable wastelands

The lands are capable or have the potential for the development of vegetative cover; however, they are not being used due to different constraints of varying degrees such as erosion, waterlogging, salinization etc. Most of these lands can be put to some productive use after proper treatment and reclamation measures. Actually these lands are problematic lands instead of wastelands.

Unculturable wastelands

The lands that cannot be developed for vegetative cover are called unculturable wastelands. *e.g.*, barren rocky areas, snow-covered glacial areas.

Classification of wastelands based on National Commission on Agriculture (1976), Ministry of Agriculture and Irrigation, Govt. of India is given in Table 9.1.

National Wasteland Development Board (1987) classified the wasteland as follows:

1. Utilizable / Culturable wastelands
   a) Eroded lands include gullied and / ravinous land
   b) Undulating upland
   c) Waterlogged land
   d) Salt-affected areas include saline and alkali soils
   e) Shifting cultivation areas
   f) Degraded forest lands
   g) Degraded non-forest plantation
   h) Sand dunes, sand bar and coastal sand
   i) Minespoils and industrial wastelands
   j) Strip lands
   k) Pasture and grazing land
2. Unculturable wastelands
   a) Barren rock/stony wastes/sheet rock areas
   b) Steep slopy area
   c) Snow covered and / glacial area

TABLE 9.1: Classification of wastelands

Category	Spread
Raverine land, Coastal sandy areas, High altitude and steep sloping areas	Coastal region, interior mountainous regions, steep slopes in Himalayas
Salt- affected areas	Semi- arid and Indo Gangetic plains and other semi-arid areas in Peninsular region
Waterlogged areas	Low- lying areas in high rainfall regions and irrigated areas
Ravine land	Gujarat, Rajasthan, Madhya Pradesh and Uttar Pradesh
Shifting cultivation	North- Eastern region
Barren hill ridges and rock outcrops	Distributed in various states of the country

MANAGEMENT OF WASTELANDS

The characteristics of the wasteland and their development vary with the categories. Agroforestry system plays greater role in the development of culturable wastelands.

Raverine land

Rivers originating from Himalayas have twin actions of erosion and deposition. Depending on the course of rivers and speed of flow, heavy load of sand and silt is carried by the gushing streams. They deposit large quantities of sediments on way to the sea. Gradually land masses are formed which remain for some part of the season atleast above the flood level. Raverine lands are called as '*khadar*' in North India, '*diara*' in Eastern Uttar Pradesh and '*char*' in West Bengal. In Punjab, and Haryana, they are called '*Rao*' and '*cho*' which are most common in branched or multiple channel rivers. Development of such land is mainly based on adoption of suitable soil conservation measures. Planting live hedge is most beneficial in controlling erosion and large deposition of sediments.

Coastal sandy areas

India has a long coastal line of about 5600 km. Wind erosion is more serious and extensive, especially during monsoon seasons. There is blowing and shifting of sands during the monsoon and cyclonic periods. This causes heavy damage to the standing crops in the neighbouring areas. The problem is acute in Eastern coast of Orissa and Western coast of Kerala. In such areas, afforestation is necessary as it acts as a moderator of the effect of cyclone. All along the coastal areas, wide forest belt is to be created for moderating the effects of cyclones. Casuarina is an important tree suitable for coastal belts as it can stand high degree of salinity and moisture stress. It also acts as windbreak and it thrives best in sandy belts. Casuarina easily grows with least attention. Casuarina plantation on the sandy foreshore should be backed by plantation of other adaptable tree species further inland. These plantations can be maintained up to 10 metres width along the coast. The inner areas can be planted with cashew trees interspaced with coconut.

The species such as *Salvadora persica, S. oleoides, Atriplex nummularia* and *Juncus regidus* are suitable for saline coastal regions. *Simmondsia chinensis* (Jojoba), *Simuruba spp* and *Prosopis spp* are highly adopted for sand dune areas. Grasses *viz., Panicum maximum, Cenchrus spp, Chloris spp, Spinifex squamosus, Sporobolus spp* and *Cynodon dactylon* are most suited.

High altitude and steep slopy areas

In high altitude region of Himalayas, the soils suffer from excessive run off during monsoon, causing floods and there is moisture deficiency during the dry period. Indiscriminate grazing by cattle, especially sheep and goat including the nomadic herds, are the major causes for soil erosion in hilly areas. Hedgerow planting is required under hilly terrain. Nitrogen fixing tree species and shrubs suitable for agroforestry may be planted at close spacing. The space between trees and within the rows may be utilized for growing hedges with perennial grasses. Tree species such as

Acaia modesta, A. catechu, Prosopis juliflora, Populus alba, P. nigra, P. ciliata and P. candicuas are best suited. In Nilgiris with land slope of above 33%, perennial vegetation preferably with silvipasture and tea plantation is recommended.

Salt-affected soils

Salt- affected soils may be classified as saline soils and alkali soils. Saline soils are predominant in arid, semi-arid and coastal areas. The alkali (sodic) soils occur in the Indo-Gangetic plain and parts of Madhya Pradesh. In peninsular semi-arid tracts, sodic soils occur where the soils are irrigated injudiciously. Most of these soils have high productivity potential due to abundant nutrient reserve and ideal moisture retaining and release characteristics. Classification based on the United States Salinity Laboratory (USDA) and Soil Science Society of America (SSSA) is given in Tables 9.2 and 9.3.

TABLE 9.2: Classification of salt affected soils (USDA)

Class of soil	EC (mmhos /cm)	ESP	pH
Saline	>4	<15	<8.5
Saline- alkali	>4	>15	>8.5
Non saline –alkali	<4	>15	8.5-10.0

TABLE 9.3: Classification of salt affected soils (SSSA)

Class of soil	EC	SAR	pH
Saline	>2	-	-
Saline -sodic	>2	>15	>8.5
Sodic	-	>15	-

Salt affected soils of India

In India, about 7.0 m. ha of otherwise productive land is salt affected and a large part of it has got out of cultivation. The problem is acute in semi-arid and sub-humid Indo-Gangetic plains. The extent of salt affected areas in India is given in Table 9.4.

TABLE 9.4: Salt affected soils in India

Group	States	Approximate area (m.ha)
Coastal salt affected soils		
Coastal salt-affected soils of arid region	Gujarat	0.714
Deltaic coastal salt affected soils of the humid region	Orissa	1.394
	Andra Pradesh	
	Tamil Nadu	
	West Bengal	
Acid -salt affected soils	Kerala	0.016

Group	States	Approximate area (m.ha)
Salt- affected soils of the medium and deep black soil region	Karnataka, Madhya Pradesh, Andra Pradesh, Maharashtra	1.420
Salt- affected soils of the arid and semi-arid regions	Gujarat, Rajasthan, Punjab, Haryana, Uttar-Pradesh	1.000
Alkali soils of the Indo-Gangetic plains	Haryana, Punjab, Uttar-Pradesh, Bihar, Madhya-Pradesh.	2.500

Characteristics of salt- affected soils

Saline soils

Soils containing excess amount of soluble salts are called saline soils. The predominant soluble salts are chlorides and sulphates of sodium, magnesium and calcium. These soils sometimes contain appreciable amount of nitrate. Presence of excess amount of soluble salts induces flocculation of the clay fraction and hence the physical properties of the saline soils are generally good. Plant growth is affected by the osmotic effects of excess soluble salts. Accumulation of specific ions such as B, Cl and Na in plants to toxic levels may often affect plant growth adversely.

Alkali soils

Alkali soils have high Exchangeable Sodium Percentage (ESP) of above 15 which is generally considered as the limit between the normal and alkali soils. The predominant salts are carbonates and bicarbonates of sodium. The soils are also termed sodic soils. In the moist situation, there are black patches due to the dissolution of organic matter and subsequent evaporation. Surface of the soil becomes very hard during drying and turns muddy with the receipt of rain. The soils are completely disbursed due to high ESP and hence water stagnation occurs in the field. The bulk density of the sodic soils is normally high (1.5-1.65 g/cm^3) and hence root penetration is hampered. The tilth of the sodic soils are poor because of high pH and ESP. Seed germination and root growth are affected due to the presence of hard surface layer. Plant growth is adversely affected due to the toxic quantities of Na or deficiency of other essential plant nutrients like Ca and Zn.

Sources of excess salt in the soil

1. The salts get deposit due to impeded drainage, as the soil may have developed from the parent material having excess salts originating from weathering.
2. Irrigation water may contain salt and by continuous use of such water, salt accumulates and is deposited in large areas.

3. Salt accumulates on the surface due to capillary movement from the ground close to the soil surface.
4. Excess salt accumulation occurs due to high sub-soil water table, aridity and poor drainage.
5. Backwater flow or intrusion of seawater also causes sodicity in the coastal areas.

Management of salt affected soils

Management of salt affected soils depends on the climate, soil characteristics, including nature of the soils, available water resources and associated features in different regions.

RECLAMATION

Reclamation of sodic soils basically requires replacing excess sodium by calcium on the soil exchangeable complex. This is done through application of amendments and leaching out of the exchanged Na from the root zone. Gypsum ($CaSO_4$-$2H_2O$) is the cheapest and the most commonly used amendment for reclamation. Gypsum dissolves to a greater extent in sodic soils due to high ESP. The solubility is also found to increase with the fineness of the particle. The quantity of gypsum to be applied will depend upon the pH of the soil and texture. Gypsum @ 15 t/ha may be required to reclaim the affected soil. Combined application of gypsum and organics like green manuring (dhaincha) is found to be better than inorganic amendments alone.

Leaching with good quality water is necessary to leach down or remove the excess salt at the surface and the sodium released from the exchange complex. Proper drainage is important to keep the salt below the root zone.

Agroforestry for salt- affected areas

Utilization of problem soils for cultivation of forest trees is a desirable alternative since the crop production on the salt affected soil is uneconomical. In places where the ground water is saline and scarce in quantity as in arid and semi-arid regions, agroforestry could be practiced. Afforestation and pasture development are the two ways of managing the salt affected lands when other measures are considered uneconomical. Putting these lands under multipurpose tree species will fulfill the twin objectives of biological amelioration and harvesting biomass to meet the fuel, fodder and timber requirements. In general, plantations for fuel wood are rated better for saline soils than timber wood species.

- **Choice of tree species:** The following tree species are recommended for sodic soils:
- *Prosophis chilensis, P. juliflora, Acacia nilotica, A. catechu, A. auriculiformis, A. tortilis, A. arabica, A. ropens, A. aneura, Tamarix articulata, Casuarina equisetifolia, Eucalyptus hybrid, Albezia lebbeck, Azadirachta indica,*

Terminalia arjuna, Dalbergia sissoo, Salbadora persica, Leucaena leucocephala.

- **Grass species:** Grasses can also be grown in saline/sodic soils for reclamation and economic returns.
  - Karnal grass- *Diplachne fusca*
  - Rhodes grass- *Chloris gayana*
  - Bermuda grass - *Cynodon dactylon*
  - Para grass- *Brachiaria mutica*
  - Blue panic - *Panicum species*
  - Hybrid Napier *Pennisetum purpureum*
  - Guinea grass - *Panicum maximum*
  - Kallar grass- *Leptochloa fusca*
  - Alkali sacaton- *Sporobolus spp.*
- **Fruit trees:** Among the fruit trees, sapota is found to be the most promising. Date palm is highly salt tolerant. Guava, ber, pomegranate and custard apple are also suitable fruit trees for salt affected areas.

Management of trees in problem soils

Tree species can be grown successfully on the sodic soils by treating the soil of the planting pit with gypsum (3-4 kg/pit), FYM (25 kg/pit) and fertilizer application. This practice gives better response than replacing the sodic soil of the pit with good soil. The pH value considerably decreases throughout the profile soon after the application of amendment. Incorporation of gypsum and farmyard manure in the soil of the planting pit also helps in checking subsequent deterioration of the soil as a result of salt movement from the surrounding salt- affected areas.

Auger hole planting

This technique has been developed for planting trees in alkali soils. In this method, 100-150 cm deep and 20-30 cm diameter auger holes are made with tractor operated auger and trees are planted. It has been found that height, girth, growth and fuel wood production of *Prosopis* were more with auger hole planting.

Sub- surface planting

In this method, saplings are planted in the trenches or furrows of 30 cm deep and these trenches are also used for irrigation. As maximum salt builds up in the surface soil, planting saplings in the furrows is found highly suitable for saline soils.

Waterlogged and marshy lands

In the waterlogged areas, stagnation of water occurs for most part of the year because of imperfect drainage. In the coastal regions, waterlogging may be caused by intrusion of sea water in the lands below mean sea level as found in parts of the West Coast. Large extent of fields in the canal irrigated areas become unproductive due to waterlogging. The Central Board of Irrigation defined waterlogging as an area where the water table rises to an extent that the soil pores in the root zone of a crop becomes saturated resulting in restriction of the normal circulation of air, decline in the level of oxygen and increase in the level of carbon-di-oxide.

Marshy lands are permanently or periodically inundated by water and characterized by vegetation which include grasses and weeds.

Proper drainage is important to reclaim these areas. Tree species suitable for the waterlogged areas are: *Eucalyptus robusta, syzygium cumini, salix spp., Populus nigra, Terminalia arjuna and Acacia nilotica.* In marshy places, trees species best adopted are: *Baringtonia spp, Bischofia javania, Eucalyptus robusta, E. rudis, Lagerstroemia flosreginea and Casuarina equisetifolia.*

Gullied and ravinous land

Gully erosion is described as 'Cancer of the land' and is considered as the severest form of erosion. A narrow deep gash formed as a result of localized and concentrated run off by running water is called gully. Very deep (>9 m) and wide gullies with steep sides are known as 'ravines'. All gullies and ravines contribute considerably to soil erosion. The ravines are characterized by the absence of vegetation of any type. Run-off is maximum; slopes are steep and gullies are of varying depth, few metres to 100 metres or more. The ravines are classified as shallow, medium and deep based on the gully depth, bed width and area. Ravinous lands are mainly confined to the states of Uttar Pradesh, Madhya Pradesh, Rajasthan and Gujarat along the banks of Yamuna, the Chambal, the Mahi and Sabarmati and tributaries. In addition to the existing areas, about 8 thousand ha are added every year due to faulty management practices.

Afforestation

Small and narrow gullies are put under agroforestry. Silvipasture is suitable for medium and shallow gullies.

The deep and narrow gullies are best controlled by putting them to permanent vegetation. Deep gullies are utilized as woodlands by planting suitable tree species. Gully heads and sides are stabilized by planting grass species. Reducing the slopes of the gullies and diverting the surface flow are essential pre-requisites for any successful afforestation programme. Constructing gully plugs in the bed of the main and branch gully is important to conserve soil and moisture. Suitable species for afforestation of gully and ravinous land are given below:

1. **Trees and shrubs:** *Acacia nilotica, Acacia catechu, Azadirachta indica, Albizia lebbeck, Dendrocalamus strictus, Dalbergia sissoo, Prosopis chilensis syn. P. juliflora, Eucalyptus* sp.,
2. **Live hedges:** *Impomea carnea, Agave americana, Arundo donax, Vitex*

negundo.

3. **Grassess and legumes:** *Cenchrus ciliaris, Pennisetum pedicellatum, Saccharum spontaneum, Dicanthium annulatum, Cynodon dactylon, Heteropogon contortus, Stylosanthes* species.

Shifting cultivation

Shifting cultivation is a primitive cultivation technique and is a transition between food gathering and food production. Shifting cultivation is dominant in the tropical and sub-tropical high land regions of the world, having high rainfall, steep slopes and shallow soils. It involves 10% of population and 30% of exploitable land of our planet. In India, this system is prevalent in several parts of the North-Eastern Hill regions of Arunachal Pradesh, Meghalaya, Mizoram, Manipur, Nagaland and Tripura. It is also prevalent in some parts of Assam, Orissa, Madhya Pradesh, Andhra Pradesh and Bihar. Shifting cultivation is popularly known as '*jhuming*' in the North Eastern zone of India. It is called as '*khallu*' or '*kurwa*' in Bihar, '*dahiya*' or '*podo*' in Orissa, Madhya Pradesh and Andhra Pradesh. Shifting cultivation is also known as 'slash and burn' or 'swidden' cultivation. It is estimated to cover an area of 4.36 million ha. Shifting cultivation is defined as the practice of cultivating clearings scattered in the reservoir of natural vegetation (forest, grass, woodland) and of abandoning them as soon as the soil is exhausted; and this includes the practice of shifting homesteads in order to follow the cultivator's search for new fertile area.

The practice of shifting cultivation consists of three phases: land clearing, cultivation phase and restoration phase.

Land clearing

Forest vegetation is felled down at various successional stages on the hill slope during winter months of December and January. The slash are then allowed to dry and burnt during February to April for nutrient enrichment, moderation of pH and charcoal. Fields are cleared of boulders and stones from surface in the process on clearing and piled-up forming bunds on slope edges and field boundary.

Cultivation phase

Minimum tillage is generally adopted and practiced on contour, using hand tools and bullock drawn implements. Hill slopes under shifting cultivation are mostly cultivated during *kharif* season, with pure or mixed crops. The crops include Indian millet, finger millet, upland rice, pigeonpea, blackgram, rice bean, niger, horsegram, etc. This cycle of cultivation varies from 3 to 5 years. The crop yield sharply declines in the successive years.

Restoration phase

A short period of cropping generally alternated with a long period of fallow ranging 5 to 50 years. Fields are allowed for natural restoration.

Impact of shifting cultivation

Burning of vegetation in shifting cultivation alters the plant nutrient supply from organic to inorganic form. Some of the nutrients, C, N and S are lost by volatilization while burning the slash. A sizable quantity of nutrients, particularly K, Ca and Mg are lost before the onset of the first rain through blown off ash due to strong winds in the drier period. During the short 'jhum' cycle, the soil fertility deteriorates to a very low level.

During the fallow period, soil fertility is lost due to erosion and other causes. Wrong tillage practices in shifting cultivation promote run off and soil erosion. Average soil loss due to shifting cultivation has been recorded to be 40.9 t/ha in Meghalaya. It is reported that erosion rates on 50-60% slope are 147 t of soil loss/ha under first year of shifting cultivation and 170 t/ha in the second year.

Under '*Jhum*' cultivation, some of the weed species, *Eupatorium odoratum* at lower elevation and *E. adenophorum* at higher elevation, become dominant.

Shifting cultivation causes large scale damage to the forests and results in deforestation and denudation of hilly slopes. During 'jhum' cycle, large number of edible vegetations are cut and burnt. Shifting cultivation and deforestation have been identified as major constraints in developing sustainable food production system in the Northeastern region. About 19.8% of the total geographical area of the region has become degraded or wastelands.

Management of shifting cultivation

It is necessary to integrate conservation measures and improved farming to stabilize production at a higher level. These measures may help in slowing down resource degradation and accelerating aggravation in the system.

Clearing and cultivation management

The land use and farm planning should depend upon the hill land classification. Area should be treated at terrace and inter-terrace level with mechanical and vegetative conservation measures. Improved vegetative cover, land configuration management and alley farming will form the base for sustained production achieving better soil and moisture conservation and improved nutrient cycling. The terrace should be protected against erosion. Contour bunds, bench terraces and half moon terraces are the conservation measures that are required for the treatment of land. Such land uses are expected to retain about 90% of the annual rainfall with negligible soil loss. Plantation of vegetative barrier could be ideal for both erosion control and improved nutrient cycling. It is possible to get higher production of finger millet by 80% under natural barrier.

Restoration management

Lack of restoration management results in slow build up of soil fertility. Normally it takes 5 years to build up vegetation and 8-10 years to restore fertility status. Retained fallow vegetation, planted vegetative barriers and integration of cultivation to restoration phase by perennial pigeonpea are successful in Orissa.

Agroforestry systems for shifting cultivation

Suitable farming systems in shifting cultivation include forestry, silvipasture/ horticulture and agriculture. Three tier system has been suggested by the ICAR centre, shillong. In this system, trees are recommended at the hill top, horticultural crops in the middle portion of the hill slopes and opening of terraces at the lower portion for cultivation of field crops. The forestry systems are primarily based on the production of fruits (pineapple, jack, mandarin) nuts (arecanut) and betel vine. These should be integrated with woody perennials which supply fuel and timber for domestic use.

Broom grass+schima systems are commonly practiced on most of the degraded boulderly lands with high slopes and shallow soil depth.

The silvipastural system comprising *Alnus nepalensis,* pine apple and forage crops like Guinea grass (*Panicum maximum)* or Nandi grass *(Setaria sphacelata)* coupled with Stylo *(Stylosanthes guyanensis)* could be the sustainable agroforestry system for hills with 30-60% slope in Meghalaya.

Lower areas of hilly slope are terraced and utilized for raising field crops according to the requirement of the farmers. Crops such as rice, maize, finger millet, mustard, sesame, blackgram, and root crops like ginger and turmeric may be grown. The terraces may be stabilized with mechanical measures and planted with fodder grasses or legumes on risers. Fodder grasses/legumes such as *Stylosanthes hamata, S. quyanensis, Clitoria ternatia, Setaria sphacelata* and thin napier are suitable for terrace rises.

Taungya system

'Taungya' is a Burmese word meaning hill cultivation. In this system, government lands are temporarily allotted to the cultivators. They are allowed to plant forest tree species and to raise agricultural crops in between the rows of forest tree species simultaneously for about 3-5 years. Thereafter, cultivators are shifted to another patch of land.

This system was practiced as early as 1856 in Myanmar by establishing teak plantations. Regular 'taungya' cultivation as a system of raising forest plantations was started in North Bengal in 1911. In India, it is now followed in Kerala, West Bengal, Uttar Pradesh, Tamil Nadu, Andhra Pradesh, Orissa, Karnataka and North Eastern Hill regions. This system is used for raising forest plantations and for regenerating forests. This system provides proper use of land and maximizes production. It also facilitates employment opportunities to unemployed rural people. Important tree species and field crops suitable for 'taungya' system are given in Table 9.5.

TABLE 9.5: Important trees and agricultural crops for 'taungya' system

Trees	Crops
West Bengal	
Tectona grandis	Paddy, maize, millets
Shoerea robusta	Turmeric, ginger
Schima wallichii	Pine apple
Cryptomeria japonica	Hemp
Michelia spp	
Uttar Pradesh	
Shoerea robusta	Paddy, maize, sorghum
Tectona grandis	Wheat, barley
Acacia catechu	Pigeonpea, soybean
Dalbergia sissoo	Rape-seed
Eucalyptus spp.	
Populus spp.	
Kerala	
Eucalyptus spp	Paddy
Tectona grandis	Tapioca
Bombex ceiba	Ginger
	Turmeric

Sand dune management

The soils of the arid zone are mostly sandy to sandy loam with excessive permeability. In India, about 22.7% of total geographical areas is occupied by sandy soils mainly in Rajasthan, Gujarat, Punjab, and Haryana. The major characteristics of these regions are severe wind erosion, high temperature, scanty and erratic rainfall, frequent droughts, high rate of evaporation, devoid of Perennial River and sparse vegetation. Most of these areas are covered by drifting or semi-established sand dunes.

The movement of sand dunes occurs particularly during dry rainless period with high wind velocity. This seriously affects the houses, buildings, farmlands, roads, railways, canals and watercourses. Sand dunes shift from one place to another due to blowing wind at high speed in regions devoid of natural vegetation. The problem is more serious in the western part of the desert in India where the vegetation is negligible and sand dune concentration is maximum. They need immediate attention for their stabilization. Some of the dunes are semi-stabilized but their crest and flanks remain active because of cultivation activity on them or due to improper management.

Afforestation

The afforestation option varies with respect to degree of aridity, wind velocity and availability of different materials. Shifting sand dunes are managed with the following methods:

1. Protection against biotic interferences
2. Mulch barrier in parallel strips
3. Planting suitable trees, grasses and shrubs to act as wind breaks

The plant species chosen should have deeply buried rhizomes or prostrate growth with stem anchored by abundant adventitious fibrous roots for rehabilitation of sand dunes. Suitable species for afforestation of sand dunes are listed in Table 9.6. Among the tree species *Prosopis cineraria* is considered as the king of trees in desert areas because of its natural spread in this area. However, under plantation condition, some initial care of the tree is required during first year of planting. *Dalbergia sissoo* is found more capable of establishing itself in desert ecosystem. Among the grass species, *Cenchrus ciliaris* performs better.

TABLE 9.6: TABLE 9.6: Species suitable for sand dunes

Trees	Bushes	Grasses
Prosopis cineraria	*Ctotalaria burhia*	*Cenchrus ciliaris*
P. chilensis	*Calligonum polygonoides*	*Lasiurus sindicus*
Acacia tortilis	*Aerva javanica*	*Panicum turgidum*
Acacia radiana	*Ziziphus* spp	*P. antidotale*
Zizyphus mauritiana		
Erianthus munja		
Dalbergia sissoo		

Wind breaks: Tall plants of the following species may be used as wind breaks for sand dune management.

Dalbergia sissoo, Albizia lebbeck, Acacia nilotica, Tamarix spp., Parkinsonia aculeata

Barren rock hill ridges and rock out crops

The rock exposure for varying lithology is often barren and devoid of soil cover and vegetation. There will be low canopy coverage at the top of the hill primarily due to poor/restricted growth as there is no soil in the hills. Extensive rock outcrops exist in the Deccan plateau, Eastern and Western ghats, the Aravallis and Vindhyan ranges. They are generally termed as skeletal areas where the soils are very shallow, coarse, poor, eroded and degraded. The selection of species depends on the rainfall and other climatic factors of the areas. The species suitable for barren rock hill ridges and rock outcrops are given in Table 9.7.

TABLE 9.7: Species suitable for barren rock hill ridges and rock outcrops

Trees species	Shrubs	Grasses
Areas of low to medium rainfall		
Ecalyptus tereticornis *Dendrocalamus strictus* *Melia azadarach* *Albizia lebbeck* *Acacia catechu* *Ailanthus excelsa* *Hardwickia binata* *Cassia siamea* *Prosopis chilensis* *Dalbergia sissoo*	*Carrisa spinarium* *Dichrostachys cinerea* *Indigofera articulata* *Inga dulcis*	*Cenchrus ciliaris* *C. setigerus* *Dicanthium annulatum* *Panicum antidotale* *Pennisetum pedicellatum*
Area of high elevation upto 2000 m		
Robinia pseudoacacia *Populus ciliata* *Pinus roxburghii*		

CHAPTER 10

Post-Harvest Management

Proper post-harvest management is required to avoid appreciable loss of agricultural produce. It has been estimated that about 10% of durable commodities and 40% of perishable commodities are lost due to improper harvest and post-harvest practices. It is necessary to adopt improved post-harvest practices starting from the harvest to consumption to reduce such losses. Proper time and method of harvesting are important to avoid yield losses in the field. Both early and late harvest is detrimental with respect to yield and quality. The harvested produce should be properly threshed, cleaned and graded. Appropriate method of drying and proper storage also is necessary.

TOOLS AND MACHINERY FOR HARVESTING AND THRESHING

Harvesting

Harvesting is traditionally done by sickles which are easily available at low cost. Their output is, however, low and effort is required for cutting the produce. The local sickles are made of mild steel and require frequent sharpening.

Serrated sickles

The serrated sickles based on Japanese and Italian designs are made of carbon or special alloy steels and have a self-sharpening edge. These require less effort and are safer to operate. It is possible to cover 18-20% more area without getting fatigued.

Mechanical reaper harvester

Machine harvest facilitates quicker coverage and timely harvest. Mechanical reaper harvester is used for various crops. These may be operated by tractor or power tiller or they are self-propelled. They have been developed based on Japanese and Chinese designs and are capable of harvesting 0.25-0.4 ha an hour. Reaper harvesting is practiced for wheat, rice, soybean and finger millet.

Combine harvester or combine

It is possible to harvest and thresh the produce simultaneously using the combine harvester. Combine harvesting of wheat, rice and soybean has been accepted in regions suffering for custom hire service. Combine harvesting costs Rs. 800/ha in North India for wheat and soybean and Rs. 1500/ha for rice in the South. Straw disposal has been a major problem where combine harvesting is in vogue. An exclusive straw collector and binder or straw combine harvester has been developed to facilitate straw disposal. More than 60% of rice and 50% of wheat in Punjab is estimated to be harvested by combines.

Threshing

Threshing of crops by animal trampling is arduous and time consuming. Traditionally, wheat and barley are threshed by bullocks which results in considerable loss and poor quality grain. A mechanical power thresher operated by 5-20 hp engine, electric motor or tractor is available for threshing wheat, rice and a few other crops. The capacity ranges from 100 kg/hour to as high as 1200-1400 kg/hour. Farmers use them on individual ownership basis or on custom hiring. About 70-80% of wheat, barley, gram, soybean, sorghum and pearl millet are threshed by mechanical power thresher.

Multi-crop threshers are suitable for threshing major cereals, oilseeds, and pulses. These threshers have provision to control concave clearance and threshing drum and blower speed independently so as to reduce grain breakage and improve cleaning. Sunflower and safflower which are difficult to thresh with traditional methods can also be threshed by the multi-crop threshers.

Rice is threshed by manual beating wherein losses are quite high. Pedal operated paddy threshers reduce drudgery. These have become popular in Eastern India. The rasp-bar type paddy thresher causes less breakage to rice stem and the straw can be put to better use. These threshers have become very popular in Andhra Pradesh, Tamil Nadu, Karnataka and Kerala.

A simple tubular maize sheller has become very popular for removing grain from dried maize. It is possible to remove 16-24 kg/hour with this tool compared to 5-8 kg/hour with a sickle or hand beating. Women can handle this machine with ease.

Groundnut kernels are removed by hand, especially for seed purposes with an output of 5-6 kg of kernel in one hour. A rocking type manual groundnut decorticator is effective for shelling the groundnut pods. About 60 kg of groundnut can be shelled in an hour with the use decorticator.

TIME OF HARVEST

Time of harvesting is important to avoid losses during harvest. It is advantageous to harvest the crop at physiological maturity. However, it is always not possible to take up harvest at this stage due to scarcity of labour and hence harvest may be taken up calculating the crop duration. Yellowing of leaves, drying of grains or pods and bursting of bolls are the general symptoms for taking up harvest. For the indeterminate type of crops like sesame, which may have both immature and mature capsules at a time, harvesting can be done when 75% of the capsules are matured. In crops like finger millet, staggered harvesting may be attempted. Criteria for harvesting of some of the important crops are given in Table 10.1.

TABLE 9.1: TABLE 10.1: Criteria for harvesting of crops

Crop	Criteria for harvesting
Rice	30-35 days after heading; 80% of the panicles are straw coloured; moisture content of grain at 20-25%.
Wheat	Hard dough grain stage; straw becomes dry and brittle.
Corn	Seed moisture content at 34%; cob dried.
Chickpea	Plants become reddish brown; leaves dry up and start shedding.
Pigeonpea	35-40 days after flowering; about 80 % pods turn brown.
Groundnut	Yellowing of leaves, shedding of older leaves, development of purple colour of the testa; dark colouring inside the shell.
Rapeseed- mustard	75 % of the silique turn yellow, seeds are firm when pressed between the fingers, seed moisture at 30%, seeds turn natural brown colour.
Sunflower	Back of heads turns to lemon yellow in colour; some of the bracts dry up.
Sugarcane	Withering of lower leaves; brix -20 %; sucrose -15 %.
Jute	50% pod stage (120-150 days)
Cotton	Bolls well -dried; fully opened; stalks dry.
Tobacco (FCV)	Leaves green to light yellow

HARVESTING TECHNIQUES

Harvesting techniques vary according to the crops. Generally the entire biomass is harvested and the economic produce is processed. In some occasions, economic produce is harvested and the stover or stalk removed later. In either case, manual labour is used in India. However, due to increasing labour shortage, machinery is nowadays engaged for harvesting. Methods of harvesting for different crops are described below:

Cereals

1. Entire crop is cut close to the ground level. The sheaves are bundled, taken to the threshing floor. Threshing is done manually beating the sheaves against any hard material like stone or wood. Grains are collected, dried and bagged. Threshing machines are used for separating the grains. Recently combine harvesters are in use to harvest and thresh the produce. *e.g.* rice, wheat.
2. Earheads are removed, dried and grains are separated manually, using cattle or machinery. Stover is harvested separately. *e.g.*, maize, sorghum, pearl millet, finger millet.
3. Whole plant is cut and transported to the threshing floor. Entire produce is dried in the sunlight and the grains are separated manually or using cattle. *e.g.* millets.

Pulses

Harvesting is done by cutting or uprooting the crop and the produce is dried in the threshing floor. Grains are separated by beating with sticks or trampling by animals. Hand picking of matured pods is also practiced. Normally hand picking is done 2-3 times.

Oilseeds

In groundnut, entire plant is pulled out manually at the optimum soil moisture. Plants are also pulled out by digging with a spade, operating plough or blade harrow. This practice is mostly followed in drylands due to moisture scarcity at the time of harvest. The pulled out plants are stacked and the pods are stripped, cleaned and dried.

Matured earheads are cut (sunflower) or capsules are collected (castor), dried and grains are separated by beating with sticks or treating under the feet of bullock.

Whole crop is cut using sickle, carried to the threshing floor and stacked. Threshing is done by beating with a stick or trampling under the feet of bullock. *e.g.* sesame, rapeseed-mustard, soybean.

Fibre crops

The produce (kapas) is hand picked from the well burst bolls in cotton. It is advisable to harvest the produce in the morning hours. Prevalence of high humidity helps to harvest the kapas clean, devoid of dry leaves and bracts. It is important to select good quality kapas. The puffy ones are separated from stained, discoloured and insect attacked kapas.

In jute and mesta, the grown up plants are cut close to the ground level or uprooted. They are bundled and stacked in the field for drying of leaves. They are processed by retting.

Sugarcane

Stalks are cut at ground level. Water shoots and top most one or two immature nodes are discarded. Dry and green trash adhering to the cane is also removed. The dry and dead canes are rejected. A minimum of binding materials of dry and green trash should be used. Harvested cane should be processed for jaggery or white sugar within 12 hours of harvest. When kept beyond this period, there is deterioration in quality.

Tobacco

One of the methods of harvesting tobacco is called 'priming'. In this method, two or three leaves which have completed their growth and turned green to yellowish green or slightly yellow in colour are detached from the plant. This method of harvesting is generally followed for cigarette tobacco. Another method of harvest is called as stalk-cut method. This method is adopted for harvesting cigar, cherroot, chewing and hookah types. In this method, plants are cut close to the ground level using sickle and generally left in the field overnight for wilting. The leaves are then processed according to the type of tobacco.

DRYING TECHNIQUES

Drying is the process of removal of moisture from the material to prevent the development of favourable environment for the growth of moulds and insects that normally cause spoilage of the grain. In the drying process, heat is used to evaporate the moisture from the grain and moving air to carry away evaporated moisture. Optimum moisture level is required for the safe storage of the grain. This depends on the grain type, climatic and storage situations. Rice can be safely stored for 2-3 months at a moisture content of 13-14%. Grains can be stored beyond 3 months with the moisture content of 12-12.5%.

Based on the mode of heat transfer, drying methods are classified into three types: (1) Conduction drying, (2) Convection drying and (3) Radiation drying

1. **Conduction drying:** Heat is transferred to the wet solid mainly by conduction through a solid surface (normally a metal). The vapourized moisture is removed independent of the heating media.
2. **Convection drying:** This method of drying is most popular in grain drying. Heat is transferred to wet solid mainly by convection. Drying agent (hot gases) is used to supply heat and carry away the vaporized moisture. Under natural air-drying, the unheated air is utilized for drying the grains. This method is generally used in the farm level for drying grains for short-term storage. However, for large quantity, heated air is used to dry the grains at a short span of time.
3. **Radiation drying:** Sun-drying is an example for radiation drying. The

radiant energy is absorbed by the grains and transformed into heat energy.

Tempering: Rice grain should not be dried too fast. The drying process should be slow and uniform to maintain the quality. Fast drying causes internal grain stress which leads to cracking and subsequent breakage during milling. To overcome internal stress and to reduce cracking, it is necessary to temper the grain. This process is done between drying periods and it permits the moisture within the grain to equalize. Tempering also increases drying efficiency.

Grain drying systems

There are two systems of drying: (i) sun drying (ii) mechanical drying.

1. **Sun drying:** This method of drying is widely practiced for drying of grains. Wet grains are spread in thin layer on flat surfaces. Constant turning is important to prevent top layers getting over dried and bottom layers to receive heat and air movement necessary for drying. Sun drying has gained popular acceptance to farmers because of its nil cost. Sun drying, however, has the following disadvantages: (i) it needs good, sunny weather; (ii) it is labour intensive; (iii) there is handling problem; and (iv) grain loss due to spillage and consumption by birds is high.
2. **Mechanical drying:** It is an alternate method to sun drying. Mechanical equipments are used for holding the grain, blowing the air through the grain mass and heating the air.

The whole process of grain drying is divided into thin layer drying and deep bed drying. In the thin layer drying, all grains are fully exposed to the drying and grain drying is uniform. "Thin" layers are widely used because of their relatively low cost and ease in operation. In the deep bed drying, all the grains are not fully exposed to drying air. The condition of the drying air changes with the grain mass and depth of grain bed. On-farm static bed batch dryers are designed on this principle.

Grain dryers

There are two broad categories of grain dryers: (i) unheated air dryers (ii) heated air dryers.

Unheated air dryers

These are also called natural air-drying. This process is commonly used for on-farm drying of small amount of grains. These are further classified as full bin drying and layer drying. Drying bins are also used as storage bins. Though natural air system alone is used, external heat source can be supplied during unfavourable weather. Round metal bin, square bin and rectangular bin are some of the natural air dryers in use. For aeration, both propeller and centrifugal types of blows are used. Various air distribution systems like perforated floor and central horizontal duct are adopted.

Heated air dryers

1. **Batch -in- bin dryers:** Small capacity (1-2 t capacity units) batch-in-bin-dryers are designed for farm or village level operation. The bin has a perforated floor with a flat or sometimes inclined bed to facilitate unloading. Rice is spread 0.6-1.2 m deep over the bin and dried. The fan and air-heater are operated until drying is complete. Grain is then removed and another batch of grain is used for drying.

   Large capacity batch-in-bin dryers are mostly round or rectangular in shape. The capacity of the bin ranges from 10 to several hundred tonnes. A maximum depth of 3 m is used for rice with moisture content upto 18%. Larger capacity (10-100 tonnes) batch-in-bin drying systems are of many forms (round vs. rectangular) and are made of prefabricated steel wood depending on economic conditions.

   Drying air temperature, depth of grain bed, airflow rate, moisture content, kind and intended use of the product are important factors to be considered while operating the batch dryer. The recommended drying air temperature for batch dryer is 43 °C when drying of rice for seed or for commercial milling is used.
2. **Recirculating batch dryers:** A batch of wet rice grain is loaded and recirculated within the dryer. The dried grain is unloaded and a new batch of grain is used for drying. Most of the recirculating dryers are portable and can be dismantled easily. The recirculating batch-in-bin dryers use a large airflow per tonne of rice grain and a much higher drying air temperature (60-80 °C). It gives fast drying and is effective because of continuous movement of rice grain during the short drying time. Though drying capacity is higher, the dryers require considerably a large investment.
3. **Continuous flow dryers:** They are commercial, multi-pass heated air columnar dryers. The drying capacity is high and a large volume of wet grain can be dried quickly. Intake is usually by bucket elevators and discharge is controlled mechanically by feed rolls or oscillating rockers. Wet grain enters at the top and flows continuously through the dryer. The heated air is blown through the grain as it moves down the dryer. The dryer is so designed that it takes rice 15-30 minutes to move through the dryer. During that time, 1-3% of moisture reduction is achieved. Continuous flow dryers have a garner or holding bin on top, followed by a tall drying section. Below that is a flow control section that controls the flow through the dryer and discharges the grain. An air heater and blower push hot air through the grains in the drying section.

The continuous flow dryers are classified into non-mixing and mixing types. The continuous flow non-mixing columnar drying bin consists of two parallel screens up to 45 cm apart in two separate columns. The space between the two columns is the plenum chamber where heated air is introduced and forced through the grain.

The mixing type drying bin is similar to columnar drying bin except that it includes louvers which cause mixing to occur as the grains flow through the system. Mixing types are of two kinds: baffle type and the Louisiana State University (LSU) design and the latter type is popular in India and USA.

Drying systems with tempering

In this system, rice grain is exposed to heated air for 15-30 minutes during which time only 1-3% of the moisture is removed. Between the drying process, rice grain is held in a tempering bin where the uneven moisture content of the grain is equalized. The tempering period usually lasts from 4-24 hours. Intermittent heating and tempering of rice during drying has the advantage of efficient heated air utilization, shorter effective drying time, increased drying capacity and equalization of moisture and stresses inside the grain. This prevents cracking of rice grain.

Warehouse dryer

A warehouse type dryer operates based on the principles of natural convection. Wind and agricultural residues are used as energy sources. In this system, a vortex wind machine creates draft for air movement in the warehouse. Combustible agricultural residues are used as a heat source for the furnace. Drying materials are held in the vertical trays which have adjustable louvers adaptable for holding different kinds of materials. The dryer is also called as multi-commodity dryer.

Solar crop dryers

Sun is the major source of energy and it is advantageous to trap this energy in countries where solar energy is abundant. Direct application of solar thermal energy conversion processes for drying crops is a recent development. Solar thermal conversion is considered as the most direct and least expensive among the processes of converting solar energy into useful form. There are two general methods of converting solar energy: air heating collectors and water heating collectors. Among them the former is less expensive.

Plate type solar collector

Solar collector is basically a heat exchange machine. Incoming radiation is trapped in one or two layers of glazing. This results in conversion of radiation to heat upon hitting an absorbing surface. The absorber can be formed as conducts through which working fluids are made to pass to bring heat losses to a minimum.

Natural convection solar dryers

The green house phenomenon is applied in the operation of these dryers.

Radiant energy which strikes the glazing are trapped and made to heat stones.

PARBOILING

Parboiling is the hydrothermal treatment of rice grain before milling. Parboiling is an age-old process of rice in parts of Asia, Africa and to a limited extent in some European countries and America. It is done to improve the milling recovery of rice, to salvage poor quality or spoiled rice grains and to meet the demands of certain consumer preferences. The varieties which are more brittle are preferred for parboiling. The long and slender varieties which are more fragile compared to short and bold grains are usually parboiled. Scented and fine grain varieties which have good milling quality are generally not parboiled. During the process of parboiling, the most important changes that occur in the rice grain are gelatinisation of starch and disintegration of protein bodies in the endosperm. Grains become translucent and hard. Breakage of grains during milling is minimized.

Three important steps in parboiling are: (i) soaking, (ii) steaming and (iii) drying.

Soaking is a diffusion process during which grains absorb water. It is also known as steeping or imbibition. With the absorption of water, grains swell and their volume increases. Swelling of rice grain depends on time and temperature of soaking.

Steaming helps to complete the gelatinization process. Moisture content of the rice grain increases to about 38% during steaming. Due to steaming, high heat can be applied at a constant temperature. Heating with non-pressurized steam (as in traditional methods) causes small variations in colour, quality of soluble starch and the amount of swelling of the milled parboiled rice. When the steaming temperature exceeds 100 °C, the colour becomes considerably deeper and the grain becomes harder. Steaming for long time also causes the rice to be harder and darker. The duration of steaming depends on the steaming arrangement. Steaming takes 2-3 minutes for small batches. In modern plant, a tonne of rice grain parboiling requires a total of 200 kg steam, at a pressure of 4-5 kg/cm^2. About 1800-2000 litres of water is used for parboiling a tonne of rice, out of which 20% is absorbed by the grain.

Parboiled rice is dried to a moisture level of 14-16 % for safe storage or milling. Parboiled rice is more difficult to dry because of its higher moisture content and hence it requires more energy than a field crop. Moisture reduction takes place rapidly during the first part of drying; particularly from 36 to 18% moisture levels and is slow from 18 to 14% moisture. The drying process should be stopped at about 18% moisture to allow the rice grain to temper or equalize for several hours before drying to 14%. Drying of the parboiled rice is mostly carried out on large paved yards in the rice mills. Drying can also be done mechanically.

Methods of parboiling

Different countries use a number of traditional and modern processes for parboiling of rice. These processes include single boiling method, Goviya, Chatty, Jadavpur University method, converted process, Avorio, Cristallo, Malek, Schule and CFTRI methods. Generally parboiling is done by any one of the following methods:

1. Soaking the grain in large concrete tanks and steaming it in small kettles;
2. Soaking and steaming the grain in a small metal tank (Goviya) without a boiler; and
3. Soaking and steaming grain in large metal tanks with a boiler.

Soaking in concrete tanks and steaming in kettles

This method is probably the most popular method of parboiling and is extensively used in India, Pakistan, Bangladesh and Sri Lanka. In this method, rice grain is soaked in hot or cold water in large concrete tanks and then steamed in small metal or concrete kettles. In some cases, a double boiling process is followed in which the grain is heated in the steam kettles prior to soaking. This method reduces time requirement for soaking; however, it is labour intensive. The grain is, then, redried on large drying floors or with mechanical dryers.

Goviya plants

Rice is hot-soaked and heat-treated in a small rectangular metal tank (Goviya tank) of 1-1.5 t capacity. Rice grain is hot soaked for 6 hours at about 45 °C and then water is drained and kept at a level below the perforated floor. Additional heat is, then, applied until the water boils and steam is produced. The steam is maintained at atmospheric pressure and takes considerably more time to penetrate the grain. Steaming is continued for one hour. The paddy is then discharged through the side openings and moved to the drying floor. This method is labour intensive but carefully parboiled rice ensures fair quality.

Soaking and steaming in large metal tanks

Large metal tanks (1-6 t capacity) are used to hot-soak the grain for 2 to 4 hours and then steamed for 20 to 30 minutes. This method was introduced into Burma and Sri Lanka in the early 1940s and became popular in India in the early 1960s. Mechanical conveying equipment is used for high operating capacity. Bucket elevators are used to load the tanks; belt or shaker conveyors are used to unload them. The tanks are unloaded into handcarts for sun-drying the paddy.

MILLING

Milling is the primary processing technique for food grains. Milling refers to the size reduction and separation operations used for processing of food grains into edible form by removing and separating the inedible and undesirable portions from them (Chakraverty, 1995). Milling includes the processes such as cleaning, husking, sorting, whitening, polishing, grinding and shifting.

Rice milling

In this process, unhulled rice grain is converted into clean rice. Rice milling has to be done with utmost care to avoid breakage of kernels. Low percentage of broken grains indicates the efficiency of the milling process. Whole grains command a higher price than broken ones.

Factors affecting milling recovery and milled rice quality

Several factors must be considered for efficient rice milling. The most critical factors are the grain condition and the method of milling.

Grain factors

1. **Moisture content:** Milling recovery is inversely proportional to moisture content of rice grain. Grain at 12% moisture content has higher milling recovery than at 18%. The optimal harvest moisture content, considering both milling head yield and total rice yield, is 18-24 %.
2. **Purity:** The presence of foreign matters such as other seeds, chaff, dust, etc. decreases the milling recovery and quality.
3. **Cracked grains:** Rice grains develop cracks or internal fissures due to various reasons, *viz.*, low harvest moisture, exposure of the mature rice grains to alternate wetting and drying conditions and increase in time from harvest to threshing. Cracked grains easily break during milling. During whitening process, the sharp corners are smoothened resulting in further breakage.
4. **Varietal characteristics:** Different varieties of rice have different proportions of husks in the kernel. The husk content of grain varies from 14 to 28.0 %. Short grains (Japonica) have husk content as low as 15% while long grains (Indica) have husk as high as 23%.
5. **Nature of the grains:** Immature and chalky kernels break easily. The shape and hardness of the kernels also influence the breakage. Immature grains have high proportion of husks in the kernel. Husk content of immature grain is as high as 40%. Long grain and soft varieties break more than short grain and hard varieties.

Machine factors

Type of machine, condition of the machines and type of milling systems affect the milling recovery. In the case of all machines adjustments, repairs and maintenance play very important role.

Processes that are followed during milling are given below:

1. **Cleaning:** Foreign materials such as particles of sand, stones, straw, other seeds, etc are removed from the grain.
2. **Dehusking and husk separation:** Removing the husk from the grain with minimum damage to the grain and separating the husk from the unhulled grain.
3. **Grain separation:** Dehusked grain is separated from the remaining grains. Most dehuskers remove about 90% of the husk.
4. **Bran removal (polishing):** All or part of the bran layer is removed from the grain so as to produce polished rice.
5. **Grading:** Separating or grading the broken from the unbroken rice. The brokens are often separated into different sizes.

Principles of rice milling

Two basic operations are involved in milling of rice: (i) removing the outer covering named the husk or hull is called as *dehulling* or *dehusking*. (ii) removal of seed coat (bran) called as *whitening* or *polishing*. These two operations are carried out using primitive manual method or with sophisticated machinery.

Manual method (Hand pounding)

Hand pounding is the manual method of milling rice. This is a primitive method of milling process employing different types of equipments. Mortar and pestle is used for hand pounding. The impact and friction action on and between the rice kernels dehulls and whitens the grain simultaneously. Excessive impact and pressure may result in high breakage of the milled rice. The whitening process is usually not thoroughly done. The resulting finished product is incidentally more nutritious than the well milled white rice since the aleurone layer containing vitamins and minerals is maintained.

Mechanized rice milling

The conventional mills in use can be categorized into three main types: huller mills, sheller-huller mills and sheller-cone polisher mills.

Single huller (Kiskisan or one-pass mill)

It is called as Engelberg rice mill bearing the name of the first popular manufacturer. The grain is husked and whitened in the huller by friction and pressure generated in the milling chamber. Both husking and whitening are done by the same machine. Milling can be carried out either in a single pass or multi-pass. This method may, in turn, result in lower total milling recovery. The total rice out-turn is 56 % for raw rice and 64% for parboiled rice depending on the rice variety and working condition of the mills.

Sheller-huller type mills

An emery coated disc sheller is used for shelling and the horizontal Engelberg type huller for polishing the rice grains. Grain is cleaned using a sieve and the cleaned grain is husked in the sheller. The stock from the sheller is fed to hullers for whitening. As compared to 'huller' mills, the out-turn is higher (1-2%). There are facilities for controlling the degree of polishing.

Two distinct machines are used: the dehuller (steel huller, stone disk or rubber roll) and the whitener (abrasive or friction type). An aspirator placed between the dehuller and whitener removes the husks from paddy and brown rice.

Sheller-cone polisher -type mills

They have the full complement of milling consisting of a cleaner, disc-sheller, aspirator, a grain-separator, one or more cone polishers and a rice grader. An under runner stone disc huller performs the dehulling process. After an aspirator removes the husk, the mixture of brown rice and unhulled grain is passed through a separator. The unhulled grain is returned to the dehuller and the brown rice proceeds to the whitening process. A multi-stage whitening operation performed by the stone coated frustum of a cone does the whitening process. Addition of the unhulled grain separator and the gradual step by step process of whitening by abrasion results in a higher total milling and head grain recovery. Of all the traditional rice mills, total rice out turn is higher (68-70 %) in these mills. The main defect, however, is that the disc sheller employed produces high breakage, especially in the milling of raw rice.

Modern rice mill

In the traditional rice mills as mentioned above, there is an avoidable loss of rice either in the form of broken or flour in the bran. This loss varies from about 1-5% from the sheller-cum-cone polisher mills to about 4-5 % in the huller type mills. The modern multiple machine rice mills were imported from Japan. A pair of rubber rolls as dehuller and combination of abrasive and friction whiteners are used. The mills are equipped with cleaners, rubber roller shellers, separator for brokens and germs from bran. These modern mills also have facilities for bulk storage of rice with mechanical handling, drying and parboiling units. Some mills also have solvent plants for oil extraction from the rice bran. An over all increase in total rice outturn due to the use of these modern mills is 2.5 % over disc sheller type units and 6.6 % over huller units in terms of raw rice. For parboiled rice, the corresponding increase in total rice yields from the modern mills is 0.8 % over the disc shell mills and 1.6 % over the huller units.

Milling of wheat

Wheat is consumed mostly in the form of flour obtained by milling the grain. Stone grain grinding is the traditional method of milling wheat in India. In the modern mills, wheat grain is cleaned from various types of impurities along with damaged kernels. Milling involves a progressive series of disintegrations followed by sievings. First, the bran and the germ are removed from the endosperm. The endosperm is pulverized and the bran and flattened germ are removed by the sieves. The pulverized endosperm is run through successive rollers and ground into fine flour. The flour is progressively milled and becomes whiter in colour, better for bread making.

Whole-wheat flour, maida and semolina are the products of wheat. Macaroni products are also called pasta or alimentary pastes. These products include macaroni, spaghetti, vermicelli and noodles.

Milling of corn

Corn is milled to remove hulls and germs. The removed parts are used as cattle feed. Germ is an important source of corn oil. Two basic ways of corn milling are dry milling and wet milling.

Dry milling

The whole grain is ground to produce flour or meal. It is done in two ways: traditional, non-degerming system and modern degerming system. In the former method, by using stone grinder, the whole corn is ground into meal of high fibre as well as high protein. In the modern degerming system, the germ and hull are removed. In this method, corn is moistened and degermed and used for milling.

Wet milling

Good kernels with moisture content of 15-16% alone are used for wet milling. In the developed countries like U.S.A., this method is predominantly followed. The wet milling process consists of cleaning, soaking, germ separation, grinding and hull removal, separation of starch and gluten. High fructose corn syrup and ethanol are the most important products of wet milling.

Milling of millets

Dehusking and debranning are done during the processes of rice milling. The wheat milling includes debranning and sizing the endosperm into semolina or flour. Milling of small millets is done by adopting both wheat and rice milling techniques. Finger millet seeds are generally powdered and the whole meal is utilized for food preparation. In other small millets, dehusking and debranning are the processes involved in milling. If desired, grinding is done. Traditionally the process of dehusking and debranning are done by hand operated pestle or denki. The seeds can be dehusked effectively by using rice milling machinery such as disc sheller, rice huller and centrifugal sheller.

Dehulling of prosomillet is often done in the rice mill. The dehulled grain can be stored for more than a month.

The traditional method of processing the small millets takes about 20-22 minutes per kg of grain. The extraction rate of kodomillet is very low (50-55 %) compared to other millets (70-80 %).

Milling of pulses

In the process of milling pulses, outer husks are removed and the cotyledons are split into two. Since the seed coat (husk) tightly envelops the cotyledons, dehusking is a problem in legumes. By adopting controlled drying, the husk can be loosened and rendered brittle and friable and easily removed by abrasion. Milling is done following wet milling or dry milling method. Dry milling is more popular and is used in commercial operations.

Wet milling

Cleaned pulse grains, after the removal of impurities, are soaked in water. The soaked grains are then mixed with red earth. The produce is then steeped and this process is known as 'conditioning'. Then dehusking and splitting are done with machinery. Dehusking is done with emery rollers. The split and unsplit pulses are separated by sieve. The split pulses are then graded. The unsplit and dehusked pulses are once again subjected to the above process. This type of wet milling is a time consuming process. Dhal prepared by wet milling is usually flat and has a small depression in the centre due to shrinkage and softens slowly during cooking.

Dry milling

Cleaned pulse grains are passed through emery machine where the husk is creaked and scratched. During this stage some portion of the pulses are dehusked and split which are separated by sieving. Pre-treatment with edible oil is an important process, particularly for 'dhal' making. The seed coat is more tightly bound to the cotyledons as compared to other grains. Oil penetrates through the cracks resulting in widening of cracks leading to breaking of the husk.

Pulse grains are subject to conditioning by alternate wetting and drying and tempering for about 3-5 days. During this process, pulse grains loose 3-5% moisture and contains 10-12% moisture at the time of processing. The conditioned pulses are dehusked and split. The dehusked pulses are graded and finally they are polished with the addition of little quantity of oil and grade one pulses are obtained. The dhal obtained by the dry method is hemispherical in shape, softens rapidly on cooking and gives good flavour.

OIL EXTRACTION

The ultimate goal of post-harvest processing of oilseed is to recover as much oil as possible and use cake/ meal as protein source for livestock and human consumption. In India, the most popular method of extraction of oil is by ghani, which is basically a large pestle and mortar. Power is supplied by one or two bullocks. Commercially, oil extraction is by one of the three basic methods:

Batch hydraulic pressing: Oil is expressed by hydraulic pressure from a mass of oil-bearing material.

Continuous mechanical pressing: Oil bearing material is squeezed through a tapering outlet, oil being expressed by increasing pressure.

Solvent extraction: Oil bearing material is taken into solution with a solvent. The solution is separated from insoluble residue and the oil is recovered from the solvent solution.

In commercial operation, one or combinations of these processes is used. Normally the process includes mechanical pressing (expelling) with continuous solvent extraction and batch hydraulic pressing and solvent extraction.

In castor, it requires special treatment, equipment and cleaning procedure for oil extraction because of the hard seed coat.

Solvent extraction is seldom used to process small amounts of oilseeds. Solvent extraction process is normally adopted where there is increasing importance of cake and meal in relation to oil.

Steps involved in oil extraction

Hulling

Hulling is recommended to provide high quality edible oil. This reduces the fibre content of the meal and increases the marketability as cattle feed. However, hulling also increases the cost of production. It has the advantage of the breaking of thin-hulled seed like safflower and elimination of unwanted principle as in rapeseed. Partial hulling of some oil seeds is possible. Disc or roller hullers may be used for hulling.

Cooking and drying

Cooking is an important process required for the materials having high protein content. This not only coagulates the protein but also frees the oil for efficient pressing. After cooking, the raw material must be dried before entering to pressing. Low protein materials with a high oil high fibre content (*e.g.*, copra) usually require drying only.

Extraction

Common method of oil extraction is by using batch hydraulic pressing followed by solvent extraction. However, the most efficient method of expressing oil is with single or double screw press either hot or cold. The screw press operates in a cage like perforated cylinder through which the oil diffuses. It has a major advantage over batch type hydraulic presses in that it need not be stopped for recharging. A screw press operates at a greater pressure than a hydraulic press, with a consequently higher oil extraction rate. The oil-bearing material is forced through a cylindrical steel cage and then through a tapered outlet by means of a powerful rotating screw. Because of the restricted discharge, an extremely high pressure is developed and oil is expelled through narrow slot around the press barrel. Compressed cake is extruded through the discharge outlet.

In the solvent extraction, the seeds are first vigorously cleaned and hulled. The seeds are then rough-milled, since too fine a material produces excessive fines in the oil. Prepared material is then extracted in a batch or continuous process. The latter process is most often used. By using solvent method, oil is removed more effectively as material comes into contact with increasingly purer solvent as it moves through the extractor. The extraction rate by this method is usually higher than from mechanical method. The most common solvent in use is hexane, a petroleum derivative with a boiling point of 65 °C. The meals from solvent extraction are with minimum oil content at commercially acceptable production levels.

Cleaning and conditioning

After the extraction is completed, the material passes through a solvent recovery plant and the oil is cleaned, bleached and filtered. Oil after pressing may contain suspended meal called 'foots' and are removed by settling, screening and filtering. There is arrangement for continuously separating, draining and feeding the foots back for reworking into the stream of fresh material. Clear oil is later conditioned and subsequently pumped through the filter press. The filtered crude oil normally contains impurities such as phosphatides, gums, resins, free fatty acids and colouring materials. These impurities from the filtered crude oil are removed. Gums, free fatty acids and some of the colouring matter are removed by alkali refining. The insoluble soap remaining is treated with sulphuric acid. These residues are known as acid oils. A high quality oil must be low in free fatty acids, pale in colour and must not deposit solid material on heating to 30 °C. Oils containing high amount of free fatty acids may produce smoke during frying. Hence frying oil must have reduced amount of free fatty acids.

Special processing

Some type of oil that is used for domestic use be stable under refrigeration when used as a base for salad dressings. For such type of oil, an operation known as winterizing is used. This involves cooling the oil to remove components with high wetting points that may settle out at low temperature. *e.g.* sunflower oil.

Deodorizing is a method necessary to produce bland oil. In this method, refined oil is treated in vacuum with steam at 200-250 °C.

Recent techniques in oil seed milling

It is now possible to introduce novel techniques in the conventional methods of oil seed milling. The value addition in the industry could be achieved to maximum extent by taking advantage of certain inherent characteristics possessed in individual seeds. Based on these, some of the relevant technologies have been developed at Central Food Technological Research Institute (CFTRI) in the recent years:

1. Preparation of high pungency mustard oil and low glucosinolate cake by aqueous conditioning of seeds;
2. Bland mustard oil by enzyme inactivation through heat or ammoniation of seeds;
3. Dehulling of sesame seed to obtain white seeds for differential use;
4. Dehulling of sunflower seed to get wax free oil and high protein cake;
5. Decortication of safflower oil seed suitable for ghani processing; and
6. Bland oilseed meals (groundnut /soybean) by secondary solvent extraction procedures.

MANUFACTURE OF SUGAR

Sugarcane contains 85% juice and 15% fibre (bagasse). The juice contains water and dissolved solids (Brix). The total sugar includes sucrose and reducing sugar. The simple sugars, glucose (dextrose) and fructose (levulose), occur free in sugarcane with lesser amount than sucrose. The sucrose content varies from 14 to 18% and reducing sugars 0.5 to 2.0%. Sugar accumulation is continuous but it obtains peak at later stage *i.e.* after vegetative stage. Sucrose occurs in all parts of the sugarcane plant and is most abundant in the stalk where it is found in the watery vacuoles of storage cells (parenchyma). The sugar of commerce is sucrose, a disaccharide. Sucrose is composed of two monosaccharides, fructose and glucose.

Removal of cane trash is important after the harvest. Cane tops have little sucrose and are high in starch and reducing sugars. Starch and reducing sugars lower the sugar yields in the boiling house. Generally trash in the range of 3-5 % is considered normal.

Rapid deterioration in the quality begins from the harvest. Sugarcane cannot be stored for processing without excessive inversion. Hence, harvesting and processing to raw sugar are concurrent.

1. **Extraction of juice:** About 90% of the juice is extracted by crushing the cane with heavy rollers. The final bagasse contains the unextracted sugar, the woody fibre and 45-55% water. Imbibition is the process in which water or juice is applied to a bagasse to enhance the extraction of juice.
2. **Neutralization:** The juice is dark-green in colour, turbid and is acidic in pH. The pH is brought to 6.8 to 7.0 by adding lime. Both soluble

and insoluble impurities are removed by employing lime and heat as clarifying agents. The objective of clarification is to remove from the juice the maximum quantity of impurities at the earliest possible time.

3. **Setting:** The clarified juice is allowed to settle and clear supernatent liquid is used for sugar manufacture. The residue is called "pressmud".
4. **Evaporation:** The clarified juice contains about 85% water. Two thirds of this water is evaporated in vacuum multiple containers. The resulting syrup has about 65% solids and 35% water. The thick syrupy structure is passed through a high-speed centrifuge when the sugar crystals come out. The recovered sugar is pure white in colour. The last portion from which no more sugar can be extracted is called "molasses". Molasses are in light brown liquid form.

Sugar yield:

Juice recovery from cane	67-80%
Cane to sugar recovery	9-10%
Cane to jaggery recovery	12-13%

Jaggery making

Jaggery is a crude form of raw sugar manufactured in several states of India. It is solidified cane after removal of the impurities suspended in the juice. In India, about 50-55% of the total cane production is converted into jaggery.

Varieties play an important role in the quality as well as the recovery of the jaggery from the cane. Varieties such as CO 997, CO 527 and CO 421 yield jaggery of light yellow colour which is very hard in consistency. Jaggery manufactured from mature cane is of the highest quality. Crop which suffered from inadequate irrigation yields poor quality jaggery because it contains soluble nitrogen in the juice. Crops that have been applied with excessive N fertilizers, those that have lodged extensively and those that have been affected by pest and diseases, in general, yield jaggery of poor quality.

It is important to use fresh cane for the manufacture of good quality jaggery. After juice extraction, it is boiled to jaggery immediately. Wide shallow pans are more suitable for making good jaggery. The pans made of iron sheets, galvanized iron or copper may help in getting jaggery of better colour. The dry leaves or trash realized at harvest time could be used for burning in the furnace.

Clarificants

The pH of the juice is acidic (5.0-5.5) and hence application of chemical clarificants like lime is important to neutralize the juice. This also facilitates flocculation of colloidal material in the juice and to remove them. Thus better-coloured juice will be obtained. The other clarificants that are being used are: bhendi juice, coconut oil, hydros (sodium bi-sulphate) and super phosphate.

Boiling

After the application of clarificants (lime), the raw juice is boiled. It is important to boil the juice at low temperature initially. This will facilitate flocculation of colloids and the scums that rises to the surface of the juice can be skimmed off. If initial boiling is rapid, it is likely that the scum that flocculates will dissolve again and impair the colour of the jaggery. After removal of the first scum, it is desirable that the juice is boiled as quickly as possible and charge brought down. The temperature of the magma when it is about to be brought down should be between 118-124 °C. Appropriate times to bring down the charge of the jaggery is determined by putting a small quantity in a shallow earthen vessel filled with cold water. If the jaggery cools quickly to a hard mass, the charge may be brought down. As soon as the charge is brought down, it is stirred slowly in the pan itself to facilitate quick cooling.

Jaggery is then moulded in different ways. The jaggery prepared from immature canes is characterized by more glucose and higher acidity in general. On the other hand, the jaggery from mature canes contains higher amount of sucrose, low glucose, ash and lime.

CURING OF TOBACCO

Curing may be described as a process by which the harvested tobacco leaf is made ready for the market. Curing is essentially a drying process whereby most of the moisture in the harvested leaf is removed. The drying process is to be conducted in such a way as to produce certain well-defined and desirable qualities in different types of tobacco. The usual curing methods adopted for different types of tobacco are flue–curing, air-curing, fire-curing, sun-curing and pit – curing.

Flue-curing

It is the quickest method of curing and takes about 5-6 days to complete. Cigarette tobacco is generally flue-cured. In this process, the moisture in the tobacco leaf is driven out with the help of radiated heat at fixed temperature and humidity. This process facilitates development of desirable colour as well as chemical and physical qualities in the product. Flue - curing process consists essentially of three distinct stages *viz.*, (i) yellowing, (ii) fixing the colour and (iii) drying of the leaf. During 'yellowing' which takes about 24-40 hours, the leaf is kept at a low temperature of 90-95°F and high humidity. Because of this process, the leaf attains a bright lemon yellow colour and the starchy matter is converted into sugars. After 'yellowing' the temperature is raised gradually and opening the ventilators lowers the humidity of the barn. This facilitates fixation of the yellow colour. If drying of the leaf is delayed, a brownish cast will develop on the yellow leaf and this is called as *'sponging'*. This occurs due to the oxidation of tannin-like substances. If drying is too rapid due to rise in temperature when the leaf is still wet, a bluish black discolouration occurs and is called *'scalding'*. These two defects reduce the market value of the produce. At the end of the second stage, the temperature is raised to 160°F to dry the mid rib.

Air curing

In India, air curing is practiced for 'hookah' tobacco in West Bengal and for 'Lanka' tobacco in Andhra Pradesh. Wrapper tobacco in West Bengal and Tamil Nadu and Burley of Andhra Pradesh and Karnataka are also air- cured.

Hoohah tobacco

Air curing consists of two stages during which yellow and brown colour development takes place. During the first stage, the leaf remains alive till necessary changes take place. Tobacco can be cured at a temperature of 60-95°F. One of the important changes takes place during curing is the disappearance of starch. If the leaf is dried too rapidly, the starch is not removed and tobacco becomes lifeless and straw. After the removal of starch, green colour changes into colourless substances and yellow colour appears. This makes the end of the first stage.

During the second stage, the colour turns into brown due to oxidation. The desired colouration will not take place till the leaf cells are dead. The development of brown colour begins in the second stage which is completed in fermentation.

Lanka tobacco

After harvesting, the leaves are separated along with some portion of the stem. The leaves are then strung on ropes in a shed for 2-2½ months. During this period, the leaves turn yellowish brown with the stems becoming completely dry. After the stems get dried, curing is often completed in pits.

The leaves are placed in a pit for 48 hours and then back again to the first for 24 to 48 hours when the curing becomes complete. Transfer of leaf is usually done at night to prevent moisture loss. Fermentation of the leaf occurs during the pit curing. It is important to frequently open the pits to replace the CO_2 and to prevent over heating. After the curing is completed, the leaf attains a dark brown colour and fruity smell develops.

Fire curing

Fire curing or smoke-curing is done for Jaffna and other dark fire-cured types of tobacco. After harvesting, the leaves are wilted for a few hours in the field, tied into bundles and hung on lathis in a hut. They are then smoke-cured for 12 hours by burning coconut husk, then stacked for 3 days and again smoked. Alternation of firing with staking at an interval of a few days helps in making the colour of the leaf even. Smoking gives a peculiar taste and antiseptic properties. After the smoke treatment, the leaf is fermented in bulk for 3-4 weeks and then given treatment with salt water or jaggery which contributes to the peculiar taste of this type of tobacco.

Sun curing

Of all the methods, sun curing is the cheapest method. It is done in different ways: (i) curing whole plants on racks as in cigar and chewing tobacco; (ii) curing leaves together with pieces of stalks on racks as in *Natu* tobacco in Andhra Pradesh; (iii) whole plant is cured on the ground as in *bidi, hookah* and chewing tobacco; and, (iv) primed leaves are cured on the ground as in chewing and *hookah* tobacco.

Pit curing

This is practiced for Lanka tobacco in Andhra Pradesh, *hookah* tobacco in Punjab and some chewing tobacco varieties in Tamil Nadu. Pit curing is similar to fermentation and is done after initially subjecting the leaf to air-curing or sun-curing.

STORAGE

Food grains are physiologically stable after harvesting and this stability as well as viability should be preserved in a good storage method. Under natural conditions, stored grains undergo chemical changes within themselves and are subjected to pest infestation and product deterioration. Most agricultural commodities are produced seasonally. Harvesting is normally done during a short period of two to three months while their consumption is spread all through the year. Hence, proper storage of agricultural produce is essential. Objectives of food commodity storage are: (i) uniform supply of food throughout the year either for domestic or export purposes; (ii) to provide a reserve for contingencies such as drought, floods and such natural calamities; and (iii) to get higher price either in domestic or in the export market.

Factors affecting losses in storage

Factors, intrinsic and extrinsic, exert their influence on grains under storage. Intrinsic factors are the constituents of grain-tissue components and enzymes. Extrinsic factors include physical (temperature and humidity), chemical (oxygen concentration and moisture), biochemical (vitamin loss, acidity and natural respiration) and biological (microbes, insects, rodents and birds).

Safe storage of food grains

Quality and quantity must be maintained during storage. Stored produce should be protected against weather, insects, rodents, birds, microorganisms, objectionable odour, moisture and any type of contamination.

Condition before storage

Rice should be cleaned and dried before storage. Rice grains get deteriorated rapidly due to the presence of foreign matter or impurities. Admixture of wet grain or straw promotes insect infestation and growth of fungi and other microorganisms. Moisture content of the cereal grain should be at 13-14% for safer storage. If the cereal grain is to be stored for a long period, moisture should be below 12%. If rice grain is stored wet, it begins to heat rapidly and mould growth follows. Odours are produced, discolouration begins and the grain begins to sour. Finally it turns brown and insects multiply rapidly.

Relative Humidity -temperature prevalence in the store house

If grains are adequately dried, storage temperature is of less importance. However, temperature also plays an important role in creating favourable conditions for multiplication of storage pathogenic fungi. The storage fungi affecting grains grow most rapidly at 30-32 °C. Prevalence of optimum temperature during storage is favourable for invasion of grains by fungi. Rice like many other grains loses or gains moisture until it is in equilibrium with the relative humidity of the surrounding air. At relative humidity above 70%, mould development commences. Bacteria generally develop on the food grains at a relative humidity of 90% and above.

Control of microorganisms

Environmental conditions existing in tropical countries are conducive for the growth of fungi and bacteria. Damage caused by microorganisms such as fungi (moulds) and bacteria in stored grain include (i) decrease in germinability, (ii) discolouration of the kernel, (iii) heating and mustiness, (iv) bad odour and off flavour, (v) toxins that may be injurious to human beings and (vi) weight loss. More than 150 species of fungi have been identified from stored cereal grains. All the storage fungi have the ability to grow in materials whose moisture content are in equilibrium with relative humidity of 70-90%. The fungi mostly comprise of the species of *Aspergillus* and *Penicillum*.

Due to the fungal activity, certain fungal metabolites are left in the grain and some of them are toxic. For example, aflotoxin B-1 is the most potent hepatocarcinogen. Quality of some of the cereal grains is affected by the bacteria.

Control of rodents

Rats and mice are serious pests of stored paddy. Rats eat food daily equivalent to about 10 % of their weight and contaminate a great deal more with their droppings and urine. Though rats are omnivorous, a significant portion of their food consists of grains. About 2.5 % of grain loss occurs due to rodents during storage. Rats are also responsible for many diseases affecting public health. Rat proof construction is necessary to minimize the damage of food grains by rat. The floor of the construction should be 0.6-0.9 m above the ground and equipped with a ledge to prevent rodents from entering the buildings. Chemicals (rodenticides) can be used to kill the rats and mice.

Control of insects

Insects are a hazard to stored grains. They not only consume stored grains and seeds but also contaminate them. Particles of insects may get into the grains and render them aesthetically objectionable. The insects affecting the stored grains are sensitive to temperature. A grain temperature of 21.1 °C is considered favourable for the insects and they cannot survive above 41.7 °C. Important insects under stored condition are:

- Lesser grain borer - *Rhyzopertha dominica*
- Rice weevil - *Sitophilus oryzae*
- Angoumois grain moth- *Sitrotroga cerealella*
- Cadelle- *Tenebroides mauritanicus*
- Sawtoothed grain beetle- *Cryptolestes pusittus*
- Indian meal moth- *Plodia interpunctella*
- Almond moth- *Cadra cautella*
- Rice moth- *Corcyra cephalonica*

Storage methods for food grains

Storage of the produce is done in bags or bulk. Normally the produce is stored in jute or gunny bags. Polythene bags are also used for grain storage. Gunny bags are easy for handling since with most polythene bags it is difficult to stake more than a few bags. The bags are stacked on wood dunnage to prevent moisture migration and to permit good sanitation practices. In such situation, the stacks should be arranged with adequate walking space around each stack.

Cereal grains are stored in bulk in many of the Asian countries. The grains are stored in bulk using the storage structures made of mud and straw as well as metal silo. Large quantities of grain are stored in bulk warehouses designed and built to withstand the load of paddy against the sidewalls. Such bulk warehouses are constructed with reinforced concrete or pre-fabricated metal sidewalls. Belt conveyors are used for loading and unloading of paddy grains.

Store structures

Grains should be stored in closed structures after drying. The material used for storing of rice grain varies from place to place. Normally the produce is heaped for a few days to a month or more. After that they are shifted to the storage structures. The traditional grain storage structures in the rural areas are *khattis, bukharis, kuthlas, kothar*-type structures, straw bins, mud bins, pitchers, etc. These are normally made with locally available materials. Structures made of metal sheets, cement, bricks and reinforced concrete are also used to a limited extent. Silo and warehouses are used for large-scale storage.

Rural storage structures

1. ***Khattis* (underground cellar):** These structures are used in places where the subsoil water level is low. The depth of the structure is about 5.0 m and may be lined with bricks or concrete. At the time of filling the grains, a layer of straw is placed on all sides. Insect infection is normally less; however, the top layers may be often infected. These structures are not suitable for high rainfall areas.
2. ***Bukari:*** These are cylindrical in shape and fabricated with the combination of bamboo and mud. The floor of the structure is made with wooden planks or bamboo stakes which are placed with wet soil mixed with cow dung and straw. Wall consists of wood or bamboo frame works and mat over which wet soil- straw plaster is applied on both the surfaces. Conical roof is constructed with bamboo frame and covered with straw or grass. At the top, 4-5 cm thick layer of mud plaster is applied for protection. Complete structure is placed on a raised platform 1.5 m above ground level and kept with a support of wooden pillars. There is provision for loading from the top and emptying from the bottom. The rat cones are provided to prevent rats from climbing up. The capacity of these structures range from 3 to 35 tonnes.
3. **Mudbins (*Kuthlas*):** They are made of unburnt clay mixed with straw and mud-cow dung or brick and masonry. The shape of the mudbin may be oval, rectangular or circular with varying diameter. The structure is provided with a small hole at the base and bigger hole at the top. Grain is transferred through the big top holes and the bottom hole is used for taking out the grain. Both the holes are plugged at the time of filling. These types of structures are commonly used in Bihar, Punjab and Uttar Pradesh.
4. ***Kothar* type structures (wooden storage structure):** These structures are similar to a timber box made of wooden planks to a capacity of 10-35 tonnes. The roof is tiled or thatched, placed over the structure for protection from the sun or rainfall.
5. **Straw bins:** These types of bins are mostly used in Eastern Humid zones of India. The bins are made of straw and the capacity may be

2-6 quintals. Dried plants are used for making temporary structure for filling the grains. Outer part of the structure is further reinforced by winding rice straw rope.

6. **Improved structures:** Bins are used for storing grain in bulk. The bins are made of M.S. steel (*Anaj kothi*) or M.S. sheet (*Kanak kothi*) and aluminium. The shape of these bins is circular with varying capacities (one to 35 tonnes). They are mostly placed outdoor. R.C.C. bin (*Dhan-kothi*) and cement masonry bin (*Anaj Ghar)* are also in use. All these structures are made airtight and there is provision for filling and taking out the grain.
7. **Silos:** A silo is a tall structure. Pre-fabricated galvanized metal silos are available in many sizes up to about 100-tonnes capacity. Flat bottom pre-fabricated metal silos are most common for rice grain storage in many countries. The height to diameter ratio of silos ranges from 1 to 12. Concrete or clay straw made silos is also used for grain storage. Silos made of concrete are widely used in India. These are durable and economical. However, there is a possibility of damage of grain due to variation in the atmospheric relative humidity and temperature during rainy season. Regular aeration should be provided for safe storage of grain in the silo. Aeration may have counter effects on high atmospheric temperature and relative humidity.
8. **Warehouses:** Large quantity of grain is stored in the warehouses. Bagged grains are stacked on wood dunnage. Modern warehouses are built of concrete or brick. The floor of building should be 1 m above ground to permit easy unloading or loading into trucks. Warehouses may be designed and constructed to the desired size and capacity. Warehouses are also designed and built for bulk storage of grains.
9. **Open plinth cap storage:** Food Corporation of India (FCI) recently introduced a storage method called as "open -plinth cap storage". In this type of storage, godown is constructed up to the floor level with a raised brick masonry platform for staking. The bags are stacked on this open plinth and covered with 600-1000 gauge polythene sheet.

CHAPTER 11

Integrated Farming System

Integration of various farm enterprises in a farm ensures growth and stability in overall productivity and profitability. It also ensures recycling of residues, optimization of resources, minimization of risk and generation of employment. Various enterprises that could be included in farming system are crops, vegetables, fruits, flower cultivation, dairy, poultry, fish, goat, pig, sericulture, mushroom cultivation, agroforestry, bee keeping, silviculture, agro-based industries and food processing. A judicious mix of enterprises complementary to cropping and suited to the given farm situation and farmer's preference would bring overall prosperity.

DEFINITION OF FARMING SYSTEM

Farming system is a complex inter-related matrix of soil, plants, animals, implements, power, labour, capital and other inputs controlled in part by farm families and influenced by varying degrees of political, economic, institutional and social forces that operate at many levels. Under farming system, the farm is viewed in a holistic manner. Farmers are subjected to many socio-economic, bio-physical, institutional, administrative and technological constraints. Farming system conceptually is a set of elements or components that are inter-related which interact among themselves. At the centre of the interaction is the farmer exercising control and choice regarding the type and results of interaction.

Farming system is a resource management strategy to achieve economic and sustained production to meet diverse requirement of farm household while preserving resource base and maintaining a high level environmental quality (Lal and Millar, 1990).

FARMING SYSTEM CONCEPT

In farming system, all the activities, decision, management, input/output, purchase/sale and resource (s) utilized make the matrix which interacts with socio-economic and bio-physical environment. Farm activities interact with market forces (socio-economic) and ecosystem (bio- physical) for purchasing inputs and disposing outputs by utilizing and degrading natural resources (land, water, air, sunshine, etc.). Sustainability is the objective of the farming system where production process is optimized through efficient utilization of inputs without infringing on the quality of environment with which it interacts.

The overall objective is to evolve technically feasible and economically viable farming system models by integrating cropping with allied enterprises for irrigated, rainfed, hilly and coastal areas with a view to generate income and employment from the farm. The specific objectives are:

1. to identify existing farming systems in specific areas and assess their relative viability,
2. to formulate farming system models involving main and allied enterprises for different farming situations,
3. to ensure optimal utilization and conservation of available resources and effective recycling of farm residues within a system and
4. to maintain sustainable production system without damaging resources/ environment.

SCOPE OF FARMING SYSTEM

Farming enterprises include crop, livestock, poulty, fish, tree crops, plantation crops, sericulture, etc. A combination of one or more enterprises with cropping, when carefully chosen, planned and executed, gives greater dividends than a single enterprise, especially for small and marginal farmers. Farm as a unit is to be considered and planned for effective integration of the enterprises to be combined with crop production activity. Integration of farm enterprises depends on many factors such as,

1. Soil and climatic features of the selected area.
2. Availability of the resources, land, labour and capital.
3. Present level of utilization of resources
4. Economics of proposed integrated farming system.
5. Managerial skill of the farmer.

INTENSIVE CROPPING

Cropping systems based on climate, soil and water availability have to be evolved for realizing the potential production levels through efficient use of available resources. The cropping system should provide enough food for the family, fodder to the cattle and generate sufficient cash income for domestic and cultivation expenses. These objectives could be achieved by adopting intensive cropping. Methods of intensive cropping include multiple cropping and intercropping. Intensive cropping may pose some practical difficulties such as shorter turn-around time lapse for land preparation before the succeeding crop and labour shortage at peak periods of agricultural activities. These practical handicaps can easily be overcome by making modifications in the cropping techniques. Alteration of crop geometry may help to accommodate intercrops without loosing the base crop population.

Terms and definitions

1. **Multiple cropping:** Two or more crops are grown on the same field in one year. Intensification of cropping is in temporal and spatial dimension.
2. **Sequential cropping:** Growing two or more crops in sequence on the same field in a year. The succeeding crop is sown/planted after the preceding crop has been harvested. Crop intensification is only in time dimension and there is no intercrop competition. Some variations of sequential cropping are:

   a) **Double cropping:** Growing two crops per year in sequence.
   b) **Triple cropping:** Growing three crops per year in sequence.
   c) **Quadruple cropping:** Growing four crops per year in sequence.
   d) **Relay cropping:** A significant part of the life cycle of the second crop overlaps with the cropping cycle of the first crop.

3. **Ratooning:** Cultivation of crop regrowth after harvest, although not necessarily for grains.
4. **Monoculture:** Repetitive growing of the same crop on the same land.
5. **Crop rotation:** Repetitive cultivation of an ordered succession of crops (or crops and fallow) on the same land. One cycle may take several years to complete.
6. **Intercropping:** Intercropping can be defined as growing two or more crop species simultaneously in the same field during the growing season. Different types of intercropping are:

   a) **Mixed intercropping:** The practice of growing component crops simultaneously with no distinct row arrangement.
   b) **Row intercropping:** The component crops are grown simultaneously in different rows.
   c) **Strip intercropping:** It is simultaneous growing of component crops in different strips to permit independent cultivation of each crop.
   d) **Relay intercropping:** Component crops are relay sown so that growth cycles overlap.

7. **Main crop or base crop:** The crop which is planted at its optimum sole crop population in an intercropping situation.
8. **Component crops:** Individual crop species that are a part of the multiple cropping system.

PLANT INTERACTIONS

Interaction between component crops

In intensive cropping, crops are grown in association (intercropping) or in sequence (sequential cropping). In such situations there is possibility of interaction between the component crops. The interaction is mainly due to response of one species to the environment as modified by the presence of another species. Interaction may be competitive or non-competitive or complementary. If the crops are grown in association and the growth of either of the concerned species is not affected, such type of interaction is called as *non-competitive* interaction or interference. If one species is able to help the other it is known as *complementary interaction. e.g.* supply of N fixed by the legumes to the associated non-legumes. (This is otherwise known as *annidation*). One species may have greater ability to use the limiting factor and will gain at the expense of the other. This is called as *competitive interaction* or *interference*. Interaction may also occur in some other manner by way of producing toxic substances and affecting the establishment and growth of the associated species. This is called *"allelopathy"*.

Interactions in intercropping

Factors such as light, water, nutrient, oxygen and CO_2 are required for plant growth. In mixed or intercropping situations, the component species compete for the growth factors. The close proximity of species causes sub-optimal utilization of the growth factors and hence there is inequitable distribution of resources among the plants. Generally competition will develop between two components or within the components. The nature of such competition may vary depending on the density and proportion of each component and planting pattern.

1. **Light:** Photosynthetically active radiation (light) is directly related to photosynthetic rates of component crops. Intercropping can increase light interception by as much as 30-40%. When one component is taller than the other in an intercropping system, the taller component intercepts most of the solar radiation. The pattern of light interception also varies according to the age of the crop. Light transmission by coconut is only about 20% at the age of 8-10 years and this remains almost constant till about 25 years of age. Subsequently the % light transmission increases progressively as the canopy coverage of ground decreases. When the palms are at about 40 years of age, light transmission increases to about 50%. In an intercropping situation where the component crops have different growth durations, the peak demand for light would occur at different times. For example, in maize + greengram intercropping, the peak light demand for maize occurs at 60 days when greengram is ready for harvest. In such combinations, competition for light is less among the component crops and there is

greater light use in intercropping than in pure stands. In general, the component crops under intercropping situations are grown in such a way that competition for light is minimized. Proper choice of crops and varieties, adjustment of planting density and pattern are the techniques to reduce competition and increase the light use efficiency.

2. **Moisture and nutrients:** Competition for moisture and nutrients may result in two types of effects on the less successful or suppressed component. First, the roots of this component may grow less on the sides towards plants of aggressive component. Secondly, plants affected by competition for soil factors may have increased root/shoot ratio. The aggressive component generally absorbs greater quantity of nutrients and soil moisture. In legume and non-legume combination, the latter takes up large amounts of P, K and S. As a result, the legume may show deficiency of these nutrients. Such effects, however, may be mitigated by appropriate fertilizer application. Among intercrops, sorghum and pearl millet are more competitive in extracting nutrients. Generally the intercropped stands remove greater amount of nutrients than sole crop stands.
3. **Allelopathy:** Allelopathy is any direct or indirect harmful effect that one plant has on another through the production of chemical substances that escape into the environment. Some crops may be unsuitable to be grown as intercrops because they may produce and excrete toxins into the soil which are harmful to the associated components. Allelochemicals produced from the leaves of *Eucalyptus globulus* drastically reduce the germination of mustard sown underneath.
4. **Annidation:** Annidation refers to complementary interaction which occurs both in space and time.

   a) *Annidation in space:* The canopies of component crops may occupy different vertical layers with taller component tolerant to strong light and high evaporative demand and the shorter component favouring shade and high relative humidity. Multi-storeyed cropping in coconut and planting shade trees in cocoa and tea plantations use this principle. Similarly, root systems of component crops may exploit the nutrients in different layers of soil and hence utilize the resources in a better way with much less competition.

   b) *Annidation in time:* When component crops of widely varying duration are planted, their peak demand for light and nutrients are likely to occur at different periods, thus reducing competition. In a combination having early and late maturing crops (sorghum + redgram), when early maturing crops are harvested, conditions become favourable for the late maturing crop (red gram) to put forth its full vigour.

5. **Other complementary effects:** In an intercropping system involving a legume and a non-legume, part of the N fixed in the root nodule of the legume may become available to the non-legume component. With the presence of rhizosphere microflora and mycorrhiza, one species may lead to mobilization and greater availability of nutrients not only to the species concerned but also to the associated species. Provision of physical support by one species to the intercropped climbing species may improve the yield of the climber. Examples are coconut + pepper and maize + beans. The taller component acts as wind barrier protecting the shorter components from lodging.

Interactions in sequential cropping

In sequential cropping, sole crops are grown in succession. Hence, competition for light, water and nutrients as found in mixed cropping does not occur. In relay cropping, a short span of overlapping occurs between two crops in sequence. Hence the relay sown crop at the seedling stage may have competition for light from the standing crop. Such type of competition may be minimized by proper choice of crops and varieties and adjustment of time and method of planting.

In intensive multiple cropping involving two or more crops in sequence, the main objective is to harvest as much solar energy per unit area per unit time as possible. In rice based cropping system, the solar energy use efficiency ranged from 1.58 to 2.02% of PAR in Uttar Pradesh. In Coimbatore, the efficiency ranged from 0.82 to 1.77% of PAR for the whole year in cotton based system. Inclusion of a C_4 plant in the summer increased the efficiency.

In sequential cropping, the preceding crop has considerable influence on the succeeding crop. This includes the complementary effects such as release of N from the residues of the previous crop, particularly legume, to the following crop and carry-over effects of fertilizer applied to the preceding crops. The adverse effects include allelopathy, temporary immobilization of N due to wide C/N ratio of the residues and carry over effect of pest and diseases. Introduction of pulses as summer crops results in improved yield of rice in *Kharif* season.

SEQUENTIAL CROPPING SYSTEMS

In India, food crop is predominantly grown in most suitable seasons and thus particular food crop is basic to the cropping system followed by the farmers. Accordingly the cropping systems are usually referred to as:

i) Rice-based cropping system
ii) Sorghum-based cropping system
iii) Pearl millet-based cropping system
iv) Wheat and gram-based cropping system

Some of the cropping systems based on commercial crops are (i) cotton-based, (ii) groundnut- based (iii) sugarcane-based, (iv) plantation crop-based and (v) vegetable-based cropping system.

The grain production potential in different regions of the country ranges from 11-18 t/ha. In maize-potato or toria-wheat-moong system followed at IARI, New Delhi, it was possible to produce 14-15 tonnes of food per ha per annum without impairing the soil health. The results of multiple cropping demonstrations under irrigated conditions showed that production potential can be as high as 19.8 t/ha in cereal-based cropping system of rice-rice-rice. The yield potential of multiple cropping varies from region to region depending upon the physical and socio-economic conditions.

Rice based cropping system

Sequential cropping is the most suitable cropping pattern in the rice paddies. Traditionally single crop of rice with long duration cultivars is planted during the rainy period. However, due to the advent of short duration, photoinsensitive varieties, multiple cropping is being now practiced. The cropping system adopted under lowland condition can be grouped into two broad categories such as all rice and mixed rice and upland crop sequential cropping systems. These can be further grouped as below:

1. All rice cropping pattern
   a) Rice- Rice (R-R)
   b) Rice - Rice- Rice (R-R-R)
2. Mixed rice and upland crop sequence
   a) Rice- upland crop (R-UC)
   b) Upland crop - Rice- upland crop (UC-R-UC)

All rice sequential cropping system

Rice crop is repeatedly grown wherein two or three crops are raised. With three crops of rice, the land is cropped atleast ten months in a year. This is possible only in irrigated areas where water is adequate even during the dry periods. Crop failure due to water stress normally does not exist. Among the three crops, productive rice crop is the one which coincides with the dry months. During this period, solar radiation is high and the occurrence of other calamities such as cyclone or pest infestation is very low.

Two rice crops are mostly cultivated in many parts of the rice growing areas in India. The first crop is a short duration crop and is cultivated during the *Kharif* season. This is followed by the second crop of rice during *rabi* season with medium duration varieties.

Single crop of rice with the medium or long duration varieties is most prevalent in the command areas. Cultivation is restricted to the period of water availability in the canal.

All rice sequence is followed in some pockets of the river command areas of Orissa, Andhra Pradesh, Karnataka and Tamil Nadu.

Mixed rice and upland crops

Only one rice crop is grown during the peak rainy period. In such situations, there is enough time left to grow a fast-maturing annual crop between the first monsoon rain and the time of transplanting. Such crops must mature early. The crops uniquely suited for these conditions are vegetables, such as green corn, cowpea, green soybean or a green manure. The crop can easily be harvested within 80 days since only cobs or pods are harvested.

In most occasions immediately after the harvest of the main rice crops, it is possible to plant another crop (rice fallow crop). Because rice crop is usually harvested at the end of the rainy season when the soil is still wet, there is usually enough moisture in the soil to support the succeeding crop. Some of the crops that are suited to this condition are greengram, blackgram, cowpea, soybean, etc. Rice-upland crop is the commonly used system. Greengram is the popular choice as upland crop after rice.

Systems with more than three crops

With ratooning or relay cropping and special cultural practices that avoid puddling in lowland rice, upto five crops can be harvested in the same rice field over 12 month period (Bradfield, 1970). In rice paddies with adequate irrigation and good water control, Bradfield experimented at IRRI, Philippines, with various cropping patterns that could maximize productivity per unit area. The most successful pattern was a sequence of five crops consisting of rice, sweet potato, soybean, sweet corn and green soybeans. The tillage pattern varied for each crop and number of days to harvest were 102, 100, 85, 66 and 60 respectively. This pattern gave three times higher gross income than normally obtained in a rice-rice pattern.

Promising rice-based cropping systems in India

Promising rice-based cropping systems with high productivity and intensive land use for diverse agro-climatic situations of India have been identified in multi-locational experiments under Cropping Systems Research Project (Table 11.1.)

TABLE 11.1: Promising rice based cropping systems in India

System	Region
Rice - Indian mustard	Kashmir valley
Rice- wheat- sorghum (Fodder)	Jammu region
Rice- wheat- greengram	Punjab, Haryana, U.P
Rice- mustard	North Konkan
Rice- field bean	South Gujarat

System	Region
Rice- groundnut	South Karnataka
Rice- blackgram/sesame/cotton	Thanjavur, Tamil Nadu Old Cauvery delta)
Rice-groundnut	Thanjavur, Tamil Nadu (New Cauvery delta)
Rice- mustard	Assam
Rice- wheat- jute	West Bengal
Rice- groundnut	Coastal Andhra Pradesh and Orissa
Rice- greengram	Eastern Madhya Pradesh

Crop sequences under irrigated upland conditions

Under irrigated uplands (garden lands), depending upon the water availability or irrigation potential, more than two crops can be grown in a year. Crop sequences and their production potential have been tested under different agro-climatic conditions. At Delhi, a four crop sequence of greengram-maize-potato-wheat gave the highest production of 13.6 t/ha. However, three crop sequence of greengram-maize-wheat was found to be the most ideal for the small and marginal farmers (Table 11.2).

TABLE 11.2: Crop sequences and their production potential, New Delhi, India

Crop sequences	Total production (Q/ha)
Two crops	
Maize-wheat	90.1
Three crops	
Greengram- maize- wheat	97.7
Greengram- pigeonpea- wheat	68.8
Cowpea – pearl millet- wheat	92.9
Four crops	
Greengram-maize - potato-wheat	135.9
Greengram- maize- toria- wheat	112.8

Under All India Co-ordinated Agronomic Experiments Project, production potentials of the crop sequences under irrigated condition were studied. Some of the important sequences and their yield potential are given in Table 11.3.

TABLE 11.3: Crop sequences, duration and yield levels in different states of India

State	Crop sequences	Duration (days)	Yield (Q/ha)		
			Grain	Fodder	Vegetable
Himachal Pradesh	Soybean - wheat	323	77	-	-
	Soybean -potato	283	34	-	72
	Maize- wheat	299	65	-	-
Haryana	Pearl millet- wheat-cowpea (f)	323	83	63	-

State	Crop sequences	Duration (days)	Yield (Q/ha)		
			Grain	Fodder	Vegetable
Uttar Pradesh	Maize- wheat- cluster bean (f)	323	82	103	-
	Pearl millet- wheat- maize (f)	232	81	126	-
	Maize- wheat - pearl millet (f)	301	108	316	-
	Sorghum- wheat - greengram	306	63	-	-
	Sorghum - wheat - cowpea	313	59	-	-
Rajasthan	Pearl millet- wheat- greengram	339	35	-	-
	Greengram - wheat- greengram	295	22	-	-
Madhya Pradesh	Maize- wheat -cowpea	323	70	-	-
	Maize - wheat - greengram	325	70	-	-

f-fodder

In multi-location experiments, under Cropping Systems Research Project, promising cropping systems with high productivity as well as intensive land use for diverse agro climatic situations have been identified (Table 11.4).

TABLE 11.4: Potential cropping systems for different agroclimatic situations

Region	System
Western Haryana	Cotton - wheat
Rajasthan	Groundnut- wheat
Madhya Pradesh	Soybean - wheat
North Gujarat	Pearl millet- mustard
Sourashtra region-Gujarat	Cotton - groundnut
Western Maharashtra	Sorghum - wheat
Western Maharashtra	Groundnut-wheat
Marathwada region of Vidarba region	Cotton- groundnut
North Karnataka	Sorghum - bengalgram
South Karnataka	Cotton - groundnut

Cropping systems in dryland

Normally only one crop is grown under dryland condition and cultivation is restricted during the rainy season. However, the intensity of cropping can be increased through sequential or intercropping, depending on the rainfall and moisture storage capacity of the soils (Table 11.5).

TABLE 11.5: Cropping pattern with varying rainfall and soil moisture storage capacity

Rainfall (mm)	Storage capacity of soil (mm)	Cropping pattern
350-625	100	Single crop in *kharif*
650-750	100	Intercropping can be attempted
780-900	150	Sequential cropping is possible
900-above	200	Sequential cropping is assured

Source: Sharma, 1980

Choice of crops: Selection of a suitable crop and genotype is important to get higher yield in dry farming conditions. Deep rooted crops extract moisture from the deeper layers and they also have slow rate of transpiration. Leguminous crops are very well adopted for rainfed conditions because of their root system. Among the cereal, barley has better ability to harvest moisture from deeper layers than wheat. Moisture loss from the plant surface is also less in barley. Similarly linseed has greater ability to trap soil moisture under water scarce situation.

Important factors such as total rainfall, soil type and water availability have to be considered while practicing a particular cropping pattern in a place/ region. Cropping systems for different regions as suggested from the results of AICARP (1970) are given in Table 11.6.

TABLE 11.6: Cropping systems for different regions of India under drylands

Regions/soil type	Crops	
	Kharif	Rabi
Northern Region		
Samba (Jammu)	Maize	Wheat
	Green gram	Barley
	Cowpea	Wheat
	Sunflower	Wheat / Barley
	Groundnut	Barley
	Pearl millet	Bengal gram
Punjab	Sorghum	Wheat
	Maize	Wheat /Potato/ Barley
Hisar (Haryana)	Pearl millet	Cluster bean/Chickpea
Arid soils (Sierozemic soils)	(Monocropping is the rule)	
Central Region		
Dehra Dun (Uttar Pradesh)	Maize	Wheat
	Rice (upland)	Wheat/Bengalgram

Regions/soil type	Crops	
	Kharif	**Rabi**
Agra (Uttar Pradesh) *Entisols (Alluvial soils)*	Gram Pearlmillet	Mustard Chickpea/Barley
Varanasi (Uttar Pradesh) *Entisols (Alluvial soils)*	Sesame Bengal gram Rice Pearlmillet	Chickpea/ Mustard Barley or Mustard Chickpea/ Mustard Chickpea / Mustard
Eastern Region		
Ranchi (Bihar) *Alfisols and related red soils*	Rice Maize	Chickpea/ Linseed/Barley Rapeseed/ Bengalgram
Bhubaneshwar (Orissa) *Alfisols and related red soils*	Rice Fingermillet Maize	Linseed or Mustard Horsegram Horsegram
Rewa region (M.P.) *Vertisols and related black soils*	Rice Sorghum Greengram	Chickpea/ Lentil Bengal gram/ Wheat Wheat/ Chickpea
Jhansi region (M.P.) *Vertisols and related black soil*	Sorghum Pearl millet Blackgram Sesame	Bengal gram Bengal gram Safflower/ Chickpea Bengal gram
Indore (M.P.) *Vertisols and related black soils*	Maize Soybean Soybean	Chickpea Safflower Wheat
Western Region		
Udaipur (Rajasthan) *(Vertisols and related black soils)*	Greengram Sorghum Pearl millet Maize Blackgram/ Sunflower	Safflower Bengal gram Bengal gram Wheat Wheat
Anand (Gujarat)	Pearl millet Pigeonpea Castor Sunflower	Wheat - - -
Akola (Maharashtra) *Vertisols and related black soil*	Green gram Sorghum	Safflower Safflower

Regions/soil type	Crops	
	Kharif	**Rabi**
Sholapur (Maharashtra) *Vertisols*	Green gram Pearl millet Black gram	Safflower Bengal gram Sorghum
Southern regions		
Anantapur (AP) *Alfisol*	Sorghum Pearl millet Black gram Green gram Cowpea Monocropping is generally adopted	Safflower/ Horsegram Cowpea/ Blackgram Sorghum Pearl millet Pearl millet / Sorghum
Hyderabad *Alfisol*	Pearlmillet Sorghum	Cowpea Horsegram
Bijapur *Vertisols*	Sorghum Greengram	Greengram/ Blackgram Sorghum/ Safflower
Bangalore (Karnataka) *Alfisols*	Cowpea Cowpea	Finger millet Chilli
Mysore (Karnataka)	Groundnut Setaria Hybrid Pearl millet	Sorghum safflower Cotton
Bellary (Karnataka)	Cotton Blackgram	Sorghum Bengalgram Safflower
Kovilpatti (TN) *Vertisols*	-	Cotton, Sorghum Pearl millet, Cowpea Horsegram, Chilli

INTERCROPPING SYSTEMS

Multiple cropping in the form of intercropping is predominant in the regions of dry, humid and semi-arid tropics. Farmers normally grow two or more crops together on the same piece of land. Different crops are cultivated in mixed cropping: simple mixture of only two or three crops is the most common.

The objectives of this practice are:

i) Insurance against total crop failure under aberrant weather conditions or pest epidemics.

ii) Increase in total productivity per unit land area.
iii) Judicious utilization of resources such as land, labour and inputs.

When two crops are to be grown together, they are chosen in such a way that there is variation in their growth duration. The peak periods of growth of the two crop species should not coincide. In such arrangements, a quick maturing crop completes its life cycle before the other crop starts. Willey (1979) described the concept as temporal complementarity. Greater the differences in maturity and growth demands of the crop components, more opportunity is provided for greater exploitation of growth factors and over yielding. This will be achieved either by genetic difference in crop species or manipulation of planting dates. Normally short and long duration crops are grown together. Food crops are usually mixed with cash crops to ensure both sustenance and cash income.

Combination of species under intercropping depends on climate, location preferences and other site specific factors. Some of the important intercropping systems are described below:

Intercropping in cereals: Intercropping with cereal is an excellent way of improving the resource utilization because the cereal utilizes the rainy season resources while late maturing crop exploits the post-rainy season resources such as residual moisture. Sorghum is most commonly inter cropped with pigeonpea on a variety of soils. Sorghum is harvested after 3 1/2 to 4 1/2 months and pigeonpea matures in about 6-9 months depending on the genotype. Grain legumes such as cowpea, greengram, blackgram and groundnut are the other recommended intercrops with sorghum.

Maize + bean (*Phaseolus vulgaris* L.) is a predominant intercropping system in Central and South America and parts of East Africa, where rainfall ranges from 700 to 1500 mm spreading over 4-5 months. Soybean is also a good compatible companion crop with maize.

Pearl millet is a quick tillering and fast growing crop that attains full canopy development within 20-30 days of seedling establishment. It can be intercropped with groundnut, blackgram or castor.

Finger millet is widely intercropped with field beans (*Dolichos lab-lab*) in Karnataka State, India, where 4-12 rows of the millet are alternated with one row of beans.

Intercropping in pulses: For pigeonpea, short duration grain legumes such as blackgram and soybean are the best companion crops in Peninsular India. Groundnut is also a suitable intercrop. Sorghum is commonly intercropped with pigeonpea.

Intercropping in cotton: Cotton is initially a slow growing crop. Any short duration and fast growing crops such as greengram, blackgram, groundnut or cluster bean are the compatible companion crops. Onion is also a preferred intercrop in cotton.

Intercropping in sugarcane: Sugarcane is slow growing upto 80-90 days. Since the crop is planted in rows 0.8-1.0 m apart, considerable space is available for intercropping. Short duration crops maturing in 80-90 days can be advocated as intercrops. Blackgram and soybean are found suitable. The green manure, dhaincha (*Sesbania aculeata*) can be sown in the interspace and incorporated at about two months of its growth.

Intercropping for dryland

Intercropping recommended for different regions of India under dryland conditions are given in Table 11.7.

TABLE 11.7: Intercropping for different regions in India

Region	Intercropping
Samba (Jammu)	Castor + blackgram/ sesame/ cowpea/ sunflower
	Maize + cowpea (fodder)
	Maize + greengram
Hissar (Haryana)	Pearl millet+ cluster bean/ greengram
Dehra Dun (U.P.)	Pigeonpea + soybean
	Maize + pigeonpea
Agra (U.P.)	Pearl millet + blackgram / green gram
	Pigeonpea + green gram / pearl millet
Varanasi (U.P.)	Pigeonpea + maize / blackgram / millet
Ranchi (Bihar)	Barley + rapeseed
	Wheat + bengalgram/ rapeseed/ lentil
Bhubaneshwar (Orissa)	Pigeonpea + blackgram/sorghum/ groundnut
Rewa region (M.P.)	Pigeonpea + sorghum / finger millet blackgram / sunflower
Jhansi (M.P.)	Sorghum + blackgram / greengram / soybean
	Wheat + bengalgram/ mustard
	Barley + bengalgram / mustard
	Bengalgram + linseed / mustard.
Indore (M.P.)	Pigeonpea + sorghum
	Cotton + soybean
Udaipur (Rajasthan)	Sorghum + blackgram
	Pearl millet + blackgram
	Sunflower + blackgram
Anand (Gujarat)	Pearlmillet + red gram / castor / sunflower
Akola (Maharashtra)	Pigeonpea + blackgram / greengram/ sorghum/ groundnut
	Cotton + sunflower / blackgram / groundnut
Sholapur (Maharashtra)	Pigeonpea + pearlmillet / sorghum/ blackgram
	Cotton + sunflower / groundnut
Anantapur (A.P.)	Pigeonpea + greengram / pearl millet / sorghum/ foxtail millet / groundnut / sunflower
Bijapur (A.P.)	Cotton + groundnut / sorghum/ pearlmillet / greengram
Mysore region	Pigeonpea + pearlmillet
(Karnataka)	Cotton + pearlmillet
	Groundnut + cotton

Region	Intercropping
Kovilpatti (T.N.)	Cotton + blackgram / greengram Sorghum + blackgram / cowpea / *Dolichos lab lab* Pearlmillet + greengram / cluster bean / cowpea / *Dolichos lab* lab

Multi-tier cropping

Intercropping is mostly prevalent in plantation crops like coconut and arecanut. There is scope for intercropping in coconut garden upto the age of 8 years and after 25 years. During this period, there is adequate light transmission to the ground which permits cultivation of intercrops. The practice of growing different crops of varying height, rooting pattern and duration is called 'multi-tier cropping'. The objective of this system of cropping is to utilize the vertical space more effectively. In this system, the leaf canopies of intercrop components occupy different vertical layers. The tallest components have foliage tolerant of strong light and high evaporative demand and the shorter component (s) with foliage requiring shade and or relatively high humidity. *e.g.*, coconut + black pepper + cocoa+ pineapple. The schematic representation of planting of these crops is shown in Fig. 11.1.

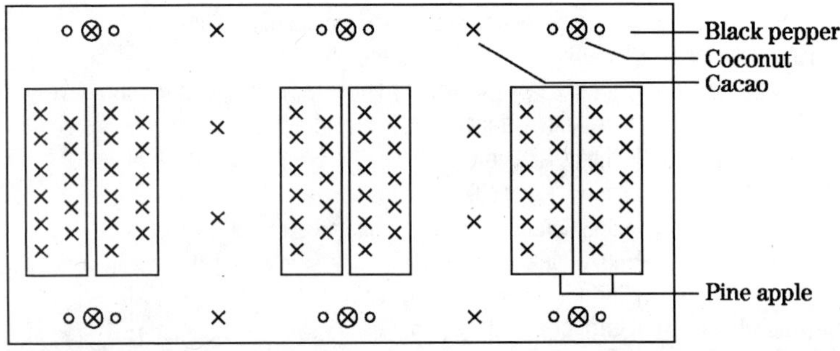

FIG. 11.1: Multi-tier cropping plan

In this system, coconut is planted with a spacing of 7.5 m. Rooted cuttings of black pepper are planted on either side of coconut about 75 cm away from the base. On the coconut trunk at a height of about one metre from the ground level, the vines of pepper are trailed. A single row of cacao is planted at the centre of space between coconut rows. Pine apple is planted in the interspace.

Coconut growing to a height of more than 10 m occupies the top floor. Black pepper growing to about 6-8 m height forms the second floor. Cacao with its pruned canopy of about 2.5 m height and pine apple growing to about 1 m height form the first and ground floors respectively.

In another multi-tier system in coconut, ginger or turmeric and partial shade loving vegetables form the first tier, banana in second tier, pepper in third tier and coconut or arecanut in the final tier.

In the arecanut plantation, tuber crops are predominantly intercropped. Elephant yam, tapioca, greater yam and sweet potato are common intercrops in humid tropics. Banana and pine apple are also cultivated as intercrops in arecanut gardens.

In coffee based multi-tier cropping system, first tier is with pine apple, second tier with coffee, third tier with cacao/mandarin orange and final tier with fast growing shade trees necessary for coffee plantation. (*e.g.*, dadaps and silver oak).

MANAGEMENT OF CROPPING SYSTEM

Management of cropping system differs from that of single cropping. This is due to inclusion of more than one crop as in intercropping or planting of crops in succession as in sequential cropping.

Water management in cropping system

The technique of water management is the same for sole cropping and inter-or sequential cropping. However, the presence of an additional crop may have an important effect on evapo-transpiration. With proper water management, it is possible to grow two crops where normally only one crop is raised under rainfed conditions. Scheduling of irrigation and method of water application have to be carefully done under intercropping situations since one of the components may be sensitive for excess irrigation. All these aspects should be carefully considered while developing water management techniques for intensive cropping system. Crop yield can be increased without significant increase in water use by selecting suitable cropping systems and adopting appropriate crop and soil management practices.

Water requirement

The total water requirement of intercropping does not increase much compared to sole cropping. At ICRISAT, the seasonal water requirement of sole sorghum and intercropping with redgram was almost similar (584 and 585 mm respectively). However, in a more competitive crop like onion as intercropped in groundnut increased the total water requirement by about 50 mm.

Water use efficiency

Water use efficiency in a cropping system can be increased by identification of appropriate crop combinations. WUE (in terms of economic produce) varied from 23 to 54 with cotton-based multiple cropping system under irrigated conditions of Coimbatore. Under wetland conditions, WUE ranged from 43 to 57 by adopting the cropping system of rice-rice-finger millet-green gram. Rice-rice-rice system was found least efficient in water use. In north Bihar, rice-potato-green gram registered highest water use efficiency (110-113 kg/ha cm).

More remunerative and less water consuming crop rotations have been standardized at different locations of India. Rice-mustard-sesame, rice-mustard-greengram, rice-potato-greengram rotations were found more water efficient systems at Memari in West Bengal. At Karaghpur (W.B.), rice-wheat, rice-mustard and rice-potato were more viable with less water input. Under higher level of irrigation in tarai region of U. P, rice-lentil and rice-wheat cropping systems were found better. In Bihar, rice-potato-greengram sequence appeared more water efficient compared to rice-wheat-greengram under adequate water supply. Under limited water supply, rice-gram-greengram and rice-mustard-greengram were found suitable. In north western plains, under annual supply of 10 irrigations, maize-wheat system used minimum water. However, with annual supply of 6 irrigations, greengram-wheat system performed better.

Irrigation methods and scheduling

Under intensive cropping, two or more crops are grown together. Scheduling of water for the component crops may vary widely and the critical periods of water requirements for the crops may not coincide. If one of the crops is irrigated based on its requirement, the other crop may suffer due to excess water or water stress, sometimes leading to total failure of the crop. In cotton + blackgram intercropping system, cotton is irrigated once in 15-20 days. The intercrop, blackgram is often affected by excess water and gives poor yield. In such situations, skip furrow method of irrigation is advocated.

In rice- wheat system, irrigation management in wheat succeeding transplanted puddled rice becomes critical due to disturbed structure of rice soils. At Varanasi and Faizabad (U.P.), pre-sowing irrigation given to wheat after harvest of puddled rice proved beneficial for crop establishment and system productivity. On the other hand, the practice of dry seed-bed preparation and irrigating wheat after sowing resulted in considerable yield loss.

Weed management in cropping system

Generally it is believed that intensive cropping reduces weed problems. Weed infestation is reduced in some situations, while it is not so in other circumstances. This depends on the crops, plant density and cultural operations done. Herbicide selectivity and residual toxicity also affect the weed problem in intensive cropping.

Intercropping and weed management

More complete crop cover and high density available in intercropping cause severe competition with weeds and reduce weed growth. The weed suppressing ability of intercrop is dependent upon the component crops selected, the genotypes used, plant density adopted, proportions of component crops, their spatial arrangement and the fertility and moisture status of the soil. Experiments carried out at ICRISAT, Hyderabad, indicated that there was 50-75% reduction in weed infestation by intercropping. Pigeonpea + sorghum intercropping system, which is extensively practiced in Karnataka, Maharashtra and Andhra Pradesh, is known to reduce weed intensity. Besides sorghum, intercropping of many short- duration legumes like greengram and blackgram with pigeonpea smother weeds to 60-70%. Quick growing non-competitive, compact legumes like greengram and blackgram act as a smother crop due to their good canopy coverage. Weed infestation in intercropping is influenced by the early growth and competitive abilities of the component crops. If one or both the components are vigorous and cover the land area rapidly, weed infestation is greatly reduced.

Though intercropping may reduce weed infestation and growth, still there is a need for some weeding in most cases. Labour requirement for weeding is greatly reduced because of limited weed growth. Normally two hand weedings are required; however, it may be restricted to one weeding under intercropping. Since the canopy coverage is almost complete, weed growth is minimal after first weeding. In sorghum + redgram or sorghum + cowpea, just one weeding is sufficient to get as high yield as in weed-free check.

The critical period of weed free condition may have to be extended a little longer in inter- cropping than in sole cropping. This is because the critical growth stages of the component crops vary temporally in intercropping. For example, the critical weed free period has to be extended to the first 7 weeks in sorghum + redgram intercropping while sole sorghum crop requires only 4-5 weeks of weed free period.

Chemical weed control is a great problem in intercropping than in sole cropping. Most herbicides are crop specific. Hence it is difficult to choose chemicals that will control a broad spectrum of weeds without causing damage to the component crops. The pre-emergence herbicides recommended for some of intercropping situations are given in Table 11.8.

TABLE 11.8: Pre-emergence herbicides for intercropping systems

Intercropping	Herbicides
Maize + green gram or cowpea	Butachlor
Maize + groundnut	Trifluraline
Sorghum + pulse	Alachlor
Sorghum + red gram	Ametryn or prometryn or terbutryn
Sugarcane + groundnut or soybean	Nitrofen

Sequential cropping and weed management

Under intensive cropping, land is cultivated throughout the year. This causes shift in the weed flora, towards more persistent perennials. The perennial sedge, *Scirpus maritimus,* is becoming a problem in lowland rice fields in Asia. Other perennials such as *Cynodon dactylon, Cyperus rotundus* and *Panicum maximum* pose a threat to crop production. When dryland crops are rotated with wetland rice without any weed control, *S. maritimus* decreased drastically during the dry period. In North Indian belt, considerable area follows the cropping system of rice-wheat system. These areas have been found heavily infested with the problem weed, *Phalaris minor* which is threatening wheat cultivation in Punjab, Haryana, Western U.P., Himachal Pradesh, parts of Madhya Pradesh, Rajasthan, Bihar and West Bengal. Wild oats is also becoming a problem in some of the areas. Adoption of sugarcane-wheat system in the place of rice-wheat decreases *Phalaris minor* infestation to almost negligible level which is, otherwise, not achieved through herbicides. In maize, Johnson grass (*Sorghum halepense)* becomes dominant which can be controlled by rotating maize with cotton.

While using herbicides for multiple cropping, it is important to consider the residual effect. Atrazine is used as a pre-emergence herbicide for sorghum. Establishment of legumes such as greengram and groundnut following sorghum is poor in atrazine applied fields. However, the succeeding cotton is not affected. To avoid residual toxicity problems, it is important to use a herbicide that leaves little residue or that is safe for the succeeding crop.

Ploughing the field well ahead of planting season, either at the end of rainy season or after summer rains helps to kill most of the weeds and reduces the weed problem in the ensuing season. For effective weed control in multiple cropping, a combination of cultural and chemical methods may be more appropriate.

Soil fertility management in cropping systems

Soil fertility management becomes more complex in intensive cropping because of the additional factors such as residual effect of nutrients applied to the previous crops, possible effect of legumes in the system, complementary and competitive interference from the component crops and influence of crop residues left in the soil. In modern agriculture, efficient nutrient management has emerged as one of the most important factors in sustaining high production levels of intensive cropping systems. Higher cropping intensity involving improved varieties, heavier inputs of fertilizer and water, increasing yields and accelerated removal of plant nutrients have added newer dimensions to the soil fertility management.

Fertilization practices for cropping system

Based on long term fertility experiments conducted in various parts of India, the following broad conclusions are drawn with respect to efficient management of nutrients.

System productivity increased with the application of P along with N, which showed further improvement at many locations with the use of N, P and K. Application of N at recommended rates and phases to each crop of the cropping system is advocated.

Phosphorus management in cropping system needs careful adjustment of P fertilizer dose taking into account the type of fertilizer, soil characteristics and their yield level, extent of P removal and growing environment. In the cropping system involving wheat, fertilizer P dose to *kharif* crop can be reduced if preceding wheat has received P in adequate amounts.

Removal of K in proportion to N is very high in cropping systems, particularly those involving cereal and fodder crops. In long-term fertilizer experiments, uptake of K by the crops even at optimal NPK dose was far in excess of K applied in almost all soils and cropping systems. It is important to apply K fertilizer at recommended rate to maintain soil fertility status.

Among micronutients, Zn deficiency is the most common as nearly 50% soils of intensively cultivated areas suffer from Zn deficiency. The crops vary greatly in their capacity to utilize Zn. Hence its application becomes more crucial for certain crops than others in multiple cropping systems. Rainy season crops like rice, maize and sorghum respond more to applied Zn than winter crops like wheat and chickpea. Application of Zn is important for enhancing the efficiency of other nutrients and the productivity levels of crops. Under long-term fertilizer experiments at Ludhiana (Punjab), significant decline in productivity of maize was recorded after 10 and 12 annual cycles, consequent to fall in Zn status. The yield losses were recovered with the application of $ZnSO_4$ @ 50 kg Zn/ha once in 4-5 years. Crops fertilized with Zn utilize only a fraction of applied Zn. In the system involving non-rice crops, residual effect of Zn lasts for several crops grown in succession. Hence it is important to decide the rate and frequency of Zn application in cropping system based on careful appraisal of the deficiency. Use of organics prevents Zn deficiency in intensive systems under normal soils.

Cropping system and integrated nutrient management (INM)

The major components of the INM are fertilizers, organic manures, green manures, crop residues and biofertilizers. In cereal- based cropping systems, about 25-50% fertilizer NPK dose of rainy season crops could be curtailed with the use of organics such as FYM, green manure and crop residues under different situations. In sugarcane-based system, integrated use of sulphitation pressmud, cane trash and biofertilizers each with inorganic fertilizer and green leaf manuring showed 20-25% economy in fertilizer N applied to sugarcane by improving the use efficiency of N, P and other nutrients. Inclusion of legumes in cropping systems for green manuring, fodder or grain purposes proved an assured agro-technique to improve nutrient use efficiency, especially that of N. Incorporation of summer greengram residues after picking pods is as effective as green manuring in rice-wheat system.

Legume effects

Legumes generally find a place in crop mixtures and rotations because of their capacity to fix atmospheric N. Legumes are reported to contribute N to the associated non-legumes. Inclusion of legumes in the cropping system helps to save upto 25% of recommended level of N application to the associated cereal and improve the soil N status. Groundnut is estimated to fix 10 to 60 kg N/ha in a single season. Hence the crop following groundnut gets benefited. Growing grain legumes in the winter season improves soil fertility and increases the yield of the following maize crop.

Besides their N fixing capacity, legumes have been reported to extract insoluble forms of soil phosphorus. Legumes also have greater root cation exchange capacity than cereals and hence they are able to absorb more of divalent cations such as Ca^{++} and Mg^{++}. Normally legumes cannot compete effectively with the cereals in the absorption of monovalent cation like K^{+}. Inclusion of legume as a component of intensive cropping system is important for maintaining soil fertility and economizing fertilizer application.

Effect of intensive cropping on soil properties

Under intensive cropping, different crops with varying rooting patterns are cultivated. This helps to explore the soil effectively for moisture and nutrients and prevent formation of compact sub-soil layer which often happens in monoculture and with repeated cultivation. At Delhi, adoption of berseem-sugarcane system was found to improve the soil structure.

Adopting intensive cultivation in the marginal soils without adequate fertilization may deplete the soil in course of time and decrease its productivity. Many intercropping and sequential cropping systems do not cause great variation in soil available N status. Continuous N application to the crops in cereal-based system is not likely to build up N status of the soil and even heavy doses of N applied to wheat. Crops like potato are found to hardly leave residual effect on the succeeding crop.

In most of the cropping systems, the quantity of added P through fertilizer is greater than the quantity removed. Hence there may be build up in soil P status. But this may or may not be reflected in the available P status since most of the added P is rapidly converted to insoluble forms. However, under lowland rice, soluble P increased due to submergence and high temperature though the magnitude may vary in different soils. Hence, in rice-wheat system, rice is found to make better use of residual P than wheat. Because of this reason, P application is advocated preferably to wheat or other rice fallow crop, which is relatively a poor user of residual P and requires direct application.

Majority of soils in India are well supplied with K. There is hardly any noticeable impact on soil available K even after continuous cropping with greater removal of K by the crops. This is mainly because of the dynamic equilibrium existing among various forms of soil K. Once the available K is depleted, it is slowly replenished by release from other forms. However, in coarse textured soils and with the use of high yielding varieties, there may be decline in soil K status.

It is possible to maintain soil organic matter to a satisfactory level with adequate fertilization and addition of crop residues to the soil.

EVALUATION OF CROPPING SYSTEMS

Various types of cropping systems are practiced in a farm/region. They are to be properly evaluated to find out their stability and relative advantage. Such a comparison may be made with reference to land use efficiency, biological potential, economic viability, etc. Some of the important indices to evaluate the cropping systems are discussed here.

Land Use Efficiency

Multiple Cropping Index or Multiple Cropping Intensity (MCI): It was proposed by Dalrymple (1971). It is the ratio of total area cropped in a year to the total land area available for cultivation and expressed in %age.

$$\text{MCI} = \frac{\sum_{i=1}^{n} a_i}{A} X100$$

Where, i = 1,2,3,...n, n = total number of crops, a_i = area occupied by i^{th} crop and A= total land area available for cultivation.

Cultivated Land Utilization Index (CLUI): Cultivated land utilization Index (Chuang, 1973) is calculated by summing the products of land area planted to each crop, multiplied by the actual duration of that crop divided by the total cultivated land area, times 365 days

$$\text{CLUI} = \frac{\sum_{i=1}^{n} a_i.d_i}{AX365} \times 100$$

Where, i. = 1,2,3,....n, n = total number of crops, a_i = area occupied by the ith crop, di =days that the ith crop occupied a_i and A = total cultivated land area available for 365 days.

CLUI can be expressed as a fraction or %age. This gives an idea about how the land area has been put into use. If the index is 1 (100%), it shows that the land has not been left fallow and more than 1, tells the specification of intercropping and relay cropping. Limitation of CLUI is its inability to consider the land temporarily available to the farmer for cultivation.

Crop Intensity Index (CII): Crop intensity Index assesses farmer's actual land use in area and time relationship for each crop or group of crops compared to the total available land area and time, including land that is temporarily available for cultivation. It is calculated by summing the product of area and duration of each crop divided by the product of farmer's total available cultivated land area and time period plus the sum of the temporarily available land area with the time of these land areas actually put into use (Menegay *et al.* 1978). The basic concept of CLUI and CII are similar. However, the latter offers more flexibility when combined with appropriate sampling procedures for determining and evaluating vegetable production and cropping pattern data.

$$CII = \frac{\sum_{i=1}^{NC} a_i.t_i}{AoT + \sum_{j=1}^{M} A_j.T_j}$$

Where, i = 1,2,3,...Nc, Nc = total number of crops grown by a farmer during the time period, T, ai = area occupied by ith crop, t_i = duration of ith crop (months that the crop i occupied an area a_i), T = time period under study (usually one year), Ao = Total cultivated land area available with the farmer for use during the entire time period, T, M = total number of fields temporarily available to the farmer for cropping during time period, T, j = 1,2,3,....M, Aj = land area of jth field and Tj = time period A_l is available. CII = 1 means that area or land resources have been fully utilized and less than 1 indicates under utilization of resources.

Biological potential

Production Efficiency (PE)

Crop Equivalent Yield (CEY): Many types of crops/cultivars are included in a multiple cropping sequence. It is very difficult to compare the economic produce of one crop to another. To cite an example, yield of rice cannot be compared with potato yield. Similarly the yield of crops grown for fodder purposes cannot be compared with the yield of grain cereals or pulse crops and so on. In such situations, comparisons can be made based on economic returns (gross or net returns). The yields of protein and carbohydrate equivalents can also be calculated for valid comparison. Efforts have also been made to convert the yields of different crops into equivalent yield of any one crop such as wheat equivalent yield (Lal and Ray, 1976 and Verma and Modgel, 1983). Verma and Modgal (1983) evolved the equation for calculating wheat equivalent yield (WEY).

$$\text{WEY} = \sum_{i=1}^{n} (Y_i \cdot e_i)$$

Where, Y_i = the economic yield of ith crop, e_i =the wheat equivalent factor of ith crop, $e_i = \frac{P_i}{P_w}$, P_i = the price of unit weight of ith crop, and P_w = the price of a unit weight of wheat.

This type of comparison is valid when considering the gross returns. However, it does not indicate the net gain obtained from a cropping system. This will not give any explanation about the land use pattern of the cropping system.

Some of the common indices have been developed to measure and compare farm land use and production potential in multiple cropping. Land Equivalent Ratio is the most important one.

Land Equivalent Ratio (LER): This is the most frequently used efficiency indicator. LER can be defined as the relative area of sole crop that would be required to produce the equivalent yield achieved by intercropping.

$$\text{LER} = \sum_{i=1}^{n} = \frac{Yab}{Yaa} + \frac{Yba}{Ybb}$$

Where, Y_{ab} = yield of crop a in intercropping, Y_{ba} = yield of crop b in intercropping, Y_{aa} = yield of crop a in pure stand and Y_{bb} = yield of crop b in pure stand.

LER of more than 1 indicates yield advantage, equal to 1 indicates no gain or no loss and less than 1 indicates yield loss. It can be used both for replacement and additive series of intercropping.

Economic viability

Gross returns: The total monetary returns of the economic produce such as grain, tuber, bulb, fruit, etc and bye- products viz., straw, fodder, fuel, etc obtained from the crops included in the system are calculated based on the local market prices. The total return is expressed in terms of unit area, usually one hectare.

The main draw back in this calculation is that the market price of the produce is higher than that actually obtained by the farmer. Generally gross returns calculated is somewhat inflated compared to the actual receipt obtained by the farmer.

Net returns or net profit: This is worked out by subtracting the total cost of cultivation from the gross returns. This value gives the actual profit obtained by the farmer. In this type of calculation only the variable costs are considered. Fixed costs such as rent for the land, land revenue, interest on capital, etc. are not included. For a realistic estimate, however, fixed costs should also be included.

Returns per rupee invested: This is also called benefit-cost ratio or input-output ratio.

$$\text{Return per rupee invested} = \frac{\text{Gross Returns}}{\text{Cost of cultivation}}$$

This index provides an estimate of the benefit derived and expenditure incurred by the farmer in adopting a particular cropping system. Anything above the value of 2.0 (meaning that the farmer can get Rs 2 as returns for every rupee invested) can be considered worthwhile.

Per day Return: This is also called as income per day and can be obtained by dividing the net returns by number of cropping period (days).

$$\text{Per day return} = \frac{\text{Net returns}}{\text{Cropping period (days)}}$$

This gives the efficiency of the cropping system in terms of monetary value. If the system is stretched over one year, the denominator can be replaced by 365 days and per day return for the whole year can be calculated.

STUDY OF ALLIED ACTIVITIES

In the integrated farming system, it is always emphasized to combine cropping with other enterprises/activities. Many enterprises are available and these include cattle maintenance, sheep or goat rearing, poultry, piggery, rabbit rearing, bee keeping, etc., Any one or more can be combined with the cropping.

Cattle maintenance

Cattle rearing in India is carried out under a variety of adverse climatic and environmental conditions. The cattle are broadly classified into three groups.

1. **Draft breeds:** The bullocks of these breeds are good draft animals, but the cows are poor milkers. *e.g.* Nagore, Hallikar, Kangeyam, Mali.
2. **Dairy breeds:** The cows are high milk yielders but the bullocks are of poor draft quality. *e.g.*, Sahiwal, Sindhi, Gir.
3. **Dual purpose:** The cows are fairly good milkers and the bullocks are with good draft workcapacity. *e.g.*, Hariana, Ongole and Kankrej.

Exotic breeds: The exotic breeds are high milk yielders, *e.g.*, Jersey, Holstein-Friesian, Aryshire, Brown Swiss and Guernsey.

Buffaloes

Important dairy breeds of buffalo are Murrah, Nili Ravi (which has its home tract in Pakistan), Mehsana, Suti, Zafarabadi, Godavari and Bhadawari. Of these Godavari has been evolved through crossing local buffaloes in coastal regions of Andhra Pradesh with Murrah.

Housing: Each cow requires 12 to 18 sq. m space and the buffaloes need 12 to 15 sq. m. It is important to provide good ventilation and an open shed of housing is always preferable. Dairy building should be located at an elevated place to facilitate easy drainage. The floor should be rough and have gradient of 2.5 cm for every 25 cm length.

Breeding and maintenance: The cows remain in milk for 9-10 months, the average calving interval being 16-18 months. A cow does not require more than 6-8 weeks of dry period. From the economic point of view, cow should ordinarily be bred during the second and third months after calving. In weak animals and heavy milkers, breeding may be delayed by 1 or 2 months. Cattle come to heat in more or less regular cycles of about 21 days which lasts for about a day. The best time to serve a cow is during the last stage of heat. If artificially inseminated, a second insemination may be given within 6-8 hours after the first insemination. The gestation period varies with individual cows and breeds and normally it is about 280 days.

In the case of buffaloes, the lactation period last for 7-9 months. She-buffalo comes to heat every 21-23 days. The gestation period is 310 days. Calf rearing is very important in the case of buffalo maintenance. Since they require abundant water, wallowing is required. Regular deworming is needed for buffalo maintenance.

Under Indian conditions, cattle commonly mature at the age of about three years. This period can, however, be reduced by six months under well managed herd.

Feeding: Cattle feed generally contains fibrous, coarse, low nutrient straw material called roughage and concentrates.

Roughages: Dairy cattle are efficient user of the roughages and convert large quantities of relatively inexpensive roughage into milk. Roughages are basic for cattle ration and includes legumes, non-legume hays, straw and silage of legume and grasses.

Concentrates: Grains and byproducts of grains and oilseeds constitute the concentrates. They are extensively used in dairy cattle ration. These include cereals (maize, sorghum, oats, barley), cotton seeds, industrial wastes (bran of wheat, rice, gram husk) and cakes of oilseeds (groundnut, sesame, rape-seed, soybean, linseed).

Vitamins and mineral mixtures: It is advisable to feed a supplement containing vitamins A and D. Mineral mixtures containing salt, Ca and P should also be provided in the ration.

The ration per animal per day normally includes concentrate @ 1 kg for 2 litres of milk yield, green fodder (20-30 kg), straw (5-7 kg) and water (32 litres).

Goat rearing

In India, activity of goat rearing is sustained in different kinds of environments, including dry, hot, wet and cold, high mountains or low lying plains. The activity is also associated with different systems such as crop or animal-based, pastoral or sedentary, single animal or mixed herd, small or large scale. Goat is mainly reared for meat, milk, hide and skin. Goat meat is the preferred meat in India. A goat on hoof (live goat) fetches a better price than a sheep on hoof.

Housing

Goats can be maintained under stall-fed conditions. Successful goat rearing depends on the selection of site. Goats do not thrive on marshy or swampy ground. Goats are to be provided with a dry, comfortable, safe and secure place, free from worms and affording protection from excessive heat and inclement weather. The kitts are kept under large inverted baskets until they are old enough to run along with their mothers. Males and females are generally kept together. The space requirement for a goat is 4.5 to 5.4 sq. m.

Breeding and maintenance

Goat matures in about 6-7 months. Breeding is allowed for buck at one year and doe after 10 months of age. Gestation period is 145-155 days. It gives birth to 1-3 kitts per time. Number of evings are three per 2 years. The kitts can be weaned after 30-45 days. Mother can be allowed for mating 45-60 days after eveing. Once in five years, the buck can be changed to avoid deterioration due to inbreeding. When the young ones attain a body weight of about 25-30 kg in about nine months, they can be sold.

Feeding

The per head requirement of nutrients in respect of goats is relatively low. Hence, they are suitable for resource poor small farmers with marginal grazing lands. They are essentially browsers and eat plants which any other animals won't touch. Goats eat 4-5 times that of their body weight. Since the profit depends on weight addition, adequate proteins and calorie should be given to goats. They eat more of tree fodder and hence 40-50% of green fodder should contain tree leaf fodder and the rest with other grass species. Goats should be fed with concentrates of maize, wheat, horsegram, groundnut cake, fish meal and wheat bran. Common salt and vitamin mixtures should also be added. Abundant clean fresh water should be made available to the goats. Water should be changed every morning and evening. Fresh water is required for digestion, blood circulation and removal of waste from the body. Water is also required for regulation of the body temperature.

Sheep rearing

Sheep are well adapted to many areas. They are excellent gleaners and make use of much of the waste feed. They consume large quantities of roughage, converting a relatively cheap food into a good cash product. Housing need not be elaborate or expensive. However, to protect the flock from predatory animals, the height of the fencing should be raised to two metres.

Breeds of Indian sheep

There are three types of sheep in India based on the geographical division of the country.

i) **The temperate Himalayan region:** Gurez, Karanah, Bhakarwal, Gaddi, Rampur- Bushiar.
ii) **Dry western Region:** Lohi, Bikaneri, Marwari, Kutchi, Kathiawari
iii) **Southern Region:** Deccani, Nellore, Bellary, Mandya, Bandur.

Breeding and maintenance

One ram can be maintained for 40-50 ewes. Rams are liable to fight when two or more of them are put in a pen. Unlike other farm animals, ewes in general do not come in heat at regular intervals throughout the year but are seasonal in this respect. The duration of the heat period will range from 1-3 days and 75% of the ewes remain in heat for 21-39 hours. The optimum time of service is towards the end of heat period. Average heat interval is 18 days during the breeding season. The gestation period will vary from 142-152 days with an average of 147 days. A normal ram is in full vigour for breeding from the age of 2 1/2 -5 years. Sheep grow fully at two years of age when the ewe is ready for breeding. Under average range condition, ewes may be expected to produce about five crops of lambs.

Feeding

A sheep requires about 1-2 kg of leguminous hay per day depending on the age of sheep and its body weight. Proteins may be supplied through concentrates such as groundnut cake, sesame cake or safflower cake when the pastures are poor in legumes or when scarcity conditions prevail. Normally 110-225 g of cake are sufficient to maintain an average sheep in good condition. Feeding a mixture of common salt, ground limestone and sterilized bone meal in equal parts is required to alleviate deficiency of minerals in the feed.

Poultry

Poultry is one of the fastest growing food industries in the world. Poultry meat accounts for about 27 % of the total meat consumed world wide, and its consumption is growing at an average of 5% annually. Poultry industry in India is relatively a new agricultural industry. Till 1950, it was considered a back yard profession in India. In the sixties, the growth rate of egg production was about 10% and it increased to 25% in the seventies. The growth rate came down to 7-8% by 1990 due to price-rise in poultry feed. By 2000, the total egg production may reach upto 5000 crores. Broiler production is increasing at the rate of 15% per year. It was 31 million in 1981 and increased upto 300 million in 1995 (Singh, 1997). Nearly 330 thousand tonnes of broiler meat are currently produced. The average global consumption is 120 eggs per person per year and in India, it is only 32-33 eggs per capita year. As per the nutritional recommendation, the per capita consumption is estimated at 180 eggs/year and 9 kg meat /year.

Breeds: Specific poultry stocks for egg and broiler production are available. A majority of the stocks used for egg production are crosses involving the strains or inbred lines of white Leghorn. To a limited extent, other breeds like Rhode Island Red, California Grey and Australop are used. Heavy breeds such as white Plymouth Rock, White Cornish and New Hampshire are used for cross-bred broiler chickens. Hence, it is essential to consider the strain within the breed at the time of purchase. Several commercial poultry breeders are selling day old chicks in India. It is best to start with the day old chicks.

Housing: Adequate space should be provided for the birds. Floor area of about 0.2 m^2 per adult bird is adequate for light breeds such as white Leghorn. About 0.3-0.4 m^2 per bird is required for heavy breeds. The house should have good ventilation and reasonably cool in summer and warm during winter. It should be located on well-drained ground, safe from flood waters.

Feed: The feed conversion efficiency of the bird is far superior to other animals. About 60-70% of the total expenditure on poultry farming is spent on the poultry feed. Hence, use of cheap and efficient ration will give maximum profit. Ration should be balanced containing carbohydrates, fats, minerals and vitamins. Some of the common feed stuffs used for making poultry ration in India are:

Cereals: Maize, barley, oats, wheat, pearl millet, sorghum, rice- broken.

Cakes/meal: Oil cakes, maize-gluten-meal, fish meal, meat meal, blood meal.

Minerals/salt: Limestone, Oyster shell, salt, manganese.

From the day old to 4 weeks of age, birds are fed on starter ration and thereafter finisher ration, which contains more energy and 18-20% protein. Feed may be given 2-3 times. In addition to the food stuffs, antibiotics and drugs may also be added to the poultry ration. Laying hens are provided with oyster shell or ground limestone. Riboflavin is particularly needed.

Maintenance: The chicks must be vaccinated against Ranikhet diseases with F_1 Strain vaccine within the first 6-7 days of age. One drop of vaccine may be administered in the eye and nostril. When chicks get the optimum body weight of 1.0-1.5 kg around six weeks, they can be marketed for broiler. Hens may be retained for one year for production *i.e.*, upto the age of about 1 1/2 years. After that they are disposed off for table purpose. It may not be economical to keep the hens beyond 1

1/2 years since egg production would get reduced. One hen is capable of laying 180-230 eggs in a year starting from the sixth month. In addition, a laying hen produces about 230 g of fresh droppings (75 % moisture) daily.

Duck rearing

Ducks account for about 7% of the poultry population in India. They are popular in coastal and water logged states like West Bengal, Orrisa, Andhra Pradesh, Tamil Nadu, Kerala, Tripura and Jammu and Kashmir. Dusks are predominantly of indigenous type and reared for egg production on natural foraging. They have a production potential of about 130-140 eggs/ bird/year. Ducks are quite hardy, more easily brooded and resistant to common avian diseases. In places like marshy river side, wetland and barren moors where chicken or any other type of stock do not flourish, duck farming can be a better alternative.

Breeds: The important Indian breeds are Sylhet Mete and Nageswari which are mostly found in the Eastern region of the country. Their annual production is 150 eggs/ bird year. Improved breeds for egg and meat production are available. Khaki Campbell and Indian Runner are the most popular breeds for egg laying. Khaki Campbell has a production potential of 300 eggs/bird/year. Indian Runner is the second best producer. White Pekin, Muscovy and Aylesbury are known for meat production. White Pekin is the most popular duck in the world. It is fast growing and has low feed consumption with fine quality of meat. It attains about 3 kg of body weight in 40 days. Indigenous types, however, still continue to dominate in duck farming. Desi ducks are robust, well adapted to local conditions and free of diseases.

Housing: Ducks prefer to stay outside day and night even during winter or rains. In mild climate, it is possible to raise ducks without artificial shelter. A light fence of atleast 1.2 m high enclosing the yard is enough to stop any predators. One nest of size 0.3 x 0.3 x 0.45 m to every 3 ducks is sufficient. In case of laying birds, a mating ratio of 1 drake: 6-7 ducks and in meat type 1:4-5 is allowed. The duck house should be well ventilated, dry, leak and rat proof. The roof may be of thatched or asbestos sheeted. A water channel of 0.5 m wide and 0.20 m deep is constructed at the far end on both sides parallel to the night shelter in the rearing or layer house.

Feeding: Ducks normally require lesser attention. They supplement their feed by foraging, eating fallen grains in harvested paddy fields, small fishes and other aquatic materials in lakes and ponds. However, for intensive rearing, pellet feeding may be given. Ducks prefer wet mash due to difficulties in swallowing the dry mash. Hence, ducks should never have access to feed without water. During the first 8 weeks, birds should always have an access to feed. Later on they may be fed twice a day in the morning and late afternoon.

Maintenance: The general management of ducks is similar to that of the chickens. The incubation period is 28 days. A broody duck or hen may be used for small scale hatching and incubator for large scale hatching. During the early part of the life, newly hatched ducklings require warm temperature under the natural or village conditions. A duck or broody hen can take care of 10-15 ducklings. Artificial brooding may be resorted for large number of ducklings. High egg-laying strains of duck come into production at 16-18 weeks of age.

Ducks are resistant to common avian diseases. Some of the common diseases in duck are duck plague, duck virus hepatitis, duck cholera and aflatoxicosis.

Turkey rearing

Turkey is a robust bird and can be reared in humid tropics. It actively feeds on a variety of crop residues and insects in the farm and hence can be raised with much ease.

Physical features: There are a few peculiar features in the physical appearance of a turkey. Male has black beard attached to the upper breast regions. This beard is small in females of white turkeys and absent in those of coloured varieties. A fleshy protuberance called snood is present near the base of the beak in both males and females. The head bears caruncles and a large flap of skin below the chin is known as dewlap. Broad Breasted Bronze breed are ordinarily seen in India. Norfolks and the Cambridge are the other important breeds.

Housing: Housing for turkeys may be of range system, confinement or a combination of both. There is a growing trend towards confinement housing. Breeds require a floor space of 0.4 m^2/bird in confinement and 32.5 m^2/bird in the range rearing.

Feeding: Turkeys have much higher growth rate compared to chickens. Hence they have relatively higher feed and nutrient requirement. Turkey can be fed with all types of dry feed comprising pellets, wet mash, grain and green feed in well balanced combination. They also need plenty of clean water.

Maintenance: Mating ratio in natural flock is 14 hens:1 tom for small and 12:1 for medium sized turkeys. The birds should be carefully segregated when they reach the mating stage. Mating take place during summer. Particular attention should be bestowed in regulating mating. The males should be kept away from their mates in the morning and selectively mated with other birds by turn. Mating in the evening increases the number of fertile eggs.

Generally turkey lays eggs on alternate days from six months onwards. In a year, they lay about 150 eggs. The bird attains a weight of 5-8 kg in a year. The birds should not be allowed to fatten too much as it would make them vulnerable for diseases. Changing the breeding stock periodically would be gainful for the farmers.

Pigeons for meat

Domestic pigeon (*Columba livia)* belonging to the sub-family Columbia can be reared for its meat. Females are smaller than the males and finer in the head. They hold their tails higher than males and their pelvic pones are spaced wide apart. The males are large, aggressive and make a loud cooling noise. They strut around females during the breeding season. There is difference in the growth rate among the males and females. The former grows faster than the latter. Thus, even at an early stage, the gender difference can be easily made based on their body weight.

Feeding: Adults feed the young ones (squabs) with 'pigeon milk', a fluid that is secreted in their crop. The pigeon milk looks like thick custard and has a high protein content. Pigeons require water for drinking and for bathing to remove external parasites. A pair of breeds drink about 500 ml of water per day.

Pigeons are not fussy eaters, but do best on diets having whole grains. Nutrient requirement of pigeons is crude protein (13.5%), carbohydrates (65%), crude fibre (3.5%) and fat (3.0%). The daily feed intake of an adult pair is about 120 g.

Maintenance: Each pair normally produces 14 squabs in a year. The incubation period of the eggs is 18 days. Both partners build their nest and take turns to sit on the eggs. The female starts laying eggs again when the squabs are two weeks old. The young ones become independent in 35 days. Squabs of 30-35 days age are best suited for meat purpose since recovery is high with the body weight of 350 g. In addition to the meat, pigeon droppings (25 g per bird per day) can be used as fish feed or enriched manure.

Japanese quail

Quail belongs to class Aves, family *Phasianidae* and genus *Coturnir*. Quails, introduced initially as experimental birds, have become popular for their eggs and meat. Efforts are being made by Central Avian Research Institute, Izatnagar, to develop the guinea fowl for meat production. Males are lighter than females and are identified by the cinnamon coloured feather on the upper throat and lower breast region. Female is similar to male in colour except that the feathers on the throat and upper breast are long pointed and much lighter cinnamon in colour.

Maintenance: Quails need small space and are highly suitable for cage rearing. Therefore, it is possible to rear them even in urban areas where space is a major constraint. They are socially and commercially more adaptable due to their small body size, shorter generation interval, highly prolific nature and simplicity in rearing and are more economical. Females lay eggs as early as at the age of 5 weeks. The average age of the first egg production is 40 days. They are in full production by 50 days. They have a capacity to lay 300 or more eggs each per annum. The shell of a typical quail's egg is a mixture of greenish black and brownish speckles or patches of varying sizes. An egg weighs about 10-12 g on an average and is comparatively thin and delicate in nature. Albumen content is 56 to 59%, yolk 28-32% and shell 12-14%. The yolk content in relation to albumen is more in a quail's egg than in a chicken's egg. Special care should be given for collecting and handling the egg.

The rapid growth rate of the Japanese quail renders it an ideal broiler. At six weeks, quails attain a body weight of 125-150 g with a feed efficiency of 3.0. Japanese quails are fairly resistant to most of the common diseases affecting chicken. However, they are sensitive to abrupt environmental changes during first and second week of their life.

Piggery

Pigs are maintained for the production of pork. They are fed with inedible feeds, forages, certain grain byproducts obtained from mills, meat byproducts, damaged feeds and garbage. Most of these feeds are either not edible or not very palatable to human beings. The pig grows fast and is a prolific breeder, farrowing 10 to 12 pigs at a time. It is capable of producing two litres per year under good management conditions. The carcass return is high at 65-70 % of the live weight.

Breeds: Imported breeds of Large White Yorkshire and Landrace are being used widely. Yorkshire is the most extensively used exotic breed in India. It is a prolific breed having good carcass quality, growth rate and feed conversion ability. For a small breeding farm or unit, the selection of a herd boar is extremely important. A good boar weighs 90 kg in about 5-6 months and is strong on feet and legs. The mother of the pig to be selected should have large litters of eight piglets or more.

Housing: Housing should provide maximum comfort to pigs so that their growth is optimum. There should not be dampness, draft and over heating. Locally available materials can be used for housing. One pig requires about 2.7 sq. m with a wall of 1.2 m height. Eight boars can be kept in 2.7-4.5 sq. m area with 2.4-6.0 sq. m open space.

Feeding: Feed plays an important role in successful pig production. Pigs are the most rapidly growing livestock and suffer more from nutritional deficiencies than the ruminants. Protein, carbohydrates, fats, minerals, vitamins and ample good water form a complete diet for pig. Pigs have a simple stomach; therefore, they must be fed with maximum of concentrates and minimum of roughage. The main ingredients of swine ration are cereals and millets and their byproducts. The fibre content in swine ration should be very low (around 5-6%) for better feed utilization efficiency. Mixed ration should also contain 0.5% of added salt. Swine requires comparatively higher percentage of Ca and P than do cattle or sheep. When pigs are maintained with agricultural/kitchen waste or fish and slaughter house waste, the cost of production remains low. On an average, the consumption of feed is 3.5 % of total weight. Feed allowance is calculated as 2.5 -3.0 kg/100 kg body weight +@ 0.25 kg feed per piglet with the lactating mothers.

Management: As a general rule, well developed gilts weighing about 100 kg, when 12-14 months old, may be used for breeding. The body weight is more important than age at breeding. Sows with low body weight show higher rate of fetal and pre-weaning mortality and have been proved as mothers with poor nursing ability. The gestation period is on an average 114 days. Litter size at birth may be 1-16 numbers with the body weight of 1-25 kg. Normal period between birth of piglets is 10-20 minutes. Time taken for the whole process of farrowing ranges from 1.5 to 4.0 hours. Sows are weaned after 40 days. It is advantageous to cull the sow after fifth or sixth litter in a commercial herd. Weaned sows come into heat in 3-10 days after weaning and may be allowed to breed. The boar-sow ratio should be 1:15. It is profitable to raise two litters from each sow each year.

Mortality in piglets is an important cause of heavy economic loss leading to failure of pig industry. In general, one fourth of piglets farrowed die before they are weaned. Another one tenth are also categorized into stunt or unprofitable group due to disease or parasite infection. Thus about 60-65 % of the piglets farrowed perform as healthy piglets at slaughter age. Death rate is high during farrowing and the first week after farrowing. The farrowing season also determines mortality rate. Mortality in new born piglets is maximum when farrowing takes place in acute cold or hot climate. Therefore, mating should be planned in such a way that farrowing could be avoided in such seasons.

Rabbit rearing

Rabbit (*Oryctologus cuniculles*) is reared all over the world in various climatic conditions. Rabbit rearing in India is of recent origin, though hunting of wild rabbits for meat is not uncommon. Rabbits can easily be reared with relatively less concentrate feed and with very high reproduction rates. Rabbit meat is pure white and is low in fat and cholesterol content. Further, rabbit meat does not have any religious taboo, unlike pork and meat from cow.

Breeds: Rabbits can be classified into two categories as meat and wool producing ones. Important meat breeds are New Zealand White, Soviet Chinchilla and Kandinrex. Breeds for wool are Angora, Polish Bolamina, Dan and Flirorida.

Housing: Rabbits can be kept in hutches outside or in cages inside. Cages should have door (30x30 cm) with welded wire mesh at floor and on sides. The area required by a rabbit depends on the body weight. For one kg weight, 1.8 sq. m area is needed. Angora rabbits cannot be kept at high temperature and should be restricted to hills. Breeding bucks and adult does are housed single. Castrated male can be kept in group. Young rabbits also live in group till the age of 4 months and thereafter they are separated. Rabbit keeping requires calm and quite areas. Sudden noise can cause death of rabbits. Disturbance by dogs, cats and humans should be kept to the minimum.

Feeding: Rabbit is a non-ruminant herbivorous animal having a simple stomach. Like any other animal, rabbit requires protein, carbohydrates, fats, minerals and vitamins in its feed. Rabbits digest the fibre fraction very poorly and a diet having 5-7% crude fibre is adequate. Alfalfa and other forages are well utilized by rabbits. The feed ingredients may constitute maize (20%), alfalfa (25%), wheat bran (40%), groundnut cake (12%), mineral mixture (2%) and salt (1%). The feed mixture should be given twice a day, in the morning and evening. Other grasses and vegetables can be given intermittently in small quantities. Water should always be provided.

Maintenance: Rabbits of 5-6 months age are ready for breeding and the body weight should not be less than 2.0 kg. The female rabbit is taken to the cage of male for mating. At the time of mating, the male produces a particular noise. After that the female rabbit is taken out of the cage of the male. Early morning is the best time for mating. Rabbits mostly breed from March to July.

Gestation period is 28-32 days. The eyes of the young ones (pups) open around two weeks and at 3 weeks, they feed themselves. During this period, the pups should not be often handled. Around four weeks, the young ones are separated from the mother. After two weeks of weaning, the female can be allowed for mating.

In an year, it gives birth five times, each time producing about six numbers. Mortality in the kindlings is the most important component that determines the economics of rabbit rearing. In general, mortality in adult rabbit is very low ranging from 3-5%. However, it ranges 10-15% in kindlings up to the age of 30-42 days. Mating during extreme hot and cold season causes high mortality of kindlings.

Bee keeping

Bee keeping is one of the most important agro-based industries which does not require any raw material from the artisan like other industries. Nectar and pollen from flowers are the raw materials which are available in plenty in nature. Bee keeping can even be started with a single colony.

Species: There are two species, *Apis cerana indica and A. mellifera* are complementary to each other but have different adaptations. *A. cerana* is better acclimatized to higher altitudes of the Himalayan region. *A. mellifera* is more profitable in the plains.

Management: The bee- keeper should be familiar with the source of nectar and pollen within his locality. The most important sources of nectar and pollen are maize, great millet, bulrush, sunflower and palm. The beginner should start with 2 and not more than 5 colonies. A minimum of 2 colonies is recommended because in the event of some mishap, such as the loss of the queen occurring in one, advantage may be taken with the other.

The hive consists of floor- board, brood chamber, super chamber, top cover, inner cover, frames and entrance rod. These parts can easily be separated. The hive may be double walled or single walled. The single walled hive is light and cheap.

The most suitable time for commencing bee keeping in a locality is the arrival of the swarming season. Swarming is a natural tendency of bees to divide their colonies under conditions that are generally favourable for the survival of both parent colony and the swarm. This occurs during the late spring or early summer.

Honey collection: Honey should have good quality to meet the national and international standards. Qualities such as aroma, colour, consistency and floral sources are important. Proper honey straining and processing are needed to improve the quality of the produce. Honey varies in the proportion of its constituents owing to the differences in the nectar produced by different plants. The nectar collected by bees is processed and placed in comb cells for ripening. During the ripening, sucrose is converted into glucose and fructose by an enzyme called invertase which is added to it by the bees. Honey is an excellent energy food with an average of about 3500 calories per kg. It is directly absorbed into the human blood stream, requiring no digestion.

Aquaculture

Ponds serve various useful purposes, *viz.*, domestic requirement of water, supplementary irrigation source to adjoining crop fields and pisciculture. With the traditional management, farmers obtain hardly 300-400 kg of wild and culture fish per ha annually. However, poly-fish culture with the stocking density of 7500 fingerlings and supplementary feeding will boost the total biomass production.

Pond: The depth of the pond should be 1.5-2.0 m. This depth will help for effective photosynthesis and temperature maintenance for the growth of zoo and phytoplanktons. Clay soils have higher water retention capacity and hence are best suited for fish rearing. Pond water should have appropriate proportion of nutrients, phosphate (0.2- 0.4 ppm), nitrate (0.06-0.1 ppm) and dissolved oxygen (5.0-7.0 ppm). Water should be slightly alkaline (pH 7.5-8.5). If the pH is less than 6.5, it can be adjusted with the addition of lime at an interval of 2-3 days. Higher pH (>8.5) can be reduced with the addition of gypsum. Application of fresh dung may also reduce high pH in the water.

Soil of the pond should be tested for N and P content. If the nutrient content is less, nitrogenous fertilizers like ammonium sulphate and urea and phosphatic fertilizers like super phosphate can be added. Organic manures such as FYM and poultry droppings may also be applied to promote the growth of phyto and zooplanktons.

Species of fish:

i) Among the Indian major carps, Catla (*Catla catla*) is the fast growing fish. It consumes a lot of vegetation and decomposing higher plants. It is mainly a surface and column feeder.
ii) Rohu (*Labeo rohita*) is a column feeder and feeds on growing plants, decomposing vegetation, large colonial algae, zooplanktens and detritus to a small extent.
iii) Calbasu (*Labeo calbasu*) is a bottom feeder on detritus. Mrigal (*Cirrhimus mrigale)* is also a bottom feeder, taking detritus to a large content, diatoms, filamentous and other algae and higher plants. Common carp (*Cyprinus carpio*) is a bottom feeder and omnivorous.
iv) Silver carp (*Hypophthalmichlthys molitrix)* is mainly a surface and phytoplankton-feeder and also feeds on microplants.
v) Grass carp (*Cyernus carpia*) is a specialized feeder on aquatic plants, cut-grass and other vegetable matter. It is also a fast growing exotic fish.

Poly fish culture: The phytophagous fish (Catla, Rohu and Mrigal) can be combined with omnivorous (Common Carp), plankton -feed (Silver Carp) and mud-eaters (Mrigal and Calbasu) in a composite fish culture system.

Management: The fish are to be nourished with supplementary feeding with rice bran and oilseed cakes. This will enable faster growth and better yield. Each variety of carps could be stocked to 500 fingerlings with the total of 5000-8000 per ha. This stocking density will enable to get a maximum yield of 2000 to 5000 kg/ha of fish annually.

Sericulture

Sericulture is defined as a practice of combining mulberry cultivation, silk worm rearing and silk reeling. Sericulture is a recognized practice in India. It plays an important role in socio-economic development of rural poor in some areas.

The climatic conditions in India are favourable for luxuriant growth of mulberry and rearing of silkworms throughout the year. The temperature in Karnataka state, major silk producing state in India, ranges from 21.2 to 30 °C. Climatic conditions in Kashmir are favourable to rear silk worm from May to October.

Moriculture: Cultivation of mulberry plants is called as 'moriculture'. There are about 20 species of mulberry, of which four are commonly cultivated. They are *Morus alba, M. indica, M. serrata* and *M. latifolia*. The crop can yield well for 12 years, after which they are pulled out and fresh planting is done. Yield of mulberry leaves is 30-40 t /ha/year.

Silk worm rearing

There are four types of silk worm:

i) Mulberry silk worm - *Bombyx mori*
ii) Eri silk worm - *Philosamia ricini*
iii) Tassar silk worm - *Antheraea mylitta*
iv) Muga silk worm - *Antheraea assami*

Rearing and maintenance: The fertilized moth is covered with an inverted funnel or cellule and eggs are allowed to be laid over a card board. Parasites may be removed by brushing the egg masses with a fine brush. This will also enable to obtain an uniform hatch. In a bamboo tray rice husk is spread. Tender chopped mulberry leaves are added to the tray. The hatched out larvae are transferred to the leaves. It is important to change the leaves every 2-3 hours during the first 2-3 days.

The cacoon is constructed with a single reelable thread of silk. If the moths are allowed to emerge from the cacoons, the silk thread is cut into pieces. Hence, the pupa are killed 2-3 days before the emergence of moth and processed. The cacoons required for further rearing are kept separately and moths are allowed to emerge from them.

A family of three can manage 0.75 ac. without engaging extra labour. Under irrigated condition one hectare of mulberry garden gives employment 13 people throughout the year. It requires 607 mandays and 827 woman days/ha.

Mushroom cultivation

Mushroom is an edible fungi with great diversity in shape, size and colour. Essentially mushroom is a vegetable that is cultivated in protected farms in a highly sanitised atmosphere. Just like other vegetables, mushroom contains 90% moisture with high in quality protein. Mushrooms are fairly good sources of vitamin C and B complex. The protein have 60-70% digestibility and contain all essential amino acids. It is also rich source of minerals like Ca, P, K and Cu. They contain less of fat (0.3%) and CHO and are considered good for diabetic and blood pressure patients. Fibre content in mushrooms is very high which in helps in excretion of waste and prevention of constipation.

Types of mushroom

i) Oyster mushroom - *Pleurotus spp.* (var CO1, APK 1, MDU 1,2, Ooty 1)
ii) Milky mushroom- *Calcybe indica* (APK 2)
iii) Button mushroom - *Agaricus gisporus* (Var. Ooty 1)

Oyster mushroom basically occur on dead woods in nature and resembles the shape of the oyster shell. It can be grown on a wide range of agricultural wastes. It can be grown on a wide range of temperature and with low investment. The production of this mushroom is being done on a small scale in different parts of the country and is most popular one.

Milky mushroom is new of its kind and was introduced for commercial cultivation in the year 1998 from TNAU with the variety, APK 2. The mushrooms are umbrella shaped, robust, attractive and milky white in nature. This variety is tropical in nature and can be grown when button and oyster mushroom cannot be grown due to high temperature.

Button mushroom is particularly suitable for winter season, in northern states. Cultivation of this mushroom requires more investment. This mushroom cannot be cultivated in paddy or wheat straw.

Method of production (Oyster mushroom)

Take fresh paddy straw and cut into small pieces of 3-5 cm length. Soak them in water for 4-6 hours and then boil for half an hour. Drain the water and dry the straw in shade till it is neither too dry or wet. Take polythene bags of 60 x 30 cm size and make two holes of one cm diameter in the centre of the bag such that they face opposite sides. Tie the bottom of the bag with a thread to make a flat bottom. Fill the bag with paddy straw to 10 cm height. Then inoculate with the spawn. Likewise prepare 4-5 layers of straw and spawn alternatively. The last layer ends up in straw of 10 cm height. Keep this in a spawn running room maintained at a temperature of about 20-25 °C and with RH 85-90%. After 15-20 days when the spawn running is completed, cut open the polythene bag and take it to cropping room and allow it to grow for 7 days and harvest the mushroom. Yield: 0.5-1.0 kg/bed.

Biogas plant

Biogas is a clean, unpolluted and cheap source of energy, which can be obtained by a simple mechanism and little investment. The gas is generated from the cow dung during anaerobic decomposition. Biogas generation is a complex biochemical process. The celluloitic material are broken down to methane and carbon-di-oxide by different groups of microorganisms. It can be used for cooking purpose, burning lamps, running pumps, etc.

Types of biogas plant:

i) **Float dome type:** Different models are available in this category, *e.g.*, KVIC vertical and horizontal, Pragati model, Ganesh model.

ii) **Fixed dome type:** The gas plant is dome shaped under-ground construction. The masonry gas holder is an integral part of the digester called dome. The gas produced in the digester is collected in dome at vertical pressure by displacement of slurry in inlet and outlet. The entire construction is made of bricks and cement. The models available in this category are Janata and Deen-Bandhu.

The selection of a particular type depends on technical, climatological, geographical and economic factors.

Size: The size of the bio-gas plant is decided by the number of family members and the availability of cattle. One cubic metre capacity plant will need two to three animals and 25 kg of dung. The gas produced will meet the requirement of a family of 4-6 members. It would suffice to have a 2 cubic metre plant to cater to the needs of a family of 6-10 members.

Site selection and management: The site should be close to the kitchen or the place of use. It will reduce the cost of gas distribution system. It should also be nearer to the cattle shed to reduce the cost of transportation of cattle dung. Land should be leveled and slightly above the ground level to avoid inflow or run-off of water. Plant should get clear sunshine during most part of the day.

Generation of dung has a direct bearing on the quantity of gas generated. The amount of gas production is considerably higher in summer followed by rainy and winter seasons. Gas production would be maximum at a temperature between 30 to 35 °C. If the ambient temperature falls below 10 °C, gas production is reduced drastically.

Bio-gas slurry: Slurry is obtained after the production of bio-gas. It is an enriched manure. Another positive aspect of this manure is that even after weeks of exposure to the atmosphere, the slurry does not attract fleas and worms.

INTEGRATION OF ENTERPRISES

In agriculture, crop husbandry is the main activity. The income obtained from cropping is hardly sufficient to sustain the farm family throughout the year. Assured regular cash flow is possible when cropping is combined with other enterprises. Judicious combination of enterprises, keeping in view of the environmental conditions of a locality will pay greater dividends. At the same time, it will also promote effective recycling of residues/wastes.

Choice of enterprise: The basic points that are to be considered while choosing appropriate enterprise in Integrated farming system (IFS) are:

1. Soil and climatic features of an area/locality
2. Resource availability with the farmer
3. Present level of utilization of resources
4. Return/income from the existing farming system
5. Economics of proposed integrated farming system
6. Farmer's managerial skill
7. Social customs prevailing in the locality

Enterprise integration

Livestock is the best complementary enterprise with cropping, especially during the adverse years. Installation of a biogas plant in crop-livestock system will make use of the wastes, at the same time provides valuable manure and gas for cooking and lighting. In a wetland farm, there are greater avenues for fishery, duck farming and buffalo rearing. Utilizing the rice straw, mushroom production can be started. Under irrigated conditions (gardenlands), inclusion of sericulture, poultry and piggery along with arable crop production is an accepted practice. The poultry component in this system can make use of the grains produced in the farm as feed. Pigs are the unique components that can be reared with the wastes which are unfit for human consumption. In rainfed farming, sheep and goat rearing form an integral part of the landscape. Sericulture can be introduced in rainfed farming, provided the climatic conditions permit it. Agro- forestry (silviculture and silvi-horticulture) are the other activities which can be included under dryland conditions. In the integrated system, selection of enterprise should be on the cardinal principle that there should be minimal competition and maximum complementary effect among the enterprises.

Integrated farming system - case studies

Wetland system

Integrated farming system components have been tested in Tamil Nadu for wet land condition at Coimbatore (Rangasamy *et al.* 1996) and at Cauvery Delta zone, Aduthurai (Govindan *et al.* 1990). Details of various components are given below:

Integrated farming system - Coimbatore

Components of integrated farming for wetland (Coimbatore) are as follows:

1. Cropping
2. Fish culture
3. Poultry
4. Mushroom production
   Allocation of area (Total 0.4 ha):
   - Cropping: 0.36 ha
   - Fish pond: 0.04 ha.

Cropping	**Area (ha)**
Rice -Rice -Maize	0.16
Rice - Rice - Groundnut	0.10
Maize- Rice- Sesame	0.10
Total	**0.36**

This farming system was compared with the conventional cropping normally followed in the region: rice-rice-greengram (0.20 ha) and rice-rice-green manure (0.20 ha).

Components description

Fish pond in an area of 0.04 ha was excavated to a depth of 1.5 m. Fifteen days old fingerlings of different fish species were stocked in varied proportions (silver carp /rohu/mrigal/grass carp at 4: 2: 3: 1 ratio with a total of 7500 fingerlings/ha). No artificial feeding was done. Harvest of fish commenced from tenth month. A poultry shed with a plinth area of 2.2 m^2 was erected at one corner of the fish pond. Bottom of the poultry shed was provided with wire mesh (3x3 m) to facilitate free fall of poultry droppings into the fish pond. Twenty Bapcock chicks (18 weeks old) were reared in the shed. The feed components were purchased in the first year of cropping. Second year onwards, poultry feed was managed with recycling of farm wastes and the produce obtained from the crop components. Alfalfa cultivated around the fish pond was also used as feed for poultry. The birds started laying eggs around 22nd week up to 72nd week, when they were culled out.

A mushroom shed with a dimension of 5x3 m was constructed with locally available materials. Oyster mushroom (*Pleurotus sp.*) was produced utilizing rice straw as the base material.

Economic returns from the system

On an average, a net profit of Rs. 11,755 was obtained in rice-poultry-mushroom system as compared to Rs. 6335 only from conventional system of cropping alone. An additional employment of 174 man days was generated due to the adoption of IFS.

Integrated farming system-Cauvery Delta zone, Aduthurai, Tamil Nadu

Farmers of this zone are practicing monocorpping of rice for two seasons (June-October and October-January) followed by a rice fallow pulse (January-March). Among the different allied activities, pisciculture plays an important role in this zone since water is available in the canal for about 7-8 months. Poultry farming is another feasible enterprise. By combing the enterprises of poultry-cum-fish culture with rice cropping system, the economic status of the small and marginal farmers could be improved.

Components description

An area of one hectare has been selected for the study. About 0.04 ha was allotted for fish pond. The improved cropping system of rice- rice -cotton (0.76 ha) and rice-rice- maize (0.20 ha) was adopted. Maize, being a major constituent of poultry feed, was included in the system. This integrated system was compared with the existing practice of rice-rice- blackgram.

Poultry component

A poultry shed measuring 4.6 x 2.4 m was constructed over the fish pond in one corner with locally available materials. The bottom of the shed was provided with weld mesh to enable the droppings to fall directly into the fish pond. The shed was covered on all four sides with chicken mesh, over which gunny bags were enclosed to prevent entry of rain water and protect the birds from excess chill during winter. Fifty Bapcock Bu 300 hybrid layer birds of 21 weeks age were maintained till 43 weeks. Each bird was fed with feed of 100-200 g/day. The feed ingredients were maize, rice bran, groundnut cake, fish meal, shell grit, dicalcium phosphate and vitamins.

Fish culture

Two fish ponds, each 400 $m^{2,}$ were excavated. The depth of the pond was 1.0 m. One pond was maintained as control without fish feed to compare the effect of poultry dropping on fish growth. Water was maintained in the fish pond at 1 m depth throughout the culture period. The ponds were fertilized with 63 kg cowdung, 1.2 kg urea, 1.6 kg super phosphate and 0.26 kg potash, two weeks before stocking of fingerlings. Poultry dropping at 2 kg/day was applied initially for 45 days and thereafter, fresh droppings were allowed to directly fall into the fish pond from the poultry shed in the treatment pond. Fingerlings belonging to the silver carp, catla, rohu, mrigal, common carp and grass carp were stocked at 1, 25, 20, 25 27 and 2 % of the total stock, respectively. The density of population maintained was 10,000 fingerlings/ha. The fish were harvested after 6 1/2 months.

Economic returns from the system

A total of 4670 eggs was obtained in 22 weeks from 50 birds. In addition, one bird on an average voided about 110 g of droppings per day (wet drops). About 794 kg of fresh droppings (260 kg dry) were recycled in the fish pond during the period of 22 weeks. The growth rate of fish was linear for each month of sampling. During the harvest at the end of 6 1/2 months, the total fish weight was 450 kg/ha in the treatment pond and 240 kg/ha in the control pond. The increased fish production in the treatment pond was due to recycling of 350 kg poultry droppings as feed.

A net return of Rs. 17,200 was obtained by integrating different enterprises. By introducing poultry-cum-fish culture with cropping, a total employment of 385 man-days was generated.

Integration of Duck+ Fish Farming

The droppings of duck are rich in non-protein nitrogenous substances (urea) which serve as readymade feed for fishes thus minimize the expenditure of artificial feeding which is about 70% of the total input. Ducks consumes weeds, grass and green algae. Ducks consume the grasshopper, beetles and snails in and the ponds as protein rich natural feed source.

Total number of ducks may vary 300-1000/ha of water area. This is best suited for Indian conditions. The dropping of ducks serves in fertilizing the pond water for more vegetation. This vegetation serve as natural food for the fish.

System for irrigated situations (Gardenlands)

A model integrated farming system to suit the small and marginal farmers of gardenland condition was studied at TNAU, Coimbatore, during 1988-1993 (Rangaswamy *et al.* 1995). An area of one ha was selected for IFS and compared with conventional cropping system (CCS).

Components of IFS:

	Cropping	Area (ha)
(i)	Cotton + greengram-maize + fodder cowpea- bellary onion	0.56
(ii)	Wheat + sunflower – maize + fodder cowpea - summer cotton + green gram	0.19
(iii)	Grass Bajra Napier (CO. I)	0.15
(iv)	Lucerne	0.05
(v)	150 trees of Leuceana (planted in the bunds)	0.05
	Total	**1.00**

Farm stead

Dairy unit	3 Jersey cows + 2 calves
Biogas unit	2 m^3 capacity
Mushroom production	1.5 -2.0 kg/day

The above integrated system was compared with the conventional cropping system of cotton - sorghum - finger millet in 0.20 ha area.

Economic returns from the system

Maize flour, cotton seed and wheat bran obtained from the crop components were recycled for preparing dairy feed from the second year. About 45.5 t of grass fodder, 2.5 t of legume fodder and 1.0 t of dry fodder were obtained from the system and fed to the animals. Dung was recycled for the biogas plant. Mean revenue of Rs 34,600/ha was realized in IFS as compared to Rs 13,950 obtained in CCS. Employment opportunity was also enhanced to the tune of 770 man days per year under IFS as against conventional cropping.

Dryland based system

Integrated farming system for drylands suggested for Coimbatore and Aruppukottai, Tamil Nadu, are described below:

Model for Coimbatore, Tamil Nadu

(Mean annual rainfall: 640 mm) Crop components for one hectare:

	Cropping	Area (ha)
(i)	Sorghum + cowpea both grain purpose	0.20
(ii)	Sorghum + cowpea both fodder purpose	0.20

	Cropping	Area (ha)
(iii)	Leucaena (tree fodder) + Cenchrus (grass fodder)	0.20
(iv)	*Acacia senegal* (tree fodder) + grass	0.20
(v)	*Prosonic cineraris* (tree fodder) + grass	0.20

Animal components: Tellicherry goat: 6 (5 female + 1 male-stall fed).

Conventional cropping system = 0.20 ha (Sorghum + cowpea-grain purpose).

The animal component, Tellicherry goat, numbering 6 (5 female + 1 male) were kept in a shed (6 x 4 m). The goats were stall fed from the cropping components. Two kg each of green and dry fodder and 100 g of concentrate were given to each animal. At the end of second year, all the male goats were disposed retaining one number. From the end of third year onwards, 20 female and one male were retained and remaining disposed. The litter from the goat shed was used for composting and recycled as manure. A farm pond was dug in an area of 300 m^2 and the rain water harvested was utilized for pot watering the tree saplings.

Economic returns from the system: Mean additional revenue of Rs 3750/ha/ year was obtained from IFS over CCS. The employment generation under IFS was 153 man days/ha/year whereas it was only 40 man days/ha/year in the CCS (Sivasankaram *et al.* 1995).

Model for Arupukottai, Tamil Nadu

Integrated farming system study for drylands was conducted (Senthivel, *et al.* 1998) from 1989-90 to 1994-95 at Regional Research Station, Arupukottai, Tamil Nadu. The soil type of the experimental site was black cotton soil (vertisol) and the annual rainfall of the region is 830 mm received in 47 rainy days. The rainfall pattern is "unimodel" with its peak during the months of October and November. The following is the integrated farming system model that has been studied (cropping - 1.6 ha, fruit trees- 0.4 ha).

Cropping	Area (ha)
Cotton + blackgram	0.5
Sorghum + cowpea	0.5
Fodder crops (*Cenchrus ciliaris*)	0.2
Fodder trees	0.4
Fruit trees	
Ber	0.2
Custard apple	0.1
Amla	0.1

This was compared with conventional system of sorghum alone.

Components description

Rainfed fruit tress viz., ber, custard apple and amla were planted and recommended package of practices were adopted for better maintenance.

The orchard areas were divided into compartments by providing field bunds and along the field bunds, vetiver slips were planted in order to conserve rain water and prevent run off and soil erosion during rainy periods. The interspace between fruit trees were sown with pulses and vegetable, cluster bean, which had, in turn, provided income as well as maintained the soil health. The fruit trees, ber and custard apple, started yielding from third year onwards. Ber yield ranged from 20-25 kg per tree during normal rainfall years and 10-12 kg per tree in the years of deficit rainfall. Custard apple yielded 10 and 5 kg of fruits per tree during normal and deficit rainfall years respectively.

One unit of the Tellicherry goats (5+1) was maintained by stall feeding in the shed (6 mx4 m). The goats were fed from the fodder crops and tree loppings planted along the border. Two kg of dry fodder, 2 kg of green fodder and 100 g of concentrate were given to each goat. The herd size of Tellicherry goats increased from 6 to 84 at the end of sixth year. At the end of second year all the male goats except one were disposed. From the end of third year onwards, 20 female + one male were retained in this system. About 10 tonnes of goat litter per year was obtained and recycled after proper decomposing in the IFS cropping area.

The fodder grass, *Cenchrus glaucus* and fodder legume, *Desmanthus* were maintained in 3:1 ratio. The fodder tree loppings of sesbania, subabul and neem were also fed to the goat and the remaining part of the feed was composted and applied to crop field.

Economics of the system

The additional net income obtained from IFS over CCS varied from Rs. 2,160 to 15,460 in different years. An increase of additional net income was noticed during each year and it was higher during the sixth year. A mean additional net income of Rs. 7100 per year was obtained in IFS over the CCS. The additional net income per day in IFS over CCS was Rs. 21. Employment generation under IFS was 131 man days per ha per year, whereas it was only 35 man days per ha per year under CCS, thus generating an additional employment of 78 man days/ha/year under IFS.

Integrated Aquaculture - Agriculture systems

Small ponds on a mixed enterprise can improve the whole farm productivity and profitability as well as produce fish. Farm ponds could at best best be an alternative to the large scale, intensive, specialized fish farms. The scientists at the International Center for Living Aquatic Resources Management (ICLARM) in the Philippines conducted a series of experiments in farmer's holdings in Africa. They have found that wide adoption of small ponds could result in sizable increase in farm fish production in Africa, in addition to facilitating increases in other produces such as vegetables, fruits and condiments from pond dikes and margins and adjacent garden and from pond bed itself in dry periods. This type of integrated farming system practices are spread to a number of other Asian countries. *e.g.*, the Mayan Chinampa system of water channels and raised beds for plants. The small farm ponds act as bio-digesters of waste, providers of fertile soil and water and help in site improvement that permit new operations for rotating and linking enterprises for risk management.

A set of six 'traditional' ponds were integrated with vegetable plots, maize gardens, banana groves, leucaena species, hedge rows and rice fields. The small ponds (50 sq.m) were undrainable and filled with runoff and underground infiltration. Waste materials from the other enterprises were used as pond inputs. Fish were periodically harvested and no special efforts made to control predation from birds and others. Pond muds and water were used to fertilize the vegetable plots. In studies using these traditional ponds, sizable yields of mustard, cabbage, hybrid maize and fish were obtained.

The total productive area of 639 sq. m (250 sq. m of ponds and 139 sq. m of vegetables and maize) yielded an equivalent of 43 tonnes of mustard-cabbage, 42,000 cobs and 454 kg fish/ha. Various combinations of farming enterprises with aquaculture have proved to be rewarding. (Fig. 11.2.)

Integrated farming system for hill regions

The North Eastern Hill Regions of India are unique in their physiographic characteristics of land, varied agroclimatic conditions, land tenure system and cultivation practices from the rest of the country. The region falls under high rainfall zone and is characterized by hilly terrain with wide variation in elevation from 100 m to 5,500 m. Majority of the farmers in the region are maintaining dairy cattle and the major source of green fodder comes from lopping of the fodder trees and locally available grasses. Crops and cropping patterns of such land uses will differ depending on the type of enterprise such as milk, beef, mutton, wool, pork and poultry production. Combination of cultivated varieties of perennial legumes, grasses, shrubs and trees can extend availability of green fodder upto February at low altitude, thereby shortening the requirement of conserved fodder for lean season feeding.

Land up to 100% slope having soil depth greater than 1 m can be used for agri-horti-silvipastoral system. This system has the potentiality of maintaining 1.18 livestock unit/ha of land use.

Integrated farming system for island ecosystems

Integrated farming system models have been developed for the Andaman and Nicobar Islands. Major part of Andaman and Nicobar Islands comes under medium slope category. The topography is mainly characterized by undulating slopy lands. Present cropping system in this region is raising of fruits trees such as banana, papaya, mango, guava, pineapple, sapota, pomegranate, lemon, lime, sweet orange, mandarin, jack fruit, custard apple etc.

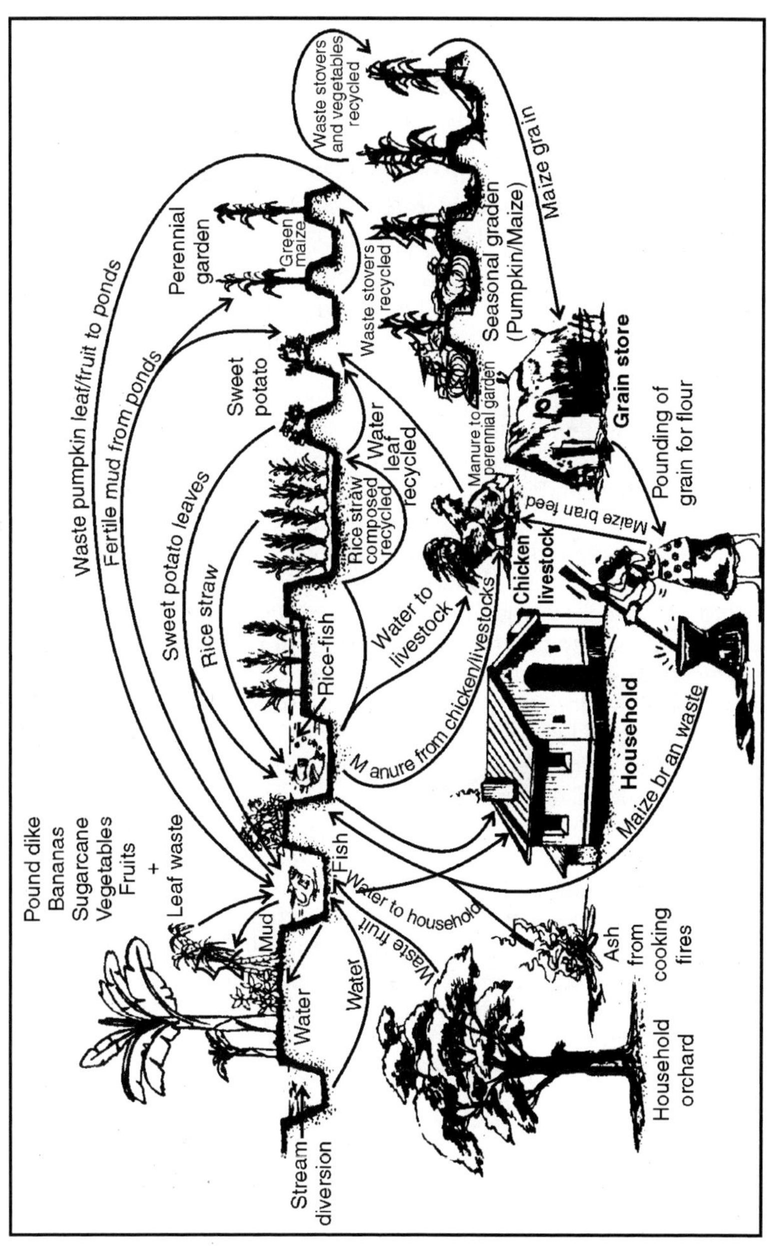

FIG. 11.2: Integrated farming system for Sub-Saharan region, Africa

Among the plantation and spice crops, coconut, arecanut, cashewnut, black pepper, nutmeg and clove are mainly grown. Rice is predominantly cultivated during the rainy season (May to December) and field crops such as greengram, blackgram, cowpea, sesame, groundnut, vegetables, etc. are grown in the dry season on a very limited scale in rice fallows. Animal husbandry is in its infant stage. Fishery resources are very rich but remain unexploited.

Some of the possible integrated farming systems (Shyam Singh and Gangwar, 1989) considered to be useful for the socio-agroclimatic conditions of Andaman and Nicobar Islands are discussed below:

1. **Coconut-cum-fodder-cum-milch cattle:** Mixed farming by raising fodder grass in coconut has been found profitable. Raising grasses such as hybrid Napier alone or with leguminous fodder crops like Stylosanthes in the coconut garden can support 4-5 dairy animals. The animals supply large quantity of cattle manure which, when applied to coconut garden, improves the soil fertility considerably.
2. **Coconut-cum-fodder-cum-fish or prawn culture:** This system is suitable for tidal marshy area. The coconut palms are grown on platforms raised upto the highest tidal level and fish and prawn in channels between the coconut plantations. On platform with coconut trees, fodder crops like Guatemala grass, thin Napier and guinea grass could be raised successfully with an average forage yield of 290, 190 and 184 q/ha respectively under high salinity conditions.
3. **Coconut-cum-fish culture in salt affected lands:** Coconut grows successfully even in salt- affected paddy fields if the fields are within the approach of brackish water. The bunds of fields at water entrance gate should be raised to maintain the required level of water. Field bunds should also be raised as per requirement. In high tides, water will be exchanged and thus fish raising can be taken up together with coconut in dry period. In rainy season, salinity-tolerant rice varieties could be cultivated in the same field with coconut and fish culture.
4. **Fruits-cum-fodder-cum-milch cattle:** The space available between the fruit trees can be utilized for growing fodder crops such as cowpea, rice bean, greengram and blackgram. The fodder could be used for feeding the cattle and cattle manure could be applied to the fruit trees and fodder crops.

CHAPTER 12

Field Experimental Techniques

Agronomy experiments are mainly field oriented. Choice of appropriate design and conduct of the experiments in a proper manner may help to get valid information. Field selection and layout of the experiments also play a vital role. It is always necessary to collect data on ancillary characteristics so as to have better interpretation of the results. Use of appropriate software package makes the job of the scientists/field workers to analyze the data scientifically and interpret the results.

Terms and definitions

1. **Population:** The entire bulk of the observational material from which samples are drawn is referred to as 'population'. It is also known as 'aggregate' or totality of all units. *e.g.*, number of plants in a unit area.
2. **Sample:** A relatively small portion of the population is called a sample. It should be a fairly true representation of the entire bulk or population. A sample must be selected in such a way that each individual in the population has an equal chance and independent opportunity of being included in the sample. The method of selecting a sample from its population is called "sampling". There are two types of sampling: (i) probability sampling (simple random sampling) and (ii) non- probability sampling (purposive sampling). Normally sampling is done randomly and is known as "random sampling". Sometimes special selection of sampling is done. For example, samples are drawn at regular intervals of 5,10,15 or 20th plant or at every 5,10,15 and 20th meter spacing.
3. **Variable:** Any character, quantitative or qualitative, which changes from observation to observation is called a 'variable'. Qualitative variable is referred as 'attributes'. The variable may be continuous or discrete. Plant height is an example of continuous variable because it takes fractional measurement on a continuous scale. The discrete variable is separated and disjoined, varying in whole numbers. It takes only the finite number of values. *e.g.*, number of bolls/cotton plant.
4. **Frequency:** The number of observations that fall within a particular class interval is called as its frequency. The manner in which the

frequencies are distributed over the different classes is called the 'frequency distribution' of the character under study. 'Frequency distribution' is nothing but the quantitative classification of the given unorganized data. In a frequency distribution, the minimum and maximum number of classes will be 5 and 12 respectively.

5. **Measure of central tendency:** For a given bulk of unorganized data, there is a tendency of values to cluster around the central value of the given data. This behaviour of the data is known as 'central tendency'. These central values are called 'averages'.
   Characteristics of good measure of central tendency are:
   a) It should be easy to calculate.
   b) It should be easy to understand.
   c) It should be based on all observations.
   d) It should not be affected by sampling fluctuations.
   e) It should be suitable for further algebric treatments.
   To measure the central values, different methods are adopted: They are mean, median and mode.
6. **Arithmetic mean or mean:** The most common measure of central tendency is the mean or the arithmetic average. It is obtained by summing the values of individuals in the data and dividing by the number of individuals in the data.

$$\mu = \frac{\sum x}{N}$$

μ = the mean,
Σx = summation of the individuals,
N = number of observations in the population.

7. **Median:** It is also called as positional average. Median is the value which is located in the middle of a series when observations are arranged in the order of magnitude. It divides the data into two halves having 50% of data below the median and the remaining 50% above the median.
   a) For raw and discrete data,

$$\text{Median} = \text{The size of } \left(\frac{N+1}{2}\right)^{th} \text{ item}$$

   Where N is the number of observations
   b) For the continuous data,

$$\text{Median} = L + \left(\frac{N/2 - CF}{F}\right) \times i$$

L = lower limit of median class
N = number of observations
CF = cumulative frequency of pre- median

class

F = frequency of median class

i = width of the median class

8. **Mode:** Mode is the value of the variate which occurs most frequently in a distribution. It is also defined as the value which has the highest frequency in a given distribution. It is not affected by the extreme values of the given distribution.
   In a distribution, if there is only one mode, it is called as unimodel distribution. If two modes exist, it is known as bimodel distribution.
   Calculation of mode for the continuous series:

$$M_0 = L + \frac{\Delta_1}{\Delta_1 + \Delta_2} \times i$$

L = lower limit of model class

Δ_1 = difference between the frequency of the model class and the pre model class

Δ_2 = difference between the frequency of the model class and the post model class

i = width of the model class

9. **Measures of dispersion:** To understand the complete picture / behaviour of the given data, the variability of the given data is to be studied in addition to the study of the measure of central tendency. There are two types of measure of dispersion: (i) absolute measure of dispersion and (ii) relative measure of dispersion.
   If the measure of dispersion is expressed by the same unit of the given data, it is called absolute measure of dispersion, *e.g.*, range, mean deviation, standard deviation etc.
   If the measure of dispersion is expressed as the ratio of an absolute measure of dispersion to an average, it is known as 'relative measure of dispersion', *e.g.*, co-efficient of variation. It is a unit free measurement.
10. **Range:** The simplest measure of dispersion is the range. It is the difference between the largest and smallest of observations in a group of observations.
11. **Mean Deviation:** The mean of the deviations of individual values from the average is known as mean deviation. The average may be either mean or median. Usually the mean is used to find out the mean deviation.
12. **Standard deviation (SD) (σ):** It is a measure of the variation between individuals in a given population and is an estimation of the dispersion of variables around the mean. It is the square root of the arithmetic average of the squares of the individual variations from the mean. It

is also called as root mean square value (RMS).

$$\sigma = \sqrt{\frac{\sum d^2}{N}}$$

σ = standard deviation
D = deviation of observation from the arithmetic mean $(x - \bar{x})$
N = number of observations

When the sample is small,

$$S = \sqrt{\frac{\sum d^2}{(n-1)}}$$

Where (n-1) is the degrees of freedom.

13. **Co-efficient of variation (C.V.):** It is the ratio of the standard deviation to the mean. It gives a measure of variation which is independent on the unit of measurement. C.V. is useful for comparison between different populations with different units. It is a percentage measure.

$$\text{C.V.} = \frac{\sigma}{\mu} \times 100$$

σ = standard deviation
μ = Mean

To test the consistency or reliability of the yield data, the range of C.V. should be 5 to 15%.

14. **Variance:** It is the square of the standard deviation.
15. **Correlation:** In an experiment, if the changes of one variable affect the changes of the other variable, then the variables are said to be correlated. *e.g.*, yield and tiller number, length of panicles and grains / panicles, etc. If the measurements of the variables are in the same direction, then the variables are said to be directly correlated or positively correlated, *e.g.*, test grain weight and grain size, leaf area and leaf size. If the movements of variables are in opposite direction, then the variables are said to be negatively correlated, *e.g.*, yield and pest incidence, germination percentage and ageing of seeds. To know the direction of movement of the variables, scattered diagram method is used.

When only two variables are involved, the correlation is termed as 'simple correlation'. If more than two variables are involved, the correlation is known as 'multiple correlation'.

To measure the degree of relationship between the correlated variables, x and y the following formula is used:

$$r = \frac{\sum xy}{\sqrt{\sum x^2 \times \sum y^2}}$$

Where, $x = (x - \bar{x}), y = (y - \bar{y})$

'r' is called as the correlation co-efficient. If the value of 'r' is positive, then the correlation is said to be a positive and r =0, then the variables are independent. If – ve, it is called as negative correlation. The correlation co-efficient always lies between -1 and +1 (*i.e.*, $-1 \leq r \leq +1$), called range of correlation co-efficient.

16. **Regression:** Regression is a simpler and more useful approach to the study of simultaneous variation of two (or more) characters. In a field experimentation, we may examine the relationship between levels of nitrogen and crop yield. The levels of N may be fixed arbitrarily and may not have any distribution. Under such condition, the method of regression is more appropriate than correlation. Of the two variables, one is known as independent variable, denoted by X. The other variable is called dependent variable, denoted by Y. The underlying relation between y and x in a bivariate population can be expressed as a function. Such functional relationship between two variables is termed as regression.

    The equation is in the following form for a straight line graphs.

    $$Yp = \alpha + \beta x$$

    Where, α and β denote the population constants and Yp, the hypothetical population mean corresponding to any x.

    The regression represented by a straight line is named a 'linear regression'. The regression line can be written as,

    $$Y = a + bx$$

    Where, Y is the value one would expect to obtain corresponding to any given value of x on the basis of the observed linear relationship, between the variables.

17. **Test of significance:** With the help of statistical measures such as mean, standard deviation, standard error, standard error of difference, it is possible to conclude whether the particular sample is representative of the population or not. It is also possible to test the difference between the sample means. While testing the difference between two sample means, we may commit any one of the two mistakes:

    a) we may conclude the difference of the mean is due to chance when it is real, or
    b) we may conclude the difference of mean is real when it is a chance

variation. Testing the difference between two means is due to chance or real is called 'test of significance' or 'testing hypothesis'.

Steps involved in testing hypothesis:

i) Null hypothesis (Ho)
ii) Alternate hypothesis (H_1)
iii) Level of significance (5% or 1%)
iv) Test statistic
v) Interpretation/conclusion

18. **Standard error (SE):** It is the measure of variability of sample mean from the population mean.

$$SE = \frac{\sigma}{\sqrt{n}}$$

Where, σ is the standard deviation and n is the sample size.
Standard error of difference SE (d): This gives the magnitude of difference between two sample means.

$$SE(d) = \sqrt{2} \times SE$$

19. **Critical difference (CD):** For dealing with significance of small samples, statisticians have constructed a table of probability integral of a quantity which is called t-statistic. It is the difference between the means of two variates under comparison measured on a scale the unit of which is the standard error of the differences. The 't' table gives for degrees of freedom upto 30 and infinity. If that probability is low, that is, if P is less than 0.01 (100 to 1 chance), or 0.05 (20 to 1 chance), it is concluded that the observed difference, d, is statistically significant. It is customary to regard the probability level of 0.05 as of sufficient value for statistical accuracy in agricultural experiments.
The critical value obtained from the table multiplied by the standard error of the difference between the means is called "critical difference". When the difference between any two means exceeds the critical differences, we may say that the sample with a higher mean is superior to the other, or in other words, the observed difference is significant.
20. **Analysis of variance:** In the statistical analysis of data of a biological experiment, the analysis of variance procedure and consequently the appropriate 'F' test of significance are often used to determine significance of treatment differences. These procedures are based on four assumptions that one must consider before doing statistical analysis and consequent statistical inferences are considered valid.

Basic assumptions:

21. The treatment effects due to environmental must be additive.
    a) The experimental errors must all be independent.
    b) The experimental errors should be normally distributed.

c) The experimental errors should be homogenous.
The degree to which the assumptions are met apparently determines the validity of inference drawn from the analysis of variance.

22. **Analysis of co-variance:** The analysis of co-variance is an indirect method of error control and is used to reduce the experimental error. For the use of co-variance analysis, it is important to take measurement on covariates or covariables (concomitant variables) which are related to the variable of primary interest. For example, in the varietal yield trial, number of plants per plot are taken as co-variates. If the number of plants in each and every plot is not uniform, it is more logical to correct the yield on the basis of the relation between the yield and plant number. This systematic procedure for adjustment of the data with respect to co-variable is known as "analysis of co-variance".

Experimental Designs

An experiment is designed based on the objectives, availability of experimental material and cost of the experiment. It is important to design the experiment carefully to test the hypothesis with acceptable degree of precision. The choice of treatments, method of assigning treatments to experimental units and arrangement of experimental units in various patterns to suit the requirement of a particular problem are combinedly known as the design of experiment. In an agricultural field experimentation, it is normally aimed to assess the performance of varieties of a crop, effect of manures, irrigation methods, new herbicides, etc. All these objects of comparison are known as treatments. The basic objects on which the experiment is done are known as experimental units. *e.g.*, a plot of land, a plant, an insect, etc.

Basic principles of design of experiments

It is important in any design of experiment to reduce the experimental error in order to increase the precision of the experiment. The means of reducing experimental error in any experimental design are (i) replication, (ii) randomization and (iii) local control of error. They are called basic principles of design of experiment.

Replication

The repetition of the treatments under investigation is known as replication. Replication is important in estimating the experimental error, increasing the precision of treatment means and in enhancing the sensitivity of the test of significance by decreasing standard error. There should be minimum error degrees of freedom of 12 to detect the given difference at the 5 % level of significance. Accordingly number of replications is to be decided. For example, to test 5 treatments, there should be 4 replications so as to achieve minimum error degrees of freedom of 12 [(5-1) (4-1)].

Randomization

It refers to the method of giving equal chance to all individual treatments to show their performance. Randomization of treatments is done by using random numbers. Randomization will help to give real comparison between the treatments by arranging them in a systematic manner. Randomization avoids personal bias in the allotment of treatments. In short, randomization helps to make an unbiased estimate (validity) of a treatment mean or experimental error.

Local control of error

It is a non-statistical device used to make the field into a homogenous one. Local control of error is necessary to have soil analysis, uniformity trial, soil profile study, formation of blocks to provide adequate number of replications and for allotting the treatments within a block by randomization so as to avoid personal bias. It also helps to reduce the experimental error without interfering the statistical requirement of randomness. Lower experimental error may help to detect the smaller real differences between the treatments to be significant.

Designs of Experiments

Completely Randomized Block Deign (CRD)

Completely randomized block design is the basic single factor design of experiment. When the experimental unit is more or less homogeneous, CRD is a suitable one. It is more applicable to laboratory or pot culture experiments where the homogeneity of the experimental unit is assured. The experimental material is equal to number of treatments and replications. The treatments are allotted to the experimental unit (plots) completely at random.

Merits and demerits

It is a flexible design with no restriction on the number of replications and treatments. Statistical analysis is simple even if the number of replications and treatments vary. If some of the observations of the treatments are missing still the analysis of variance can be carried out by using CRD with unequal replications.

The CRD is rarely used in the field experiments where there is generally a large variation among the experimental plots. If the number of treatments and replications are increased, the experimental error will be increased which reduces the accuracy of results.

Lay out in CRD

In a CRD, if there are' t' treatments, (T_1, T_2....T_t), each replicating 'r' times; there will be r x t number of plots (n). Hence, entire field is to be divided into 'n' number of plots. If there are 5 treatments with 5 replications, there will be totally 25 plots. The field is divided into 25 plots and numbered serially starting from one end and proceeding in a serpentine manner, as given below:

1	2	3	4	5
10	9	8	7	6
11	12	13	14	15
20	19	18	17	16
21	22	23	24	25

We have to draw 25 three-digit random numbers from the random number table. These numbers are then assigned ranks from the lowest to the highest. The first 5 ranks go to treatment T_1 and similarly by subsequent ranks are allotted to other treatments (Table 12.1).

TABLE 12.1: The random numbers, their ranks, and allotment of treatments.

Random number	Rank	Treatment to be allotted
642	16	T_1
790	22	
435	11	
218	3	
263	5	
296	6	T_2
835	23	
058	1	
452	12	
757	21	
149	2	T_3
639	15	
648	17	
573	13	
879	25	
676	18	T_4
235	4	
749	20	
364	8	
406	10	
355	7	T_5
392	9	
627	14	
709	19	
876	24	

T_1 is allotted to the plots 3, 5, 11, 16 and 22. T_2 is allotted to the plots

1, 6, 12, 21 and 23. Similarly other treatments (T_3, T_4, T_5) are allotted to the experimental unit (plots) completely at random (Fig. 12.1).

1 T_2	2 T_3	3 T_1	4 T_4	5 T_1
10 T_4	9 T_5	8 T_4	7 T_5	6 T_2
11 T_1	12 T_2	13 T_3	14 T_5	15 T_3
20 T_4	19 T_5	18 T_4	17 T_3	16 T_1
21 T_2	22 T_1	23 T_2	24 T_5	25 T_3

FIG. 12.1: Layout plan for CRD

Analysis of variance

In CRD, total variation can be split into treatment variation and experimental error variation. The ANOVA model for CRD is:

$$Y_{ij} = \mu + t_i + e_{ij}$$

Y_{ij} = yield of ith treatment in jth replication

μ = over all mean

t_i = treatment variation

e_{ij} = experimental error variation

The analysis of variance table for 't' number of treatments and 'n' number of plots is given in Table 12.2.

TABLE 12.2: Analysis of variance in CRD

Source of variation	Degrees of freedom	Sum of squares	Mean square	F_c
Treatment	(t-1)	TrSS	TrMS	TrMS / EMS
Error	r (t-1)	ESS	EMS	
Total	**(n-1)**	**Total SS**		

CD is computed as:

$$CD = t.\,SE(d)$$

$$SE(d) = \sqrt{\frac{2EMS}{r}} \quad \text{(for equal replication)}$$

$$SE(d) = \sqrt{EMS + \frac{1}{r_i} + \frac{1}{r_j}} \quad \text{(for unequal replication)}$$

Bar chart can be drawn arranging the treatment mean values in ascending or descending order and results interpreted.

Randomized Block Design (RBD)

The general assumption in an experimental field is that the fertility variation runs from one direction to another. The direction of fertility variation is called 'Fertility Gradient'. When the fertility gradient runs in one direction, the field is made to homogenous by forming blocks perpendicular to fertility gradient (Fig. 12.2). Thus, the fertility status in one block will be more or less same from one end to the another of a particular block.

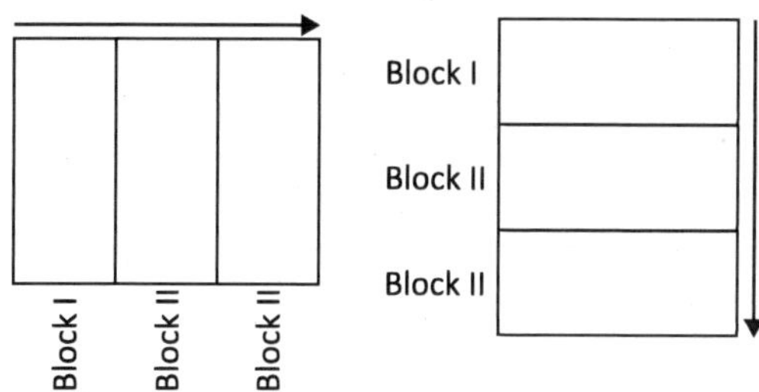

FIG. 12.2: Blocking the field

In RBD, the experimental area is divided into blocks of equal area. Each block is further divided into number of plots equal to the number of treatments, which are distributed at random, each treatment occurring only once in each block. The nature of RBD provides equal replications for all the treatments. The individual blocks can be distributed parallel to each other across the field. Each block is a replication and the total number of replications will be equal to the number of blocks.

By doing blocking, the plots (experimental units) are made homogenous. Since the treatments are allotted at random, randomization is followed. Soil variation between the different blocks could be distinguished since the total yield of any block is comparable with that of other block as each block includes one plot of each treatment.

Merits and demerits

RBD is suitable for field experiments and this design is most widely adopted in agricultural research. Statistical analysis is easy since each treatment replicates equal number of times. It is possible to analyze the data even if one of the plots is damaged by using the missing plot technique.

The demerit is that if the fertility gradient runs in two directions, RBD is not suitable.

Layout in RBD

The general layout plan for RBD with 4 varieties (V_1, V_2, V_3, V_4) and 5 replications for each variety is given below:

V_3	V_2	V_1	V_4	Rep 1
V_4	V_2	V_1	V_3	Rep 2
V_1	V_3	V_2	V_4	Rep 3
V_4	V_2	V_3	V_1	Rep 4
V_1	V_2	V_4	V_3	Rep 5

Analysis of variance and interpretation

The total variance in RBD is divided into three source of variation viz., between replications, between treatments and error.

$$Y_{ij} = \mu + t_i + r_j + e_{ij}$$

Where,

μ = overall mean

t_i = i th treatment effect

r_j = j th replication effect, and

e_{ij} = error term

The analysis of variance table for RBD with 't' treatments and 'r' replications is given in Table 12.3.

TABLE 12.3: Analysis of variance for RBD

Source of variation	Degrees of freedom	Sum of squares	Mean square	F_c
Replication	(r-1)	RSS	RMS	
Treatment	(t-1)	TrSS	TrMS	TrMS/EMS
Error	(r-1) (t-1)	ESS	EMS	
Total	**(rt-1)**	**Total SS**		

Critical difference can be calculated as follows:

$$CD = t.\ SE\ (d)$$

$$SE\ (d) = \sqrt{\frac{2EMS}{r}}$$

Based on the CD value, bar chart is drawn and interpretation made.

Latin Square Design

This design is commonly referred to as row blocking and column blocking. The experimental material is divided into rows and columns. The treatments are allotted in such a way that each treatment occurs only once in each row and once in each column. The number of rows and columns are equal to the number of treatments and the arrangement of layout will be as a square. According to the number of rows and columns, LSD is identified as 5x5 latin squares, 6x6 Latin squares, etc. Each row and each column is a complete block or replication.

Merits and demerits

The design is applicable to the fields having the fertility gradient in two directions. Since the variations are estimated in two directions due to columns and rows, the treatment effect is estimated more precisely. It is possible to analysis the data even if one of the plots is damaged, by using missing plot technique. The design is simple to layout and easy for analysis of the data.

It is not possible to test a large number of treatments in LSD. Randomization procedure is difficult when compared to RBD. There is restriction that number of columns and treatments should be the same. The design is in limited use for agricultural research as compared to other designs.

Layout LSD

Before proceeding to the layout plan, it is important to know some of the terminologies connected with randomization of the treatments.

1. **Standard Latin Square**: In a Latin square, the treatments of first row and first column are ordered alphabetically (square 1)
2. **Conjugate Latin Square:** Two standard squares are said to be conjugate squares when the rows of one square are the columns of the other square (square 2,3).

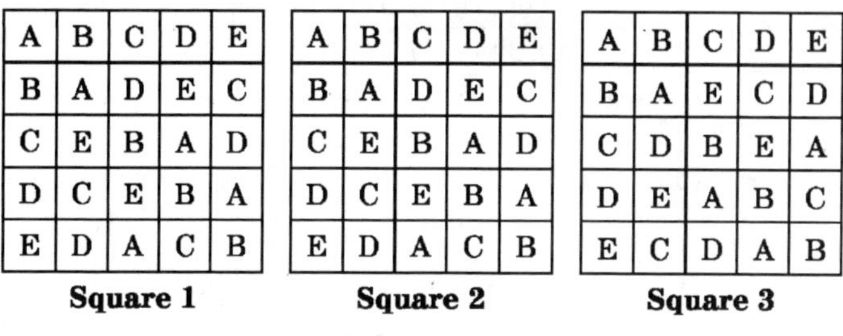

A	B	C	D	E
B	A	D	E	C
C	E	B	A	D
D	C	E	B	A
E	D	A	C	B

Square 1

A	B	C	D	E
B	A	D	E	C
C	E	B	A	D
D	C	E	B	A
E	D	A	C	B

Square 2

A	B	C	D	E
B	A	E	C	D
C	D	B	E	A
D	E	A	B	C
E	C	D	A	B

Square 3

Standard Square **Conjugate Square**

3. **Self Conjugate Latin Square:** A standard Latin Square is said to be self conjugate, if it remains the same 000000 after changing the rows into columns or columns into rows. (Fig. 12.3).

A	B	C	D	E
B	C	E	A	D
C	E	D	B	A
D	A	B	E	C
E	D	A	C	B

Self Conjugate Square

A	B	C	D	E
B	C	E	A	D
C	E	D	B	A
D	A	B	E	C
E	D	A	C	B

Changing Row into Columns

A	B	C	D	E
B	C	E	A	D
C	E	D	B	A
D	A	B	E	C
E	D	A	C	B

Changing Columns into Rows

FIG. 12.3: Self conjugate square

In a statistical table, there are 25 standard Latin squares each having two numbers (1,2) (3,4) … (49,50). In addition, there are six conjugate Latin squares (51 to 56).

Randomization: First the square is chosen randomly. Suppose the chosen random number is even and below 50, the given standard Latin square is changed into its conjugate. If the number is odd, the standard Latin square can be chosen as such from the table. If the number is between 51 and 56, the corresponding self-conjugate square can be chosen as such. For our purpose the square chosen is 10 and conjugate form is drawn as below:

A	B	C	D	E
B	C	D	E	A
C	E	B	A	D
D	A	E	B	C
E	D	A	C	B

Standard Square

A	B	C	D	E
B	C	E	A	D
C	D	B	E	A
D	E	A	B	C
E	A	D	C	B

Conjugate

Column randomization: Choose one digit random numbers, *e.g.*, 3,2,1,5,4. The third column of the above conjugate Latin square becomes the first column, the second column becomes the second, first column becomes third, fifth column as the fourth and the fourth column as the fifth. The resultant square is as follows:

C	B	A	E	D
E	C	B	D	A
B	D	C	A	E
A	E	D	C	B
D	A	E	B	C

Row randomization: From the resultant standard Latin square, the first row is kept as such. One digit random number is drawn from 2-5, *e.g.*, 3,2,4,5. The third row of the square becomes the second; the second row becomes the third, fourth row as fourth and the fifth row as the fifth. The final layout will be as in Fig. 12.4.

C	B	A	E	D
B	D	C	A	E
E	C	B	D	A
A	E	D	C	B
D	A	E	B	C

FIG. 12.4: FIG. 12.4: Final layout of Latin square

Analysis of the variance

The analysis of variance model for LSD is given below:

$$Y_{ijk} = \mu + r_i + c_j + t_k + e_{ijk}$$

Where,

μ = over all mean

r_i = i th row effect

c_j = j th column effect

t_k = k th treatment effect

e_{ijk} = error term

The analysis of variance for LSD is given in Table 12.4.

TABLE 12.4: Analysis of variance for LSD.

Sources of variation	Degrees of freedom	Sum of squares	Mean square	F_c
Column	(t-1)	CSS		
Row	(t-1)	RSS		
Treatments	(t-1)	TrSS	TrMS	TrMS/EMS
Error	(t-1) (t-2)	ESS	EMS	
Total	**(t^2-1)**	**TSS**		

The critical differences can be calculated as follows:

$$CD = t.\ SE\ (d)$$

$$Sed = \sqrt{\frac{2EMS}{r}}$$

The means can be compared from the bar chart and interpreted.

Factorial Experiments

In an experiment, if only one factor is involved, it is called single factor experiment. *e.g.*, varieties, irrigation levels, manurial levels, etc. On the other hand, if more than one factor is involved, it is called factorial experiment. *e.g.* irrigation and N levels, varieties and levels of manure, etc.

Factor: It is a type of treatment. e. g. varieties, irrigation, spacing, etc.

Levels of factor: The components of a treatment factor are called levels of treatment factor. *e.g.*, N at 0, 50, 100, 150 kg/ha.

The factors are denoted by capital letters (Nitrogen -N, Irrigation -I) and the levels of the factors by small letters (n_0, n_1, n_2, n_3)

In a factorial experiment, the levels of the factors are combined to form the treatment combinations. Any one of the designs such as CRD, RBD or LSD can be used to test the set of treatments. Hence, factorial experiment itself is not a design. It is a concept in designing an experiment. In the field experiments, factorial RBD (FRBD) is commonly used.

In a factorial experiment, if two factors are involved, it is called 2-factorial experiment. Like this, it is named 3-factorial experiment if three factors are involved. In a two factorial experiment, if each factor has two levels, it is denoted as 2^2 factorial experiment. In general, if there are *n* factor each at p levels, it is designated as p^n factorial experiment.

In a factorial experiment where the levels of different factors are same, it is called as symmetrical factorial experiment. If the levels of different factors are different, it is termed as asymmetric factorial experiment. Symmetrical factorial experiment can also be represented as a^n where the power '*n*' indicates the number of factors and the base, the levels of each factor.

Merits

1. Two or more factors can be combined and tested easily.
2. It takes less time, labour and capital to conduct the factorial experiment.
3. Interaction effect of the factors can be precisely determined.

Different effects in a factorial experiment

There are three effects exist in a factorial experiment: (i) simple effect, (ii) main effect, (iii) interaction effect.

1. **Simple effect:** The difference in response between two consecutive levels of a given factor at each level of other factor or combination of level of other factor.
2. **Main effect:** Average of the simple effects of a factor is known as main effect.
3. **Interaction effect:** The failure of simple effect of a given factor to remain consistent at various levels of the other factor is known as interaction effect. In a 2x2 factorial experiment, the interaction effect can be determined by taking the average of the difference between the two simple effects of a given factor. The interaction may be positive or negative and accordingly the interpretation will be drawn.

For example, two factors N and K each at two levels viz., nitrogen - no, n_1, and potassium - ko, k_1, the treatment combinations will be as follows:

	K_0	k_1
n_0	$n_0 k_0$	$n_0 k_1$
n_1	$n_1 k_0$	$n_1 k_1$

If the mean values are put in the corresponding cells of the above table,

	k_0	K_1
n_0	20	23
n_1	25	30

Simple effect of N at k_0	=	25-20	=	5
Simple effect of N at k_1	=	30-23	=	7
Simple effect of K at n_0	=	23-20	=	3
Simple effect of K at n_1	=	30-25	=	5
Main effect of N = (5+7) /2	=	12/2	=	6
Main effect of K = (3+5) /2	=	8/2	=	4
Interaction effect = (7-5) /2 or (5-3) /2	=	2/2	=	+1

2^n Factorial Experiment

In 2^n factorial experiment, effects of 2 or more factors each at two levels are involved. In general, if there are '*n*' factors in a 2^n series, number of factor interactions would be equal to nc_r. In an experiment of 2^n series, where each factor occurs at only two levels with *n* factor, there are n main effects, *n (n-1) /2* two factor interactions, *n (n-1) (n-2) /6* three factor interactions and so on.

Layout

For example, if there are three factors N, P and K each at two levels, the treatment combinations will be as given below:

	n_0		n_1	
	p_0	p_1	p_0	p_1
k_0	$n_0p_0k_0$	$n_0p_1k_0$	$n_1p_0k_0$	$n_1p_1k_0$
k_1	$n_0p_0k_1$	$n_0p_1k_1$	$n_1p_0k_1$	$n_1p_1k_1$

These 8 treatment combinations will be randomly allotted in any basic design such as CRD, RBD or LSD. In agricultural experiments, RBD is commonly used.

Analysis of variance

In the factorial experiment, the analysis of the results will be same as that of the basic design. However, the treatment degrees of freedom and treatment sum of squares will be split up according to the components. The analysis of variance (Table 12.5) for the above treatments with 'r' replications is given below:

TABLE 12.5: Analysis of variance for factorial RBD

Source of variation	Degrees of freedom	Sum of squares	Mean square	F_c
Replications	(r-1)	RSS		
Treatments	(t-1)			
N	(n-1)	NSS	NMS	NMS/EMS
P	(p-1)	PSS	PMS	PMS/EMS
K	(k-1)	KSS	KMS	KMS/EMS
NxP	(n-1) (p-1)	(NxP) SS	(NxP) MS	(NxP) MS/EMS
NxK	(n-1) (k-1)	(NxK) SS	(NxK) MS	(NxK) MS/EMS
PxK	(p-1) (k-1)	(PxK) SS	(PxK) MS	(PxK) MS/EMS
NxPxK	(n-1) (p-1) (k-1)	(NxPxK) SS	(NxPxK) MS	(NxPxK) MS/EMS
Error	(r-1) (t-1)	ESS	EMS	
Total	**(rt) -1**	**Total SS**		

Critical difference can be computed by following the steps as that of single factor experiments. The general formula for SE (d) is,

$$\text{SE (d) for x} = \sqrt{\frac{2EMS}{r.D}}$$

Where,

X = Main factors or interactions

D = Product of the levels of the left out factors other than x

r = Number of replications

Bar chart can be drawn for the main factors as usual. For the interactions which are significant, the bar chart for each factor is drawn at each level of the other factors.

For example, for NK interaction, the bar chart may be as follows:

At level n_0 = k_1, k_0

At level n_1 = k_1 k_0

Factorial experiments involving dummy treatments

In certain situations, factorial experiments are conducted with a number of identical treatments among the treatment combinations. For example, in a factorial experiment involving two factors, sources of nitrogen (s) at 3 levels (s_1, s_2, s_3) and N at 4 levels (n_0, n_1, n_2, n_3), the treatment combination will be s_1n_0, s_1n_1, s_1n_2, s_1n_3, s_2n_0, s_2n_1, s_2n_2, s_2n_3, s_3n_0, s_3n_1, s_3n_2 and s_3n_3. Out of the 12 treatment combinations, three combinations, s_1n_0, s_2n_0 and s_3n_0, are identical (it is not possible to have source of N at 0 level). Differences between such treatments can only be due to error and they are called "dummy treatments". The error contributed by the dummy treatments is known as "pure error". The variations due to dummy comparisons should be included in the error since its presence in the treatment sum of squares will mask the genuine treatment effects. In the statistical analysis of such experiments, care should be taken in partitioning the degree of freedom of treatments in the main effects and interactions. If the above experiment is conducted in RBD with r replications, the skeleton analysis of variance will be as in Table 12.6.

TABLE 12.6: Analysis of variance for dummy treatments in RBD

Source of variation	Degrees of freedom	Sum of squares	Mean square	F_c
Replication	(r-1)			
S	(s-1)	SSS	SMS	SMS/EMS
N	(n-1)	NSS	NMS	NMS/EMS
S X N	(n-2) (s-1)	(SxN) SS	(SxN) MS	(SxN) MS/EMS
Pure error	r (d-1)			
Experimental error	(r-1) (t-1)	ESS	EMS	
Total	**(snr) -1**			

Confounding

In the factorial concept of experimentation, a large number of factors are studied at a time. Whenever a large number of factors or a large number of levels of each factor or both are included in a trial, it is difficult to control the size of the block. The only way of overcoming this difficulty and of retaining simultaneously the comprehensiveness of the factorial concept and the advantage of increased precision through local control by having homogeneous blocks is to adopt the principle of 'confounding'. Thus by way of confounding, the restriction in randomized block design that each block should form a complete replication is avoided. Instead, each replication is divided into two or more incomplete blocks of small size, which are obtained by making the experimental material more or less homogenous in the blocks, and thus precision is increased.

As along as the treatments occur in the same block (as in complete block), the real differences from any two treatment comparisons can be easily identified. When the treatments occur in two different blocks within a replication the real differences get mixed with the block effects and are not distinguished or detected.

Generally the interaction of a high order (involving three or more factors) seldom turns out to be significant. More over, it becomes very difficult to attach any physical interpretation to the higher order interaction. Because of the reason of least interest in estimating the effects due to high order interaction, they are generally confounded with block differences.

Thus, confounding can be defined as a device by which the precision on the main effect and certain interactions is increased by sacrificing the precision on certain high order interactions by reducing the block size.

The number of elements to be confounded will depend upon the number of factors under study and the block size (number of plots per block). Generally in a 2^n experiments, 2^{n-1} elements can be confounded, where n=1,2...n-1 and where '*n*' represents the number of factors under study.

Split plot design

In a factorial experiment, if any one of the factors need larger plot and the other requires more accuracy, the split plot design is suitable. In a spilt plot design, the given field will be divided into a number of blocks equal to the number of replications of treatment combinations. Further each block will be divided into number of larger plots equal to number of main plot (whole plot) treatments and each larger plot will be divided into number of sub plots (split plot) equal to the number of sub plot treatments. The treatment combinations will be allotted to the ultimate experimental unit (plots) completely at random.

Factors such as irrigation methods, sowing methods, plant population, etc. may require larger plots. Similarly some of the factors such as manurial levels, time of fertilizer application, etc. may require more precision which may be allotted to the sub-plots.

Merits and demerits

The split plot design is adopted whenever two factors are involved with one factor requiring larger area for operation. Whenever the experimental results require more precision on the interaction effect, split plot design is applicable.

If the number of factors and the levels are increased, statistical analysis will become complex in the split plot design.

Layout

Let there are two factors, the varieties (V) with four levels (v_1, v_2, v_3, v_4) and nitrogen (N) with three levels (n_1, n_2, n_3) with four replications. The levels of varieties are allotted to the main plots at random. Similarly, levels of N are allotted to the sub-plots at random in each main plot. The final layout plan is given in Fig 12.5.

v_3	v_2	v_1	v_4
n_3	n_2	n_2	n_1
n_2	n_1	n_3	n_3
n_1	n_3	n_1	n_2

R_1

v_2	v_3	v_1	v_4
n_3	n_2	n_2	n_1
n_1	n_3	n_1	n_2
n_2	n_1	n_3	n_3

R_2

v_1	v_3	v_4	v_2
n_3	n_2	n_3	n_2
n_2	n_1	n_2	n_1
n_1	n_3	n_1	n_3

R_3

v_3	v_1	v_2	v_4
n_3	n_3	n_1	n_1
n_1	n_2	n_2	n_3
n_2	n_1	n_3	n_2

R_2

FIG. 12.5: Layout plan for spilt plot design

Analysis of variance

In split plot design, there are two types of plots viz., main plots and sub-plots. Hence variation among the main plots will produce one type of error and the variation among the sub-plots, will constitute another type of error. In other words, the interaction of larger plots with block will be different from that of interaction of sub plots with blocks. Hence, there will be two separate errors in the split plot design. The first error (Error 1) is for larger plots and the second error (Error 2) for smaller plots. As the sub-plot treatment and the combinations receive the same smaller plot size, the main effect of sub-plot treatments and interaction of sub-plots with the whole plots will be treated with the Error (2). The analysis of variance model for the spilt plot experiment is as follows:

$$Y_{ijk} = \mu + r_i + m_j + m_{ij} + s_k + (ms)_{jk} + e_{ijk}$$

Where,

Y_{ijk} = the observation of i th replication, j th main plot and k th sub-plot

μ = over all mean

r_i = i th replication effect

m_j = j th main plot treatment effect

m_{ij} = main plot error *i.e.* Error (1)

s_k = kth sub-plot treatment effect

$(ms)_{jk}$ = interaction effect

e_{ijk} = error component for sub-plot and interaction *i.e.* Error (2)

The analysis of variance for the above example is given in Table 12.7.

TABLE 12.7: Analysis of variance for spilt plot design

Sources of variation	Degrees of freedom	Sum of squares	Mean square	F_c
Replication	(r-1)			
V	(v-1)	VSS	VMS	VMS / E_1MS
Error (1)	(r-1) (v-1)	E_1SS	E_1MS	
N	(n-1)	NSS	NMS	NMS / E_2MS
V x N	(v-1) (n-1)	(V x N) SS	(V x N) MS	(V x N) MS / E_2MS
Error (2)	(v-1) (n-1)	E_2 SS	E_2MS	
Total	**(rvn) – 1**	**TSS**		

SE (d) for the main plot treatments is computed with the formula:

$$SE\ (d) = \frac{\sqrt{2E_1MS}}{rs}$$

r - replication

s - levels of sub-plot treatments

CD = t. SE (d)

Where 't' is the table value of Students 't' distribution for a specified level of significance and the Error (1) degrees of freedom.

SE (d) for comparing two sub-plot treatment means is computed with the formula:

$$SE\ (d) = \frac{\sqrt{2E_2MS}}{r\,m}$$

r – replication; m – levels of main plot treatment

CD = t. SE (d)

Where, table 't' value corresponds to Error (2) degrees of freedom.

To work out SE (d) for interaction, there are two formulae. For comparing two sub-plot treatment means at a given main plot treatment,

$$SE\ (d) = \sqrt{\frac{2E_2MS}{r}}$$

The CD is calculated with the 't' value taken against Error (2) degrees of freedom.

The following formula can be used for comparing two main plot treatment means at each level of sub-plot treatment.

$$SE\ (d) = \sqrt{\frac{2[E_1 + (s-1)E_2]}{rs}}$$

The CD is worked as:

CD = tw-.SE (d)

Where, $$\text{tw-} = \frac{t_1 E_1 + t_2[(s-1)E_2]}{E_1 + (s-1)E_2}$$

in which

t_1 = table 't' value for error (1) df at 5% level of significance

t_2 = table 't' value for error (2) df at 5% level of significance

E_1 = Error (1) means square (E_1 MS)

E_2 = Error (2) means square (E_2 MS)

Strip-plot design

In a factorial experiment involving two factors with both the factors requiring larger plots, strip plot design is suitable. *e.g.*, irrigation and tillage. In the strip plot design, the field is divided into number of replications of each treatment combination. Each block is divided into number of horizontal strips equal to the level of the one factor and the same block is further divided into number of vertical strips equal to the levels of the other factor. The treatment combinations are allotted to the ultimate experimental units completely at random.

Randomization

Let A and B are the two factors having 3 (a_1, a_2, a_3) and 5 levels (b_1, b_2, b_3, b_4, b_5) respectively in a strip plot design. Each treatment combination replicates 3 times.

1. **Step I:** The field is divided into 3 blocks equal to the number of replications.
2. **Step II:** The first block is divided into 3 horizontal strips equal to the levels of the first factor A. Draw a set of 3 random numbers of three digits like 807, 186, 410 from the random number table. The ranks of this random numbers may be assigned from the lowest to the highest. The ranks of the above random numbers are 3,1,2. According to these ranks, the levels of the factor A are allotted to the horizontal plots as a_3, a_1, and a_2 respectively. Same process may be continued to the other blocks.
3. **Step III:** Divide the same block into 5 vertical strips equal to the levels of the second factor, B. A set of 5 three digited random numbers are drawn like 270, 608, 099, 326, 225 and ranked from the lowest to the highest as 3, 5, 1, 4 and 2. The levels of factors B may be allotted to the vertical plots as per the ranks (b_3, b_5, b_1, b_4 and b_2). Similarly the treatments are alloted to other replications at random. The final layout is given in Fig. 12.6.

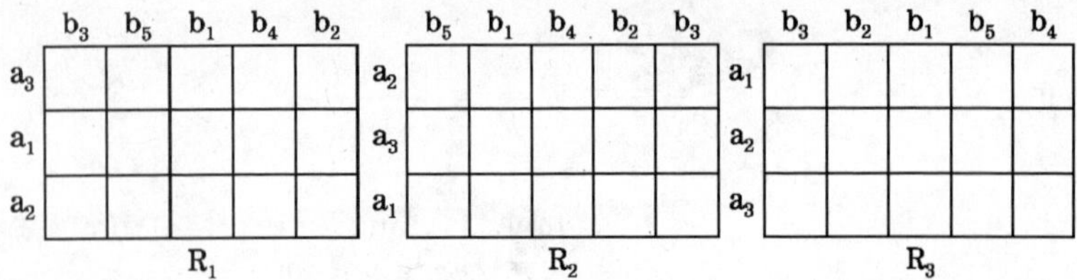

FIG. 12.6: Layout plan for strip plot design

Analysis of variance

In strip plot design, there are three types of plot sizes. The horizontal plots are different from the vertical plots and these two are different from the ultimate plots. For example, let the plot size of the levels of factor A is 9 x 1 m² and the plot size for the levels of the factor B is 3 x 1 m². Hence, the ultimate plot size for interaction will be 3 x 1 m². Hence, there may be 3 errors in the strip plat design. They include error due to interaction of horizontal plots with blocks, the interaction of vertical plots with blocks and the interaction of ultimate plot with block. Hence, the total variation can be split as follows: The analysis of variance is given in Table 12.8.

Total variation = block variation + factor (A) variation + error (1) + factor (B) variation + error (2) + interaction (A x B) variation + error (3).

Total Sum of square = RSS +ASS+E_1SS+BSS+E_2SS + (A xB) SS + E_3 SS.

TABLE 12.8: The analysis of variance for strip plot design

Source of variation	Degrees of freedom	Sum of squares	Mean square	F_c
Block	(r-1)	Block SS		
A	(a-1)	ASS	AMS	AMS/E_1MS
Error (1)	(a-1) (r-1)	E_1SS	E_1MS	
B	(b-1)	BSS	BMS	BMS/E_2MS
Error (2)	(b-1) (r-1)	E_2SS	E_2MS	
A xB	(a-1) (b-1)	(A x B) SS	(A x B) MS	(Ax B) MS/E_3MS
Error (3)	(a-1) (b-1) (r-1)	E_3SS	E_3MS	
Total	**(abr) -1**	**TSS**		

Calculation of SE (d) for the factors and interaction is as follows:

$$\text{SE (d) for A} = \sqrt{\frac{2E_1}{rb}}$$

$$\text{SE (d) for B} = \sqrt{\frac{2E_2}{ra}}$$

$$\text{SE (d) for A at levels of B} = \sqrt{\frac{2[E_1 + (b-1)E_3]}{rb}}$$

$$\text{SE (d) for B at levels of A} = \sqrt{\frac{2[E_2 + (a-1)E_3]}{ra}}$$

Where, E (1), E (2) and E (3) are the corresponding error mean squares.

The critical t value may be computed by using the weighed mean method as in the case of split plot design.

Split-split plot design

In this design, the given field is divided into number of blocks equal to the number of replications of each treatment combination. Each block is divided into number of larger plots equal to the number of main plot treatments. The main plot treatments are allotted completely at random. Each larger plot is further divided into number of sub-plots equal to the sub-plot treatments. The sub-plot treatments are allotted completely at random. Each sub-plot is further divided into a new set of smaller plots equal to the number of split-split plot treatments which are allotted completely at random.

For example, let 'a' be the number of main plot treatments, 'b' be the number of sub-plot treatments and 'c' be the number of sub-sub-plot treatments (or split-split plot treatments). Let 'r' be the number of replications of each treatment combination. Total number of treatment combinations will be abc and the total number of plots will be abcr. The analysis of variance for the split-split plot design is given in Table 12.9.

TABLE 12.9: Analysis of variance for split –split plot design

Sources of variation	Degrees of freedom	Sum of squares	Mean square	F_c
Replication	(r-1)	RSS		
Main plot (A)	(a-1)	ASS	AMS	AMS / E_1MS
Error (1)	(a-1) (r-1)	E_1SS	E_1MS	
Sub plot (B)	(b-1)	BSS	BMS	BMS / E_2MS
A x B	(a-1) (b-1)	(A x B) SS	(A x B) MS	(A x B) MS / E_2MS
Error (2)	a (b-1) (r-1)	E_2 SS	E_2MS	
Sub-sub plot (C)	(c-1)	CSS	CMS	CMS/E_3MS
A x C	(a-1) (c-1)	(A x C) SS	(A x C) MS	(A x C) MS/ E_3MS
B x C	(b-1) (c-1)	(B x C) SS	(B x C) MS	(B x C) MS/ E_3MS
A x B x C	(a-1) (b-1) (c-1)	(A x B x C) SS	(A x B x C) MS	(A x B x C) MS/ E_3MS
Error (3)	ab (c-1) (r-1)	E_3 SS	E_3MS	
Total	**(abc) r**	**TSS**		

Planning field experiments

It is important to plan the experiment with specific objectives. It is also possible to combine two or more objectives in a single experiment. While fixing the treatments, care is necessary to ensure that the treatments are really capable of achieving the declared aim of the experiment.

The site selected for conducting the field experiment should be representative of the particular region/locality.

The choice of the experimental design largely depends on the nature and number of treatments to be included in the experiment. Single factor can be tested in a Randomized Block Design. More than one factor can be tested with factorial experiments. In an experiment involving irrigation and fertilizers as the factors, split plot design may be preferred. A standard design should be chosen to fulfil the objectives.

Uniformity trials

The field chosen for conducting the experiment should be as uniform as possible. Uniformity of the field means uniformity in fertility and not simply uniformity in topography. At the same time, the evenness of the surface topography of the field is also to be considered. Variation in the fertility of a field can easily be judged from the stand of the crops grown in a field. If the experimental field is more or less homogeneous, the experimental error will be smaller which will give greater precision of the treatment comparisons.

Uniformity trial is to be conducted in the proceeding season to get a reasonably accurate idea of the uniformity of the land. The field is divided into a number of plots and a common crop is raised in all the plots. Same cultivation practices are followed for all the plots. The yield is recorded in each plot separately. The yields are plotted on a map and the plots having the same yields are joined by lines called as 'isoyield lines'. The resultant diagram is known as the 'contour map'. This map will indicate the area of equal fertility as well as the type and extent of variation. Usually the variation does not follow any systematic pattern. The fertility does not increase or decrease uniformly in any direction. The fertility variations may distribute over the field in an erratic manner. Standard deviation gives an index of the inherent variability of the land. Such variations from plot to plot caused by uncontrolled factors is known as 'experimental error'.

Experimental error can be minimized by replicating the treatments while conducting the experiment.

Uniformity trial thus gives the information about the direction of the fertility gradient. It is easier to find out the optimum size and shape of the plots to be used in an experiment by conducting such trails.

Size and shape of plots

Some of the points to be considered while determining the size of the plot are: (i) the character to be studied; (ii) treatments to be compared and (iii) number of replications. The shape of the plot normally depends on the homogeneity of the soil. The plot size should be large enough to have the convenience for normal cultural operations.

While fixing the plot size, it is important to consider the border effects and the consequences of leaving non-experimental margins. Normally the plants nearer to the border rows will give more yield than the plots in the center portion of the plot. In the varietal trial, the border plants grow vigorously than the plants in the central portion of the plots and hence there is possibility of over-estimating the differences between the varieties. In the fertilizer trails, the nutrients may permeate upto some distance beyond the border of the fertilized plots. This may result in benefiting the border plants of the unfertilized plots. It becomes necessary to have non-experimental margins around the experimental plots. This may be done by leaving one or more rows or a narrow strip of the crop, depending on the magnitude of the border effect on either side of the experimental plot. There should be adequate number of plants in a plot so that the sample dwawn will be representative of the population.

The size of the plot depends on the type of crop to be cultivated. Wide spaced crops like sugarcane may require larger area than narrow spaced crops like rice. For rice crop, 20-40 m^2 areas may be adequate while for sugarcane, 80-100 m^2 may be required. Whenever, implements are to be tested, a larger plot size of more than 400 m^2 is required. The plot size should be generally larger under rainfed condition since the variability is greater than under irrigated situation. Square shape of plot is preferred to long and narrow plots since the margin effects are minimum.

Ancillary observations and data collection

The yield of a crop is the principal character; in addition other observations such as growth and yield parameters, pest and disease incidence are also to be observed.

The unit of sampling is important and it varies with the nature of crop. In crops like maize or cotton, individual plants are distinct and hence serve as the sampling unit. However, for crops like wheat and sugarcane which are grown in continuous rows and the individual plant cannot be distinguished, a unit length of row (0.5 m) may be taken as the sampling unit. In each plot, an equal number of units is selected for observation. The data obtained from all units in a plot are pooled for analysis. In the case of observation on herbicides effects, ratings may be used to assess its effect on crop plants and weed species.

Data transformation

The most generally accepted and useful method to treat many kinds of data is to transform the original data to a scale in which all assumption of analysis of variance are fulfilled. The most commonly used transformations in analysis of biological experiments are: (i) square root transformation, (ii) logarithmic transformation and (iii) angular (or arcsine) transformation.

Square root transformation

When the data consist of small whole numbers, for example. number of bacterial colonies in a plate count, number of plants or insects of a specified species in given area, the square root transformation can be used. This type of data often follow the poisson distribution for which the mean and variance are equal. The analysis of such enumeration data is often best accomplished by first taking the square root of each observation before proceeding with the analysis of variance. When very small counts below 10 are involved, $\sqrt{x}$ can be used as a satisfactory transformation. However, $\sqrt{x+0.5}$ is recommended as an appropriate transformation especially when zeros and less than 10 are present.

Logarithmic transformation

Logarithmic transformation is used on the positive integers of a wide range. It cannot be used directly for zero values. It is desirable to have a transformation which will act as square root for smaller values and logarithmic for larger values. Addition of 1 to each number prior to taking logarithms is useful. That is Log (x + 1) behaves like the square root transformation for numbers upto 10 and differs little from log x thereafter.

Angular, Arcsine or Inverse sine transformation

This transformation is applicable to data where the variable follows a binomial distribution and is expressed as decimal fractions or percentages. This is recommended especially when the percentages cover a wider range of values. This method is appropriate when the percentages are less than 100. If the percentage value lies between 30 and 70, transformation is not needed. With n< 50, zero % should be counted as (1/4 n) 100 % before transforming to angles, and a 100% proportion as (n-0.25) 100/n. This empirical device improves the equality of variance in the angles.

When data are transformed, comparisons among the means are made on the transformed scale. Thereafter the treatment means only should be given in original scale. When the results of such an analysis with transformed means are presented along with the means in the original scale of measurement, this should be clearly stated (in the proper place). It is not appropriate to retransform the standard error (S.E.) of means and the critical differences (CD) to original scale.

Biometric observations in field crops

It is important to collect data on various growth and yield parameters which may facilitate to interpret the results in a better way. Generally growth parameters such as plant height, tiller production, leaf area index and dry matter production are recorded. In addition, yield parameters may also be recorded. The growth and yield parameters may be recorded at different growth stages viz., tillering, primordial initiation, flowering and at harvest. Observations can also be taken at 20,40,60,80 and 100 days after planting or sowing. Whenever simultaion modeling is to be attempted, readings may be taken at narrow interval. Appropriate method of sampling and proper measurement are important to get valid data. The growth and yield parameters that should be recorded for important field crops are given below:

Rice

1. Plant height,
2. Leaf area index (LAI),
3. Tiller production,
4. Drymatter production,
5. Number of panicles/ m^2,
6. Number of spikelets/panicle,
7. Filled grain %,
8. Test grain weight,
9. Grain yield and
10. Straw yield.

Wheat

1. Plant height,
2. LAI,
3. Tillers/m row length,
4. Effective tilllers/m row length,
5. Spikelets/panicle,
6. Grains/panicle,
7. Test grain weight,
8. Grain yield and
9. Straw yield.

Maize

1. Cobs/plant,
2. Cob weight,
3. Grains/cob,
4. Test grain weight
5. Grain yield, and
6. Stover yield.

Millets

1. Number of effective tillers/hill,
2. Spikes/panicle,
3. 1000 grain weight,
4. Grain yield, and
5. Straw yield.

Pulses

1. Number of pods/plant,
2. Number of grains/pod
3. weight of pods/plant,
4. 1000-grain weight, and
5. Grain yield.

Groundnut

1. Number of pods/plant,
2. Mature pods / plant,
3. Immature pods / plant,
4. Pod weight/plant,
5. 100 kernel weight,
6. Pod yield, and
7. Haulm yield.

Rapeseed-mustard

1. Number of branches/plant,
   a) Primary,
   b) Secondary,
   c) Tertiary,
2. Siliquae/plant,
3. Seeds/siliqua,
4. 1000 seed weight,
5. Seed yield, and
6. Stover yield.

Sunflower

1. Head diameter,
2. Seed weight/plant,
3. 100 seed weight, and
4. Seed yield.

Soybean

1. Number of pods/plant,
2. Pod weight/plant,
3. Number of seeds/pod
4. 100 seed weight, and

5. Seed yield.

Cotton

1. Number of monopodials and sympodials
2. Number of bolls/plant,
3. Seed cotton weight/boll,
4. Seed cotton yield,
5. Lint yield.

Sugarcane

1. Length of milleable cane,
2. Number of internodes/cane,
3. Diameter of the cane,
4. Cane weight,
5. Number of milleable canes/sq.m., and
6. Cane yield.

Forages

1. Green forage yield

Green manure

1. Biomass production/unit area

Tabacco

1. Total cured leaf yield,
2. First grade leaf, and
3. Bright leaf yield.

Information Technology and field Experimentation

The increasing power and access to computers and improvements in computer software have led to many advances in methodologies and application to agriculture systems. Computer application in agronomy is very large. Normally computer is used in analyzing the experimental data with many variables. It is often used in analyzing the correlation and regression and fitting equations. Computer application in dry farming situation is very vital since it is used to forecast rainfall which is the only source of soil moisture. Under farming systems, computer application is helpful in taking decisions on optimum combination of enterprises to maximize farm family income. Computer application is very useful for crop modeling and predicting crop yields.

Crop simulation models

Simulation models are necessary (i) for interpreting experimental results, (ii) as agronomic research tools and (iii) as agronomic grower tools.

Many crop models or parts of crop models have been built to help the researcher to understand the operation of some part of crop production such as photosynthetic rate, stomatal control, etc. These attempts may help in quantifying the plant growth process. Other crop models are built as research tools. These models help in knowing what could happen, if some changes are made in the system. Field experiments are very expensive, especially as the number of variables and/or treatments increase. Also a lot of time is required to complete the experiments and to draw inferences. A proven model, however, would help to evaluate the treatments and indicate which ones could be expected to give the desired results at the earliest period.

Types of models

i) Empirical (or correlative) models describe relationships between variables without referring to any underlying biological or physical structure that may exist between the variables.
ii) Mechanistic (or explanatory) models attempt to explicitly represent casuality between variables. The mathematical functions represent the known or hypothesized mechanism that relates the variables and explains their observed behaviour.
iii) Phenological models are a broad class of models that predict crop development from one growth stage to another. These predictions are generally based upon accumulated heat units, with development being delayed by various stresses.
iv) Stochastic simulation models are based upon the probability of occurrence of some event or exogenous variable. Weather variables are often treated in a stochastic manner or probability of occurrence and as such may be combined with a mechanistic crop model.

Model application

Comprehensive, mechanistic crop models such as GOSSYM have been developed to test the effects of different soil management strategies and/or natural occurrence such as erosion.

Using software application, management decision is made annually or daily by the cotton growers in USA. On an annual basis, decisions are taken with respect to area to be planted, selection of varieties, etc., On a daily basis the farmer is able to decide whether to irrigate, apply herbicide or insecticide, use of fertilizer, growth regulator or a boll opener.

Artificial intelligence/expert systems

An expert system is a computer system which is capable of performing at the level of a human expert. The objective is to allow an unavailable human expert to be replaced with a computer. Under certain circumstances, it has been possible to create expert systems which perform better than human experts. The Agricultural Research Service of the USDA has developed the crop management expert system for cotton called COMEX/GOSSYM.

It advises the cotton growers regarding applications of nitrogen, irrigation and growth regulators. COMEX informs the grower about the crop maturity. COMEX was designed to run at the farm site on a PC-type computer.

Yield estimation of field crops

It is important to estimate the yield of crops in advance so as to take a decision at micro- and macro level. Yield estimations of various crops have been attempted with the use of computers. An attempt was made in West Bengal to estimate rice yield from combined effects of individual weather elements viz., temperature, sunshine, evaporation, rainfall and number of rainy days for different overlapping periods, ranging from one week to nine weeks. Those particular periods which give high correaltions for a weather element are called "sensitivity periods".

Yield is assumed to be directly related to the weather elements. It is assumed that the effect of weather elements on rice yield in each period is independent of the effect of weather elements in some other time period. Different weather elements are selected and the periods are subjected to linear multiple regression analysis with yield as dependent and weather element as independent variables. The regression equation has the form:

$$Y = a+b_1x_1+ b_2x_2+\dots\dots\dots\dots+.b_k x$$

where, a, b_1, b_2,...bk are all constants and x_1, x_2....xk are the weather elements during different phenological periods of crop growth, and Y is yield. Numerous combinations and permutations have been tried. The combination which gave significant and high multiple correlation combinations-efficient is selected.

Rainfall prediction and forecasting

Monsoon is a complex system. An attempt has been made to develop a parametric and power regression models to predict monsoon rainfall by utilizing signals from 15 parameters known to be related with the Indian summer monsoon rainfall. Some of the parameters are global and others are regional in nature. These parameters also have physical links with the Indian summer monsoon. Some of these parameters are inter-related. The parametric model (Vasant Gowriker *et al.* 1989) which analyses the monsoon rainfall vis-à-vis the 15 parameters for 37 years (1951-87) has shown encouraging results. It is observed that whenever more than 70% parameters showed favourable signals, the monsoon rainfall in India was not only normal (percentage departure of rainfall ±10% of normal) but it was towards the positive side of the normal.

Weed management

It is important to know how weed species spread over a period of time. The model INVADE was used to simulate spreading population of weed species, *Avena fatua*. The model accurately predicted total population, area occupied and gross distribution of *A. fatua* in wheat cultivating regions (Auld and coote, 1990).

A mechanistic dynamic simulation model for crop–weed competition was introduced in 1983 by Spitters and Aets. In this model, competition effects were explained from the underlying process. The basis of the approach was the distribution of the growth - determining and limiting resources of light, water and nutrient over the species. From the amount of resources (light, water and/or nutrient) acquired by the competing species and the efficiency of the species in using these resources, drymatter production by the species could be computed.

Studying plant growth

A model developed by Andres (1987) was an attempt to relate the growth of plants to the magnitudes of soil and atmosphere intensive variables-temperature, soil solution concentration of N, P, K, water potential, light intensity and CO_2 level in the atmosphere. The mathematical analysis of plant growth is based on the assumption that the influence of deficiencies in water, N, P and K is to reduce the fraction of the plant mass denoted to photosynthesis by increasing the root fraction, thereby diminishing the rate of growth of the total plant.

The crop growth model WOFOST (World Food Studies) was developed by the Centre for World Food Studies in Wageningen, Netherlands, in co-operation with the Agricultural University and the DLO Center for Agrobiological Research (Van Diepen *et al.* 1988, 1989). The model has been further developed at the DLO Winand Staring Center (Guiking, 1993). The model simulates phenological development and growth of a field crop from emergence to maturity as determined by the crop's response to environmental conditions.

Fertilizing field crops

It is now widely acknowledged that fertilizer application should be done on a cropping system basis. This is more important in the case of phosphorus as it can have considerable residual effect, which can also be accounted while recommending its application to the crops grown in sequence. To describe the recovery of fertilizer application in the year of application and its after effects in the following years, a model operating with time interval of one year was described by Wolf *et al.* (1987). It can be used to calculate the long term recovery of fertilizer P and to establish long term fertilizer recommendations for a target P uptake.

To optimize N fertilizer application strategy, the model ORYZA - O has been applied (Ten Berge *et al.* 1994). The model simulates rice production as limited by radiation and nitrogen. It is the simplest of currently available ORYZA models. A set of sub-routines is wrapped around this model to identify the best N fertilizer application curve, given a total amount of N input and number of varietal and environmental characteristics. The calculation of the best N application curve is done by parameter optimization. The resulting curve is named the 'fertilizer recommendation curve'.

Data collection for crop simulation modeling

The data that are to be collected for modeling depends on the type of model. The required data can be broadly grouped into (i) meteorological data, (ii) crop data, (iii) soil data and (iv) management data.

Meteorological data

Latitude and altitude of the location of the study are required. Daily meteorological parameters are recorded. They include solar radiation, rainfall, maximum and minimum temperature, sunshine hours, wind speed and relative humidity.

Crop data

1. **Phenological observations:** Date of sowing, emergence, floral initiation, anthesis, physiological maturity, etc.
2. **Agronomic observations:** The agronomic observations to be recorded at all the phenological stages of crop include plant population, number of leaves/plant, maximum leaf area of individual leaf, LAI, diurnal leaf water potential, diurnal leaf temperature, PAR, plant height, leaf weight, culm weight, drymatter, head/ear weight, grain weight, etc.
3. Final grain yield and yield components.

Soil data

Soil type, soil depth, structure, texture, water holding capacity, soil profile structure, bulk density, salinity, alkalinity, pH, EC, microbial content, soil fertility, soil productivity, available soil moisture at field capacity, wilting point, permanent wilting point and available soil moisture at different stages of crop.

Management data

Amount of irrigation, fertilizer quantity, herbicide quantity, date and mode of application, insecticide quantity and date of application, etc.

Precision Farming

Precision farming is the application of technologies and principles to manage spatial and temporal variability associated with all aspects of agricultural production for the purpose of improving crop performance and environmental quality (Pierce and Nowak, 1999).

Basic components of precision farming

- Measurement and understanding of variability.
- Manage the variability by matching inputs to conditions within fields using site-specific management recommendations and mechanisms to

control the accuracy of site-specific inputs.

- Measurement and recording the efficiency and efficacy of the site-specific practices in order to assess valve on and off-farm. Thus, precision farming is technology enabled, information based and decision focused.

Enabled technologies

The enabling technologies of precision agriculture can be grouped into five major categories: computers, geographic information system (GIS), global positioning systems (GPS), sensors and application control.

Selected References

Abrol, I.P. and Dhruva Narayana, V.V. (Eds.) 1998. Technologies for Wasteland Development. Indian Council of Agricultural Research, New Delhi.

Agarwal, M.C. and Khanna, S.S. 1983. Efficient Soil and Water Management in Haryana. Haryana Agricultural University, Hissar.

Agarwal, R.R., Jadav, J.S.P. and Gupta, R.N. 1982. Saline and Alkali Soils of India. Indian Council of Agricultural Research, New Delhi.

Alan, R. Putnam and Chung Shih Tang. 1986. The Science of Allelopathy. John Wiley and Sons. Canada.

Alden S. Crafts and Wilfred W. Robbins. 1973. Weed Control - A Text Book and Manual. Tata McGraw- Hill Publishing Co. Ltd., New Delhi.

Anandeshwari Awasthi. 1995. Indian Climatology. APH Publishing Corporation, New Delhi.

Arnon, I. 1972. Crop Production in Dry Regions. Vol I. Leonard Hill, London.

Ashawa, G.L. 1996. Irrigation Engineering. New Age International Publishers, New Delhi.

Auld, B.A. and Kim, K.U. 1998. Weed Management in Rice. Oxford and IBH Publishing Co. Pvt. Ltd., New Delhi.

Barwale, B.R. 1993 (Ed.). Hybrid Rice. Food Security in India. MacMillan India Ltd., Madras, India.

Beldev Sahai and Ajai. 1988. Application of Remote Sensing Techniques in Agriculture. Fert. News 33(4): 59-65.

Chakraverty, A. 1995. Post Harvest Technology of Cereals, Pulses and Oilseeds. Oxford and IBH publishing Co. Pvt. Ltd., New Delhi.

Chandha, K.L. (Ed.).2002. Handbook of Animal Husbandry. Indian Council of Agricultural Research, New Delhi.

Chatterjee, B.N. and Bhattacharya, K.K. 1986. Principles and Practices of Grain Legume Production. Oxford and IBH publishing Co. Pvt. Ltd., New Delhi.

Chatterjee, B.N. and Das, P.K. 1989. Forage Crop Production- Principles and Practices. Oxford and IBH publishing Co. Pvt. Ltd., New Delhi.

Chatterjee, B.N. and Maiti, S. 1984. Cropping System- Theory and Practice. Oxford and IBH publishing Co. Pvt. Ltd., New Delhi.

Chidda Singh, 1984. Modern Techniques of Raising Field Crops. Oxford and IBH publishing Co. Pvt. Ltd., New Delhi.

Crafts, A.S. 1975. Modern Weed Control. University of California Press,

California.

CSSRI. 1979. A Decade of Research. Central Soil Salinity Research Institute (ICAR), Karnal, India.

Daniel Sundaraj, D. and Thulasidas, G. 1993. Botany of Field Crops. (Second Edition). Mac Millan India Ltd., New Delhi.

Dargan, K.S., Singh O.P. and Gupta I.C., 1982. Crop Production in Salt-Affected Soils. Oxford and IBH Publishing Co. Pvt. Ltd., New Delhi.

De Datta, S.K. 1981. Principles and Practices of Rice Production. John Wiley and Sons, New York.

Desai, B.B., P.M. Kotecha, D.K. Salunkha. 1999. Science and Technology of Groundnut: Biology, Production, Processing and Utilization. Naya Prokash, Culcutta.

Dev, G. and Sanders, L.L. (Eds.). 1989. Maximum Yield Research. Proceedings of Symposium on Maximum Yield Research, Nov. 16-18, 1988, New Delhi. Potash and Phosphate Institute of Canada, India Programme, Potash Research Institute of India, Haryana, India.

Dhruva Narayana,2002. Soil and Water Conservation Research in India. Indian Council of Agricultural Research, New Delhi.

Donn, W.C. 1965. Meteorology. Mc Graw Hill Book Co., New York.

Donnell Hunt. 1997. Farm Power and Machinery Management. Iowa State University Press. IOWA, USA.

Dwivedi, A.P. 1992. Agroforestry - Principle and Practices. Oxford and IBH Publishing Co. Pvt. Ltd., New Delhi.

Eugene P. O. 1996. Fundamentals of Ecology. Natraj Publishers, Dehra Dun.

FAO. 1988. Sericulture Manual. Vol. I, II and III. Mulberry Cultivation, Silkworm Rearing and Silk Reeling. Oxford and IBH Publishing Co. Pvt. Ltd., New Delhi.

FAO. 2003. FAO Statistics, 2003. Food and Agricultural Organization of the United Nations, Rome. (www.fao.org.).

Francis, C. A. 1986. Multiple Cropping System. MacMillan Publishing Co. New York.

Franklyn W. Cole. 1970. Introduction to Meteorology. John Wiley and Sons, Inc., New York.

Gallagher, E.J. 1984. Cereal Production. Butter Worths and Co. Ltd., London.

Gaur, A.G., Neelakandan S. and Dergan. K.S. 1984. Organic Manures. Indian Council of Agricultural Research, New Delhi.

Glenn T. Trewartha, 1968. An Introduction to Climate. McGraw Hill Book Co., New York.

GOI, 2003. Agricultural Statistics at a Glance, 2003. Directorate of Economics & Statistics, Government of India, New Delhi. (www.agricoop.nic.in).

Gomez, K.A. and Gomez, A.A. 1984. Statistical Procedures for Agricultural Research with Emphasis on Rice. John Wiley and Sons Inc., New York.

Gopal Chandra De. 1989. Fundamentals of Agronomy. Oxford and IBH Publishing Co. Pvt. Ltd., New Delhi.

Gopalachari, N.C. 1984. Tobacco. Indian Council of Agricultural Research,

New Delhi.

Gopalswamy, N. 1994. Agricultural Meteorology. Rawat Publications, New Delhi.

Govindan, R., Chinnasami, K.N., Chandrasekaran, B., Budhar M.N. and Prince J. 1990. Poultry-cum-Fish Culture in Rice Farming System in Cauvery Delta Region of Tamil Nadu. Indian J. Agron. 35 (1& 2): 23-29.

Gupta, O.P, 1999. Modern weed Management. Agrobios (India), Jodhpur, India.

Gupta, O.P. 1993. Weed management- Principles and Practices. Agrobios (India), Jodhpur, India.

Gupta, P. K. 2003. Handbook of Soil, Fertilizers and Manure.(2nd Ed.). Agrobios (India), Jodhpur, India.

Gupta, U.S. 1982. Physiological Aspects of Dryland Farming. Oxford and IBH Publishing Co. Pvt. Ltd., New Delhi.

Gurmel Singh, Arora, Y.K., Pratap Narain and Grewal, S.S. 1990. Agroforestry Research. Surya Publications, New Delhi.

Gurmel Singh, Venkataramanan, C., Sastry, G. and Joshi, B.P. 1990. Manual on Soil and Water Conservation Practices. Oxford and IBH publishing Co. Pvt. Ltd., New Delhi.

Gururaj Hunsigi and Krish, K.R. 1998. Science of Field Crop Production. Oxford and IBH publishing Co. Pvt. Ltd., New Delhi.

Hiran, K.S., Jaspal Singh and Acharya, M.S. 1990. Irrigation Scheduling. CBS Publishers and Distributors, New Delhi.

Howard Critchfield, J. 1962. General Climatology. Prentice Hall of India, Pvt. Ltd., New Delhi.

Hridai Ram Yadav (Ed.). 1988. Dimensions of Wasteland Development. Proceedings of the National Seminar on Wasteland Development, New Delhi, 1986. Concept Publishing Company, New Delhi.

IARI. 1972. Recent Research on Multiple Cropping. A Bulletin. Indian Agricultural Research Institute, New Delhi.

IARI. 1977. Water Requirement and Irrigation Management of Crops in India. Water Technology Centre. Indian Agricultural Research Institute, New Delhi.

ICAR. 1960. Indigenous Agricultural Implements of India - An All India Survey. Indian Council of Agricultural Research, New Delhi.

ICAR. 1981. Indian Farming -Special number on Pulses Vol. 31: No. 5.

ICAR. 1982. A Decade of Dryland Agricultural Research in India 1971-80. All India Co-ordinated Research Project for Dryland Agriculture. Hyderabad, India.

ICAR. 1982. Indian Farming - Special number on Oil Seeds. Vol. 32. No. 8.

ICAR. 1985. Rice Research in India. Indian Council of Agricultural Research, New Delhi.

ICAR. 1996. Indian Farming Special Issue. XXth World's Poultry Congress 2-8 Sep, 1996, New Delhi. Indian Council of Agricultural Research, New Delhi.

ICAR. 1997. Hand Book of Agriculture (Revised). Indian Council of Agricultural Research, New Delhi.

ICAR. 2002. Hand Book of Animal Husbandry. Indian Council of Agricultural Research, New Delhi.

ICRISAT. 1975. Proceedings on International Workshop on Farming Systems. 18-21, Nov. 1974. International Crops Research Institute for Semi- Arid Tropics, Hyderabad, India.

ICRISAT. 1981. Proceedings of the International Workshop on Intercropping, 10-13 Jan., 1979. International Crops Research Institute for Semi- Arid Tropics, Hyderabad, India.

ICTC. 1960. Indian Tobacco. Indian Central Tobacco Committee, Ministry of Food and Agriculture, Government of India, Madras.

IJAS. 1998. Indian Journal of Agricultural Sciences 68(8), Special Issue. August 1998.

IRRI. 1988. Green Manuring in Rice Farming. International Rice Research Institute, Manila, Philippines.

ISA. 1972. Multiple Cropping. Proceedings of a Symposium. Oct 7-8, 1972. Haryana Agricultural University, Hissar and Indian Society of Agronomy and Indian Council of Agricultural Research, New Delhi.

ISA. 1986. Proceedings of the National Symposium on Cropping System. 3-5 April, 1985. Central Soil Salinity Research Institute, Karnal and Indian Society of Agronomy, New Delhi.

ISOR. 1993. National Seminar on Oilseeds Research and Development in India: Status and Strategies- Extended Summaries. Indian Society of Oilseeds Research, Hyderabad.

Isrealsen, O.W. and Hansen, V.E. 1962. Irrigation - Principles and Practices. John Wiley and Sons, Inc., New York.

Jagdishwar Sahay. 1971. Elements of Agricultural Engineering Vol I. Agro Book Agency. Patna, India.

James, E. Wimberly. 1983. Technical Hand Book for the Paddy Rice Post Harvest Industry in Developing Countries. International Rice Research Institute, Philippines.

Jasbir Singh and Dhillon S.S. 1994. Agricultural Geography. Tata McGraw Hill Publishing Co. Ltd., New Delhi.

Jeswani, L.M. and Baldev, B. 1990. Advances in Pulse Production Technology. Indian Council of Agricultural Research, New Delhi.

Jha, L.K. 1995. Advances in Agroforestry. APH Publishing company, New Delhi.

John C. Gordon, William R. Bentley, Salleh Md. Noor and Hashim Md. Noor. 1990. A Hand Book on the Management of Agroforestry Research. Winrock International USA and Oxford and IBH Publishing Co. Ltd. New Delhi.

John Milton Poehlman. 1991. The Mungbean. Oxford and IBH Publishing Co. Pvt. Ltd., New Delhi.

John. F. Griffiths and Dennis M. Driscoll. 1982. Survey of Climatology. Charles

E. Merrill Publishing Co. Columbus, Ohio.

Josef berger. 1969. The World's Major Fibre Crops. Their Cultivation and Manuring. Centre d' Etude de I' Azote, Switzerland.

Josef D. Zimmerman. 1996. Irrigation. John Wiley and Sons Inc., New York.

Joshi, N.C. 1987. Manual of Weed Control. Researchco Publications, New Delhi.

Kakde, J.R. 1985. Agricultural Climatology. Metropolitan Book Co. Pvt. Ltd., New Delhi.

Kanitkar, N.V. 1963. Dry Farming in India. 3rd Edition. Indian Council of Agricultural Research, New Delhi.

Kanwar, J.S. (Ed.), 1978. Soil Fertility -Theory and Practices. Indian Council of Agricultural Research, New Delhi.

Klingman, G.C. 1981. Weed Science. Principles and Practices. John Wiley and Sons Inc., New York.

Kondap, S. and Upadhyay, U.C. 1985. A Practical Manual of Weed Control. Oxford and IBH publishing Co., New Delhi.

Kumar, D., Rai, M. 1992. Advances in Oilseeds Research. vol. 1. Rapeseed and Mustard. Scientific Publishers, Jodhpur, India.

Lawrence J. King. 1966. Weeds of the World- Biology and Control. Interscience Publishers, Inc. New York.

Mahendra Pal, Jayanta Deka and Pai, R.K. 1996. Fundamentals of Cereal Crop Production. Tata Mc Graw Hill publishing Co. Ltd., New Delhi.

Maiti, S., Hedge, M.R. and Chattopadhyay, S.B. 1988. Hand Book on Annual Oilseed Crops. Oxford and IBH publishing Co. Pvt. Ltd., New Delhi.

Mandal, R.C. 1999. Weeds, Weedicides and Weed Control: Principles and Practices. Agrobios (India), Jodhpur, India

Mavi, H.S. 1986. Introduction to Agrometerology. Oxford and IBH Publishing Co. Pvt. Ltd., New Delhi.

Menon, P.A. 1989. Our Weather. National Book Trust, New Delhi.

Michael Haines, 1982. An Introduction to Farming System. Tien Mab lither Printing Co. Pvt. Ltd., London.

Michael, A.M. 1978. Irrigation- Theory and Practice. Vikas Publishing House Pvt. Ltd., New Delhi.

Micra, R.D. and Ahmed, M. 1987. Manual on Irrigation Agronomy. Oxford and IBH Publishing Co. Pvt. Ltd., New Delhi.

Morachan, Y.B. 1980. Crop Production and Management. Oxford and IBH Publishing Co. Pvt. Ltd., New Delhi.

Nagarajan, S., Gyanendra Singh and Tyagi, B.S. (Eds.). 1998. Wheat: Research Needs Beyond 2000 AD. Narosa Publishing House, New Delhi.

Nair, P.K.R. 1985. Classification of Agroforestry System. Agroforestry systems. 3:97-128.

Ninan, K.N. 1989. Edible Oilseeds. Growth, Area, Response and Prospects in India. Oxfords and IBH Publishing Co. Pvt. Ltd., New Delhi.

Norman N. Potter and Joseph H. Hotchkiss. 1996. Food Science. CBS Publishers and Distributors, New Delhi.

NWDP. 1991. National Wasteland Development Project for Rainfed Areas-Guidelines. 1991. Ministry of Agriculture, Department of Agriculture and Co-operation. Govt of India, New Delhi.

Nyle, C. Brady. 1990. The Nature and Properties of Soils. (Tenth edition) MacMillan Publishing Co. Inc., New York.

Palaniappan, SP. and Sivaraman, K. 1996. Cropping System in the Tropics. Principles and Management (Second Edition). New Age International Pvt. Ltd., New Delhi.

Pandey, S.N. and Ajanta Chandha. 1996. Economic Botany. Vikas Publishing House Pvt. Ltd., New Delhi.

Panse, V.G., and Sukhatme, P.V. 1967. Statistical Methods for Agricultural Workers. Indian Council of Agricultural Research, New Delhi.

Papendick, R.I., Sanchez, P.A. and Triplett, G.B. (Eds.). 1976. Multiple Cropping. American Society of Agronomy. spl. Publ. 27, USA.

Paul J. Kramer. 1969. Plant and Soil Water Relationship: A Modern Synthesis. Tata McGraw-Hill Publishing Co. Ltd., New Delhi.

Pillaiyar, P. 1988. Rice- Post Production Manual. Wiley Eastern Limited, New Delhi.

Pratap Singh, Jaspal Singh and Mathur. 1995. Technology for Dryland Agriculture. Himanshu Publications, New Delhi.

Prihar, S.S. and Sandhu, B.S. 1987. Irrigation of Field Crops - Principles and Practices. Indian Council of Agricultural Research, New Delhi.

Punjab Singh, Pathak, P.S. and Roy, M.M. (Eds.) 1994. Agroforestry Systems for Degraded Lands. Paper Presented at the International Conference on Sustainable development of Degraded Lands Through Agroforestry in Asia and the Pacific. New Delhi. Nov 25-30, 1994, Vol. I. Oxford and IBH Publishing Co. Pvt. Ltd. New Delhi.

Radha Vasiraju, and Murty Krishna. 1995. Practical Mannual on Agricultural Meteorology. Kalyani Publishers, New Delhi.

Rajendra Prasad (Ed.).2002. Textbook of Field Crop Production. Indian Council of Agricultural Research, New Delhi.

Raju, R. A. 2000. Glimpses of Rice Technology. Agrobios (India), Jodhpur, India.

Raju, R.A. 1996. Ecology of Aquatic Weeds and their Control. Kalyani Publishers, New Delhi.

Rama Rao, M.S.V. 1962. Soil Conservation in India. Indian Council of Agricultural Research, New Delhi.

Rangasamy, A., Venkitaswamy, R., Purushothaman, S. and Palaniappan SP. 1996. Rice - Poultry – Fish - Mushroom Integrated Farming Systems for Lowlands of Tamil Nadu. Indian J. Agron. 41(3): 344-348.

Rangaswamy, R. 1995. A Text Book of Agricultural Statistics. New Age International Publishers Limited, New Delhi.

Rao, V.S. 2000. Principles of Weed Science (Second Edition). Oxford and IBH Publishing Co. Pvt. Ltd., New Delhi.

Rathore, P. S. (Ed.). 2000. Techniques and Management of Field Crop

Production. Agrobios (India), Jodhpur, India.

Ratikanta Maiti, 1996. Sorghum Science. Oxford and IBH Publishing Co. Pvt. Ltd., New Delhi.

Reddy, S. R. 1999. Principles of Agronomy. Kalyani Publishers, New Delhi.

Rengaswamy, A., Premsekhar, M. and Venkitaswamy, R. 1995. Integrated Farming System for Gardenlands. Madras Agric. J. 82 (6,7,8): 464-466.

Rosenberg, N.J. 1974. Microclimate - The Biological Environment. John Wiley and Sons, Inc., New York.

Samuel, L. Tisdale, Warner. L. Nelson and James D. Beaton. 1990. Soil Fertility and Fertilizers (Fourth edition). MacMillan Publishing Co. Inc., New York.

Sankaran, S. and Subbiah Mudaliar, V.T. 1992. Principles of Agronomy. The Bangalore Publishing Co. Ltd., Bangalore, India.

Sankaran, S., Jayakumar, R. and Kempuchetty, N. 1993. Herbicide Residues. Gandhi Book House, Coimbatore, India.

Sarkar, R.P. and Biswas, B.C. 1988. Weather Forecasting and its Application in Agriculture. Fert. News. 33(4): 73-76.

Seetharam, A., Riley, K.W. and Harinarayana, G. 1989. Small Millets in Global Agriculture. Oxford and IBH publishing Co. Pvt. Ltd., New Delhi.

Sharma, B.C. 1991. Dryland Farming- Perspectives and Prospects. Daya Publishing House, New Delhi.

Sharma, P.N. and Kampen. 1977. Watershed Based Land and Water Management Technology - Some Tentative Guidelines. ICRISAT, Hyderabad, India.

Shippen, J.M., Ellin C.R. and Clover, C.H. 1980. Basic Farm Machinery. Pergamon Press. Oxford, London.

Singh, G., Venkataramanan, G. and Sastry, G. 1981. Manual of Soil and Water Conservation Practices in India. ICAR Bull. No T-13/ D-10, Centre for Soil and Water Conservation Research and Training Institute, Dehradun.

Singh, R.P. 1991. Farm Ponds. All India Co-Ordinated Research Project for Dryland Agriculture. Hyderabad. India.

Singh, R.P. and Subba Reddy, G. 1986. Identifying Crops and Cropping Systems with Greater Stability of Production in Deficient Environment. International Consultants Meetings on Research on Drought Problems in Arid and Semi-Arid Tropics. ICARISAT, Patancheru, Andhra Pradesh, India.

Singh, R.P., Das, S.K., Bhaskara Rao, U.M. and Reddy, M.N. 1990. Towards Sustainable Dryland Agriculture Practices. Central Research Institute for Dryland Agriculture, Hyderabad, India.

Singh, R.P., Padmanabhan, M.V., Das, S.K. and Mishra, P.K. 1990. Field Manual on Watershed Management. Central Research Institute for Dryland Agriculture, Hyderabad, India.

Singh, S.P. 1994. Hand Book of Agroforestry. Agrotech Publishing Academy. Udaipur, India.

Singh, S.P. and Prasad, C. (Eds.) 1991. Technologies for Minimizing Risk in

Rainfed Agriculture. Indian Society of Extension Education and Indian Council of Agricultural Research, New Delhi.

Singh, S.S. 1996. Principles and Practices of Agronomy. Kalyani Publishers, New Delhi.

Singh, S.S. 1996. Soil Fertility and Nutrient Management. Kalyani Publishers, New Delhi.

Singh, S.S. 1997. Crop Management under Irrigated and Rainfed Conditions. Kalyani Publishers, Ludhiana, India.

Sivanappan, R.K. and Karai Gowder, K.R. 1977. Irrigation and Drainage. Popular Book Depot. Madras, India.

Sivasankaran, D., Venkitaswamy, R., Chinnusamy C. and Shanmugasundaram. V.S. 1995. A Sustainable Integrated Farming System for Drylands. Madras Agric. J. 82 (6,7,8): 458-460.

Snedecor, G.W. and Cochran, W.C. 1967. Statistical Methods. Oxford and IBH publishing Co. Pvt. Ltd., New Delhi.

Somani, L.L. 1992. Dictionary of Weed Science. Agrotech Publishing Academy. Udaipur, India.

Somani, L.L., Chowdhary, G.R. and Kumar, D. (Eds.) 1990. Current Practices in Dryland Resources and Technology. Vol. 5. Divyajyotic Prakashnan, Jodhpur, India.

Somani, L.L., Vittal, K.P.R. and Venkateswarlu, 1992. Dryland Agriculture in India- State of Art of Research in India. Scientific Publishers, Jodhpur, India.

Sree Ramulu, V.S. 1995. Dry Farming in India. Oxford and IBH Publishing Co. Pvt. Ltd., New Delhi.

Srilakshmi, B. 1997. Food Science. New Age International Pvt. Ltd., Publishers, New Delhi.

Srivastava, H.C., Bhaskaran, S., Menon, K.K.G., Ramanujam, S.and Rao, M.V. 1984. Pulse Production Constrains and Opportunities. Oxford and IBH publishing Co. Pvt. Ltd., New Delhi.

Srivastava, S.C., Johari, D.P. and Gill, P.S. 1988. Manual of Sugarcane Production in India. Indian Council of Agricultural Research, New Delhi.

Steel, R. G.D. and Torrie J.H. 1960. Principles and Procedures for Statistics. McGraw Hill Book, Inc., New York.

Stephen O. Duke, 1987 (Ed.). Weed Physiology Vol II. Herbicide Physiology. CRC Press, Inc. Boca Raton, Florida.

Subramanian, S., Kothandaraman, G.V., Natarajan, S. and Ramaswami, P.P. (Ed.). 1987. Soil Survey and Land use Planning for Watershed Management. Directorate of Soil and Crop Management Studies, TNAU, Coimbatore, India.

Sunith, C.P. 1975. Methods in Agricultural Meteorology. Elsevier Scientific Publishing Co., Amstardam, India.

Susil Malhotra, N.A. 1992. Rural Energy Planning. Oxford and IBH publishing Co. Pvt. Ltd., New Delhi.

Tadulingam, C. and Venkatanarayanan, G. 1985. A Handbook of Some South

Indian Weeds. Periodical Expert Book Agency. New Delhi.

Thakur, C. 1980. Scientific Crop Production. Vol. I and II. Metropolitan Book Co. Pvt. Ltd., New Delhi.

Tripathi, R.P. and Singh, H.P. 1993. Soil Erosion and Conservation. Wiley Eastern Limited, New Delhi.

Venkataraman, V., Subramanian, S., Kulandaivelu, R., Srinivasan, N., Balasubramanian, N. and Veerabadran, V. 1983. Integrated Farming System - An Experience and Case Studies. TNAU, Coimbatore, India.

Venkateswarlu, J. 1986. Contingent Crop Production Strategy in Rainfed Areas under Different Weather Conditions. Project Bulletin No. 5. Central Research Institute for Dryland Agriculture, Hyderabad.

Venkateswarlu, J. 1987. Efficient Resource Management System for Drylands of India. Advances in Soil Science. 7: 165-221.

Vishwa Nath and Chhotey Lal. 1995. Oilseeds in India- An overview. Westvill Publishing House, New Delhi.

Waller, G.R. (Ed.). 1987. Allelochemicals Role in Agriculture and Forestry. American Chemistry Society. Washington D.C., U.S.A.

Weiss, E.A. 1983. Oil Seed Crops. Longman Group. Ltd., London.

Wild, A. 1988. Russell's Soil Conditions and Plant Growth (Eleventh Edition). Longman Group, London.

Yadava, R.L. 1993. Agronomy of Sugarcane. Principles and Practices. International Book Distributing Co. Lucknow, India.

Yellamada Reddi, T. and Sanka Reddi, G.H. 2002. Principles of Agronomy. Kalyani Publishers, New Delhi.

Yohida, S. 1981. Fundamentals of Rice Crop Science. International Rice Research Institute, Philippines.

Young, A. 1989. Agroforestry for Soil Conservation. CAB International, Walling Ford, U.K.

Index

A

B

E

F

G

H

N

O

P

Q

R

S

Y

Z